P9-CDF-129

D0015320

The CEREMONIES *of* THE ROMAN RITE DESCRIBED

OMNIA AVTEM HONESTE ET SECVNDVM ORDINEM FIANT.—1 COR. XIV, 40.

In accordance with the Rubrics of the Liturgical Books, the Decrees of the Congregation of Sacred Rites, the Code of Canon Law, and approved authors.

Containing all such ceremonies as may occur in a Parish Church, the Rules for some Pontifical Functions and Directions for the Administration of the Sacraments, with Plans and Diagrams by the Author.

THE CEREMONIES
OF THE ROMAN RITE
DESCRIBED

BY

ADRIAN FORTESCUE

EIGHTH EDITION FURTHER
REVISED THROUGHOUT AND
AUGMENTED BY

J. C. O'CONNELL

With additional notes about
United States Practice in the Reception
of Converts and Matrimony

THE NEWMAN PRESS
WESTMINSTER, MARYLAND

1949

Eighth Edition • • • • *1948*

Nihil Obstat:

Raymond B. Meyer, S.S.
Censor Deputatus

Imprimatur:

Francis P. Keough, D.D.
Archbishop of Baltimore

February 28, 1949

CONTENTS

PART V

OCCASIONAL FUNCTIONS

BIBLIOGRAPHY

Aertnys (Jos.)–Dankelman (A.) : *Compendium Liturgiae Sacrae* (Marietti, 1936).

Ahearne (P.)–Lane (M.) : *Pontifical Ceremonies* (Burns, Oates, 1942).

Alphonsus M. de Liguori (St.) : *Liber de Caeremoniis Missae* (edition of G. Schober, Pustet, 1882).

(Ab) Appeltern (B. Victorius): *Sacrae Liturgiae Promptuarium* (Beyaert, 1913).

Amicis, De (P.) : (1) *Caeremoniale Parochorum* (Artero, 1910). (2) *Il Cerimoniale Completo* (Pustet, 1921).

Attwater (D.) : *The Catholic Encyclopaedic Dictionary* (Cassell, 1931).

Augustine (C. A.) : *Liturgical Law* (Herder, 1931).

Barin (L. R.) : *Catechismo Liturgico* (1932, 1934, 1935).

Bauldry : *Manuale Sacrarum Caeremoniarum* (Venice, 1778).

Bootsma (G.) : *Tractatus de Officio Divino et Missa* (Herder, 1928).

Braun (J.) : *I Paramenti Sacri* (Marietti, 1914).

Brehm (F.) : *Synopsis Additionum et Variationum in Editione Typica Missalis Romani Factarum* (Pustet, 1920).

Britt (M.) : *How to Serve in Simple, Solemn and Pontifical Functions* (Bruce, 1934).

Caeremoniale Romano-Seraphicum (1927).

Callewaert (C.) : (1) *Caeremoniale in Missa Privata et Solemni* (Beyaert, 1934). (2) *De Missalis Romani Liturgia* (Beyaert, 1937). (3) *De Exsequiis* (1935).

Cappello (F. M.) : *Tractatus Canonico-Moralis de Sacramentis* (Marietti, 1928).

Carpo, De (A. M.)–Moretti (A.) : *Caeremoniale juxta Ritum Romanum* (Marietti, 1932).

Catalani (G.) : (1) *Rituale Romanum . . . Commentariis Exornatum* (Rome, 1757). (2) *Caeremoniale Episcoporum . . . Commentariis Illustratum* (Jouby, 1860).

Ceremonial for the Use of the Catholic Churches in the United States of America, Ninth Edition (revised by Rev. W. Caroll Milholland, S.S., Kilner, 1935).

Clergy Review (1930–1943).

Coelho (A.) : *Corso di Liturgia Romana* (Marietti, 1936–1940).

Collins (H. E.) : *The Church Edifice and its Appointments* (Dolphin Press, 1936).

Croegart (A.) : (1) See *Stappen*. (2) *Tractatus de Rubricis Missalis Romani* (Dessain, 1935).

Deodati (G.)–Toscano (A.) : *Manuale Pratico di S. Cerimonie* (Scuola Tipografica Salesiana, Catania, 1926, 1928).

Dictionnaire D'Archéologie Chrétienne et de Liturgie (Letouzey et Ané, 1907–).

Dictionnaire de Droit Canonique (Letouzey et Ané, 1924–).

Dictionnaire de Théologie Catholique (Letouzey et Ané, 1909–).
Directions for Altar Societies and Architects [J. O'Connell] (Burns, Oates and Washbourne, 1936).
Dubosq (R.) : *Le Guide de l'Autel* (Desclée, 1938).
Dunne (W.) : *The Ritual Explained* (A. Hickling, 1940).
Duret (D.) : *Mobilier, Vases, Objets et Vêtements Liturgiques* (Letouzey et Ané, 1932).
Ephemerides Liturgicae [1] (1887–1939).
Eucharistia (Encyclopédie Populaire ; Bloud et Gay, 1934).
Favrin (B.) : *Praxis Sollemnium Functionum Episcoporum* (Pustet, 1926).
Gatterer (M.) : (1) *Annus Liturgicus* (Rauch, 1935). (2) *Praxis Celebrandi Functiones Ordinarias Sacerdotales* (Rauch, 1926).
Gavanti (B.)–Merati (C. M.) : *Thesaurus Sacrorum Rituum* (Venice, 1744 and 1762).
Gemert (P. A.) : *Rubricarum ac Caeremoniarum Promptuarium* (1935).
A Grammar of Plainsong (Stanbrook Abbey, 1926).
Hanin (A.) : *La Législation Ecclésiastique en matière de Musique Religieuse* (Desclée, 1933).
Hébert (L.) : *Leçons de Liturgie* (Berche et Pagis, 1937).
Herdt, De (J. B.) : (1) *Praxis Pontificalis* (Van Linthout, 1873). (2) *Sacrae Liturgiae Praxis* (Van Linthout, 1902).
Hove, Van (A.) : *Tractatus de Sanctissima Eucharistia* (Dessain, 1933).
Irish Ecclesiastical Record (1865–1943).
Kieffer (G.)–Guillaume (R.) : *Précis de Liturgie Sacrée* (Salvator-Casterman, 1937).
Kuenzel (L.) : *A Manual of the Ceremonies of Low Mass* (Pustet, 1923).
Lane (J.) : *Notes on Some Ceremonies of the Roman Rite* (Burns, Oates and Washbourne, 1937, 1938).
Liturgia (Encyclopédie Populaire, Bloud et Gay, 1930).
MacMahon (M.) : *Liturgical Catechism* (Gill, 1927).
Martinucci (P.)–Menghini (J. B.) : *Manuale Sacrarum Caeremoniarum* (Pustet, 1911–1915).
Menghini (J. B. M.) : (1) *Liturgia Eucharistica* (Desclée-Lefebvre, 1906). (2) *Manuale Novissimo di S. Ceremonie* (Pustet, 1927).
Moretti (A.) : *Caeremoniale Juxta Ritum Romanum* (Marietti, 1936–1937).
Müller (J. B.) : *Handbook of Ceremonies* (Herder, 1927).
O'Callaghan (M.)–Sheehy (J. S.) : *The Sacred Ceremonies of Low Mass* (a translation of Zualdi's book). (Browne and Nolan, 1935.)
O'Connell (J.) : (1) *How to Serve Mass* (Brepols, 1928). (2) *The Clementine Instruction* (a Translation and Commentary). (Burns, Oates and Washbourne, 1927). (3) *The Celebration of Mass* (Burns, Oates and Washbourne, 1940–1942).

---

[1] The issue of January–February, 1939, contains the text of decisions of S.R.C. from 1927 to 1938 (many of which did not appear in *Acta Apostolicae Sedis*).

O'Kane (J.)–Fallon (M. J.) : *Notes on the Rubrics of the Roman Ritual* (Duffy, 1932).

O'Leary (P.) : *Pontificalia* (Browne and Nolan, 1895).

Oppenheim (P.) : *Institutiones Systematico-Historicae in Sacram Liturgiam* (Marietti, 1938–1940).

Perardi (G.) : *La Dottrina Cattolica—Culto* (Torino, 1938).

Periodica de Re Morali, Canonica, Liturgica (1922–1939).

Questions Liturgiques et Paroissiales (Les) (Louvain, 1910–1939).

Romita (F.) : *Jus Musicae Liturgicae* (Marietti, 1936).

Schober (G.) : *Caeremoniae Missarum Solemnium et Pontificalium* (Pustet, 1909).

Stappen (J. Van Der)–Croegaert (A.) : *Caeremoniale* (Dessain, 1933 and 1935).

Stehle (A.) : *Manual of Episcopal Ceremonies* (1916).

Sunol (G.) : *Text Book of Gregorian Chant* (Desclée, 1930).

(Le) Vavasseur (L.)–Haegy (J.)–Stercky (L.) : (1) *Manuel de Liturgie et Cérémonial* (Gabalda, 1935). (2) *Les Fonctions Pontificales* (1932).

Veneroni (P.) : *Manuale di Liturgia* (Artigianelli, 1933 and 1936).

Vismara (E. M.) : *Le Funzioni della Chiesa* (Torino, 1934 and 1935).

Wapelhorst (I.) : *Compendium Sacrae Liturgiae* (Benziger, 1931).

Webb (G.) : *The Liturgical Altar* (Burns, Oates and Washbourne, 1939).

Wuest (J.)–Mullaney (T. W.) : *Matters Liturgical* (Pustet, 1931).

Zualdi (F.)–Capoferri (S.) : *Caeremoniale Missae Privatae* (Marietti, 1922).

FOREWORD TO THE EIGHTH EDITION

DURING the first World War (1914-1918) the late Dr. Adrian Fortescue wrote "Ceremonies of the Roman Rite Described" to replace Dale's translation of Baldeschi's Ceremonial. It was published in 1917. It proved a very popular book and has already gone through seven editions, five of which were prepared by me. In April, 1941, the stereotype plates of the sixth edition were destroyed by enemy action and so a completely new edition, fully revised, was issued in 1943.

Another edition (the eighth) has now been called for. I have taken the opportunity to make some minor changes to eliminate any inaccuracies or ambiguities that I have noticed, and to bring the book fully up to date.

A new section has been added (p. 376) to deal with the administration of Confirmation by a parish priest, in accordance with the decree of September 14, 1946, of the Congregation of the Sacraments.

J. O'CONNELL.

June 1947.

SOURCES

Missale Romanum (typical edition, 1920).
Caeremoniale Episcoporum (typical edition, 1886).
Memoriale Rituum Benedicti XIII (typical edition, 1920).
Rituale Romanum (typical edition, 1925).
Instructio Clementina (1731).
Codex Juris Canonici (published 1917).
Decreta Authentica Congregationis Sacrorum Rituum (1588–1926).
Acta Apostolicae Sedis (1909–1943).
Motu Proprio " Inter Pastoralis Officii Sollicitudines " (Pius X, 1903).
Graduale Sacrosanctae Romanae Ecclesiae (typical edition, 1907).
Cantorinus seu Toni Communes (typical edition, 1911).
Ordo Administrandi Sacramenta et Alia Quaedam Officia Peragendi
(1915).
Ritus Servandus in Solemni Expositione et Benedictione Sanctissimi
Sacramenti (1928).

ABBREVIATIONS

A.A.S. = Acta Apostolicae Sedis.
Addit. = " Additiones et Variationes in Rubricis Missalis " (to be
found at the beginning of the Missal, after *Rubricae
Generales*, since the reform of the Missal by Pius X in the
bull *Divino afflatu* of 1911).
C.E. = Caeremoniale Episcoporum.
C.J.C. = Codex Juris Canonici.
D. = Decretum (of the Congregation of Sacred Rites).
I.C. = Instructio Clementina (of Clement XII regarding the Forty
Hours' Prayer).
M.P. = Motu Proprio of Pius X (regarding the reform of Church
music).
M.R. or *Mem. Rit.* = Memoriale Rituum.
O.M. = *Ordo Missae* (found, normally, in the centre of the Missal
after Holy Saturday).
R. = *Ritus Servandus in Celebratione Missae* (found at beginning
of the Missal).
R.G. = Rubricae Generales Missalis.
R.R. = Rituale Romanum.
R.S. = Ritus Servandus in Expositione et Benedictione Sanctissimi
Sacramenti.
S.R.C. = Decrees of the Congregation of Sacred Rites.

LIST OF PLANS

SYMBOLS USED IN THE PLANS

The Bishop, even when he wears no mitre

The Celebrant wearing a chasuble

The Celebrant in cope

The Deacon

The Subdeacon

Master of Ceremonies

Assistant Priest

} Assistant Deacons

Thurifer with incense

Thurifer not bearing incense

Aspersory-bearer

Cross-bearer

} First and Second Acolytes with their candles

} Acolytes without candles

Server (at Low Mass)

} Torch-bearers

} Assistants in copes (pluvialistae) at the Divine Office

Cantor

Mitre-bearer

Crozier-bearer

Book-bearer

Candle-bearer

Train-bearer

PART I

GENERAL PRINCIPLES CONCERNING CEREMONIES

CHAPTER I

THE CHURCH AND ITS FURNITURE

IT is not necessary, in a book of ceremonies, to give a full account of rules for building and furnishing churches. Yet, to understand the ceremonies, one must have some idea of the dispositions of the building, and one must know the names of the vestments, vessels and ornaments used. We begin, then, with a summary account of these,[1] as far as they concern the ceremonies.

Normally a Catholic church or public oratory should be consecrated by a bishop, according to the form in the Pontifical ; or at least it should be solemnly blessed.[2] When a church is consecrated, at least one altar (which should be the High Altar, if not already consecrated[3]) must be consecrated with it. The essential condition for consecration is that the building be a permanent church, both in construction and purpose ; that is, it must be solidly built and must be intended to be used always as a church. To turn a consecrated church to another use is sacrilege, unless it had previously, in accordance with the provisions of Canon Law[4] (cf. 1170 and 1187), been converted to profane use. It follows that consecration is not allowed till the building is free of debt and mortgage.

In Great Britain and Ireland many churches are not consecrated, but merely blessed. Canon Law makes no provision for temporary churches. A building to be used as a church for a time only should receive the simple " Benedictio loci."[5] A church may be blessed at first, then consecrated later, when it is free of debt.

It makes no difference to any later ceremony whether the church be consecrated or only blessed.

Plan of a Church. According to the old principle churches were ORIENTATED, that is, the High Altar was at the East end[6] and the

---

[1] *Directions for Altar Societies* (see Bibliography, p. xi) deals in detail with church appointments.

[2] The blessing is a reserved one and is found in R.R. VIII. xxvii. A semi-public oratory *may* receive this blessing, or may be given the common blessing of a place (cf. C.J.C. 1196). There is a new form of blessing (R.R. Appendix, n. 16) for a private oratory.

[3] C.J.C. 1165, § 5.

[4] Cf. C.J.C. 1170, 1187.

[5] S.R.C. 4025 [6] (cf. C.J.C. 1196.)

[6] It is a very old Christian principle that people turn to the East at prayer; so the priest saying Mass should normally face the East.

main entrance at the West. In describing ceremonies we speak of the Gospel and Epistle sides of the church and altar. The GOSPEL SIDE is where the Gospel is read at Mass ; it is the left side as you face the altar ; the EPISTLE SIDE is the right. If the church is orientated properly, the Gospel side will be the North, the Epistle side the South.[1]

The plan of a church varies very considerably according to its size, the architect's design, and so on. There is much latitude in planning a church. A large church will probably have a number of side chapels, each with its own altar.[2] In this case, too, the normal principle would be that each altar faces the East, so that the priest looks that way when saying Mass. There may also be two or more aisles and a transept.

For the purpose of ceremonies we distinguish five parts of the church. Every church, however small, will have these, at least as theoretic divisions. They are the nave, baptistery, porch, choir and sanctuary. The NAVE is that part of the church where the people attend the services. Generally it is arranged in two groups of seats, one on either side, with a passage down the middle. It is not now usual in English-speaking countries to separate men from women, though this ancient arrangement is desired by Canon Law.[3]

The BAPTISTERY should be a separate chapel, or at least railed off from the rest of the church.[4] It may contain an altar,[5] as well as a font. The font[6] should stand in the middle of the baptistery. It is covered when not in use (see p. 379).

Beyond the main entrance to the nave is the NARTHEX, or PORCH (sometimes called *vestibulum*). This has important liturgical uses, and should never be wanting. At the church doors are holy-water stoups.

In front of the nave, generally raised by one or more steps, is the CHOIR. This is where the clergy or singers attend in cassock and surplice. It should have seats or stalls on either side, facing each other across the church. In cathedral and collegiate churches the canons have their stalls arranged in this way.

If the Blessed Sacrament is reserved at the High Altar there is generally a COMMUNION RAIL between the nave and the choir. This should be of a convenient height, so that people can kneel at it to receive Holy Communion. Hanging from it, on the altar side, is the

---

[1] In heraldic language the Gospel side is the *dexter* of the altar, the right of the crucifix as it faces down the church. The Epistle side is *sinister*.

[2] Subsidiary altars should never be within the sanctuary, and, when feasible, each real altar should have a separate chapel.

[3] C.J.C. 1262, § 1.

[4] In the rite of Baptism the first part takes place in the Narthex (" ad limen ecclesiae," R.R. II. i, 68). Then, after the child has entered the church, an exorcism is said " antequam accedat ad baptisterium " (*ib.*, II. ii, 12). Similarly, churching is begun *ad limina* (R.R. VII. iii, 1).

[5] The old liturgical books constantly suppose Mass said in the baptistery (for instance, the *Gelasian Sacramentary*, ed. H. A. Wilson, pp. 142–143). The great baptisteries in Italy all have altars.

[6] The Roman Ritual sometimes calls the font " baptisterium."

COMMUNION CLOTH of white linen, which rests on the top of the rail while Communion is distributed.[1]

Beyond the choir is the SANCTUARY. Often there is no mark in the building to show the line of separation between the choir and sanctuary. The sanctuary is merely the end (normally the east end) of the choir near the High Altar. If it is not on a higher level than the choir it is counted as beginning about where the seats or stalls of the choir end on that side.

The chief object in the sanctuary is the ALTAR [2] in the middle ; this will be the High Altar of the church. All others are counted as side altars.

Altars. There are two kinds of altar, the fixed (*altare fixum*) and portable altar (*altare portatile*).

A FIXED ALTAR must be of stone with the table and base permanently united. A relic of at least one martyr is buried in it. The whole top (the " mensa ") of the altar is of stone and joined by stone to the ground ; it is all consecrated as one thing.

In the case of the PORTABLE ALTAR the only real altar is the ALTAR STONE. This is a stone in which relics are placed and sealed up. It is comparatively small,[3] perhaps about one foot square or so, and an inch or two thick. Mass is said on this. The altar stone may be placed on a table of any material. It is not fixed to the table. So in many churches there is what looks like a large wooden altar. Really this is only the framework or stand. In the middle (generally sunk into the wood) is the altar stone, which alone is consecrated. The framework may also be of stone. In this way an altar may be built of stone, used as a portable one, having on it the consecrated altar stone, till the whole can be consecrated as a fixed altar. There is no difference in the ceremonies between a fixed and a portable altar.[4]

There should be some kind of canopy over the altar.[5] This may hang from the roof of the church (a baldachin or tester) or may stand on columns (a ciborium or civory). It should cover not only the altar, but also the foot-pace, or at least the priest celebrating. The altar should not stand immediately against the wall of the church ; at the consecration of an altar the rubrics require that the consecrating bishop go round it.

The altar is raised above the floor of the sanctuary by steps. Every

---

[1] The Congregation of the Sacraments in an Instruction to Ordinaries, dated 26 March 1929, directs a Communion plate *also* to be used for the Communion of the people.

[2] Cf. C.J.C. 1197–1202.

[3] " Quae tam ampla sit, ut Hostiam et majorem partem Calicis capiat " (R.G. xx).

[4] The older principle was that, as no church may be consecrated unless a fixed altar be consecrated with it, so, on the other hand, an altar may not be consecrated except in a consecrated church. Thus consecrated church and consecrated altar always went together. But the S.R.C. 3059[15], and the Code (1165, § 5) allow an altar to be consecrated in a merely blessed church.

[5] C.E. I. xii, 13 ; xiv, 1. S.R.C. 1966, 2912, 3525[2] (cf. *Index Generalis*, vol. v, p. 35).

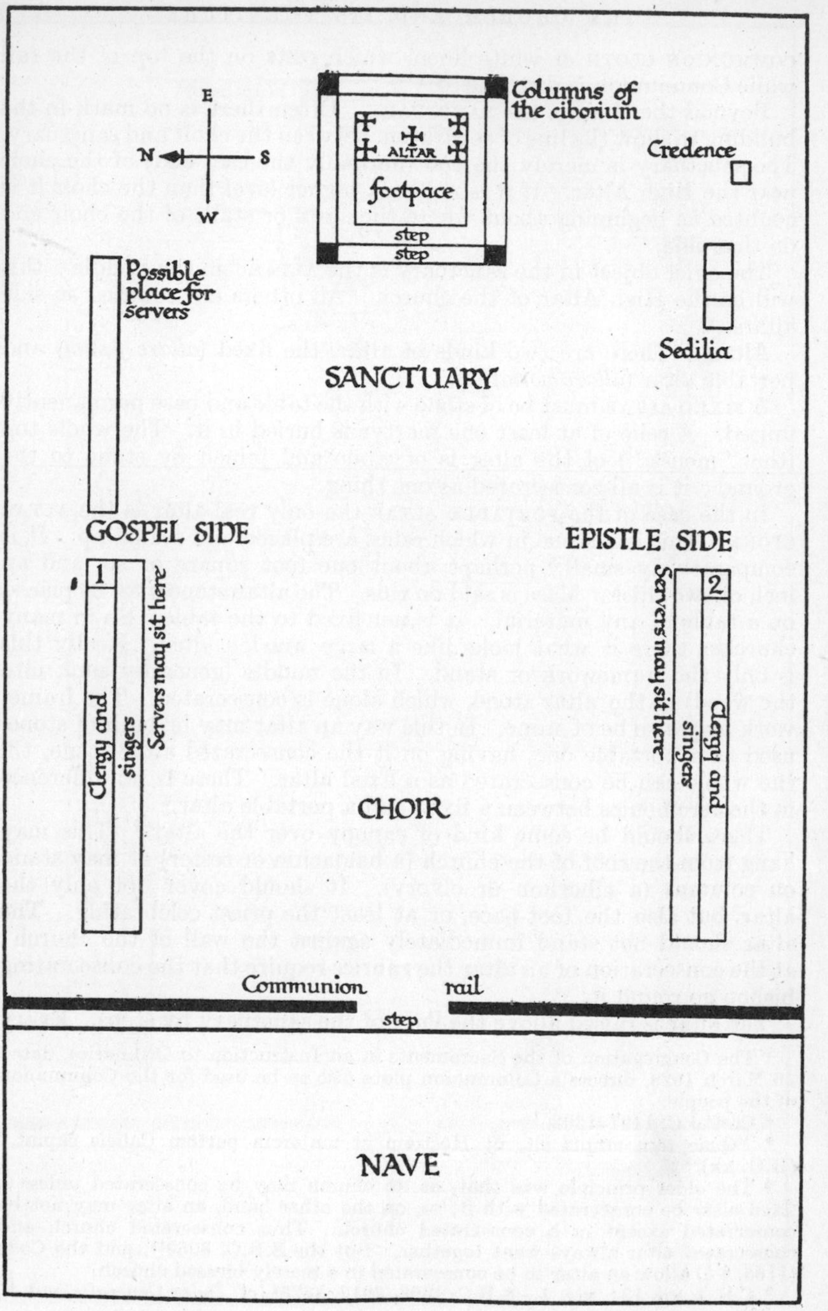

FIG. 1. PLAN OF A PARISH CHURCH: CHOIR AND SANCTUARY

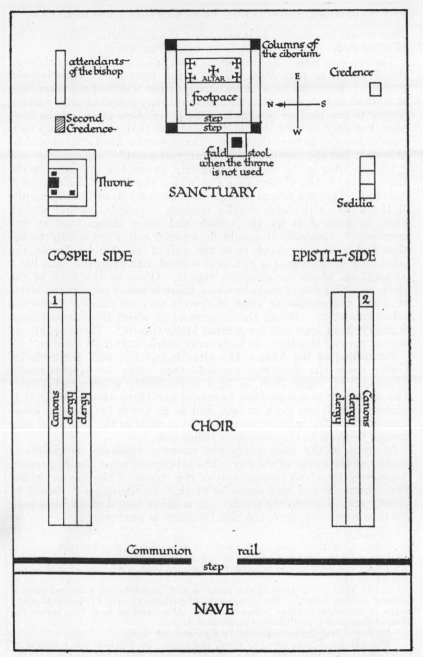

attendants of the bishop

Columns of the ciborium

ALTAR

footpace

step
step

N ← → S

E

W

Credence

Second Credence

faldstool when the throne is not used

Throne

SANCTUARY

Sedilia

GOSPEL SIDE

EPISTLE-SIDE

1

Canons | clergy | clergy

2

Canons | clergy | clergy

CHOIR

Communion rail

step

NAVE

FIG. 2. PLAN OF A CATHEDRAL CHURCH : CHOIR AND SANCTUARY

5

altar should be raised at least one step ; the High Altar will have three or more steps. There should be an uneven number.

The top step before the altar forms a platform on which the celebrant stands while he says Mass. This is the FOOT-PACE (*suppedaneum, predella*). It should be as long across as the width of the altar, and at least so wide in front that the celebrant may genuflect on it without having to put his foot outside it. The lower steps go round the foot-pace, not only in front, but at the sides, so that one can go up to it from either side as from the front. The steps of a fixed altar should be of stone ; but the foot-pace is preferably of wood.[1]

On one altar in the church (ordinarily, in smaller churches, on the High Altar) is the TABERNACLE [2] in which the Blessed Sacrament is reserved. This is a safe or casket—permanently fixed [3] in the middle of the altar—with doors usually opening outwards, leaving enough room in front of it for the vessels and other things used at any ceremony.[4] Generally it should be an iron safe fixed solidly to the altar and so to the ground, or to the wall of the church. Inside, the tabernacle is either gold or gilt, or it is lined with white silk ; and has a corporal on which the ciborium stands. Often at the back of the altar, on either side of the tabernacle, there is one or more raised steps, on which the candles or vases of flowers may be placed. These are called GRADINES. Before the tabernacle in which the Sanctissimum is reserved, at least one lamp must always burn.[5] There ought—at least in greater churches—to be several lamps, uneven in number.

Furnishing of the Altar. The altar is covered with three cloths. Under these the Pontifical requires that there be a CERE-CLOTH (*chrismale*) of waxed linen, at least immediately after consecration.[6] The cere-cloth is not counted as one of the three altar-cloths. It is allowed to fold one cloth in two, and so to use it for the two lower altar-cloths. The upper cloth should be as wide as the altar, and long enough to reach to the ground on either side.

In front of the altar hangs the FRONTAL (*pallium, antependium*) usually of the colour of the day. The tabernacle must also be covered completely by a veil (*conopaeum*) of the colour of the day or white. The tabernacle veil may never be black. At Requiems it should be violet,[7] and so should the frontal. It is never lawful to dispense with the tabernacle veil where the Sanctissimum is reserved.

---

[1] Cf. S.R.C. 3576[1].

[2] C.J.C. 1268–1269; Instr. of S. Congr. of Sacraments, May 26, 1938.

[3] But not embedded in a reredos or in gradines.

[4] Hence the door should be split into two, so that when opened it does not project too far.

[5] C.J.C. 1271. The glass of the lamp should be white but coloured glass is *tolerated* (S.R.C. 3576[5]). The Ceremonial of Bishops (I. xii, 17) requires many lamps in the church, three before the High Altar and at least five before the Blessed Sacrament, at all events on greater days.

[6] No law orders the cere-cloth to be a permanent thing.

[7] The rubrics always use the word *violaceus*. In English the meaning of violet as a colour is not clear. As a liturgical term it means not the colour of the flower (which is blue-violet) but the colour (in varying shades) of a prelate's robes, i.e., red-violet.

On the altar stands a CROSS—with the figure of the Crucified—sufficiently large to be seen by the celebrant and people.[1] It should stand in the middle of the large candlesticks, its base as high as these, and the entire cross itself higher than the candlesticks. If there is a tabernacle the cross may not stand before it, nor should it stand on it,[2] nor may it stand in the throne (if there be one) used for exposition of the Blessed Sacrament. On every altar on either side are at least two candlesticks with candles. The High Altar of a church will normally have six larger candlesticks with candles, and in front of these two or four smaller ones.[3] Other candles for Benediction, Exposition, and so on, should be placed there for the occasion only and taken away afterwards.

Candles. The rules about candles on the altar are these. At Low Mass (when strictly private) two candles burn all the time ; according to the rubric of the Missal, a third should be lit from the Consecration to the Communion.[4] At High Mass, solemn Vespers and all such more solemn functions six candles are lit, three on either side of the altar cross. At Pontifical High Mass of the living by the Ordinary a seventh candle is lit (p. 154). At a Sung Mass without ministers there may be four or six candles. During Exposition or Benediction of the Blessed Sacrament twenty, or at least twelve, candles must burn on the altar. There may be more. When the Sanctissimum is exposed candles at other altars or before statues and pictures should be put out, at least those which can be seen from the altar.

For other rites celebrated at the altar, such as marriage, blessings, distribution of Holy Communion not in Mass, and for non-liturgical prayers and devotions, two or more candles are lit on the altar.

The proportion of beeswax in church candles is regulated by law. The Paschal candle, the two candles for Low Mass, six for High Mass, and the twelve necessary for Exposition and Benediction must have at least 65 per cent of real beeswax. All other candles used on an altar must have at least 25 per cent of beeswax.[5] The firms which provide candles for Catholic churches stamp the percentage of beeswax on their candles.

Flowers on the altar are not necessary. They are not used in the great churches of Rome. But there is no law against them at certain times [6] ; and in England and Ireland custom is in favour of their use. They should, however, be used with the greatest restraint.

[1] If immediately behind the altar there is a large representation of the crucifixion, this may count as the altar cross. (S.R.C. 1270[2].)

[2] Cf. *Directions for Altar Societies and Architects*, p. 24, n. 5.

[3] These smaller candlesticks, which are used for private Masses, are not part of the normal furniture of the high altar and it is better to remove them when Mass is over. [4] See p. 37.

[5] So the bishops of England and Wales on 4 December 1906, following S.R.C. 4147. The bishops of Ireland, in October 1905, directed "that the Paschal candle and the two principal candles on the Altar at Mass should contain at least 65 per cent of beeswax and that all the other candles used on the Altar should contain at least 25 per cent of beeswax."

[6] C.E. (I. xii, 12) expressly suggests "vascula cum flosculis" as an ornament

When the altar is not in use the altar-cloths are covered with another cloth of some coloured material (sometimes called vesper-cloth),[1] to keep off dust. This should be removed before every service at which the altar is used.

Furniture of the Sanctuary. Near the altar, on the Epistle side, stands the CREDENCE (credentia, abacus). During Mass this should be covered with a white linen cloth which reaches to the ground all around.[2] The vessels and books, and sometimes vestments used at Mass, are placed on the credence when they are not in use.

On the same side of the sanctuary is the SEAT (sedile or sedilia) for the celebrant and sacred ministers. This should be a bench with room for three persons, and covered with cloth, green or violet according to the season or occasion. The use of domestic chairs is not allowed. In cathedrals the bishop's THRONE is on the Gospel side facing the sedile. The canopy over it, its covering and cushion are of the colour of the Mass or Office, namely, white, red, green or violet.[3] They should be of silk.[4]

Instead of the throne, a bishop who is not the Ordinary, and sometimes the Ordinary,[5] uses a FALDSTOOL (faldistorium). This is a stool without a back. It consists of a frame of gilt metal or wood, shaped like the letter X, with a seat of leather or cloth stretched across its upper extremities. It can be folded flat. *When used as a seat* the faldstool has a covering and cushion of the liturgical colour of the Office, namely, white, red, green, violet, or black. These are of silk for a cardinal, cloth for a bishop.

The bishop kneels, on various occasions, before the altar. According to the Ceremonial of Bishops he kneels at a GENVFLEXORIVM (kneeling-desk, prie-dieu).[6] This has a covering and two cushions, one on which he kneels, the other on which he rests the arms. This covering and the cushions (silk or cloth, as before) are, for a cardinal red, or violet for mourning and times of penance; for a bishop green, or violet for occasions of mourning and times of penance.[7]

For this genuflexorium the faldstool may be, and often is, used. A carpet should be spread beneath; there are two cushions, one placed before the faldstool, on which the bishop kneels; the other lies on the seat, so that he rests the arms on it. The cushions are of silk for a cardinal; of cloth for a bishop. They should be of red, green or violet, according to the occasion as explained above for the kneeling-desk.

In cathedrals and churches which possess a faldstool, it is generally

on the altar on greater feasts, and Benedict XIII's *Memoriale Rituum* suggests their use " if customary " on certain days (pp. 254, 287, 330.).
[1] Green is the correct colour, but any colour (except black) is permissible.
[2] Except on Good Friday (C.E. II. xxv, 2).
[3] Violet is used at the throne when the vestments are black.
[4] C.E. I. xiii, 3.
[5] In presence of a higher Prelate (C.E. I. xiii, 4)., at Confirmation, etc.
[6] C.E. III. iv, 1 and *passim*.
[7] For the colour worn by cardinals and bishops at times of penance and mourning, see p. 13.

convenient to use it for a genuflexorium. When the bishop visits a small church which does not possess a faldstool a chair with a low back, with a cushion, is prepared on which he will sit, and a kneeling-desk with two cushions. They should be covered with red, green or violet, according to the rank of the bishop and the occasion (as above).

There may be seats for the servers at Mass and other services on either side of the sanctuary ; or they may sit in front of the stalls in the choir.

The LECTERN (*legile*) and seats for cantors in the middle of the choir, used for parts of the Divine Office, are put in their place before each such service and taken away afterwards. A lectern may be used for the Epistle and Gospel at High Mass. It should be covered with cloth of gold or with silk of the colour of the Office.[1]

The SACRISTY (*sacristia, sacrarium*) is a large room on one side of the sanctuary, or behind it, separated by a door. There should be a stoup of holy water and a bell at this door. There may be two sacristies, an outer one for the choir and servers, an inner one for the sacred ministers. In the sacristy are cupboards and presses in which are kept the vessels, instruments and vestments. There must be at least one large table on which the vestments are laid out. The celebrant and ministers vest at this table. It may form the top of presses for vest-ments. Over this table, or in the middle of the sacristy, a crucifix or sacred image should hang. All who enter or leave the sacristy in procession bow to this on arriving and before leaving. A card should be hung up in a conspicuous place, showing the names of the reigning Pope, the Bishop, the Titular of the church, and indicating the " oratio imperata," if there be one.

C.E. II. viii, 45.

CHAPTER II

THE VESTMENTS OF THE ROMAN RITE

THE common dress for servers and all who assist at any function in choir is a black CASSOCK (*vestis talaris*) with a white linen SURPLICE (*superpelliceum*).[1] Certain prelates and dignitaries wear a violet cassock. The two chaplains or servers at pontifical functions who hold the mitre and crozier have scarves of thin white silk (VIMPA) rather like broad stoles, worn round the neck and tied in front. Through these they hold the mitre and crozier.[2] Clerics have, in choir, a BIRETTA (*biretum*), a square cap of black cloth with three ridges. Some dignitaries also wear a SKULL-CAP (*pileolus*).[3] Canons in chapter [4] have a cape (MOZZETTA or CAPPA PARVA) over their surplice or rochet. Prelates sometimes wear a tunic called MANTELLETTUM,[5] having slits at the side through which the sleeves of the rochet pass.

Vestments for Mass. The celebrant at Mass, if he is a simple priest, wears over his cassock;[6] first the AMICE (*amictus*), a rectangular piece of linen with strings to tie it. He lays this on the head, then passes it around the neck. Then he puts on the ALB (*alba*), a long garment of linen reaching to the feet. This is tied round the waist by the GIRDLE or cincture (*cingulum*), which may be of the colour of the day, but is generally white. On the left arm he wears the MANIPLE (*manipulus*), a band of silk of the colour of the day. The STOLE (*stola*) is a longer band of coloured silk worn round the neck, crossed in front and secured by the ends of the girdle. The CHASUBLE (*casula, planeta*) is the last garment covering all the others. It has a hole through which the head is passed and (generally) strings on the inner side to tie around the body. The maniple, stole and chasuble are usually of silk and of the colour of the Mass to be celebrated.

A set of vestments for Low Mass also includes the burse (to hold the corporal) and veil to be put on the chalice.

[1] Italian, "cotta." The ROCHET (*rochettum*) is a garment like the surplice, but shorter, fitting the body more closely, with narrow sleeves. It is worn by cardinals, bishops, prelates, sometimes (by indult) by canons. It is generally worn under other vestments.

[2] They and the manner of wearing them are described in the C.E. I. xi, 6. But here provision is made only for the mitre-bearer's veil. The crozier-bearer is to hold the crozier with the right hand covered by part of his surplice and to hand it, with bare hand, to the bishop. Instead of this, a veil similar to that of the mitre-bearer is now usual.

[3] Italian, "zucchetto." The skull-cap of a cardinal is red; of a bishop and some abbots violet. Others may wear only a black skull-cap.

[4] Namely, normally, in their own cathedral or collegiate church (cf. p. 31).

[5] This is the name in the C.E.; Italian, "mantelletta."

[6] The rubrics of the Missal (R. I. 2) say that the priest should wear all the other vestments over a surplice, "if it can be had conveniently." This direction is now generally considered obsolete.

At Mass the deacon wears the amice, alb, girdle, maniple and stole. But he wears the stole differently from the priest. He lays it across the breast so that the middle is on the left shoulder, and the two ends under the right arm. It is fixed in this position by the ends of the girdle. Then he puts on the DALMATIC (*dalmatica*). This is a kind of tunic (often open a little up the sides from the bottom) with short sleeves, with an opening through which the head is put. It is usually of silk of the colour of the Mass.

The subdeacon at Mass wears the amice, alb, girdle, maniple, no stole, but a TUNICLE (*tunicella*) made in much the same shape as the deacon's dalmatic, but with longer and narrower sleeves.[1]

During part of High Mass, namely from the Offertory to the Fraction, the subdeacon wears a HUMERAL VEIL (*velum humerale*) under which he holds the paten. This is an oblong of silk, of the colour of the vestments, often with strings to tie it. It is worn like a cape over the shoulders. The object of the humeral veil is to cover the hands when something is held in them.

On certain days [2] the deacon and subdeacon do not wear the dalmatic and tunicle. Instead of these, in greater churches, they wear FOLDED CHASUBLES.[3] The chasubles are now generally folded up in front about half-way and so fixed. They are taken off during the principal parts of the Mass, as will be explained (p. 245). When the deacon takes off the folded chasuble in Mass, according to the rubrics of the Missal he should fold it again lengthwise and wear it, like the stole, over the left shoulder. Instead of this he generally puts on a garment made specially to represent this folded chasuble, namely a long piece of silk, violet, or black on Good Friday. This is popularly called the BROAD STOLE (Italian *stolone*). It is not really a stole at all.[4] "Greater churches" are cathedrals, collegiate churches, parish churches and the chief churches of Regulars. They include therefore nearly all churches in England. In others the ministers wear simply the usual vestments without the dalmatic or tunicle.[5] As a rule the celebrant wears the chasuble only at Mass. Normally also, the maniple is not worn except at Mass. One exception to this is when, on Palm Sunday, the ministers read lessons during the blessing of the palms before Mass. Then, although the celebrant has the cope and no maniple, they wear the maniple while reading the lessons.

The Cope. During the solemn blessings in the Missal (as on Candlemas, Ash Wednesday and Palm Sunday), in processions, at the Asperges

[1] C.E. I. x, 1. The deacon and subdeacon also wear dalmatic and tunicle at the Asperges, in processions and at Exposition and Benediction, but not at the Divine Office.

[2] See p. 245.

[3] R.G. xix, 6.

[4] The only reason for the so-called " broad stole " is that the modern chasuble is rarely so made that it can be folded into a long strip, as the rubrics say. The rubrics provide for the alternative use of the " broad stole " (*aliud genus stolae latioris, in modum planetae plicatae*).

[5] R.G. xix, 7. They may wear folded chasubles in any church.

ceremony before Mass, at funerals, at Benediction of the Blessed Sacrament, at Vespers and Lauds sung solemnly, at Matins from the ninth lesson, the celebrant wears a COPE (*pluviale*). This is a large semicircular garment reaching to the feet behind, with a band [1] (having a large hook and eye) to join it in front.

Usually the cope is of the colour of the day. At Benediction of the Blessed Sacrament it is white,[2] at funerals always black. For the more solemn blessings the colour is violet (e.g., the blessing of candles, ashes, palms). Except in the Divine Office the celebrant wears a stole of the same colour under the cope.

At the Divine office he wears either a surplice only, or surplice and cope. At processions and Benediction of the Blessed Sacrament he will generally wear a surplice, stole and cope. When he holds the monstrance or ciborium he has a white humeral veil. At blessings before Mass he has the amice, alb, girdle and stole. When he wears the girdle he crosses the stole before the breast. With a surplice it hangs straight down from the neck.

Other persons besides the celebrant wear the cope. The assistant priest at Mass (when there is one, see p. 134) does so. At Mass by a simple priest no one else may wear a cope except at a priest's first Mass when it is solemnly sung. Then the practice of·having an assistant priest in cope is tolerated.[3] At the Divine Office (Vespers and Lauds) the cantors may wear copes of the colour of the Office. At certain pontifical functions and at the procession of the Blessed Sacrament at Corpus Christi some of the clergy wear copes.

When preaching the preacher, if a secular priest, wears a surplice. He may wear a stole of the colour of the day, if this is the custom. Regulars who have a habit wear no surplice as a rule. In administering sacraments and sacramentals the priest normally wears a surplice and stole.

The Dress of a Bishop. The usual dress of a BISHOP is a cloth cassock, violet in colour, with a train, fixed up at the back so that it does not trail on the ground. The train is let down at functions. The cassock is edged with and has buttons of a lighter colour, now almost red. The bishop wears a violet silk belt. Over the cassock he wears a white linen rochet. Over this a bishop in his own diocese wears the mozzetta. Auxiliaries and all bishops where they have no jurisdiction wear the mantellettum (p. 10) instead.[4] Bishops wear a pectoral cross, which should hang from the neck by a green and gold

---

[1] A morse (*formale, pectorale*), i.e., a metal clasp ornamented with jewels, etc., may be used only by the Bishop or a higher prelate (C.E. I. vii, 1; II. i, 4; cf S.R.C. 2425[9]) in the place of his jurisdiction.

[2] When Benediction immediately follows Mass or Vespers and the celebrant does not leave the sanctuary, the colour of the cope will be that of the Mass or Office, unless this be black (S.R.C. 1615[6], 2562, 3175[3], 3799[2], 3949[7]).

[3] S.R.C. 3564[2].

[4] The mozzetta alone over the rochet is always understood to signify jurisdiction. In the presence of superiors, bishops, even in their own diocese, wear the mantellettum, and sometimes over this the mozzetta.

silk cord when the bishop is wearing choir dress. They use a violet skull cap [1] and a violet biretta.[2] On certain days of penance or mourning it is becoming that the cassock, mozzetta and mantellettum should be of black cloth, the cassock edged with violet. These days are all fast days (except Quarter Tense of Pentecost), and in addition the season of Advent and from Septuagesima to Lent (except on great feasts).[3] Black is laudably used also at Requiem functions.

At functions, instead of the mozzetta, the Bishop of the diocese may wear the " cappa magna." [4] This is a great cloak with a long train, of violet cloth. It has a cape and hood, which in winter is of ermine, in summer of almost red silk. When the Bishop wears the cappa magna he needs a train-bearer. Regular bishops have the cappa, and its fur, of the colour of their order (if it has a special habit).

Pius IX instituted a kind of undress for prelates, called after him " habitus pianus." It consists of a black cloth cassock with no train, crimson facings, a violet belt and ferraiolo, violet stock and stockings. This is now used constantly at non-liturgical functions.

CARDINALS have the same dress as bishops, but always bright red instead of violet, and violet instead of black for mourning. Round their hat bishops have a green [5] cord, archbishops green and gold,[6] cardinals red and gold.

For Low Mass a bishop wears the same vestments as a priest, over the rochet.[7] The only difference is that he wears the pectoral cross over the alb, under the stole. He wears the stole not crossed, but hanging straight down. He does not put on the maniple till after the prayer " Indulgentiam," except at Requiem Masses (p. 67).

At High Mass [8] and at certain Low Masses which sometimes take the place of a solemn Mass (e.g., at Ordinations or the consecration of a bishop) the bishop wears special stockings and shoes [9] of the colour of the Mass. Over the rochet he wears the amice, alb, girdle pectoral cross, stole, tunicle, dalmatic, gloves, chasuble, mitre. On certain occasions a Metropolitan will wear the pallium over the chasuble. The manner of putting these on will be described (pp. 160 sqq.).

The tunicle and dalmatic worn by a bishop are made of very thin silk. They are of the colour of the Mass.

There are three kinds of MITRE (mitra). The " precious mitre "

---

[1] Conceded by Pius IX, 17 June 1867.

[2] Conceded by Leo XIII, 3 February 1888.

[3] C.E. I. iii, 2 ; S.R.C. 4355[1].

[4] See p. 158, n. 1.

[5] Green, not violet, is a bishop's heraldic colour.

[6] The Congregation of Ceremonial granted (3 November 1826) the use of a green *and gold* cord to the four Latin Patriarchs. This privilege was not, it would seem, extended to archbishops, but it is adopted by some of them ; and its use is recognized by some authorities (e.g., Martinucci II. i, p. 6, n. 3 ; Favrin, *Praxis Sollemnium Functionum Episcoporum* (1926), p. 9).

[7] R. I. 2.

[8] But not if it is a Requiem Mass.

[9] These look more like gaiters and slippers. In Latin they are " caligae et sandalia," in English generally " buskins and sandals."

(*mitra pretiosa*) is generally of cloth of gold or of silver with embroidery and ornaments of gold and precious stones. Since this is supposed to be heavy and burdensome if worn all the time, its place is taken during parts of the services by the " gold mitre " (*mitra aurifrigiata*) made of cloth of gold with no additional ornament. The " simple mitre " (*mitra simplex*) is of plain white linen, without ornament. This is worn at certain functions (e.g., at funerals). The bishop also has a RING (*annulus*). In his own diocese the Ordinary carries a CROZIER (*baculus pastoralis*). He has a train to the cappa magna, which is borne by a train-bearer (*caudatarius*). During parts of the Mass a silk veil, called a GREMIAL (*gremiale*), of the colour of the day is laid over his knees while he sits.

On other occasions a bishop wears amice, alb, girdle, pectoral cross, stole, cope and mitre.

Certain other prelates, abbots and protonotaries, may on occasions share some of the marks of a bishop's rank (see pp. 31–36).

Linens.   Besides the vestments, the following cloths are used. The CORPORAL (*corporale*) is a square piece of linen spread on the altar during Mass. The chalice and paten stand on the corporal. When it is not used the corporal lies in the BURSE (*bursa*), a pocket of silk, of the same colour as the vestments, strengthened with cardboard. The PURIFICATOR (*purificatorium*) is a linen cloth folded in three lengthwise, used by the celebrant to wipe the chalice during Mass. The PALL (*palla*) is a small square of stiffened linen, used to cover the chalice at Mass.

The TOWEL (*manutergium*) is also a small linen cloth, not unlike a purificator, used to dry the fingers after the washing at Mass.

Liturgical Colours.   The colours of the silk vestments and insignia (that is, of the chasuble, stole, maniple, dalmatic, tunicle, humeral veil, cope, bishop's gremial, shoes and stockings) vary according to the feast or occasion on which they are used.

The colours of the Roman rite are white, red, green, violet, black, rose-colour.

WHITE (*albus*) is used for all feasts of our Lord, except those of his Cross and Passion, for Trinity Sunday, for all feasts of the Blessed Virgin Mary, of the angels, and of all saints who were not martyrs ; as a colour *de tempore* it is used from Vespers of Christmas to the octave-day of Epiphany, from Easter to the vigil of Pentecost.

RED (*ruber*) is used on Whitsun eve (for Mass), on Whitsunday and during its octave, for the feast of the Precious Blood (1 July), the two feasts of Holy Rood (3 May and 14 September), and for martyrs. It is used on Holy Innocents' Day (28 December) if it fall on a Sunday, and on its octave-day always.

GREEN (*viridis*) is the neutral colour. It is used on Sundays and weekdays from the end of the Epiphany octave to Septuagesima, and on Sundays (except Trinity Sunday and the Sunday within the octave of Corpus Christi and of the feast of the Sacred Heart) and weekdays (except vigils and Quarter Tense) in the season after Pentecost.

VIOLET (*violaceus*) is the colour of penance. It is used on Sundays and weekdays of Advent and from Septuagesima to the Wednesday of Holy Week, except (in some churches) on the third Sunday of Advent and the fourth of Lent. Violet is also used on vigils (except those of Epiphany, Ascension and, in part, Pentecost), when the Office is of the vigil; on Ember days, except those in Whitsun week; on the Greater and Lesser Litanies; on the feast of the Holy Innocents, if it does not fall on a Sunday; for the more solemn blessings and for many votive Masses. On Holy Saturday and Whitsun eve the lessons and collects before the Mass with the Litanies are said in violet vestments, the Mass itself in white (Easter) or red (Whitsun).

BLACK (*niger*) is used on Good Friday, for Masses for the dead and at funerals.

ROSE-COLOUR (*color rosaceus*) may be used on two occasions, the third Sunday of Advent (called *Gaudete* Sunday) and the fourth of Lent (*Laetare* Sunday). If the church does not possess vestments of this colour violet is used in its stead.

The Congregation of Sacred Rites tolerates the use of real cloth of silver to replace white and real cloth of gold in place of white, red or green (not of violet or black).[1]

When Vespers are so divided that the second half, from the Chapter, is of the following feast, then the frontal and copes are of the colour of the second half throughout Vespers.

The colour for processions and Benediction of the Blessed Sacrament is white. But if Benediction or procession follows immediately after Mass or Vespers, and the celebrant does not leave the sanctuary, the colour of the day may be kept.[2] Only, in any case, the humeral veil must be white. The vestments worn by the celebrant and ministers at Mass must be blessed by a bishop or by a priest to whom this faculty has been given.[3] It is not strictly necessary to bless the cope. The burse, chalice veil, humeral veil and surplice need not be blessed but may be and often are.

[1] S.R.C. 3145, 3191[4], 3646[2, 3].
[2] See above, p. 12, note 2, and S.R.C. 1615[6], 2562, 3175[3].
[3] R. I, 2; cf. C.J.C. 1304.

CHAPTER III
LITURGICAL VESSELS, INSTRUMENTS AND BOOKS

§ 1. VESSELS

THE chief sacred vessels used in the Liturgy are the CHALICE (*calix*) and PATEN (*patena*), the forms of which are well known. The chalice, if it is not of gold, must be at least gilt inside the cup ; the paten, too, must be gilt at least on the upper side.

The CIBORIUM is a vessel like a chalice with a cover, at least gilt inside. It is used to contain the consecrated particles in the tabernacle. When it contains the Blessed Sacrament, or when exposed to public view [1] (e.g., on the altar before Mass awaiting consecration), it should be covered with a veil of white silk. At the Consecration, if used, it stands open on the corporal by the chalice.

In the tabernacle there is also generally a PYX (*pyxis, custodia*), a small box of silver or other metal, gilt inside, which contains the Host used for Benediction. This Host is usually held by a little instrument, shaped like a new moon, called the LUNETTE (*lunula*). This, too, must be at least gilt. The general principle is that the Sanctissimum may rest only on gold or white linen. The MONSTRANCE (*ostensorium*) is a vessel for exposing the Blessed Sacrament. It is so made that the Host may be placed in it and can then be seen by the people. Often the place where the Host rests is surrounded by rays. The Sanctissimum may not touch glass.

There is also a small pyx or ciborium used when the Holy Communion is taken to the sick. This, too, must be at least gilt inside.

The chalice and paten are consecrated by a bishop or other cleric having the necessary faculty. The pyx, ciborium and lunette are blessed by a bishop or by a priest having the faculty.[2] There is no law that the monstrance be blessed but it often is.[2]

Other vessels, not counted as sacred and not blessed, are :

For Mass the CRUETS (*ampullae, hamulae*). These are two little jugs to hold the wine and water. They should be of clear glass ; but other material is tolerated. Sometimes their purpose is marked on them ; the one having the letter V (for " vinum," wine), the other A (" aqua," water). Otherwise, since they should be always washed out and kept perfectly clean, it does not matter which is used each time for the wine or water. The cruets should have stoppers or lids or at least be covered, when filled, with the finger towel to keep out dust, insects, etc. With

---

[1] So some rubricians on the principle that sacred vessels exposed to view, and not in use are to be veiled (e.g., the chalice, the monstrance). The rubrics are not explicit, and other rubricians teach that the ciborium is veiled only when it contains the Sanctissimum.

[2] The form of blessing is in R.R. VIII. xxiii.

them is the DISH (*pelvicula*) on which they stand when not in use. This is not merely used as a stand for the cruets ; when the celebrant washes his hands at Mass, the water may be poured by the server over his fingers into this dish, or, more conveniently, there is a separate bowl for this purpose. With the cruets and dish a TOWEL (*manutergium*) is laid on the credence. The celebrant dries his fingers with this after washing them.

A bishop uses a larger jug (*bacile*) of water and a dish of silver or other metal (gold or gilt for a cardinal). His towel is generally larger too.

§ 2. INSTRUMENTS

For the sprinkling with holy water before Mass (the Asperges ceremony) and for blessing any object a portable HOLY-WATER STOUP (*vas aquae benedictae*) and SPRINKLER (*aspersorium*,[1] *aspergillum*) are used. The stoup is of metal, the sprinkler has a brush at the end, or a hollow globe with holes in it.

The THURIBLE (*thuribulum*) is a vessel, round in shape, hanging by three long chains from a disk. Held by this disk it can be swung. It has a cover which hangs by a fourth chain from a ring passing through the disk. By pulling up this ring the thurible may be opened. Generally there is another ring round all the chains to keep them together. The INCENSE-BOAT (*navicella*, *navicula*, *acerra*) is a little vessel, shaped like a boat, in which the incense is kept. It has a SPOON (*cochlear*) with which the incense is put on the burning charcoal in the thurible. In the sacristy are kept the ACOLYTES' CANDLES in tall candlesticks.[2] These are so made, with a foot, that they can stand without being held, for instance on the credence. There are also TORCHES (*funalia*) held by the torch-bearers (*caeroferarii*) at Mass and Benediction. In theory these should be long torches. It is now usual to make them in the form of a separate case (practically a candlestick) into which a candle is placed. But the idea of a torch is so far preserved that they have no foot, and cannot stand alone. When not in use they are kept in a rack in the sacristy.

The PROCESSIONAL CROSS is fixed to a long staff, also so made that it cannot stand alone. In Catholic churches it now always has a figure of our Lord crucified.

For processions of the Blessed Sacrament a portable CANOPY (*baldachinum*, *umbraculum*) is used. It has four or more poles.[3] For short processions in the church, as when the Sanctissimum is carried from one altar to another, a smaller canopy (*umbella*) with one rod, like an umbrella, is used. For the Blessed Sacrament both must be white [4] or cloth of gold.

The SANCTUS BELL (*campanula*, *squilla*) is a small hand-bell (not a

---

[1] " Aspersory " is used also for the holy-water container.

[2] In pontifical functions, while the prelate reads, a server holds a small hand-candle in a portable candlestick (*scotula*, *palmatorium*), near the book.

[3] C.E. I. xiv, 1, says it has six or eight poles, borne by " noble laymen."

[4] C.E. I. xiv, 1.

gong) [1] rung during Mass at the moments appointed in the rubrics of the Missal. It is placed on the credence before Mass and taken away afterwards. A STAND or cushion [2] is needed, on which to rest the Missal at Mass.

For the kiss of peace, instead of the more usual way of giving it (p. 26), sometimes a little disk is used (cf. p. 64). This is the PAX-BREDE (*pax, instrumentum pacis, tabella pacis*). It is generally a disk of silver or gilt, with a handle to hold it. On the face it has some such symbol as the cross, the Agnus Dei, a pelican in her piety. If this pax-brede is used it should have a cloth of linen to wipe it each time after it has been kissed.

Near the tabernacle where the Sanctissimum is reserved a little vessel should be kept, generally of glass, with water.[3] The priest uses this to purify the fingers when he gives Holy Communion not in Mass ; or sometimes when he cannot make the ablutions at Mass in the usual way, because he will say Mass again the same day. It has a small purificator by it.

§ 3. BOOKS

THERE are six chief liturgical books of the Roman rite.

The MISSAL (*Missale Romanum*) contains all that is needed for Mass, and for certain other functions which take place immediately before Mass, such as the blessings at Candlemas, on Ash Wednesday, Palm Sunday, the morning services on the last three days of Holy Week, certain blessings (of lustral water, etc.). It also has the preparation and thanksgiving of the celebrant before and after Mass.

The BREVIARY (*Breviarium Romanum*) contains all the Divine Office for the year.

The MARTYROLOGY is a calendar, giving the names and a short statement about martyrs and other saints, each on his day. It is read or sung, where the Divine Office is said in choir, during Prime.

The RITUAL (*Rituale Romanum*) has the administration of the Sacraments, many blessings, prayers for processions and such liturgical functions, as far as they are used by a priest. There is less uniformity in the Ritual than in any other liturgical book. Many provinces and dioceses still have their own Ritual book, based on the Roman one. Throughout England the official Ritual, approved by the English hierarchy, is the ORDO ADMINISTRANDI SACRAMENTA (see p. 377).

The PONTIFICAL (*Pontificale Romanum*) is the book for bishops. It contains the Sacraments and other functions performed by a bishop, such as Confirmation and Ordination, the consecration of a church, and so on.

---

[1] The use of an Indian (hanging) gong is not permitted (S.R.C. 4000³).

[2] C.E. I. xii, 15, says it is a cushion of silk, of the liturgical colour, or a small silver or ornamented wooden stand (*legile*). A stand is far more convenient and also looks better than a cushion.

[3] This water, and all water used for ablutions, must be put in the piscina (*sacrarium*), a channel leading to clean earth, generally behind the altar.

The CEREMONIAL OF BISHOPS (*Caerimoniale Episcoporum*) is a directory of ceremonies for bishops and others who take part in public services.[1]

The MEMORIALE RITUUM of Benedict XIII describes functions for six days of the year—Candlemas, Ash Wednesday, and Holy Week—as performed in small parish churches (see pp. 252 *sqq*).

There are other books consisting of parts of these official books printed separately for convenience. There is no reason why any special service should not be printed in a separate book, so long as it conforms to the text in the book from which it is taken.

From the Missal the BOOK OF LESSONS is taken. This contains the Epistles and Gospels for the year, to be used by the deacon and sub-deacon at High Mass. There may be two such books, one of epistles and one of gospels (*Epistolarium* and *Evangeliarium*). If the church does not possess this book, a Missal may always be used in its stead. The GRADUAL (*Graduale Romanum*) contains the parts of the Missal needed by the choir, with music. The Masses for the dead are often printed in a separate book (*Missale Defunctorum*).

There are many excerpts from the Breviary. The DAY HOURS (*Horae Diurnae*) contains all the Office except Matins. For use in the choir various extracts are made, with the music, such as the VESPERAL (*Vesperale Romanum*) and DIRECTORIVM CHORI. A HOLY WEEK BOOK (*Officium Hebdomadae Maioris*) contains what is needed for the services of Holy Week, taken from the Missal and Breviary.

In England we have a book, RITVS SERVANDVS, approved by S.R.C. and by the hierarchy, which contains directions and the prayers for Benediction of the Blessed Sacrament and some non-liturgical services.[2] In Ireland there is a similar but unofficial publication entitled " Benedictionale." [3]

The Ceremonial (I. xii, 15) says that, at pontifical functions, and, at other solemn functions too,[4] all the liturgical books used (the Missal, book of lessons, Vesperal, Pontifical Canon,[5] etc.) are covered with silk of the liturgical colour.

The ALTAR-CARDS (*Tabella Secretarum*) contain certain prayers from the Missal, printed separately for the convenience of the celebrant. There are usually three altar-cards. The largest, containing the words of consecration and other prayers, stands in the middle of the altar,

[1] This book (C.E.), although intended in the first place for bishops, contains very full directions for all people at most functions ; so that, in spite of its title, it is really a book of ceremonies in general.

[2] *Ritus servandus in solemni expositione et benedictione sanctissimi Sacramenti adiectis hymnis et litaniis et orationibus quae in ipsa expositione et in aliis quibusdam sacris ritibus adhiberi solent* (Burns and Oates, new edition, 1928), see p. 231.

[3] " *Benedictionale* " *seu Ritus in Expositione et Benedictione SS. Sacramenti cui adjunctae sunt quaedam preces in piis exercitiis per annum occurrentibus adhibendae*, compiled by Rev. J. O'Connell (Brepols, Turnhout, 1930). There is a special edition for Great Britain (1930) and for U.S.A. (1930).

[4] Cf. C.E. I. xii, 22.

[5] A book containing the Ordinary and Canon of the Mass and some liturgical forms proper to prelates. At Mass it is used, instead of altar cards, by prelates.

leaning against the cross or tabernacle during Mass. The altar-card which contains the prayer at the blessing of water (" Deus qui humanae substantiae ") and the Lavabo psalm stands at the Epistle end ; the third, containing the last Gospel, at the Gospel end.[1] The altar-cards are used only at Mass. They should be put in their places on the altar, as part of the preparation for Mass, and taken away afterwards.

A card with the prayers ordered by Pope Leo XIII to be said after private Mass (and so sometimes called the Leonine prayers) is placed on the credence.

[1] This chart need not be put on the altar when the last Gospel is a proper one.

CHAPTER IV

COMMON CEREMONIAL ACTIONS

THERE are many actions, such as bowing, genuflecting, and so on, which occur constantly during all services. In order not to have to explain these each time, it will be convenient to say here, once for all, how they should be done.

On changing from sitting to kneeling first stand, then kneel. Never slide directly on to the knees.

To make a GENUFLECTION, first stand upright facing the object or person to whom it is to be made. Unless something is held, the hands are joined palm to palm before the breast. Then, without bending the body or the head, touch the ground with the right knee at exactly the place where the right foot was. Rise again at once.

A PROSTRATION or double genuflection is made by first genuflecting as above ; then, before rising, touch the ground with the left knee where the left foot stood. Now, kneeling on both knees, bow the head and shoulders slightly.[1]

Everyone who passes the altar where the Sanctissimum is reserved, unless forming part of a procession, genuflects to the Sanctissimum as he passes. Where It is reserved on the High Altar, on entering the church genuflect before It, either as soon as you enter or before going to your place. Genuflect again before going out. In ceremonial entrances everyone except the celebrant genuflects to the altar on entering and before leaving. But the celebrant genuflects only when the Sanctissimum is reserved at the altar ; otherwise he bows low.[2]

If the Blessed Sacrament is exposed, that is, during the rite of Exposition, on entering or leaving the church make a prostration. At a function everyone makes this prostration on entering and before leaving the church ; during the service normally they genuflect only. When the Sanctissimum is reserved at the so-called " altar of repose " on Maundy Thursday and Good Friday morning It is treated as if It were exposed.

A genuflection is made to a relic of the true cross, if it is exposed, also to the cross when unveiled on Good Friday. A cardinal everywhere (outside Rome), a bishop in his own diocese, a metropolitan in his province, a Papal Legate or a Nuncio or an Apostolic Delegate in the place of his jurisdiction, an abbot in his own church, is saluted by a genuflection when he is present in vestments or in choir dress. But the genuflection is not made to a bishop or other prelate in the presence of his superior or outside the place of his jurisdiction. Prelates,

---

[1] Prostration in this sense must not be confused with the " prostratio " (lying prostrate), e.g., on Good Friday (p. 292) and Holy Saturday (p. 320).

[2] This rule applies also to canons in their own cathedral or collegiate church and prelates.

canons in their official dress, the celebrant at Mass or other services, do not genuflect to anyone. Instead they bow low.

If the head is covered it is always uncovered before genuflecting except when the priest is carrying the chalice.

If one is about to kneel immediately at the same place as a general rule one does not first genuflect nor make a prostration. But if one is to kneel on a step, then the genuflection is first made on the ground. Rising from this one then kneels on the step.

At the beginning and end of Mass the genuflection is made on the ground (this is called *in plano*). During Mass it is made on the lowest step of the altar by those in sacred vestments (*parati*).

The cross-bearer, while holding the processional cross, never genuflects.[1] When the acolytes accompany him they do not genuflect either. When an archbishop gives his blessing, then only does his cross-bearer kneel before him, holding the archiepiscopal cross turned towards him (p. 150).

Bows. The rubrics prescribe several kinds of BOWS (*reverentia, inclinatio*). Thus sometimes they say that the person is *profunde inclinatus*, sometimes that he is *aliquantulum inclinatus*, sometimes merely *inclinatus ;* or they say *caput inclinat*. Generally three bows are distinguished. A LOW BOW (*profunda inclinatio*) is made by bending the head and body so that the hands might touch the knees if they hung down ; though, as a matter of fact, they are kept joined before the breast. The MEDIUM or MODERATE BOW (*media inclinatio*) is made by bending the head and shoulders less low than before. The SIMPLE BOW is made by bending the head either in a marked way [2] (which involves a slight bending of the shoulders) or not so deeply (a bow of the head alone).

The general rules for bowing are these :

In bowing always keep the hands joined before the breast, unless they hold something. The celebrant bows low to the cross at the beginning and end of services. When one does not genuflect to a prelate, then he receives a low bow. The medium bow is usually made to persons of higher rank than one's own. The head alone is bowed to greet persons of equal or less dignity. The head is bowed deeply when certain words are said : for instance, at the Holy Name ; when the three Divine Persons are named *Pater et Filius et Spiritus Sanctus ;* at *Oremus ;* and during the *Gloria in excelsis*, and the Creed at the verses so indicated in the Missal. The head is bowed less deeply at the name " Mary " of the Blessed Virgin, at the mention of the name of the saint of the day,[3] at that of the Pope and of the Bishop.[4] When one bows at the Holy Name or at *Oremus* one should—if standing—turn to the altar cross (except during the Gospel). In other cases of a bow at a word recited or sung, it is done straight in front of one, without turning. People who are already bowing during any part of a

---

[1] M.R. I. ii, § III, 5.
[2] This is called a deep bow of the head.   [3] Cf. p. 48, n. 3.
[4] When a prayer for him is said aloud.

service make no further motion on these occasions. Neither does anyone bow when he is impeded (e.g., while he is making the sign of the cross) Everyone bows, before and after being incensed, to the person who incenses him ; and he bows, before and after, to the person incensed (see p. 26).

While standing or kneeling, when the hands are unoccupied, they should be joined before the breast ; that is, they are extended and joined palm to palm, the fingers pointing upward, the thumbs crossed. When sitting the hands should be extended one on each knee. In genuflecting at the altar the celebrant alone lays the hands on it while doing so ; the ministers and all others keep the hands joined. When something is held in one hand the other should be extended on the breast ; but the celebrant at the altar and facing it lays the other hand on it. In bowing, the head is always first uncovered. When one takes off the biretta it is held in the right hand by the raised edge on its right side. When standing hold the biretta against the breast with both hands. When sitting rest the biretta on the right knee, while the left hand lies extended on the left knee. If several names or texts, at each of which a bow should be made, follow one another immediately it is more seemly to bow once and to remain bowing till all have been said. Those who wear a skull-cap [1] in choir take it off whenever they genuflect or bow to the altar, when they receive the sprinkling of holy water, while they say the *Confiteor, Misereatur, Kyrie eleison, Gloria in excelsis*, Creed, *Sanctus, Agnus Dei* at Mass, while the Gospel is sung, while they are incensed, from the Preface to the Communion (inclusive), at the Blessing. Also whenever the Sanctissimum is exposed ; during the Gospel at Matins, at the Confession at Prime and Compline. No one wears the skull-cap when he intones the antiphons and the psalms, sings the Invitatorium, lessons, short responsories, or Martyrology.

In the Roman rite the SIGN OF THE CROSS is made thus : Place the left hand extended under the breast. Hold the right hand extended also. At the words *Patris* raise it and touch the forehead ; at *Filii* touch the breast at a sufficient distance down, but above the left hand ; at *Spiritus Sancti* touch the left and right shoulders ; at *Amen* join the hands if they are to be joined. When the sign is made with other words the same order is kept. In making the small sign of the cross, the left hand is laid flat under the breast, the right, fully extended (palm inwards) and pointed towards the left, is carried to the forehead and with the left corner of the fleshy part of the thumb (separated from the fingers) a small sign of the cross with equal arms (+) is traced on the forehead, touching the skin. The same action is repeated on the closed lips and in the middle of the breast.

Ceremonial Kisses. The ceremonial KISS (*osculum*), which occurs frequently, should be made by merely touching the object with the closed lips. The rule is that every time anyone hands anything to

---

[1] When celebrating Mass only a cardinal, a bishop or a blessed abbot may— apart from Apostolic indult—wear a skull-cap (C.J.C. 811, § 2).

the celebrant one kisses first the object, then the celebrant's hand. On taking things from the celebrant, first his hand, then the thing is kissed. But blessed candles and palms are kissed first when they are taken. When the Sanctissimum is exposed, only the kiss at the Epistle, Gospel and for the chalice and paten and of the celebrant's hand when presenting them remain.[1] The thurible is then not kissed, nor the incense spoon. If the Ordinary assists at his throne the thurible is not kissed when handed to the celebrant, nor the incense spoon, nor the celebrant's hand at the Epistle and Gospel, nor his biretta. At Masses for the dead and at funerals nothing is kissed (except the altar and the paten by the celebrant).

The Thurible. To handle a THURIBLE neatly is a thing that requires some knowledge. This knowledge is acquired most easily by seeing the actions done by someone who already knows. It is one of the many things, not really difficult or complicated, that require many words to explain.[2]

Except when the Sanctissimum is exposed (including the Elevation at a solemn or sung Mass), incense is always blessed by the celebrant before it is used.[3] When the Sanctissimum is exposed and will *alone* be incensed, incense is put in the thurible by the celebrant without blessing ; but if both the Sanctissimum and, e.g., the altar are to be incensed the incense is then blessed.

When the thurifer merely holds the thurible, while waiting for it to be used, he does so by the chains, just under the disk at top ; if incense has not yet been put in ceremonially, he holds it in the left hand, otherwise in the right.[4] When the thurible is not in use the lid should be raised slightly to allow more ventilation to the burning charcoal and to keep the lid cool. To raise the lid the ring at the end of the middle chain joined to it should be pulled up.

In holding the thurible the thumb may be passed through the ring of the disk, the middle finger through the movable ring, or the thumb through this and the little finger through the disk ring. With the thumb the ring may be drawn up easily, so as to open the thurible below. Holding the thurible in this way the thurifer swings it gently, to keep the charcoal alight. The other hand, holding the boat,[5] should be laid on the breast. But when he is kneeling the chains are so long that, if he held the thurible this way, it would be on the ground. So, when kneeling, he holds the chains under the disk in the left hand

---

[1] Martinucci-Menghini, I. i, pp. 11–12. These kisses are an intrinsic part of the solemnity of the rite of High Mass of the living, and are not mere acts of liturgical politeness.

[2] Cf. O'Connell, *The Celebration of Mass* (III, p. 29).

[3] Except also the cases when it is blessed by a higher dignitary present, as will be noted in place.

[4] So many rubricians teach.

[5] In some churches it is usual to employ another server as " boat-bearer." There is no provision for such a server in any official book ; nor do the authors of books on ceremonies say anything about him. If he is employed the boat-bearer will stand or kneel at the thurifer's left, and will always hand him the boat before he approaches the celebrant and he himself will stand aside.

held against the breast, takes the chains about half-way down in the right and so swings the thurible.

When the thurifer brings the incense to be blessed he first hands the boat to the deacon (or M.C. if there is no deacon). Then he takes the chains under the disk in the left hand. With the right hand he pulls the ring up, to open the thurible sufficiently, so that the celebrant may conveniently put in the incense. He takes the chains more than half-way down in the right hand, holding them close to the top of the cover of the thurible, and so holds up the thurible in front of the celebrant at a convenient height. At the same time he lays the left hand, holding the disk, on his breast. He should not stand too near the celebrant. The celebrant needs a certain amount of room to put out his hand and put in the incense.

Meanwhile the deacon (or, if there is no deacon, the M.C.) opens the incense-boat, takes the spoon and hands it to the celebrant, with the usual kiss of the spoon and the celebrant's hand. At the same time he says *Benedicite, Pater reverende.* The celebrant takes the spoon; with it he takes a little incense from the boat and puts it on the live charcoal in the thurible. He repeats this a second and third time. Meanwhile the deacon (or M.C.) holds the boat open, that he can do so conveniently. While putting on the incense the celebrant says *Ab illo benedicaris in cuius honore cremaberis. Amen.* (Only on one occasion, at the Offertory in Mass, is there another formula : *Per intercessionem bcati Michaelis archangeli,* etc., as in the Missal.) Then he hands the spoon back to the deacon (or M.C.), who receives it with the usual kisses. The celebrant, having joined his hands for a moment, makes the sign of the cross over the thurible, saying nothing. While he does so he lays the left hand on his breast.

On occasions when the incense is not blessed, namely, when the Sanctissimum is exposed, and It *alone* is to be incensed, neither the deacon nor the celebrant say anything ; nor does the celebrant make the sign of the cross.

The thurifer waits till the incense is put in and the sign of the cross made (if it is to be made). Then he lowers the thurible. He shuts down the cover ; if there is a ring round the chains he puts this down over the cover to hold it firm. Then he hands the thurible to the deacon (or M.C.). To do this he holds the upper part of the chains under the disk in his right hand and presents the ring at the top to the deacon. The deacon takes it and hands it to the celebrant, who proceeds to incense the altar, or whatever is to be incensed.

Incensation. The particular directions for incensing the altar, persons or things will be given at their place in the ceremonies. Here we note only the manner of incensing any person or thing in general.

To INCENSE anything or anyone take the top of the chains of the thurible in the left hand and place it against the breast. Take the chains close above the shut cover in the right. It is important not to hold the chains far from the cover, or the thurible will swing out too far and will perhaps get entangled in the chains. The most convenient way of holding the chains in the right hand is to pass them all together between the first and second fingers. The second, third and fourth fingers, lying together, are then under the chains. By moving the hand upwards the thurible is cast outwards towards the thing incensed.

There are two ways of incensing : with a SIMPLE swing (*ductus simplex*) and with a DOUBLE swing (*ductus duplex*). The simple swing is made in this way : lift the right hand to the level of the breast only, at the same time swing the thurible out towards the thing to be incensed and let it fall at once towards one's self. The double swing is made by raising the thurible to the level of the face, then swinging it out towards the object or person to be incensed, repeating this outward swing and then lowering the thurible.

When incensing, the person who incenses should as a rule bow to the person (or object) incensed before and after. The person incensed normally bows each time in return, but stands upright with joined hands, facing the incenser, while he is incensed.

The thurible is handed back to the deacon or other person who is to receive it. He, as usual, kisses first the hand, then the disk of the thurible when it is handed back by the celebrant.

The Kiss of Peace. The KISS OF PEACE at Mass is given in this way. The two persons stand facing each other with hands joined. The one who is to receive the kiss bows. Then the one who gives it lays his hands on the shoulders of the other ; the receiver clasps the arms of the other, holding them at the elbows. Each bows the head forward, so that the left cheeks of the two persons almost touch. The one who gives the kiss says *Pax tecum*. The other answers *Et cum spiritu tuo*. Then they withdraw a little and stand again with joined hands facing each other, and both bow.

CHAPTER V

THE CHOIR AND ASSISTANTS AT CEREMONIES

§ 1. THE LITURGICAL CHOIR

WE must note first that the " choir " during a service does not necessarily mean those who sing. It was so originally. In theory, no doubt, it should be so still, namely, that the singers have their places right and left of the altar and sing there. But there are often practical difficulties against this. In singing part-music especially it is often difficult to produce a good artistic effect when the singers are arranged in two rows facing each other, perhaps at some distance, across the church. Often, therefore, the actual singers are placed elsewhere, in a space together at the side behind a grating, behind the altar, or in a gallery at the other end of the church. In such cases no notice is taken of them during the ceremonies.

There remains, however, the possibility that a liturgical " choir " may assist at the service ; even if they sing only part, or none, of the chants.

Thus canons in cathedral and collegiate churches, Regulars in the churches of their Order, clergy of any kind, may assist in the seats or stalls on either side, before the altar. These then form " the choir " from the point of view of ceremonies.

They are dressed in cassock and surplice with biretta, or in their special " choir dress." Dignitaries wear the dress appropriate to their dignity (p. 10). Regulars generally wear the habit of their Order [1]; and do not wear the surplice over it in choir.

Choir Ceremonies. On entering the choir its members may come in procession (with or without a processional cross), the celebrant wearing vestments.[2] In this case the younger or inferior members walk in front of the elder or superior ones. But when they enter, not in solemn procession, that is, without either a cross or celebrant vested, the more dignified walk before the others.

They walk two and two, at equal distances from each other, with head covered till they come into the church.[3] At the entrance to the church they uncover and take holy water (unless the Asperges is to take place), the one nearer the stoup giving it to his companion by dipping his own fingers and holding them towards the other, who touches them. Both then make the sign of the cross.

---

[1] Namely if their Order has a recognized habit.

[2] To wear vestments (chasuble, cope, dalmatic or tunicle) is what liturgical books mean by being " paratus." To wear even a surplice and stole (as when, e.g., going to administer Holy Communion) is regarded as being " paratus."

[3] Within the church and not seated no one—whatever his rank—may wear the biretta unless he is *paratus*. A preacher wears it in the pulpit.

Before the altar each pair genuflects in turn,[1] taking care to do so exactly together. They then salute one another with a bow. So they go to their places.

In their places they either stand or kneel or sit, as will be said in the case of each function. The general rule is that when they sit they cover the head, except when the Blessed Sacrament is exposed. They never stand or kneel with covered head. Before standing they take off the biretta ; they put it on again after they have sat down. Those who wear a skull-cap wear this while standing. They take it off on the occasions noted at p. 23.

While members of the choir assist at a service at the High Altar they should take no notice of anything that happens in any other part of the church, for instance, private Mass said at a side altar. If, however, Mass is being celebrated at an altar in sight of the choir, and the bell be rung at the Elevation (it ought not), then those in choir uncover, but do not kneel nor interrupt the Office in which they are engaged.

If anyone has to leave the choir or come to it alone, he must take care not to do so while any text is being said or sung, at which the others have to perform a ceremonial act, such as bowing. Thus, no one should leave the choir or enter while the verse *Gloria Patri* at the end of a psalm is sung, nor while those in choir are sprinkled with holy water, nor while they say the *Confiteor, Kyrie, Gloria in excelsis*, Creed, *Sanctus, Agnus Dei* at Mass, nor while the Collect(s), Gospel, Post-communion(s) are sung, nor while his side of the choir receives the Pax or is being incensed, nor during any short verse at which they bow or genuflect.

If a person has to enter the choir alone it is usual to kneel first in the middle, say a short prayer, then rise, genuflect (or bow if a canon or prelate and the Blessed Sacrament be not present), bow to the celebrant if he is at the sedile, bow to either side of the choir, beginning with the side of greater dignity, and go to his place.

When anyone has to leave the choir alone he uncovers and rises ; holding his biretta in his hands he goes to the middle, reverences to the cross, bows first to the celebrant, if he is sitting at the sedile, then to each side of the choir, beginning with the side of greater dignity, and goes out. As a general rule, the Gospel side is considered that of greater dignity. This side will then generally be incensed before the other, will receive the kiss of peace first, and so on. The exception is that, if a person of higher rank be present, the side on which he sits is considered the one of greater dignity. Such a person would be a prelate, the hebdomadary,[2] and so on.

At many functions, such as, for instance, High Mass following Terce, the choir will already be in their places when the procession for Mass

---

[1] If the Sanctissimum be not present, canons and prelates make a low bow to the cross of the altar.

[2] A choir official, i.e., the canon or religious appointed to act for a week (*hebdomada*) as the officiant at the choral recitation of the Canonical Hours and the celebration of the Capitular or Conventual Mass.

enters. In this case on the approach of the procession the clergy in choir stand and the clergy and servers in the procession bow to the choir, first to the side of greater dignity, then genuflect to the altar, as will be noted (p. 96).

In standing and kneeling the members of the choir face each other across the church. They do not turn to the altar, except on the special occasions when the rubrics direct them to do so.

We shall note in each case the particular rules for the choir as to standing, kneeling, bowing and so on. Here occur only certain occasions in general when the choir always bow. They are the *Gloria Patri* verse after the psalms (not the verse *Sicut erat in principio*) whenever the three Divine persons are named,[1] and whenever the Holy Name occurs. In this case they bow during the words *Iesus Christus*, not merely during the first of these. They bow the head slightly at the name *Maria* (of the blessed Virgin), at the name of the Saint of the day, of the reigning Pope, of the Ordinary. They bow in return whenever anyone bows to them.

It is important that when there is any common action to be performed by all, such as rising, kneeling, bowing, they should do so uniformly together.

All text books of ceremonial insist on certain obvious points of deportment in choir. It goes without saying that the members of the choir should know what they have to do beforehand, so as to be ready to act at once when the time comes. Although their part of the ceremony is comparatively small, nevertheless they have a part in it. They must know this part, as the servers know theirs. They should kneel, stand and sit straight, behaving always with such reverence as to give edifying example to the people in church. They should not spend the time in choir reading irrelevant books, even pious ones. They should not, for instance, say their Office during Mass nor anticipate their own Matins during Vespers.

They should attend to the public service at which they assist, making this their prayer. When they recite or sing any text of the service they should mean what they say ; *Orabo spiritu, orabo et mente : psallam spiritu, psallam et mente* (1 Cor. xiv, 15). Otherwise their attendance would not be really an act of religion at all, and they would deserve the words : *This people honours me with its lips ; but its heart is far from me* (Is. xxix, 13).

§ 2. MINISTERS AND SERVERS

IN the case of each service or function the exact number of servers required will be stated. Here a note as to the number generally needed in the average Catholic church in England or Ireland may be useful.

For a private Low Mass one server only attends. For High Mass,

---

[1] When the Divine Persons are named " distincte et cum glorificatione " (Martinucci I. i, pp. 2–3), e.g., in the conclusion of a hymn.

solemn Vespers, solemn Benediction, processions carried out with some pomp, and the more solemn offices generally, besides the priest who celebrates, there are the sacred ministers, that is, deacon and sub-deacon.[1] At Vespers on the greater feasts there may be four or six assistants in copes. For High Mass, solemn Vespers and such functions the servers required are : A Master of Ceremonies (M.C.), thurifer, two acolytes. At High Mass two, four or six torch-bearers are needed ; though there may be two only, and these, if others are not available, may be the acolytes (see p. 89). At Benediction a thurifer, two, four or six torch-bearers—according to the degree of solemnity of the occasion—and at least one other server (here called M.C., see p. 233) attend. For processions a cross-bearer is needed, except in the cases where a subdeacon carries the cross. A sung Mass (*Missa cantata*) can be celebrated with two servers only ; or there may be as many as at High Mass (p. 127).

Pontifical functions require many more assistants and servers. Generally there are two Masters of Ceremonies. An Assistant Priest (A.P.) is required ; and in the case of the Ordinary using his throne there are two assistant deacons there, besides the ministers of Mass. Three or four servers (called chaplains) hold the hand-candle, book, mitre and crozier. If the Bishop wears the cappa he has a train-bearer. Six servers are needed to vest a bishop, though this can be managed with a less number. Altogether some twenty-three persons attend the Ordinary when he sings Mass using the throne (p. 155). Not quite so many are required by a bishop who uses the faldstool (p. 177).

At solemn processions (as for Corpus Christi) canopy-bearers, clergy in vestments, the choir and clergy in surplices may increase the number indefinitely.

As a general rule, except in the case of processions and funerals (when an indefinite number of clergy, supposed to be the choir, stand around the hearse holding lighted candles), not more servers should attend than those really needed, who have some office to perform. It does not add to the dignity of a rite that a crowd of useless boys stand about the sanctuary doing nothing. Nor is it in accordance with the tradition of the Roman rite to add useless ornamental attend-ance.[2] The servers needed for the ceremonies are sufficient to make the procession coming in and going out. " Entia non sunt multi-plicanda sine necessitate."

A remark by Martinucci about the behaviour of servers in church may be noted with advantage here : " They should avoid too much precision or affectation, or such a bearing as befits soldiers on parade

[1] In the great majority of cases in England the deacon and subdeacon, as a matter of fact, are also ordained priests. At Vespers the assistants, who wear copes, need not be in Holy Orders (see p. 190).
[2] It is remarkable how few people they use in Rome itself for functions, never more than are strictly necessary. There seems a strong tendency to keep down the number as much as possible.

rather than churchmen. They must certainly do all gravely and regularly ; but if they behave with too punctilious a uniformity the sacred functions look theatrical." [1]

Yet perhaps in England the danger is in the other direction, lest servers (generally young boys [2]) behave carelessly and irreverently. Considerable tact and good taste are needed in the priest or M.C. who trains the boys, to find the right mean between slovenliness and affectation.

§ 3. ECCLESIASTICAL RANK

CEREMONIES are sometimes modified according to the rank of the person who performs them or assists at them. It is therefore important to understand such rank, as far as it affects ceremonial.

Most cases are so obvious as to require no special notice. The celebrant at Mass, Vespers, Compline, Benediction and all such functions must be ordained priest. The deacon and subdeacon must have received those Orders. The one exception to this is that a cleric, at least tonsured, may, for a reasonable cause, perform part of the office of subdeacon at High Mass and other functions (cf. p. 103). In such a case he must omit certain duties performed only by a subdeacon (see p. 103). No one may act as deacon unless he has received that Order.

The rubrics suppose that the servers and even the members of the choir be (tonsured) clerics. The acolytes and thurifer should be ordained acolyte, the others should be in Minor Orders, or at least be tonsured. According to the Ceremonial of Bishops, the Master of Ceremonies should be a priest, or at least in Holy Orders.[3] Often, however, this rule cannot be observed. It is now recognized that laymen may serve at Mass or at any function, and may form the choir.

Above the rank of the simple priest are CANONS (*canonici*) in Chapter. This means, when they are present, in a body, in the church of which they are canons ; or at another church at which, for some reason, the whole Chapter assists. A canon may now wear his robes and special insignia throughout the diocese to which his Chapter belongs, even when the Chapter is not present, but ordinarily not elsewhere.[4]

A PRELATE (*praelatus*) is, in the first case, a bishop. But not all bishops receive the same honours at every ceremony they may attend. There is, for instance, considerable difference between a bishop where he has jurisdiction (as the Ordinary in his own diocese), and an auxiliary or a strange bishop visiting a place.

The liturgical books frequently speak of GREATER PRELATES (*maiores praelati, maiores praesules*). Under this term the following persons are understood : Cardinals [5] everywhere out of Rome, and in their

[1] Martinucci-Menghini II. ii, pp. 550–551, § 21.
[2] It is much to be desired that young men should, when possible, minister at the altar, instead of small boys.
[3] C.E. I. v.
[4] C.J.C. 409, § 2.
[5] For privileges of cardinals see C.J.C. 239.

titular churches at Rome, Patriarchs and Archbishops throughout their Patriarchate or Province, Ordinary bishops in their own diocese, Papal Legates in the territory where they are Legates.[1]

Below these in rank come archbishops or bishops who have no jurisdiction in the place where the function occurs.

Abbots. Below bishops are the so-called LESSER PRELATES (*praelati inferiores*).   The first case of these is that of ABBOTS.[2]

A decree of the Congregation of S. Rites, in 1659 (D. 1131), lays down rules as to the use of pontifical vestments, and other distinctions, by lesser prelates.   Many of these rules are now abrogated by the later legislation of Pius X in 1905 and 1906 (D.D. 4154, 4182), in regard to prelates of the Roman court (see below, p. 34) ; but the rules of 1659 still obtain in the case of abbots,[3] except in so far as D. 1131 has been modified by C.J.C. (323, 325, 625, 782, 811, 812, 964) and the revised rubrics of the Missal (R. i, 4, 5 ; xii, 8).

While abbots *nullius* have almost the full liturgical privileges of a diocesan bishop, the privileges of abbots *de regimine* are curtailed.   In general, having been blessed by the diocesan Bishop, they have the right to use within the place of their jurisdiction the pontifical insignia,[4] with throne and canopy, and there celebrate the Divine Offices with pontifical rite.[5]   They have the right to wear everywhere the pectoral cross and a gemmed ring [6] ; to have an assistant priest when celebrating pontifically [7] ; to use everywhere the skull-cap and ring even during the celebration of Mass.[8]   Even in a private Mass an abbot now wears the pectoral cross and the stole hanging straight down, and assumes the maniple (except in a Requiem Mass) at *Indulgentiam* ; and he blesses at the end of Mass with a triple sign of the cross. [9]

Some of the restrictions expressly placed on the liturgical privileges of abbots by S.R.C. 1131 and not modified—it would seem—by subsequent legislation are these :

They may not have a seventh candle on the altar. They may not have a fixed throne in the sanctuary. They must use a chair, to be

---

[1] Under this title are included Nuncios and Apostolic Delegates (C.J.C. 267).

[2] An abbot is the head of a monastery of monks or of a congregation of regular canons.   The following religious Orders have abbots : Canons of the Lateran (Augustinian Canons), Premonstratensian Canons, Canons of the Immaculate Conception, Benedictines of all congregations, Cistercians.   All monks of Eastern rites have Archimandrites or Hegumenoi, who are equivalent to Western abbots. An abbot " nullius (scil. dioecesis) " is one who is in no bishop's diocese, having himself quasi-episcopal jurisdiction over clergy and people within a certain territory.   There is no such abbot in the British Isles.   Rules for abbots and other lesser prelates are given in C.J.C. 319–327.

[3] This is the view of modern rubricians who treat of the liturgical privileges of abbots at any length (e.g., Vavasseur-Stercky, Moretti).   Abbots are not mentioned in D.D. 4154, 4182.

[4] These are mitre, crozier, ring, dalmatic and tunicle, Pontifical Canon, hand-candle, ewer and basin, gremial, gloves, buskins and sandals.

[5] C.J.C. 625, 325.   This privilege is no longer limited to certain days as it was by D. 1131.

[6] *Ib.*

[7] C.J.C. 812.

[8] C.J.C. 811, § 2

[9] R. i, 4 ; xii, 7, 8.

removed afterwards.[1] Over this chair, placed on the Gospel side
(unless the Ordinary be present), they may have a canopy, not of cloth
of gold or other precious material, but of simpler stuff than the altar
frontal. The chair may be covered with silk of the colour of the day ;
it may be raised two steps only above the floor of the sanctuary. They
may not be accompanied by the body of monks or canons, as the Bishop
is, on coming to the church or on going away ; neither may they bless
the people on the way, nor the clergy or ministers during the function,
as the Bishop does. Nor may abbots bless a preacher before his
sermon. At High Mass they are assisted by the deacon and subdeacon
of the Mass, by two other deacons in dalmatics, by an assistant priest
in a cope. Six other monks or canons may attend, two in copes, two
in chasubles, two in tunicles ; but these may not sit in the choir stalls ;
they must have seats, benches without a back, covered with green
cloth, which are taken away afterwards. Abbots may not wear the
precious mitre, without a special indult of the Holy See. Under their
(gold or linen) mitre they wear a black skull-cap. They carry their
crozier only in their own church, not in public processions. As Regulars
they wear no rochet, unless it is part of the habit of their Order. They
may take the vestments from the altar only when they are about to
celebrate pontifically.[2] They may bless the people in the pontifical
form, making the sign of the cross three times, at pontifical functions
and also in private Masses. In the presence of a Bishop they are not to
give blessings without special indult. If the Bishop [3] is present he
is to have his seat on the Gospel side ; it is to be raised by one step
higher than that of the abbot on the Epistle side. Canons of the
cathedral sit around the Bishop, monks or canons of the abbot's
Chapter around his seat. The Bishop puts incense into the thurible
and blesses it ; he kisses the Gospel book after the Gospel ; he blesses
the people at the end of Mass.

When an abbot says a private Mass, he will vest in the sacristy
(wearing his pectoral cross and the stole uncrossed). He puts on the
maniple (except in Requiem Masses) at *Indulgentiam*. He does not
use a silver vessel and basin to wash his hands. He will have one
server only ; ordinarily two candles only will be lit on the altar.

In view of the authority given to abbots by C.J.C. 325, 625 to celebrate the Divine Offices with pontifical rite in their own churches, only
the authority of the Holy See can decide how far some of the restrictions
imposed by S.R.C. 1131 now hold. In practice, in England (presumably
by privilege or legitimate custom) abbots use the rochet, the precious
mitre and the crozier without a veil attached to the top. They
give a triple Blessing with the Blessed Sacrament at Benediction
(detached from a pontifical function) and are " associated " with their

---

[1] Abbots do not use a faldstool, except when celebrating (*a*) in the presence
of the Ordinary, (*b*) outside their own territory by pontifical indult.

[2] S.R.C. 1131[11]; cf. R. 1. 5.

[3] The Ordinary or other greater prelate (S.R.C. 1131[15]). Another bishop has
only the first place in choir.

monks at pontifical functions. Some abbots, by privilege, consecrate altars.

Besides abbots there are other " lesser prelates," namely, real or titular officials of the Papal court. These are the priests commonly called " Monsignori." [1] A decree, " motu proprio," of Pope Pius X [2] defines exactly who these are and establishes their rights.

Protonotaries Apostolic. First among these are PROTONOTARIES APOSTOLIC (*protonotarii apostolici*). These are divided into four classes : (I.) There are seven Protonotaries " de numero participantium," who form a college, still representing the old Notaries of the Apostolic See.[3] Now they have duties chiefly in connection with the cause of canonization and beatification of Saints. Their ceremonial privileges are that they may celebrate pontifically [4] out of Rome, but only having asked and obtained the permission of the Ordinary. They may not, however, use crozier, throne or cappa magna ; nor may they have a seventh candle on the altar, nor an assistance of several deacons. They do not say *Pax vobis*, as a bishop does, instead of *Dominus vobiscum ;* nor may they sing the verses *Sit nomen Domini* and *Adiutorium nostrum* before blessing. They do not bless with the triple sign of the cross. Wearing the mitre, they bless (singing the usual form for priests, *Benedicat vos*), unless the Ordinary or a greater prelate be present. In this case, according to the general rule (p. 149), he gives the blessing at the end of Mass. Coming to the church to celebrate they wear the mantellettum, and over it a pectoral cross. They are not to be received at the door of the church as a bishop is. Their pectoral cross (worn only when they have the mantellettum) is to be of gold with one gem ; it hangs from a cord of ruddy violet (*color rubinus*) mixed with gold thread and with a tassel of the same kind. They use a cloth of gold mitre and a simple mitre. Under this they may have a black skull-cap. They use the hand-candle and Pontifical Canon ; and a silver vessel and dish to wash the hands. At an ordinary Low Mass they have no special privilege, except the use of the hand-candle. These seven protonotaries have precedence over abbots. All who attend Mass said by one of them, even in a private oratory, satisfy the obligation of hearing Mass on Sundays and feasts.

The choir dress of these Protonotaries is the " habitus praelatitius,"

[1] The title " Monsignore " is not given as such. Certain offices of the Papal court, often granted as honorary offices to priests living away from Rome, involve that their holder be called " Monsignor." This general title is used for dignitaries of various ranks, as will be seen from the description above. Like the stars, one Monsignore differeth, and very considerably, from another Monsignore in glory (cf. C.J.C. 328).

[2] *Inter multiplices*, 21 February 1905. (S.R.C. 4154.) Cf. C.J.C. 106, 70.

[3] Originally they were the Pope's legal advisers, who drew up documents, settled questions of Canon Law according to the " usus forensis," and so on.

[4] This means always the " usus pontificalium," namely with the same ceremonies and vestments as a bishop, save where an exception is made. These Protonotaries use all a bishop's vestments and insignia (except the crozier), the shoes, ring, pectoral cross, tunicle, dalmatic, mitre.

namely a violet cassock with a train (which, however, is never let down), a violet silk belt, rochet and violet mantellettum, a black biretta with a ruddy tassel. They may wear the " habitus pianus " (p. 13), like a bishop, but without pectoral cross and with a ruddy cord round the hat.

(II.) PROTONOTARII APOSTOLICI SVPRANVMERARII are the canons of the three Patriarchal basilicas at Rome, the Lateran, Vatican and Liberian (St. Mary Major), also canons of certain other cathedrals to which this privilege is granted.[1] Honorary canons are excluded.

These prelates have various privileges, according to three cases : when they are present together in Chapter in their own cathedral, or alone but in their diocese, or in another diocese. The two former cannot occur in England. In the third case they have the same rights as the next class.

(III.) PROTONOTARII APOSTOLICI AD INSTAR PARTICIPANTIVM consist of the canons of certain cathedrals [2] and a great number of other priests, on whom the Pope has conferred this dignity.[3]

These share the rights of the first class (the " Participantes ") somewhat diminished. They may wear prelate's dress and the " habitus pianus." Out of Rome, with the consent of the Ordinary, they may celebrate pontifically (but not a Requiem Mass). In this case they use neither a faldstool nor the gremial (p. 14) : they sit at the sedilia with the ministers. They wear a white damask silk mitre, having no further ornament than ruddy fringes at the end of the infulae. If the church is not a cathedral, and if no greater prelate be present, they may be assisted by a priest in a cope. They wear a pectoral cross of plain gold, without jewels, hanging by a violet cord. They say all the Mass at the altar, and wash their hands only at the Lavabo. They have a ring. They may—with permission of the Ordinary—celebrate pontifically the Vespers of the feast of which they celebrate pontifical Mass, or, by special commission of the Ordinary, other Vespers. In this case they wear the mitre, pectoral cross and ring. At Low Mass said with solemnity they conduct themselves as supernumerarii, otherwise they may use only the handcandle.

(IV.) PROTONOTARII APOSTOLICI TITVLARES are appointed by the Pope or by the college of the " Participantes." Every Vicar General or Vicar Capitular, during his time of office, is a Protonotary of this class.[4] Outside Rome they may use prelate's dress, but all black ; that is, a black cassock with a train (that may never be let down), a black silk belt with two tassels, rochet and black mantellettum, a black biretta. They take precedence of other clergy, of canons not in Chapter, but not of canons in Chapter nor of Vicars General and

[1] For example, the canons of Concordia Iulia (prov. of Venice), Florence Görz, Palermo, Padua, Treviso, Udine, Venice.
[2] For example, the canons of Bologna, Cagliari, Malta, Strigonia.
[3] The list, each year, will be found in the *Annuario Pontificio*.
[4] C.J.C. 370, § 2 ; 439.

Capitular, nor of Superiors General of religious Orders or abbots, nor of prelates of the Roman curia. Outside Rome, at solemn Mass and Vespers, and at Low Mass and other functions when on occasion they are celebrated more solemnly, they may use the hand-candle.

Domestic Prelates and Chamberlains. Other prelates of the Roman court are the *Antistites urbani,* generally called DOMESTIC PRELATES. These may wear prelate's dress of violet, with a rochet and mantellettum. They may never let down the train. They have a violet tassel in their biretta. In ceremonies their only privilege is the use of the hand-candle, and this only on occasions of solemnity.

There are CHAMBERLAINS (*cubicularii*) [1] of the Papal court in various orders, " Cubicularii intimi " (*camerieri segreti*), who may be active or " supranumerarii," and " Cubicularii honoris " ; also " Capellani secreti " and " Capellani secreti honoris." These titles are given to many priests as a compliment.

Papal Chamberlains are not prelates.[2] They wear a violet cassock not the rochet nor the mantellettum. Instead of this they have a long violet robe [3] of the same kind as the mantellettum, but reaching to the feet. It has slits at the sides for the arms and false sleeves which hang down behind. They have no liturgical privileges. As private dress (*habitus pianus*) they wear a black cassock with violet piping or edging and a violet belt and stock.

None of these persons, neither prelates, canons, nor Papal chamberlains, genuflect, but bow only to a bishop, even when he gives his blessing. A Vicar General, as such, has no liturgical privilege ; but all Vicars General are now Titular Protonotaries ; they have precedence over all the clergy of the diocese.[4] In choir, whereas normally the Gospel side is the side of greater dignity, receives incense and the kiss of peace first, if a prelate or canon be present, the side at which he has his place becomes of greater dignity.[5] No civil distinction affects any ceremony in church, except that the Pontifical and Ceremonial grant certain privileges to " princes." [6]

---

[1] Italian " camerieri." There are also lay " camerieri di spada e cappa," who have no special rights at ceremonies.

[2] They are sometimes called prelates, with a qualification, " praelati honorarii," " inferiores," " prelati di mantellone." They have an honorary prelature, an honour attached to their office, which does not affect their person. Hence they are not prelates in reality, but may be described as prelates " secundum quid " (in their office, not personally).

[3] Called in Italian " mantellone." On duty at the Vatican they have a great red cloth cloak with a cape.

[4] C.J.C. 370.

[5] For the rights of prelates see Le Vavasseur, *Fonct. Pont.* ii, pp. 383 *seq.*

[6] A " maximus princeps " may have a place in the sanctuary. He is given a book of the Gospels to kiss (not the one used) after the Gospel. He is incensed with three double swings after the Bishop (but Kings and the Emperor—the Roman Emperor—before) ; he is given the kiss of peace. " Magistrates, barons, and nobles " receive this after all the clergy by means of a pax-brede (cf. p. 18). A " mulier insignis " is incensed (C.E. I. iv, 6 ; xxiii, 30, 31 ; xxiv, 5, 6).

PART II

THE HOLY SACRIFICE

CHAPTER VI

LOW MASS SAID BY A PRIEST

§ 1. PREPARATION

ALTHOUGH High Mass, historically, is the original rite, so that Low Mass is really only a shortened form of that, nevertheless, in practice, the first thing a priest must learn is how to say Low Mass.[1] He does so constantly, generally every morning. The ceremonies of normal Low Mass form, as it were, the background for all other Eucharistic rites. It is possible to describe these others more shortly, supposing that the priest is familiar with those of Low Mass. Then we need note only the differences on other occasions.

Nothing is said here about the rite, as far as the prayers, etc., are concerned ; that is another matter and is extremely complicated.[2] Here we describe only the ceremonies.

Preparation of the Altar. Before Mass the following preparations must be made. The altar must be uncovered of the dust-cloth, leaving the three altar-cloths of white linen. It must have a cross and three, or at least two, candles, which two are lighted. They should stand at either side. The third candle, ordered by the rubrics for the Consecration,[3] should stand at the Epistle end of the altar, outside the others, or it may be fixed to a bracket near the altar. The frontal and tabernacle veil (if there is a tabernacle containing the Sanctissimum) may always be of the colour of the day for a Low Mass ; or—if the colour of the Mass be different from that of the day, e.g., at a votive Mass—they may conform to the colour of the Mass. When vestments are black the conopaeum and frontal (if the Sanctissimum be present) may not be black. They must either be violet or of the colour of the day. The missal-stand or cushion is placed at the Epistle side of the altar, straight, so that its front line is parallel with the front of the altar. The Missal lies on it, with its edges towards the cross, unless the server bring this with him from the sacristy (which is the

---

[1] For the ceremonies of Low Mass the first norm is, of course, the rubrics of the Missal (*Rubricae Generales* and *Ritus Servandus*).

[2] This aspect of the Mass is fully dealt with in *The Celebration of Mass*, by Rev. J. O'Connell, Vol. I, " The General Rubrics of the Missal " (see Bibliography (p. xi).

[3] (R.G. xx ; R. viii, 6.) There is a widespread custom of not using this third candle and S.R.C. has declared that this custom may be retained. The Ordinary may, however, order the observance of the rubric (4141[6]).

more correct practice). In any case, all the places should be found
and marked in it before Mass begins. The altar-cards will be in their
place on the altar (cf. p. 19).

On the credence [1] the cruets stand, filled with wine and water,
with the dish and towel (pp. 16, 17), the communion-plate, the bell
and the card with the prayers to be said after Mass, if this be needed.

The Vestments. In the sacristy the vestments are laid out on the
vesting table, in the order in which the priest will put them on, so
that the one he takes first will be on the top. First the chasuble is
laid out, conveniently so that the priest can take it at once. It is
laid on the table with the front part down. On the chasuble the stole
is laid, then the maniple, the girdle, the alb and amice, in that order.

Each priest uses his own amice and purificator ; so that these are
kept apart for him. The other vestments are the same for any
celebrant.

By the side of the vestments the chalice is prepared with the purificator, the paten, having on it the altar bread, the pall, veil and
burse, with a corporal inside, as described below.

Unless the Missal is already on the altar, it will be placed near the
vestments, so that the priest may first find and mark the places in it.
All these preparations are made by the sacristan, or partly by the
server, according to the custom of the church.[2] In any case the server
should look to see that all is ready in order before Mass begins.

The time for beginning Mass is not earlier than an hour before dawn
nor later than 1 p.m.[3]

Preparation of the Celebrant. The priest who is about to celebrate
must be in a state of grace and fasting from midnight. According to
the rubric, he should have said at least Matins and Lauds.[4]

The rubric of another rite applies very well to that of Rome too.
" The priest who is about to celebrate the holy mysteries must have
confessed his sins, must be reconciled to all men and have nothing
against anyone. He must keep his heart from bad thoughts, be pure,
and fasting till the time of sacrifice." [5]

Before Mass the priest will spend some time in saying preparatory
prayers, and will make the intention for which he is to offer the sacrifice.
He is not bound to use the prayers given for this purpose in the Missal [6] ;
but they certainly form the best preparation.[7]

---

[1] The more correct usage is to have the prayer-card, bell and all such things
on the credence. That is what the table is for, while the altar steps are not
intended—except in a passing way—for this purpose.

[2] The rubrics (R. I, 1) direct the priest to prepare the chalice himself. A
cleric or sacristan may do this (S.R.C. 4194[1], 4198[15] ; cf. C.J.C. 1306, § 1), but
the priest is recommended to do it himself (S.R.C. 4198[15] ; cf. S. Congr, Sacram.
26 March 1929).

[3] R.G. xv, 1 ; C.J.C. 821. Any system of calculation (e.g., sun time or
" summer time ") may be followed.   [4] R. I, 1.

[5] Rubric of the Byzantine *Euchologion* before the " Order of the Holy Liturgy."

[6] The " Praeparatio ad Missam pro opportunitate Sacerdotis facienda "
at the beginning of the Missal.

[7] Generally he will make this preparation in the church or sacristy.

Vesting for Mass. Then, when he is ready, about five minutes before the time fixed for Mass to begin, in the sacristy he goes to the vesting table. It is supposed that he already wears the cassock.[1] If he does not wear this habitually, he will put it on before saying the preparatory prayers.[2] The rubric directs that first he find the places in the Missal.[3] Then he washes his hands at the place prepared for that purpose, saying the prayer appointed. He prepares the chalice [4] (or sees that it has been duly prepared) : the purificator laid across the mouth of the chalice, on it the paten containing a host or hosts to be consecrated, on the paten the pall, and covering all fully the chalice veil. On top of that is laid the burse containing the corporal. Then he puts on the vestments. First he takes the amice, kisses the cross which is in the middle of it, places it for a moment on the head, then slips it over the shoulders, inserts the amice all round the neck, inside his collar, and ties the strings that keep it in place, passing them around the body. He puts on the alb (inserting his right arm into its sleeve before the left) and sees that it does not trail on the ground, but does extend to the ankles, and falls evenly all around. He fastens it round the body with the girdle folded double (having the part with the tassels on his right), and then lets the two ends of the girdle hang down in front. He takes the maniple, kisses the cross in the middle, puts it on the left arm and fastens it there if necessary. He takes the stole, kisses the cross in its middle, puts it over the shoulders,[5] crosses it in front (the part on the right over that on the left) and fixes its ends on either side with the ends of the girdle. He puts on the chasuble, passing the head through the opening, and fixes it by tying the strings attached to it around the body. Finally he puts on his biretta.

As he puts on each vestment he says the prayer appointed for that purpose in the Missal.[6] The server should assist the priest in vesting by handing him each vestment, or by at least helping to arrange the alb,[7] and stole.

It is fitting that the priest be ready a minute or two before the time appointed for Mass. He will then stand at the vesting table and say his prayers till that moment arrives.

From the time he has begun the prayers before Mass, he should not speak to anyone, except in case of strict necessity.

Going to the Altar. At the time for beginning Mass the priest takes the chalice in the left hand, and lays the right on the burse. The

---

[1] No one may wear a skull-cap while saying Mass without express permission of the Holy See. Only cardinals, bishops and blessed abbots have this right normally (C.J.C. 811, § 2). If anyone else has the privilege he must observe their rule (p. 23).

[2] C.J.C. c. 811, § 1.   [3] R. I, 1.

[4] Cf. p. 38, n. 2.

[5] It is a much disputed question as to the position of the stole on the back. The best solution of the difficulty seems to be that the stole should lie between the shoulders at the base of the neck (covered by the chasuble) neither up around the neck (C.E. II. viii, 14) nor yet down low on the back (R. I, 3).

[6] In the beginning, after the " Praeparatio."

[7] R. I, 3.

veil should cover the chalice at least in front, so that it cannot be seen. If the veil has a cross or ornament on one side, the chalice should be held so that this be in front. The opening of the burse is to be towards the priest. Holding the chalice before his breast, with head covered,[1] he bows his head to the cross or principal image in the sacristy, then follows the server into the church. At the door of the sacristy it is usual that the priest take holy water and make the sign of the cross with it, though this is not prescribed. It is also the practice in many churches that, on leaving the sacristy door, the server ring a bell there, to warn the people that Mass is about to begin.

If, on going to the altar where he will say Mass, he pass before the Blessed Sacrament, he, with the server, genuflects to it in passing. He bows his head to the High Altar if he passes it, if the Blessed Sacrament is not reserved there. In neither case does he take off the biretta to do so. If he pass before the Blessed Sacrament exposed (e.g., during the distribution of Holy Communion), he takes off the biretta and makes a prostration. This does not apply to the case of passing an altar at which Mass is being said, between the Consecration and Communion.[2] In this case he is to take no notice unless his attention is drawn to the part of the Mass by, e.g., the ringing of the bell. If it is so drawn he is to genuflect without uncovering. But if he pass at the moment of elevation, he kneels uncovered till the Elevation is finished.

On the way to the altar the priest does not greet anyone, except the Bishop or another priest in vestments coming from an altar. In this case he bows without uncovering.

On arriving at the altar where he will say Mass he stops before its lowest step and first hands his biretta to the server. If the Blessed Sacrament is reserved here, he genuflects on the ground, not on the step. Otherwise he bows low to the cross.[3] If the Sanctissimum is exposed he makes a prostration.

Then he goes up to the altar, puts the chalice covered on the Gospel side, takes the burse, opens it, takes out the folded corporal and puts it on the altar. He puts the burse on the Gospel side, leaning against the gradine or a candlestick. Then he spreads the corporal in the middle of the altar (about an inch from the front edge) and puts the chalice on it, with the chalice veil covering the whole chalice. He must take care to do this so that ample room is left in front of the chalice for him to kiss the altar. With joined hands he then goes to the Missal at the Epistle side and opens it at the Introit of the Mass.[4]

---

[1] At Low Mass the celebrant bows to the cross in the sacristy with covered head, because he already holds the chalice. At High Mass the celebrant and sacred ministers bow with uncovered head.

[2] S.R.C. 4135[2].

[3] All such reverences as this are intended for the altar. He bows to the altar; but, in practice, he always does so towards the cross, as being in the centre of the altar.

[4] At Low Mass by a priest he must always open the book and find the places himself (S.R.C. 2572[5]).

He comes back to the middle, bows to the cross, turns by the Epistle side,[1] and comes down to the ground in front of the steps in the middle. Here he again bows low, or, if the Blessed Sacrament be present, genuflects, this time on the lowest altar step.

§ 2. TO THE GOSPEL

THREE tones of voice are used at Low Mass. All that, at High Mass, would be sung by the celebrant or others, at Low Mass is said ALOUD, so as to be heard distinctly by all who assist.[2] The preparatory prayers are said in the same clear voice. All that at High Mass would be said secretly is said at Low Mass SILENTLY, that is, articulated in a whisper, so as not to be heard by bystanders ; but the priest should hear himself.[3] There is a third, medium voice, namely AUDIBLE BUT LOWER than the clear or loud voice. It is heard only by those near the celebrant. It occurs four times only : at the words *Orate, fratres*, during the whole *Sanctus* and *Benedictus*, at the words *Nobis quoque peccatoribus*, at the words *Domine, non sum dignus*, said thrice.

Preparatory Prayers. The celebrant makes the sign of the cross, standing before the lowest altar step, saying at the same time : *In nomine Patris*, etc Then he says the antiphon *Introibo ad altare Dei* and the psalm *Iudica me*, the server answering the alternate verses. He bows his head to the cross at the verse *Gloria Patri* and makes the sign of the cross again at *Adiutorium nostrum* While he says the *Confiteor* he bows profoundly He strikes his breast (with the open palm) three times at the words *mea culpa, mea culpa, mea maxima culpa*. He does not turn to the server at the words *vobis fratres, vos fratres*. He remains profoundly bowed while the server says the prayer *Misereatur*. Then he stands erect. He makes the sign of the cross again as he says *Indulgentiam*. . . . He bows moderately during the verses *Deus, tu conversus*, to *Oremus* inclusive.

During all this time, except when he makes the sign of the cross or strikes his breast, the priest holds the hands joined before the breast.

As he says *Oremus* before the prayer *Aufer a nobis* he separates the hands and joins them again, but does not raise them. Having said *Oremus* he stands erect and goes up to the altar, saying *Aufer a nobis* silently. Arrived at the middle of the altar he bows moderately, laying the joined hands on the altar, so that the ends of the longer fingers rest on it. So he says the prayer *Oramus te, Domine*. At the words *quorum reliquiae hic sunt* he bends down, separates the hands,

---

[1] With the exceptions to be noted, the celebrant at Mass always turns from the altar and back to it by the Epistle side, that is, on turning from the altar by his right hand, on turning back to it by his left. At High Mass the deacon stands on that side, so that the celebrant does not turn his back to him.

[2] But not so loud as to disturb other celebrants (R.G. xvi, 2) should they be near.

[3] R.G. xvi, 2.

laying each palm downwards on the altar, outside the corporal,[1] on each side of him, and kisses the altar in the middle. This position of the hands is to be observed every time he kisses the altar. To do so conveniently he should stand slightly away from it, so that, when he bends his head, he can just touch the altar with the closed lips, a little way in from its outer edge.

Then, making no further reverence to the cross, he goes with joined hands to the Missal at the Epistle side. As he goes he continues the prayer *Oramus te, Domine.*

Introit. Here he reads the Introit of the Mass in a clear voice. As he begins it he makes the sign of the cross, laying, as always, the left hand under the breast.[2] Joining the hands again, he continues the Introit. At the verse *Gloria Patri* he turns and bows his head towards the altar cross. In repeating the antiphon of the Introit he does not again make the sign of the cross. When the Introit is finished, he comes to the middle, makes no reverence to the cross [3] and here says the *Kyrie, eleison* alternately with the server. If the *Gloria in excelsis* is to be said, he begins it as soon as the *Kyrie* is ended, standing at the middle of the altar. As he says the first words, he separates the hands, extends them, elevates them to about the height of the shoulders, joins them and bows his head at the word *Deo.* With joined hands he continues the *Gloria in excelsis*, reading it (if necessary) from the altar·card in the middle. He bows the head at the words *Adoramus te, Gratias agimus tibi, Iesu Christe, suscipe deprecationem nostram.* At the last words, *Cum Sancto Spiritu*, he makes the sign of the cross on himself, then lays the hands on the altar and kisses it.

If the *Gloria in excelsis* is not said, he kisses the alter, in the same way, as soon as the *Kyrie, eleison* is finished.

Prayers, Epistle, etc. With joined hands and eyes cast down he turns, by the right, to face the people. He says *Dominus vobiscum*, at the same time extending the hands and joining them again, not lowering them meanwhile. Turning back by the left he goes to the Missal. While he says *Oremus* he extends the hands and joins them again, and he bows his head to the cross. Then he reads the Collect, holding the hands uplifted and extended, at about the height and width of the shoulders, the palms facing one another. When he says *Per Dominum nostrum*, etc., he joins the hands. If the prayer ends *Qui tecum* or *Qui vivis* he joins his hands when saying *in unitate.* He bows his head again to the cross at the Holy Name, *Iesum Christum.* In the same way he says the following collects, if there are several.

After the last collect he either holds the book or lays his hands on it,

---

[1] During Mass, except from the Consecration to the Communion, whenever the celebrant lays his hands on the altar, he places them, not on the corporal, but one on each side of it. Between the Consecration and the Communion, when the forefingers and thumbs are joined all the time, he lays his hands on the corporal.

[2] This is the rule whenever he signs himself, that the other hand rest meanwhile under the breast. He must place the left hand below the lowest point of the cross he will form on himself.   [3] S.R.C. 2682[27].

one on each side, the palms downwards, so that his thumb or the ends
of the fingers rest on the edges, while he reads the Epistle. It is usual to
give a sign to the server when the Epistle is ended, that he may answer
Deo gratias. This may be done by raising slightly the left hand for a
moment, or by lowering the voice at the concluding words and turning
slightly towards the server.

On certain days, notably the Ember days, there is a series of lessons,
each preceded by a collect, before the Gospel. In this case *Dominus
vobiscum* is said only before the collects preceding the last lesson.
Immediately after the *Kyrie, eleison* the celebrant, instead of saying
Dominus vobiscum, goes at once to the Missal. He says each collect
and the following lesson in the usual way. Then, at the place marked
in the Missal, he comes to the middle, says *Dominus vobiscum,* returns
to the book and continues as above.

If *Flectamus genua* is to be said, as soon as the celebrant has said
Oremus he lays his hands on the altar and genuflects while he says
Flectamus genua. The server at once answers *Levate ;* the celebrant
rises and goes on with the Collect.

After the Epistle, the priest goes on at once to read, in the same tone
of voice, the Gradual, Tract, *Alleluia* or Sequence, as these occur in
the Missal. Meanwhile he still holds his hands on the book.

In the Collect, Epistle, Gradual, etc., if such a word occurs as is
noted above (p. 22), that is, the Holy Name, name of the Blessed
Virgin, of the Saint of the day, he makes a reverence, as there described.
At the Epistle or Gradual, he will genuflect, laying his hands on the
altar in the usual way, when the rubric directs this.

He then comes to the middle of the altar with hands joined, leaving
the book open at the Epistle side. In the middle he looks up to the
cross,[1] then bows low, without laying the hands on the altar, and so
says *Munda cor meum* and *Iube, Domine,*[2] *benedicere. Dominus sit
in corde meo,* etc. [If for any reason the server does not carry the Missal
across to the Gospel side, the priest does so himself, bowing to the
cross as he passes.[3] He lays the Missal on its stand or cushion at the
Gospel end diagonally, so that he will turn somewhat towards the
people when reading the Gospel, then comes back to the middle and
says *Munda cor meum.*]

§ 3. FROM THE GOSPEL TO THE PREFACE

WHEN the celebrant has said the prayer *Dominus sit in corde meo,*
he goes with joined hands to the book at the Gospel side. He does not

---

[1] See p. 45, n. 2.

[2] At Low Mass the celebrant says " Domine," addressing God. By a curious
development the mediæval form " domnus," really nothing but a mispronuncia-
tion, is now looked upon as the correct one when a merely human superior is
addressed. So the rubrics in the R. vi, 2, and *Ordo Missae* give the form, " Iube,
domne, benedicere " when the deacon at High Mass addresses the celebrant ;
but " Iube, Domine, benedicere " when, at Low Mass, the celebrant prays to God
(See Ducange, *Glossarium med. et inf. Latinitatis,* c.v. " Domnus.")

[3] R. vi, 1 ; S.R.C. 3975[2].

here turn his back to the people, but he faces half towards them looking across the Gospel corner diagonally. Without separating the hands he says *Dominus vobiscum.* Then *Sequentia* (or *Initium*) *sancti Evangelii secundum N.*, adding the name of the Evangelist, in the accusative case. As he says these words he lays the left hand on the book. He holds the right stretched out, the fingers joined, the palm downwards and so makes the sign of the cross with the thumb on the book at the beginning of the text of the Gospel that he is about to read. Then, still holding the hand stretched out in the same way, he makes the sign of the cross with the front part of the thumb on his forehead, lips and breast, laying the left hand under the breast (below where he will sign the cross). He must be careful not to make the cross on his lips while he is speaking. If he is saying the words *Sequentia sancti Evangelii*, etc., he must pause while signing his lips. More probably he will have finished that formula by the time he signs his lips. When the server has answered *Gloria tibi, Domine*, the priest reads the Gospel, with hands joined. If in the Gospel the Holy Name occurs, or any other word at which he bows, he does so towards the book. If he has to genuflect at any words, he lays his hands on the altar and does so also towards the book, unless the Sanctissimum be exposed. In this case he turns and genuflects towards the Blessed Sacrament.[1]

While reading the Gospel, if he has to turn a page, then, as always, he does so with the right hand, laying the left meanwhile on the altar or on the Missal.

When the Gospel is finished he raises the book with both hands, and kisses it at the beginning of the text, saying *Per evangelica dicta*, etc.[2] He stands erect and replaces the book on the stand. Then he brings the Missal to the middle of the altar, raising its stand with both hands. He places it here at the middle, but on the Gospel side of the corporal, turning diagonally towards the middle ; it should not stand on the corporal, but as near to it as possible.

Creed. If the Creed is to be said, he begins it at once in the middle of the altar. As he says *Credo in unum Deum* he extends his hands, lifts them to the height of the shoulders, joins them as he says the words *in unum Deum* and bows the head. He says the Creed with joined hands, reading the text, if necessary, from the altar-card. At the Holy Name he bows his head. As he says the words *Et incarnatus est*, etc., he lays his hands on the altar outside the corporal and genuflects on one knee. He does not rise from this genuflection till he has said *Et homo factus est*. He should make the whole genuflection slowly, and not rest with one knee on the ground. He does not bow the head at these words. He bows his head at the word *adoratur* (of the Holy Ghost). As he says the last words *et vitam venturi saeculi*, he makes the sign of the cross, laying the left hand on the breast.

---

[1] See p. 62.
[2] Many rubricians suggest that the celebrant say the first half of this verse (" Per evangelica dicta "), then kiss the book, then say the rest.

After the Creed he does not join the hands, but lays them on the altar at once and kisses it. Then he turns, by the Epistle side, and says *Dominus vobiscum* in the usual manner.

If there is no Creed in the Mass, he kisses the altar and turns to say *Dominus robiscum* as soon as he is at the middle, after the Gospel.

Offertory. Facing the altar again, opening out, joining the hands and bowing, he says *Oremus*. In the same tone he then reads the Offertory verse.

The Offertory act now follows. The celebrant takes the chalice veil from the chalice with both hands, folds it and lays it on the altar at his right, just outside the corporal.[1] He lays his left hand on the altar, outside the corporal. With the right he takes the chalice by the knob of its stem and stands it outside the corporal, at his right side. He takes the pall from the chalice and lays it on the folded veil. He takes the paten, having on it the altar bread, and holds this, with both hands, over the middle of the corporal, at about the height of his breast. He should hold it with the thumb and first finger of each hand touching its edge, the other fingers under it. Holding it thus he looks up,[2] and then down at the bread, and says silently the prayer *Suscipe, sancte Pater*. If other altar breads are to be consecrated at the Mass, they must be placed on the corporal before this Offertory prayer is said. If they are in a ciborium, it is put on the corporal, unveiled and opened, then covered again after the priest has made the sign of the cross with the paten. If he has forgotten the other breads to be consecrated, he repeats the prayer or makes a mental offering.

When the prayer *Suscipe, sancte Pater* is finished, the celebrant lowers the paten ; still holding it as before he makes the sign of the cross with it over the corporal, tracing first a line towards himself, then one from left to right. He slides the altar bread on to the corporal in the middle, in front, without touching it. Then he lays the left hand on the altar, as always in such cases, outside the corporal. He puts the paten on the altar, at his right, and slips about half of it under the corporal.

Putting in Wine and Water. With joined hands he comes to the Epistle corner. He takes the chalice at its knob with the left hand, and the purificator (which lies on it) with the right. With this he wipes the inside of the chalice. Then, still holding the knob of the chalice in the left, he puts the purificator so that it hangs over the left thumb by the side of the chalice. He takes the cruet of wine from the server in his right hand and pours as much as is needed into the chalice,[3] saying nothing. The server holds up the water cruet.

---

[1] The rubric seems to suggest that the priest himself folds the veil. Some authors say that he may hand it to the server to fold. For more than one practical reason it is better that the priest should himself fold and put aside the veil.

[2] In looking up the celebrant always looks at the altar cross, unless it stands beneath his eyes (S.R.C. 2960[2]). This is only a practical direction, that the action may be done uniformly. In principle he looks up to heaven, as so often in the New Testament (e.g., John xi, 41).

[3] Rather less than half of what is in the cruet (see p. 56).

The priest makes the sign of the cross over it, as he begins to say the prayer *Deus, qui humanae substantiae*. He continues this prayer ; as he says the words *da nobis per huius aquae et vini mysterium* he takes the cruet in the right and pours a little water into the chalice, a few drops only. In some churches a little spoon is used to measure the water. In this case he takes the spoon, dips it into the cruet,' and so puts one spoonful into the chalice. Then he may wipe away any drops there may be on the sides of the chalice. As he says the Holy Name at the end of the prayer he bows towards the cross. He puts the chalice near the corporal, with the left hand. He either lays the purificator at its place on the paten, or puts it near there and comes to the middle with joined hands ; or he may come while folding the purificator and lay it on the paten on arriving at the middle of the altar. At the middle he arranges the purificator so that, folded lengthwise, it shall cover the half of the paten not already under the corporal. Meanwhile he lays the left hand on the altar. With the right he takes the chalice by its knob ; he holds its foot with the left hand, lifts it so that the top does not exceed the level of the eyes, and so holding it says the prayer *Offerimus tibi, Domine*, with his eyes raised to the cross. When this is said, he makes the sign of the cross over the middle of the altar with the chalice ; as he did before with the paten. To do so he lowers the chalice ; he should take care not to extend the cross over the bread. He then puts the chalice in the middle of the corporal, behind the bread. Laying the left hand on the foot of the chalice, he takes the pall with the right hand and covers the chalice. He bows moderately, lays the hands, joined, on the altar in front of him, and so says the prayer *In spiritu humilitatis*, silently. He stands erect, looks up for a moment, extends and raises the hands, then lowers the eyes and joins the hands before the breast. While doing so he says the prayer *Veni, sanctificator*. At the word *benedic* he lays the left hand on the altar and with the right makes the sign of the cross over the bread and chalice together.

Washing of Fingers. With joined hands he now goes to the Epistle end of the altar. Facing the server, who stands there, he holds his hands over the dish, so that the server pours water over the ends of the thumb and forefinger of each hand. Then he takes the towel and dries them. In doing this he should hold the hands, not over the altar, but outside and in front of it. As soon as he begins to wash his fingers he says silently the verses of the psalm *Lavabo inter innocentes* and continues while drying them. He stands at that end of the altar while saying these verses ; if necessary he may read them from the altar-card. He bows his head towards the cross as he says the verse *Gloria Patri*. Then he comes to the middle with joined hands, while saying *Sicut erat*, etc. At the middle he looks up and then lowers the eyes. Laying the hands joined on the altar before him, and bowing moderately, he says silently the prayer *Suscipe, sancta Trinitas*. Then, laying the hands palm downwards on each side, outside the corporal, he kisses the altar. Joining the hands and with downcast eyes he turns by his right to the people. Facing them he opens out the hands and joins them again, as at the *Dominus vobiscum.* Meanwhile he says *Orate, fratres* in an audible voice.[1] He turns back to the altar, by his right (completing the circle), while he continues, *ut meum et vestrum sacrificium*, etc., secretly. The server answers *Suscipiat Dominus*, etc. If the server does not say this, for any reason, the celebrant says it himself, altering the form to *de manibus meis* instead of *tuis.* At the end of this answer he says *Amen* in the medium voice.

Secret(s). Then he extends the hands and holds them with palms facing one another as at the Collects. But he does not say *Oremus.* So he says the Secrets, reading them from the Missal. He says these silently. Only the first and last Secrets have the conclusion *per Dominum nostrum*, etc., which is said with the usual joining of hands and bow of head as at the Collects. At the end of the last Secret (therefore of the first, if there is only one) he says the words of the conclusion as far as *in unitate Spiritus Sancti Deus*, like all the rest, silently. Then he pauses, lays the right hand on the altar, and with the left finds the place of the Preface in the Missal.[2] When it is found he lays the left hand also on the altar and says aloud *Per omnia saecula saeculorum.* The server answers *Amen*, and answers each verse of the following dialogue.

Preface. The celebrant, keeping the hands on the altar, says *Dominus vobiscum.* Then he raises the hands to the height of the shoulders or breast, holding them with the palms facing one another, as during the Collects and Secrets. So he says *Sursum corda.* He joins the hands as he says *Gratias agamus ;* as he says *Deo nostro* he looks up to the cross, then bows his head. As he begins the Preface he holds the hands again extended on each side and remains in that position till it is ended.

At the end of the Preface he joins his hands, bows over the altar moderately, not resting the hands on it, and says the *Sanctus* aloud, but less loud than the Preface.[3] As he says *Benedictus qui venit* he stands erect and makes the sign of the cross. Then, laying the right hand on the altar, he finds with the left the beginning of the Canon in the Missal.

§ 4. THE CANON TO THE COMMUNION

The celebrant looks up to the cross,[4] extends and lifts the hands, then looks down, joins the hands, bows low, lays the joined hands on the altar and so begins *Te igitur.* When he has said *supplices rogamus ac petimus* he lays the hands on the altar, one on either side, outside the corporal, kisses the altar, then stands erect, joins the hands, lays

---

[1] " Voce aliquantulum elata " (R. VII, 7) (cf. p. 41).
[2] The rubric does not determine how this is to be done. Most authors mention the way given in the text. In practice it will be found more convenient to use the right hand to seek the place in the Missal, or to use both hands.
[3] "Voce mediocri " (cf. p. 41).
[4] See p. 45, n. 2.

the left hand on the altar, and with the right makes the sign of the cross thrice over the chalice and bread as he says *haec+dona, haec+ munera, haec+sancta sacrificia illibata.* After the third cross he does not join the hands, but holds them extended and uplifted before the breast, exceeding the shoulders neither in width nor height. This is the normal position of the hands throughout the Canon.

At the words *una cum famulo tuo Papa nostro N.* he adds the name of the reigning Pope in the ablative case,[1] and bows his head slightly towards the book. If the Holy See is vacant at the time, he omits this clause altogether. At the words *et Antistite nostro N.* he adds the name of the Bishop of the place where he says Mass. If the see is vacant he omits this clause.

Memento of the Living. As he says *Memento, Domine, famulorum famularumque tuarum* he raises his hands and joins them before his face or breast. He then stands a moment in this position, bowing his head, while he remembers any persons for whom he wishes here to pray. The words *N. et N.* are not expressed in practice ; or rather, instead of them, he names as many persons as he likes. He may make the remembrance either verbally (in the secret voice), or entirely mentally. It is usual here to renew also the special intention for which he offers the sacrifice. He should not delay too long at the Memento.[2]

Then, standing again erect with the hands extended, he continues *et omnium circumstantium.* In the prayer *Communicantes,* he bows his head slightly towards the book at the name *Mariae ;* he bows his head towards the cross at the words *Iesu Christi.* If the name of the saint whose feast is being celebrated or commemorated that day [3] is one of those in this list he bows again, slightly, towards the book as he says it. At the words *Per eundem,* etc., he joins the hands. As he begins the next prayer, *Hanc igitur oblationem,* he opens the hands without disjoining them ; that is, he separates the lower part of the hands, keeping the thumbs and forefingers joined, the thumbs crossed, right over left, till the hands are spread out in the same horizontal plane. So he stretches them over the *oblata,* so that the extremity of the fingers is over the middle of the pall. He does not touch the pall. He keeps this position while saying the prayer and joins the hands again at the conclusion *Per Christum Dominum nostrum.* So he continues the next prayer, *Quam oblationem.* He makes the sign of the cross thrice, as before, over the *oblata,* at the words *bene+dictam, adscri+ptam, ra+tam, rationabilem, acceptabilemque facere digneris.* It will be convenient to prolong this last sign of the cross a little, so that it takes as long to make as it does to say these words. Then he

---

[1] Without the number of the Pope : " Papa nostro Pio."

[2] Nor should he make the memory of the living (and later, of the dead) too quickly. Gavanti says : " tu memento ne Memento fiat in momento " (Pars II, tit. viii, n. 3 ; *ed cit.,* i, p. 159).

[3] The head is also bowed at the name of the saint on the vigil of his feast, or during the octave of his feast (and this even though the octave be not commemorated) but not at a votive Mass in honour of a saint. The head is bowed fter the consecration (if the name occur in *Nobis quoque*) as well as before.

makes the sign of the cross over the bread only as he says *Cor+pus* and over the chalice only as he says *San+guis*. He raises his hands and joining them before his breast continues, bowing the head as he says *Iesu Christi*. If he is to consecrate other hosts besides the one he will receive in Communion, he may here renew his intention of doing so. He will uncover the ciborium, if there is one on the corporal, covering it again after the Elevation of the Host. All bread to be consecrated must be on the corporal at the time.

If necessary, he wipes the thumb and forefinger of each hand on the fore corners of the corporal. In any case it is well to rub these slightly together, so as to dispel any particles of dust on them.

Consecration of the Bread. As he says *Qui pridie quam pateretur* he takes the host between the thumb and forefinger of each hand. To do this more easily he may first lay the forefinger of the left hand on the upper part of the bread ; then he takes it by the lower extremity of the circle with the thumb and forefinger of the right, then in the same way with those of the left. He so lifts the host a little from the corporal and places the other fingers of each hand, joined and extended, behind it. He does not rest the hands on the altar. Still standing erect he continues the words *accepit panem*, etc. As he says *elevatis oculis in caelum* he looks up to the cross and at once looks down. As he says *gratias agens* he bows his head. At the word *bene+dixit* he holds the bread in the left only, and makes the sign of the cross over it with the right. In doing this he does not keep the thumb and forefinger joined, but holds the hand straight out, in the usual way when blessing. Then, at once, he again holds the bread in both hands as before, and continues, *fregit, deditque discipulis suis dicens : Accipite et manducate ex hoc omnes*. He now bows over the altar, leaning the forearms on it. Holding the bread before him, he says, " secretly, distinctly, and attentively," [1] the words of consecration, *HOC EST ENIM CORPUS MEUM*.

He should say these words in the secret voice, but so that he can hear himself.[2]

He does not touch any other hosts that may be present to be consecrated.

While saying the words of consecration it is usual to look at the bread he holds in his hands.

When the words have been said, without delay he stands erect, then genuflects on one knee ; still holding the Host with both hands over the altar, as before. He rises at once and holds up the Blessed Sacrament, so that It may be seen by the people.[3] He lifts It straight up before him to such a height that It may be seen from behind, over

[1] Rubric in the Canon.
[2] For the form of the sacrament is part of the visible, or audible, sign.
[3] When asked if the celebrant may say in a low voice the words " My Lord and my God " at the elevation of the Sacred Host—a practice to which Pius X attached rich indulgences for the faithful—the S.R.C. replied (6 November 1925, D 4397[1]) : " No, according to Canon 818 of the Code of Canon Law and the rubrics of the Roman Missal."

his head. He does this slowly, taking care to hold It over the corporal all the time. He lowers It again and places it reverently on the corporal, with the right hand, at the same place as before. He leaves It there, lays his hands on the altar and genuflects again.

From this moment till the ablutions at the end the celebrant keeps the thumb and forefinger of each hand joined, except when he touches the consecrated Host. In turning over pages, holding the chalice, or doing any other such action, he must be careful to use the other fingers in such a way as not to separate the thumb and index.

From now till the Communion every time he lays his hands on the altar he does so on the corporal.

Consecration of the Wine. Rising from the second genuflection he takes the pall from the chalice and lays it on the Epistle side. Meanwhile he touches the foot of the chalice with the left hand.[1] Then— if necessary—he rubs the thumb and forefinger of the hands over the chalice, to let any particle there may be fall into it. He does this every time after he has touched the Host. Standing erect he says *Simili modo postquam coenatum est.* Then he takes the chalice in both hands, holding it between the knob and the cup by the stem ; he lifts it a little above the altar and sets it down again at once. He continues the words, still holding the chalice with both hands. As he says *gratias agens* he bows his head. As he says *bene+dixit* he makes the sign of the cross over the chalice with the right (keeping the thumb and forefinger always joined) and holds it, still in the same way, with the left. Then he holds the knob with the right hand and the foot with the left as he says *deditque discipulis suis dicens : Accipite et bibite ex eo omnes.* He bends over the altar, leaning the forearms on it. He lifts the chalice a little from the altar, putting the second, third and fourth fingers of the left hand joined under its foot, the thumb and forefinger of the same hand over the foot. So, in the same secret voice as before, he says the words of consecration over the chalice, "attentively, continuously and secretly," holding it a little lifted : *HIC EST ENIM CALIX SANGUINIS MEI NOVI ET AETERNI TESTAMENTI MYSTERIUM FIDEI QUI PRO VOBIS ET PRO MULTIS EFFUNDETUR IN REMISSIONEM PECCATORUM.* He sets the chalice on the altar, stands erect and says, *HAEC QUOTIES-CUMQUE FECERITIS IN MEI MEMORIAM FACIETIS.*

Taking the hands from the chalice he lays them on the altar on each side (on the corporal) and genuflects. He stands, takes the chalice with both hands, holding the knob with the right and the foot with the left partly under it as before. So he elevates it to a height where it can be seen by the people above his head, lifting it slowly and straight up, so that it is always over the corporal. He sets it on the corporal, covers it with the right hand, the left laid on the foot of the chalice. Then he genuflects again as before.

Standing erect and holding the hands extended on either side, but now always keeping the thumbs and forefingers joined, he continues

[1] This he may do every time he covers or uncovers the chalice to steady it.

to say the Canon at the words, *Unde et memores*. As he says *de tuis donis ac datis* he joins the hands before his breast ; then as he says *hostiam+puram, hostiam+sanctam, hostiam+immaculatam* he lays the left hand on the corporal and with the right makes the sign of the cross thrice over both the Sacred Host and the chalice. Then as he says *Panem+sanctum* he makes the sign of the cross over the Host only. At *calicem+salutis* over the chalice only.

He extends the hands, as before, and says the prayer, *Supra quae.*

He bows profoundly, lays the joined hands on the altar before him, and so says *Supplices te rogamus* to the word *quotquot*. Here he lays his hands on the corporal on each side, and kisses the altar once in the middle. He stands erect, joins his hands and continues *ex hac altaris participatione*, etc. At the word *Cor+pus* he makes the sign of the cross over the Host ; at *San+guinem* over the chalice, as before. As he says *omni benedictione caelesti*, he signs himself with the cross, holding the left hand at the breast, but so that the thumb and fore-finger do not touch the chasuble. Then he joins the hands. He extends them again slowly as he says *Memento etiam, Domine.* The words *N. et N.* are omitted. As he says *in somno pacis* he joins his hands, raising them arcwise to meet before the lower part of the face, bows his head, looks at the Blessed Sacrament before him and so prays silently for the faithful departed whom he wishes to commemorate. Then he stands erect again with hands extended and continues the prayer at the words *Ipsis, Domine, et omnibus in Christo quiescentibus*. At the conclusion, *Per Christum Dominum nostrum*, he joins his hands and bows his head.

As he says *Nobis quoque peccatoribus* he raises his voice so as to be heard by anyone near.[1] At the same time he lays the left hand on the corporal and strikes his breast once with the right. He does so with the second, third and fourth fingers extended, not touching the chasuble with the thumb or forefinger. He continues *famulis tuis*, etc., erect, with hands extended. If the Saint whose vigil, feast or octave is kept or commemorated be named among those of this prayer, he bows his head slightly towards the book as he pronounces it. He joins the hands at the conclusion, *Per Christum Dominum nostrum*.

Little Elevation. *Amen* is not said here. With joined hands he says, *Per quem haec omnia ;* then at the words *sancti+ficas, vivi+ficas, bene+dicis*, he makes the sign of the cross with the right over the Host and chalice together, laying the left on the corporal. With the right hand he uncovers the chalice and lays the pall on his right. Placing the hands on the corporal on each side, he genuflects and rises at once. He takes the Sacred Host with the right hand between the thumb and forefinger ; with the left he holds the chalice by its knob. He makes the sign of the cross thrice with the Host over the chalice, not extending this sign beyond the cup, as he says *Per ip+sum, et cum ip+so, et in ip+so*. Still holding the chalice in the same way with the left hand, he makes the sign of the cross twice over the corporal between himself

---

[1] " Vocem aliquantulum elevat " (R. IX, 3) (cf. p. 41).

and the chalice, beginning at the edge of the chalice, as he says *est tibi Deo Patri+omnipotenti, in unitate Spiritus+Sancti.* Then he holds the Host over the chalice upright, holding it still with the forefinger and thumb of the right hand, by the lower edge. He may rest the lower part of the hand on the edge of the chalice. With the left he continues to hold the chalice at its knob. So, with both hands, he elevates the Host and chalice together a little above the altar, as he says *omnis honor et gloria.* Then he places the chalice back on the altar, and the Host in the place where it was before, in front of the chalice, still holding the chalice with the left hand. He rubs the fingers of both hands over the chalice, lays the left on its foot, while the right covers it with the pall ; then genuflects, laying both hands on the corporal as usual.

Pater Noster. He stands erect, his hands still on the corporal, and says aloud *per omnia saecula saeculorum.* When the server has answered *Amen,* he joins the hands before his breast, and bowing his head to the Sanctissimum says *Oremus.* Erect, with hands joined, he says the introduction to the Lord's prayer, *Praeceptis salutaribus moniti,* etc. As he begins *Pater noster* he extends the hands and looks at the Sanctissimum. In this position he says the prayer. When the server has answered *Sed libera nos a malo,* the celebrant answers *Amen* in the subdued voice. With the left hand on the corporal he takes the paten in the right from under the corporal and purificator. He wipes it with the purificator (using the left hand to aid him if required), then lays the purificator back on the Epistle side near the corporal. He holds the paten in the right hand between the joined forefinger and thumb together and the second finger. He holds it outside the corporal on his right, upright, so that the concave side faces the middle. So he says silently the Embolism, *Libera nos, Domine.* As he says *et omnibus Sanctis,* he lays the left hand on the breast. As he says *da propitius pacem in diebus nostris,* he makes the sign of the cross on himself with the paten. As soon as he has made this sign he kisses the paten, not in the middle, but at its upper edge. Then he slips the paten under the Host (laying meanwhile the forefinger of the left hand on the farther edge of the Host), continuing the prayer, and lays the paten against the foot of the chalice.

He uncovers the chalice in the usual way and genuflects with the hands on the corporal. Rising, he takes the Sanctissimum in the right hand, holding its lower edge between the thumb and forefinger, and assisting, if necessary, with the left. He holds It over the chalice ; then with both hands he breaks It reverently in a straight line down the middle,[1] using both hands to do this, holding each half between the forefinger and thumb of each hand. Meanwhile he continues *Per eundem Dominum nostrum,* etc. Still holding one fragment in the left hand over the chalice he lays the other with the right on the paten.

---

[1] Altar-breads are generally made with a line down the middle and another, marking the division for the fragment to be put in the chalice, at the back.

With the right hand he now breaks off a small part of the half of the Host he holds over the chalice in his left. Holding this Particle in the right hand over the chalice, with the left he lays the rest of the fragment on the paten by the side of the half already there, saying *in unitate Spiritus Sancti Deus*. He grasps the knob of the chalice in the left hand, and still holding the Particle in the right over the chalice, he says aloud *Per omnia saecula saeculorum*. He makes the sign of the cross thrice with the Particle in his right hand over the chalice from edge to edge of the cup, not going outside this, as he says *Pax+Domini sit+semper vobis+cum*. When the server has answered *Et cum spiritu tuo*, he says silently *Haec commixtio*, etc., and lets the Particle fall into the chalice. He rubs the fingers over the chalice, then at once joins the forefinger and thumb of each hand. He covers the chalice with the pall and genuflects.

Agnus Dei. Rising and bowing moderately towards the Sanctissimum, with hands joined before the breast, but not on the altar, he says aloud *Agnus Dei*, etc. He lays the left hand on the corporal ; with the second, third and fourth fingers of the right he strikes his breast as he says *miserere nobis*. He does not join the hands after this, but holds them in the same position, the left on the corporal, the right resting on the breast,[1] till he says the second time *miserere nobis ;* then he strikes the breast again. So, in the same way, till and while he says *dona nobis pacem*.

Then he joins the hands and lays them on the edge of the altar, not on the corporal. Bowing moderately and with his eyes fixed on the Sacred Host he says the three prayers before Communion, *Domine Iesu Christe, qui dixisti ; Domine Iesu Christe, Fili Dei vivi* and *Perceptio Corporis tui*. Then he stands upright, genuflects, and says *Panem caelestem accipiam*, etc.

He now takes the Host in the left hand. The most convenient and reverent way to do this is thus :

The Host lies on the paten in two halves, side by side, the half on the celebrant's left being without the small fragment which has been put into the chalice. On these he lays the forefinger and thumb of the left hand, one on either fragment. So he pushes them gently forward till their upper edge projects a little beyond the upper part of the paten. He takes the two fragments here, at their upper part, between the thumb and forefinger of the right hand. The fragments are side by side, so as to form a circle, as if the Host were not broken in the middle. So he can hold them between the right thumb and forefinger together, just at the place where they are divided. Taking the two fragments thus in the right he places them in the left hand. The left hand receives them at the bottom in the same way, holding them together, just at the line of fraction, between the thumb and forefinger. Then, with the right hand, he takes the paten at the top (not separating the thumb and forefinger) and puts it under the forefinger of the left between

---

[1] Or being moved slowly away from him in preparation for the subsequent striking of the breast, or laid on the altar.

that and the second finger. He now holds the Host in the left hand between the thumb and forefinger, and the paten under It between the forefinger and second finger. So he keeps them in front of him, not resting the forearm on the altar. Bowing moderately, he strikes the breast with the second, third and fourth fingers of the right hand as he says, in the medium voice,[1] *Domine, non sum dignus.* Then silently he continues *ut intres sub tectum meum*, etc. He does this thrice in the same way.

Communion of the Priest. He stands erect ; with the right hand he takes the fragment of the Blessed Sacrament at his right at its upper edge, and places It beside and slightly overlapping the other half. Then he takes the two fragments, lying one on the other, at the lower edge, with the right hand. The left hand still holds the paten as before ; its thumb and forefinger are now joined over the paten. With the Sanctissimum he makes the sign of the cross in front of himself over the paten, not going beyond its edge, as he says silently *Corpus Domini nostri*, etc. At the Holy Name he bows his head. He leans over the altar, resting the forearms on it, and receives his Communion. In doing so he does not extend the tongue. It is convenient to break the Sacred Species against the roof of the mouth ; but he should, as far as possible, not touch them with the teeth. He then lays the paten on the corporal, rubs the fingers lightly over it, stands upright and " rests a little, meditating the most holy Sacrament," [2] holding the hands raised and joined before his face. It is usual here to shut the eyes. The object of this moment of pause is that he may have time to swallow the holy Species.[3] It should not be prolonged. Then he separates the hands, and lays the left on the foot of the chalice ; with the right he takes the pall, lays it on the Epistle side and genuflects. Meanwhile he says *Quid retribuam . . . mihi ?* silently. Rising he takes the paten in the right hand, inspects it to see if he can discern any fragments of the Sacred Host and wipes them into the chalice if he does. He then inspects the corporal, and collects the fragments on it, if there are any, with the paten. He may lift the edge of the corporal with the left hand while doing this. He then holds the paten over the chalice with the left hand, and with the thumb and forefinger of the right wipes it, so that any particles may fall into the chalice. Having purified the paten, he rubs his thumb and forefinger together over the chalice to detach any fragments that may adhere to them. Saying *Calicem salutaris*, he takes the chalice in the right hand, holding it by the knob between the forefinger and the other fingers, and continues to hold the paten in his left. He makes the sign of the cross before him with the chalice, saying *Sanguis Domini nostri*, etc., again bowing his head at the Holy Name. He holds the paten in the left hand under the chin. Raising the chalice he drinks all the Precious Blood with the Particle in it, with one or at most two draughts, not

---

[1] See p. 41.
[2] Rubric in the Canon.
[3] That is why there is no such pause after Communion in the form of wine.

taking the chalice from the mouth meanwhile and not throwing back the head nor making a sucking noise.

There is no authority for making a pause to say private prayers after the Communion under the form of wine.

If no one else receives Holy Communion the celebrant omits all in the following paragraph and goes on at once as directed in § 6.

§ 5. DISTRIBUTION OF HOLY COMMUNION

IF anyone receives Holy Communion [1] at the Mass the server may begin to say the *Confiteor* before the celebrant has finished making his own Communion, thus indicating that there are communicants. [2]

The celebrant first covers the chalice with the pall and places it (if there be a ciborium) towards the Gospel side on the corporal.

He then genuflects, if he distributes Communion with Hosts consecrated at the Mass. They will be on the corporal. If they are in a ciborium he uncovers this. If they lie immediately on the corporal he puts them on the paten, using the thumbs and forefingers only. He genuflects again.

If he is to take the Sanctissimum from the tabernacle, as soon as he has covered the chalice he removes the altar-card from before the tabernacle, draws aside the tabernacle veil, takes the key, opens the tabernacle, genuflects, takes the ciborium from it with the right hand and places it in the middle of the corporal. [3] He shuts the doors of the tabernacle, not locking them, unveils the ciborium, then uncovers it [4] and genuflects again.

When the server has finished the *Confiteor* the priest turns partly towards the people, facing somewhat towards the Epistle corner so as not to turn his back to the Sanctissimum ; with joined hands he says the prayer *Misereatur*, then *Indulgentiam*. As he begins this second prayer he makes the sign of the cross over the people with his right hand and placing his left on his breast, not separating the thumb and forefinger of either. Both these prayers are always said in the plural form, even if there be but one communicant.

He turns back to the altar, genuflects, takes the ciborium in the left hand at its knob, or the paten at its edge between the forefinger and second finger (keeping, as all this time, the thumb and forefinger

---

[1] The rules for Communion are in the C.J.C. 845–869. The priest who is celebrating may not during Mass give Holy Communion to persons so distant that he would lose sight of the altar when going to communicate them (C.J.C. 868).

[2] The rubrics do not determine at what point exactly the *Confiteor* is to be said. It should be concluded by the time that the priest is ready to turn around to say *Misereatur*. It is best said *immediately* after the consumption of the Precious Blood, while the priest is getting ready the ciborium ; but it should be recited a little earlier if the Hosts for Holy Communion are already on the altar.

[3] This is the moment to put into the tabernacle a (second) ciborium of Hosts that have been consecrated at the Mass or a Benediction Host that has just been consecrated in the lunette. It is also the moment to change the Benediction Host (consuming the old one) if this is to be done.

[4] The veil is placed outside the corporal, the ciborium cover on it.

joined). With the forefinger and thumb of the right hand he takes one Host and holds It above the ciborium or paten, upright, and so turns to the people by the right, and stands with his back to the middle of the altar.

Looking at the Sanctissimum he says aloud *Ecce Agnus Dei*, etc., and *Domine, non sum dignus* (this last three times). When he has completed this the third time, not before, he walks to the Communion rail, or place where the communicants kneel, holding the one Host above the ciborium or paten. If there are many people, he goes first to the person at the end of the Epistle side. Here he says the form of administration, *Corpus Domini nostri*, etc., making the sign of the cross in front of the person with the Host he holds in his right. In making this cross he should not carry the Sanctissimum beyond the edge of the ciborium or paten. Then he lays the Host on the communicant's tongue. He repeats the sign of the cross and form of administration to each person, however many there may be. When all have received Holy Communion, he takes the Communion-plate from the last communicant,[1] and goes back directly to the middle of the altar, not genuflecting, saying nothing. He places the paten or ciborium on the corporal. If any Particles remain in it, he genuflects. He inspects the Communion-plate, and if there are any particles of the Sacred Species on it, he purifies it into the chalice.[2]

If there are any consecrated Particles from the ciborium or paten to be consumed he does so at this moment.[3] He receives the consecrated Species reverently, saying nothing.

If he has to replace the ciborium in the tabernacle, he covers it with its lid and veil, puts it back in the tabernacle, genuflects, then closes and locks the tabernacle.

He then removes the chalice to the middle of the corporal again, takes the pall from it, drinks any drops that may be in it and holds it with the right hand to the server, who approaches on the Epistle side.

§ 6. FROM THE ABLUTIONS TO THE END OF MASS

IF no one but the celebrant has received Communion, as soon as he has drunk the Precious Blood he holds out the chalice over the altar to the server on the Epistle side. Meanwhile he lays the left hand, still holding the paten, on the corporal. The server pours wine into the chalice for the ablution. Meanwhile the celebrant says the prayer *Quod ore sumpsimus*, etc. He may make a sign to the server when enough wine has been poured, by raising the chalice. The quantity of wine at this ablution should be about equal to the amount conse-

---

[1] Unless a server holds the plate for the communicants; he then may take it back to the altar and there hand it to the celebrant.

[2] Instruction of the Congregation of the Sacraments, 26 March 1929.

[3] In no circumstances may the celebrant consecrate one Host at Mass, reserve that and receive another for his Communion. He must always break and receive the Host consecrated at the Mass he says. In the case of renewing the Sacred Species in the lunette, he must consecrate two hosts. The other then lies on the corporal till he, after his Communion, puts it in the lunette.

crated. The priest turns the chalice about gently, so that the wine of the ablution may gather up any drops of the Precious Blood remaining in the chalice. Then he drinks the ablution, using the same side of the chalice from which he received Communion, holding the paten with the left hand under his chin, not making the sign of the cross with the chalice, saying nothing. He lays the paten on the corporal, towards the left side of it, and sets the chalice in the middle. He now puts the thumbs and forefingers of both hands over the cup of the chalice and grasps the cup with the other fingers. He goes to the Epistle side, rests the chalice on the altar there, still holding it as before. The server pours first a little wine, then water, over the celebrant's fingers into the chalice. More water than wine should be poured. Meanwhile the celebrant says the prayer *Corpus tuum, Domine,* etc. If any other finger has touched the Sanctissimum, this too must be purified by having the wine and water poured over it. The celebrant sets the chalice on the altar, near, but not on, the corporal, on the Epistle side, rubs the fingers a little over it, then takes the purificator and dries them. From this moment he no longer holds the thumbs and forefingers joined. He holds the purificator in the left hand under his chin, takes the chalice in the right, and drinks the ablution, saying nothing. Then replacing the chalice on the altar he grasps it by the stem in the left hand,[1] and with the right wipes it out thoroughly with the purificator.

He places the chalice near the corporal on the Gospel side, lays the purificator over it, as it was at the beginning of Mass, and the paten and pall on this. He takes the corporal, folds it and puts it back into the burse. He covers the chalice with the veil, then lays the burse on the top of all (the opening away from him). He sets the chalice in the middle of the altar, and sees that the veil covers it completely in front. If there is a cross or other ornament on the veil, this will be to the front.

Communio. With joined hands he goes to the Epistle side and there reads the Communio, the hands still joined.

If he has to move the book himself, he will take it after he has arranged the chalice and carry it to the Epistle side, bowing his head to the cross as he passes it.

After the Communio he comes to the middle, kisses the altar, turns and says *Dominus vobiscum* in the usual way. He goes again to the Epistle side, says *Oremus,* bowing toward the cross, and says the post-Communion prayers exactly as he said the collects, with hands extended, observing all that is said at p. 42.[2]

---

[1] The most convenient way to do this is to pass the stem, just under the cup, between the first and second fingers, and to close all the fingers around the outside of the cup.

[2] During Lent in ferial Masses the *Oratio super populum* occurs. The celebrant having finished the conclusion of the last post-Communion prayer, standing before the book, extending and joining his hands as usual, and bowing towards the cross says *Oremus, humiliate capita vestra Deo.* Then turning to the book and extending his hands he says the *Oratio.*

If the last Gospel is the prologue of the fourth Gospel, he shuts the Missal when he has finished the conclusion of the last post-Communion, leaving it so that the edges of the pages face the middle of the altar. If there is a proper last Gospel, he leaves the book open at the place where this Gospel is printed.

He comes to the middle, kisses the altar, turns and says again *Dominus vobiscum*, as usual. Without turning back to the altar, still facing the people, he says *Ite, missa est*, with hands joined.

But if he says *Benedicamus Domino* he first turns back by his left to face the altar, and says this versicle in that position·

Facing the altar, bowed moderately and with the hands joined on the altar before him, he says the prayer *Placeat tibi, sancta Trinitas* silently. Then he lays the hands, palms downwards, on each side, kisses the altar, stands upright, looks up at the cross, extends, raises and joins the hands, and says *Benedicat vos omnipotens Deus*. As he says this last word he bows his head to the cross and with downcast eyes turns by the Epistle side, lays the left hand on the breast and with the right makes the sign of the cross over the people, saying, *Pater et Filius+et Spiritus Sanctus*. He makes this sign holding the right hand upright, with the fingers joined, the little finger towards the people. He joins the hands, turns, this time by the Gospel side, completing the circle, goes straight to the altar-card at the Gospel side and there says *Dominus vobiscum* partly facing the card, that is, half turned towards the people, as at the first Gospel.

If there is a proper last Gospel, and if he himself moves the Missal, he does so after having given the blessing, and he bows his head to the cross as he passes it.

Having said *Dominus vobiscum* he lays the left hand on the altar ; with the right thumb he makes the sign of the cross on the altar, then on his own forehead, lips and breast. While he signs himself he lays the left hand on the breast. Meanwhile he says *Initium sancti Evangelii secundum Ioannem*. As he says the words *Et Verbum caro factum est* he genuflects where he stands, laying his hands on the altar.

If the last Gospel be proper, he lays the left hand on the Missal, and makes the sign of the cross with his thumb on the page at the beginning of the text of the Gospel before signing the crosses on himself. He does not kiss the book at the end, but, with the right hand, closes it (in either direction) when he has finished.

He then may either go straight to the foot of the altar steps, or to the centre of the step immediately beneath the foot-pace, or he may first go to the middle, bow, and then turn by the Epistle side and so go down.[1] In either case he does so with hands joined.

Leonine Prayers. According to the present law, after a private Mass the celebrant with the people must say the prayers prescribed by Pope Leo XIII in 1884 and 1886 ; which law was renewed by Pius X (1903), by Benedict XV (1915), and by Pius XI (1930, for Russia). To say these he kneels either on the foot-pace or on the lowest step

[1] Cf. S.C.R. 3637⁸.

and says them from memory or reads them from a card provided. In England they are generally said in the vulgar tongue. Since these prayers are not part of the Mass, according to the strict principle the celebrant should take off his maniple before saying them. If he does so, he may take it off at the middle of the altar and leave it there. But it seems that the general usage is not to take off the maniple.[1]

These Leonine prayers may be omitted after Low Masses which take the place of a solemn Mass and are not strictly private, e.g., a conventual or capitular Mass ; or which have the privileges of a solemn Votive Mass, e.g., the votive Mass of the Sacred Heart on the First Friday ; or which are celebrated with certain solemnity, e.g., Mass for a first Communion, for a general Communion, for a marriage. They may also be omitted if any sacred function or pious exercise (e.g., Benediction, Absolution for the dead) immediately and duly follows Mass and the celebrant does not leave the sanctuary between the Mass and this added ceremony.[2]

When these prayers are finished [3] he goes up to the altar, takes the chalice, holding it in the left hand by the knob and laying the right on it (if he has taken off the maniple, he may lay this on the burse). He comes again to the foot of the steps, makes a profound inclination to the altar, or a genuflection if the Sanctissimum is there reserved, takes the biretta from the server, covers himself and so follows the server to the sacristy.

On the way to the sacristy he says silently the antiphon *Trium puerorum* (doubled on double feasts and with *Alleluia* at the end in Paschal time), the canticle *Benedicite*, the psalm *Laudate Dominum in sanctis eius*, etc., as prescribed in the Missal to be said after Mass.[4]

In the sacristy he first bows his head to the cross, then lays the chalice on the vesting table, takes off the biretta and unvests, in the inverse order to vesting. The server usually assists. When the priest takes off the stole and maniple he kisses the cross in the middle, as when he puts them on.

In some churches it is usual to give the server a blessing after Mass.

Having invested, the celebrant goes to some convenient place to make his thanksgiving. " Having adored and thanked God for everything, he goes away."[5]

§ 7. RULES WHEN THE SAME PRIEST CELEBRATES MORE THAN ONCE ON THE SAME DAY [6]

EVERY priest may say Mass three times on Christmas Day, and now on All Souls' Day. Moreover, in case of necessity, the Ordinary may

---

[1] Regarding the prayer for the king, see p. 133.

[2] S.R.C. 3697[7], 4177[2], 4271[2], 4305.

[3] If any other prayers are said after Mass, with the consent of the Ordinary, those ordered by Leo XIII must be said first (S.R.C. 3682 and 3805).

[4] The *Gratiarum actio post missam* after the *Praeparatio ad missam*.

[5] Rubric at the end of the Byzantine Liturgy of St. John Chrysostom.

[6] Cf. rubrics of the Missal on Christmas Day and All Souls' Day and R.R., Appendix (S.R.C. 3068).

give leave to a priest to say Mass twice on Sundays and holy days of obligation.[1]

Each Mass must be said entirely, including the preparatory prayers at the foot of the altar. The only difference to be observed is with regard to the purification of the chalice. If the celebrant is to say Mass again the same day he may not purify the chalice in the usual way, because to do so would break his fast. At the Offertory of the first Mass it is better to pour all the contents of the wine cruet into the chalice. This will prevent him from taking the ablutions afterwards through oversight. After the consumption of the Precious Blood he replaces the chalice on the corporal and covers it with the pall. He takes no ablutions ; he says the prayer, *Quod ore sumpsimus*, with hands joined, at the middle of the altar ; then purifies his fingers in the little glass vessel containing water,[2] which should stand on the gradine or altar, saying *Corpus tuum, Domine.* Then he covers the chalice, unpurified, with the purificator (not wiping it inside), paten, pall, veil. But he does not put the corporal into the burse. The chalice remains standing on the corporal, the burse at the side. If there is an interval between the Masses the unpurified chalice—which must all the time stand on a corporal—may be left on the altar, or brought to the sacristy, or even put (without the veil) into the tabernacle. If a solemn Mass is to follow it may be brought to the credence and placed there on a corporal.

Before veiling the chalice or before the next Mass, or even at its Offertory, he must put an altar bread, to be consecrated, on the paten. At the next Mass he does not wipe the chalice inside at the Offertory, nor does he then place it on the altar outside the corporal. He places it a little to the Epistle side within the corporal and there, raising it slightly, puts in the wine and water.

Second Mass at Another Church. If he will say the next Mass at another church, the chalice must be purified. In this case the priest proceeds as he does in the case of Masses at the same altar. But when Mass is over he unveils the chalice and first consumes any drops of the Precious Blood that may have flowed down from the sides of the chalice and have collected at the bottom. Then, at the centre of the altar, he pours a little water into the chalice, turns the chalice about gently, that the water may gather up any drops of the Precious Blood, and pours the water into a vessel prepared for that purpose, pouring it over that part of the chalice where he had drunk the Precious Blood. He then wipes the chalice with the purificator and veils it as usual. The water used for the purification should afterwards be poured into the sacrarium, or it may be kept and consumed at the second ablution of a subsequent Mass. The chalice is thus purified and may be put

---

[1] To say Mass twice on the same day is called *binatio*. It may not be done without an apostolic indult or without special faculty from the Ordinary, given only when otherwise, because of a shortage of priests, a notable number of people (say, twenty at least) would be unable to hear Mass on days of obligation (C.J.C. 806, § 2).

[2] The water in this vessel is poured eventually into the sacrarium (p. 18, n. 3).

aside in the usual way. It is not necessary to use the same chalice for the next Mass he says.

§ 8. MASS BEFORE THE BLESSED SACRAMENT EXPOSED

WITHOUT necessity, grave cause or special indult, Mass may not be said at an altar on which the Sanctissimum is exposed. It is forbidden, to distribute Holy Communion at the altar of Exposition.

In all Masses (sung or low) during Exposition, for a public cause lasting some time, even on the more solemn feasts of the Universal Church, the prayer of the Blessed Sacrament is to be added (unless the Mass or an occurring commemoration be of a mystery identical with the M. H. Sacrament) after the prayers prescribed by the rubrics and before *orationes imperatae.* This added collect gives no right to the Creed or to the Preface of the Nativity nor to the gospel from the votive Mass of the Blessed Sacrament as the last gospel.[1]

At Mass said before the Blessed Sacrament exposed these differences must be made :

On approaching the altar the celebrant takes off the biretta as soon as he is in sight of It ; nor does he cover himself again till he is away from the altar. Before and after Mass he prostrates (p. 21) on the ground, not on the step. He makes no prostration during Mass. When he has placed the chalice on the altar he genuflects, laying the hands on the altar. He goes to the Missal and finds the places. Coming back he again genuflects in the middle, before going down to the foot of the altar. He genuflects in this way every time he goes up to, or down from, or passes before, the middle of the altar. In coming down he must take care not to turn his back directly to the Sanctissimum.[2] At the foot of the altar he genuflects again on one knee on the lowest step, makes the sign of the cross, and begins Mass.

The general rule is this : every time the celebrant goes from the middle of the altar to either side, and every time he comes to the middle, he genuflects. He makes this genuflection the last thing before leaving the centre and the first thing on arriving there. Whenever he has to turn to the people, for the *Dominus vobiscum* or other verse, he genuflects before and after turning. If he is already at the centre he makes this genuflection last, immediately before turning (therefore after having kissed the altar or performed any other such ceremony). But when he comes to the middle in order then to turn towards the people, he observes the rule above and genuflects as soon as he is at the centre.

Whenever he turns, he does so, not quite in the middle, but a little towards the Gospel side, and does not turn fully around facing the people, so as not to turn his back to the Sanctissimum. At the *Orate, fratres* and the blessing he does not turn back to the altar by the

---

[1] S.R.C., 11 January, 1928.
[2] So he comes down not in the middle, but towards the Gospel side.

Gospel side, completing the circle ; but he turns by the Epistle side, as at the *Dominus vobiscum.*

At the Holy Name in the Gospel he turns and bows, at the text *et Verbum caro factum est* in the last Gospel he genuflects, towards the Sanctissimum. When he washes his hands at the *Lavabo,* he goes down from the foot-pace either to the step immediately below the foot-pace or *in plano* [1] and turns by his left towards the people, having the altar at his right hand, so that he does not turn his back on the Sanctissimum.

At the ablutions at the end he need not go to the Epistle side. Standing in the middle he holds the chalice towards the server ; then he puts it on the altar just outside the corporal and there receives the wine and water in it over the fingers.

At the verse *Flectamus genua* in ferial Masses he genuflects towards the Missal.

Having imparted the Blessing—partly turned to the people—the celebrant turns back to the altar by his left and, without any further genuflection, goes to the Gospel corner for the last Gospel.

S.R.C. 2682[48].

CHAPTER VII

LOW MASS FOR THE DEAD

AT Requiem Masses the following points are to be observed :
The vestments are always black. If the Blessed Sacrament be present the colour of the conopaeum will be white or violet ; that of the frontal violet.[1] In the preparatory prayers the psalm *Iudica* is omitted. The antiphon, *Introibo ad altare Dei*, is said as usual, then at once the verse *Adiutorium nostrum in nomine Domini* and all that follows.

At the Introit the celebrant does not make the sign of the cross on himself. He lays the left hand on the altar and with the right makes the sign of the cross over the Missal.

Neither *Gloria in excelsis* nor the Creed is said.

After the prayer *Munda cor meum*, before the Gospel, the form of blessing, *Iube, Domine, benedicere* and *Dominus sit in corde meo* are omitted.

After the Gospel the celebrant neither kisses the book nor says *Per evangelica dicta*, etc.

While pouring the water into the chalice the prayer, *Deus qui humanae substantiae*, is said as usual ; but the priest does not make the sign of the cross over the water.

He omits the verses *Gloria Patri* and *Sicut erat in principio* at the end of the *Lavabo* psalm.

The text of *Agnus Dei* is changed. The last clauses are *dona eis requiem* twice ; then, the third time, *dona eis requiem sempiternam*. While saying this the priest does not strike the breast. He holds the hands joined before him, not placed on the altar.

He omits the prayer *Domine Jesu Christe, qui dixisti Apostolis tuis* before Holy Communion.

At the end, instead of the verse *Ite, missa est*, he says *Requiescant in pace*. This is always in the plural, even when the Mass is offered for one person. He turns towards the altar after the *Dominus vobiscum* before this verse, and says it at the middle, facing the altar, with hands joined in front of the breast. No blessing is given at the end of Mass. The celebrant says the prayer *Placeat tibi* as usual, kisses the altar, then goes at once to the Gospel corner and begins the last Gospel.

[1] When the Blessed Sacrament is not present the frontal may be black.

CHAPTER VIII

MASS BY A PRIEST IN THE PRESENCE
OF A PRELATE

IF a priest says Mass in the presence of a Greater Prelate,[1] the following rules are observed :
  A faldstool or kneeling-desk is prepared before the altar,[2] and is adorned as described at p. 8.

The pax-brede [3] is prepared, covered with a veil of the colour of the day, at the credence. If possible, the celebrant should arrive at the altar before the prelate. Here he arranges the chalice and Missal, then goes down to the ground on the Gospel side and stands there, facing the Epistle side across the sanctuary.

When the prelate arrives at his place, where the faldstool or kneeling-desk is prepared, the celebrant bows low to him. The prelate gives a sign that Mass may begin ; the celebrant bows again to him; then makes the usual reverence to the altar, a profound bow, or he genuflects on the step if the Sanctissimum is reserved there. The server kneels at the left of the celebrant. The priest begins Mass as usual, but standing at the Gospel side.

In the *Confiteor*, instead of *vobis, fratres* and *vos, fratres*, he says *tibi, Pater* and *te, Pater*, turning and bowing towards the prelate.

Before going up to the altar he bows again to the prelate.

Mass proceeds as usual, with these differences. After the Gospel the celebrant neither kisses the Missal nor says the verse *Per evangelica dicta*, etc. Instead, the server takes the book to the prelate. He kisses it and says that verse. The server makes no reverence to the prelate when he brings him the book. He brings it open at the place of the Gospel. When the prelate has kissed the book, the server genuflects to him. The celebrant should wait to continue Mass till the server has brought back the book and has replaced it on its stand. The celebrant, not the prelate, blesses the water at the Offertory.[4]

After the *Agnus Dei* the celebrant says the first of the three prayers before his Communion. Meanwhile the server brings the pax-brede from the credence with the veil. He kneels at the right of the celebrant and holds the pax towards him. The celebrant kisses the altar in the middle, then with joined hands kisses the pax saying : *Pax tecum ;*

---

[1] See p. 31. It is supposed that the prelate is present officially in his robes. (See p. 66.)

[2] It may be at the Epistle side, or in another part of the sanctuary, if this is more convenient (C.E. I. xxx, 1). In this case the celebrant says the preparatory prayers in front of the altar, as usual, so long as he does not turn his back to the bishop.

[3] Cf. p. 18.

[4] C.E. I. xxx, 3.

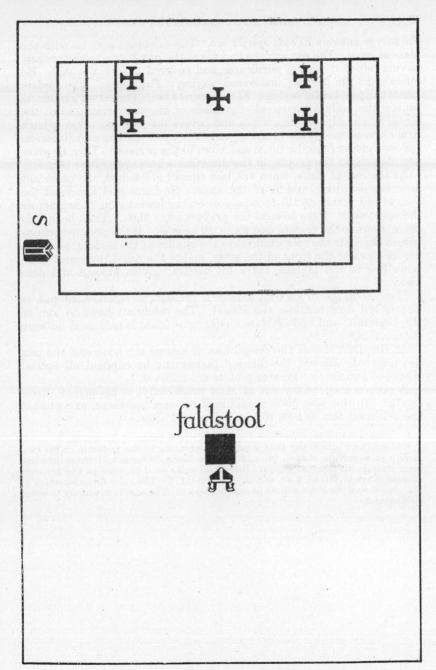

S

faldstool

FIG. 3. LOW MASS BEFORE A GREATER PRELATE
THE CONFITEOR.

R.R.   65   F

the server answers *Et cum spiritu tuo*. The celebrant goes on with the Mass at once. The server rises and takes the pax-brede to the prelate, having wiped it with a purificator and covered it with the veil. He offers it to the prelate, uncovered, saying : *Pax tecum*. The prelate kisses the pax-brede, saying : *Et cum spiritu tuo*. The server genuflects (unless the prelate be outside the place of his jurisdiction, when the server bows only) to him, wipes and covers the pax and takes it back to the credence. At the blessing, when the celebrant has said *Benedicat vos omnipotens Deus*, he turns and bows to the prelate.[1] Then he gives the blessing to the people, in the direction where the prelate is not.

At the end of Mass, when the last Gospel is finished, the celebrant does not go to the middle of the altar. He turns and kneels at the Gospel end, either on the foot-pace or on the lowest step, facing across the sanctuary. Here he says the prayers after Mass. Then he stands there, bows to the prelate and waits till he goes. If the prelate remains before the altar the celebrant takes the chalice at the middle, as usual, comes down to the front of the altar, makes the usual reverence to it, bows low to the prelate, takes his biretta, covers himself and goes away.

If a bishop not in his own diocese is present, he receives the pax as above, but does not kiss the Missal. The celebrant bows to him at the beginning and end of Mass. Otherwise Mass is said as if he were not present.[2]

At Requiem Masses the ceremonies of kissing the book and the pax are omitted. Should the Blessed Sacrament be exposed all special marks of honour to a greater prelate are omitted.

A prelate may be present at Mass unofficially, in his private dress (p. 13). In this case Mass is said as if he were not there, except that the celebrant should bow to him before and after.

[1] " Capite inclinato, quasi licentiam benedicendi petens " (R. xii, 3).

[2] Merati and others say that a priest, celebrating in the presence of his own bishop in a private chapel, no one but the bishop's household being present, even outside his diocese, should observe all rules as if he were in the bishop's diocese (Pars II, tit. iii, § 4 ; *ed. cit.*, vol. i, p. 111). The rules for celebrating in the presence of the Pope will be found there (*ib.*). The case is not likely to occur in England.

CHAPTER IX

LOW MASS SAID BY A BISHOP [1]

WHEN a bishop celebrates Low Mass with some solemnity, in addition to two or three servers, there should be two assistants (*capellani* [2]), one of whom should be in major Orders. They wear cassocks and surplices only, not stoles. The altar-cards are not put on the altar. The vestments (except the maniple) should be laid out on the altar.[3] On the credence are placed the chalice prepared as usual, the maniple, the larger vessel for water (*bacile*) and the dish used by a bishop, one or more finger towels, a silver salver for the skull-cap. A faldstool or kneeling-desk is prepared before the altar ; on this are the Pontifical Canon (p. 19, n. 5) and near by the hand-candle (p. 17, n. 1).

If the celebrant is a bishop in his own diocese, he comes to the church in choir cassock, belt, rochet, mozzetta (p. 10) and biretta. In the case of a bishop not in his own diocese he wears the mantellettum instead of the mozzetta. On greater feasts four candles should be lighted on the altar, otherwise two are sufficient.

The bishop makes his preparation for Mass at the faldstool. While he reads the prayers the Canon lies on the kneeling-desk, one chaplain holds the hand-candle, lighted, at his side.

Vesting. When the time comes for Mass to begin the bishop takes off the pectoral cross and mozzetta or mantellettum. He puts on the the biretta and washes his hands. Every time he washes the hands the water should be poured and the dish held, not by the chaplains, but by a servant or server ; the chaplains hold the towel.[4] The bishop takes off the biretta and hands it to a chaplain,[5] then goes to the altar and vests, assisted by the chaplains. He uses the same vestments as a priest, except that he puts on the pectoral cross over the alb, immediately before taking the stole (the ends of which he wears hanging straight down). He also wears the skull-cap and his ring. When the bishop has vested, a chaplain puts the Pontifical Canon open at *Oramus te, Domine* on the altar, where the central altar-card would stand.

The bishop (except at Requiem Masses) does not take the maniple before Mass, but puts it on after he has said *Indulgentiam* [6] at the foot of the altar. The maniple, therefore, is taken by the chaplain who

[1] C.E. I. xxix. It is presumed in this chapter that the bishop celebrates Mass with some solemnity, and not in the way he would celebrate in his private oratory.

[2] C.E. I. xxix, 2.

[3] If the Blessed Sacrament is exposed, the bishop vests in the sacristy.

[4] C.E. I. xxix, 10 : " semper in lotione familiaris aliquis ministrat aquam et pelvim : capellani vero mantile."

[5] A bishop does not normally wear the biretta with vestments.

[6] C.E. II. viii, 32.

kneels at the Gospel side while these prayers are said, as far as the *Indulgentiam*. Then the chaplain kisses the maniple at its side, not at the cross, hands it to the bishop, who kisses its cross ; the chaplain puts it on the bishop's left arm and then kisses the bishop's hand.

The Chaplains. The two chaplains answer the prayers at Mass and one of them transfers the Missal. At the Offertory the chief chaplain brings the chalice [1] to the altar and ministers the cruets. Having poured in the wine he holds the water cruet up to the bishop saying *Benedicite, Pater reverendissime*. He hands the chalice to the bishop with the solita oscula, but does not recite *Offerimus* nor hold up the chalice ; and also hands him the paten at the Embolism, kissing it and his hand, as usual. After the ablutions one of the chaplains [2] dries and veils the chalice and takes it to the credence, as the subdeacon does at High Mass.

During Mass the chaplains stand one on either side of the bishop, at least when he is at the middle of the altar. When he is at the side they may either stand in the same way, one on either side of him, or, according to some authors, they should then stand together at his farther side, so that the bishop is nearer the middle of the altar. Whenever the bishop reads the hand-candle is held near the book by one of the chaplains or by a server. When the bishop is at the Epistle corner it is held, normally, on his right ; when he is at the centre or at the Gospel corner it is held at his left.[3] Throughout Mass the chaplain nearest the book turns over its pages.

The chaplains kneel at the beginning of Mass till the bishop goes up to the altar. They genuflect each time with the bishop. They kneel during the Elevation, the Communion act and blessing at the end of Mass.

If they are canons, they do not kneel, but bow, at the preparatory prayers, when the bishop bows, and at the blessing.

Preface. All bishops may now wear the skull-cap while saying Mass, except from the Preface to the Communion, both included.[4] The second chaplain takes it from the bishop at the beginning of the Preface and puts it on again after the Communion. While the bishop does not wear the skull-cap, it is put on the silver salver on the credence.

At the end of the Secrets the Missal is shut, taken from its stand and placed aside on the altar or on the credence. The Pontifical Canon is taken from the centre of the altar and put on the missal-stand.

---

[1] Unless at least one of the chaplains is a cleric the chalice must be placed ready on the altar before Mass begins.

[2] Provided he is in major Orders.

[3] The chaplain who holds the candle never kneels nor genuflects while doing so. At the prayer " Qui pridie " he puts the candle on the altar and goes to kneel on the edge of the foot-pace by the side of the other. As soon as the Elevation is ended he goes back to the bishop's side, by the book, genuflects, and again holds the candle.

[4] Cf. C.J.C. 811, § 2. The bishop must also remove the skull-cap whenever the Sanctissimum is exposed.

After the ablutions the Canon and Missal are put back in their places as before.

When a bishop distributes Holy Communion the communicant kisses his ring before opening the mouth to receive the Blessed Sacrament [1] if the bishop thinks fit to present his ring to be kissed.[2]

After the ablutions the bishop again washes his hands.

Blessing. At the end of Mass the bishop gives his blessing in the episcopal form. Facing the altar he says the versicles, *Sit nomen Domini benedictum.* Rʲ. *Ex hoc nunc et usque in saeculum.* Ỿ. *Adiutorium nostrum in nomine Domini.* Rʲ. *Qui fecit caelum et terram.* Then he says : *Benedicat vos omnipotens Deus,* bows to the cross and turning around makes the sign of the cross over the people thrice. Rʲ. *Amen.*

At Low Mass the bishop never uses mitre or crozier, except at ordinations ; nor does an Archbishop use an Archbishop's cross.

When Mass is finished, the bishop unvests before the altar at the foot of the steps ; the vestments are carried by the chaplains to the altar and are laid there. He puts on the mozzetta or mantellettum, resumes the pectoral cross and receives his biretta. Then, at the desk or faldstool he says the prayers after Mass, the Canon lies on the kneeling-desk ; a chaplain or server holds the hand-candle on ·his right.

If there are several servers, two of them hold candles or torches, kneeling before the altar, during the Elevation, that is, from the *Sanctus* to after the Elevation of the chalice. If servers are not available, servants of the bishop,[3] may hold these candles ; or two large candles in candlesticks standing on the ground before the altar may be lit at this time and should be extinguished after the Communion.

At a Requiem Mass the bishop puts on the maniple with the other vestments, as a priest does at the vesting. Nothing is kissed by the assistants (except the vestments).

Prelate Present. If a cardinal, prince or prelate of higher rank than the celebrating bishop be present, another faldstool or desk is prepared for him before the altar. At a bishop's Mass no other prelate kisses the Missal from which he has read the Gospel ; the celebrant always does this himself. But after the Gospel another Missal or book of Gospels is taken to a cardinal or a sovereign prince who may be present ; he kisses it, and the server who brings it to him observes what is said above at p. 64.

The pax-brede is taken to any prelate or prince assisting, as described above, p. 64.

---

[1] This kissing of the bishop's ring is a remnant of the old kiss of peace before Communion, as the ministers at pontifical High Mass kiss his cheek before receiving.

[2] S.R.C. 4395.

[3] C.E. I. xxix, 7, says : " Si vero non adsint tres capellani, poterunt ad cereos supplere duo scutiferi aut alii familiares, arbitrio episcopi, decenter vestiti." Scutiferi are not often met in the households of English bishops to-day. Practically these persons " decenter vestiti " will mean servers in cassock and surplice.

CHAPTER X

THE MANNER OF SERVING LOW MASS

§ 1. GENERAL DIRECTIONS

W HEN the server is doing nothing with the hands he keeps them joined before the breast, unless he hold a book.
Whenever he hands anything to the celebrant, he kisses first the thing, then the celebrant's hand. In taking anything he kisses first the hand, then the thing. These are the so-called "solita oscula" [1]. They are omitted in Masses for the dead an l when the Blessed Sacrament is exposed. While serving one Mass the server must take no notice of anything that may be done at ano'her Mass, for instance, the Elevation at a neighbouring altar. If he se¹ ves a private Mass at a side altar while High Mass or a Sung Mass is celebrated at the High Altar, he does not ring the bell at all. Nor does he do so when the Blessed Sacrament is exposed in the church.

The normal place for the server is, kneeling, on the lowest altar step at the side opposite to that where the Missal is. [2]

Whenever in the course of Mass the celebrant while speaking aloud bows, genuflects, or makes the sign of the cross, the server, as far as possible, does the same.

At the beginning and end of Mass, and when passing before the altar, he genuflects, whether the Sanctissimum be reserved there or not. [3] If It be exposed he genuflects on both knees and bows on arriving at the altar and before departing from it.

§ 2. PREPARATION

BEFORE Mass the server vests in cassock and surplice, [4] and (if this is needed) goes to prepare everything at the altar. [5]

He takes the two cruets, one containing wine, the other water, with the dish and towel for the washing of hands, to the credence. He sees that the altar is uncovered, showing the altar cloth, that the altar-cards are in their place, that the stand for the Missal is at the Epistle side.

---

[1] By custom these oscula are frequently omitted altogether by laymen.

[2] At the last Gospel when it is the pericope from S. John, the altar-card replaces the Missal.

[3] S.R.C. 4193¹.

[4] The rubrics of the Missal (R. II, 1) and the S.R.C. (4194²) both require that the server who wears a cassock, whether a tonsured clerk or not, should wear a surplice at Mass. Yet in many countries, including England, it is a common custom that he serve in lay dress and this usage is now recognised (S.R.C. 4271¹). In case of necessity a woman may kneel outside the sanctuary and answer (C.J.C. 813, § 2). The priest himself moves the book, and so on.

[5] All or part of this preparation may be made by the sacristan.

If he does not bring the Missal with him at the beginning of Mass,[1] he will see that it is already on the stand closed.[2] He lights the two smaller candles used at Low Mass, beginning with the one on the Epistle side.

In the sacristy he then assists the celebrant to vest. He takes the Missal, closed, bows with the celebrant (standing behind him) to the cross in the sacristy, and leads him to the altar at which Mass will be said. In many churches it is usual that the server ring a bell near the sacristy door as he passes, to warn the people that Mass is about to begin. He may take holy water at the sacristy door and offer it to the priest. If they pass an altar at which the Sanctissimum is reserved, the server genuflects with the celebrant. He bows to the High Altar of the church, if they pass it, unless the Sanctissimum be there. At the altar at which the Mass will be said the server goes to the Epistle side, takes the celebrant's biretta, with the usual oscula, genuflects as the celebrant either does so or bows. He puts the biretta on the credence or at another convenient place. He places the Missal on the stand or cushion (parallel to the front edge of the altar) at the Epistle side, going round in plano to do so, not ascending the front steps.

He comes back and kneels in front of the altar at the Gospel side, on the ground, not on the step.

§ 3. FROM THE BEGINNING OF MASS TO THE PREFACE

KNEELING here a little behind the priest he answers the preparatory prayers. He does not bow while the celebrant says the Confiteor. He bows slightly towards the celebrant while he himself says the prayer Misereatur tui omnipotens Deus. He bows moderately towards the altar while he says the Confiteor, and remains so while the celebrant says Misereatur vestri. At the words tibi, pater and te, pater in the Confiteor he partly turns towards the priest. He strikes his breast three times at mea culpa, mea culpa, mea maxima culpa. He bows again slightly at the versicles, Deus, tu conversus, and remains bowing till the celebrant has said Oremus.

As soon as the celebrant goes up to the altar the server rises too. Then he kneels again, this time on the bottom step of the altar. In future he always kneels on this bottom step.

At the Introit he makes the sign of the cross with the priest. He answers Kyrie, eleison and says Amen after the first and last collect, which have the conclusion. At the end of the Epistle he says Deo gratias,[3] and then goes at once to the Epistle corner of the altar. He goes round in plano, genuflecting in the middle, and stands at the foot of the altar.

[1] At Low Mass the server may never open the Missal, nor turn over its pages. This is done by the celebrant himself (S.R.C. 3448[14]).

[2] The rubrics of the Missal suppose that the server bring the Missal with him when the priest comes out to begin Mass, and that he take it back with him to the sacristy afterwards (R. II. 1 and XII. 6).

[3] The priest usually gives a sign at the end of the Epistle, turning towards the server or lifting his left hand (p. 43).

On certain days, for example on Ember days, there are several collects and lessons. The celebrant will not say *Dominus vobiscum* until these extra prayers and lessons are finished. The server remains kneeling at his place for these, answering *Levate* if the priest (while genuflecting) says *Flectamus genua, Amen* at the end of each collect, and *Deo gratias* at the end of each lesson. When the celebrant has said *Dominus vobiscum* the Mass continues as on ordinary days.

Gospel. The server waits at the Epistle corner during the Gradual or Tract. When the celebrant goes to the middle the server takes the Missal across to the Gospel side (carrying it down and up by the middle of the steps), and puts it here at the corner of the altar diagonally, so that its pages face half-way towards the middle of the altar. He stands by the book. The priest comes to read the Gospel. The server answers the versicles at the beginning, and makes the sign of the cross with the thumb on forehead, lips and breast with the priest. If the Holy Name occurs in the opening words of the Gospel the server bows his head. Then he goes to the Epistle side *in plano* and stands at that corner facing the priest, while the Gospel is read. If the priest genuflects during the Gospel, the server does so too. At the end he answers *Laus tibi, Christe.* If the Creed is said, the server kneels during it [1] and bows moderately at the verse *Et incarnatus est*, etc.

Offertory. When the priest has said *Dominus vobiscum* and *Oremus* at the Offertory, the server goes to the credence, takes the dish with the cruets which stand on it and the towel. The practice at Rome is that he spread the towel on the altar at the Epistle corner, put the dish and cruets as they are, on the towel, then take the wine cruet in the right hand, the water cruet in the left, stand at that end of the altar and there wait till the celebrant come. [2] He bows and hands the wine cruet to the priest and takes the water cruet in the right hand. He takes back the wine cruet with his left hand. He kisses both before handing them to the celebrant, and on receiving them back, but, this time, not the celebrant's hand. Then he sets down the wine cruet either on the altar or on the credence (if he goes there to get the special bowl for the washing of the fingers), lays the towel on the altar or on his left arm, takes the dish or bowl in the left and the water cruet in the right hand. The priest comes to wash his hands. The server holds the dish under the celebrant's hands and pours a little water over his fingers from the cruet. He must be careful to hold the dish under the priest's hands, so that the water poured over the fingers may go into it. Before and after washing the priest's fingers he bows to him.

He puts all back on the credence, takes the bell and goes to his place at the lowest step on the Epistle side and kneels there.

When the priest says *Orate, frates* the server should wait till he has again turned to the altar ; then, kneeling (wherever he may be), he

---

[1] The rubric (R.G. xvii, 2) supposes those assisting at Low Mass to kneel during the Creed. Should they stand, as is the custom in many places, the server must still obey the rubrics and kneel.

[2] Cf. Martinucci, I. i, p. 338.

says the answer, *Suscipiat Dominus*, etc. He answers the versicles before the Preface. As the celebrant says the *Sanctus* the server rings the bell gently three times. He then goes to the Epistle side and lights the third candle there. This remains alight till after the Communion.[1] He comes back to his place.

§ 4. FROM THE CANON TO THE END OF MASS

WHEN the celebrant spreads his hands over the host and chalice at *Hanc igitur,* the server rings once the warning bell, where this is customary. When the priest makes the signs of the cross after having stretched his hands over the bread and wine the server comes to kneel on the top step or on the foot-pace at the Epistle side, but near the middle. He takes the Sanctus bell with him. At each Elevation he holds up slightly the end of the chasuble in his left hand,[2] and rings the bell with his right, either continuously or three times. He may arrange this so that he ring once when the celebrant genuflects, once when he elevates, once again when he genuflects. Since there are two elevations the bell will be rung altogether six times. After the Elevation of the chalice and the priest's genuflection following, the server goes back, without genuflecting, to the place where he was before, at the end of the lowest step on the Epistle side, and kneels there. He strikes his breast when the priest does so at *Agnus Dei*. He rings the bell thrice, if customary, at *Domine, non sum dignus.*

Communion. He bows while the priest makes his Communion. If anyone now come to the Communion rail, or if the server himself intend to receive Holy Communion, he rises as the priest gathers the fragments from the corporal with the paten and kneels on the lowest step at the Epistle side, sideways, facing the Gospel side across the sanctuary. Here, kneeling and bowing moderately, he says the *Confiteor*, beginning *immediately* after the priest has consumed the Precious Blood. He should begin the *Confiteor* thus soon, so that the priest may not have to wait when he has opened the tabernacle, put the ciborium on the altar and is ready to begin the prayer *Misereatur*.[3] The server answers *Amen* after this and the next prayer, *Indulgentiam*. If the server himself receive Holy Communion, ordinarily he does so before anyone else. If he is a cleric he will receive after clerics of a higher order than himself ; if a layman, all clerics will receive before him. The server may receive Communion kneeling either on the foot-pace at the Epistle side facing the Gospel side, or kneeling on the edge of the foot-pace in front of the altar, rather to the Epistle side. He will bring with him from the credence the Communion-plate and hold it under his chin.

When the priest goes to give Holy Communion to the people the server will take the Communion-plate and hand it to the first person

---

[1] See p. 37.

[2] Only as the priest elevates, not as he genuflects.

[3] If the Hosts for Holy Communion are already on the altar the *Confiteor* should be begun sooner.

to receive on the Epistle side.[1]   After Communion the priest or the server will take the plate back to the altar and there the celebrant purifies it.   When it has been purified the server will replace it on the credence.

For whatever reason the tabernacle be opened, the server always kneels till it is closed.   After Communion he will take the cruets to the altar for the ablutions.

Ablutions.   If no one but the celebrant receive Communion, the server will take the cruets at once, when the priest has made his Communion in the form of bread and begins to cleanse the corporal with the paten.   He takes the cruets from the credence, the wine in his right hand and the water in his left.   He genuflects at the foot of the altar steps (if the priest has not already consumed the Precious Blood), and stands on the highest step outside the foot-pace at the Epistle corner, at the place where he handed the cruets to the priest at the Offertory.   When the celebrant holds the chalice towards him the server draws near him and bows.   He pours some of the wine into the chalice, until the priest makes a sign.   Then he bows and goes back to where he was before.   The priest, when he has drunk the wine, comes to the server.   The server bows and pours into the chalice a little wine, then water, both over the priest's fingers.   The priest will usually make a sign when enough has been poured.   The server then bows again to the priest, puts the cruets back on the credence and extinguishes the third candle lit after the *Sanctus.*   At the ablutions the server does not kiss the cruets nor the celebrant's hand.

The server then goes to the Gospel side, genuflecting, as always, in the middle as he passes, takes the Missal and brings it to the Epistle end of the altar, again genuflecting as he passes the middle.   He places the Missal straight on the altar, facing the people, as it was at the Introit.   Then he goes to kneel at the lowest step on the Gospel side. He answers the post-Communions, *Dominus vobiscum, Ite, missa est,* or other versicle in its stead.   [During the Easter octave the priest adds *Alleluia* twice to the *Ite, missa est* ; the server does so, too, after the response, *Deo gratias.*]   He makes the sign of the cross at the blessing, then stands.

Last Gospel.   If there is a proper last Gospel the celebrant leaves the Missal open after the post-Communions.   This is the sign for the server.   In this case, as soon as he has answered *Ite, missa est,* he brings the book again to the Gospel side.   He may arrange so that his genuflection in passing the middle with the book coincide with that for the blessing.   In this case he will kneel on both knees at the middle.   Or he may·bring the book to its place, then kneel for the blessing at the Gospel side.

He remains standing at the Gospel side, where he was before, while he makes the responses at the beginning of the last Gospel.   Then he goes over to the Epistle side and stands there, turning towards the

---

[1] It is also permitted to have the plate held for the communicants by the server.

priest. He genuflects with him at the verse *Et Verbum caro factum est*, and answers *Deo gratias* at the end.

He waits for the celebrant at the Epistle side. If necessary he hands him the card from which the prayers after Mass are said. During these he kneels on the lowest step at the Epistle side and answers the prayers aloud.

When the celebrant ascends the altar to get the chalice, the server fetches the Missal from the altar and the biretta from the credence. He hands the biretta to the celebrant with his right hand, making the solita oscula ; genuflects when the celebrant genuflects or bows, and then goes in front of him to the sacristy. He may extinguish the altar candles before doing so.[1]

In the sacristy he bows, with the priest, to the cross, lays down the Missal, assists the celebrant to unvest, and bows to him.[2]

Then, if he is to do so, he goes back to the altar, extinguishes the candles (beginning with the one on the Gospel side), and brings the cruets to the sacristy.

Lastly, he takes off his surplice and cassock.

§ 5. AT REQUIEM MASS

AT Masses for the dead the server omits all kisses. The *Judica* psalm is not said. If the Sequence, *Dies irae*, is said, the server does not rise to move the Missal till the concluding verses. At the end of Mass, instead of *Ite, missa est*, the celebrant says *Requiescant in pace*. To this the answer is *Amen*. There is no blessing.

§ 6. TWO SERVERS AT LOW MASS

ON great feasts there may be two servers at Masses which are not strictly private. In this case one of the two is the first server ; he does nearly all as above. The other may answer with him ; he must take care to bow and genuflect with the first. The second server (who is on the Gospel side) moves the Missal for the Gospel and after the Communion.

At the Offertory the two servers genuflect at the centre and go to the Epistle side. The first serves the cruets. At the Lavabo the first server takes the towel on the right, the second the cruet and dish. While the first goes to carry anything from one place to another the second stands. They both go up and hold the end of the chasuble at the Elevation. The first server will hand the Communion-plate to the first person who is to receive. They may hold the cloth extended between them at the Communion of the clergy or people, if these come to the altar.

At the ablutions the first server alone goes to the credence and serves the celebrant ; the other stands at his place, until he goes to transfer the book.

[1] The Missal supposes that the candles are extinguished before the priest leaves the altar (R. xii, 6). However, this is not the usage now in many places.

[2] In some churches it is the custom for the celebrant to give the server his blessing after Mass at this point.

CHAPTER XI

HIGH MASS

IN the case of High Mass sung by a priest it will be convenient to describe the functions of each assistant separately. Figures, showing the position of each person at various moments of High Mass, are given at pp. 115–118.

§ 1. THE CHOIR AT HIGH MASS

FOR general directions for the choir at all liturgical functions see chapter V, pp. 27 *seq.*

The choir may enter with the celebrant and his ministers, or they may already be in their places before the altar, as when one of the canonical Hours (generally Terce) is sung immediately before Mass.

If the choir enters with the celebrant the members genuflect to the altar and go to their places, in pairs, as described at pp. 27, 28.

If they are already in their places when the celebrant enters with the ministers and servers, they stand during that entrance and bow in return when the celebrant bows to them.

Standing and Sitting. They do not genuflect when the servers and ministers do so before the altar. They stand during the entire Asperges ceremony, bow and make the sign of the cross as they are sprinkled with holy water.[1] All (except prelates and canons) kneel during the preparatory prayers, said by the celebrant at the altar steps. While he and the ministers say the *Confiteor* the members of the choir also say it to each other, in pairs. They should say the *Kyrie, eleison* in the same way, in pairs, while the celebrant says it. If the celebrant sits during the sung *Kyrie, eleison,* the choir sits too. They stand while he says the *Gloria in excelsis,* then sit when the celebrant has done so. They rise as he rises at the end of the *Gloria ;* stand during *Dominus vobiscum* and the Collects ; sit during the Epistle and the chants (Gradual, Tract, Sequence or Alleluia verse) that follow. They stand for the sung Gospel, genuflect if the deacon does so, and stand while the celebrant says the Creed. At the verse, *Et incarnatus est,* etc., they genuflect with the celebrant, as he says it. They then sit as soon as the celebrant does so ; they do not kneel, but uncover and bow, while *Et incarnatus est* is sung.[2] When the celebrant rises, at the end of the sung Creed, the choir stand. They sit again when he has sung *Oremus* at the Offertory. After the celebrant has been incensed, they stand, and remain standing till those of their order have been incensed. They bow before and after being incensed. When the incensation is finished they sit till the celebrant has finished the Secrets.

[1] All stand bareheaded at this time ; those who wear a skull-cap take it off (p. 23).

[2] Cf. C.E. II. viii, 53 ; S.R.C. 1421³ 1476²,³, 1594², 2960.²

They stand when he sings *Per omnia saecula saeculorum* before the Preface. They say the *Sanctus* with the celebrant. After that they kneel till after the Elevation of the chalice, then stand till the end of the celebrant's Communion (except at ferial Masses and on fast days ; see below). They say the *Agnus Dei* with the celebrant. After the Communion they sit. They stand again when the celebrant sings *Dominus vobiscum* before the post-Communion, till the blessing. They kneel for the blessing at the end of Mass, except prelates and canons in chapter, who stand. All make the sign of the cross at the blessing. They stand during the last Gospel (genuflecting at the words *Et verbum*), and so till the end of Mass. They stand as the procession of ministers and servers goes out, if they do not form part of it.

At ferial Masses of Advent, Lent, Ember days, fasting vigils and at Masses for the dead the members of the choir kneel during the Collects, post-Communions and *Oratio super populum*, also from the *Sanctus* to *Pax Domini sit semper vobiscum* inclusive. The exceptions to this rule are the eves of Christmas, Easter, Pentecost and the Ember days in Whitsun week.

Bowing. The members of the choir bow on all the occasions noted at p. 22. Further they bow, at High Mass, during the *Gloria in excelsis* at the words *Adoramus te, Gratias agimus tibi, Iesu Christe, suscipe deprecationem*. During the sung Creed they bow at the Holy Name and at the words *Et incarnatus est. . . homo factus est, simul adoratur*. Before the Preface they bow at *Gratias agamus Domino Deo nostro*. For rules for removing the skull-cap, in the case of those who wear it, see p. 23. For the manner of giving and receiving the kiss of peace, see p. 26.

On Christmas Day at all Masses and on Lady Day [1] the choir kneels at the Creed during the verse *Et incarnatus . . . homo factus est*. They genuflect at the words *Flectamus genua* on fast days, rising when *Levate* has been sung. They kneel at the sung verse, *Adiuva nos, Deus salutaris noster*, in the Lenten Tract,[2] at the verse, *Veni, Sancte Spiritus*, in the Gradual of Whitsunday and its octave, during the Gospel of the Epiphany at the words *Et procidentes adoraverunt eum*, at the Epistle of the feast of the Holy Name, during the words *In nomine Iesu , . . infernorum*, and on all other occasions when the rubric of the Missal says *Hic genuflectitur*. They do not genuflect when the celebrant says these words, only when they are sung. For the order of receiving Holy Communion by members of the choir see pp. 119–121.

§ 2. THE PROCESSION TO THE ALTAR. PROCESSIONAL CROSS

AT Rome it is not the custom that a processional cross be borne before the procession to the altar when a priest sings High Mass ; so the

---

[1] On the day when the Mass of the Annunciation is said.

[2] The Tract " Domine non secundum peccata," in which these words occur, is sung at ferial Masses on Mondays, Wednesdays and Fridays in Lent.

Roman books of ceremonies do not usually speak of it.   The rubrics of the Missal, as Gavanti observes,[1] are incomplete in describing the preparation for High Mass. When the Bishop celebrates, the Ceremonial of Bishops orders that the cross of the Chapter be borne in front of the procession by a subdeacon in tunicle, behind the thurifer.[2]

There is no rule against the cross being carried in front of the procession when a priest celebrates ; in many churches this is the custom. If the cross is carried there will be a cross-bearer wearing, normally, a cassock and surplice.   He has only to bear the cross in the procession on coming to the altar, and again when the procession leaves the church at the end of Mass.   When a priest celebrates, the cross is carried with the figure of our Lord facing forward.   The cross-bearer walks between the acolytes.   He has no other office.   When the procession has arrived at the altar he stands the processional cross in some convenient place in the sanctuary,[3] and goes to a place appointed for him, generally in front of the choir, where he attends Mass, standing, kneeling and bowing as the members of the choir do.   During the last Gospel, when the procession is formed to go out, he will take the cross, place himself between the acolytes before the altar, stand when the others genuflect, turn and so go out as he came.

Note that the cross-bearer, while he carries the cross, never genuflects.   Neither do the acolytes at his side.[4] According to the general rule, the thurifer goes in front of the procession, whether he has the thurible or not.   The cross-bearer and acolytes follow him.

If it is the custom of the church that the thurifer precede the procession with incense,[5] the celebrant will put the incense in the thurible and bless it in the usual way, the deacon assisting, in the sacristy before the procession goes out.

The order of the procession to the altar will be thus, if there are a processional cross, torch-bearers and members of the choir who enter with it :

(Verger or Mace-bearer).

Thurifer.

Second Acolyte.   Cross-bearer.   First Acolyte.

Torch-bearers in pairs (without torches).

Choir in pairs.

Master of Ceremonies.

Subdeacon.

Deacon.

Celebrant.

This order will be modified according to the persons who take part in the procession.   The simplest order is :

[1] Gavanti-Merati, Pars II, tit. ii, ad rubric. V. (ed. cit., vol. i, p. 106.
[2] C.E. I. xv, 8.
[3] There should be a stand for it on the Epistle side.
[4] Cf. p. 22.
[5] This should be done really only at a Pontifical Mass.

Thurifer.
Second Acolyte.   First Acolyte.
Master of Ceremonies.
Subdeacon.
Deacon.
Celebrant.

But if the celebrant wear the cope, then the ministers walk on either side of him, the deacon at his right, the subdeacon at his left, holding the ends of the cope.[1]

The M.C. may walk at the side of the ministers, instead of in front of them, or he may go in front of the procession, if it be necessary to clear a way.

§ 3. THE ASPERGES CEREMONY

By universal Church law, in all cathedral and collegiate churches the ceremony of sprinkling the clergy and people with lustral water should take place before the chief Mass on Sundays. In England the bishops order this in all parish churches before the principal Mass, even if this be a Low Mass only.

The ceremony is in no sense part of Mass. Therefore the celebrant wears for it the cope, not the chasuble.[2] Neither is the maniple worn. If the Asperges is to be performed before Mass, the chasuble for the celebrant will be laid out at the sedilia with the maniples for him, the deacon and subdeacon. When the procession enters the church the celebrant wears all the Mass vestments, except the maniple and chasuble. Instead he has a cope of the colour of the day.[3] The sacred ministers wear the Mass vestments, except the maniple. On the days when the ministers wear folded chasubles (p. 245), they generally wear these during the Asperges; or they may put them on before Mass.

The holy water is usually blessed by the celebrant, but it may be done by another priest,[4] before Mass in the church or in the sacristy. He does this according to the form in the Missal or Ritual, before he puts on the cope.

Procession to the Altar. On going to the altar the thurifer walks first, carrying the vessel of holy water and the sprinkler. The ministers walk on either side of the celebrant holding the ends of the cope. In this case no one takes holy water at the sacristy door. On arriving before the altar the thurifer goes to the right of where the deacon will be, the acolytes to each corner of the altar-steps, the sacred ministers

---

[1] It is a good thing to turn in the orphreys so that the lining does not show unduly.

[2] The celebrant of the Mass that is to follow, and not another priest, must perform the Asperges.

[3] If a cope be not available, he will perform the ceremony in alb and stole.

[4] The celebrant wears (crossed) the stole of the Mass, another priest a violet stole, to bless the water.

stand between the thurifer and the second acolyte. All make the usual reverence,[1] that is, all genuflect, the celebrant bows low, unless the Blessed Sacrament be reserved there, in which case he, too, genuflects. All (except the acolytes who carry their candles to the credence and then kneel before it) kneel, even in Paschal time.[2] The deacon takes the sprinkler from the thurifer, dips it into the holy water and hands it, with the usual kisses, to the celebrant. The celebrant takes the sprinkler and intones the antiphon. *Asperges me, Domine.* The choir continues this, the first verse of the psalm *Miserere,* the verses *Gloria Patri* and *Sicut erat* and repeats the antiphon. [In Passiontide *Gloria Patri* and *Sicut erat* are omitted. In Paschal time, instead of *Asperges me,* the celebrant begins *Vidi aquam.* This is continued, according to the text in the Missal and Gradual.]

Sprinkling the Altar. As the celebrant intones the first words, he sprinkles the altar [3] three times, first in the middle, then on the Gospel side, then on the Epistle side. He signs himself with the holy water on the forehead,[4] then rises, sprinkles first the deacon, then the subdeacon, who sign themselves. The ministers, servers and all who have been kneeling then rise. The celebrant hands the sprinkler back to the deacon, who receives it, as always, with the solita oscula. He gives it to the thurifer.

The celebrant, ministers (on the lowest step) and thurifer (*in plano*) genuflect and go to face the choir on the side of greater dignity (normally, the Gospel side, see p. 28). The deacon again takes the sprinkler from the thurifer and hands it to the celebrant, as before. They bow to the choir, who bow in return ; the celebrant sprinkles them. If there are but few persons in choir, he may sprinkle each one. If there are many, he should rather sprinkle all together three times, once in the middle, once to his left, lastly to his right. He and the ministers bow again, go to the other side of the choir (making due reverence to the altar as they cross the centre) and do as before.

If canons are present in chapter, each is sprinkled separately with one sprinkling, and the celebrant and ministers bow to each before and after and are saluted in return.

After the choir, the celebrant sprinkles the servers, who stand by the credence or altar (with the triple aspersion for all together).

Sprinkling the People. Then he goes to sprinkle the people. To do this he goes, with the ministers, to the entrance to the sanctuary, and facing the people, bows, sprinkles them in the middle, to his left, and to his right and bows again. He may (if customary) go down the church. If he goes down and returns by the centre passage, it is better to sprinkle the people on both sides alternately on his way down, and

---

[1] If there is a liturgical choir, all bow to it, to the side of greater dignity first, on arriving at the entrance to the choir.

[2] Rubric of the Missal.

[3] If the Sanctissimum is exposed the altar is not sprinkled.

[4] He may sign his forehead with the sprinkler, or may touch his thumb with it and make the sign of the cross with the thumb.

not at all on his return (it is not becoming to sprinkle the backs of some of the congregation and unseen by them). But if, in a large church, he goes down on one side and returns by the other, he will go down on the Epistle side (turning to his left outside the sanctuary) and return by the Gospel side,[1] sprinkling the people all the while, either on both sides alternately or on one side only according to the position of the people.

During the singing of the *Gloria Patri*, the sacred ministers may stand and bow towards the altar.

During this ceremony the celebrant recites the psalm *Miserere* (in Paschal time, *Confitemini*) with the ministers, in a low voice. When all are sprinkled, the celebrant may cease the recitation of the psalm, terminating it with *Gloria Patri*. He then repeats in full the antiphon *Asperges* (or *Vidi aquam*). Meanwhile he returns the sprinkler to the deacon, who gives it to the thurifer.

The Prayer. When they have returned to the altar they make the proper reverence to it, and stand there. The M.C. hands the book containing the versicles and prayer, and the ministers hold this before the celebrant. When the choir have finished the repetition of the antiphon, the celebrant, with hands joined, sings the versicles (in Paschal time *Alleluia* is added to the first one), and the prayer to the second ferial tone (inflexion d'l). The choir answer.

When *Amen* after the prayer has been sung, the deacon hands the book to the M.C., who puts it on the credence. The celebrant and ministers make the usual reverence to the altar (those in vestments who genuflect do so on the lowest step), and go to the sedilia. The choir sit, and the servers, if this be the custom of the church.

The thurifer should now go to the sacristy to see that the charcoal is ready in the thurible for the beginning of Mass.

At the sedilia the celebrant takes off the cope and puts on the chasuble and maniple, assisted by the M.C. or a server. The ministers put on the maniple.

All stand as the celebrant and ministers come to the altar.

Here they again make the usual reverence, and so begin Mass.

In churches which have a font, on Easter Day and Whit-sunday, the ceremony of sprinkling the people before Mass is done, not with the usual holy water, but with water from the font, taken from it before the holy Oils were put in, when the font was blessed the day before.

At a Sung Mass all is done as above, except, naturally, that the deacon and subdeacon are absent. Either the M.C. walks at the left of the priest and holds the holy-water stoup, handing him the sprinkler and doing all the deacon does at High Mass, or the thurifer does so, while the M.C. holds back the cope on the right. If there is no choir to sing the celebrant says the antiphon and the rest in an audible voice ; the server answers the versicles.

[1] S.R.C. 3114[2].

R.R.   G

§ 4. THE THURIFER AT HIGH MASS

THE thurifer[1] should come to the sacristy in good time before Mass begins, and vest in cassock and surplice. Usually he will then prepare the thurible and (if necessary) assist the celebrant to vest. During Mass (except from the Consecration to the Communion inclusive) each time that the thurifer leaves the choir or returns to it he bows to the clergy, normally to those on the Gospel side first.

If there is a boat-bearer, he has merely to accompany the thurifer at his left side, holding the boat, and to hand it to the thurifer when it is wanted. He genuflects and bows with the thurifer, and stands aside at all ceremonies with the thurible. No rubric supposes the presence of a boat-bearer. The Ceremonial always supposes that the thurifer carries the incense-boat himself.[2] But Merati allows for a boat-bearer.[3]

Asperges. If the Asperges ceremony is performed before Mass, the thurifer leads the procession into the church, carrying the holy-water vessel. He stands at the right of the deacon before the altar, genuflects each time with the others, hands the sprinkler to the deacon and accompanies him, on his right, down the church, as described above (p. 80). As soon as the holy-water vessel is put back on the credence, and the celebrant and ministers go to the sedilia to put on the chasuble and maniples, the thurifer should go to the sacristy, genuflecting as usual before the altar if he passes it, to get the thurible. He will bring the thurible, carrying it in his left hand, with the incense-boat in the right, to the church. He should arrive in the sanctuary before the end of the *Confiteor.* Genuflecting if he passes the altar, he goes to stand in the sanctuary on the Epistle side.

If there is no Asperges the thurifer—usually carrying the thurible and boat—leads the procession to the church, and stands on the Epistle side of the sanctuary during the preparatory prayers.[4]

For the manner of handling the thurible and of holding it while incense is blessed, see pp. 24, 25.

Incensation of Altar. He comes up to the altar, on the foot-pace, at the Epistle side, as soon as the celebrant goes up to it. Here he hands the boat to the deacon, holds the thurible before the celebrant while incense is put in and blessed, hands the thurible to the deacon (taking the boat from him) and goes down from the foot-pace to the floor of the church. He may have to remove the Missal while the altar is incensed if the M.C. does not do so. When the deacon incenses the celebrant the thurifer stands near him, a little behind, on his right, and

---

[1] The thurifer is really one (the first) of the acolytes. He is called so constantly in C.E. (e.g., I. xxiii, 2, " ipso acolythus thuribulum deferens ").

[2] E.g., C.E. I. xxiii, 1.

[3] Gavanti-Merati, Pars II, tit. ii, § 21 (*ed. cit.*, vol. i, p. 107).

[4] Or he may not come out until towards the end of the *Confiteor.* If he comes out at the beginning it is not clear whether he should stand or kneel during the opening prayers and confession. Some authorities say that he should kneel. Others suggest that he should stand. This seems the more convenient, since he is carrying the thurible.

bows with him (see fig. 6, p. 115). He takes the thurible from the deacon and carries it back to the sacristy. Then he comes to his place, between the acolytes before the credence. He stands here, waiting, till the end of the Collects or Epistle.[1]

Then he goes back to the sacristy, sees that the charcoal is burning in the thurible, if necessary renews it, and comes out, with the thurible, before the reading of the Gospel has terminated. When the celebrant has finished reading the Gospel the thurifer takes the boat from the credence and comes up to the altar on the Epistle side, as before. The celebrant puts in incense and blesses it in the usual way. The thurifer takes the thurible (open) in the right hand and the boat in the left. He goes down on the Epistle side, leaves the boat on the credence as he passes and leads the acolytes to the middle of the sanctuary before the altar steps, stands some distance from the steps in front of the acolytes and waits there.

Gospel. The deacon and subdeacon come and stand in front of the thurifer and acolytes.[2] When the M.C. gives the sign, the thurifer genuflects with the others, and bows, with them, to the choir, first to the Epistle side and then to the Gospel side. He then, with the M.C., leads the procession to the place where the Gospel is sung. He stands here at the deacon's left, allowing the acolytes to pass before him. For the group at the Gospel, see fig. 12, p. 117.

When the deacon has announced the title of the Gospel, the thurifer shuts down the thurible and hands it to the M.C., who gives it to the deacon to incense the book. The M.C. hands it back to the thurifer. He raises the lid a little and stands in the same place as before. He should not swing the thurible while the Gospel is sung. When the Gospel is finished the subdeacon goes directly to the celebrant while the thurifer (with the M.C.) leads the deacon and acolytes to the foot of the altar. There he genuflects when the deacon does so, and handing him the thurible stands at his left, and, with him, bows to the celebrant before and after the incensation. He takes the thurible back (on the deacon's right) when this is done. He genuflects with the M.C. and acolytes and goes to put aside his thurible—and renew the charcoal—for the sermon or Creed. If there is neither sermon nor Creed he does not leave the sanctuary (unless he must get charcoal) but stands between the acolytes before the credence.

If he leaves the sanctuary he comes back at once, without the thurible, and goes to his usual place.

[1] He must go to fetch the thurible in time to be at hand with it as soon as the celebrant has finished reading the Gradual, Tract, Alleluia, or Sequence. The moment when he goes out depends on the length of these. If there is only a short Gradual he should go as soon as the last collect is sung. If there is a long Tract or Sequence he may wait till the subdeacon has finished singing the Epistle. Should the thurible not need fresh charcoal the thurifer may remain standing with the acolytes near the credence.

[2] See fig. 11, p. 117. Should a M.C. not take part in the Gospel group, the thurifer may stand between the acolytes at the foot of the altar before the Gospel group is formed, and in this group may stand at the deacon's right, a little behind him.

Offertory. Towards the end of the sung Creed he goes again to fetch the thurible from the sacristy. He brings it out and waits at the Epistle side of the sanctuary. As soon as the subdeacon comes down from the altar, the thurifer goes up to it, first taking the boat from the credence, and assists, as usual, while incense is put in and blessed. When he receives the boat back from the deacon, he takes it to the credence. He stands there, on the ground, at the Epistle side, with joined hands, while the celebrant incenses the altar, unless he has to move the Missal (p. 91, n. 2).

When the deacon takes the thurible from the celebrant and comes down to incense him, the thurifer goes to his side at the left, but a little behind. He accompanies the deacon in this way while the celebrant, choir and subdeacon are incensed, bowing and genuflecting each time with him.

After he has incensed the subdeacon the deacon returns the censer to the thurifer. He then incenses the deacon (who goes to his place behind the celebrant and turns round) with two double swings (see p. 26), then he incenses the M.C., the acolytes and other servers, with one double swing for each, facing each where he stands, and bowing before and after.[1] He comes to the entrance of the choir, genuflects turns to the people, bows, and incenses them with three simple swings, one down the middle, the next towards the Epistle side, lastly towards the Gospel side. Then he bows, turns, genuflects again, and takes the thurible to the sacristy. Usually, when he goes out the torch-bearers follow him (p. 89). If so, they should form up in a line with him before the altar, all genuflect together, bow to the choir (first to the side of greater dignity)[2] and follow him to the sacristy.

Elevation. The thurifer in the sacristy renews the fire in the thurible, if necessary. He comes back to the sanctuary, after the recitation of the *Sanctus* by the sacred ministers, leading the torch-bearers. They all genuflect together in the middle, and then bow to the choir on the Gospel side, normally, and then on the Epistle side. Then the thurifer goes to the Epistle side and stands there, facing across the sanctuary. Just before the Consecration the M.C., or an acolyte puts incense into the thurible. The thurifer incenses the Sanctissimum,[3] kneeling on the lowest step at the Epistle side. He makes three double swings of the thurible at each Elevation (in practice, one each time the bell is rung), and bows before the first and after the third of these.

After the incensing of the Blessed Sacrament at the Elevation, the thurifer makes a simple genuflection and takes the thurible to the sacristy and puts it back in its place. Except when the torch-bearers remain,[4] he genuflects with them and leads them out. The thurible is

---

[1] Making only one common bow—a slight one—before and after, to each group of servers. If he incenses them collectively it will be with three single swings (centre, to his left, to his right).

[2] Cf. p. 28.

[3] See p. 94, n. 2.   [4] See p. 89.

not used again and so the thurifer's office ends at this point. Usually he returns to choir and takes his place with the other assistants for the rest of Mass. When the Mass is ended the thurifer may lead the procession in, walking before the acolytes, with joined hands.

If the thurifer replaces an acolyte : Sometimes, however, the thurifer may have to replace an acolyte, e.g. if the acolytes take the place of torch-bearers, on those days when the torch-bearers remain till after the Communion. In this case, then, the thurifer will take the humeral veil from the subdeacon at the words *Dimitte nobis* in the Lord's Prayer. He folds it and carries it to the credence. Also, when he has received the pax from the M.C., or the person standing next to him, he takes the chalice veil round to the Gospel side of the altar ; then he brings the cruets to the altar for the ablutions, takes them back afterwards to the credence and goes back to his place before the table.

Communion. If the clergy go to Communion (see § 11, p. 119) the thurifer, when he has laid the humeral veil aside, takes the Communion cloth, goes over to the Gospel side and there kneels on the ground. After the prayer *Indulgentiam* he comes to meet the M.C. in the middle. They genuflect together, each takes one end of the Communion cloth, they separate and go one to either end of the altar (the thurifer back to the Gospel side), stretching the cloth between them. They kneel, facing one another, on the two ends of the foot-pace, and hold the cloth across between them. The clergy come to this cloth and receive Communion over it. Then the M.C. and thurifer come again to the middle, fold the cloth there ; the thurifer takes it to the credence, then brings the cruets to the altar for the ablutions.

§ 5. THE ACOLYTES

THE two acolytes should be, as far as possible, of the same height.[1] In due time before Mass they come to the sacristy, and vest in cassock and surplice. Unless someone else has this duty, the acolytes light the candles on the altar, each lighting those on one side. They begin lighting the candle nearest the altar cross. If one acolyte light all the candles he begins on the Epistle side.[2] They then see that their candles in the sacristy are lighted. The first acolyte assists the deacon to vest, the second acolyte the subdeacon. When the celebrant is vested they hand the maniples to the deacon and subdeacon to kiss, then put them on the left arm of each. If the Asperges comes before Mass, the maniples are not put on in the sacristy.

The normal place for the acolytes, when they are not occupied, is in front of the credence. At High Mass, when the celebrant and ministers sit, the acolytes, thurifer and other servers may sit too. They may sit on the steps of the altar ; [3] often special places are appointed for them, a bench or seats in front of the choir. When they are not occupied they

[1] C.E. I. xi, 8.
[2] S.R.C. 4198[9].
[3] S.R.C. 2515[5]. They may never sit at the sedilia.

join the hands before the breast. When sitting they lay the hands flat on the knees. Whenever they pass before the altar they genuflect together in the middle.

Procession. The acolytes go at the head of the procession, following the thurifer, having bowed to the cross or image in the sacristy with the sacred ministers. If the processional cross is carried, they go on either side of it. The first walks to the right of the second. He carries his candle, holding it under its knob, in the right hand and puts his left under its foot. The second holds the left hand under the knob of his candle and puts the right under its foot. It is important that they should hold their candles straight and at exactly the same height. The acolytes can verify this, without looking up, by seeing that the feet of the candlesticks are level.

When they arrive in front of the altar, they do not at first genuflect, but go at once to either side, at the corners of the altar steps. There they turn to face one another, if the clergy are in the procession, and so now going to their places in choir.[1] When the celebrant and sacred ministers arrive at the foot of the altar, the acolytes turn and face the altar, genuflect with them and then carry their candles to the credence. They put them down there, one at each corner at the back, then kneel side by side in front of the credence.

During a function (unless attending the cross-bearer) they always genuflect when passing the centre of the altar, whether the Sanctissimum be reserved there or not.

Asperges. If the Asperges ceremony takes place before Mass, the acolytes stand when the deacon and subdeacon rise. They bow and make the sign of the cross when they are sprinkled. They remain standing before the credence till the celebrant and ministers go to the sedilia. Then they go to assist them. The first acolyte hands the maniple to the deacon, the second to the subdeacon, while the M.C. assists the celebrant (p. 81). It may be necessary for one of the acolytes to carry the cope to the sacristy. They then go back to their place before the credence. They kneel there during the preparatory prayers, making the responses, bowing and signing themselves as the deacon and subdeacon do, and they stand when the celebrant goes up to the altar. When they are not engaged in some duty they will normally stand at the credence, facing across to the Gospel side.

Gloria in Excelsis. Whenever the celebrant and sacred ministers go to sit down, as at the *Gloria* or Creed (perhaps during the singing of the *Kyrie, eleison* or Sequence) the acolytes go to assist them at the seats. They go to the sedilia, the first acolyte to the side nearer the altar, where the deacon will sit, the second acolyte to the subdeacon's place. When the celebrant has sat down the first acolyte hands to the

---

[1] If the clergy be already in choir the acolytes will arrive there immediately in front of the sacred ministers. On arriving at the entrance to the choir they separate, stand in a line with the sacred ministers and reverence to the choir, first on the Gospel then on the Epistle side. They then proceed with the sacred ministers to the foot of the altar.

deacon his biretta,[1] while the second acolyte hands the biretta to the subdeacon. The acolytes may arrange the dalmatic and tunicle, if feasible, over the back of the sedilia. If they pass before the celebrant they bow to him The acolytes may themselves then sit, at some bench prepared for them.

Folded Chasubles. On the days when the ministers wear folded chasubles,[2] while the last collect is chanted the second acolyte goes to the subdeacon, helps him to take off the folded chasuble, and takes it to the credence. When the subdeacon has kissed the celebrant's hand, after reading the Epistle, the second acolyte helps him to put it on again. In the same way he takes the folded chasuble from the deacon while the celebrant reads the Gospel ; the first acolyte helps the deacon to put on the so-called " broad stole." [3] At the end of Mass, when the deacon has moved the book for the post-Communion, the first acolyte helps him to take off the broad stole, takes it to the credence, brings the folded chasuble and assists him to put it on.

Gospel. Before the sung Gospel, while the celebrant puts incense in the thurible, the acolytes take their candles from the credence. The thurifer comes down on the Epistle side, and as he comes around on his way to the centre he is joined by the acolytes coming from the credence. They follow him to the centre near the foot of the altar ; and stand there on either side of him or behind him and M.C. Then, some time after the deacon and subdeacon have come to stand in front of them, the M.C. gives a sign ; all genuflect together to the altar and bow to the choir right [4] and left. They then go to the place where the Gospel is sung. The M.C. and thurifer go first, then the two acolytes side by side, then the deacon and subdeacon. The acolytes swing round, the second keeping his place to the left of the first, and stand facing the deacon, on either side of the subdeacon, slightly behind him, the first acolyte on his right (fig. 12, p. 117). They stand while the Gospel is sung and do not genuflect or bow if the deacon does so, nor make the sign of the cross.

When the Gospel is ended they precede the deacon to the middle, and genuflect behind him when he does so. After the incensation of the celebrant, at a signal from the M.C., they genuflect again, with the thurifer, and take their candles back to the credence. They stand here, at their usual place, while the celebrant says the Creed ; they genuflect with him. They go to the seats to make ready for the sacred ministers, as at the *Gloria*. But this time they stay there till the deacon comes back from having spread the corporal on the altar. They kneel while the choir sings the words *Et incarnatus est*, etc., unless they are sitting, when they bow only. The first acolyte assists the deacon when he sits ; they then go back to their place, bowing to the celebrant, if they pass before him.

---

[1] If there is no M.C. he first hands the celebrant's biretta to the deacon.
[2] See p. 245.   [3] See p. 245.
[4] I.e., first to the Epistle side this time, as the procession is to go towards the Gospel side.

Offertory. When the subdeacon comes for the chalice at the credence the first acolyte assists him to put on the humeral veil ; the second acolyte folds up the chalice veil when handed to him. The first takes the towel, dish and cruets, and follows the subdeacon to the altar. Here he spreads the towel at the Epistle end, and stands the dish and cruets on it. He hands the cruets to the subdeacon ; [1] when the wine and water have been poured into the chalice he takes the towel, dish and cruets back to the credence.

While the deacon incenses the celebrant the first acolyte takes the towel, the second takes the cruet with water in his right hand, and the bowl in his left. As soon as the celebrant has been incensed they come to him at the Epistle end, the first at the right of the second, and bow. The second acolyte pours water over the celebrant's fingers into the bowl, the first hands him the towel. When he gives back the towel they bow again, take the cruet, etc., back to the credence and stand before it in their usual place. When they are incensed they bow to the thurifer before and after.

Consecration. The acolytes stay by the credence during the Canon [2] and attend, if necessary, to the ringing of the bell, and to putting in incense for the thurifer before the Elevation (fig. 13, p. 118). Like the choir, they kneel from the beginning of the Canon till after the Elevation, then stand. But on the days when the choir remains kneeling till the Pax (see p. 77), the acolytes do so too.

When the celebrant sings the words *Et dimitte nobis debita nostra* in the Lord's Prayer, the first acolyte goes to the subdeacon near the foot-pace, takes the humeral veil from him and puts it on the credence, having genuflected with the subdeacon before and after the removal of the veil.

Communion. The acolytes bow at the celebrant's Communion under both species.

If there is Communion of the clergy, and if the acolytes do not bear torches, they hold the Communion cloth as described at pp. 120–121. If the acolytes receive Holy Communion, they do so after the deacon, subdeacon, and any clergy who may communicate. They genuflect on one knee before and after their Communion.

When the celebrant gathers up fragments of the Sacred Host, the first acolyte takes the cruets to the altar and hands them to the subdeacon. On the way he genuflects to the Sanctissimum at the foot of the steps on the Epistle side. The second acolyte meanwhile takes the chalice veil to the Gospel side, genuflecting as he passes the altar in the middle at the same time as the deacon and subdeacon when changing places. He comes back to his place, again genuflecting at the middle.

The acolytes kneel at their place for the blessing at the end of Mass, stand for the last Gospel, and make the signs of the cross with the celebrant at its beginning.

---

[1] He does not kiss the cruets at High Mass, since he does not hand them directly to the celebrant.

[2] If the acolytes have to act as torchbearers, see *infra*, p. 90.

Last Gospel. During the last Gospel the acolytes take their candles, come to the middle—arriving just before the words *Et verbum caro*, when the Gospel is that of S. John—genuflect and go to the entrance to the choir. They genuflect again when the sacred ministers reverence to the altar, and lead the procession back to the sacristy, following the thurifer. If there is no procession of clergy, the acolytes go during the last Gospel to their places at the corners of the foot of the altar ; genuflect with the sacred ministers at *Et verbum* (if these words occur) and to the altar, reverence with them to the clergy in choir to left and right and lead them to the sacristy.

In the sacristy they bow to the cross, extinguish their candles and put them away and take the maniples from the deacon and subdeacon. When the celebrant has taken off his vestments they help the ministers to do so. Lastly they go back to put out the candles on the altar. They do this in the inverse order to lighting them (see p. 85).

§ 6. TORCH-BEARERS

IF servers other than the acolytes [1] are torch-bearers they may be two, four or six, according to the solemnity of the Mass. They come to the church in the procession, after the acolytes, with joined hands. They go, after the common genuflection, to the place prepared for them in the sanctuary, generally a seat in front of the choir. Here they attend Mass, having no special office, behaving as the members of the choir, till the Preface.

Then they come to the middle of the sanctuary, genuflect together, bow to the clergy (normally to those on the Gospel side first) and go to the sacristy in pairs with joined hands. It is usual to combine this with the moment when the thurifer goes to the sacristy after the incensing at the Offertory (p. 84). In this case the torch-bearers stand in a line with him in the middle, genuflect with him and follow him out.

In the sacristy they take the lighted torches. At the Sanctus they follow the thurifer back to the sanctuary in pairs—each holding his torch in the outside hand, the other being laid flat on the breast—genuflect with the thurifer, bow to the choir on either side then to one another, separate and kneel in line either facing the altar (fig. 13, p. 118) or at the sides facing one another.

At most Masses they go out again as soon as the Elevation of the chalice is ended. They rise, come together, genuflect together with the thurifer, who leads them out (p. 84), but do not now bow to the choir. So they go out two and two, put the torches back in the sacristy, come back, genuflect and go to their places, as before. They have no further function. At the end of Mass the torch-bearers come to the middle with joined hands, genuflect with the others, and take their place in the procession back to the sacristy.

But on certain occasions the rubric orders that the torches remain

---

[1] Sometimes the acolytes have to act as torch-bearers (cf. R. viii, 8). They then use torches, not their candlesticks.

till after the Communion.   These are fast days [1] (when the ferial Mass is said), when a Requiem Mass is celebrated, and when other persons besides the celebrant will receive Communion.

On the days when the torches remain, the torch-bearers stay on their knees in the sanctuary till after the Communion ; then they rise, genuflect, bow to the choir and go out two and two.

If the torch-bearers receive Holy Communion they must meanwhile hand the torches to someone else to hold while they do so.

In the other case, when the acolytes of the Mass are the torch-bearers, they must go out with the thurifer at the Preface, perform this function as described, then come back and go to their place at the credence.

If the acolytes hold torches, and if it is a day on which the torches remain till the Communion, it follows that they cannot perform their usual service between the Consecration and Communion.   In this case their place is supplied by others, normally by the M.C. and thurifer.'

§ 7. THE MASTER OF CEREMONIES

The Master of Ceremonies (M.C.) or ceremoniar [2] should know not only what he has to do himself, but also the function of everyone else.   It is his business to see that the ceremony is carried out correctly by all who take part in it.[3] He must, if necessary, guide the other servers by some sign, as little noticeable as possible.   If the mistake is unimportant it is wiser to let it pass at the time and to point it out afterwards.

He comes to the sacristy in good time before Mass begins and vests in cassock and surplice.   He prepares the chalice and paten, also a ciborium, if it will be wanted, and puts these on the credence.   He finds the places in the Missal—which should be on the Missal-stand open at the Mass which is to be sung—and marks them.   On the credence he prepares the book of lessons, marked at the Epistle and Gospel.   With the acolytes he sees that the cruets, towel and bowl for the Lavabo and the bell are on the credence ; that the thurible, torches and everything else that will be needed are ready.   He tells the celebrant and ministers when the time has come for them to vest and sees that this is done properly.   The ministers should not put on the maniple (or the folded chasuble, when this is used) till the celebrant is fully vested.

Procession.   The M.C. at the proper time gives the signal for the procession to go to the sanctuary.   He sees to it that each person walks in his proper place.   He himself goes with the sacred ministers, immediately in front of the subdeacon or to their right (p. 78).   During the whole service he remains uncovered.

[1] Except Christmas Eve, Holy Saturday, the eve of Pentecost and the Ember days of Whitsuntide.

[2] " Magister caeremoniarum," " caeremoniarius."   According to the Ceremonial (I. v, 1), the Bishop should have two masters of ceremonies, the first a priest, the second at least a subdeacon, who must know all functions performed by each person.

[3] " Si quid erroris accidat, aut incaute fiat, ipsi uni Caeremoniario imputari solet " (C.E. I. v, 2).

When the celebrant and ministers take off their birettas the M.C. will take them from the deacon and subdeacon,[1] not kissing them ; he genuflects and puts the birettas on the sedilia. Then he kneels at the deacon's right, behind him, facing the altar, or at the side facing towards the Gospel corner. He answers the celebrant during the prayers at the altar steps, in a low voice, and he makes the usual signs of the cross and inclinations.

The M.C. oversees from a distance the putting in of incense, ready to intervene if necessary. While the celebrant is incensing the cross the M.C. removes the Missal and stands *in plano* with it, facing towards the Gospel side ; he puts it back as soon as that end of the altar has been incensed.[2] In neither case does he genuflect. While the deacon incenses the celebrant the M.C. stands at the Epistle corner (fig. 6, p. 115). The M.C. must remember that, throughout the service, his normal place is at the celebrant's side, so that he may assist him in any way needed.[3] As soon as the celebrant begins the Introit of the Mass, the M.C. stands at his right, forming a semicircle with the ministers. He points out the Introit with the open palm of the right hand. Whenever he is at the celebrant's side, and the deacon is not there, while the celebrant reads or sings, he will attend to the Missal, indicating the place and turning the pages.

Kyrie and Gloria. If the choir take long to sing the *Kyrie*, so that the celebrant and ministers sit while they finish it, then, as soon as the celebrant has said the *Kyrie*, the M.C. will conduct the sacred ministers to the sedilia.

Whenever the celebrant and ministers sit, the M.C. first hands the celebrant's biretta to the deacon and then stands, at the right hand of the deacon, facing down the church, with joined hands (fig. 8, p. 116). When the choir sings the last invocation of the *Kyrie, eleison,* the M.C. bows to the celebrant, as a sign that he should go back to the altar. He leads the sacred ministers to the foot of the altar (seeing that they salute the choir on the Epistle side and then on the Gospel side), genuflects when they reverence to the altar, and goes to the Epistle corner.

If the celebrant and ministers do not go to sit during the *Kyrie,* then, shortly before the last invocation is sung, the M.C. gives the sign to the deacon and subdeacon that they should stand in line behind the celebrant. When the choir begins the last *Kyrie* the M.C. bows to the

---

[1] This will occur at the entrance to the choir if the clergy are already in choir.

[2] In some churches, both at this moment and at the incensing at the Offertory, the thurifer removes the Missal. Liturgical authorities hold different views as to whether he or the M.C. should do so. The question is not decided by the rubrics and so remains an open one.

[3] What is set out in this whole section is simply a general guide to a M.C. Just because he is M.C. it is supposed that he has accurate knowledge of the entire function, and in the discharge of his duties he has no fixed place nor act. Much will depend on circumstances. He must be considered quite free in his movements in order that he may secure the most perfect possible carrying out of the ceremonies. In general, of course, the (first) M.C. is to be regarded as chiefly concerned with the celebrant at any function.

sacred ministers as an indication to proceed to the middle of the altar. When the celebrant has intoned the first verse of *Gloria in excelsis*, the M.C. signs to the ministers to go up on either side and to say the *Gloria* with him. When they have finished saying it, the M.C. leads them (after a due reverence to the altar) by the shorter way, to the seats. He must take care that they do not move while any of the verses are being sung at which an inclination is to be made (p. 77). If necessary, they must wait till such a verse is ended. But, if they have started, they go on. He stands by their side while they sit, as already explained, and bows to the celebrant as the sign when he is to uncover at the verses. Then the M.C. will himself bow towards the altar while the verse is sung.

Towards the end of the sung *Gloria in excelsis* the M.C. bows to the celebrant as a sign that he should go to the altar. He leads the sacred ministers back, as described above. He then goes to the Missal at the Epistle side, points out the place for the Collects, and turns the page (fig. 9, p. 116).

Epistle. As soon as the celebrant begins the last collect, the M.C. goes to the credence. Here he takes the book of lessons in both hands, the openings of the pages being on his right ; so he hands it to the subdeacon,[1] bowing once before he gives him the book. He then stands a little behind the subdeacon, at his left. As the last collect is ending (having bowed to the cross at the words *Jesum Christum*, if they occur), he accompanies the subdeacon to the middle, genuflects with him, reverences to the clergy left and right, and goes with him to the place where the Epistle is sung at a distance from the altar. He stands at the subdeacon's left while the Epistle is chanted and gives a sign to the choir (by bowing to them), if there is any place at which they should bow or genuflect. He bows or genuflects with the subdeacon at such places.

As soon as the subdeacon has read the Epistle, the M.C. at the middle genuflects towards the altar and bows to the choir with him ; they go to the Epistle side, where the subdeacon is blessed by the celebrant. The M.C. takes the book of lessons from the subdeacon.[2] The celebrant at the middle says the *Munda cor meum*, the subdeacon carries the Missal to the Gospel side. When the celebrant has begun the reading of the Gospel the M.C. bows to the deacon and hands him the book of the Gospels [3] at the foot of the altar on the Epistle side. He waits at the Epistle side while the celebrant reads the Gospel and while incense is put in and blessed.

On certain weekdays of Lent (p. 77, n. 2) the celebrant and ministers kneel on the edge of the foot-pace while the choir sings the entire

---

[1] Unless the subdeacon prefers to take it himself from the credence.

[2] Should there be a long Sequence or Tract, after the subdeacon has been blessed, the M.C. may lead the ministers (without any previous reverence to the altar) to the sedilia, and conduct them back—as after the *Gloria*—towards the end of the chant.

[3] Unless the deacon prefers to take it himself from the credence.

verse, *Adiuva nos, Deus . . . nomen tuum.* In this case the incense is blessed after that verse is sung. Then the deacon says *Munda cor meum.*

Gospel. While the deacon says *Munda cor meum* the M.C. will lead the thurifer and acolytes to the middle and wait there with them. He stands either to the left of the subdeacon or behind the subdeacon to the left of the thurifer, so that he may be in a convenient position to lead the procession to the place of the singing of the Gospel.

All genuflect together, bow to the choir right and left, and so go in procession to the place where the Gospel is to be sung. They go in this order : first, the M.C., and the thurifer, then the acolytes together and lastly the subdeacon and deacon.

The group at the place where the Gospel is sung is arranged as fig. 12, p. 117.

The M.C. makes the sign of the cross on forehead, lips and breast, with the thumb, as the deacon signs *Sequentia* (or *Initium*) *s. Evangelii,* etc.

Then he takes the thurible from the thurifer and hands it to the deacon ; when the book has been incensed he passes it back to the thurifer. During the Gospel he stands at the deacon's right and turns the pages. If the deacon genuflects at any verse, the M.C. does so too. In this case, and when the deacon makes the sign of the cross at the beginning, or bows at the Holy Name, it is better that M.C. should bow slightly towards the celebrant at the altar, so as to give him the sign to do so also.

As soon as the Gospel is ended, the M.C., following the subdeacon, leads the acolytes, thurifer and deacon to the foot of the altar in the middle, where they all genuflect on a signal from the M.C. when the subdeacon is ready. After the incensation of the celebrant the M.C. receives the book of lessons from the subdeacon, bowing to him. He then genuflects again with the thurifer and acolytes and leads them to the credence, where he lays aside the Evangeliarium.

If a sermon follows here, the M.C., having led the sacred ministers to the sedilia, may accompany the preacher to the pulpit ; he will then go and sit in a place prepared for him.

Creed. If there is no sermon (or when the sermon is finished and he has led back the sacred ministers) he goes to the Epistle side and stands there, facing across the sanctuary. During the recitation of the Creed he bows and makes the sign of the cross with the celebrant, and genuflects with him at the words *Et incarnatus est,* etc. When the celebrant has finished saying the Creed, the M.C. gives a sign to him and the ministers, that they should go to the seat. He arranges everything needed as they sit, and himself stands by them, as during the *Gloria.* When the choir is about to sing *Et incarnatus est,* the M.C. bows to the celebrant (as a sign that he should uncover), then kneels, facing across the sanctuary and bows.

At the three Christmas Masses, and on Lady Day, the celebrant and ministers kneel and bow at *Et incarnatus* (p. 114), on the lowest altar step, in front or at the Epistle side. If the music is short the ministers may remain at the altar and kneel on the edge of the foot-pace for the *Et incarnatus*. A cushion is placed for a prelate. On these occasions the M.C. will give the sign and arrange everything required, then kneel behind them.

As soon as the verse *Et incarnatus est* has been sung, the M.C. signs to the deacon to go to the credence for the burse. While the choir sings *Et vitam venturi saeculi. Amen,* the M.C. signs to the celebrant and ministers to go to the altar. They go by the longer way, bow to the choir, genuflect at the altar steps. The M.C. bows and genuflects with them and goes to his place at the Epistle corner of the altar.

Offertory. When the celebrant has sung *Oremus* at the Offertory, the M.C. gives a sign to the subdeacon, who will then genuflect, go to the credence to put on the humeral veil and bring the chalice to the altar.

The M.C. may assist at the uncovering of the chalice. He supervises the blessing of the incense in the usual way. While the altar is incensed the M.C. first waits at the Epistle side ; but when the celebrant, incensing, comes to that side, the M.C. goes over to the Gospel side. removes the Missal [1] and holds it, standing *in plano*, until the Gospel corner of the altar has been incensed. He then replaces the Missal close to the corporal and stands by it, assisting the celebrant. He stays by the Missal while the celebrant washes his hands. He turns round when the thurifer incenses him, and bows before and after. When the celebrant is ready to begin the Preface the M.C. may give a sign to the organist, by turning and bowing, that the organ be silent.

Towards the end of the Preface the M.C. signs to the deacon and subdeacon to join the celebrant for the recitation of the *Sanctus*.

Canon. At the beginning of the Canon the deacon takes the place of the M.C. at the Missal ; the M.C. may go to the Epistle side. He stands at this corner (fig. 13, p. 118). At the words *Qui pridie quam pateretur* he, or an acolyte, puts incense into the thurible. Then he kneels with the thurifer at that side,[2] or he may kneel at the Gospel side, or on the foot-pace at the left of the deacon (holding the chasuble with him).

The bell is to be rung at the *Sanctus* before the Consecration and at the Elevation.[3] It may be rung by the M.C. or, more correctly, by one of the acolytes.

After the Elevation the M.C. rises and stands at the Epistle side to the words *Per quem haec omnia*.[4] Then he goes round to the Missal, passing behind the subdeacon, and genuflecting in the middle. He now stands again by the Missal at the celebrant's left, and turns the

---

[1] Or the thurifer may do this while the M.C. accompanies the celebrant on his left during the incensation of the altar.

[2] The M.C. may incense the Sacred Host and Chalice (C.E. II. viii, 70), but this is generally done by the thurifer as R. VIII. 8, directs.

[3] S.R.C. 4377.

[4] If he had been on the foot-pace or at the Gospel side for the Elevation, he remains at the foot on the latter side until he replaces the deacon at the Missal.

pages of the book. He genuflects each time with the celebrant. Before the *Pater noster*, when the celebrant sings the words *audemus dicere*, the M.C. gives a sign to the deacon that he go to stand behind the celebrant. Towards the end of the *Pater* (at the words *Et dimitte nobis*) he again signs to the ministers that they both genuflect and go to the Epistle side of the altar. He gives the sign again that the subdeacon genuflect and go to the left of the celebrant for the *Agnus Dei*. He then steps back to make room for the subdeacon. While the deacon receives the pax the M.C. goes down to the floor of the sanctuary, and stands at the right of or behind the subdeacon. When the deacon has given the pax to the subdeacon, the M.C. accompanies at his left the subdeacon, who gives it to the choir. When this is done, he comes back to the middle, before the altar steps, with the subdeacon, genuflects there with him (on his right), receives the pax from him, genuflects again and goes to the credence to give the pax to the thurifer (or to the first acolyte if the thurifer be not there). He then goes to the Epistle side and waits there bowing while the celebrant communicates. He may assist at the ablutions.

Communio. At the reading of the Communion antiphon and the post-Communions the M.C. turns the pages of the Missal and indicates the places. If there is a last Gospel proper to the day he leaves the Missal open, finds the place of this Gospel and signs to the subdeacon to transfer the Missal, when the *Ite, missa est* has been sung. Otherwise he closes the Missal after the last post-Communion. During the Blessing he kneels at the Epistle side on the lowest step. Towards the end of the last Gospel he arranges the procession that will go out. He gives the sign to the acolytes to take their candles (and to the cross-bearer, if there be one, to get his cross) and to go to the middle before the altar steps. He takes the birettas from the sedilia, gives them to the ministers (giving the deacon both his own and that of the celebrant), genuflects with the ministers, bows to the choir, and so goes out, as the procession came in.

§ 8. THE SUBDEACON

IN due time before the Mass begins the subdeacon will come to the sacristy, look over the Epistle, see that the chalice is correctly prepared (unless the M.C. does this), wash his hands and vest, assisted by the second acolyte. He does not put on the maniple (nor the folded chasuble, if it be used) till the celebrant is vested. He assists the celebrant to vest. He puts on the biretta after the celebrant has done so. When the M.C. gives the sign, he uncovers, bows to the cross, then to the celebrant, and so takes his place in the procession, immediately before the deacon. If the Asperges precede the Mass, or for any other reason the celebrant wear a cope, he walks on his left, holding the edge of the cope with the orphrey turned in. If, on entering the church, the M.C. gives him holy water,[1] he uncovers to

---

[1] This is not done if the " Asperges " takes place.

make the sign of the cross. If on entering the choir they are to bow
to its members, the ministers stand right and left of the celebrant and
bow with him (first to the side of greater dignity). In this case they
uncover on entering the choir and hand their birettas to the M.C.
Otherwise they keep in their rank, with head covered, till they stand
before the altar. On arriving at the altar the subdeacon goes to the
left of the celebrant. He genuflects [1] with the deacon

For the Asperges ceremony, see § 3 (pp. 79–81).

Whenever the subdeacon stands holding nothing, he joins the hands
before the breast. When he sits he rests them on the knees, palm
downwards. When he holds anything in the right the left hand is laid
under the breast.

Beginning of Mass. Standing before the lowest altar step the subdeacon joins the deacon in answering the prayers. He makes the sign
of the cross with the celebrant. He does not bow while the celebrant
says the *Confiteor*. He turns slightly to the celebrant, with a moderate
inclination, when he says the *Misereatur*. While he says the *Confiteor*
he bows low to the altar, and partly turns to the celebrant at the words
tibi, pater and *te, pater*. He stands upright and signs himself when the
celebrant begins the *Indulgentiam* prayer, and bows moderately during
the versicles, *Deus, tu conversus*, etc.

As the celebrant goes up to the altar the sacred ministers accompany
him. They do not genuflect when the celebrant kisses the altar at the
beginning of Mass.

While the celebrant blesses the incense the subdeacon remains in
his place at the celebrant's left partly facing him.

Whenever the celebrant incenses the altar, the subdeacon accompanies him on his left, supporting him a little by putting his right hand
under the celebrant's left arm.[2] With the deacon he genuflects each
time they pass the middle of the altar.

When the celebrant gives the thurible to the deacon, the subdeacon
goes straight to the deacon's side. Here, standing on his left, he bows
to the celebrant, with the deacon, before and after the celebrant is
incensed (fig. 6, p. 115). Then he goes with the deacon to the Epistle
side, behind the celebrant. He stands on the altar step below that
of the deacon, or on the ground, forming a semicircle with him and the
celebrant (see fig. 7, p. 115).[3]

Introit. With the celebrant and deacon he makes the sign of the
cross at the beginning of the Introit ; he answers the invocations of the
Kyrie with the deacon. If the celebrant and ministers sit while the
choir sings the *Kyrie, eleison*, at the sign of the M.C. they go straight to
the seats. When they are at the side of the altar they do not first go

---

[1] The first genuflection on arriving in the sanctuary, and the last before
leaving it at the end of Mass, are made *in plano ;* all other genuflections are
made on the step (because the subdeacon is *paratus*, i.e., in sacred vestments).

[2] C.E. I. ix, 1, 5 ; x, 2.

[3] Most authors say that they form a semicircle. The rubric of the Missa I says
only : " diacono a dextris eius (sc. celebrantis), subdiacono a dextris diaconi
stantibus in cornu Epistolae " (R. iv, 7).

to the middle before going to the seats, nor do they make any reverence to the altar. They turn so that, in going to their seats, the subdeacon will be on the right of the celebrant, the deacon on his left. Then turning again at the sedilia they find themselves in the normal order. At the sedilia the subdeacon first holds the celebrant's chasuble over the back of the seat while he sits down. When the deacon has given his biretta to the celebrant, both ministers take theirs from the acolytes, they bow, not to the celebrant, but slightly to each other, sit and put on the biretta. While sitting they rest the hands on the knees. This is the rule each time they sit at the seats (fig. 8, p. 116). They rise and go to the altar by the longer way, at the sign of the M.C. First they uncover and hand their birettas to the acolytes, then they rise before the celebrant, wait till he has risen, then accompany him to the altar. They form in line to bow to the choir, first on the Epistle side,[1] then, after going some steps further, on the Gospel side. The ministers genuflect on the lowest step. All this is to be observed every time the celebrant and ministers sit.

Gloria. If they have not gone to the seats, when the choir approaches the last *Kyrie, eleison*, the ministers form a straight line behind the celebrant, when directed by the M.C. to do so, and then go with him to the middle. The subdeacon keeps his place on the ground or on the step below the deacon. He stands thus at the middle while the celebrant intones *Gloria in excelsis Deo ;* he bows at the word *Deo*, then goes to the left of the celebrant, not genuflecting, and joins the celebrant and deacon in saying the *Gloria*, bowing with them and making the sign of the cross at the end. When they have finished the *Gloria*, the celebrant and ministers (having genuflected when the celebrant reverences) go to the seats and sit there, observing everything noted above. The subdeacon bows with the celebrant and deacon at a sign from the M.C. at the verses so marked.[2] In bowing he will always first uncover, lay the biretta in the right hand on the knee, and the left hand extended on the left knee. Towards the end of the singing of the *Gloria* the celebrant and ministers return to the altar as noted above. The subdeacon stands behind the others, so as to be in line behind the deacon. Thus they stand while the celebrant sings *Dominus vobiscum*.[3] Keeping this rank they go to the Epistle side for the Collects. Here they stand in line (fig. 9, p. 116). They bow each time with the celebrant.

If the verse *Flectamus genua* is sung by the deacon, the subdeacon then genuflects with him. The subdeacon at once sings *Levate* and he himself rises first. If he wear the folded chasuble he takes it off while the last collect is being sung. He hands it to the second

---

[1] Because in going towards the altar, in front, they approach the Epistle side of the choir first.

[2] See p. 77.

[3] If the *Gloria in excelsis* is not sung, the *Dominus vobiscum*, as above, follows at once after the *Kyrie, eleison*, when the celebrant and ministers come to the middle of the altar.

acolyte, who lays it on the credence or on the sedilia. He puts on the folded chasuble again after he has been blessed at the end of the Epistle.

Epistle. At the beginning of the last collect the M.C. brings the book of lessons to the subdeacon at his place.[1] The subdeacon bows to the M.C. and takes it. He holds the book, shut, against the breast, having the opening of the pages towards his left. So he waits till the celebrant has sung *Iesum Christum* in the conclusion of the last collect. Then he bows to the altar, if and when the words *Iesum Christum* occur, goes to the middle of the sanctuary, genuflects, bows to the choir on either side (beginning on the Gospel side), goes and stands on the right-hand side of the choir, some distance from the altar steps,[2] opens the book and sings the Epistle.[3] If a verse occur at which the rubric tells us to kneel, as he sings that he genuflects where he is, facing the altar. When he has finished the Epistle he shuts the book, goes again to the middle of the choir, genuflects and bows to the choir, as before; he goes round to the Epistle corner of the altar, kneels there on the edge of the foot-pace, holding the closed book upright. The celebrant (when he has finished reading the Gradual, etc.) lays his right hand on the top of the book ; the subdeacon kisses it and is blessed. With a bow he hands the book to the M.C. and takes the Missal round to the Gospel side, descending the front steps of the altar and genuflecting on the lowest step as he passes the middle. He sets the Missal here in its place, and stands by it, facing across the sanctuary. So he waits for the celebrant. The celebrant comes to read the Gospel (fig. 10, p. 116). The subdeacon at his left answers the versicles, makes the signs of the cross, bows with him and answers *Laus tibi, Christe* at the end. He then moves the Missal towards the middle of the altar.

If the choir sing a verse in the Gradual at which all kneel, the subdeacon does so with the celebrant, at his left hand. He waits at the celebrant's left while the incense is blessed, then goes down and waits again before the lowest altar step, rather to the left.

Gospel. The deacon comes with the book of lessons and joins him here (fig. 11, p. 117). The subdeacon genuflects and bows to the choir with the deacon, this time beginning on the Epistle side. He goes at his left,[4] to the place where the Gospel is sung. Here he turns to face the deacon, standing between the acolytes (fig. 12, p. 117). The deacon hands him the book of lessons. He holds it open before his

---

[1] Or the subdeacon may himself take it from the credence.

[2] Cf. O'Connell, " The Celebration of Mass," Vol. III, p. 97, n. 3.

[3] If it is the custom of the church that the Epistle be sung from a lectern (C.E. II. viii, 40, 45), the lectern will be put on the right hand side of the sanctuary before the Epistle (by one of the acolytes). The subdeacon lays the book, open, on it ; while singing the Epistle he rests the hands on the edge of the pages. The lectern is moved away afterwards.

[4] R. says (VI, 5) " a sinistris," while C.E. II. viii, 44, directs the subdeacon to precede the deacon. Hence the former arrangement should be followed in an ordinary Mass ; the latter in a pontifical one.

breast [1] at a convenient height, so that the deacon may sing from it. While the deacon sings the Gospel the subdeacon neither bows, nor genuflects, nor makes any other sign.

If a lectern is used, it is put in place first and taken away afterwards. The subdeacon stands behind it, resting his hands on the upper edge of the book. If the Gospel is sung at an ambo, the subdeacon stands at the deacon's right, hands him the thurible and turns the pages.[2]

As soon as the Gospel is ended the subdeacon takes the book to the celebrant. Holding it open, he walks by himself straight to the celebrant at the Epistle side of the altar, making no genuflection on the way, even if the Sanctissimum be exposed. Arriving in front of the celebrant he holds the book before him, pointing with the open palm to the place where the Gospel begins. When the celebrant has kissed the book the subdeacon stands aside to the right, shuts the book, bows to the celebrant, genuflects towards the cross when the deacon and others genuflect at the foot of the altar, goes down the altar steps on the Epistle side and stands there during the incensation of the celebrant. He then goes to his place at the foot of the altar or to the left of the celebrant and on his way he returns the Evangeliarium to the M.C., bowing as he does so.

Creed. If there is to be a sermon at this point the subdeacon goes to the left of the celebrant at the middle of the altar, genuflects there with the deacon, who has come up to the celebrant's right ; so the celebrant and ministers go to the seat. Otherwise the subdeacon goes to his place behind the deacon for the Creed. He bows at the word *Deum*, then goes to the left of the celebrant, making no genuflection, and with him says the Creed. The celebrant and ministers go to sit at the seat, when they have said the Creed, exactly as they do at the *Gloria in excelsis.* They uncover and bow at the words *Et incarnatus est.*[3] They also bow at the other verses noted at p. 77. When the deacon, during the Creed, rises to put the corporal on the altar, the subdeacon rises too, first uncovering and then holding the biretta on his breast with both hands. He will either stand the whole time till the deacon comes back to the seat, or sit as soon as the deacon has gone, then rise again when he comes back.[4] When the deacon comes back he bows to him and sits as before.

Towards the end of the Creed he goes with the celebrant and deacon back to the altar, in the way already indicated (p. 97). If there is no Creed the ministers stand in line behind the celebrant as soon as he has been incensed after the Gospel.

Offertory. The subdeacon stands behind the deacon while the celebrant sings *Dominus vobiscum* and *Oremus* at the Offertory. He

---

[1] C.E. I. x, 3 ; II. viii, 44. The usual practice—approved by many authors— is to lean the top of the book against the forehead, thus entirely covering the subdeacon's face.

[2] C.E. II. viii, 45. Both cases are here provided for.

[3] On certain days they kneel for this verse (see p. 114).

[4] C.E. II. viii, 54.

bows at the word *Oremus*, then genuflects on the lowest step and goes to the credence.   Here he receives the humeral veil on his shoulders from an acolyte.   He takes the chalice veil from the chalice,[1] then he holds the chalice at its knob in the left hand bare (not through the humeral veil).   On the chalice are the purificator, paten, host and pall.   He lays the right end of the humeral veil over the pall, lays his right hand on the chalice so covered, and takes it to the altar direct by the shortest way, making no genuflection.[2]   He puts the chalice on the altar ; the deacon removes the pall and paten.   The subdeacon, still wearing the humeral veil, cleans the inside of the chalice with the purificator, then gives it to the deacon.   He takes the cruets from the acolyte and hands the cruet of wine to the deacon.   When the deacon has poured wine into the chalice, the subdeacon holds the cruet of water up, bows to the celebrant and says to him, *Benedicite, Pater reverende*.   When the celebrant has blessed the water, the subdeacon pours a little into the chalice and hands the cruet back to the acolyte.   The deacon gives the subdeacon the paten.   He takes this in his right hand, bare, covers it with the right end of the humeral veil, and so rests it against the breast.   He goes straight to his place in the middle, in front of the lowest altar step, genuflects [3] on the step and stands there, now holding the paten aloft (before his face [4] or before his breast), supporting his right elbow with the left hand, and letting the veil fall over it in front. Except when he has some special office this is now his normal place till the end of the *Pater noster*.

At the *Orate fratres*, if the deacon is not yet back at his place behind the celebrant, the subdeacon should answer.   When the deacon comes to incense him (after the choir) he turns to face the deacon on his right, bows before and after being incensed, then turns to face the altar again.   He does not genuflect.

Sanctus.   At the *Sanctus*, when the deacon goes to the right of the celebrant, the subdeacon, without first genuflecting, goes up to the left.[5]   Bowing, they say the *Sanctus* with the celebrant.   The subdeacon does not sign himself at the *Benedictus* as he is holding the paten.[6]   He returns to his place at the foot of the altar without any genuflection or bow.   When the deacon kneels for the Consecration, the subdeacon also kneels, in his place (fig. 13, p. 118).   At the Elevation he looks up at the Sacred Host and at the chalice, bowing before

---

[1] It is a moot point whether the small chalice veil should cover the chalice when it is on the credence covered by the humeral veil.   If it is not used, it must lie folded on the credence, as it will be needed to veil the chalice at the end of Mass.

[2] If there is no Creed the subdeacon brings up the burse also and the deacon spreads the corporal, while the subdeacon is wiping the chalice.

[3] R. vii, 9.   This genuflection is anomalous.

[4] If it is held face high, he lowers it to his breast if he replies to *Orate, fratres*, when he is incensed, if he says the *Sanctus* and when he kneels for the Consecration.

[5] R. vii, 11.   In some places the subdeacon does not go up at the " Sanctus." The S.R.C. (2682[30]) allows this custom.

[6] S.R.C. 4057[5].

and after. He rises and stands again after the Elevation of the chalice.

Pater Noster. When the celebrant sings the verse *Et dimitte nobis debita nostra* in the Lord's Prayer, the subdeacon genuflects with the deacon and goes to the altar, on the Epistle side, to the right of the deacon. He hands the paten to the deacon ; then the acolyte, or thurifer, takes the humeral veil from him. He genuflects and goes back to his place at the middle; in front of the steps. Here, without again genuflecting, he stands with joined hands. When the celebrant sings *Pax Domini*, etc., he genuflects, goes to the left of the celebrant. After the *commixtio* he genuflects with the celebrant and deacon. Bowing towards the altar he joins them in saying *Agnus Dei*, etc. He strikes the breast at the words *miserere nobis* and *dona nobis pacem*. Then he genuflects and goes back to his former place, not genuflecting on arrival there.

Pax. At this place the deacon comes to give him the Pax. He turns towards him, on the Epistle side, bows before and after, and receives the Pax in the usual manner. Accompanied by the M.C. he then goes to give the Pax to the members of the choir, first genuflecting with the deacon on the lowest step. He gives the Pax first to the person of greatest dignity. If there is no such person present, he will begin with the one nearest the altar, in the farthest row, on the Gospel side. Then he goes to the corresponding person on the Epistle side. He comes across to him who stands nearest the altar in the second row on the Gospel side ; then to the corresponding person on the Epistle side ; and so on for each row, however many there may be.[1] Each time he passes the altar he genuflects in the middle. In giving the Pax, first he stands in front of him who will receive it, while this one bows to him. The subdeacon does not bow in return. Then, leaning forward he puts his hands on the shoulders of the other and almost touches the other's left cheek with his own while he says *Pax tecum*. The other answers *Et cum spiritu tuo*. Both then join the hands and bow to each other. But if he has to give the Pax to a " greater prelate " (p. 31) it is a common practice to put his arms under those of the person who receives it. When he has given the Pax to the head of each line in the choir he comes back to the foot of the altar with the M.C. Here he genuflects, gives the Pax to the M.C., genuflects, goes up to the right hand of the celebrant, and stands there. At *Domine, non sum dignus* he bows to the Sanctissimum, not striking his breast.

Communion. During the celebrant's Communion in each form the subdeacon bows low towards the Sanctissimum. Before the celebrant's Communion in the form of wine he uncovers the chalice. The usual sign for him to do this is that the celebrant touches the foot of the chalice. He genuflects each time with the celebrant. After the Communion the subdeacon pours the wine into the chalice for the ablution, then he pours wine and water over the celebrant's fingers and

[1] " Dat pacem primo cujusque ordinis, dignioribus prius, deinde minus dignis " (R. x, 8).

hands him the purificator. He gives the cruets back to the acolyte ;
then he changes places with the deacon. The deacon carrying the
Missal now comes to the Epistle side, the subdeacon to the Gospel
side. They genuflect, once only, in the middle together, the subdeacon
behind the deacon. At the Gospel side the subdeacon dries the chalice
with the purificator and then arranges this across the chalice, puts on it
the paten and pall, folds the corporal and puts it in the burse, veils the
chalice and lays the burse on it as at the beginning of Mass. He takes
the chalice so arranged in his left hand, laying the right on the burse,
and carries it to the credence, genuflecting as he passes the middle.

Postcommunion. He comes back from the credence and takes his
place behind the celebrant and deacon, on the ground, in front of the
lowest altar step. If the celebrant is at the centre of the altar the
subdeacon genuflects on arriving at his place in the middle, but not
if he has to go at once to the Epistle side. He stands with joined hands
behind the deacon, goes with him and the celebrant to the middle, and
back to the Epistle side. He stands facing the altar while the deacon
sings *Ite, missa est,* or other versicle. Then, while the celebrant says
the prayer *Placeat tibi,* he goes up to the Gospel side, to the same level
as the deacon and to his left. He kneels on the edge of the foot-pace.[1]
with the deacon for the blessing, signing himself. Then he rises, goes
to the end of the altar at the Gospel side and assists the celebrant at
the last Gospel, holding the altar-card or turning the pages of the
Missal.

Last Gospel. If the last Gospel is proper to the day, after the *Ite,
missa est* the subdeacon goes to the Epistle side, takes the Missal from
the altar and carries it to the Gospel side, genuflecting as he passes the
middle. Then he comes back to the middle and kneels at the deacon's
left on the foot-pace for the blessing. During the last Gospel he stands
on the celebrant's left and makes the responses. If he is holding the
altar-card he neither makes the sign of the cross at the beginning nor
genuflects at the verse *Et Verbum caro factum est.* When the last
Gospel is finished, he answers *Deo gratias,* puts back the altar-card or
shuts the book (facing either way), comes down [2] to the floor of the
sanctuary with the celebrant and deacon, genuflects on the ground
with the deacon, receives and puts on his biretta and goes to the
sacristy in front of the deacon. He will bow to the choir, if this is to
be done, with the celebrant and deacon, as he did on coming in, beginning with the side of greater dignity (p. 28).

In the sacristy he stands at the celebrant's left, bows with him to
the clergy, then to the cross and the celebrant. He first takes off (the
folded chasuble, if this is used, and) the maniple and then assists the
celebrant to unvest if this is the custom.

If after Mass prayers for the sovereign, or other prayers, are to be

---

[1] It is better that the deacon and subdeacon should kneel apart, so as not to
cut off the celebrant from the people as he blesses them.
[2] Should the celebrant first go to the middle to reverence to the cross, the
subdeacon on his left, genuflects when the celebrant bows.

said before the altar, the subdeacon stands there with the others and assists the celebrant, holding the book with the deacon.[1]

Substitute for Subdeacon. For a reasonable cause the place of the subdeacon may be taken by a cleric in minor Orders, or by one who is at least tonsured.[2] In this case he does not wear the maniple ; he may not wipe the chalice nor pour water into it at the Offertory, but leaves this to the deacon ; after he has brought the chalice to the altar at the Offertory he does not touch it, nor does he cover or uncover it ; nor does he clean the chalice after the ablutions. This is done by the celebrant. The cleric does, however, arrange the chalice and veil it and carry it back to the credence. Otherwise he fulfils all the office of a subdeacon.

§ 9. THE DEACON

THE deacon comes to the sacristy in due time before Mass begins, looks over the Gospel and the *Ite* (or *Benedicamus*), washes his hands and vests. He does not put on the maniple, nor the folded chasuble (if this is to be used) till the celebrant has vested. He stands at the right of the celebrant and assists him to vest. At the sign of the M.C. he bows with uncovered head to the cross, then to the celebrant. So he walks in the procession to the sanctuary, wearing the biretta, behind the subdeacon. But if the celebrant wears the cope, the deacon goes on his right holding the edge of the cope, with the orphrey turned in. If he receives holy water from the M.C. or subdeacon, he first uncovers, receives the water, presents it to the celebrant, and then signs himself and puts on his biretta. If on entering the choir they are to bow to its members, the deacon uncovers first, waits for the celebrant, takes his biretta, kissing the celebrant's hand and the biretta, and hands it to the M.C. Otherwise he goes to the right of the celebrant before the altar and here takes his biretta in the same way. Before the lowest altar step he genuflects [3] when the celebrant genuflects or bows, then stands to begin the Mass. If before Mass there is the Asperges ceremony, see pp. 79–81.

Throughout the service, when the deacon stands he joins the hands before the breast, unless he has to hold anything. When he holds something in the right he lays the left extended on the breast. When he sits he lays the hands extended on the knees. When he is by the side of the celebrant he genuflects with him whenever he genuflects.

Beginning of Mass. When Mass begins the deacon joins in the prayers at the altar steps, answering the celebrant with the subdeacon. He makes the sign of the cross each time with the celebrant. While the celebrant says the *Confiteor* the ministers do not bow. They bow to the celebrant while they say the prayer *Misereatur*. They bow low towards the altar while they say the *Confiteor*, and partly turn towards the celebrant at the words *tibi, pater* and *te, pater*. They still bow

---

[1] See p. 110, n. 1. [2] S.R.C. 4181.

[3] See p. 96, n. 1.

while the celebrant says *Misereatur ;* they stand upright at the prayer *Indulgentiam.* They bow again moderately at the versicles *Deus, tu conversus,* etc.

Whenever he hands anything to the celebrant he first kisses the thing, then the celebrant's hand. When he takes anything from him, he first kisses the hand, then the thing. These are the " solita oscula."

Incensation. He goes up to the altar with the celebrant. At the altar he takes the incense-boat from the thurifer, kisses the spoon, hands it to the celebrant, and kisses his hand as he does so. As he hands the spoon to the celebrant he says *Benedicite, Pater reverende,* bowing slightly to him. Only if the celebrant is a bishop does he say *Pater reverendissime.* The deacon takes back the spoon from the celebrant in the way described. When the incense has been blessed he takes the thurible, holding the chains low down in the left hand ; high up, just under the rings at the top, in the right. So he hands it to the celebrant, again with the " solita oscula." [1]

While the celebrant incenses the altar the deacon accompanies him at his right, supporting him by putting his left hand under the celebrant's right arm,[2] and genuflecting whenever he genuflects or bows. Then he takes the thurible from the celebrant, with the " oscula," first taking in his right hand the lower part near the cover, and then the top of the chains in his left. He comes down on the Epistle side, and there incenses the celebrant with three double incensings, bowing before and after (see fig. 6, p. 115). He hands the thurible to the thurifer and goes to the right of the celebrant on the highest step below the foot-pace. Here he will stand by the celebrant during the Introit. The M.C. points to the place and turns the pages (fig. 7, p. 115). The deacon answers the *Kyrie, eleison.* If the celebrant and ministers are to sit while the choir finishes the *Kyrie,* at a sign from the M.C. the deacon turns so as to be now at the celebrant's left, and goes with him and the subdeacon (without any previous reverence to the altar) to the seats. Here he takes the celebrant's biretta from the M.C. and gives it to the celebrant with the " solita oscula." Then he takes his own, waits till the celebrant sits, bows slightly to the subdeacon, sits and puts on his biretta. When they rise, the deacon first uncovers, stands, places his biretta on the sedile, takes the celebrant's biretta with the " oscula," hands it to the M.C. and goes back to the altar by the longer way at the celebrant's right, bowing to the choir on either side (beginning on the Epistle side) and genuflecting with him in the middle before they go up the steps.

Gloria in Excelsis. If they do not sit during the *Kyrie,* towards the end of the singing of this, on a signal from the M.C., the deacon stands behind the celebrant, on the top step, and at another signal, goes with him to the centre, where the *Gloria* is intoned. He bows at the word *Deo,* then goes up to the celebrant's right, not genuflecting. Here he says the *Gloria* with the celebrant, bowing and making the sign of the

---

[1] The thurible is kissed at the disk to which are fixed the chains at the top.
[2] C.E. I. ix, 1, 5.

cross with him. When they have said the *Gloria* the ministers genuflect at the middle where they stand, go with the celebrant to the seats and sit there, observing all that has been noted above (p. 97). With the others, the deacon uncovers and bows at the verses so marked (p. 77). Towards the end of the *Gloria* they come back to the altar as above at a sign from the M.C. The deacon stands behind the celebrant on the highest step while the *Dominus vobiscum* [1] is sung and then goes to the Epistle side behind the celebrant. He stands there during the Collects (fig. 9, p. 116), bowing to the cross or towards the Missal when the celebrant does so.

If the verse *Flectamus genua* is to be sung, the deacon sings it, at the same time genuflecting. He rises again when the subdeacon sings *Levate*. When the last collect is finished the deacon goes to the right hand of the celebrant, assists him at the Epistle, and answers *Deo gratias* at the end. He stands there while the celebrant reads the Gradual, turning back, to give the subdeacon room to receive the blessing, at the end of the Epistle. As soon as the celebrant has begun the Gospel the deacon—having signed his forehead, lips and breast—at a sign from the M.C., descends *in plano*, and, bowing, takes from him [2] the book of lessons. He holds this, closed, before his breast, with both hands, so that the opening of the pages be to the left. So he goes to the middle in front of the lowest altar step, genuflects and goes up the steps. He lays the book of lessons on the middle of the altar, steps back a little, and stands there facing towards the celebrant (fig. 10, p. 116).

Folded Chasuble. If he wear the folded chasuble, before he takes the book from the M.C., he goes to the credence, takes off the folded chasuble, assisted by an acolyte, and puts on the so-called " broad stole " (p. 245). He wears this through the Mass till he has taken the Missal across the altar, to the Epistle side, for the Communion antiphon. Then he goes to the credence, takes the broad stole off, and puts on the folded chasuble again.

Gospel. When the incense is blessed before the Gospel the deacon assists in the usual manner. Then at once he goes and kneels on the edge of the foot-pace, and says the prayer *Munda cor meum*. Rising, he takes the book of lessons from the altar, kneels [3] on the foot-pace towards the celebrant, and says *Iube, domne, benedicere*. The celebrant turns towards the deacon, gives his blessing, lays his hand on the top of the closed book, and the deacon kisses his hand.

The deacon now rises, bows to the celebrant, and comes down the altar steps to the floor of the church, where the subdeacon awaits him. He stands here, at the right of the subdeacon, still holding the closed book of lessons (fig. 11, p. 117).

On a signal from the M.C. they genuflect on the step, bow to the choir

---

[1] The deacon and subdeacon do not make such responses as are sung by the choir.

[2] Or he may take the Evangeliarium himself from the credence.

[3] Stands bowed if he is a canon ministering in his own church.

—beginning this time on the Epistle side—and go to the place where the Gospel is to be sung. In this procession the deacon walks by the subdeacon's side on his right.[1] When they arrive at the place (fig. 12, p. 117), the subdeacon turns and faces the deacon, who puts the book into his hands,[2] opens it, and with joined hands sings *Dominus vobiscum.* When he sings *Sequentia* (or *Initium*) *sancti Evangelii* he makes the sign of the cross on the book with the thumb of the right hand at the place where the Gospel begins, laying the left hand meanwhile palm downwards on the book ; then he lays the left hand on the breast and makes the sign of the cross with the right thumb on his forehead, mouth and breast. He now takes the thurible from the M.C., and incenses the book with three double incensings, in the middle, to his left and to his right—bowing his head to it before and after—gives back the thurible to the M.C., joins his hands, and sings the Gospel. He bows or genuflects towards the book if any verse is so marked.

At the end of the Gospel he lays the open right hand (palm upwards) at the place where it begins, to show it to the subdeacon. He then follows M.C., thurifer and acolytes back to the foot of the altar and there genuflects on the step at a sign from the M.C. Then receiving the thurible, when the celebrant has kissed the book he incenses him with three double swings, bowing before and after, and gives back the thurible to the thurifer. He now goes and joins the celebrant. If there is to be a sermon he goes to the celebrant's right, genuflects with him, and so accompanies him to the sedilia, where they sit in the usual manner.

Creed. If there is no sermon, the deacon goes to his place behind the celebrant on the highest step and stands while the *Credo in unum Deum* is intoned. He bows at the word *Deum*, goes, without genuflecting, to the celebrant's right, and there joins him in saying the Creed. He makes the sign of the cross, bows and genuflects with the celebrant. Then, when they have said the Creed, the celebrant and ministers reverence to the altar and go to sit at the seats in the usual way. If there is no Creed the deacon goes to stand behind the celebrant at *Dominus vobiscum* and *Oremus* and all follows as below (p. 107). After the choir has sung the verse *Et homo factus est,* the deacon rises, leaves his biretta at his seat, and going to the credence takes the burse containing the corporal. He holds this in both hands at about the level of the eyes, with the opening towards himself, and takes it to the altar. If he passes the celebrant he bows to him ; he genuflects on the lowest altar step, goes up and puts the burse on the altar. Then he takes out the corporal and puts the burse leaning against a candlestick or the gradine, near the middle on the Gospel side. He spreads the corporal before the altar cross, arranges the Missal conveniently, genuflects there before the altar, not laying his hands on the table when he does so, and comes back by the shorter way to his seat. Here he takes his biretta, bows slightly to the subdeacon, sits and covers

---

[1] See p. 98, n. 4.
[2] Unless he puts it on the lectern or ambo (p. 99).

himself. Towards the end of the Creed, at the sign from the M.C., the deacon, with the others, goes back to the altar by the longer way, with the usual bows to the choir.

Offertory. The deacon stands behind the celebrant while *Dominus vobiscum* and *Oremus* are sung. At the word *Oremus* he bows and goes at once to the celebrant's right. The subdeacon brings the chalice and paten and hands them to the deacon.[1] The deacon takes off the pall and puts it near the corporal. He takes the paten, with the altar-bread on it, hands it to the celebrant, kissing first the paten, then the celebrant's hand. [If there is a ciborium with breads to be consecrated he uncovers this and holds it near where the celebrant holds the paten. When the offertory prayer is ended he covers the ciborium.] He takes the chalice in his left hand, receives the wine cruet in his right from the subdeacon and pours in the wine, holding the purificator with the thumb of the left hand against the stem of the chalice. Usually the celebrant gives a sign to show how much wine should be poured. The subdeacon then pours in the water. The deacon wipes away any separate drops on the sides of the chalice, takes it by the stem in the right, holding the foot in the left, and so hands it to the celebrant, kissing first the foot of the chalice, then the celebrant's hand. He has left the purificator on the altar near the corporal. As the celebrant lifts the chalice, to offer it, the deacon also holds it, touching the foot with his right hand. He lays his left under the breast. Looking up towards the crucifix, he says the offertory prayer, *Offerimus tibi*, with the celebrant. When the celebrant sets the chalice on the corporal, the deacon covers it with the pall, hands the paten to the subdeacon, and covers it with the right end of the humeral veil. He then lays the purificator, folded in two, beside the corporal.

Incensation. He next assists at the blessing of incense in the usual way. He accompanies the celebrant while the altar is incensed, supporting him under his right arm. At the incensing of the *oblata* he places his right hand on the foot of the chalice and afterwards he removes it towards the Epistle side, but not outside the corporal, while the altar cross is incensed. Then he puts the chalice back in the middle. He genuflects each time when the celebrant bows or genuflects. At the end of the incensing of the altar he takes the thurible, with the usual oscula, goes down and incenses the celebrant as he did at the beginning of Mass, the thurifer standing at his left. Accompanied by the thurifer, he now incenses the choir, if there are clergy present. First they genuflect in the middle, then the deacon incenses the choir on the Gospel side.[2] He bows once to all on that side, incenses each person with one double swing of the thurible, then bows again.[3]

---

[1] If there has been no Creed the subdeacon brings the burse on the chalice. The deacon then first spreads the corporal, leaning the burse against a candlestick or the gradine. While he does this the celebrant stands away a little, towards the Gospel side.

[2] Or the side of greater dignity (see p. 28).

[3] If prelates or canons in chapter be present, the deacon incenses them (each with two double swings) first and bows to each separately before and after

He turns, genuflects at the middle and goes, in the same way, to incense those on the Epistle side. On his return to the altar he genuflects, comes to the right of the subdeacon, turns and incenses him with two double incensings. He hands the thurible to the thurifer, goes up to his place on the highest step behind the celebrant (not genuflecting again), turns and is himself incensed, bowing to the thurifer before and after. He turns towards the altar and does not genuflect. If he is at his place in time he answers the *Orate, fratres ;* otherwise the subdeacon does so. During the Preface he stands behind the celebrant. At its last words (*supplici confessione dicentes*) he goes, without genuflecting, to the right of the celebrant ; bowing he says the *Sanctus* with him. He makes the sign of the cross at the word *Benedictus*. Then he goes to the left of the celebrant, genuflecting on the step as he passes the middle.

Canon. During the Canon the deacon stands at the celebrant's left, by the Missal, points out the places and turns the pages. It is usual that he stand back a step or two at the commemoration of the living and of the dead, that he may not hear the names spoken by the celebrant. At the words *Quam oblationem* he goes to the other side of the celebrant, genuflecting in the middle. If there is a ciborium on the corporal he opens it. He kneels on the edge of the foot-pace, bowed, during the Consecration, lifts the end of the chasuble at the Elevation of the Host and looks up at It (fig. 13, p. 118). He rises at once, as the celebrant rises after his genuflection at the end of this Elevation, covers the ciborium, if there is one, and uncovers the chalice. Then he kneels, bowed, as before, and again lifts the chasuble and looks up at the chalice. Immediately after the Elevation of the chalice he rises again and covers it with the pall. Then he genuflects with the celebrant. He goes round to the left of the celebrant, genuflecting not in the middle but in the place at which he arrives. Here he stays pointing the places and turning the leaves.

At the words *Per quem haec omnia* he genuflects and goes to the right of the celebrant again, not genuflecting in the middle. When the celebrant says *praestas nobis*, the deacon uncovers the chalice, genuflects with the celebrant, and places the index and middle fingers of his right hand on the foot of the chalice. He covers it again after the Little Elevation when the celebrant has cleansed his fingers over the chalice and genuflects with the celebrant.

Pater Noster. When the celebrant begins *Pater noster* the deacon genuflects, turns to the left and goes behind the celebrant, on the highest step. Here he does not again genuflect, but stands there with joined hands during the Lord's Prayer. At the words *Et dimitte nobis* he genuflects with the subdeacon ; both go to the Epistle side, at the celebrant's right, the deacon nearer to the celebrant. He takes the paten from the subdeacon, cleans it with the purificator and hands it

incensing him. When the choir is made up of clergy of different ranks, divided between the two sides, the dignitaries and canons on *each* side must be incensed before the clergy of lower rank.

to the celebrant, with the " solita oscula." He uncovers the chalice, genuflects, as always, with the celebrant, covers the chalice again when the Particle has been put into it and repeats the genuflection. Standing there on the right, he joins in saying the *Agnus Dei*, bowing and striking his breast. When that prayer is ended he kneels on the right of the celebrant. When the celebrant has said the first Communion prayer *Domine Iesu Christe, qui dixisti Apostolis tuis*, the deacon rises ; with joined hands he kisses the altar at the same time as the celebrant, but outside the corporal, turns to the celebrant, bows, clasps his arms, holding them at the elbows, and receives the pax from him in the usual manner (p. 26). He bows again, genuflects to the Sanctissimum, goes to the subdeacon and gives him the pax. According to the general rule, he bows only after having given it. Then—having again genuflected with the subdeacon—he goes up to the celebrant's left, and stays there till after the ablutions. He bows low at the celebrant's Communion. If Holy Communion is distributed during Mass, see pp. 119–121.

Post-communion. After the ablutions the deacon takes the Missal to the Epistle side, genuflecting in the middle only.[1] He then takes his place on the highest step behind the celebrant for the *Communio*. He follows the celebrant to the middle for the *Dominus vobiscum* and goes behind him to the Epistle side for the post-Communions.[2] After these he goes with the celebrant and subdeacon to the middle. The celebrant sings *Dominus vobiscum*. The deacon turns towards the people, with his back to the celebrant, and sings *Ite, missa est*. If the Sanctissimum be exposed he does not turn his back to it, but steps back towards the Gospel side and looks across the sanctuary towards the Epistle side. If he has to sing either *Benedicamus Domino* or *Requiescant in pace*, he does not turn, but sings the versicle facing the altar. When the celebrant has said the prayer *Placeat tibi*, the deacon steps a little towards the Epistle side facing the altar and kneels on the edge of the foot-pace for the blessing.[3] At the Blessing he makes the sign of the cross. During the last Gospel he stands at the place where he is with joined hands (or he may stand at the right or left of the celebrant). He makes the sign of the cross with the right thumb on forehead, lips and breast, and genuflects with the celebrant at the words *Et Verbum caro factum est*. If he is at the right of the celebrant he turns by his left and comes down to the ground with the celebrant and the subdeacon.[4] He genuflects with them, takes the celebrant's biretta and

---

[1] If he wears the broad stole he now goes to the credence, takes it off, and dons the folded chasuble. He then takes his place behind the celebrant (genuflecting if the latter be at the centre of the altar).

[2] In Lent when *oratio super populum* is to be sung the deacon turns towards the people by his left when the priest sings *Oremus* for the third time and chants *Humiliate capita vestra Deo*. He then turns back to the altar without completing the circle.

[3] If he is a canon ministering in his own church he will not kneel, but bow low for the blessing.

[4] Should the celebrant go to the middle and bow to the cross the deacon should genuflect to it on his right.

hands it to him, with the usual oscula, takes his own, covers himself after the celebrant has done so, and so goes to the sacristy behind the subdeacon, bowing (uncovered) to the choir, if this is to be done, as when they came in. If, on occasion, prayers are said after Mass, he stands with the others before the altar and holds the book with the subdeacon.[1] In the sacristy he takes off the biretta, bows to the clergy and celebrant and takes off the maniple (and folded chasuble, if he wears it). He assists the celebrant to unvest and then he himself unvests.

§ 10. THE CELEBRANT OF HIGH MASS

THE priest who is to sing High Mass, after having made his preparation, comes to the place of vesting, looks over the prayers and Preface, washes his hands and vests (the ministers having already done so), saying the prayers in the Missal as he puts on each vestment. He waits there, between the deacon and subdeacon, wearing the biretta, till the M.C. gives the sign. Uncovering he then bows to the cross in the sacristy, to the deacon and subdeacon, and follows the rest of the procession in the last place.[2] If the deacon give him holy water on leaving the sacristy, he uncovers to make the sign of the cross. If the procession passes an altar where the Sanctissimum is reserved the celebrant uncovers and genuflects to it. If the members of the choir are in their places, and are to be saluted, he uncovers at the entrance of the choir, gives his biretta to the deacon, and bows as described at p. 80, n. 1. Otherwise he goes straight to the altar steps. Here he uncovers. If the Sanctissimum is reserved at the High Altar he genuflects,[3] if not he bows low to the altar. For the Asperges ceremony see pp. 79–81.

Voice. At High Mass the celebrant uses three tones of voice. Some parts of the Mass are sung aloud, to the plain-chant melody provided. This is the *vox clara* (clear voice). All the other prayers said aloud at Low Mass (the *Gloria in excelsis*, Gospel, Creed, *Sanctus*, etc.) are spoken at High Mass *voce submissa* (medium or subdued voice). This means loud enough to be heard by those around, but not so loud as to disturb the singing. The form of blessing the people, however, is specially noted as said " voce intelligibili." [4] The third tone is *vox secreta* (secret voice), quite low, yet so that he can hear himself. The prayers said secretly at Low Mass (the Offertory prayers, Canon, Communion prayers, etc.) are said in this same tone at High Mass.

Beginning of Mass. Standing before the lowest altar step, between the ministers, the celebrant begins the Mass. He bows low while he says the *Confiteor*. At the words *vobis, fratres* and *vos, fratres* he turns first towards the deacon, then to the subdeacon. He remains bowed

---

[1] Strictly speaking, the celebrant and ministers should take off the maniple before these prayers.
[2] If he wears the cope he walks between the ministers, who hold its ends.
[3] See p. 96, n. 1.
[4] R. xii, 1, 7.

while the ministers say the *Misereatur*. He does not bow to them when they bow to him during the *Confiteor*. He goes up to the altar saying *Aufer*, etc., and kisses it in the middle. The deacon presents the spoon saying *Benedicite, Pater reverende* and the celebrant puts incense into the thurible three times, saying *Ab illo benedicaris in cuius honore cremaberis. Amen.* He returns the spoon to the deacon, joins his hands momentarily, and makes the sign of the cross over the thurible. While he puts the incense into the thurible and blesses it, he lays the left hand on the breast. This is the invariable way in which incense is blessed. The deacon hands him the thurible and he proceeds to incense the altar. If the Sanctissimum be reserved in the tabernacle, he first genuflects (resting the three extended fingers of his left hand on the table of the altar), otherwise he bows low towards the altar cross. He incenses the altar cross with three double incensings.[1] Then he either genuflects or bows, as he did before. If there are relics or images between the candlesticks he next incenses these, first those on the Gospel side, making two double swings of the thurible for all of them together, without moving himself from the middle of the altar, or bowing to them. He again bows to the cross, or genuflects to the Blessed Sacrament, and incenses in the same way those on the Epistle side. Then, without again bowing or genuflecting, he continues the incensing of the altar. He walks before the altar to the Epistle side ; as he does so he incenses it over the inner part of the mensa or table, with three single swings of the thurible, one opposite each of the altar candles.[2] At the Epistle corner he lowers his hand and swings the thurible twice along the side, first low down, then higher up and then returns to the middle, again making three single swings along the front part of the table, bows or genuflects. He now does the same on the Gospel side, first three single swings towards the candlesticks, and then two at the Gospel end. Having finished this, he remains standing still at the Gospel end and incenses the front of the table of the altar at that side with three single swings. Then, still at the Gospel corner, he lowers the thurible and incenses the front of the altar itself three times at the Gospel side and three at the Epistle side, meanwhile walking towards the Epistle corner and genuflecting or bowing as he passes the middle. So he arrives at the Epistle end of the altar ; here he hands the thurible to the deacon. In incensing the altar he swings the thurible in single, not double, swings. For all this see fig. 4.[3] The manner is the same, whenever the altar is incensed. At the Epistle end of the altar, having given the thurible to the deacon, the celebrant stands facing him with hands joined and his left side to the altar and is incensed, bowing slightly before and after.

Introit. Turning to the altar he says the Introit and *Kyrie, eleison,*

[1] S.R.C. 4057[2].

[2] The candles are only convenient directions. Not they, but the altar is incensed. It is incensed three times on either side, whatever the number of candlesticks may be. The thurible is swung out in a straight line, not in semi-circles.

[3] p. 113.

the deacon and subdeacon answering. If the singing of the *Kyrie* takes much time, so that the celebrant and ministers sit during it, the M.C. gives a sign, the celebrant goes to the seat, without genuflecting or bowing, between the deacon and subdeacon. He sits first, takes his biretta from the deacon, and puts it on. While he sits he lays the hands stretched out, with the palms downwards, on the knees. When they rise, the ministers rise first ; the celebrant uncovers, hands his biretta to the deacon, then stands. He goes back to the altar by the longer way, bowing to the choir (first on the Epistle side), bows to the altar at the foot of the steps, or genuflects on the step if the Sanctissimum be reserved there, goes up the steps. This is the invariable rule for sitting at the seats and returning to the altar.

At the altar the celebrant intones *Gloria in excelsis Deo*, and then continues with the ministers in the subdued voice. At the end he bows, or genuflects, and they go to the seats as before. The celebrant uncovers and bows during the sung *Gloria* at the special verses so noted.

Collect(s). When he returns to the altar he kisses it in the middle, turns to the people and sings *Dominus vobiscum*. Then he goes to the Epistle side and sings the Collect(s).[1] After the last collect he reads in the subdued voice the Epistle, Gradual, Tract, Sequence or *Alleluia* verse.

Blessing Subdeacon. When the subdeacon has sung the Epistle he comes to the celebrant, at the Epistle side, holding the book of lessons. The celebrant turns partly to him and lays the right hand on the top of the closed book, the left being placed under his breast. The subdeacon kisses the celebrant's hand ; the celebrant makes the sign of the cross over the subdeacon, saying nothing.

If there is a long Sequence the celebrant finishes it before blessing the subdeacon, and then he may go, with the ministers, to sit at the sedilia. Otherwise he goes to the middle, says the prayer *Munda cor meum* and reads the Gospel, as at Low Mass. At the end he does not kiss the Missal ; nor does he say *Per evangelica dicta*, etc. He comes to the middle of the altar, puts incense into the thurible, and blesses it in the usual way.

Gospel. The deacon, having recited *Munda cor meum*, kneels sideways before him. The celebrant turns to the deacon, gives him the blessing with the form in the Missal, *Dominus sit in corde tuo*, etc., and makes the sign of the cross over him, at the invocation of the Holy Trinity. He lays his hand on the top of the book of lessons and the deacon kisses it.

He goes to the Epistle corner and stands there with joined hands facing the altar, till the deacon sings *Dominus vobiscum*. Then he turns and faces the deacon. When the latter sings *Sequentia sancti Evangelii*, etc., the celebrant also makes the sign of the cross with the thumb on forehead, lips and breast. If the Holy Name is sung, he bows towards the altar cross ; at the name of the Blessed Virgin or of

[1] Should *Flectamus genua* be sung by the deacon the celebrant does not genuflect.

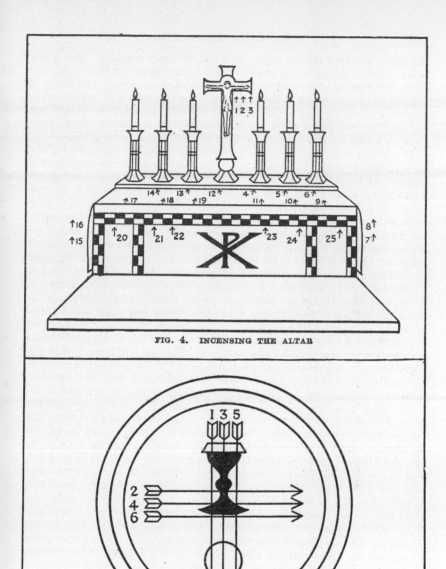

FIG. 4.   INCENSING THE ALTAR

FIG. 5.   INCENSING THE OBLATA

the Saint of the feast he bows his head without turning.   If a genuflection is to be made, he faces the altar and rests his hands on it.

At the end of the sung Gospel the subdeacon brings the book of
lessons to the celebrant and shows him the place where it begins.   The
celebrant, holding the book with both hands, kisses it at this place,
saying *Per evangelica dicta*, etc.   Standing at the same place, he is
then incensed by the deacon, bowing slightly before and after.

If there is a sermon he goes to the middle, bows or genuflects, and
goes to the sedilia in the usual way ; at the end he comes back by the
longer way to the altar.[1]

Standing at the middle he intones *Credo in unum Deum*, and continues in a low voice with the ministers.   He genuflects slowly while
saying the verse *Et incarnatus est*, etc.   At the end of the recitation of
the Creed, with the ministers, he goes to the seat and sits as before.
He uncovers and bows at the special verses and at the words *Et incarnatus est*, etc.[2]   If there is no Creed, as soon as he is incensed after the
Gospel he goes at once to the middle and continues Mass, as follows.

Offertory.   On returning to the altar after the Creed he kisses it,
turns and sings *Dominus vobiscum*, then, turning back, *Oremus ;* he
reads the Offertory verse.   He takes the paten from the deacon and
says the prayer for the offering of the bread,· *Suscipe, sancte Pater*.
He indicates to the deacon when sufficient wine has been poured into
the chalice and then blesses the water, held by the subdeacon, with the
usual form, laying meanwhile the left hand on the altar.   He continues
the prayer with hands joined.   The deacon hands him the chalice ;
holding it up he says the prayer *Offerimus tibi* with the deacon.

At High Mass the celebrant never covers nor uncovers the chalice
himself.[3]   When this is to be done he usually gives the sign to the
deacon by touching its foot.   When he has said the prayers *In spiritu
humilitatis* and *Veni, sanctificator*, he puts incense into the thurible in
the usual way.   But this time there is a special formula for blessing it,
Per intercessionem beati Michaelis, etc.   He takes the thurible and
incenses the *oblata*.   In doing this he makes the sign of the cross
jointly over the bread and chalice three times with the thurible ; he
then forms two circles round them from right to left, and one circle
from left to right (i.e. clockwise).[4]   Meanwhile he says the prayer
Incensum istud a te benedictum, etc., as in the Missal.   Then he proceeds
to incense the cross and the altar, as before, the Introit, saying mean-

[1] If the celebrant himself preaches, he may do so at the altar at the Gospel
side or he may go to the pulpit (conducted there by the M.C.).   The ministers
sit at the sedilia.   At the end of the sermon they join the celebrant when he
arrives from the pulpit and go with him, in the usual (longer) way, to the altar.

[2] At the three Masses on Christmas Day and at Mass on the feast of the
Annunciation (or on the day to which it may be transferred) the celebrant and
sacred ministers kneel on the lowest step at the Epistle side or in front and bow
during the singing of these words.   Cf. p. 93.

[3] Except the one case when a clerk, not ordained subdeacon, acts as such and
the deacon is not at hand (see p. 103).

[4] See fig. 5, p. 113.

FIGURES

OF

HIGH MASS

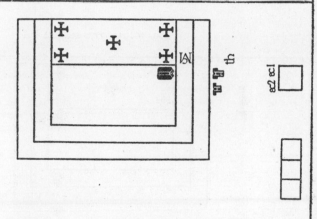

FIG. 6. INCENSING THE CELEBRANT BEFORE THE INTROIT

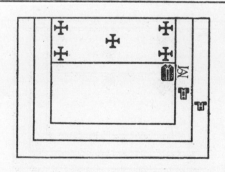

FIG. 7. THE INTROIT

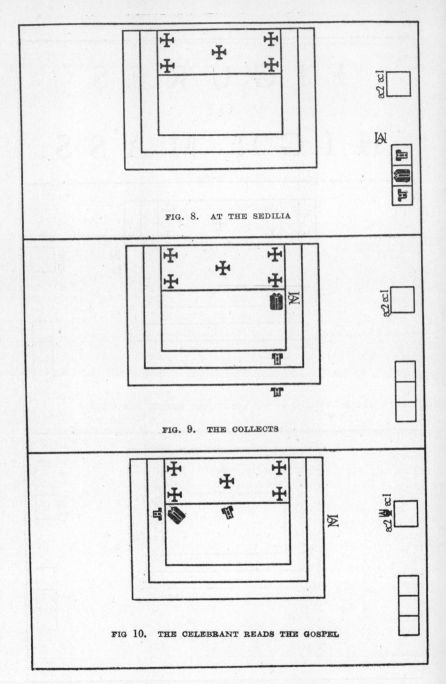

FIG. 8.   AT THE SEDILIA

FIG. 9.   THE COLLECTS

FIG 10.   THE CELEBRANT READS THE GOSPEL

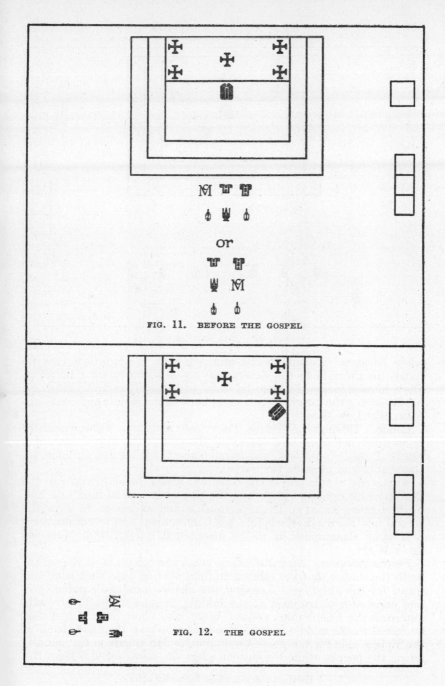

FIG. 11.   BEFORE THE GOSPEL

FIG. 12.   THE GOSPEL

117

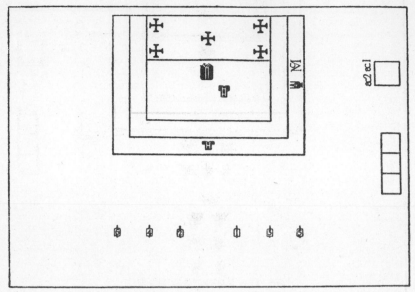

FIG. 13.   THE ELEVATION

while *Dirigatur, Domine, oratio mea,* etc.   At the Epistle corner he hands the thurible to the deacon, saying *Accendat in nobis Dominus.* He is himself incensed ; then he turns to the acolytes and washes his hands, saying the *Lavabo.*   He comes back to the middle and continues Mass as at Low Mass.

Canon. He sings the Preface, *Pater noster* and *Pax.*   Otherwise there is no difference from Low Mass, till the end of the first Communion prayer *Domine Iesu Christe qui dixisti* (except that the deacon uncovers the chalice and presents the paten).

At the end of this prayer the celebrant kisses the altar, turns to the deacon at his right and gives him the pax in the usual form [1] (p. 26). Then, turning again to the altar and bowed as before, he says the second and third prayers before his Communion, and so continues.

If Holy Communion is to be distributed during High Mass see pp. 119–121.

Postcommunion. After his Communion the celebrant at the centre holds the chalice that the subdeacon may pour in wine, then wine and water for the ablutions.   Leaving the chalice (undried), paten, pall and purificator unarranged at the middle, he goes to the Epistle side and reads the Communion verse.   When the choir has finished this he comes to the middle for the *Dominus vobiscum,* then goes back to the Epistle side for the post-Communions.   He stands in the middle, facing the people, while the deacon sings *Ite, missa est,* but faces the

---

[1] He does not genuflect before or after.

altar if the form be *Benedicamus Domino* or *Requiescant in pace*.[1]
Bowing he says the prayer *Placeat tibi*. If there is a last Gospel special
to the day, the celebrant should wait before giving the blessing, that
the subdeacon may have time to carry the Missal across. He turns to
give the blessing [2] and says the last Gospel in a low tone. Then he may
descend at once to the foot of the altar or he may first go to the middle
and bow to the cross. At the foot he bows or genuflects, takes his
biretta from the deacon, bows to the choir (if this is to be done), covers
himself (when outside the choir if the clergy remain) and follows the
procession, himself last, to the sacristy. If prayers are to be said or
sung after Mass, the celebrant stands for them and bows or genuflects
when they are finished.[3]

In the sacristy he uncovers and with the ministers bows to the clergy,
if they are present, on either side, beginning normally with those on
the right, bows to the cross and to the deacon and subdeacon, and
unvests.

§ 11. HOLY COMMUNION DURING HIGH MASS

ON Maundy Thursday there is a distribution of Holy Communion at
High Mass. This does not often occur on other days; but any
Catholic has normally a right to present himself for Communion at any
Mass, on condition that he is in a state of grace and fasting from
midnight. Should then there be a distribution of Communion at High
Mass the following rules are to be observed.

After the *Pax* the M.C. gives a sign to the members of the choir, if
they will make their Communion. Priests and deacons wear a stole
of the colour of the Mass or white. The communicants come to the
middle of the sanctuary two and two, without birettas, the hands
joined, and kneel there.

The torch-bearers do not go away after the Elevation, but stay
kneeling till after the Communion.

The members of the choir who do not make their Communion remain
in their places and stand during the *Confiteor*, *Indulgentiam*, etc. They
kneel during the distribution of Holy Communion. When the celebrant has received Communion in the form of wine, the subdeacon
covers the chalice and puts it aside towards the Epistle side, but not
outside the corporal. The deacon and subdeacon genuflect and change
places, the deacon going to the right of the celebrant, the subdeacon
to his left. The celebrant and ministers genuflect,[4] the deacon opens

---

[1] The celebrant does not say *Ite missa est* while the deacon sings it; but he
does say in a low voice *Benedicamus Domino* or *Requiescant* (S.R.C. 2572[22]).

[2] He should wait till the sung response, " Deo gratias," is finished. He says
the formula of blessing just as at Low Mass, that is loud enough to be heard by
all (R. XII, 1, 7).

[3] Strictly speaking, he ought to take off the maniple before these prayers.
Regarding the Prayer for the King, see p. 133.

[4] Supposing that the ciborium is on the altar, as when the particles have been
consecrated at the Mass. If it is in the tabernacle, the deacon first opens the
tabernacle, then they genuflect.

the ciborium and moves it to the middle of the corporal ; all three genuflect. The deacon goes to the top step on the Epistle side (facing towards the Gospel corner) and bowing, sings the *Confiteor* or says it in a loud tone.[1] The celebrant faces the Epistle corner, partly turned towards the communicants ; the subdeacon stands behind him and bows low during the *Confiteor*.

As soon as the *Confiteor* is begun, the acolytes, or, if they hold torches, the M.C. and the thurifer, take the Communion cloth, come with it to the middle before the lowest step, genuflect, separate, each holding one end of the cloth, and go to kneel at the ends of the foot-pace, facing each other and holding the cloth stretched across between them.

The celebrant says *Misereatur* and *Indulgentiam*, then turns towards the altar. He genuflects, takes the ciborium in his left hand, holds a consecrated Particle in the right above it, and says *Ecce Agnus Dei*. Meanwhile the deacon and subdeacon, if they are to receive Holy Communion, come round to the other side of the Communion cloth, and kneel there. So the celebrant gives them Communion over the cloth. The deacon and subdeacon, if they make their Communion, always do so before anyone else. The ministers then go the celebrant's side, the deacon at his right, on the Gospel side, the subdeacon at the Epistle side. The deacon takes the paten and holds it under the chin of each communicant while Communion is given. The subdeacon stands with joined hands. If the two who hold the Communion cloth make their Communion, they do so immediately after the ministers. In this case they take away the cloth for the time, kneel together on the edge of the foot-pace, and there receive Communion. Then they again spread out the cloth.

At the *Indulgentiam* the members of the choir in the middle of the sanctuary—who have been bowed during the *Confiteor* and *Misereatur* —kneel upright and make the sign of the cross. They look at the Sacred Host at *Ecce Agnus Dei* and strike the breast at each *Domine, non sum dignus*. After the third *Domine, non sum dignus* the communicants all rise. As soon as the ministers have made their Communion, the first two members of the choir genuflect, come forward and kneel on the edge of the foot-pace, or on the highest step below it. While they are receiving the second two come to the foot of the altar, genuflect and wait there. When the first pair have received Communion, they rise and stand aside to make room for the next two, who then ascend while the first pair descend. The third pair come forward ; all four genuflect together. This is repeated as long as Communion is distributed. Those who have made their Communion go back to their places in choir and there kneel until *Dominus vobiscum*. If the torchbearers receive Communion they do so after the clergy of the choir. If there is no one in holy Orders, they do so before the members of the choir. When they are about to come up for Communion they hand their torches to others, to hold till they come back to take them again.

[1] At Requiem Masses the deacon does not sing the *Confiteor*, but says it aloud (S.R.C. 4104[2]).

If the number of communicants is uneven, at the end three approach together. If there are many communicants, and if there is room, they may approach four at a time, instead of two.

If laymen are to communicate, when the members of the choir have done so, the acolytes, or those who hold the Communion cloth, come to the middle, genuflect, fold it, and take it back to the credence. The celebrant and ministers then go to the Communion rail and give Holy Communion to the people, and may be accompanied by two torch-bearers, who kneel one at each end of the Communion rail.

After Communion the celebrant consumes what may remain of the holy Species, if the altar has no tabernacle. The ciborium is then purified by the celebrant and wiped by the subdeacon, with the chalice. If there is a tabernacle, the deacon may put the ciborium into it, the celebrant and both ministers genuflecting before and after.

CHAPTER XII

SOME SPECIAL FORMS OF HIGH MASS

§ 1. HIGH MASS FOR THE DEAD

AT Mass for the Dead certain special rules are observed.[1] The vestments are black. The altar frontal should also be black. If the Sanctissimum is reserved on the altar the conopaeum of the tabernacle must be violet. (It is never allowed to use a black conopaeum on the tabernacle.) The frontal should then be violet also.[2] It is becoming that the altar candles be of unbleached wax. The carpet—which is violet or black—in front of the altar covers only the foot-pace, not the altar steps. The seats are bare or covered in violet. On the credence are placed the chalice, cruets and all that is needed for High Mass, also candles to be given to the clergy ; and the holy-water vessel and sprinkler, if the Absolution will follow. No humeral veil is required. Incense is not wanted till the Offertory. The processional cross may be put near the credence ; not at the head of the coffin, if this is present.

The prayers are sung in the simple ferial tone.[3] The organ may not be played, except it be necessary to sustain the chant at Mass, then it should be silent when the singing ceases.

All kisses of hands or things (except, of course, that of the altar and of the paten by the celebrant) are omitted.[4] The salutations to the choir are as usual.

Beginning of Mass. The acolytes carry their candles as usual in the procession to the altar and back to the sacristy, and leave them lighted on the credence during the Mass. While the celebrant and ministers say the confession the M.C. kneels on the ground at the Epistle side. The altar is not incensed at the beginning of Mass, but the ministers go up to the altar with the celebrant, as usual, and stand at his sides. They do not genuflect when the celebrant kisses the altar. They go, with the celebrant, to the Epistle side for the Introit. At the Introit the celebrant does not make the sign of the cross on himself. He lays the left hand on the altar and makes the cross over the book with the right. The ministers do not make the sign at all.

During the Collects and post-Communion prayers the clergy in the choir kneel and the acolytes at the credence. After the Epistle the subdeacon does not go to be blessed by the celebrant, but gives the book of lessons to the M.C. or thurifer and joins the deacon. After the Epistle candles may be distributed to the clergy in choir by the

---

[1] R. XIII ; C.E. II. xi.
[2] S.R.C. 3201¹⁰, 3562, and Index Generalis (p. 357).
[3] Cf. p. 259, n. 1.
[4] R. XIII, 2 ; C.E. I. xviii, 16 ; II. xi, 5.

122

acolytes. They light these just before the Gospel, and the clergy hold them lighted during the Gospel, and then extinguish them. They also hold them lighted from the *Sanctus* till the end of the Communion.

Sequence. When the celebrant has read the Epistle, Gradual, Tract and Sequence (which he alone [1] reads) should he wish to sit he goes, without a reverence, and by the shortest way with the ministers to the bench. They go back to the altar (by the front) at about the verse *Qui Mariam absolvisti* of the Sequence. The celebrant at once says the *Munda cor meum* and goes to read the Gospel, the subdeacon having transferred the book. The deacon leaves the book of the Gospels on the table of the altar as usual.

Before the Gospel the deacon kneels as usual to say the *Munda cor meum*, but he does not go to receive the celebrant's blessing.

No incense is blessed before the Gospel, nor is the book incensed. In the procession the order is : the M.C., then the deacon, next the subdeacon and last of all the acolytes (not carrying their candles).

After the Gospel the celebrant is not incensed, nor does the subdeacon take him the book to be kissed. Instead he hands it at once to the M.C., who takes it later to the credence. The ministers return in procession and go to their places behind the celebrant, genuflect there and stand while he sings *Dominus vobiscum* and *Oremus*.

Offertory. Then the deacon, not genuflecting, goes to the right of the celebrant. The subdeacon genuflects, goes to the credence, takes the chalice covered by the chalice veil and burse (without the humeral veil) and carries it to the altar. The deacon spreads the corporal ; the subdeacon uncovers the chalice, handing the chalice veil to the second acolyte. He pours water into the chalice, not asking for the blessing. The subdeacon does not hold the paten at Requiem Masses, so he goes at once to the left of the celebrant, genuflecting on the lowest step as he passes the middle. After the offering of the chalice, the deacon puts the paten so that part of it lies under the corporal, as at Low Mass ; he covers the other part with the purificator. Incense is blessed as usual ; the *oblata* and altar are incensed. But then the celebrant only receives incense, not the ministers nor choir. The ministers may wash the celebrant's hands,[2] the deacon taking the towel, the subdeacon the water cruet and dish. Or this may be done, as usual, by the acolytes, in which case the ministers stand in line behind the celebrant as during the collects. In any case they will be in line behind the celebrant after the washing of hands. The deacon answers *Orate, fratres*. At the end of the Preface the deacon goes to the right of the celebrant, the subdeacon to his left, to join with him in saying the *Sanctus*, as usual. Then the subdeacon goes down to the middle in front of the lowest step, and stands there with joined hands. The deacon goes to the book and assists the celebrant. Those in choir may hold lighted candles from the *Sanctus* to the Communion (inclusive). At the words *Quam oblationem* the deacon, as usual, goes round to the celebrant's right ;

---

[1] S.R.C. 2956[7].
[2] Cf. O'Connell, " The Celebration of Mass," III, p. 174, n. 1.

the subdeacon, without genuflecting, goes to the Epistle side, there kneels on the lowest step facing the Gospel side of the sanctuary, takes the thurible from the thurifer (who has already had incense put in by M.C.) and incenses the Sanctissimum with three double swings of the thurible at each Elevation. He then rises, hands the thurible back to the thurifer, goes to his place in the middle, genuflects and stands there till *Pax Domini sit semper vobiscum*. The acolytes, or other servers, who have come to kneel with torches before the Elevation, stay kneeling until after the Communion. The members of the choir kneel from the *Sanctus* to *Pax Domini*, etc., inclusive.

Pater Noster. Towards the end of the Lord's Prayer (at *Et dimitte nobis*) the deacon genuflects, goes to the celebrant's right and hands him the paten without kissing it. He remains standing there. Just before *Agnus Dei* the subdeacon genuflects and goes to the celebrant's left. They say *Agnus Dei* (in the special form for Requiems) with the celebrant, not striking the breast. There is no kiss of peace ; so the ministers change their places at once, each genuflecting before and after.

After the last *Dominus vobiscum* the deacon, not turning round, sings *Requiescant in pace* (always in the plural). The celebrant should say this in a low voice. He, too, does not turn. There is no blessing. The subdeacon goes at once to the place where is the altar-card for the last Gospel.

If the Absolution follows,[1] the thurifer must prepare the thurible during the last Gospel.

Sermon. If a sermon or panegyric about the dead person is preached, it comes at the end of Mass, before the Absolution. The preacher wears no surplice, but only a cassock and "ferraiolo." A bishop or prelate may wear the rochet and either the mozzetta or the mantellettum according to circumstances.

§ 2. HIGH MASS BEFORE THE BLESSED SACRAMENT EXPOSED

HIGH Mass before the Blessed Sacrament exposed is allowed during the octave of Corpus Christi and on the third day of the Forty Hours' Prayer. The Mass will proceed as usual except for the rules given on pp. 61–62 and for the following points. If the Asperges be done (*a*) the altar is not sprinkled ; (*b*) if the people are sprinkled from the entrance to the sanctuary, the sacred ministers will stand somewhat to the Gospel side (not to turn their backs on the Sanctissimum).

All who arrive in the sanctuary make a double genuflection and do the same before departing from it. During the function, within the sanctuary, all genuflections are single. The salutations to the choir are omitted (except for the incensation and the kiss of peace). The biretta is not worn and the clergy and sacred ministers sit as little as possible, if at all.

---

[1] See pp. 411–413. There is no law that Absolution at a catafalque must follow a Requiem Mass when this Mass is not the Exequial one.

The deacon and subdeacon omit such oscula as are not inherent in the rite of solemn Mass.[1] They follow these rules for their genuflections: they genuflect (i) *at the middle* of the altar (only) : (*a*) when they arrive there or pass it when not coming from the side of the celebrant ; (*b*) when they leave it to go to the side of the celebrant or of the altar ; (ii) *on leaving, but not on arriving*, when they leave the side of the altar, or of the celebrant to go to the centre, and vice versa ; (iii) *on leaving and on arriving*, when they pass from one side of the altar to the other.

The incensation of the altar and choir is as usual, but (*a*) on each occasion before incensing the altar (after the incensation of the *oblata* at the Offertory) the celebrant, kneeling on the edge of the foot-pace, incenses the Sanctissimum (with three double swings), bowing before and after [2] ; (*b*) the cross (if there) is not incensed ; (*c*) the thurifer stands somewhat to the Gospel side to incense the people.

To be incensed and to wash his fingers the celebrant leaves the foot-pace and stands (on a step or *in plano*) facing the congregation.

The bell is not rung at all. The kiss of peace is as usual. The deacon genuflects before turning to sing *Ite*, turns only partly, and genuflects again on turning back to the altar.[3] At the Blessing the celebrant having said *Benedicat . . . Deus*, genuflects, then partly turns for *Pater*, etc. and turns back the same way. He does not sign the altar at the beginning of the last Gospel if the Sanctissimum is on the table of the altar.

---

[1] Hence the kissing of the altar, book, hand of the celebrant after the Epistle and before the Gospel, of the paten and chalice are *not* omitted.

[2] The clergy in choir need not kneel for this. The subdeacon (holding the paten at the Offertory incensation) does not kneel.

[3] For *Benedicamus* he does not genuflect.

CHAPTER XIII

SUNG MASS (MISSA CANTATA) WITHOUT DEACON AND SUBDEACON

§ 1. THE SIMPLER FORM

THERE are two ways of celebrating a Sung Mass without sacred ministers. The rules for the choir are the same as those for High Mass in any case.[1]

The first way supposes no servers but two acolytes, or even one. In this case the ceremonies are almost the same as at Low Mass (for which see pp. 40 *sqq.*). The only differences are these : The servers do not say those responses which the choir sings. When the celebrant sits at the seat, that is during the sung *Gloria in excelsis*, Creed (and possibly the *Kyrie, eleison* and Sequence) the acolytes go to the middle, genuflect, go to the seat. The first acolyte arranges the chasuble over the sedile, then hands the biretta to the celebrant with the usual kisses. They stand on either side of the celebrant, facing each other, with joined hands.[2] The first acolyte takes the biretta from the celebrant before he rises, with the same " solita oscula," and lifts the chasuble from the seat. They follow him to the altar. At the verses so marked in the sung *Gloria* and Creed they bow to the altar. They kneel (if not sitting), facing the altar, and bow at the verse *Et incarnatus est*, etc.

The ceremonies performed by the celebrant differ but little from those of Low Mass. He sings all that is sung at High Mass, including the Gospel and *Ite, missa est* or other versicle. He may sit while the choir sings *Gloria*, Creed or Sequence. The Epistle must [3] be read by a clerk (i.e., one who has received at least Tonsure [4]) if such be available. He wears a surplice and stands at the place where the Epistle is usually sung. He does not go to the celebrant for the blessing, but to the middle, genuflects, then takes the book of lessons back to the credence. If a cleric be not present the celebrant himself reads [5] the Epistle aloud or chants it. There may be torch-bearers (normally two) at the Elevation. If so, they observe the rule of High Mass. They go to fetch their torches at the Preface, come out with them at the *Sanctus*, genuflect in the middle, then kneel, one on either side, in the middle of the sanctuary till after the Elevation. They genuflect again before the altar and take the torches back to the sacristy. But at Masses for the dead, on fast days and when others besides the celebrant will receive Holy Communion they stay till after the Communion.

---

[1] *Mutatis mutandis,* since there is no kiss of peace and may be no incense.
[2] Or they may sit at a bench different from the celebrant's.
[3] R. VI, 8.   [4] Cf. S.R.C. 4181[1] and [2].
[5] Cf. S.R.C. 3350[1].

§ 2. THE MORE SOLEMN FORM

THE other form of Sung Mass without deacon and subdeacon is more solemn. It supposes a M.C.,[1] acolytes, thurifer, torch-bearers, and partakes more of the nature of High Mass, except for the absence of the sacred ministers. This form is not used at Rome, where there is no difficulty in celebrating High Mass. It is indeed expressly forbidden to use incense at Mass without deacon and subdeacon except by an indult of the Holy See.[2] In England, in the great majority of churches, it is impossible to provide sacred ministers. In such churches, therefore, High Mass is hardly ever celebrated. As a substitute for High Mass it has long been the custom to celebrate this kind of Missa Cantata, as the principal Mass on Sundays and feasts.

In this Sung Mass the same server can perform the function of both thurifer and M.C.; but it is better to have two persons.

Preparations. The manner of celebration is as follows : [3]

The servers vest in good time in the sacristy. At least four (and not more than six) candles are lighted on the altar. The chalice is placed on the table of the altar (unless there be an assistant who is a cleric, then it will be left on the credence). The Missal is left open on the bookstand. Another Missal is placed on the credence if a cleric is to sing the Epistle. The M.C. assists the celebrant to vest. All bow to the cross, at a sign from the M.C., and go to the sanctuary in procession, in this order. The thurifer goes first, with joined hands ; he is followed by the acolytes carrying their candles, any other servers who may, later, be torch-bearers, the M.C., lastly the celebrant wearing the biretta.

Before the altar the celebrant uncovers and hands the biretta to the M.C., who receives it with the solita oscula and takes it to the sedile. The acolytes go to the corners of the altar and after the reverence go and put their candles on the credence and stand there. All genuflect when the celebrant genuflects or bows.

Asperges. If the Asperges ceremony is to take place, the celebrant will come from the sacristy in a cope of the colour of the day,[4] the

---

[1] Cf. S.R.C. 3377. In addition to his functions as a server at Low Mass the chief assistant to the celebrant at a sung Mass may perform the following offices : (i) if he is a layman he may assist at the Missal (turning the leaves, etc.) and may hold the hand-candlestick for prelates who are entitled to its use ; (ii) if he is a cleric (i.e., initiated by the reception of Tonsure) he is to sing the Epistle, and may at the Offertory carry the chalice to the altar, and after the ablutions—when it has been wiped by the priest—he may re-veil it and carry it to the credence ; (iii) if he is in major orders (i.e., at least a subdeacon) he may at the Offertory wipe the chalice and pour in the wine and water, he may during the Canon remove and replace the pall whenever this is required, and after the ablutions he may wipe the chalice, re-veil and remove it as he would at solemn Mass (S.R.C. 3377[1], 4181).

[2] S.R.C. 3328[1], 3611[6], etc.

[3] There is a good deal of difference of opinion among liturgical authorities about the rite of a Missa Cantata. One form is the one given in the text.

[4] In this case the chasuble and maniple must be laid out on the sedile beforehand.

M.C. or thurifer carries the holy-water vessel and sprinkler. Two servers may hold the ends of the cope, one at either side. At the altar the celebrant and servers kneel. The M.C. is at the right and hands the sprinkler to the celebrant, with the solita oscula. The celebrant takes it, intones *Asperges me, Domine*, or, in Paschal time, *Vidi aquam*, and sprinkles the altar in the middle, on the Gospel side, on the Epistle side. If necessary, a server holds a book before him. The celebrant touches his forehead with the sprinkler,[1] then rises and sprinkles the servers on the Epistle and Gospel sides. He and the M.C. reverence to the altar and go to sprinkle the clergy, if there are any in choir, and then to the entrance to the sanctuary, where the celebrant sprinkles the people, in the centre, to his left, and to his right (or he may go down the church).[2] Meanwhile he recites the psalm *Miserere*, terminating it with *Gloria Patri* when he finishes the sprinkling. He then repeats the antiphon *Asperges me*. On arrival back at the foot of the altar the celebrant and M.C. reverence to the altar and the celebrant sings the versicles and the prayer.

The celebrant, after the Asperges ceremony, goes to the seat with the M.C. The M.C. puts down the vessel of holy water and the sprinkler. Assisted by him, the celebrant takes off the cope and vests in the maniple and chasuble. The first acolyte takes the cope to the sacristy. The thurifer should now go to fetch the thurible.

Beginning of Mass. The celebrant and M.C. come to the foot of the altar and make the proper reverences. Mass begins, the M.C. answering the preparatory prayers. When the celebrant goes up to the altar, the M.C. and thurifer come to him. He puts incense in the thurible, and blesses it as at High Mass,[3] the M.C. saying *Benedicite, Pater reverende*. The celebrant incenses the altar.[4] The M.C. moves the Missal when the celebrant is about to incense that part of the altar. Or the M.C. may accompany the celebrant at his right, the thurifer at his left, while he incenses the altar. In this case the first acolyte removes the Missal. When the altar is incensed, the M.C. takes the thurible from the celebrant, with the solita oscula, descends to the pavement on the Epistle side and incenses the celebrant with three double swings of the thurible. The thurifer meanwhile stands at his left, and both bow before and after. The M.C. gives the thurible to the thurifer, who takes it to the sacristy. The M.C. stands by the Missal and assists the celebrant, and then answers the *Kyrie, eleison*, which the celebrant says at the centre as in Low Mass.[5] If the celebrant goes to sit during the sung *Kyrie*, after he has said the *Kyrie* he genu-

---

[1] See p. 80, n. 4.
[2] See p. 80.
[3] P. 111.
[4] P. 111. If incense is used, by indult, at a *Missa Cantata* it must be used exact as at solemn Mass. It is not lawful to use it only at the Offertory, as in the rite of a Requiem Mass.
[5] The *Kyrie* may be recited (it is a Roman usage) at the Epistle corner. In this case should the celebrant go to sit he does not first make any reverence to the altar.

flects or bows at the centre and then goes to the seat ; the M.C. accompanies him, hands the biretta with the oscula, arranges the chasuble over the back of the seat and stands at the celebrant's right, facing down the church, with joined hands. This same rule is observed every time the celebrant sits, except during the sermon when the M.C. sits. If the celebrant has gone to the seat while the *Kyrie* is sung, he goes back to the altar towards its end. He gives the biretta to the M.C., who takes it, as usual, with the oscula, and puts it on the seat. The celebrant goes to the altar by the longer way, bowing low at the foot of the steps or genuflecting on the lowest step. The M.C. goes back to his place by the Missal. He stays there while the celebrant goes to the middle, to intone the *Gloria in excelsis*. Having recited this prayer the celebrant goes to sit as before. At the verses at which everyone is to bow the celebrant uncovers and bows. The M.C. gives him a sign to do so, by bowing to him ; then the M.C. turns and bows towards the altar. The celebrant comes back to the altar, as before, towards the end of the *Gloria*, at the verse *Cum Sancto Spiritu*.[1] The M.C. goes to the Missal and stands there at the Epistle side. If a cleric is to read the Epistle, he takes the book from the credence during the last collect, goes to the middle in front of the lowest step, there genuflects, goes to the place of the Epistle (away from the altar) and waits. .

Epistle. When the last collect is finished he chants the Epistle.[2] (Meanwhile the celebrant reads it and the Gradual, etc., in a low voice.) Then he again genuflects in the middle and takes the book back to the credence. He does not go to the celebrant for the blessing. If there is no cleric to sing the Epistle, the celebrant himself may chant it or read it in a clear voice at the Epistle corner.[3]

During the Epistle the thurifer goes to the sacristy to prepare the thurible. If there is a Sequence or a long Tract the celebrant may go to sit while it is sung, after he has read it himself.[4]

Gospel. The celebrant goes to the middle towards the end of the sung Gradual or Sequence. The thurifer and M.C. come to him ; he puts in and blesses the incense. Then he says the prayer *Munda cor meum*. Meanwhile the M.C. moves the Missal to the Gospel side. The acolytes take their candles from the credence and are led by the thurifer to the middle before the altar. All three genuflect, the thurifer between the acolytes.

It is convenient so to arrange that their genuflection should coincide with that of the M.C. as he carries the Missal across the altar. In this case they will genuflect behind him. The acolytes go to the Gospel side of the altar and stand on the ground, side by side, facing the

[1] If the *Gloria in excelsis* is not sung immediately after the *Kyrie, eleison*, the celebrant, at the middle, sings *Dominus vobiscum*, then goes back to the Missal at the Epistle side to sing the Collects.

[2] R. VI, 8.

[3] S.R.C. 3350[1]. (Cf. p. 253, n. 4.)

[4] In this case the thurifer may go later to prepare the thurible, towards the latter part of the Sequence.

Epistle side, holding their candles, behind the Missal. The M.C. stands near, at the left of the celebrant, when he comes to the Missal, the thurifer between the acolytes. The celebrant sings *Dominus vobiscum* and *Sequentia sancti Evangelii*. Then the M.C. takes the thurible from the thurifer and hands it to the celebrant with the usual kisses. The celebrant incenses the Missal, as the deacon does at High Mass. He gives the thurible back to the M.C., who receives it again with the oscula and hands it to the thurifer.

At the end of the Gospel the M.C. goes down to the ground, on the Gospel side, and takes the thurible from the thurifer. The celebrant turns towards him and is incensed by him, as at the Introit. The thurifer leads the acolytes to the centre before the altar steps, where all three genuflect. The acolytes carry their candles to the credence, the thurifer his thurible to the sacristy.

If there is a sermon the celebrant goes to sit as usual. During the sermon all the servers sit in some convenient place. If the celebrant himself preaches he may be accompanied to the pulpit by the M.C.

The celebrant intones the Creed, at the middle of the altar, and continues it in a low voice. When he genuflects at the words *Et incarnatus est*, etc., all the servers genuflect with him. Then he goes, by the shorter way, to sit. The M.C. assists him as before. When the verse *Et incarnatus est*, etc., is sung, the M.C. and all the servers (if standing) kneel at their place. The celebrant uncovers and bows. He goes back to the altar in the usual way.

Offertory. When the celebrant has sung *Oremus* at the altar, the M.C., if he is a cleric, will bring the chalice, covered with the veil, to the altar from the credence. Otherwise it should be on the altar from the beginning of Mass. The celebrant uncovers the chalice and offers the bread. The acolytes bring up the cruets and they or the M.C. hand them to the celebrant,[1] as at Low Mass.

As soon as the Creed is finished, the thurifer goes to the sacristy and prepares the thurible. He comes out when the celebrant sings *Oremus*, or soon after, so as to be ready after the offering of the bread and wine. The M.C. and thurifer come to the celebrant after the prayer *Veni, sanctificator ;* he puts incense into the thurible (the M.C. assisting), blesses it and incenses the *oblata* and the altar.[2] The thurifer goes to the Gospel side and removes the Missal, when that part of the altar is to be incensed. If the M.C. and thurifer accompany the celebrant during the incensing, the first acolyte will remove the Missal. At the end of the incensing of the altar, the M.C. takes the thurible from the celebrant and incenses him, as at the Introit, the thurifer standing at his left and bowing with him. The M.C. now goes to stand by the Missal till the Consecration.[3] The thurifer genuflects in the middle and goes to

---

[1] See p. 72.   [2] See pp. 111, 114.

[3] The M.C. at the Missal turns the pages and assists the celebrant. It may be convenient that he give a sign to the organist (by bowing to him) before the Preface and Lord's Prayer. He should stand back a step at the commemorations of the living and of the dead, so as not to overhear their names.

incense the clergy, if any are present. He bows to the choir on the side where are those of greater dignity, or on the Gospel side, and incenses those in the farthest row with one double swing of the thurible for each, bowing at the beginning and end of the whole row. Then he does the same for those on the Epistle side. He returns to the Gospel side and incenses in the same manner those in the next row, then those in the corresponding row on the Epistle side, and so on, according to the number of rows in the choir. Each time, on passing in front of the altar, he genuflects. He next incenses the M.C. with one double swing ; then the acolytes, with a double swing for each, but bowing once only to the two, before and after (if there is no liturgical choir on either side, he incenses the M.C. first). Then, genuflecting, he turns and incenses the people. He bows once down the church, makes three single swings, one down the middle, one towards his left (i.e., the Epistle side of the altar), one towards his right, then bows again. He turns to the altar, genuflects and goes to the sacristy. If there are special servers to be torch-bearers, it is convenient that they form in line at the middle with the thurifer before he goes out, genuflect and go with him.

As soon as the celebrant has been incensed, the acolytes come to the Epistle corner of the altar with the water cruet and bowl, held by the second at the left, the towel by the first at the right. Here they wash the celebrant's hands, as at Low Mass. They then stand at their place by the credence. If the acolytes are to bear torches at the Elevation they go to fetch them in the sacristy at, or just before, the beginning of the Preface. They may join the thurifer, genuflect and go out with him. If the torches are at the credence they take them towards the end of the Preface.

Canon. At the *Sanctus* the thurifer comes from the sacristy, accompanied by the torch-bearers, if they have been there. All genuflect in the middle together, the thurifer in the middle of the torch-bearers, who genuflect in a straight line across the sanctuary. The thurifer goes to the foot of the steps on the Epistle side of the altar. The torch-bearers separate, bow to one another and kneel facing the altar, in line along the middle of the sanctuary. They stay here till after the Elevation. The thurifer at the Epistle side waits till just before the Consecration. After the warning bell the first acolyte puts incense into the thurible. The thurifer kneels on the lowest step on the Epistle side, facing the Gospel side. At the Elevation he incenses the Sanctissimum with three double swings at each Elevation, bowing once before and after each group of three incensings. It is convenient that he time the incensings so as to correspond with the celebrant's genuflection, elevation, genuflection. Before the Consecration the M.C. kneels. He may kneel on the edge of the foot-pace at the celebrant's left, behind him, and raise the end of the chasuble as the celebrant holds up his arms. The first acolyte will ring the bell at the *Sanctus* ; once when the priest spreads his hands over the *oblata*,[1] and three times at

[1] Cf. S.R.C. 4377.

each Elevation. After the Elevation the M.C. rises, goes to the side of the celebrant by the book, genuflects and stands there, turning the pages. He will again stand back a step at the commemoration of the dead. The thurifer rises, comes to the middle, genuflects and takes the thurible to the sacristy. His office is now ended. The torch-bearers, if they are to take the torches to the sacristy, rise and genuflect with him, then follow him to the sacristy. But at Requiems, at Masses on certain fast days, and when people will receive Communion, the torch-bearers stay kneeling till after the Communion.

The thurifer and the torch-bearers (unless these be the same persons as the acolytes) have no more duties after they come back from the sacristy, where they have left the thurible and torches. They go to kneel and stand at some convenient place prepared for them. It may, however, be convenient to delegate one or two further duties, otherwise belonging to someone else, to the thurifer, in order to avoid haste or confusion. This is so especially if there are to be people other than the celebrant who receive Holy Communion.

The ordinary *Pax* is not given, but the kiss of peace may be given by means of the pax-brede (cf. pp. 18, 64).

Communion. If there is Communion the M.C. may go to the Epistle side and there say the *Confiteor*. Or this may be done by the thurifer. Either of these may hold the Communion plate.

The acolytes spread the Communion cloth across the front of the foot-pace (if persons in the choir or sanctuary are to communicate) as described at p. 120. If the acolytes hold the torches, this should be done by the M.C. and thurifer.

After the Communion the first acolyte presents the cruets to the celebrant, as at Low Mass. The second acolyte carries the Missal to the Epistle side. As the M.C. and acolyte cross in front of the altar they genuflect together, the M.C. passing in front of the acolyte. If the M.C. has the right to do so,[1] he carries the chalice to the credence. He then takes his place at the Epistle side by the Missal and assists the celebrant by pointing the place and turning the leaves.

Conclusion of Mass. After the last post-Communion the M.C. shuts the Missal, unless there be a proper last Gospel. In this case he leaves it open and carries it to the Gospel side, as soon as the *Ite, missa est* or corresponding versicle has been sung. He may arrange this so that he makes his genuflection in the middle as the celebrant gives the blessing, and so receive the blessing there. Otherwise (and this is more correct) he will kneel for the blessing at the Gospel side. The acolytes and thurifer kneel for it where they are.[2]

During the last Gospel the procession is formed to go back to the sacristy. The thurifer will go first (he stands behind the others so as to be in front when all turn round) ; the acolytes with their candles, stand before him, the torch-bearers before them, so that they can take their place behind the acolytes in the procession. Meanwhile the M.C.

---

[1] See p. 127, n. 1.
[2] For the choir and organ at the blessing, see p. 119, n. 2.

stands by the altar-card or Missal, answers the verses at the beginning of the last Gospel and then goes to fetch the celebrant's biretta and stands at the foot of the altar. At the end of the last Gospel the M.C. answers *Deo gratias ;* the celebrant comes down to the ground before the altar steps. The M.C. hands him his biretta with the usual *oscula.*

If the prayer for the sovereign, or any prayer ordered by the Bishop, is to be said,[1] strictly speaking the celebrant should take off the maniple and hand it to the M.C. before this prayer. He and the servers stand in their places in front of the altar during the prayer. Then all genuflect when the celebrant genuflects or bows and go out as they came in.

If there is no prayer after Mass, as soon as the celebrant comes down before the altar, all reverence to the altar and go out.

THE PRAYERS FOR THE KING

IT is of obligation,[2] on Sundays, after the principal Mass—whether sung or not—in all churches and oratories (other than private) to sing or recite, in Latin, or in the vernacular, the prayers for the King [3] which are printed in *Ritus Servandus.*[4] If the Mass be one after which the prayers for Russia must be recited, these are to be said first.

---

[1] The prayers in the vernacular ordered by the Pope which are usually said after private Mass are omitted after a sung Mass.

[2] The obligation arises from diocesan law and from custom (cf. *Clergy Review,* March, 1936, p. 249).

[3] The structure of these prayers is curious ; there is no antiphon, but only a versicle and response and prayer. The versicle and response (without the name of the King, of course) form the tenth verse of the nineteenth psalm—a psalm which is a prayer for a king. The versicle is found among those in *Ordo ad Recipiendum Processionaliter Regem,* in the Roman Pontifical (Part III). The prayer is that *Pro Rege* found among the *Orationes Diversæ* of the Roman Missal (No. 6), with the addition of the words for wartime, and those for the Queen and Royal Family. This prayer, which is Gallican in origin, dates from at least the eighth century. It is found (adopted from the Missal) in the Roman Pontifical (Part I) for use in the Mass celebrated at the sacring of a Catholic sovereign.

The *Gloria Patri* does not form part of the correct text of the Prayers for the King.

[4] P. 76 ; " Benedictionale," p. 85.

CHAPTER XIV

THE ASSISTANT PRIEST

§ 1. AT HIGH MASS

IT is not lawful for any celebrant—except bishops and other prelates enjoying the use of pontifical privileges—to be assisted by another priest, on the sole ground of honour or solemnity.[1] The canons of certain chapters have this privilege, either by indult or immemorial custom. When a priest says or sings his first Mass, or first three Masses, he may be assisted by another priest. If it is a High Mass, the assistant priest may wear a cope. In this case many of the ceremonies performed by the ministers are modified, as follows.

A seat, a stool without a back, is prepared for the assistant priest (= A.P.) at the sedilia, to the right of the deacon's place, facing down the church ; or it may be at the left of the subdeacon, so that the A.P. faces the altar.

The A.P. wears a surplice, or a rochet (if he have this right). He should also wear the amice over the surplice or rochet and a cope of the colour of the Mass. When he sits he covers the head with his biretta, as do the celebrant and ministers.

Asperges. If the Asperges ceremony is performed before Mass, the A.P. has no function at that time. He should go to his place in the choir, without the cope, and put on the cope when Mass begins. Otherwise he vests with the celebrant and ministers, putting on the surplice and amice first, the cope when the celebrant has vested.

Beginning of Mass. He comes to the altar at the left but a little in front of the celebrant, the deacon and subdeacon walking, as usual, in front. If there is a choir, when they come to it, the A.P. passes behind the celebrant, goes to his right and there bows with him. The deacon goes to the celebrant's left, the subdeacon to the left of the deacon. Before the altar they stand in this order.[2] The A.P. takes the celebrant's biretta (with solita oscula) and answers the preparatory prayers with the ministers. When the celebrant goes up to the altar, the A.P. goes round to the Epistle corner, and stands there at the foot during the blessing of incense. When the altar is incensed at that side the A.P. removes the Missal, then replaces it. When the deacon incenses the celebrant the A.P. stands at the deacon's right and bows with him. Then he goes up to the celebrant's right by the Missal and points out the Introit. He answers *Kyrie, eleison* with the ministers. If they go to sit during the *Kyrie, eleison* the A.P. observes the general rule for such occasions, as below, at the *Gloria*.

Gloria. When the celebrant intones *Gloria in excelsis*, the A.P. may go with him to the middle and point out the intonation in the

[1] C.J.C. 812.　　　　　　　　　　[2] See fig. 14, p. 135.

Missal, which he will bring with him if it be required ; then he goes back
to the Epistle corner, and facing the Gospel corner, standing on the top
step, he recites the *Gloria* with the celebrant.   Or he may stay at the
Epistle corner while the *Gloria* is intoned.   At the end of the *Gloria* he
makes the sign of the cross with the celebrant.   Then, without genuflecting, he goes straight to his seat by the sedilia, sits here with the
others and puts on the biretta.   At the end of the sung *Gloria* he rises
and uncovers with the others, goes by the longer way to the middle, at
the celebrant's right, while the ministers are both at his left.[1]   The

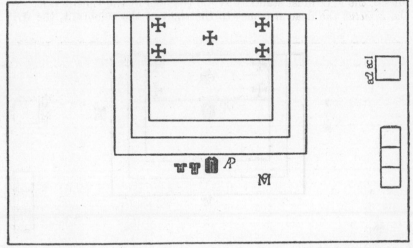

FIG. 14.   HIGH MASS WITH ASSISTANT PRIEST : " IUDICA ME "

A.P. bows to the choir with the celebrant and genuflects when he bows.
This is the rule every time they go to sit.

Gospel.   The A.P. now goes again to the Epistle corner and points
out all that is to be sung or said and makes the responses.   He carries
the Missal to the Gospel side, making the usual genuflection on the top
step in the middle as he passes.   The subdeacon accompanies him.
He stands by the Missal between the celebrant and subdeacon while
the celebrant reads the Gospel, points out the place, turns the pages,
and makes the responses.   After the celebrant has read the Gospel, the
A.P. goes to the Epistle side and waits there.   When the celebrant
comes to that side he stands at his left and faces the deacon who sings
the Gospel, with the celebrant.   When the deacon has incensed the
celebrant after the Gospel, the A.P. may go to the middle, put the Missal
in its place near the centre of the altar and point out the place for the
celebrant to intone the Creed.   If this is not necessary, he will stay at

---

[1] Whenever both ministers are at the left of the celebrant the deacon stands
nearer to him, the subdeacon on the other side of the deacon.

the Epistle corner.   He recites the Creed with the celebrant and genuflects with him at the text *Et incarnatus est*, etc.   Then he goes to his
seat by the sedilia as before.   While they sit, the A.P. does not rise
when the deacon carries the corporal to the altar.   He goes back to the
altar, as after the *Gloria* ; but this time he passes behind the celebrant
as they go up to the altar, so as to be on his left by the Missal.   He
stays here and moves the book when the altar is incensed.   The deacon
incenses the A.P. with two double incensings immediately before he
incenses the subdeacon.

Canon.   Since the A.P. now takes the place of [the M.C. by the
Missal, the M.C. must stand away, on the floor at the Epistle side.   At
the *Sanctus* the deacon comes to the right of the celebrant, the A.P.

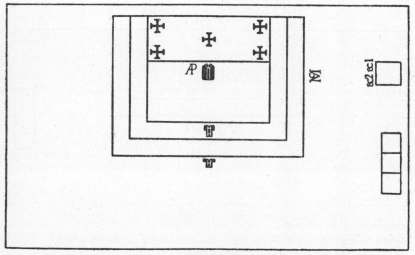

FIG. 15.   HIGH MASS WITH ASSISTANT PRIEST : THE BEGINNING
OF THE CANON

stays at his left, the subdeacon may remain at the foot of the altar steps.
During the Canon the A.P. is by the Missal at the celebrant's left.   He
stands back a step at each *Memento*.   The deacon meanwhile stands
at the right behind.   At the Elevation the A.P. kneels on the foot-pace
at the Gospel side ;   or he may kneel behind the celebrant at the
deacon's left and hold up the chasuble with him.   Then he comes back
to the book, genuflects and stands there, turning the pages and genuflecting each time the celebrant does so.   At the *Agnus Dei* the subdeacon may stay at the foot of the altar steps.   The A.P. and deacon
say the *Agnus Dei* with the celebrant.   Then they genuflect and change
places.   The A.P. genuflects on arriving at the celebrant's right ;   he
rises immediately, kisses the altar (outside the corporal) with the celebrant, not laying his hands on it.   He receives the kiss of peace from

the celebrant.   The A.P. gives the pax to the members of the choir. Returning, he gives it to the deacon, who gives it to the subdeacon. The A.P. goes to the celebrant's left, the deacon to his right.   They bow low at the celebrant's Communion.

Post-communion.   When the time comes, the A,P. moves the book to the Epistle side.   He then stands there, by the Missal, and assists the celebrant, as before.   He shuts the book after the last Postcommunion, or moves it to the Gospel side, if there is a proper last Gospel. He receives the blessing kneeling alone on the edge of the foot-pace at the Gospel side.   He stands there between the celebrant and subdeacon, and assists at the last Gospel.   He comes down, so as to be at the right of the deacon before the altar steps.   The deacon gives the celebrant his biretta ;   the A.P. receives his from the M.C.   All genuflect together.   The A.P. returns to the sacristy walking on the left of the celebrant, a little in front of him.

§ 2. THE ASSISTANT PRIEST IN A SURPLICE ONLY

IT may be, especially in the case of the first three Masses of a newly ordained priest, that another priest assist, not wearing the cope.   In this case he does not perform all the ceremonies described above.   His office is really only to see that the celebrant makes no mistake ;   his ceremonial function is reduced to a very simple one.

The A.P. wears a surplice only, even if he otherwise have the right to some distinction of dress.   If it is a High Mass, the A.P. walks (uncovered) to the altar at the celebrant's left, or he comes to the altar when Mass begins, if it is preceded by the Asperges ceremony.   During the prayers before the altar steps he kneels on the ground at the Epistle side.   He then goes to the Epistle corner by the Missal and assists the celebrant here, instead of the M.C.   The M.C. meanwhile must stand aside, near the credence.   The A.P. sits near the sedilia, when the celebrant sits there. At the altar he stands by the celebrant, sees that he makes no mistake, turns the leaves of the book and points out the places, as otherwise would be done by the M.C.   At the Offertory he is incensed by the thurifer with one double swing, before the M.C.   He stands by the book during the Canon ;   the deacon remains behind the celebrant.   When the subdeacon carries the Missal across before the Gospel, and when the deacon carries it back to the Epistle side after the Communion the A.P. walks with them and genuflects with them in the middle.   He does not receive the kiss of peace from the celebrant ; instead he goes down to receive it from the subdeacon, after it has been given to the members of the choir.   The A.P. gives it to the M.C.

§ 3. THE ASSISTANT PRIEST AT LOW MASS

THE liturgical books give no special directions for this case.   It may, however, occur at the first three Masses said by a newly ordained priest, if they are Low Masses.

It is not difficult to understand, from the rubrics in general, what the A.P. has to do. He will accompany the celebrant to the altar, kneel at the Epistle side during the preparatory prayers, answering with the server. He will then go to the Epistle corner and stand by the book. During all the Mass he stands at the celebrant's side, by the book. Only at the moment of the Elevation he steps back and kneels on the edge of the foot-pace, at the Gospel side. His office is only to be near and to guide the celebrant throughout. He must attend to what the celebrant does and says, pointing out places and correcting any serious mistake.[1]

---

[1] A stole is not necessary, but the A.P. may wear one of the colour of the day— either all the time or from the beginning of the Canon to the consumption of the Precious Blood—if it be the custom (S.R.C. 3515[7]).

CHAPTER XV

HIGH MASS IN THE PRESENCE OF A GREATER PRELATE [1]

§ 1. IN PRESENCE OF A BISHOP IN COPE AND MITRE

BY a " greater prelate " is meant a cardinal anywhere (outside Rome), a Papal Legate (including a nuncio) in the place of his jurisdiction, an archbishop in his province, a bishop within his diocese. A genuflection is the normal reverence paid to a greater prelate, but canons, prelates and the celebrant of Mass bow only to him.

No one ever genuflects to any other bishop, for instance, an auxiliary or an extern bishop ; nor to an abbot, except in churches of his jurisdiction. To these they bow.

The first case is when the prelate assists with more solemnity, wearing cope and mitre. The Ordinary should assist in this manner on the chief feasts, if he does not himself celebrate.

Preparations. The following preparations must be made :

If there is a chapel or altar of the Blessed Sacrament, distinct from the High Altar of the church, a faldstool or kneeling-desk is prepared in front of the tabernacle. It is draped and has two cushions of the appropriate colour.[2]

By the High Altar the Bishop has his throne. In the cathedral this will be a fixed ornament of the church. In other churches a throne is prepared in the sanctuary, normally on the Gospel side. Over the seat is a canopy, of which the draperies are, as far as this is possible, of the colour of the Mass. The seat is raised three steps above the floor of the sanctuary. These steps are covered with a carpet and the seat itself is normally covered with silk material. Near by is a cushion on which the Bishop will kneel. All these cloths and coverings should be of the colour of the Mass. On either side of the throne, on its platform, is a stool for the assistant deacons ; at the Bishop's right is a third stool for his assistant priest [3] (see fig. 2, p. 5).

In front of the altar is another faldstool or kneeling-desk—arranged as described above—at which the Bishop will say prayers before Mass.

At the entrance of the sanctuary four or six large candlesticks stand, with burning candles.

---

[1] C.E. II. ix, xviii ; I. vii, 7 ; viii, 4.

[2] Red or violet for a cardinal, corresponding with the colour he wears (namely, violet for fast days and mourning) ; green for a bishop in violet, violet when he wears black (fast days and mourning). One cushion is on the faldstool for his arms, the other to kneel on, on the ground before it. The covering of the " genuflexorium " should be of silk for a cardinal, cloth for a bishop. The cushions may be silk for a bishop ; for a cardinal they may be fringed with gold (cf. p. 8).

[3] The place of the A.P. may be on the other side, facing down the church.

The Bishop's vestments are spread on the altar. In the middle are the cope, with its morse, stole, pectoral cross,[1] girdle, alb, amice. These are covered with a veil of the colour of the day. On the Gospel side stands the precious mitre and by it the veil to hold it (p. 10). The golden mitre is on the Epistle side. Both mitres are so placed that their lappets hang over the frontal. The crozier stands near the altar. The chalice with paten, veil, etc., the cruets, bell, book of lessons, humeral veil for the subdeacon and other things needed for Mass, are put on the credence. On this also or on another[2] are prepared the Pontifical Canon, another Missal [3] for the Bishop, the hand-candle, and a book containing the formula of the indulgence, if this is to be proclaimed. [A stand for the cross is prepared near the altar on the Gospel side, if the prelate who is to assist be an archbishop in his province.]

All the vestments for the celebrant, ministers and servers are prepared in the sacristy. The vessel of lustral water and the sprinkler should also be ready.

General Rules. The persons who assist at the ceremony are, besides the ministers and servers required for High Mass, an assistant priest and two deacons " at the throne," to wait on the Bishop. These should be, if possible, canons ; but others may supply their place. They are dressed in their canonical robes, or choir dress, not in vestments. A train-bearer [4] and four other servers or chaplains are needed, one to hold the mitre, one for the crozier, one for the book, one for the hand-candle.[5]

There is a first M.C. to guide the whole service (with particular attention to the Bishop) and a second M.C. to assist him. Other servers assist at the Bishop's vesting and unvesting. He has an attendant who carries away and brings back the cappa magna. When the Bishop is at the throne, the normal place of the first M.C. is standing at his left. There is a place for the Bishop's servants and attendants (his " familiares "), generally east of the throne, or by the credence.

During the ceremony, the celebrant and ministers do not salute the choir, but only the Bishop and the altar.[6] All servers and others who approach the Bishop for any purpose make a reverence to him both

[1] The rubrics speak about preparing the cross with the vestments, but in practice the Bishop arrives wearing his cross.

[2] In practice, the things needed for the Bishop at the throne are often prepared at a second credence placed near the throne on the Gospel side of the sanctuary.

[3] The Missals should be covered with a silk covering of the colour of the Mass. The book of lessons has a similar covering (see p. 19).

[4] Whenever the Bishop is vested the train-bearer wears violet cassock and surplice. When the Bishop wears the cappa, the train-bearer has a violet cassock only and a black cloak (*ferraiolo*).

[5] The bearers of mitre and crozier will wear the white silk scarves described at p. 10, through which they hold them. For these four chaplains see pp. 156 *sqq*.

[6] So most authors arguing from the silence of *Caeremoniale*, e.g., II. v, 5 and 6 ; II. viii, 40, as compared with its directions when the Bishop is absent, e.g., II. vi, 12 and 14.

before and after they bring anything to him.[1] This reverence is a genuflection, except in the case of canons and the celebrant of the Mass, who bow low.

Whenever the Bishop wears the cope or chasuble and mitre his skull-cap is taken off only when he genuflects or kneels before the Sanctissimum, and during Mass from the Preface to the Communion. At all other times he keeps it on, even when kneeling or bowing. But when he is not in vestments, but wears the cappa, mantellettum, or mozzetta and the biretta, he (himself) takes off the skull-cap at other times (p. 151).

The first of the assistant deacons always puts on the Bishop's mitre, the second always takes it off. Each takes it from, or gives it to, the mitre-bearer, who holds it through his scarf (the lappets towards himself). Whenever one assistant rises to do anything, the other rises also. Before sitting, they bow the head to each other.

The Bishop reads from the Missal four times during Mass, namely, the Introit ; Epistle, Gradual and other verses and Gospel ; the Offertory ; the Communion. He reads these at his throne ; the book-bearer holds the Missal before him ; the bearer of the hand-candle is normally on the book-bearer's right [2] holding it. The Missal is not held before the Bishop at the *Kyrie eleison, Gloria in excelsis*, Creed, *Sanctus, Agnus Dei*. He recites these from memory. Nor is it used in this way at all, if a higher prelate be present.

Four times during the Mass the canons (of the cathedral), if they are present, come to form a circle around the Bishop. These occasions are, when he says the *Kyrie* and *Gloria*, the Creed, the *Sanctus*, the *Agnus Dei*. Each time they come from their stalls, those of less dignity in front of the others ; they make the usual reverence (a low bow) to the altar in passing, and to the Bishop. The A.P. takes his place among them. They stand before the throne in a wide circle (not, however, turning their back to the altar) and say the text with the Bishop. Those of lower rank are before the Bishop somewhat to his left, while those of higher rank are on his right hand. In going back to their stalls these go first. When they bow to the Bishop on retiring he gives them his blessing, making the sign of the cross. This circle of the canons is not made in Masses for the dead, nor on Good Friday, nor when a higher prelate is present ; and it is made only to the Bishop of the diocese.[3]

During Mass the deacon omits the ceremonial kisses of mere politeness (e.g. of the thurible) but not those that form an intrinsic part of the solemnity of High Mass, such as those of the chalice and paten at the Offertory, and of the paten and celebrant's hand after *Pater noster*.[4]

[1] The exception to this rule (when the subdeacon brings the book of lessons after the Gospel) is noted at p. 146.
[2] C.E. I. xx, 1.
[3] C.E. I. xxi, 5.
[4] For some general rules for the clergy in choir at a pontifical function, see p. 158.

At the beginning of the ceremony the celebrant, ministers and servers come to the altar in the usual way and go to the sedilia ; the acolytes put their candles on the credence.

Arrival of Bishop. When the Bishop arrives at the church the bells should be rung and the organ sounded.[1] He is met at the door by the highest dignitary of the Chapter or by the rector of the church who offers him holy water. The Bishop signs himself with this, then sprinkles those around. He arrives in rochet, cappa magna and biretta. He goes, accompanied by the deacons of the throne and other attendants and servers, his train borne behind, to the chapel of the Blessed Sacrament, if there is one ; there, kneeling at the faldstool, he makes a short prayer. The front of the cappa is spread over the faldstool by the M.C.[2] His attendants kneel behind him. Then he comes in procession to the High Altar. All in choir stand, then kneel to receive his blessing as he passes. The celebrant and ministers stand up at the sedilia. The A.P. is at the first stall, in choir.[3] When the Bishop arrives at the faldstool or kneeling-desk, before the High Altar, he first turns to the celebrant and ministers and blesses them. The celebrant bows low, the others genuflect, unless they are canons. The Bishop bows to the altar, kneels at the faldstool and says a prayer, his attendants kneeling behind him. He then repeats the reverence to the altar and goes to the throne. There he vests. Meantime the celebrant and ministers sit ; all others stand.

Vesting. He takes off the biretta and cappa, which are laid aside by his M.C. or by the Bishop's valet. Servers bring the vestments from the altar ; the deacons at the throne assist the Bishop to put on these. Finally, the first assistant deacon puts the precious mitre on the Bishop and he then takes the crozier in his left hand. So he goes to the altar, blessing the choir as he passes ; the deacons at the throne hold the ends of the cope, the train-bearer carries his train behind, the bearers of the mitre and crozier follow.

Asperges. If the Asperges ceremony comes before Mass, the Bishop's mitre is taken off and he stands at his throne. The celebrant sprinkles the altar, then comes to the throne, accompanied by the second ceremoniar and the acolyte who carries the aspersory. The celebrant presents the sprinkler to the Bishop with the usual reverences and oscula. The Bishop signs himself, then sprinkles the celebrant and his own assistant deacons. The celebrant having received back the sprinkler and bowed low again to the Bishop returns to the altar. He sprinkles the ministers, then the choir and people, accompanied by his M.C. and the aspersory-bearer. The ministers stand meanwhile before the altar. The celebrant finishes the Asperges as usual and vests for Mass at the sedilia.

Beginning of Mass. When the Bishop arrives before the altar steps

---

[1] C.E. I. xv, 4.

[2] This is the general rule when the Bishop kneels at a faldstool or kneeling-desk in cappa.

[3] This is his place always when he is not at the throne.

to begin Mass he gives the crozier to its bearer ; [1] the second deacon takes off the mitre and all reverence to the altar.

Meanwhile the celebrant of the Mass comes to the altar with his ministers ; he stands at the Bishop's left before the steps, a little back. The deacons of the throne stand behind the Bishop, the deacon and subdeacon of the Mass to the left of the celebrant and a little behind him [2] ; the other chaplains or servers of the Bishop behind these.

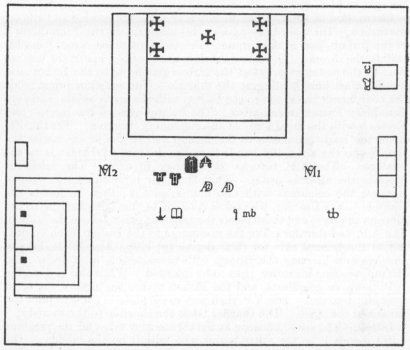

FIG. 16. HIGH MASS BEFORE A GREATER PRELATE : " IUDICA ME "

The first M.C. is on the Epistle side, the second on the Gospel side. The train-bearer stands aside on the Epistle side. All, except the Bishop and celebrant and canons (including the ministers), kneel. The Bishop and celebrant say the prayers at the altar steps, the celebrant answering the Bishop. All the others also say these prayers two and two, according to the usual rule (p. 76). After the prayer *Indulgentiam* the celebrant, having bowed to the Bishop, turns back and stands between the ministers of Mass ; the deacons at the throne come

---

[1] The crozier-bearer always receives the crozier directly and—from a " greater prelate "—kneeling.

[2] If the deacon and subdeacon are canons they stand between the deacons of the throne (S.R.C. 1583⁶), the deacon on the right of the subdeacon.

and stand on either side of the Bishop. So they say the verses *Deus, tu conversus*, etc.[1] As soon as the Bishop has said *Oremus*, adding no prayer, he bows to the altar, the first assistant deacon puts the mitre on the Bishop, who takes the crozier, blesses the celebrant and his ministers, and goes to the throne, blessing the choir as he passes. The train-bearer comes behind him and holds the train. The celebrant (having bowed when blessed) then goes up to the altar, kisses it, says the usual prayers, *Aufer a nobis*, etc., and waits there till the incense is brought to him.

Incensation of Altar. The Bishop lays aside the crozier and sits on his throne. The train-bearer goes to his place among the " familiares " of the Bishop, east of the throne. The assistant priest comes from his stall to the throne. The thurifer brings the thurible, hands the incense boat to the assistant priest at the throne genuflects to the Bishop and kneels before him, holding up the thurible. The assistant priest holds the boat, hands the spoon to the Bishop with the solita oscula, and says *Benedicite, Pater reverendissime.* The Bishop puts on the incense and blesses it with the usual formula and one sign of the cross. The thurifer takes the boat, genuflects to the Bishop and to the altar, carries the thurible to the altar and hands it to the deacon, who gives it to the celebrant. The A.P. returns to his place in choir. The celebrant incenses the altar as usual. When the altar is incensed, the deacon incenses the celebrant with two double swings ; then he hands the thurible to the thurifer, who takes it to the throne (genuflecting to the altar on the way) and there meets the assistant priest before the Bishop. The A.P. and thurifer make the reverences to the Bishop, each according-ing to the general rule for their degree (p. 140). The A.P. takes the thurible and incenses the Bishop with three double incensings. The Bishop, wearing his mitre, rises to be incensed. When this is done the A.P. bows, or genuflects, and the Bishop makes the sign of the cross over him, and sits. The A.P. then goes to his place in choir or joins the canons in the circle. The thurifer takes the thurible to the sacristy.

Introit. The second deacon at the throne now takes off the precious mitre, hands it to the mitre-bearer who puts it on the credence ; he takes the golden mitre, brings it to the throne and waits there. The Bishop rising, uncovered, says the Introit of the Mass, the book-bearer standing (having on his right the candle-bearer) holds the Missal before him. The Missal and candle are then taken away ; the Bishop says *Kyrie, eleison*, etc., with the canons.

Meanwhile, if the Chapter is present, the canons come to form a circle around, as described above (p. 141). The A.P. is among them.[2] If the sung *Kyrie* will take some time, the Bishop signs to the canons (blessing them) that they may go back to their stalls ; he sits and is covered with the golden mitre by the first deacon assisting. If the *Kyrie* is not long, and if *Gloria in excelsis* follows, the canons do not go to their stalls ; they stay, and the Bishop unmitred, remains standing

---

[1] S.R.C. 3213[8].
[2] It is always supposed that he is a canon.

to recite the prayer. The celebrant at the altar intones the *Gloria* and the choir continues it, as at every High Mass. Meanwhile the Bishop and the canons in a circle say it together. Then the Bishop sits and the first assistant deacon puts on him the golden mitre. The deacons at the throne sit in their places ; the A.P. does not return to his place in choir, but sits on the stool placed for him at the throne on the Bishop's right ; the servers who carry the mitre, crozier, book and candle sit on the steps of the throne or in some convenient place east of it. During the words *Adoramus te*, etc., the Bishop bows with mitre on, all others uncover and bow.

Collect and Epistle. When the *Gloria* has been sung all (except the Bishop) rise, and the second deacon at the throne takes off the Bishop's mitre. The Bishop stands while the Collects are sung. Towards the end of the last collect the subdeacon takes the book of lessons, but does not move from his place. The Bishop sits, the first deacon puts on him his golden mitre. The subdeacon (accompanied by the second M.C.) comes to the middle, genuflects to the cross, then to the Bishop and going to the usual place for the chanting of the Epistle sings it. He should stand not quite facing the altar, but turned half towards the Bishop. At the end of the Epistle the subdeacon genuflects [1] to the altar, comes before the Bishop, genuflects to him, goes up the steps of the throne and kneels.[1] The Bishop lays his hand on the book, the subdeacon kisses it, and the Bishop makes the sign of the cross over him. The subdeacon comes down the steps, again genuflects to the Bishop, then in the middle before the altar, gives the book of lessons to the ceremoniar at his side, and goes to carry the altar Missal to the Gospel side.

Gospel. The A.P. and assistant deacons stand as the subdeacon comes to the throne ; the bearers of the Bishop's Missal and hand-candle come to him as the subdeacon leaves. Seated and covered the Bishop reads the Epistle, Gradual and other verses, then, with joined hands, he says the prayers *Munda cor meum* and *Iube, Domne, benedicere*, and reads the Gospel.

While the celebrant reads the Gospel the deacon takes the book of lessons and puts it on the altar—genuflecting to the Bishop [1] and altar —and waits at the altar until M.C. gives him a sign to come to the throne. The celebrant, when he has read the Gospel, comes to the middle of the altar and stands there between the deacon and subdeacon. When the Bishop has read the Gospel, the bearers of his book and candle stand aside.

The deacon, at a sign from the M.C., genuflects to the cross, comes to the throne, genuflects [1] to the Bishop, goes up the steps and kneeling [1] kisses the Bishop's hand ; coming down the steps he genuflects again to the Bishop, goes to the lowest altar step in the middle,[2] kneels there and says the *Munda cor meum*. The thurifer follows the deacon to the throne, so that he is ready there when the deacon comes down. As the

---

[1] If he is a canon he bows only.
[2] C.E. I. ix, 2 ; II. viii, 42.

deacon genuflects after kissing the Bishop's hand, the thurifer does so too, then he goes up the steps. Here he hands the incense boat to the assistant priest, who comes to the Bishop's right. The Bishop puts on incense and blesses it. The thurifer rises, takes back the boat, genuflects to the Bishop and goes and stands before the altar, waiting till the others come. When the deacon has said *Munda cor meum* he takes the Gospel book, bows to the celebrant, not kneeling for his blessing, and goes with the subdeacon and acolytes to the throne. Before leaving the altar they all genuflect to it. The deacon, preceded [1] by the thurifer, acolytes and subdeacon, goes to the Bishop. Before the throne they form up as at the foot of the altar before going to sing the Gospel. All kneel before the Bishop ; the assistants at the throne stand. The deacon kneeling [2] before the throne says *Iube, Domne, benedicere.*

The Bishop gives him the blessing with the usual formula. Meanwhile the acolytes and the thurifer as well as the subdeacon,[2] kneel. All rise, genuflect again to the Bishop, and go for the Gospel to be sung as usual, except that the subdeacon must so stand as not to turn his back to the Bishop. As soon as the deacon leaves the throne, the second deacon takes off the Bishop's mitre. The four chaplains of mitre, crozier, book and candle stand in line facing the deacon (on the east side before the throne). The Bishop stands at his throne and takes his crozier. This he holds with both hands during the singing of the Gospel (except while he makes the small signs of the cross at *Sequentia*, etc., then he holds the crozier in the left hand). If, during the Gospel, a genuflection is to be made, a server puts a cushion before the Bishop, that he may kneel on that, and the Bishop genuflects towards the book of the Gospels. When the Gospel is finished, the Bishop lays aside the crozier ; the subdeacon comes straight to him, without any genuflection or reverence, holding the open book. The Bishop lays his hands on it and kisses it, saying *Per evangelica dicta*, etc. The thurifer follows the subdeacon to the throne. The deacon, with the acolytes, goes to the altar, genuflecting to the Bishop, then to the altar. The acolytes put their candles on the credence and stay there. The deacon goes to the celebrant's side. The celebrant is not incensed. The subdeacon leaves the Bishop, with the usual genuflection, hands the book to the second M.C., and goes to stand by the deacon. The A.P. takes the thurible from the thurifer and thrice incenses the Bishop with the usual reverences. At the end the Bishop makes the sign of the cross over him.[3]

Creed. If the Creed is said, the canons (including the A.P.) come to make their circle around the Bishop, and say it with him. All genuflect at the text, *Et incarnatus est*, etc. The Bishop kneels on a cushion put

---

[1] Cf. C.E. II. xxi, 19 ; viii, 44.

[2] If he is a canon he bows only.

[3] For sermon and indulgence, see pp. 167, 168. But when the Bishop does not celebrate the Mass (a) *Confiteor* is sung at the foot of the altar ; (b) the prayers *Precibus*, etc., are said (not sung), and (c) the book is held by the book-bearer.

before him by a server. Then the canons go back to their stalls, the Bishop dismissing them with a blessing. The A.P. goes to his place by the throne. The Bishop sits, and is covered with the golden mitre while the rest of the Creed is sung. When the words *Et incarnatus est*, etc., are sung, those who are standing kneel; those who are sitting uncover and bow; the Bishop bows, not taking off the mitre. When the deacon goes to spread the corporal, he bows first to the celebrant, then genuflects to the Bishop and to the altar. On going back to the altar the celebrant and his ministers make a reverence to the Bishop and to the altar in the usual way.

Offertory. The second deacon at the throne takes off the mitre, the Bishop rises while the celebrant sings *Dominus vobiscum* and *Oremus*. Standing, he reads the Offertory verse, the servers holding the book and candle. Then he sits and the first assistant deacon puts on the mitre. The thurifer comes to the throne, genuflecting as always to the Bishop, and hands the boat to the A.P. The Bishop puts on and blesses incense with the formula *Per intercessionem*. When the water is to be blessed the subdeacon, at his usual place by the altar, genuflects (or bows if he be a canon) to the Bishop, holds up the cruet and says *Benedicite, Pater reverendissime.*[1] The Bishop at his throne blesses it, saying *In nomine Patris et Filii + et Spiritus Sancti. Amen.* The celebrant says the prayer *Deus qui humanae substantiae*, not blessing the water. The thurifer brings the censer to the deacon, who hands it to the celebrant. The altar is incensed as usual, then the deacon incenses the celebrant with two swings only. He comes before the throne, where the A.P. awaits him. He genuflects to the Bishop and hands the thurible to the A.P. The Bishop stands, wearing the mitre, and is incensed by the A.P. with three double swings. Then he blesses the A.P. and the A.P. hands the thurible to the deacon, and goes to his seat by the throne; the deacon (not standing directly before the Bishop) incenses the A.P., then the deacons at the throne, each with two double swings, genuflecting to the Bishop when he passes before him.

The rest of the incensing proceeds as usual. (Cf. pp. 84, 107.)

Preface. Towards the conclusion of the Secret(s) the assistants at the throne all stand; the second deacon takes off the Bishop's mitre, the first his skull-cap. The Bishop stands when the celebrant chants the conclusion of the last Secret. The mitre-bearer takes away the golden mitre and brings the precious one. After *Gratias agamus* the canons and the A.P. form their circle around the throne and say the *Sanctus* with the Bishop. He dismisses them, as usual, with a blessing and he sits. The A.P. goes to his stall in choir.

Meanwhile the faldstool, or kneeling-desk, is brought to the middle of the choir before the altar. The first deacon puts on the Bishop's skull-cap and precious mitre. The Bishop rises, takes the crozier in his left hand and comes down from the throne to the faldstool, blessing

---

[1] The more correct procedure is to follow the usual order of the Mass, i.e., to bless the water before blessing the incense; most authors, however, suggest the order given above.

the choir as he passes. The deacons hold the ends of his cope, the train-bearer holds the train behind.

Meanwhile the torch-bearers have taken their torches ; they come to the sanctuary, genuflecting to the altar, then to the Bishop (if he is still at his throne). They kneel in two rows, facing each other on either side, the faldstool between them (fig. 17, p. 149).

Consecration. At the faldstool the Bishop hands his crozier to its bearer and kneels.[1] The second assistant deacon takes off his mitre and skull-cap ; the deacons spread out the ends of his cope. They kneel on either side ; the train-bearer, chaplains or other servers behind. Meanwhile the subdeacon, holding the paten at the foot of the altar steps, moves somewhat towards the Epistle side and turns slightly, so as not to stand with his back to the Bishop. When the Elevation is over the Bishop rises and genuflects. The two deacons holding the ends of his cope also genuflect, as do all the servers. The first deacon replaces the Bishop's skull-cap and precious mitre ; the Bishop takes the crozier in his left hand and goes back to the throne ; he does not bless the choir as he passes. As soon as he has left, the faldstool is removed ; the subdeacon returns to his place at the centre. At the throne the Bishop hands the crozier to its bearer and sits for a moment while the second deacon takes off his mitre and skull-cap.[2] Then the Bishop stands again, turning towards the altar. At the end of the Lord's Prayer the canons come to form their circle around the Bishop. In the middle they genuflect before the altar. They say the *Agnus Dei* with the Bishop, then go back, genuflecting before the altar as before.[3]

Pax. When the celebrant and his ministers have said *Agnus Dei*, the deacon goes to stand by the Missal, the subdeacon near the A.P.'s place in choir. The A.P., as soon as he, with the other canons, has said the *Agnus Dei*, goes to the altar without any genuflection and kneels there on the foot-pace, at the right of the celebrant. After the prayer *Domine J.C. qui dixisti* he (instead of the deacon) receives the kiss of peace from the celebrant. He then genuflects to the Sanctissimum and goes to the throne. Here, making no reverence to the Bishop, he gives him the pax (placing his arms under those of the Bishop, if this be the custom.)[4] Then he steps down, bows low to the Bishop and goes to his stall in the choir. The first assistant deacon goes before the Bishop, bows, receives the pax from him, bows low and goes back to his place. Then the second assistant deacon does the same. The A.P. at his place in the choir gives the pax to the subdeacon. After this he has no further duty. The subdeacon, accompanied by the M.C. of the Mass, gives it to the first dignitary. Then he gives it to the highest

---

[1] When the Bishop, mitred, is to kneel, the mitre is removed after he has knelt ; but put on when he has risen (C.E. I. viii, 3).

[2] He may, if customary, retain his skull-cap (S.R.C. 3188).

[3] C.E. I. xxi, 3, prescribes a double genuflection, but a decision of S.R.C. (4135[1]) modifies this rubric.

[4] Cf. O'Connell, " The Celebration of Mass," III, p. 45, n. 9.

canon on the other side, returns to the altar, gives the pax to the deacon, then to the second ceremoniar (who had accompanied him). The kiss of peace passes through the choir in the usual way.

Postcommunion. After the Communion the Bishop sits; the first assistant deacon puts on his skull-cap and the precious mitre. The bearers of the book and hand-candle approach, the Bishop reads the Communion verse. Then the second deacon takes off his mitre, the Bishop stands while the celebrant sings *Dominus vobiscum*, and the deacon of the Mass sings *Ite, missa est*, or *Benedicamus Domino*. When

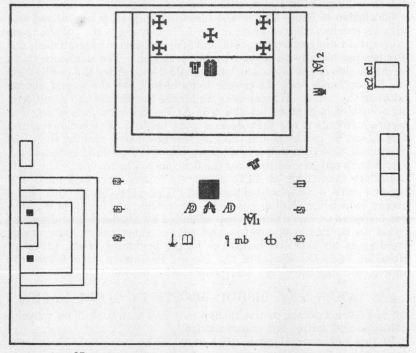

FIG. 17. HIGH MASS BEFORE A GREATER PRELATE : THE CANON

the celebrant has said the prayer *Placeat tibi* he kisses the altar and goes to stand at the Epistle corner, facing the Bishop. The deacon and subdeacon stand on their steps below him, also facing the Bishop. The first assistant deacon puts on the Bishop's precious mitre (the Bishop sits momentarily for this), the bearer of the crozier is at hand, the bearers of the book (who now has the Pontifical Canon) and of the candle stand before the Bishop. He sings the verses *Sit nomen Domini* (signing his breast) . . . and *Adiutorium nostrum* (making the sign of the cross) . . . ; then *Benedicat vos omnipotens Deus*, extending his arms and looking up. He takes the crozier in his left, makes the sign of the cross three times as he continues *Pater et Filius et Spiritus Sanctus*. The assistant deacons standing (being canons) hold the ends of the cope. All present kneel except the bearers of book and candle ; and the celebrant and canons, who bow low.

[If the pontiff is an archbishop, the cross-bearer brings the archi-episcopal cross, while the answer to *Ite, missa est* is sung. He carries this before the throne and kneels there on the lowest step, holding the cross so that the figure of our Lord faces the archbishop. In this case the mitre is not put on ; an archbishop blesses without it, because of the cross before him. He bows to the cross after the word *Deus* and before making the first sign of the cross at *Pater*.]

Conclusion of Mass. After the blessing the Bishop sits mitred and with his crozier ; the celebrant or the A.P., turning to the people, reads the form of Indulgence (cf. pp. 168 and 366), if this is to be published, and if it has not already been read by the preacher.[1] The ministers stand on either side of the celebrant while he does so. After the publication the Bishop hands back the crozier to its bearer, and the second deacon takes off the mitre. He stands again for the last Gospel and genuflects, on a cushion put there, at the text *Et Verbum caro factum est,* if it occurs. He sits ; the first deacon puts on him the precious mitre. The celebrant, ministers and their servers now leave, making the usual reverences, first to the altar and then to the Bishop (who blesses them). The Bishop unvests, assisted by the deacons at the throne. The vest-ments are carried by the M.C. or servers to the altar, laid on it and covered with a veil, as before Mass. The valet brings the cappa magna, which the Bishop puts on. Meanwhile the faldstool is again put before the altar. The Bishop attended by his deacons and servers comes to it, kneels uncovered and says a short prayer, the others kneeling at his side and behind as at the beginning of the function. He again visits the chapel of the Blessed Sacrament, then leaves the church, blessing the clergy and people as he passes.

§ 2. WHEN THE BISHOP ASSISTS IN CAPPA MAGNA

On less solemn occasions the Bishop may assist at High Mass wearing not cope and mitre, but cappa manga.[2]

In this case everything is done as when he presides in vestments (pp. 139 *sqq.*), with the exceptions here noted. No vestments are spread on the altar ; the Bishop does not vest at the throne nor does he use mitre or crozier. Four or six candles may burn at the sanctuary rails. The celebrant, ministers and servers come to the sanctuary first, and wait there. The Bishop enters wearing rochet, cappa magna, pectoral cross (if customary), skull-cap and carrying his birctta.[3] He wears these latter all the time at the throne, when seated.

---

[1] If there is a sermon at the Mass, the preacher announces the Indulgence after he has preached (p. 168).

[2] C.E. II. ix, 4.

[3] No one who is not in sacred vestments (*paratus*) may wear the biretta in church, except when seated.

He blesses the celebrant and ministers, kneels at the faldstool, or kneeling-desk, rises after a short prayer, reverences to the altar and then goes at once to the altar steps and says the prayers at the beginning of Mass, as described above (p. 143). Then he goes to the throne. All proceeds as in the last section ; the Bishop says the same parts of the Mass from a Missal, the servers holding the book and hand-candle. The canons come to form their circles around the throne. The Bishop blesses the incense each time, assisted by his A.P. He blesses the subdeacon after the Epistle and the deacon before the Gospel. He kisses the book at the end of the Gospel, as when *paratus*. He receives the kiss of peace from the A.P. He comes to the faldstool at the middle for the Consecration and Elevation. The Indulgence is published as usual ; the Bishop gives the blessing at the end.

Meanwhile two deacons at the throne in choral dress attend him, the assistant priest is by them.[1]

The following further differences are to be noted. The chief is that the Bishop in cappa is incensed (by the A.P.) only at the Offertory, not at any other time. The celebrant is incensed on three occasions (as at any solemn Mass), but with only two double swings each time. Whenever the Bishop stands or kneels he takes off the biretta, except while he gives his blessing.[2] [If an archbishop, he does not wear his biretta at the blessing, because of the cross held before him.] He wears the skull-cap all the time, even when he has taken off his biretta, except while the Gospel is sung, while he is being incensed, and from the beginning of the Preface to the Communion inclusive. At these times he takes off both biretta and skull-cap. The Bishop takes them off himself and hands them to the first assistant deacon. When both are taken off, the skull-cap is held by the deacon on the top of or put inside the biretta.

The Bishop puts both on himself, taking them from the first assistant deacon.

§ 3. HIGH MASS FOR THE DEAD BEFORE THE BISHOP

In this case the following special rules are observed.[3]

The Bishop may assist either in a black or violet cope and the simple mitre, or in cappa magna. If he wears the cope and mitre, the vestments are spread on the altar beforehand, the one (simple) mitre stands on the Gospel side. The crozier is not used. The throne, in any case, is covered with violet cloth. Its platform may be covered with a violet carpet, like the foot-pace of the altar. The faldstool or priedieu is covered with violet and has violet cushions. The candles are of

---

[1] These three assistants are in choir dress ; the train-bearer has no surplice, but only *ferraiolo*.

[2] And except during the chanting of the *Confiteor* before the indulgence, if this be given.

[3] C.E. II. xii. In § 3 above a knowledge of the rubrics which regulate a solemn Mass of Requiem (pp. 122 *sqq.*) and High Mass in presence of a greater prelate (pp. 139 *sqq.*) is presumed.

unbleached wax, except the hand-candle. When the Bishop arrives, the bells are not rung joyfully; they may be tolled. The organ is silent throughout.

The ceremony proceeds as usual (pp. 122, 139), with the following exceptions:

The Bishop gives no blessing at any time; he does not bless the choir in passing nor the celebrant. According to the rule for all Requiem Masses, no blessing is given to the ministers after the Epistle nor before the Gospel, nor does the deacon go to kiss the Bishop's hand. The canons do not come to form a circle around the Bishop.

Towards the end of the singing of the *Kyrie*, the Bishop comes from his throne, wearing the mitre, goes to the faldstool before the altar and kneels there without mitre[1] during the Collects. All kneel except the celebrant and ministers.[2] The assistant priest does not go to the throne till the Bishop has returned to it after the Collects.

The Bishop puts on incense and blesses it at the Offertory; he is incensed by the A.P. at this point only.

The Bishop kneels at the faldstool from the Consecration till the *Pax Domini* has been sung. Everyone in choir kneels during this time (p. 77). The Bishop comes again to the faldstool for the Postcommunion, as he did at the Collect. No blessing is given, no Indulgence published.

If there is a sermon after the Mass, the preacher does not go to the Bishop for his blessing. If the Absolutions follow, see pp. 416–419.

If the Bishop wears the cappa, the differences noted above (pp. 150–151) are observed.

§ 4. HIGH MASS BEFORE A BISHOP NOT IN HIS DIOCESE

WHEN a bishop who has no jurisdiction in the place—and is, therefore, not a " greater prelate " (p. 139)—assists at High Mass, he takes no special part in the ceremony. He assists in choir dress, that is, in violet cassock, rochet, mantellettum, pectoral cross, violet biretta, and takes the first place in the choir.[3] The canons are not to go to meet him at the door of the church in full procession, as they meet the Ordinary; but some of them may meet him, of whom the highest in rank offers holy water.[4] The side of the choir on which the bishop sits then becomes that of higher dignity. The celebrant and ministers bow to him at the beginning and end of the Mass. He is incensed (at the Offertory only) after the celebrant [5] before anyone else, with three double incensings. He receives the kiss of peace from the deacon before anyone else. He does not give the blessing at the end of Mass, and takes no further part in the function than do others in choir.

---

[1] See p. 148, n. 1.
[2] If the Bishop is in cope, he wears the mitre while returning to the throne.
[3] S.R.C. 442[1], 3540.
[4] S.R.C. 442[2]. The bishop takes holy water but does not sprinkle others.
[5] In such a case the celebrant is incensed with three double swings (cf. C.E. I. xxiii, 32).

CHAPTER XVI

PONTIFICAL HIGH MASS AT THE THRONE [1]

§ 1. PREPARATION

A THRONE is used by a bishop where he has jurisdiction, therefore by the metropolitan throughout his province and the Bishop throughout his diocese (except in the presence of a cardinal), also by a cardinal everywhere outside Rome and in his titular church at Rome.[2]

A chapel—other than that of the Blessed Sacrament—should be set apart (called the secretarium) in which Terce is sung and the Bishop vests.

If the Sanctissimum is reserved on the High Altar of the church, It should be removed, if possible, before the ceremony to a side chapel or altar. In the chapel of the Blessed Sacrament a faldstool or a kneeling-desk (*genuflexorium*) is placed before the altar. This kneeling-desk is covered with a cloth, green or violet according to the occasion ; either has two cushions of the same colour, one for the Bishop's arms, one on the ground, on which he will kneel. Six candles should be lit on this altar during the time the Bishop is there.

In the Secretarium. There is also an altar in the secretarium. On this are six candles, lit, and the usual altar cross. The altar is vested in the colour of the Mass ; on it are laid the Bishop's vestments, namely (inversely to the order in which they are taken) : the chasuble, gloves on a salver (to one side), dalmatic, tunicle, the morse (*formale*) of the cope on a plate (small salver), the cope, stole, pectoral cross,[3] girdle, alb, amice. All are covered with a veil of the colour of the Mass. The gremial may be used for this purpose. The precious mitre stands on the altar at the Gospel side, the golden mitre at the Epistle side. [If the prelate is an archbishop, on the days on which he may use the pallium,[4] this is laid on the altar at the Gospel corner, on a salver, and covered with a small veil of the colour of the day. The three pins to fix it lie on another salver near.] The crozier stands near the altar,

---

[1] C.E. II. viii ; I. vii, viii, ix, x.

[2] The Ordinary may now allow the use of his throne to another bishop, provided this is not his own auxiliary, nor vicar general, nor a dignitary or canon of his cathedral (C.J.C. 337, § 3 ; S.R.C. 4023 and 4355). A metropolitan may use a throne throughout his province ; but in the cathedral of one of his suffragans it is erected, temporarily, on the Epistle side of the sanctuary. The same rule holds for an Apostolic Delegate in the place of his legation. A Cardinal, however, occupies the throne of the Bishop on the Gospel side (C.E. I. xiii, 4, 9, 10). If the Bishop *pontificates* in presence of a higher prelate he does so at the faldstool.

[3] In practice, normally, the Bishop will use the cross he wears on entering, taking it off and putting it on again over the alb.

[4] The rules about the pallium are in the C.J.C. c. 275–279. A list of the days on which the pallium may be worn is given in *Pontificale Romanum* (Part I).

also the processional cross. [But if he is an archbishop he will enter with his cross. In this case there should be a stand for it near the altar on the Gospel side.] On the Epistle side is a bench for the ministers of the Mass and on it their maniples. A throne with a canopy is prepared in this chapel at either side of the altar according to convenience, and stools at its sides for the A.P. and the assistant deacons. There is a faldstool before the altar covered as above ; and seats for the canons and others in the part of the secretarium that corresponds to the choir. On the credence of the chapel the Bishop's ceremonial shoes (with a shoe-horn) and stockings are laid on a plate, covered with a cloth. There is another cloth to hold this plate when it is brought to the throne. On the same credence[1] is laid a book of Gospels (or Missal). In this at the place of the Gospel of the day the Bishop's maniple is placed. Further, the acolytes' candles, the Pontifical Canon, a Breviary or other book containing the prayer for Terce, hand-candle lighted, the vessel with water and the dish for the Bishop to wash his hands and towels, are on the credence of the secretarium. The thurible and incense boat are there, and the fire with charcoal near at hand, unless these are prepared in the sacristy.

In the Sanctuary. In the sanctuary of the church the High Altar is vested for Mass with a frontal of the colour of the Mass. On the mensa are seven candles, the six as usual, and a seventh, higher than the others, in the middle. The altar cross stands in front of this.[2] The altar cards are not put on. On the credence are placed the chalice with two purificators, the paten with two altar breads, the pall, corporal in the burse and chalice veil, as usual. Further, a vessel for the tasting of the wine, the book of lessons (Epistolary), the stand or cushion with the Missal of the altar, a second Pontifical Canon, the Bishop's gremial of the colour of the vestments, a second hand-candle (if available), the subdeacon's humeral veil (covering the chalice, etc.), the vessel and dish with which the Bishop will wash his hands and two towels, the form of the Indulgence to be proclaimed, and the pax-brede, if it will be wanted. The torches for the Elevation, six or eight, are placed near. If there is to be Communion, the pyx with particles to be consecrated and the Communion cloth are put on the credence.[3]

The throne in the sanctuary should be covered with cloths of the colour of the Mass ; a cushion lies near on which the Bishop will kneel during the Creed. On either side is a bare stool for the deacons at the

---

[1] See note 3.

[2] C.E. I. xii, 12. The seventh candle is used only at Pontifical High Mass of the living sung by *the* Bishop (at his throne or—if circumstances require—at a faldstool).

[3] In practice it is found better to have *two* credence tables, both in the secretarium and in the sanctuary. It is inconvenient to place things required at the throne on the credence at the Epistle side—especially in a large sanctuary. On the credence near the throne will be a Pontifical Canon, a Breviary (it would be well to have a second Breviary at the other credence for the singing of the *capitulum* of Terce), the hand-candle, and the ewer and basin with the towels, and a salver.

throne ; on the Bishop's right (or left [1]) a third bare stool for the assistant priest.

East of the throne is the place for the Bishop's attendants (*familiares*) (p. 140). Opposite the throne, on the Epistle side, are the sedilia for the sacred ministers. At the entrance of the sanctuary, four, six or at most seven candlesticks stand, with burning candles.

In the Sacristy. In the sacristy the vestments for the deacon and subdeacon (without the maniples) are laid out ; also vestments for the canons : copes for the dignitaries, chasubles for the canons who represent priests, dalmatics and tunicles for the canons who represent deacons and subdeacons ; two dalmatics for the deacons at the throne,[2] a cope for the A.P. Amices are made ready for all these vestments. Four copes (if customary) for the chaplains or servers who will hold the book, hand-candle, mitre and crozier ; the veils for the crozier and mitre-bearers ;[3] an amice, alb, girdle and tunicle for the subdeacon who will carry the processional cross. All the vestments are of the colour of the Mass. The lustral water, with its sprinkler, is also prepared for the reception of the Bishop.

§ 2. THE MINISTERS AND SERVERS

THE following persons take part in the ceremony :

The deacon and subdeacon of the Mass, who should be canons ; two canons (the two senior canons-deacon) who will serve as assistant deacons at the throne ; the assistant priest, also a canon, who should be the highest dignitary of the choir, or the canon who will preach the sermon ; four chaplains for the mitre, crozier, book and hand-candle [4] ; a train-bearer. Six other servers are needed for the vesting of the bishop ; these may afterwards serve as torch-bearers. There are also the (second) M.C. of the Mass, and another (first) M.C. at the throne, who regulates the whole ceremony. The acolytes and thurifer of the Mass take part as usual. The Ceremonial of Bishops enumerates the servers in this way : first, seven, namely, the bearers of the mitre, crozier, book and candle, then the thurifer and two acolytes. Further, it requires six others : one to have charge of the gremial, one of the cruets, the other four [5] assist in cassock, but without surplice, standing by the credence. This makes thirteen servers, besides the two masters of ceremonies, cross-bearer and train-bearer. Add to these the sub-deacon (not a canon) who is to be cross-bearer, the deacon and sub-deacon of the Mass, the assistant priest and two deacons at the throne, and we have altogether twenty-three persons in attendance on the

[1] See p. 139, n. 3.
[2] These they will wear over surplice (or rochet if they have the right to it) and amice (C.E. I. viii, 2). The A.P. likewise wears his cope over surplice (rochet) and amice (C.E. I. vii, 1). The ministers wear neither stole nor maniple.
[3] C.E. (I. xi, 6) does not suppose a veil used, if a cope is worn.
[4] " Those four, if it be the custom, may wear copes " (C.E. I. xi, 1).
[5] " Cubicularii sive familiares Episcopi " (C.E. I. xi, 2), i.e., chamberlains and attendants.

Bishop when he sings High Mass at the throne. There may be other attendants or servants, such as the Bishop's valet, who wait east of the throne when not occupied. The Chapter should be present to sing Terce and assist at Mass; other clergy and seminarists should, if possible, also attend.

General Rules for Assistants. It will be convenient to add at once some general directions about the functions of these persons.

The ASSISTANT PRIEST hands the towel whenever the Bishop washes his hands and after the washing (or later) replaces his ring with the solita oscula. Hands are washed four times: before Mass, at the Offertory, at the *Lavabo*, after the ablutions. The A.P. holds the boat when the Bishop (at the throne) puts on incense. At the altar he moves the Missal. When the Bishop sings anything at the throne the A.P. holds the book; when he recites the book-bearer holds it.

Ordinarily the first ASSISTANT DEACON puts on the Bishop's mitre (at the throne,[1] when the deacon of the Mass is not at hand) and gremial, the second takes them off. The Bishop wears the mitre while he walks in procession (e.g. from the throne to the altar, or back), while he sits, while he is incensed (except after the Gospel), while he washes his hands if he is vested at the time, while he gives his blessing.[2] He uses the precious mitre from the beginning to the Introit, golden mitre from the Introit to the end of the Creed, then precious mitre to the end of the whole service.

Normally the assistant deacon(s) removes the Bishop's ring when he is about to wash his hands. The A.P. replaces it.

The gremial is spread over the Bishop's knees while he sits during the sung *Kyrie, eleison, Gloria in excelsis,* Epistle, etc., Creed. While he washes his hands at the Offertory a towel may be spread.

His crozier is handed to him and taken back directly by the crozier-bearer with solita oscula. The Bishop holds it in his left hand in procession (including from throne to altar and back), while the Gospel is sung,[3] while he gives his blessing at the end.

When the Bishop is at the throne, ordinarily the place of the first M.C. is at his left, standing.

The Congregation of Rites allows, in case of necessity, that the deacon and subdeacon of Mass supply for the assistant deacons at the throne.[4]

When the Bishop himself celebrates, the canons do not come to form the circles around the throne.

General Rules for Servers. A special feature of pontifical functions is the assistance of four servers (called " capellani " in the Ceremonial), who carry the mitre, crozier, book from which the Bishop reads, and

---

[1] When the Bishop is *at the altar* the deacon of the Mass puts on and takes off the mitre (unless he be engaged, as after the incensation of the altar—C.E. I. viii, 3).

[2] An archbishop is not covered when he blesses, because of his archiepiscopal cross held before him.

[3] Then he holds it with both hands.

[4] S.R.C. 3114[3].

the hand-candle. This is the order of their rank : mitre-bearer, crozier-bearer, book-bearer, hand-candle-bearer. When the bishop has no jurisdiction (therefore in the case of an auxiliary or of an extern bishop) he will not perhaps use the crozier,[1] so the three others only attend. At solemn functions, when the Bishop is vested, these four chaplains may wear, over their surplices, copes of the colour of the Office. The mitre-bearer and crozier-bearer have scarves (*vimpae*). If they wear a cope, the scarf is under it. They hold the mitre or crozier [2] through the scarf.

The CROZIER-BEARER always hands the crozier to the Bishop and takes it from him direct, each time with the solita oscula. He hands it with the crook towards himself (so that the Bishop may have it facing forward), but carries it with the crook facing forward.

The MITRE-BEARER hands the mitre to the deacon (the first assistant deacon or the deacon of the Mass) who puts it on the Bishop. He takes it back from the second assistant deacon or from the deacon of the Mass. In the case of the mitre there are no oscula. The mitre-bearer holds the mitre with the lappets towards himself ; but when he places it on the altar or credence the lappets are to be turned outwards.

The BOOK-BEARER holds the book open before the Bishop (except when the A.P. does so, see p. 156). He kneels before a greater prelate (p. 139), otherwise he stands. He holds the book at the bottom with both hands, leaning it against his forehead. But when the Bishop sits and he stands he leans it against the breast. When the Bishop uses a book on the altar the book-bearer has no function and stands away, generally on the Gospel side, on the ground.

The CANDLE-BEARER holds the candle, lighted, in the right hand by the book. Normally at the throne he should be at the right of the book-bearer.[3] He and the book-bearer genuflect together to a greater prelate, or bow to another bishop, on arriving and retiring. When the Bishop uses a book on the altar the candle bearer stands at the side of the A.P., holding the candle. At the incensing of the altar he stands aside taking the candle with him. When he goes to kneel at the Elevation, he leaves the candle on the altar. He stands or kneels as does the book-bearer.

Neither the book-bearer when holding the book for the Bishop, nor the candle-bearer when holding the candle genuflects, even when all others do so.

These four chaplains follow the Bishop in procession. When he is at the altar the mitre-bearer and crozier-bearer are towards the Epistle side, for convenience in handing these. The candle-bearer and book-

---

[1] A bishop outside the place of his jurisdiction when he pontificates will use a crozier in functions which require its use and may use it at any function with the consent of the Ordinary (cf. C.J.C. 337, § 2, and S.R.C. 4355, iii, 3).

[2] According to C.E. I. xi, 5, the crozier-bearer holds the crozier with the end of his cotta, and hands it " nudum, nulloque panniculo appenso " to the Bishop.

[3] C.E. I. xx, 1. So placed he is less likely to incommode the A.P and is in a more convenient position to hold the candle in the right hand.

bearer are sometimes in the same line as the others, on the Gospel side (as during the prayers at the foot of the altar) ; or, more often, the candle-bearer is on the foot-pace on the Gospel side, the book-bearer stands away on the ground, on that side, not holding a book.

A greater prelate has a TRAIN-BEARER. Other bishops (an auxiliary or visitor) do not use a train ;[1] so this server does not attend them. Whenever the Bishop with train goes in procession, even from one part of the altar to the other, the train-bearer goes behind him holding the train with both hands. When the Bishop does not go in procession, the train-bearer stands or kneels aside, but near. His place then is at the east side of the throne ; or near the credence, when the Bishop is at the altar.

Choir Ceremonies. The clergy in choir at a pontifical function stand when the Bishop arrives in or departs from the choir, and whenever he passes from the altar to the throne or *vice versa*. They kneel momentarily, when he blesses as he goes by. Prelates and canons bow low. The clergy kneel while the Bishop prays for a brief space (at the faldstool) on his arrival and before his departure at the beginning and end of the function. They stand while the Bishop vests and unvests. While he is at his throne, vested, they stand or sit according as the Bishop does.

§ 3. THE VESTING OF THE BISHOP

THE service begins while the canons sing Terce in the choir of the secretarium. First, the bells of the church are rung, the organ is played. The canons proceed in choral dress to meet the Bishop. The ministers of the Mass who are canons go also to meet the Bishop or they may vest beforehand in the sacristy and then await the Bishop in the secretarium.[2] The four bearers of the mitre, crozier, book and candle wait near the credence or throne in the secretarium. The cross-bearer and other servers are there too, vested, unless they accompany the procession to meet the Bishop at the door of the church.

Arrival of Bishop. The Bishop arrives in the church in rochet and cappa. He receives the aspergill from the senior canon, signs himself and then sprinkles (thrice) the canons, and after them all present (thrice). Accompanied by his attendants, and by the canons, he goes first to the chapel of the Blessed Sacrament, kneels at the faldstool[3]

---

[1] A bishop in the place of his jurisdiction may wear his *cappa magna* even in the presence of his superior. In deference to the latter he does not allow the train to flow but carries it folded up. He will, however, allow it to flow if he is about to pontificate, but even then not when he walks with his superior or performs any act of deference towards him (S.R.C. 4355, II. 2).

[2] C.E. (I. ix, 1) says deacon is to assume his vestments in the same place as the other canons, i.e., *extra secretarium* (II. viii, 4). Though C.E. supposes him and the subdeacon to vest at the same time as the other canons, some authors (e.g., Martinucci, Schober) advise that they vest beforehand and at the sedilia await the arrival of the Bishop in the secretarium.

[3] The M.C. spreads the front of the cappa over the faldstool and sets it free when the Bishop rises. This is the rule always when a bishop in cappa kneels at a faldstool.

there prepared and says a short prayer. He comes to the secretarium, bows to the altar, kneels at the faldstool again for a few moments. Then he goes to the throne, sits, and puts on his biretta. Here the deacons assisting and the A.P. await him, in choir dress. Meanwhile the canons (except those assisting at the throne) vest in the sacristy or in some other convenient place outside the secretarium and then return to their stalls in the secretarium. The chaplains of the book and candle take these from the credence and come before the Bishop.

Beginning of Terce. The Bishop takes off his biretta, hands it to the first assistant deacon, rises, turns to the altar and says the *Pater noster* and *Ave Maria* silently. He then intones *Deus in adjutorium meum intende* (signing himself) while the A.P. holds the book. The canons answer ; the hymn *Nunc Sancte nobis Spiritus* (intoned by chanters) is sung, the antiphon intoned and the psalms of Terce begin. Then the Bishop sits, puts on his biretta and begins the prayers before Mass, *Ne reminiscaris* and the psalms. The assistant priest and deacons (standing uncovered) say these with him. The canons sit at their places and continue Terce slowly, so as not to finish before the Bishop is vested.[1]

The subdeacon goes to the credence and takes the Bishop's shoes and stockings, on their plate covered with a veil. He holds the plate by another veil, which covers his hands, and carries the plate with both hands and raised to the height of his eyes. He comes to the throne and kneels before the Bishop ; assisted by the Bishop's servant (who removes the Bishop's ordinary shoes and afterwards takes them away hidden under his cloak) he puts on the liturgical shoes and stockings, beginning with the right foot. The subdeacon then takes the plate back to the credence, and goes to the sedilia, where he waits by the deacon.

Prayers of Preparation. Meanwhile, the Bishop says the prayers of the preparation.[2] When he arrives at *Kyrie, eleison,* he uncovers, rises and finishes the prayers facing the altar. He then sits, puts on his biretta and may, for greater convenience, read all the vesting prayers. Meantime the servers receive the vestments from the second M.C. at the altar and bring them near the throne, and the four chaplains go to the sacristy and put on their copes (if they use them). When the Bishop has finished reading the prayers an attendant takes off the cappa (the first assistant deacon having removed the pectoral cross if the Bishop wears it over the cappa), lays it aside and loosens the train of the Bishop's cassock. The deacon and subdeacon of the Mass come to the throne ; the assistant deacons (the first one having removed the Bishop's ring [3] for the washing of the hands) retire, put on their amices

---

[1] If necessary the organ may play between the psalms (C.E. II. viii, 8).

[2] A bishop who is about to celebrate pontifical Mass satisfies the obligation of the canonical hour (Terce or None) by reciting these prayers which are prescribed by the Ceremonial (S.R.C., 9 April 1921).

[3] Kissing both the hand and the ring, as always. The ring is not replaced until after the vesting for Mass, when the precious mitre has been put on (S.R.C.)

and dalmatics, return and stand back, so as not to hinder the others. The Bishop, with his biretta on, now washes his hands. The A.P. spreads one of the towels over the Bishop's knees. An attendant, kneeling before the Bishop, holds the dish and pours the water, the A.P. hands the towel.[1] He then goes to put on his amice and cope, and comes back to the throne when vested.

Vesting the Bishop for Terce. The servers who hold the vestments now come to the throne ; the Bishop's biretta is taken away and put with his cappa. Meanwhile the other persons in choir, canons, prebendaries or chaplains, continue Terce. The Bishop vests in order, saying each prayer (if he has not already said the vesting prayers) assisted by the ministers of the Mass. The pectoral cross is put on after the cincture and the deacon kisses it before presenting it to the Bishop to kiss. When the cope is put on the morse is added. Lastly the Bishop sits and the deacon puts on him the golden mitre. The ministers of the Mass go to the sedilia and are replaced by the assistant deacons.

Conclusion of Terce. When the psalms of Terce are finished, the subdeacon of the Mass takes a Breviary, goes to the place at a distance from the foot of the altar where the Epistle is read and chants the Chapter, taking care not to turn his back or shoulder to the Bishop, who rises, not taking off the mitre ; all rise with him. After the Chapter the subdeacon returns to his place at the sedilia. Cantors sing the Short Responsory and the versicles of Terce. The acolytes bring their candles to the throne and stand at the bottom of its steps, on either side facing each other. The chaplains of the book and candle approach. The Bishop sits while the second assistant deacon takes off his mitre. Then he rises and sings *Dominus vobiscum* and the prayer (*in tono festivo*), the A.P. holding the book before him. He repeats *Dominus vobiscum*, the acolytes and chaplains retire ; the cantors sing *Benedicamus Domino*. The verse *Fidelium animae* is not sung, since Mass will follow at once.

Vesting Bishop for Mass. The servers return to the throne, bringing the Mass vestments, the tunicle, dalmatic, gloves and chasuble. The deacon and subdeacon of the Mass come to the throne. The deacon takes off the Bishop's morse and cope. The Bishop puts on the tunicle and dalmatic. Then he sits while the deacon puts on the right glove, the subdeacon the left, each kissing first the Bishop's hand and then the glove. Then the Bishop rises and puts on the chasuble. Meanwhile the thurifer prepares the thurible. [If the prelate is an archbishop, and if it is a day on which he wears the pallium, this is brought by a subdeacon-canon from the altar, handed to the deacon of the Mass, who puts it on the Bishop and fixes the pins, assisted by the sub-

---

3747[1] and cf. C.E. II. viii, 22 ; § 11 of C.E. does not refer to the pontifical ring, but to other rings, no longer worn by bishops). The M.C. will have at hand a salver (held by a server) to receive the pectoral cross or the ring when they are taken off momentarily.

[1] While the Bishop washes his hands those ministering near the throne (except canons) kneel ; but if a prelate of higher rank be present, all stand.

deacon.[1]] The Bishop sits and the deacon puts on the precious mitre, the subdeacon aiding by lifting the lappets.[2] The servers who held the vestments now retire. The ministers of the Mass go to their seats and put on their maniples ; the assistant deacons take their place. The subdeacon takes the Bishop's Missal, with the maniple between its leaves. The A.P. with the solita oscula puts on the bishop's ring over the glove.

Procession to the Sanctuary. The thurifer comes to the throne, the Bishop puts on incense and blesses it, the A.P. assisting.[3] Meanwhile

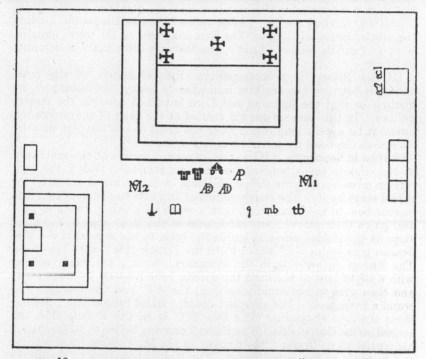

FIG. 18. PONTIFICAL HIGH MASS AT THE THRONE : " IUDICA ME "

the thurifer, as always in such cases, kneels. The subdeacon who carries the cross [4] now takes it, the chaplain brings the crozier to the Bishop. The Bishop rises and bows to the cross on the altar of the

---

[1] C.E. II. viii, 20, gives detailed instruction about the arrangement of the pallium and the pins.

[2] C.E. II. viii, 21.

[3] The A.P. uses the form *Benedicite, Pater Reverendissime* ; for a cardinal *Benedicite, Eminentissime et Reverendissime Pater.*

[4] Not, of course, the subdeacon of the Mass. The subdeacon cross-bearer is vested in amice, alb, cincture and tunicle.

secretarium [an archbishop bows to the metropolitan cross] ; the M.C. forms the procession.[1] The thurifer goes first, unless there are servants of the Bishop in lay dress to go in front of all. Then comes the sub-deacon with the cross between the acolytes. He holds the cross so that the figure of our Lord is turned forward, in the direction of the procession. The clergy follow in order, two and two, then the canons (wearing their birettas, as they are vested) : subdeacons, deacons, priests and dignitaries. The subdeacon of the Mass follows, holding before his breast the Evangeliarium closed and containing the Bishop's maniple ; then the A.P. with the deacon of the Mass at his left ; then the Bishop between his two assistant deacons, followed by the train-bearer who carries his train. As he passes he blesses the people, holding the crozier in his left hand. The four chaplains of the mitre, crozier, book and candle follow. Lastly, the Bishop's attendants or servants in livery.

[If the Bishop is a metropolitan, the subdeacon of the cross carries it between the acolytes immediately before the canons ; [2] he holds it so that the figure of our Lord is turned towards the metro-politan. In this case no cross is carried at the head of the procession unless it be a very long one. Then the cross of the Chapter may be carried at the head by a cleric wearing a surplice.[3]]

Arrival in Sanctuary. When the procession arrives at the sanctuary of the church, the attendants or servants remain outside ; the sub-deacon cross-bearer puts the processional cross in a stand prepared for it and stays by it. The clergy genuflect and bow to one another ; the canons bow to the altar cross, then bow to each other, two and two, and go to their places ; the subdeacon of the Mass goes to the altar steps at the Gospel side and hands the book to the second M.C. ; the deacon goes to his side, the A.P. to the Epistle side before the steps. The Bishop on arriving in the sanctuary, wearing his mitre, salutes with a slight bow of the head the canons (who respond by a low bow) and then goes to the middle between the A.P. and the deacon, who stand a little back. His assistant deacons stand behind him ; behind these the four chaplains. The first M.C. is on the Epistle side, the second on the Gospel side. The Bishop, arriving before the altar, hands his crozier to its bearer ; the deacon (of the Mass) takes off the mitre and hands it to the mitre-bearer. The Bishop bows low to the altar ; all the others genuflect, except canons. So Mass begins.

---

[1] If Terce is sung in choir and the Bishop vests in the sanctuary, incense is not put in and there is no procession (C.E. II. viii, 25 ; S.R.C. 3228[1]). In going from the throne to the foot of the altar the subdeacon (with the book) precedes the A.P. and deacon (on A.P.'s left) ; the Bishop, between the assistant deacons, follows them and last of all come the bearers of the Bishop's insignia.

[2] Whenever the Chapter is present the canons—if preceding—go between the archiepiscopal cross and the archbishop. Otherwise the cross is carried imme-diately before the archbishop.

[3] Cf. S.R.C. 2684[16].

§ 4. FROM THE BEGINNING OF MASS TO THE GOSPEL

In all that follows the usual ceremonies of High Mass (pp. 76 *sqq*) are supposed, except where a difference is noted.

The Bishop says the preparatory prayers at the foot of the altar, as usual.[1] The A.P., the deacon and subdeacon answer him.[2] When he begins the prayer *Indulgentiam*, the deacon steps back, the subdeacon takes the Bishop's maniple and when he has finished the prayer puts it on his left arm, kissing first the maniple (at the side), then the Bishop's hand. When the Bishop goes up to the altar the A.P. passes behind him to his left, the deacon goes to his right. The subdeacon, taking the book of Gospels, goes up to the altar with the Bishop on the left of the A.P. The assistant deacons remain where they are *in plano*. The Bishop kisses the altar, then the Gospel book presented by the subdeacon open at the Gospel of the Mass (the beginning of which A.P. will indicate to the Bishop), laying both his hands on it. The subdeacon hands it to a server ; the A.P. goes down and stands *in plano* at the Gospel corner during the incensation.[3] The thurifer comes up and kneels and the Bishop puts on and blesses incense as usual, the deacon handing the spoon and saying *Benedicite, Pater reverendissime*. The Bishop incenses the altar, assisted by the deacon and subdeacon (each placing the nearer hand to him under his arm).[4]

The deacon takes the thurible from the Bishop. The first deacon of the throne comes and puts on the precious mitre. The deacon of the Mass, with the subdeacon at his left, standing at the foot of the altar on the Epistle side, incenses the Bishop with three double swings. When he has done so the Bishop gives him a blessing.[5]

Bishop goes to Throne. The Bishop from the Epistle corner bows, with all his assistant sacred ministers, to the altar-cross, takes his crozier from its bearer, and accompanied by the two assistant deacons, with the A.P. before him, goes directly to the throne, blessing the choir as he passes. His train-bearer follows holding the train. The ministers of the Mass go to the sedilia. They stand whenever the Bishop stands. At the throne the Bishop hands his crozier to its bearer, and sits momentarily while the second assistant deacon takes off the mitre. The train-bearer goes to his place east of the throne. The chaplains of the book and candle come to the throne, genuflect to the Bishop and hold the book and candle. The Bishop, wearing only the skull-cap, stands, makes the sign of the cross, and reads the Introit. The chaplain of the mitre puts the precious mitre on the credence near the throne,

---

[1] One of the M.C. must see that the Pontifical Canon (open at *Oramus te, Domine*) is on the table of the altar at the centre. If a second Canon is used, it may be placed so ready before the function begins.

[2] In the *Confiteor* A.P., deacon and subdeacon say, as usual, *tibi Pater* and *te Pater*, bowing towards the Bishop.

[3] C.E. I. vii, 4. Some authors direct him to stand between the assistant deacons.

[4] C.E. I. ix, 1, 5 ; x, 2.

[5] The Bishop answers all incensing and reverences made by the canons or sacred ministers by making the sign of the cross over them.

and takes the golden mitre. The Bishop says *Kyrie, eleison* with those around him ; the deacon and subdeacon say it to one another.

Gloria. If the sung *Kyrie* will take a long time, the Bishop may now sit, with mitre and gremial (put on by the first assistant deacon), as he will at the *Gloria*. When *Kyrie, eleison* has been sung, the A.P. holds the book, the Bishop standing—without mitre or skull-cap [1] and facing the altar—intones *Gloria in excelsis Deo*, disjoining and elevating his hands at *Gloria*, joining them and bowing his head at *Deo*. The chaplain

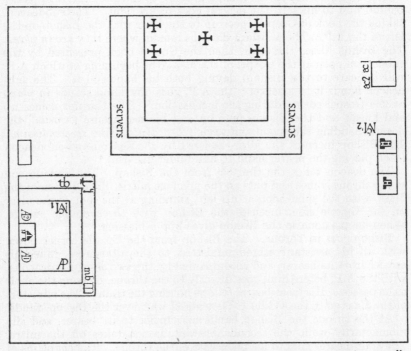

FIG. 19. PONTIFICAL HIGH MASS AT THE THRONE : DURING THE " GLORIA "
AND CREED

of the book takes it from the A.P., who goes back to his stool. The Bishop recites the hymn with his assistants, the deacon and subdeacon say it at the bench. When the Bishop has finished saying the *Gloria* the bearers of book and hand-candle take these to the credence, leave them there and come back. The Bishop sits ; the first assistant deacon puts on the skull-cap and the golden mitre, then takes the gremial from the server who has brought it and spreads it on the Bishop's knees. The assistants at the throne sit on their stools, the four chap-

---

[1] C.E. II. viii, 37 ; the second assistant deacon removes the gremial and mitre, the first the skull-cap.

lains on the steps of the throne [1] (genuflecting first to the Bishop), the ministers of Mass at the sedilia. The other servers may sit on the altar steps on either side ; the train-bearer on the step of the throne at the east side. When the words *Adoramus te*, etc., are sung the Bishop,

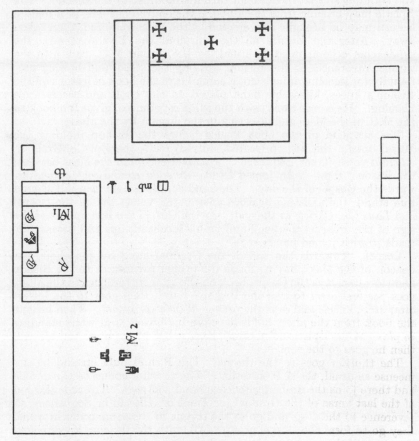

FIG. 20. PONTIFICAL HIGH MASS AT THE THRONE : THE GOSPEL.

with mitre on, bows ; ¯all others uncover and bow. Towards the end of the *Gloria* sung by the choir, all stand, except the Bishop.

Collect(s). The chaplains bring the book and candle, the second assistant deacon removes the gremial and hands it to the server, then he takes off the mitre.[2] The A.P. holds the book, the Bishop stands,

[1] Having laid aside the candle, book, etc.
[2] This is always the order. The mitre is put on before and taken off after the gremial.

turns towards the people, sings *Pax vobis* ; then turned to the altar he sings the Collect or Collects. He sits again and is covered with the mitre, and the gremial is laid over his knees. The subdeacon sings the Epistle as usual, making first the reverences to the altar and Bishop, and standing so that he does not turn his shoulder to the Bishop. The Epistle may be sung from the ambo, if the church has one, or a folding lectern may be brought out, erected at the place required, then taken away. After the Epistle all those around the Bishop stand ; the subdeacon, accompanied, as usual, by the second M.C., comes to the throne, reverences to the Bishop, goes up the steps, and bowing profoundly (or kneeling if he is not a canon) lays the book of lessons on the Bishop's knees, kisses his hand placed on the book and receives his blessing. He comes away with the same reverences, gives the book to the M.C. of the Mass and goes to join the deacon by the altar.

The chaplain of the book kneels before the Bishop, holding the Missal open ; the Bishop (seated, mitred) reads the Epistle, Gradual, *Alleluia* verse, Tract, Sequence or whatever occurs in the Mass between the lessons, then—with joined hands—*Munda cor meum* [1] and afterwards the Gospel of the day. The hand-candle is held near, all around him stand, the assisting deacons answer the verses before the Gospel and *Laus tibi, Christe* at the end. At the Gospel the Bishop makes the sign of the cross on the book and on his forehead, lips and breast ; he reads it with joined hands.

Gospel. Towards the end of the Gradual sung by the choir, the deacon of the Mass, having made the proper reverences to the Bishop and the altar, lays the Gospel book on the altar, reverences to the altar, goes *per breviorem* to kiss the Bishop's hand, then goes to the lowest altar step, kneels and says the prayer *Munda cor meum*. Then he gets the book from the altar, holds it before his breast, and waits standing *in plano* at the Epistle corner until incense has been put in and blessed, then he goes to the centre.

The thurifer goes to the throne. The Bishop puts on and blesses incense as usual, the A.P. assisting. The thurifer comes to the middle and there joins the deacon, subdeacon and acolytes. Towards the end of the last verse of the Gradual (or Tract or *Alleluia* or Sequence), all reverence to the altar and go to the throne in the same order in which they go to form the Gospel group. All, with the deacon, kneel before the steps (if the subdeacon is a canon, he does not kneel, but bows low). The deacon kneeling (if he is a canon he bows low instead) asks the Bishop's blessing with the usual form *Iube, domne, benedicere*. When the Bishop has given the blessing,[2] all who are kneeling rise ; the deacon and subdeacon genuflect (bow low, if canons) to him, the others genuflect and all go to the place where the Gospel is sung, first the M.C. of the Mass, then the thurifer, the acolytes together, then the subdeacon, and after him the deacon holding the Gospel book. The Gospel is sung

---

[1] The Bishop adds *Iube, Domine*, etc., and *Dominus sit in corde meo*, etc.
[2] He does not present his hand to be kissed as the deacon has already given this mark of respect.

as usual. The four chaplains stand in line before the throne on the east side facing the place where the Gospel is sung.

The ambo may be used as at the Epistle, or the lectern brought out and set up.[1] Before the deacon sings *Dominus vobiscum* the mitre and gremial are taken from the Bishop, he stands, takes his crozier in his left hand, makes the sign of the cross on his forehead, lips and breast as the deacon does so, and stands holding the crozier in both hands while the Gospel is sung. Then he lays it aside. The subdeacon goes to the Bishop with the book open at the page of the Gospel, making no reverence either to him or the altar, and points the place of the Gospel. The Bishop says *Per evangelica dicta*, etc., laying both hands on the book, and kisses it. The subdeacon goes down, making the usual reverence to the Bishop (genuflecting or, if he be a canon, bowing low) ; the A.P., standing before the throne, incenses the Bishop (who remains without his mitre). The thurifer stands by the A.P. and holds the end of his cope meanwhile ; when he has been incensed the Bishop blesses the A.P. In the meantime the deacon, M.C. and acolytes return in procession (in the order in which they came) to the altar, reverence to it and go to their places.

§ 5. FROM THE GOSPEL TO THE COMMUNION

Sermon. If the Bishop preaches, he may do so from the throne, or from a faldstool placed for him before the altar, facing the people. If at the faldstool placed on the foot-pace the A.P. sits at his right meanwhile ; behind the A.P. sit the deacon of the Mass and first assistant deacon, the subdeacon and second assistant deacon at the Bishop's left (a little behind him). If the sermon is preached by a canon or priest,[2] he wears his choir dress ; if he be a Religious his habit. It is customary (outside Rome) to wear a stole of the colour of the Mass. Before the sermon the preacher comes to the throne, genuflects, kneels before the Bishop (a canon bows only), kisses his hand and says *Iube, domne, benedicere.* The Bishop answers *Dominus sit in corde tuo et in labiis tuis, ut digne et fructuose annunties verba sancta sua. In nomine Patris + et Filii et Spiritus Sancti. Amen*, making the sign of the cross over him. Then the preacher asks for the Indulgence, saying *Indulgentias, Pater reverendissime.*[3] The Bishop answers *Consuetas*, or he names the number.[4] Without again kissing the Bishop's hand, the

---

[1] If there is an ambo, the subdeacon stands at the deacon's right, hands him the thurible, turns over the pages. If there is a portable lectern (which should be ornamented and have spread over it a covering of cloth of gold or of silk of the colour of the vestments) the subdeacon stands behind it, resting his hands on the edges of the book, as if he were holding it.

[2] C.E. II. viii, 48 prefers that the Bishop preach himself. If not the preacher should be a canon and he should be A.P. for the occasion (C.E. I. xxii, 1). But this rule is often not observed. If the A.P. does preach he retains his cope.

[3] To a cardinal he says : " Pater eminentissime ac reverendissime."

[4] A cardinal may concede an indulgence of 300 days to be gained (i) *toties quoties* in places or institutions or by persons under his jurisdiction or protection, (ii) in other places, by those present only ,and once on each occasion. In places

preacher rises, genuflects (or bows) to the Bishop and goes to the pulpit or place where he will preach, making the usual reverence to the altar as he passes it. When he enters the pulpit he kneels towards the altar and recites aloud the *Hail Mary*,[1] then he rises, covers and begins. Should he address himself to the Bishop during his discourse he uncovers and bows to the prelate.

Indulgence. At the end of the sermon the preacher kneels in the pulpit (a canon bows) towards the altar. The deacon of the Mass comes before the throne [2] (with the usual reverences to the altar and the Bishop) and bowing his head chants the *Confiteor*. At the words *tibi Pater* and *te Pater* he genuflects to the Bishop (a canon bows). Meanwhile the Bishop rises and stands at the throne wearing the mitre, and all the choir stand. The deacon goes back to the sedilia. The Bishop sits (all others remaining standing) and the preacher stands and reads the form of Indulgence, as it is in the Ceremonial [3] (see p. 366). Then he comes down from the pulpit. The bearers of the book and candle come to the throne; the Bishop rises, the mitre having been taken off, and chants the prayers *Precibus et meritis* and *Indulgentiam*.[4] All kneel, except canons and prelates, who bow standing. The Bishop sits for a moment while the mitre is put on; then he stands and gives the blessing, holding the crozier.[5] [If he is an archbishop, the subdeacon cross-bearer comes and kneels before him, holding his cross with the figure towards him and the archbishop does not wear the mitre.] Then Mass continues. If the Bishop himself has preached, the form of Indulgence is read by the A.P.,[6] and it is he who holds the book for the Bishop to sing the absolution and blessing.[7]

Creed. The Bishop, uncovered, turned towards the altar, intones the Creed, the A.P. holding the book. Then the book is handed back to its bearer, who continues to hold it before the Bishop while he says the Creed. The hand-candle is held near. The deacon and subdeacon recite the Creed at their places. When the Bishop says the words

under his jurisdiction an archbishop may grant an indulgence of 200 days; a residential bishop, a Vicar or Prefect Apostolic, or an Abbot or Prelate *nullius*, one of 100 days. (C.J.C. 239, § 1, 24°; 274, 2°; 349, § 2, 2°; 294; 323. S. Penitentiary, July 20, 1942.)

[1] C.E. I. xxii, 3.

[2] C.E. II. xxxix, 1. Should the Bishop have preached from the foot-pace the deacon, for the *Confiteor*, stands before the lowest step or on the highest (a little to one side) (C.E. I. xxv, 1).

[3] C.E. I. xxv, 1.

[4] *Ib.*, § 2, and II. xxxix, 3 (see p. 366).

[5] The form is given in C.E. I. xxv, 3 (see p. 366). If there is no sermon the Indulgence is announced after the blessing at the end of Mass (C.E. I. xxv, 8).

[6] If the Bishop preaches he does so in vestments with mitre and gremial on. The deacon sings the *Confiteor* at the foot of the throne if the Bishop has preached there; at the left of the Bishop if he has preached at the faldstool (C.E. I. xxv, 1; II. xxxix, 1; S.R.C. 2682[14]).

[7] If the Bishop is to give the Papal Blessing with plenary indulgence (which he may do thrice a year, on Easter Sunday and on two other solemn feasts at choice—C.J.C. 914; S. Penit., July 20, 1942) at the end of Mass, the partial indulgence and blessing are not given after the sermon.

Et incarnatus est, etc., he genuflects on the cushion placed before him by the M.C. All genuflect with him, except the bearers of book and candle. Then the Bishop sits, is covered with the gold mitre and gremial. When the choir sings the verse *Et incarnatus est*, etc., the Bishop bows towards the altar, still covered ; all the others who are sitting bow also, while those who are standing kneel and bow (p. 75).

On Christmas Day and Lady Day the Bishop kneels at the throne wearing the mitre, and bows.

After *Et incarnatus* the deacon takes the corporal to the altar, as usual, genuflecting (or bowing low, if he be a canon) to the Bishop and the altar on his way.

Offertory. When the Creed is over, the Bishop's gremial is removed and his mitre taken off. He stands, turns towards the people, sings *Dominus vobiscum* and—turned to the altar—*Oremus*. He reads the Offertory verse, the book-bearer holding the book. He sits and the first deacon puts on him the precious mitre. A server comes with the salver for the ring and gloves. The assistant deacons take off the Bishop's ring and gloves, putting them on the salver. The servers approach with the vessel, dish and towels. The assistant deacons spread one towel over the Bishop's knees, the A.P. holds the other. The servers kneel while the Bishop washes his hands. Those near the throne kneel too, except canons, who stand. The Bishop makes the sign of the cross over the servers ; they go away. The A.P. replaces the ring on the Bishop's bare hand, with the solita oscula.[1]

The A.P. takes the Missal on its stand,[2] and—accompanied by the (second) M.C.[3]—goes to the altar and arranges it there on its stand or cushion, and then at the Gospel side of the foot-pace awaits the arrival of the Bishop. The bearers of book and candle follow him. The subdeacon goes to the credence ; the acolytes put on him the humeral veil ; he takes the chalice to the Epistle corner at the same time as the Bishop arrives at the altar.

Bishop goes to Altar. The Bishop rises at the throne, takes his crozier and goes to the altar, blessing the choir as he passes. His train is carried behind as usual and he is followed by the mitre and crozier bearers. At the foot of the altar he gives up the crozier ; the mitre is removed by the deacon of the Mass ; the Bishop bows low to the cross and goes up to the foot-pace. The A.P. is then on his left,[4] the deacon of the Mass on his right. The assistant deacons go on either side of the Bishop towards the altar, they stand on the ground before it, at the

---

[1] The gloves are not worn after this, unless the Papal blessing is given.

[2] Or A.P. may send the book-bearer, immediately after the Bishop has read the Offertory, to the altar with the Missal (C.E. II. viii, 57). In this case A.P. will accompany the Bishop (on his left) to the altar. Some authors say that A.P. is also to take the Canon to the altar. C.E. is silent about this, and so the (second) ceremoniar may see to it (placing it, open at the Offertory, against the cross or tabernacle).

[3] C.E. II. viii, 57.

[4] From the Offertory to the *Agnus Dei* the A.P. is at the Bishop's left, by the book (and turns the pages), except at the Lavabo and Elevation.

foot of the steps, the bearers of crozier and mitre stand behind them. The candle-bearer goes up to the foot-pace and stands there at the left of the A.P.   This is now his place while the Bishop reads.   He stands aside at the censing of the altar, taking the candle with him.   The first M.C. stands on the ground at the Epistle side, the second on the Gospel side, and the book-bearer near him.   All in choir sit.   The Bishop kisses the altar.   The subdeacon brings up the chalice and consigns it to the deacon of the Mass.   The latter takes the chalice, uncovers it,

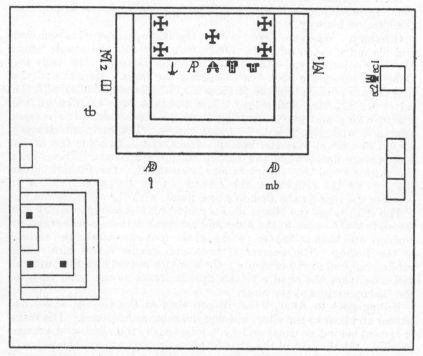

FIG. 21.   PONTIFICAL HIGH MASS AT THE THRONE : THE OFFERTORY

takes one of the two altar breads, touches with it the other bread, the paten, and the chalice within and without, and gives it to the sacristan, who eats it.   The other altar bread on the paten he gives to the Bishop, who makes the Offertory as usual and then puts the paten under the corporal.   The deacon pours a little of the wine and water into the vessel prepared and gives it to the sacristan to drink.[1] The deacon [2] wipes the chalice and pours in the wine, the subdeacon— having held up the water cruet to the Bishop and asked his blessing,

[1] This is the " praegustatio " ceremony, a curious relic of early times.   It is obviously a precaution against poison.   The ceremony is now often omitted.
[2] Not the subdeacon (C.E. II. viii, 62).

saying *Benedicite, Pater reverendissime*—pours in the water. Meanwhile the Bishop recites *Deus, qui humanae*, etc. The deacon hands the chalice to the Bishop who offers it.

Incensation. The deacon, having given the paten to the subdeacon, assists at the putting in of incense and incensation, as usual. The Bishop incenses the *oblata* and the altar ; the A.P. removes the Missal and, having replaced it after the incensation of the Gospel side, goes to the Epistle side for the washing of the fingers. The train-bearer comes up and holds the train, then goes back to his place on the ground near the credence. When the Bishop has incensed the altar, the first assistant deacon comes to him, at the Epistle side, with the bearer of the mitre. He puts on the precious mitre [1] ; the Bishop is incensed by the deacon of the Mass and blesses him. Then the first assistant deacon removes the ring and the Bishop washes his hands, the A.P. presenting the towel and the servers kneeling. The Canon, taken from the centre of the altar, is held before the Bishop (if necessary) by the M.C. or book-bearer while he recites the *Lavabo* psalm. The A.P replaces the ring and the second assistant deacon (or the M.C.) takes off the Bishop's mitre before he says *Gloria Patri* at the end of the psalm. The deacon of the Mass, when he has incensed the Bishop, incenses the A.P. and the two deacons of the throne, each with two double swings. Then he incenses the choir, according to the usual rule (p. 107). He goes up to stand behind the Bishop.

Preface. Meanwhile the Bishop continues Mass as usual. After the Secrets the A.P. changes the Missal for the Pontifical Canon on the stand or cushion.[2] Before the Bishop sings *Per omnia saecula saeculorum* the M.C. takes off his skull-cap and hands it to the mitre-bearer. The deacon of the Mass stands on the right and the A.P. on the left side of the Bishop, to say the *Sanctus* with him ; the subdeacon does not go up to the foot-pace. All this time, unless they are otherwise occupied, the two assistant deacons stand on the ground before the altar steps, the subdeacon standing between them.

The torch-bearers [3] come before the altar, genuflect, bow to each other and kneel, either behind the subdeacon or at the sides of the altar, holding their torches. All in choir and sanctuary kneel, except the A.P., M.C., assistant deacons, deacon and subdeacon, thurifer, bearers of book, candle, mitre and crozier. The subdeacon has received the paten from the deacon at the Offertory ; he stands holding it before the altar steps. The deacon (once he has recited the *Sanctus*) is on the top step behind the Bishop, the A.P. at the Bishop's left.

Consecration. Before the Elevation incense is put in the thurible by the M.C. (or by an acolyte), the M.C. or the thurifer (cf. p. 84) incenses

---

[1] Should the first assistant deacon be impeded, the M.C. may put on the mitre (C.E. II. viii, 64).

[2] He hands the Missal to the M.C. or book-bearer who lays it on the credence till it is wanted again after the ablutions. It is rubricians who direct the A.P. to replace the Missal by the Canon for the Preface. C.E. is silent on the point.

[3] There should be four, six, or at most eight torches (C.E. II. viii, 68).

the Sanctissimum, kneeling on the lowest step at the Epistle corner. At the words *Qui pridie* the deacon and A.P. kneel at the edge of the foot-pace, the others at their places ; at the Elevation they hold the end of the chasuble. The deacon uncovers the chalice, as at every High Mass.[1] After the Elevation the deacon stands behind the Bishop, the A.P. is at the book, the torch-bearers retire unless Holy Communion is to be given (p. 89). The A.P. and deacon genuflect with the Bishop whenever he genuflects during the Canon.[2] The deacon comes to the Bishop's right to uncover the chalice at *Benedicis et praestas nobis* and to put his hand on it at *Per ipsum*, etc. He then returns to his place behind the Bishop. Towards the end of the *Pater noster* the deacon comes to the Bishop's right, the subdeacon to the deacon's right ; the paten is handed to the Bishop as usual, the subdeacon has the humeral veil taken off by the second M.C. or an acolyte, genuflects to the Sanctissimum and goes to the foot of the altar steps.

Agnus Dei and Pax. At the *Agnus Dei* the deacon is at the Bishop's right ; the subdeacon does not go up to the altar. The deacon and A.P. say the *Agnus Dei* with the Bishop. They then genuflect and change places ; the deacon goes to the Missal and assists there ; the A.P. to the Bishop's right. When the Bishop has recited the prayer *Domine J.C.*, the A.P. genuflects, rises at once and, with the Bishop, kisses the altar, not laying his hands on it. The Bishop gives the kiss of peace to the A.P. He genuflects and goes to give it to the dignitaries and canons in choir accompanied by the second M.C. (p. 101). The first and second assistant deacons, the deacon and subdeacon of the Mass, now come up in turn to the Bishop's right, each (genuflecting before and after, but not kissing the altar) receives the pax from him. The subdeacon stands at the Bishop's right and uncovers the chalice at his Communion, the deacon is by the book, till the A.P. returns from giving the pax. When the A.P. comes back to the altar he gives the pax to the M.C. who had accompanied him (and he in turn goes to give it to the clergy in choir who are not canons). Then he stands at the Bishop's left and the deacon at the Bishop's right. The subdeacon now goes down to his place in the middle.

If the ministers receive Holy Communion, they do not take the kiss of peace from the Bishop before his Communion but later, immediately after their own. The *Confiteor*, etc., is not said. They make their Communion kneeling, first kissing the Bishop's hand, then they rise and kiss his left cheek, while he says *Pax tecum*. They answer *Et cum spiritu tuo*.[3]

---

[1] The bell should be rung as usual at the *Sanctus*, before the Consecration, and at each Elevation (S.R.C. 4377).

[2] C.E. I. vii, 5 ; II. viii, 69.

[3] The C.E. II. xxxi, 5 says that it is " very becoming " that the deacon and subdeacon should make their Communion at the Bishop's Mass on Sundays (cf. *Conc. Trid.*, Sess. XXIII. cap. xiii). Indeed C.E. I. ix, 6 says the sacred ministers are to communicate, when they are not priests desirous of saying Mass. For the rite see C.E. II. xxix, 3.

§ 6. FROM AFTER THE COMMUNION TO THE END OF MASS

As soon as the Communion act is over the M.C. replaces the Bishop's skull-cap. The deacon [1] pours in the wine, and the wine and water for the ablutions ; the subdeacon comes to the Gospel side of the altar, wipes the chalice,[2] and takes it to the credence. The A.P. puts the Pontifical Canon in the middle of the altar, replaces the Missal (brought to him by the book-bearer) on its stand, moves it across, then stands at the Epistle corner ready for the washing of hands. The precious mitre is put on the Bishop by the deacon of the Mass and the ring removed. Standing at the Epistle corner the Bishop washes his hands, the A.P. presenting the towel and replacing the ring. The Bishop blesses the servers, the precious mitre is taken off by the deacon.

Postcommunion. The Bishop reads the Communion verse, says *Dominus vobiscum*, sings the Postcommunion(s), as the celebrant at every High Mass. The deacon sings *Ite, missa est*, as usual. When the Bishop has said the prayer *Placeat tibi*, the deacon of the Mass puts on his precious mitre. Facing the altar the Bishop sings the versicles, *Sit nomen Domini*, etc. As he sings the end of the formula of blessing, before the word *Pater*, he turns, takes the crozier in his left hand and gives the blessing, making the three signs of the cross. All kneel, except canons and prelates, who bow. [If he is an archbishop, the subdeacon who carries the cross brings it before him, and kneels with the cross facing him. An archbiship is uncovered when blessing, but holds his crozier.]

If the Indulgence has not been proclaimed after the sermon it is proclaimed now. The A.P., standing at the Epistle corner, reads the form appointed,[3] while the Bishop, mitred, remains standing, facing the people before the altar, holding his crozier. Then the procession is formed, by the second M.C., in the same order as at the beginning (p. 162). The Bishop gives up the crozier, his mitre is removed by the deacon of the Mass. [If it is an archbishop who has worn the pallium this is now taken off by the deacon, aided by the subdeacon, laid on the salver on which it was brought at the beginning, covered with its veil and placed on the altar.]

Last Gospel. The Bishop, at the centre turned towards the Gospel corner, says in a low voice *Dominus vobiscum*, and signs the altar saying *Initium sancti Evangelii secundum Ioannem*. He is then covered with the precious mitre by the deacon, takes the crozer and follows the procession out, continuing the last Gospel as he goes.[4] The procession goes to the secretarium,[5] where the canons and others take their places.

---

[1] Not the subdeacon (C.E. I. ix, 5).

[2] An acolyte brings him the chalice veil from the credence.

[3] *Confiteor* and prayer *Precibus* are not said.

[4] If there is a proper last Gospel the Bishop (uncovered) reads it all at the altar ; an archbishop after his pallium has been taken off. A.P. transfers the book, before the Blessing, and bows for this, standing on the foot-pace at the Gospel corner.

[5] C.E. I. xvii, 8 ; II. viii, 80. Some authors direct the Bishop to unvest at the throne and Vavasseur-Stercky (I. 122) says this is the usage of Rome. If he

The Bishop, entering the secretarium, blesses the choir as he passes. He bows to the altar, goes to the throne, and the deacon of the Mass takes off his mitre. Genuflecting at the throne on a cushion, towards the altar, he says the verse *Et Verbum caro factum est,* and so finishes the Gospel. He then hands his crozier to its bearer and sits.

Unvesting. The deacon and subdeacon of the Mass take off their maniples, which are carried away by a server. The subdeacon takes off the Bishop's maniple, hands it to a server, who lays it on the altar. The rest of the Bishop's vestments are taken off in order, by the deacon and subdeacon, as they were put on. They are all laid on the altar and covered with a veil. Meanwhile the A.P. and assistant deacons unvest and then return to the throne when the deacon and subdeacon leave it. The chaplains go to the sacristy, take off their copes and return. The canons in vestments take these off and resume choir dress. The ministers of the Mass, having unvested the Bishop, go to sit at the sedilia. The Bishop's attendant brings the cappa and puts it on him. The chaplains of the book and candle come to the throne. Sitting,[1] the Bishop says the prayers after Mass. During this the subdeacon brings from the credence the plate and veil and takes off the liturgical shoes and stockings, puts them on their plate, covers them, and takes them to the credence.[2] The servant puts on the Bishop's ordinary shoes. The Bishop goes to the faldstool in the middle, says a short prayer there, goes to visit the chapel of the Blessed Sacrament, and finally leaves the church with his attendants. The canons may accompany him. They should then return to sing Sext and None.

§ 7. IF THE BISHOP DOES NOT VEST IN THE SECRETARIVM

IF there is no chapel that can be used as a secretarium, or if for any reason the Bishop does not wish to use it, there are two other ways in which he may vest before Mass, at the throne in the sanctuary, or in the sacristy. Neither case presents any special difficulty :

(1) If he vests at the throne in the sanctuary, he will come to the church in rochet and cappa, visit the Blessed Sacrament, then kneel at a faldstool in the sanctuary, go to the throne and do everything as described above. But when he is vested there there will not be the great procession from the secretarium. Instead, the Bishop, in precious mitre and holding his crozier, goes from the throne to the altar,[3] blessing the clergy in choir as he passes.

(2) If he vests in the sacristy, a faldstool will be prepared in the middle for him. The vestments will be laid out on a vesting table.

does he goes to the throne between the assistant deacons preceded by the subdeacon, whom the A.P. with the deacon on his left follow, and followed by the bearers of the insignia (cf. p. 162, n. 1).

[1] He stands for the versicles and prayers.

[2] The deacon and subdeacon, with the acolytes, may then retire (with the usual reverences) or may wait until the Bishop has departed.

[3] See p. 162, n. 1.

At this faldstool the Bishop vests in the same way as at the throne. Then the procession (with incense) is formed to the church and altar.

§ 8. IF THE CHAPTER IS NOT PRESENT

THE Ceremonial supposes, as the normal custom, that the Ordinary sings High Mass in his cathedral, his Chapter assisting.

It may, however, frequently happen that he sings Mass in another church of his diocese, where the Chapter is not present. In this case a temporary throne is erected beforehand, on the Gospel side, and is vested in the colour of the Mass. Terce is not said beforehand ; the secretarium is not used. The Bishop vests either in the sacristy or at the throne. The ministers of Mass and assistants at the throne need not be canons. All else proceeds as described above, except, of course, that there are no canons to be incensed or to receive the kiss of peace.

CHAPTER XVII

PONTIFICAL HIGH MASS AT THE FALDSTOOL

§ 1. PREPARATION

EXCEPT a " Greater Prelate " (see p. 139), every other bishop (an extern bishop or auxiliary) uses, not the throne, but a faldstool in front of the altar.[1] It may also happen that the Ordinary uses this faldstool, instead of his throne, as when, for example, a cardinal is present.[2] For Mass at the faldstool the following alterations are made in the ceremony.[3]

The bishop may begin his preparation for Mass in the sacristy. If he does so, the usual vestments for the deacon and subdeacon are laid out there, but not their maniples, which are put on the sedilia in the church. A carpet is laid in the middle of the sacristy with a chair on it. The bishop makes his preparation there. The Pontifical Canon and hand-candle are at hand ; and the bishop's liturgical shoes and stockings are laid out in the sacristy near the chair.

Preparations. At the High Altar of the church the Sanctissimum should be removed, if It is reserved there. Six candles are lighted, not a seventh. There are no altar-cards. The bishop's vestments are laid on the altar as described above (p. 153).[4] His gloves lie on a salver. All are covered with a veil, which may be the gremial. The precious mitre stands on the Gospel side, by it the mitre-bearer's veil. The golden mitre is on the Epistle side ; their lappets hang over the frontal.[5]

On the credence two candles (the acolytes') burn. Between them the following are placed : the chalice and paten, prepared as usual for Mass, the cruets and bell. The Evangeliarium (Missal), with the bishop's maniple, between the leaves at the place of the Gospel of the day, the Epistolary or book of lessons,[6] the missal-stand or cushion, the ewer, basin and towels for washing the bishop's hands, a small salver, the gremial (if it is not covering the vestments) and the humeral veil. If there is not room for all this on the credence, another should stand by its side. On the ministers' bench are left amice and cope for A.P., and the maniples of the deacon and subdeacon.

The Roman books suppose that the thurible, incense boat, the fire and charcoal and the torches for the Elevation all stand in the sanctuary near the credence. It may, however, be more convenient to prepare these in the sacristy.

On the Epistle side at the foot of the altar, a little away from the

---

[1] See p. 8.
[2] This case lies outside the scope of this book.
[3] C.E. I. vii, 4 ; viii, 2 ; ix, 3, 4 ; xix, 4, 5.
[4] Without morse (cf. p. 12, n. 1), unless the celebrant be the Ordinary.
[5] If the bishop uses the golden mitre only, this stands on the Gospel side.
[6] The books should be covered with silk of the colour of the day (see p. 19).

bottom step, is placed the faldstool.[1] It is covered with cloths of the colour of the Mass.

On the Epistle side of the sanctuary—on the right of the faldstool and nearer to the nave of the church—is the sedile.

In the centre of the lowest step of the altar is a cushion on which the bishop will kneel to say prayers before Mass.

§ 2. MINISTERS AND SERVERS

THE following persons assist the bishop : an assistant priest, the deacon and subdeacon of the Mass, two Masters of Ceremonies, the three servers who carry the mitre, book and hand-candle,[2] the thurifer and acolytes, four or six torch-bearers, who will also assist at the vesting. The bearers of mitre, book and candle do not wear copes. There are no assistant deacons. The deacon and subdeacon supply their places.[3]

§ 3. THE BEGINNING AND THE VESTING OF THE BISHOP

THE bishop arrives in the sacristy and sits (with biretta on) on the chair prepared, the A.P., in surplice, standing on his right. The book-bearer stands before the bishop, holding the Pontifical Canon open at the preparation for Mass. The bearer of the candle stands on the book-bearer's right,[4] holding it lighted. The bishop begins to say the psalms appointed for the preparation.[5] While he does this a servant takes off his ordinary shoes and puts on the liturgical shoes and stockings, kneeling before him to do so. The bishop finishes the preparation standing, uncovered, and turned towards the cross of the sacristy. The Canon and hand-candle are then taken to the credence in the sanctuary.

Meanwhile the deacon and subdeacon vest, assisted by the acolytes. Vested, but without maniples, they bow to the cross in the sacristy and to the bishop. They go to the church, the second M.C. before them, followed by the acolytes and other servers. In church they all salute the clergy in choir and genuflect to the altar, the acolytes and servers stand aside near the credence, the ministers stand behind the faldstool facing the people, the deacon on the Gospel side, the subdeacon on the Epistle side.

---

[1] The faldstool may be placed on a raised platform covered with a carpet (cf. C.E. I. xii, 11) when the celebrant is a " greater prelate " (p. 139).

[2] There is no crozier-bearer, since the crozier is not, ordinarily, used in this case. If the bishop has a train he will have a train-bearer who carries it whenever he walks, at other times stands aside among the " familiares." But a bishop who is not a " Greater Prelate " should not let down his train when proceeding to the altar, but only when he is vested.

[3] C.E. I. viii, 2.

[4] Cf. C.E. I. xx, 1.

[5] It is convenient if the bishop, having finished the prayers of preparation, recites also the vesting prayers before he leaves for the altar. Should a bishop celebrate Mass in presence of the Ordinary or his superior, the bishop vests in the sacristy and goes (between the A.P. and deacon) to the sanctuary. There, seated at the faldstool, he awaits the arrival of the presiding prelate (unless he be already at his throne).

Arrival of Bishop. Then the Bishop comes from the sacristy. He wears the rochet and mantellettum, and holds his biretta in his hand. The first M.C. goes in front of him, the A.P. at his left. At the entrance to the church the A.P. presents the sprinkler, which the bishop touches and then signs himself but does not sprinkle anyone. They come before the altar, the deacon and subdeacon bow to the bishop ; he bows to the clergy in choir and to the altar. Then he kneels for a short prayer on the cushion at the foot of the altar. When he rises, this cushion is taken away.

The bishop, rising, again bows to the altar and to the choir and goes to the faldstool. Here he sits. The deacon takes off the pectoral cross, then holds it to the bishop, that he may kiss it, and hands it to the M.C. ; he removes the mantellettum and gives this, too, to the M.C. The bishop puts on his biretta. The deacon removes the bishop's ring. A server comes with the ewer, basin and towel. Standing before the bishop the server pours water over his hands. The A.P. hands the towel to the bishop. The M.C. or an attendant loosens the bishop's train.

All this supposes that the bishop begins the preparation in the sacristy. If he does so in the church, the liturgical shoes and stockings are put first on the credence. The bishop enters the church, and after a prayer at the foot of the altar, goes to the faldstool [1] and there begins the psalm, while his servant puts on the prelate the ceremonial stockings and shoes.

Vesting. The vesting now begins. The second M.C. goes to the altar and there hands each vestment to the server, who will bring it to the bishop. If there are not enough servers, they may, after having handed a vestment to the ministers, return to the altar to bring another. The bishop stands and the book-bearer stands before him, still holding the book.[2] The bishop takes off his biretta before rising and hands it to the M.C., who puts it away with the mantellettum. The deacon vests the bishop, the subdeacon assisting. The pectoral cross (first kissed by the bishop,) is put on after the cincture. When the bishop has put on the dalmatic he sits, the ministers put on his gloves (each one glove, kissing first his hand and then the glove) and the chasuble. The deacon puts on him the precious mitre, bowing before and after. The ministers then retire to put on their maniples. The A.P. meanwhile goes to the sedilia [3] and puts on amice and cope (over a rochet or surplice) ; he comes to the bishop, carrying the ring on a salver, and puts it on the bishop's finger, kissing first the ring, then the hand. He bows before and after doing this, then stands at the bishop's right. When all the vestments are taken from the altar the

---

[1] If the bishop puts on the buskins and sandals in the sacristy (which he should do unless he arrives in his cappa, S.R.C. 2010[1]) he may complete his vesting there. In this case the celebrant's vestments, the acolytes' candles and the book containing the celebrant's maniple are all prepared in the sacristy.

[2] If the bishop has not already read in the sacristy the vesting prayers.

[3] When he has nothing special to do during the vesting he sits, covered, at the sedilia.

second M.C. removes the golden mitre and the veil which had covered the vestments and puts them on the credence. He hands the Evangeliarium (containing the maniple) to the subdeacon and he places the Canon—open at *Aufer a nobis*—at the centre of the table of the altar leaning against the cross or tabernacle.

The bishop rises and goes to the altar ; the A.P. is at his right, the deacon at his left ; the subdeacon, who now carries the Evangeliarium (Missal) with the maniple in it, at the deacon's left. The other servers and Masters of Ceremonies follow. All reverence to the choir (if the clergy are there) on the way.

§ 4. THE MASS

AT the altar the deacon takes off the mitre and hands it to the mitre-bearer ; the bishop bows low, the others genuflect. Mass begins as usual. The A.P. is at the bishop's right, the ministers at his left. After the prayer *Indulgentiam*, the subdeacon puts the maniple on the bishop's arm, as described above (p. 163). Before doing so he hands the Missal to the M.C. The A.P. and deacon change places. When they go up to the altar, the subdeacon holds the Missal open at the Gospel of the day ; the A.P. points out the beginning of the Gospel [1] ; the bishop, having kissed the altar, kisses the page. The A.P. descends *in plano* and stands (facing the altar) near the faldstool to the right of it. The second M.C. takes the Missal and removes the Canon and hand-candle from the altar. The altar and bishop are incensed as usual,[2] except that the deacon says *Benedicite, Pater reverendissime.* The bishop gives the thurible to the deacon, the M.C. puts on his precious mitre.

The deacon, with the subdeacon at his left, goes down the altar steps, and incenses the bishop. The bishop goes *per breviorem* to the faldstool, bowing first to the cross. The deacon on his right and the subdeacon on his left accompany him. Before the faldstool the A.P. (on the right), the deacon (in the centre) and the subdeacon on his left face the bishop. He sits on the faldstool and the deacon removes the mitre. The bishop rises and turns to the altar by his left.[3] The book-bearer, standing before the bishop, holds up the Missal, the candle-bearer is at the book-bearer's left, the A.P. at the bishop's right points to the places. The deacon is at the bishop's right (behind the A.P.), the subdeacon at his left, but a little back. The bishop reads the Introit, then says the *Kyrie, eleison* with the ministers. If the sung *Kyrie* takes much time he may now sit (with mitre on), as he will at the *Gloria*.

Gloria. The bishop (uncovered), facing the altar, intones the *Gloria in excelsis* ; the A.P. at his right, partly facing him, holds the book for

---

[1] Some authors (e.g. Martinucci, Vavasseur-Steroky) say that it is the subdeacon who does this at Mass at the faldstool.

[2] The thurifer does not kneel when presenting the thurible.

[3] As the celebrant does at the altar. Cf. C.E. I. xix, 4, 5.

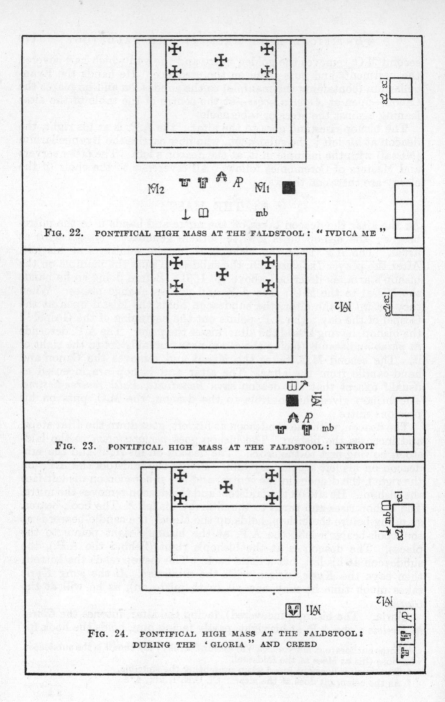

FIG. 22. PONTIFICAL HIGH MASS AT THE FALDSTOOL: "IVDICA ME"

FIG. 23. PONTIFICAL HIGH MASS AT THE FALDSTOOL: INTROIT

FIG. 24. PONTIFICAL HIGH MASS AT THE FALDSTOOL:
DURING THE 'GLORIA" AND CREED

the intonation,[1] then hands it to the book-bearer; the book-bearer and candle-bearer stand before him. While the bishop intones the hymn the ministers stand behind him in line; then they come one on either side and say the *Gloria* with him. When he has said the *Gloria*, the bishop—turning by his right—sits on the faldstool; the deacon puts on the golden mitre and spreads the gremial over his knees.[2] All then bow to him and go to sit at the sedilia in this order: the deacon is in the middle, the A.P. at his right, the subdeacon at his left.[3] They receive their birettas from the second M.C. and cover themselves. The second M.C. stands near the seat at the usual place, as at every High Mass. The first M.C. stands behind the bishop at his left.

Towards the end of the *Gloria in excelsis* the ministers rise, come

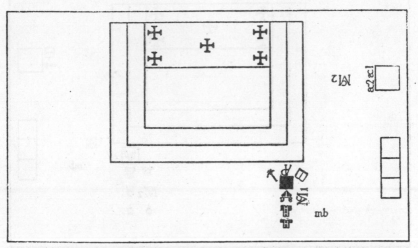

FIG. 25. PONTIFICAL HIGH MASS AT THE FALDSTOOL : THE COLLECTS

before the bishop, stand in line and bow to him. The deacon removes the gremial and hands it to a server, who puts it on the credence. He then removes the mitre. The bishop stands facing the people and sings *Pax vobis*; the deacon and subdeacon stand between him and the people in line, the A.P. is at his side (on the Epistle side) facing the altar.

Collect(s). Then the bishop turns to the altar and sings the Collect(s) the A.P. holding the book, with the candle-bearer at his right.[4] The first M.C. stands by the A.P., the second is at the credence by the

[1] Cf. C.E. I. vii, 4.

[2] Whenever the A.P., deacon, and subdeacon stand before the bishop seated on the faldstool, the deacon is in the centre, the A.P. on his right, the subdeacon on the deacon's left.

[3] The A.P. will sit nearest the bishop (cf. C.E. I. vii, 4); therefore whether he will be on the right or left of the deacon will depend on the position of the sedilia.

[4] See p. 157, n. 3.

acolytes. During the last collect the subdeacon takes the book of
lessons, goes, with the second ceremoniar, to the centre, genuflects to
the altar, bows to the choir, then goes to the place of the Epistle,[1]
away from the altar. When the collects are finished, the bishop sits
again, and receives the mitre and gremial from the deacon, as before.
The A.P. and deacon bow to him and go to sit. The subdeacon bows
to the bishop, and standing before him a suitable distance away, sings
the Epistle. Then he goes to the middle, genuflects to the altar, bows
to the choir, comes to the bishop, bows, kneels,[2] kisses his hand and
receives his blessing. He then rises and holds the Missal, that the
bishop may read the Epistle, Gradual, *Alleluia* verse or other texts

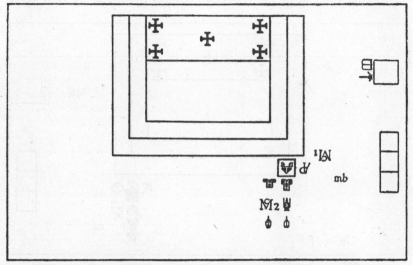

FIG. 26. PONTIFICAL HIGH MASS AT THE FALDSTOOL : BEFORE
THE GOSPEL

which occur between the lessons, sitting on the faldstool. The A.P.
rises and comes to the bishop's left to assist him as he reads and make
the responses. Before the Gospel the bishop with hands joined reads
the *Munda cor meum* prayer, for which the M.C. may bring the Canon
from the credence. Meanwhile the bearer holds the hand-candle, at
the bishop's left. When the bishop has read the Gospel, the A.P. stays
where he is. The subdeacon hands the Missal to a server and stands
opposite the bishop, at a little distance from him.

  Gospel. Towards the end of the sung *Alleluia* verse (or whatever
text may take its place) the deacon, who has been sitting at the sedilia,

---

[1] See O'Connell, *The Celebration of Mass*, III, p. 97.
  [2] Obviously the usual rule, not to kneel except to a Greater Prelate, does not
apply to the blessing at Epistle and Gospel, when the ministers would kneel to a
priest.

rises, takes the Evangeliarium (or Missal) and carries it to the altar, closed. He bows to the clergy on the Epistle side, then to the bishop in passing, then to the clergy on the Gospel side and genuflects to the altar before and after laying the book on it ; then comes straight to the bishop's right, where he assists at the imposition and blessing of incense. For this the thurifer approaches, bows and stands before the bishop. The deacon ministers the incense. Meanwhile the acolytes take their candles from the credence and led by the second ceremoniar come and stand before the bishop at some distance.

When the incense is blessed the deacon goes to say the prayer *Munda cor meum*, kneeling on the lowest step at the centre of the altar ; [1] the thurifer stands before the acolytes with the second M.C. on his left. The deacon then takes the Missal from the altar, genuflects, comes to the bishop, bows, kneels and says *Iube, domne, benedicere*. The bishop blesses him, and he kisses the bishop's hand in the usual way. Then he stands before the bishop, in front of the second M.C. and the thurifer ; the subdeacon is at his left. All bow to the bishop, go to the centre, genuflect, bow to the choir (first on the Epistle side) and go to the place where the Gospel is sung. As soon as they have gone, the first M.C. removes the bishop's gremial and mitre ; the A.P. stands a little behind the bishop at his left. The bishop stands and faces the deacon. The deacon should be careful not to begin to sing the Gospel till the bishop is thus ready.

If a genuflection is to be made at any text in the Gospel, the M.C. places a cushion, on which the bishop genuflects, towards the Gospel book.

After the Gospel the subdeacon comes up immediately and brings the book to the bishop, making no genuflection nor inclination to him. He points to the beginning of the Gospel text,. which the bishop kisses, saying *Per evangelica*, etc., and laying both hands on the text. He then shuts the book, bows to the bishop, hands the book to the first M.C. and stands at the left of the A.P. As soon as the Gospel is finished the second M.C. leads the deacon, followed by the thurifer and acolytes, back in procession to before the faldstool. They genuflect to the altar as they pass the centre. The deacon takes the thurible and incenses the bishop (still unmitred) with three double swings ; he, the thurifer at his side, and the second M.C. bow before and after. The thurifer takes the thurible to the sacristy or other place where it is kept. Meantime the acolytes go and place their candles on the credence.

If there is a sermon at this point, the ministers form in line before the bishop, bow to him, and go to sit at the sedilia. The bishop sits at the faldstool. If he preaches himself, he may do so standing before the faldstool, or sitting on it, or he may go to the pulpit, conducted by the first M.C. The ministers do not sit nor cover themselves till the bishop is ready to begin the sermon.

Creed. When the Creed is intoned the deacon and subdeacon stand

[4] Cf. C.E. I. ix, 2 ; II. viii, 42. Some authors say that the deacon is to kneel on the edge of the top step in the centre of the foot-pace.

in line behind the bishop.   He stands uncovered facing the altar ; the
Pontifical Canon is held by the A.P., with the candle-bearer on his right.
After the intonation the A.P. hands the book to the book-bearer.   The
deacon and subdeacon come to the bishop's side and say the Creed
with him, as at the *Gloria*.

The bishop then sits, the deacon puts on the gremial and golden
mitre ; the ministers bow to the bishop and go to sit, as at the *Gloria*.
At the words *Et incarnatus est*, etc., the bishop bows, wearing the mitre,
the ministers uncover and bow; all the others kneel, unless they are
sitting, when they only bow.

On Christmas Day and Lady Day the bishop kneels on a cushion at
these words before the faldstool, not uncovering ; the ministers kneel
at the sedilia.

After this text the deacon rises, takes the burse from the credence,
and spreads the corporal on the altar, making the usual inclination to
the A.P., to the bishop, to the clergy on the Epistle side, and to the
clergy on the Gospel side [1] and genuflections to the altar.   He goes back
to his place by the shortest way, bowing to the other ministers before
he sits again.   The second ceremoniar or book-bearer places the Missal-
stand on the altar in position for the Offertory.

Offertory.   Towards the end of the sung Creed the ministers come
before the bishop, stand in line and bow to him, the deacon takes off
the gremial and mitre ; the deacon and subdeacon form in line between
the faldstool and the people, the A.P. stands at the side on the Epistle
side.   The bishop rises, sings *Dominus vobiscum* facing the people, then
turns by his left to the altar, sings *Oremus* and reads the Offertory.
The book-bearer and candle-bearer stand before him, the ministers at
his sides.

The bishop sits again, the deacon puts on his precious mitre, the
three ministers bow to the bishop, the A.P. and the deacon go to his
right, the subdeacon to his left.   Servers bring a salver to hold the ring
and gloves, and the vessels and towel to wash the hands.   The deacon
takes off the ring and right glove, the subdeacon the left glove, with
the usual oscula.   The ring and gloves are put on the salver.   The
servers who hold the ewer and dish come before the bishop and bow.
He washes his hands, the A.P. presents the towel and then puts the
ring on the bishop's bare hand, again with the solita oscula.   The
subdeacon brings the chalice from the credence and carries it up to the
altar as the bishop ascends thither.

After the bishop has washed his hands, the A.P. takes the Missal
from the credence, and the Canon, and carries them to the altar.[2]   The
second M.C. goes with him, and the server bearing the candle.   They
bow to the clergy on the Epistle side, to the bishop in passing, to the
clergy on the Gospel side, genuflect before the altar steps and the A.P.
arranges the Missal and Canon on the altar and places the hand-candle

---

[1] Cf., however, O'Connell, *The Celebration of Mass*, III, p. 113, n. 6.
[2] Or this may be done by the book-bearer.   Then the A.P. accompanies the
Bishop (on his left) from the faldstool to the altar (cf. p. 169, n. 2).

near them. He then stays by the book. The bishop rises and goes to the altar between the deacon (on his right) and the M.C., mitre-bearer and train-bearer following; all salute the choir on the way. Before the altar the deacon takes off the mitre, the bishop bows low, the others genuflect. The bishop, with the deacon on his right, goes up to the altar. The A.P. meets the bishop on the foot-pace; the subdeacon has gone to the credence to bring the chalice.

From now to the end of Mass everything continues as in the case of Pontifical High Mass at the throne (see above, pp. 170 *sqq*), except that (*a*) the deacon incenses the A.P. and the subdeacon (each with two double swings) *after* the incensation of the choir, (*b*) in the case of a bishop not in his own diocese, no Indulgence is published, (*c*) the bishop recites the last Gospel at the Gospel corner. The subdeacon holds the Canon. The candle-bearer holds the candle at the left of the A.P. (who stands between the bishop and the subdeacon).

Conclusion of Mass. At the end of Mass the bishop may go with the ministers and servers in procession[1] to the sacristy and there unvest. Or he may go to the faldstool (having saluted the altar and clergy) and unvest there. In this case, when he arrives at the faldstool, he sits and the three ministers bow to him, go to the credence, where the A.P. takes off the cope, the others their maniples. The deacon and subdeacon come back to the bishop; the subdeacon takes off the bishop's maniple, the deacon his mitre. Then they assist him to unvest, handing each vestment to a server who carries it to the altar and consigns it to the second M.C. When the bishop has unvested the M.C. loops up his train. The mantellettum is put on, the deacon hands him the pectoral cross to kiss and puts it on him and then hands him his biretta. The deacon and subdeacon now bow to the bishop and retire to the sacristy. The bishop sits at the faldstool and says the prayers after Mass (uncovering and rising and turning to the altar for *Kyrie* and the subsequent prayers), the book-bearer holding the book standing before him, the candle by the book.[2] Meanwhile an attendant takes off the ceremonial shoes and stockings. Finally, after a concluding prayer said kneeling in the centre on the lowest step of the altar, the bishop retires, accompanied—as at his coming—by the A.P. and M.C.

[1] The acolytes with their candles will be at the head; the subdeacon precedes the bishop, who walks between the A.P. (on his right) and the deacon (all vested and covered).

[2] Or the bishop may read the prayers of thanksgiving and take off the ceremonial shoes and stockings in the sacristy.

CHAPTER XVIII

PONTIFICAL HIGH MASS FOR THE DEAD

§ 1. PREPARATION

WHEN a bishop sings Mass for the dead, whether he do so at the throne or at a faldstool, the following changes must be made.[1]

The Bishop uses neither crozier, gloves, nor ceremonial shoes and stockings. He has the gremial, of black silk. He wears only the simple mitre, of white linen, with ruddy fringes to its lappets.

The vestments are kissed during the vesting and unvesting ; there are no solita oscula during Mass. The Bishop gives no blessing to anyone. The Sanctissimum should not be at the High Altar, according to the general rule for Pontifical Mass (p. 153).

Preparations. In the chapel of the Blessed Sacrament a kneeling-desk or faldstool is prepared, as usual. Its coverings and cushion are in violet.

In the sacristy are prepared the vestments (black) for the deacon and subdeacon ; on the benches of the choir are laid the vestments for the canons, including the black dalmatics (with amices) for the two assistant deacons.

On the altar of the Blessed Sacrament six candles are lit, at least during the time the Bishop kneels there, before and after the ceremony. On the High Altar are six candles (never seven) of unbleached wax, and the altar cross. The candlesticks should be of bronze or brass, not gilt nor of silver. No other ornament should stand on the altar or retable. The frontal is black.[2] The foot-pace is covered with a violet carpet, the rest of the sanctuary is bare. The Bishop's vestments, black—the maniple included—are laid out on the altar as usual (p. 153). The simple mitre, only, stands on the Gospel side. Before the altar is the faldstool on a small carpet. It is covered with violet and furnished with two violet cushions.[3] The usual vessels are put on the credence, namely, the acolytes' candles (lighted and of unbleached wax), the chalice prepared (with two hosts and two purificators), the ewer, dish and towels for washing hands, the Missals, the Epistolary (book of lessons), and the Pontifical Canon which should be covered with black, the hand-candlestick with a candle of white wax, the cruets and the gremial. At the sedilia an amice and black cope for the assistant priest, the maniples for the ministers. A black cope with simple morse

---

[1] C.E. II. xi, xii.

[2] Should the Blessed Sacrament be present the frontal and the conopaeum will be violet (cf. S.R.C. 3035[10], 3201[10], 3562).

[3] For Mass at the throne. But for Requiem Mass at the faldstool it is covered in black (cf. p. 8).

(*formale*) is prepared nearby for the Bishop, if he will give the Absolution. In this case the Pontifical will also be wanted. Candles of white wax to be distributed to the clergy, if this is the custom, are made ready and tapers to light them. The four torches are of unbleached wax.

If the Absolution is to follow, the processional cross should be ready near the credence and the aspersory and sprinkler at hand.[1] [If the celebrant be an archbishop within his province, the processional cross will not be needed, but a stand for the archbishop's cross should be prepared.]

The sedilia are bare or covered in black or violet. If there is a throne it will be covered in violet cloth ; the stools for the assistants will be bare. If the Absolution is to be made at the catafalque, this will stand before the sanctuary. At its foot is another faldstool (covered in black) if available.

§ 2. REQUIEM MASS AT THE THRONE

THE same ministers, assistants and servers attend as at all such Pontifical Masses (p. 155), except that there is no crozier-bearer. The Mass is sung after None. When the Bishop enters the church the bells are not rung joyfully. They may be tolled. The organ is not used at all.[2]

All proceeds as is usual in Pontifical Mass at the throne, except the following points :

The Bishop vests at the throne. He omits the prayers of preparation ; he says the vesting prayers (beginning with *Exue me, Domine*) omitting those for the ceremonial shoes and for the gloves. The maniple is put on him after the girdle, before the pectoral cross.[3] [An archbishop does not wear the pallium at Requiem Masses.] When the Bishop is vested, the A.P. puts on his ring ; the deacon and subdeacon put on their maniples.

Beginning of Mass. All then go to the altar,[4] the Bishop with joined hands, since he does not use the crozier. The subdeacon does not bring the Gospel book with him. After the prayers at the foot of the steps the Bishop, between the deacon and subdeacon, goes up and kisses the altar, not the Gospel book. The deacon puts on the mitre. The altar is not incensed ; the Bishop, preceded by the A.P. and accompanied by the assistant deacons, goes back to the throne at once. The deacon and subdeacon go to the sedilia. After the sung *Kyrie, eleison* the Bishop says *Dominus vobiscum*, not *Pax vobis*. During the Collects (which are sung in the simple ferial tone) all in choir kneel,

---

[1] These will be needed at the church door if the Bishop is to be received ceremonially.
[2] C.E. I. xxviii, 13 ; S.R.C. 4265[2]. (In case of necessity, the organ may be used to sustain the singing, and so must not be played by itself.)
[3] Because of the practical difficulty it may be put on immediately after the dalmatic.
[4] For the order see p. 162, n.

except the sacred ministers and the candle-bearer. After the Epistle the subdeacon reverences to the altar and to the Bishop, but is neither blessed nor kisses the Bishop's hand. During the Sequence candles (if they are to be used) are given to all in choir by servers and are lighted by them.[1] They hold these burning during the Gospel, and then again from the *Sanctus* to the ablutions. During the last verse of the *Dies irae* [2] the deacon carries the book to the altar, but does not kiss the Bishop's hand nor seek a blessing. He says the *Munda cor meum* kneeling on the top step. The procession to the place of the Gospel proceeds in this order : first the M.C., then the deacon followed by the subdeacon, lastly the acolytes.[3] If it passes the throne all (except canons) genuflect to the Bishop. At the Gospel there is no incense, nor do the acolytes hold their candles. They stand on either side of the subdeacon with joined hands.

Offertory. After the Gospel the subdeacon does not take the book to be kissed by the Bishop, but. hands it at once to the second M.C. Those taking part in the Gospel group return to the altar in the same order in which they came. The Bishop goes to the altar, having read the Offertory and washed his hands. At the foot of the altar the deacon takes off the mitre. The subdeacon brings the *oblata*, not wearing the humeral veil. The water is not blessed. The Bishop blesses incense and incenses the altar as usual ; then he alone, wearing the mitre, is incensed by the deacon. The deacon removes the mitre after the Bishop washes his fingers. The torch-bearers (four in number) kneel before the altar till the ablutions ; and all in choir kneel until *Per omnia saecula* before *Pax Domini*, etc.[4] (inclusive). The subdeacon does not hold the paten. He assists the Bishop (on his left) during the incensation. Then he returns to his place at the foot of the altar. He incenses the Sanctissimum at the Elevation,[5] kneeling on the lowest step at the Epistle side. The kiss of peace is not given, nor do the sacred ministers strike their breasts at *Agnus Dei*. When the deacon, facing the altar, sings the verse *Requiescant in pace* the Bishop says it to himself.[6] There is no blessing at the end of Mass, nor is the Indulgence published. The Bishop begins the last Gospel at the altar, continues it as he goes back, wearing his mitre, to the throne, and ends it there, genuflecting at the throne at the words *Et Verbum caro factum est*. He then sits, and the ministers take off the maniples ; the A.P. takes off his cope.

The Bishop is unvested by the deacon and subdeacon at the throne. They then depart and are replaced by the two assistant deacons (who

---

[1] Candles are not handed to the assistant deacons as they could not conveniently hold them and assist the Bishop. It is a moot point as to whether the Bishop himself holds one at the Gospel.

[2] C.E. II. xi, 6.

[3] *Ib.*

[4] *Ib.* § 7 (cf. R.G. xvii, 5 and S.R.C. 3624[10]).

[5] The Sacred Host is not elevated until the singing of the *Sanctus* (to *Benedictus* exclusively) has concluded (S.R.C. 4364).

[6] S.R.C. 2572[22].

meantime have taken off their vestments) for the Bishop's thanksgiving. If the Absolution follows at once,[1] the deacon and subdeacon aid the Bishop to vest in cope and mitre. The subdeacon then departs to act as cross-bearer and the deacon (with the A.P.) takes his part in the Absolution.

§ 3. REQUIEM MASS AT A FALDSTOOL

No special directions for this are necessary. All is done according to the normal rules for Pontifical High Mass at the faldstool (for which see pp. 176 *sqq.*), with the exceptions and particular rules for Requiems in general and those noted in the last paragraph for Pontifical Requiems. In this case, too, the Bishop wears only the simple mitre ; he gives no blessing (except that of incense), the altar is incensed only at the Offertory and so on, as already explained.

[1] For the Absolution, see pp. 416–419.

PART III

EVENING SERVICES

CHAPTER XIX

VESPERS

§ 1. GENERAL DIRECTIONS

ALTHOUGH the Ceremonial of Bishops is intended primarily for pontifical functions, its directions and rubrics apply, with the necessary modifications, for all celebrations of the services it contains. For Vespers, therefore, the Ceremonial, Lib. II, cap. i–iii, and the other places at which Vespers are described, forms the final standard, as far as its directions go.

In the descriptions of the ceremony which are given here, account is taken of the different circumstances which are likely to arise. The rubrics of the Ceremonial have been followed as closely as possible. Necessary modifications have been made and details added in accordance with the decisions of the Congregation of Sacred Rites and the opinions of the best rubricists, and account has been taken of local usages which are not contrary to the rubrics.

General Rules. Vespers may be solemn or not solemn. On weekdays which are not great feasts the celebrant uses no cope, the altar is not incensed, there are practically no ceremonies. On Sundays and feasts the Vespers should be solemn, that is, with cope, incense, acolytes. There should further be assistants to the celebrant (who must always be a priest) who wear copes. On ordinary Sundays there should be two such assistants, in some sort corresponding to the deacon and subdeacon at Mass. On greater feasts there may be four or six. Since they wear the cope, according to the general rule these assistants should be at least tonsured. They must not be canons. In addition to the assistants in cope there should be (on greater days) two cantors, in surplice. They may sit with the other clergy in choir (on either side or on the same side) or have a place behind the assistants in cope in the sanctuary, near its entrance. Their business is to intone the psalms, the *Magnificat*, and (if the choir does not do it) the antiphons for the commemorations (if any). If there are only two assistants in cope, the cantors will also sing the versicles and *Benedicamus Domino*, and will pre-intone the antiphons to the clergy in choir. If there be no assistants in cope, the cantors will, in addition, pre-intone to the celebrant the first antiphon, the hymn, and the antiphon of the *Magnificat*.

It is supposed, normally, that where Vespers are sung there is a liturgical choir placed in seats or stalls on either side of the altar, though it is possible to celebrate Vespers without such a choir.

Preparations. In the sacristy a cope of the colour of the Office [1] and a surplice are prepared for the celebrant,[2] surplices and copes for the assistants, surplices for the cantors, the M.C., and servers. The acolytes' candles are ready. The thurible will be needed towards the end of the chanting of the psalms.

In the sanctuary the sedile or bench on the Epistle side is ready for the celebrant.[3] In front of it is laid a carpet, and a lectern (covered with a silk cloth of the colour of the Office, and having on it a Vesperal or Breviary—also covered in silk) may be placed there. Near the sedile, on the right, is put a stool for the M.C. For the assistants in cope benches (covered in green) or stools in the middle of the choir, on the side, facing the altar.[4] If it is customary another lectern may be placed in the middle of the choir, at which the cantors will intone the psalms. On it a Vesperal (covered in silk of the colour of the Office) should lie.

The cover which protects the altar cloths may remain on the table of the altar (as it does for Pontifical Vespers), or it may be removed. Often Benediction will follow Vespers and then the cloth ought to be removed, but candle branches and flowers (if permitted and used) should be kept as far as possible off the table of the altar, leaving it unencumbered for the incensation. The frontal and conopaeum (if the Sanctissimum be present) are of the colour of the Office (of the Chapter). For solemn Vespers on greater days the six large candles are lighted : four suffice on ordinary Sundays. If other altars are to be incensed (p. 197), at least two candles should be lighted on them.

§ 2. RULES FOR THE CHOIR

Whether the Vespers be celebrated solemnly or simply the rules for the liturgical choir are the same. Its members generally enter the church in procession following the acolytes, unless they are already in their places for some preceding service. They come in pairs, genuflect to the altar, bow to each other, and go to their places in the stalls, as at High Mass (p. 27). Here they stand till the celebrant and his assistants come before the altar. All kneel then to say the silent prayer *Aperi, Domine.* They stand to say silently the *Pater noster* and

---

[1] If the Vespers are " a capitulo de sequenti," the colour from the beginning is that of the Office whose Chapter is sung.

[2] If he has the right to wear the rochet he will use it instead of the surplice and wear over it an amice.

[3] He may, however, sit in the first stall of the choir (on either side, according to custom). If he does, there is practically no difference in the ceremony, the assistants and acolytes will go to him there as they would to the sedile. In this case a cushion is placed on the seat of the stall and one on the kneeler in front, which should be covered with a (green) cloth.

[4] The first two assistants generally sit beside the celebrant on the sedile (or on stools, if the sedile be short) and the first, on his right, ministers to the celebrant.

Ave Maria. When the first psalm has been intoned they sit (at the asterisk of the first verse).

They uncover and bow (towards the altar, if standing) at the verse *Gloria Patri* at the end of each psalm, at the Holy Name, the name of Mary,[1] of the Saint of the Office [1] or commemoration, or at the names of the three Divine Persons, at the last stanza of hymns when this stanza is a real doxology, at *Oremus,* and, if it is customary, at verse 2 (*Sit nomen Domini benedictum*) of Psalm 112 (*Laudate pueri*). As each antiphon is intoned all stand meanwhile.[2] All stand during the Chapter, hymn and to the end of Vespers, except that they sit again while the antiphon of the *Magnificat* is sung before (if doubled) and after. They kneel if the *Preces feriales* are said and then remain kneeling for the subsequent commemorations and the Suffrage. They kneel during the anthem of the Blessed Virgin, at the end, except on Saturdays, Sundays and during all Paschal time. They kneel during the entire first stanza of the hymns *Ave maris stella* and *Veni, Creator,* during the entire stanza *Tantum ergo* of the *Pange lingua,* if the Sanctissimum is present on the altar,[3] during the whole stanza *O crux ave spes unica* in the hymn *Vexilla regis.* At the *Magnificat,* when they are incensed, they bow as at Mass (p. 26).

§ 3. SOLEMN VESPERS WITH TWO ASSISTANTS IN COPE

It will be convenient first to describe what should be the normal ceremonies on Sunday, when clerics in cope assist the celebrant, then to add how the modifications should be made, when the rite is more solemn or when it is impossible to carry out the whole of this rite.

Vesting. In the sacristy the celebrant vests in a surplice (or rochet with amice), and over it a cope of the colour of the day.[4] On Sundays he should have two assistants who wear surplice and cope also, but a cope that is less ornate than the celebrant's. They and the celebrant wear the biretta. The first assistant or the M.C. assists the celebrant to vest. The procession is formed and all (uncovered) bow to the cross in the sacristy. The acolytes holding their lighted candles go first, then the members of the choir (lay members if in soutane and surplice, and the clergy after them), the cantors, the M.C.[5] and the celebrant between the two assistants who hold the edges of his cope (turning in the orphreys). The acolytes go to the foot of the altar, and stand one at each corner before the steps. The members of the choir genuflect

---

[1] For these the bow is not towards the altar.

[2] C.E. II. iii, 8. But the S.R.C. 3781[2], allows the custom that only those on the side where it is intoned stand.

[3] Certainly if the Sanctissimum is exposed; if it is in the tabernacle the custom, either way, may be observed (S.R.C. 1280[2]).

[4] The celebrant may wear a stole only if Benediction will immediately follow the function (S.R.C. 2956[5], 4162[1], 4269[11]). The assistants may not wear dalmatic and tunicle, not even if a procession is to follow (S.R.C. 4271[3]).

[5] The thurifer has no function until the end of the psalms. He may go out in any convenient place in the procession (even on the left of the M.C.) and take his place near the credence or in choir.

in pairs, salute one another and go to their places ; so do the cantors. The M.C. stands aside at the Epistle side, and the celebrant and assistants go to the foot of the altar. There they bow profoundly [1] (or genuflect *in plano* if the Sanctissimum is reserved there) ; the M.C. and acolytes genuflect. The celebrant and assistants (holding their birettas in their hands) kneel on the lowest step and say silently the prayer, *Aperi, Domine.* Meanwhile the acolytes go to the sides of the altar, set down their candles (on the ground or on the lowest step) at each side, and extinguish them (unless the Blessed Sacrament be exposed). Then they go to their places at the credence or in choir, genuflecting at the centre as they pass.

Beginning of Vespers. When the celebrant has finished the prayer, he rises, again bows or genuflects to the altar with the assistants ; they bow to the choir on either side, first to the side opposite the place to which they will now go. They go to the sedile. The assistants stand here, facing each other, on the floor of the sanctuary or go to the sides of the celebrant ; the M.C. is at his right. The celebrant says silently the *Pater noster* and *Ave Maria.* The first assistant (or M.C.) lifts the right end of the celebrant's cope ; he makes the sign of the cross, singing *Deus in adiutorium meum intende.* All in choir make the sign of the cross with him. The choir continues, answering the verse. At the words *Gloria Patri*, etc., all bow towards the altar.

While the *Sicut erat* is sung, the first assistant (accompanied by the M.C.) comes before the celebrant, facing him, bows and pre-intones the first antiphon to him, i.e. sings in a low tone the opening words (as far as the asterisk). The celebrant repeats the same notes in a louder tone, and the choir continues the antiphon, if it is a double, so that the antiphon is sung in full before as well as after the psalm. When the celebrant has intoned the antiphon the first assistant bows again and returns to his place at the celebrant's right.[2]

Psalms. Meanwhile the cantors come to the middle of the sanctuary (before the lectern, if there is one), bow to each other, genuflect, and when the antiphon ceases, intone the first psalm. They sing either the whole first verse or up to the asterisk only, according to custom, and then bow to that side of the choir that is to continue the psalm [3] ; they genuflect, bow to each other, and return to their places.

When the psalm has been intoned (at the asterisk of the first verse,

---

[1] When the assistants *in cope* reverence to the altar (at which the Sanctissimum is not reserved) with the celebrant they bow profoundly, but when not with the celebrant they genuflect *in plano.* If the Sanctissimum be present all three genuflect *in plano* at each arrival at and before each departure from the foot of the altar.

[2] If the two assistants sit in the centre of the sanctuary (and this they must do if the celebrant be not at the bench, but in the first stall in choir) both will go before the celebrant for the pre-intonation, genuflecting as they go and return.

[3] See p. 200. In some churches the rule is that the second verse of this psalm is to be sung by the side on which the first dignitary or the hebdomadarian sits. If the entire antiphon (in an office of double rite), or its beginning, consist of the opening words of the psalm, the intonation of the psalm will begin where the antiphon terminated.

to secure uniformity) all sit and put on their birettas, the first assistant [1] hands his biretta to the celebrant with the *solita oscula*. The choir continues the psalm. At the last verse of each psalm the M.C. rises and bows to the celebrant to uncover. All uncover and bow (the M.C. towards the altar since he is standing) for *Gloria Patri*. After this verse the M.C. bows to the celebrant to resume his biretta and sits. After *Sicut erat* the whole choir sings the entire antiphon. During this the cantors again come to the middle, genuflect, and go to stand before

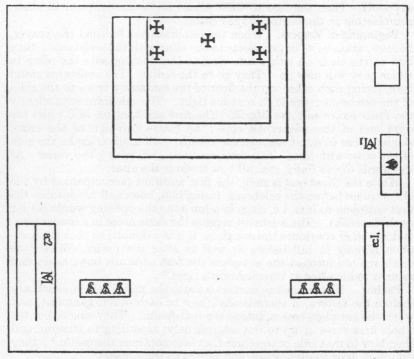

FIG. 27.   VESPERS WITH SIX ASSISTANTS : DURING THE PSALMS [2]

the person of highest rank in the choir (no matter what side he be on), to pre-intone the next antiphon to him. If there is no person of higher rank, they go to him whose place is nearest the altar, in the farthest row, on the Gospel side. They pre-intone the antiphon to him as before, singing its first words in a low voice. He repeats what they have sung, the choir continues. The cantors go back to their places,

---

[1] The M.C., if the assistant does not sit beside the celebrant.

[2] In figures 27 and 28, the first two assistants are shown with the others. They may, however, in each case be at the sides of the celebrant (the first assistant on his right).

again genuflecting before the altar. The same process is repeated at the antiphon of each psalm ; the cantors go then to the person of next highest rank (on the opposite side to the person to whom they had intoned the second antiphon), or to the one nearest the altar on the Epistle side, then to the second on the Gospel side and so on. When they come before him who is to intone and bow to him, he rises, and all the choir with him,[1] but not the celebrant nor the assistants in copes.

Hymn. Towards the end of the fifth psalm the acolytes go to the altar, light their candles and stand by them. During *Sicut erat* they come before the altar, with their candles, genuflect, go before the celebrant, where they are joined by the assistants, bow in a line with them to the celebrant, and then go and stand at each side of the lectern that is before the celebrant, and facing each other. The assistants come before the celebrant, bow with the acolytes, and stand before him.[2] When the last antiphon is finished, the celebrant rises, and all the choir with him. He first hands his biretta to the M.C., who receives it, as always, with the solita oscula. Standing he sings the Chapter ; the choir answer *Deo gratias.* The first assistant bows and pre-intones the hymn to the celebrant, singing its first line in a low tone. The celebrant repeats this in a louder tone and the choir continues it.[3] The assistants and acolytes (who come into line with them) bow to the celebrant, and the assistants return to their places beside the celebrant (if in the sanctuary, they go with the acolytes genuflecting on the way). The acolytes set down their candles at the sides of the altar as before, not extinguishing them, and stand before them, until the end of the *Magnificat.*[4]

Magnificat. During the hymn the thurifer goes to the sacristy and prepares the thurible, comes out with the thurible and incense boat, genuflects to the altar, bows to the celebrant, and waits standing in the sanctuary by the altar at the Epistle side. While the last verse of the hymn is sung the cantors come to the middle, salute each other, genuflect, and, when the hymn is finished, sing the versicle of the Office, the choir answering. They go back to their places, the first assistant comes to the celebrant, bows to him and pre-intones the antiphon of the *Magnificat.* The celebrant intones the same words, then, if the antiphon is doubled, sits and puts on his biretta. All sit with him ; the choir continues the antiphon and the assistant returns to his place. The cantors come to the middle and sing the first verse of the *Magnificat.*

---

[1] See note 2, p. 192.

[2] If the assistants do not sit beside the celebrant, but in the middle of the sanctuary, they will join the acolytes before the middle of the altar, genuflect with them and go to the celebrant.

[3] If alternate stanzas are sung by each side of the choir, that on which the celebrant is will take up the first stanza of the hymn when it has been intoned by the celebrant. If the first verse be *Veni, Creator* or *Ave maris stella,* all (except the acolytes) kneel in their places until the end of the first stanza.

[4] If the altar table be covered, just before the *Magnificat* the acolytes are to roll back the cover (towards the gradine) for the incensation, and afterwards replace it.

As soon as they begin, the celebrant and all in choir rise and may make the sign of the cross. The celebrant goes to the altar, accompanied by the assistants and the M.C. (if other altars are to be incensed, the M.C. brings the celebrant's biretta) ; they bow to the choir on either side, beginning on the Epistle side (on their way to the altar). The celebrant and assistants bow to the altar (or genuflect *in plano* if the Sanctissimum is reserved there) ; the thurifer also comes up, he and the M.C. genuflect in any case. The assistants on either side of the celebrant hold the ends of his cope ; between them he goes up to the altar, kisses it, turns to the Epistle side, puts on and blesses incense. The first assistant holds the incense boat and says *Benedicite, Pater reverende,* ministering the spoon, as the deacon at Mass, with the solita oscula. The second holds aside the right end of the cope. The celebrant blesses the incense with the usual form *Ab illo benedicaris,* etc. He incenses the altar as at Mass (p. 111), the assistants on either side holding up the cope.[1] At the Epistle corner he hands the thurible to the first assistant, who receives it with the solita oscula and hands it to the thurifer. The celebrant comes to the middle bows, descends between the assistants, bows or genuflects with them at the foot, and goes back to his seat, bowing to the choir first.[2] The assistants follow him and stand facing him, the first takes the thurible and incenses the celebrant with three double swings, bowing before and after. He gives the thurible back to the thurifer ; both assistants go to their places. The thurifer incenses the choir as at Mass (p. 107), then the assistants, giving two double swings to each, the acolytes, and lastly the people, as at Mass (p. 84).[3] The singers must take care not to end the *Magnificat* too soon. For this reason, if the incensing takes long (and especially if other altars are incensed), the organ should play—when permissible— between the verses, or at the end of the last verse, before the *Gloria Patri.* The *Gloria Patri* of the *Magnificat* should not begin till the thurifer has incensed the people. While it is sung, unless he has already finished and has gone back to the sacristy, he will stand facing the altar and bowing, at the place where he has last incensed. Then he genuflects and goes to put away the thurible in the sacristy. He comes back to his place, and has no further duty. After the verse *Sicut erat* has been sung, all sit during the antiphon at the end.

Prayer. Meanwhile the acolytes take up their candles and go to the altar, the assistants in copes [4] also rise and go to the place just before the acolytes (unless the assistants are already by the celebrant). All genuflect to the altar, come to the celebrant, and bow to him. The

[1] If it be customary he may, during the incensation, recite the *Magnificat* alternately with the assistants. He will say *Gloria Patri* bowed at the centre of the altar before descending.

[2] Beginning with the side opposite to the one to which he is to return.

[3] Rubrical authorities are not in agreement about the order of the incensation. That most commonly adopted by them is : (1) canons, (2) the clergy, (3) the assistants, (4) the M.C. and acolytes, (5) the people. Some prescribe the incensation of the assistants before that of the clergy in choir.

[4] If not already beside the celebrant.

acolytes again stand one on either side as before, the assistants are by the celebrant. When the antiphon is ended the celebrant uncovers, rises and all rise with him. He sings *Dominus vobiscum*, and the collect of the Office in the solemn tone (as at Mass). If there are commemorations (including the Suffrage), the cantors go to the middle, at the lectern. The choir sing the antiphon of each commemoration, the cantors the versicle, the celebrant the collect (each preceded by *Oremus*, the last alone with its conclusion). Then the celebrant sings *Dominus vobiscum*, and the cantors *Benedicamus Domino*. While they sing this the acolytes bow to the celebrant, go to the altar (not genuflecting this time) and stand there on either side.[1] When the choir has answered *Deo gratias* to the verse *Benedicamus Domino*, the celebrant in a lower voice says *Fidelium animae*, etc. He says silently the Lord's Prayer, then in the medium voice [2] and on one note, *Dominus det nobis suam pacem*. He begins, in a low voice, the anthem of the Blessed Virgin for the season, standing or kneeling (p. 192); the choir continues in the same way.[3] The celebrant says, in the medium (or subdued) voice,[4] the versicle and (standing) collect of that anthem, then *Divinum auxilium maneat semper nobiscum*. The choir answers *Amen*, and Vespers are ended.

Unless another service follows, all form in procession before the altar, make the usual reverence to it, and go out, as they came.

§ 4. ON INCENSING OTHER ALTARS AT VESPERS

IF the Sanctissimum is exposed on the altar of the choir where Vespers are sung, no other altar may be incensed. Otherwise, if the Sanctissimum is reserved at another altar, this altar must be incensed first, before that of the choir. If it is the custom, other altars in the church (e.g., an altar dedicated to a Saint whose feast occurs) may then be incensed also. If the Sanctissimum is not at the altar of the choir, this latter is incensed last. Candles (six, or at least two) should be lit on each altar, at least for the time while it is incensed. The celebrant puts on and blesses the incense once only, at the first altar incensed. The thurifer may afterwards add more incense himself if this is necessary.

In going to incense other altars the celebrant may be accompanied by some canons or members of the choir if this is the custom. In this case the M.C. must give them a sign in time, so that they come out from their places and form in the procession. In going to the other altars (all having first formed up before the High Altar and reverenced

[1] If no other service is to follow they may go and stand at the entrance of the sanctuary.
[2] C.E. II. iii, 15.
[3] It is, however, permitted and a common practice to sing the anthem ; and (by custom) the celebrant may go to the foot of the altar for this (see below, p. 201). If another canonical Hour (Compline) is to follow the anthem is omitted, and Vespers end with *Fidelium animae*.
[4] C.E. II. iii, 15.

to it) the thurifer leads ; the acolytes follow with their lighted candles (all three having gone to the entrance of the choir during the antiphon preceding the *Magnificat*), next the M.C. and then the celebrant between the assistants,[1] who hold the ends of his cope. The accompanying canons or clergy follow him. The celebrant and assistants wear their birettas while going from one altar to the other. At each altar they make the usual reverences ; the celebrant kisses the altar and incenses it, as already described in the case of the High Altar. When all have been incensed the procession comes back to the choir, all go to their places, and the celebrant is incensed.

§ 5. VESPERS WITH MORE THAN TWO ASSISTANTS IN COPES[2]

THE Ceremonial orders that Vespers should be celebrated with two assistants (as described above) on Sundays and feasts observed by the people. It adds that on certain greater days there should be four to

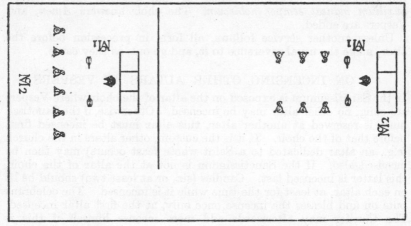

a. First Position.　　　　　　　*b.* Position after Bowing.

FIG. 28. VESPERS WITH SIX ASSISTANTS : THE CHAPTER

six assistants. Naturally this is possible only when a number of clerics (i.e. men who are at least tonsured) are available.

On the following feasts six assistants take part : Christmas, Epiphany, Easter Sunday, Ascension Day, Whit Sunday, Corpus Christi, the feast of the Sacred Heart and of Christ the King ; the Immaculate Conception and Assumption of Our Lady ; the feast and

---

[1] Should there be several assistants in cope they—except the first and second who are with the celebrant—walk in pairs before the celebrant.

[2] The function of Vespers has been described above in detail (§ 3), only the differences when more than two assistants in cope take part are described here.

solemnity of St. Joseph ; SS. Peter and Paul ; All Saints ; the Titular of the church ; the Patron of the place ; the Dedication of the church.

Four assistants take part on the three days following Christmas ; on the two days following Easter and Whitsunday ; on the Circumcision and Candlemas ; on Trinity Sunday ; on Lady Day and Our Lady's Birthday ; on the Birthday of St. John the Baptist and on the Dedication of St. Michael, Archangel.[1]

Rules for Assistants. The first two assistants may sit at each side of the celebrant (when he is at the bench) or with the others in the middle of the choir.[2] The position of the assistants is indicated by the diagram on p. 194.

The first two assistants are with the celebrant when he walks and

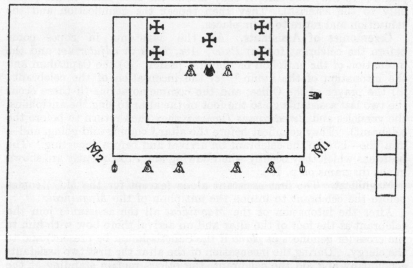

FIG. 29. VESPERS WITH SIX ASSISTANTS INCENSING THE ALTAR

raise the edges of his cope. The first of them pre-intones to the celebrant the antiphon of the first psalm,[3] the hymn and the antiphon of the *Magnificat*, and incenses the celebrant. The last of the assistants (the fourth or sixth) announces the antiphons to the clergy in choir [4] (accompanied by a M.C.), and incenses the clergy and the other assistants (accompanied by the thurifer). He is himself incensed by the thurifer, who then incenses the M.C., the acolytes and the people.

---

[1] Cf. C.E. II. iii, 16, 17.

[2] In this case it is the M.C. who will assist the celebrant at his place.

[3] This is the usual practice. C.E. II. iii, 6 says, " unus ex dictis presbyteris paratis."

[4] " Canonicis ab utraque parte chori per ordinem, incipiendo a dignioribus " (see p. 194). Or this pre-intoning may be done by the two cantors (C.E. II. iii, 8).

The two last assistants (standing before the altar in the middle and genuflecting before and after) sing the verse after the hymn, the verses of the commemorations, and *Benedicamus Domino*.

Rules for Cantors. Two cantors (who occupy convenient places in choir, either together or on opposite sides), in surplice, should intone the psalms (the entire first verse of each or as far as the asterisk only, according to custom), the *Magnificat*, and the antiphons of the commemorations.[1] They go to the centre of the choir, near the entrance (behind the assistants in cope), bow to one another, genuflect, and intone. At the end of the intonation they bow to the side of the choir that is to continue the psalm (i.e. to the side opposite to that to which the antiphon was intoned if they intone the entire first verse of the psalm ; to the same side, if they intone the first verse of the psalm only to the asterisk). They then repeat the genuflection and the salutation and retire to their places.

Ceremonies of Assistants. All the assistants in copes come before the celebrant for (*a*) *Pater, Ave, Deus in adjutorium* and the intonation of the antiphon of the first psalm ; (*b*) the Capitulum and the intonation of the hymn [2] (*c*) the incensation of the celebrant ; (*d*) the prayer of the Office, and the commemorations (if these occur the two last assistants go to the foot of the altar to sing the antiphons, the versicles and *Benedicamus Domino*, they then return to before the celebrant). They genuflect before the altar,[3] coming and going, and— in a line—bow to the celebrant on arrival and before departing. The positions which they occupy when bowing and subsequently are shown in the diagrams on p. 198.

Magnificat. The first assistant alone (except for the M.C.) comes before the celebrant to intone the antiphon of the *Magnificat*.

After the intonation of the *Magnificat* all the assistants join the celebrant at the foot of the altar and on arrival there bow with him to the cross (or genuflect *in plano* if the Sanctissimum be present) and to the clergy. During the incensation of the altar the first two assistants accompany and aid the celebrant, the others remain standing at the foot of the altar [4] (diagram, p. 199). After the incensation of the altar, the assistants reverence with the celebrant to the altar and choir, and accompany him to his place. They stand in line before him while the first assistant incenses him (bowing when the first assistant bows) and then return to their places, the last of them taking the thurible from the first and going to incense the clergy and afterwards the other assistants in the order of their rank.[5]

When the celebrant has sung *Dominus vobiscum* (the second time),

---

[1] When these are not intoned by the choir.

[2] If the hymn be *Veni, Creator* or *Ave maris stella*, they kneel where they are by the celebrant until the end of the first stanza, and only then depart.

[3] If the first two assistants are beside the celebrant they do not go to the centre to genuflect but take their place in the middle of the others when these arrive before the celebrant.

[4] If other altars are incensed all the assistants go in procession with the celebrant for the incensation.   [5] Two double swings to each.

after the final prayer, the two last assistants sing *Benedicamus Domino* at the foot of the altar and then rejoin the other assistants before the celebrant. He recites *Fidelium animae* in a low tone and Vespers are at an end. If Compline follows, the celebrant and his assistants with the M.C. and acolytes, having saluted the altar and clergy, depart in procession as they entered.

Anthem of Our Lady. If, however, Compline does not immediately follow, the celebrant says silently *Pater noster*, then (in the same tone as for *Fidelium*) *Dominus det nobis suam pacem*, and then begins the antiphon of Our Lady, according to the season. He continues this " submissa voce " standing or kneeling according to the time,[1] and at the end recites the verse, the prayer and *Divinum auxilium*.

It is permitted, however, to sing the antiphon of Our Lady, and (by custom) the celebrant and his assistants may go to the foot of the altar for it.[2] The celebrant sings *Dominus det nobis* in the same tone as he had sung *Fidelium*, and without any inflexion at the end, and then he intones the antiphon which the choir continues. The chanters sing the verse, and the celebrant (standing, if he had been kneeling for the antiphon) the prayer in the second ferial tone (i.e. with the inflexion d'l at the end of the prayer and of its conclusion). He then adds in a low tone and without inflexion *Divinum auxilium*.

§ 6. VESPERS WITHOUT CEREMONIES

DURING the week, on weekdays and lesser feasts, there are no assistants ; the celebrant sits at the first place in the choir, he wears no cope ; there are neither acolytes nor thurifer, the altar is not incensed. There are no ceremonies at all, except observerance of the rules for the choir as to rising, bowing, and so on. There may be cantors or precentors. The Office is sung straight through, as, for instance, Compline.

§ 7. BEFORE THE BLESSED SACRAMENT EXPOSED [3]

IF the celebrant is to expose the Sanctissimum immediately before Vespers he will assume a stole with the surplice and cope, and he may retain it during Vespers, if Benediction will immediately follow.[4] But if the Sanctissimum be already exposed, it is more correct not to use the stole at Vespers, but to assume it after Vespers if Benediction follows.[5] If another priest exposes the Sanctissimum he wears a stole, only while so doing.

In the case in which the Sanctissimum is exposed immediately before Vespers, two torch-bearers at least will come out in the procession. They kneel before the altar. The thurifer carries the thurible

---

[1] See p. 192.
[2] C.E. supposes them to stay at the celebrant's place.
[3] This case will occur especially on Corpus Christi and during the Forty Hours' Prayer.
[4] S.R.C. 3593², 4269¹².
[5] S.R.C. 4084².

with lighted charcoal. The acolytes place their candles, as usual, on the lowest step but leave them lighted.

The Blessed Sacrament is exposed on the throne and incensed as usual (pp. 234 *sqq*). Then, kneeling before the altar, the celebrant says the prayer *Aperi, Domine*. He genuflects on both knees on the floor and goes to his seat. The acolytes leave their candles burning on the lowest step before the altar. The thurifer and torch-bearers, having made a double genuflection, go back to the sacristy.

If the Sanctissimum is already exposed, the procession comes out without incense or torches. As soon as they are in sight of the throne of exposition all uncover. All make a prostration on both knees on the ground before the altar. Vespers proceed as usual. But the acolytes leave their candles burning before the altar ; all kisses and reverences to persons are omitted, even to a bishop if he be present. All should stand the whole time. If this is found too fatiguing, at least no one when seated covers the head during any part of the service.[1] At the *Magnificat* the celebrant, having kissed the altar, puts on incense and blesses it standing on the foot-pace a little towards the Gospel side. Then without genuflecting he comes down to the second altar step and kneeling on the edge of the foot-pace incenses the Sanctissimum with three double swings, bowing low before and after. He incenses the altar, but not the cross (if it be there). He and others are incensed as usual ; but no one should turn his back to the altar. No other altar may be incensed.[2]

§ 8. SOLEMN VESPERS FOR THE DEAD[3]

SOLEMN Vespers for the dead (for one deceased person, or for many or for all the faithful departed) may be sung the evening before any day on which a Requiem Mass is allowed, under the same conditions. Naturally this Office is not permitted if the Blessed Sacrament is exposed.

The altar is clothed in black, but if the Sanctissimum be present the conopaeum and the frontal should be violet. The celebrant wears a surplice and a black cope—with or without a black stole.[4] There are no assistants in copes and incense is not used, but (if possible) there will be two cantors, and the acolytes will have their candles, as usual, but of unbleached wax. They place them at the sides of the altar at the beginning as usual and extinguish them, as they are not needed until after the *Magnificat*. The salutations to the choir are not omitted.[5] but the solita oscula are. The antiphons are not pre-intoned (and they are always doubled when the Vespers are " solemn ")[6] but are sung straight through by the choir. *Pater* and *Ave* are recited silently at

---

[1] C.E. II. xxxiii, 33.
[2] S.R.C. 2390[6].
[3] The Office of the Dead and the rubrics for it are to be found not only in the Breviary, but also in the Roman Ritual (Tit. VI. cap. 4).
[4] " Aut saltem stola nigra " (C.E. II. x, 10 ; S.R.C. 3029).
[5] S.R.C. 3059[27].   [6] Cf. R.R. VI. iv.

the beginning, unless the Vespers immediately follow (a) the arrival of a corpse in the church and the responsory *Subvenite*, (b) or the Office of the day. The cantors intone the psalms. After the intonation of the first psalm all sit and remain seated until the *Magnificat*, when they stand. The altar is not incensed. All sit again while the *Magnificat* antiphon is repeated. Meanwhile the acolytes light their candles and come to stand beside the celebrant.[1] When the antiphon is finished all kneel for the *Pater noster*, etc., sung by the celebrant. He alone rises for *Dominus vobiscum* and the prayer. This will be selected for the occasion from the prayers given in the Breviary or Roman Ritual, will be sung to the simple ferial tone (without inflection) and will have the long conclusion.

The *Requiem aeternam* at the end of each psalm and of the *Magnificat*, and that which follows the prayer are always to be in the plural, even where the Office is for one person ; but the versicles between the *Pater* and the prayer will be in the singular, if the Office is for one person only.

After the prayer the celebrant chants *Requiem aeternam* and the chanters *Requiescant* (both in the plural, because these last prayers are for the souls of all the faithful departed).

§ 9. VESPERS IN SMALL CHURCHES

IN many churches it is not possible to provide a liturgical choir on each side of the altar, nor assistants in copes. In this case Vespers should be celebrated with as much of the ceremonies of the Ceremonial as possible.

A simple ceremony is given here [2] which supposes the presence of two acolytes and a thurifer. Generally it will be possible to add a M.C. and sometimes two cantors. In the absence of assistants in cope the cantors will not only intone the psalms but one of them will pre-intone the first antiphon, the hymn, and the antiphon of the *Magnificat* to the celebrant. If no cantors are available the celebrant himself may intone the antiphons and psalms and sing the versicle and *Benedicamus Domino*.

In the procession out the cantors may accompany the celebrant, holding the ends of his cope. If there are no cantors the M.C. and thurifer may do this.

Beginning of Vespers. On arrival before the altar the celebrant bows low (genuflects, if the Sanctissimum be present), his assistants all genuflect. The acolytes place their candles at the sides of the altar and

---

[1] Some authors (e.g. Vavasseur-Haegy-Stercky, Britt, Callewaert, Stappen-Croegaert) follow Martinucci's view (which, it would seem, was based on the Roman usage of his day) that the acolytes do not take part in Vespers for the Dead. But for Pontifical Vespers of the Dead, C.E. (II. x, 4) expressly speaks of them, and there seems to be no sufficient reason for departing from its directions when the Vespers, though not Pontifical, are solemn. This is the view of such good authorities as *Caeremoniale Romano-Seraphicum*, de Amicis, Baldeschi, Augustine, Hébert, Vismara.

[2] For a more detailed treatment of the ceremony, see §§ 3 and 5 above.

extinguish them.   After *Aperi, Domine* the M.C. will accompany the
celebrant to the sedile and there assist him (taking his biretta, etc.).
The celebrant, having recited *Pater, Ave* intones *Deus in adjutorium,*
etc., and the choir continues.   The antiphons are sung by the singers,
wherever they may be placed.   If there are no cantors to intone them,
it will be convenient if one or two leaders in the choir begin them (as far
as the asterisk).   If there are cantors they will sit, one at each side,
in the sanctuary facing the altar, go to the celebrant for the pre-
intonations, and to the centre for the intonation of the psalms, etc. ;
they genuflect together in the middle each time, going and coming.
If there are no cantors the choir will begin the psalms (one or two
leaders may intone each one, up to the asterisk).   A good arrangement is that the special singers chant alternately with the whole
congregation.

The celebrant uncovers and bows at the verse *Gloria Patri* each time,
also (if it is the custom) at the verse *Sit nomen Domini benedictum* in
the psalm *Laudate pueri*, at the Holy Name, the name of Mary and of
the Saint of the Office or commemoration.

Chapter.   Towards the end of the fifth psalm the first acolyte lights
the acolytes' candles ; during the last antiphon the acolytes come to
the middle, take their candles, genuflect together before the altar,
come to the celebrant, bow to him, then stand one on either side, facing
one another.   The celebrant uncovers, gives his biretta to the M.C.,
who lays it on the sedile, then rises and standing at his place chants the
Chapter.   The acolytes then bow to him, go to the altar, genuflect and
set down their candles on the lowest altar step, one on each side, not
extinguishing them.   They stand before the candles.

At the first stanza of the hymns *Veni, Creator* and *Ave maris stella*
the celebrant, M.C. and servers in the sanctuary kneel.   In this case
the acolytes do not kneel, but stay standing on each side of the celebrant
till the stanza is ended.   All kneel also during the stanza *Tantum ergo*
in the hymn *Pange lingua*, if the Sanctissimum is exposed, or if It is
reserved in the tabernacle ;[1]   also during the stanza *O Crux ave spes
unica* in the *Vexilla regis*.   In these two cases, since the acolytes are
before the altar, they kneel there.   The cantors, or the celebrant, sing
the versicle after the hymn.

Magnificat.   The altar must be incensed when the celebrant wears
the cope, even if there be no assistants in copes.[2]   The thurifer goes out
towards the end of the hymn and prepares the thurible.   He comes
back with it, genuflects and stands waiting in the sanctuary at the
Epistle side.   If the antiphons are doubled the celebrant sits while the
antiphon of the *Magnificat* is sung first.   Then he rises and makes the
sign of the cross (all in the sanctuary doing the same) as the initial
words of the canticle are sung.   He goes to the altar, genuflects or
bows (according to the usual rule), goes up and kisses the altar.   The
thurifer and M.C. join him here.   He puts on and blesses incense as usual.

---

[1] See p. 192, n. 3.   [2] S.R.C. 3844[2].

Incensation. While he incenses the altar the M.C. may hold the end of the cope on his right and the thurifer on his left. He returns the thurible to the M.C., bows to the cross at the centre, descends to the foot of the altar, reverences there to the Sanctissimum or to the cross and goes to the sedile. The M.C. incenses him with three double swings, bowing before and after. The thurifer incenses the clergy (if any are present), the singers (if present in surplice in the sanctuary),[1] the M.C. (who has gone to his place by the celebrant's side), the acolytes and people. The clergy, the M.C. and acolytes receive each one double swing ; in incensing the people the thurifer bows, incenses with one simple swing straight down the church, then with one swing to his left, one to his right, then again bows, turns round, genuflects to the altar and goes out. He comes back without the thurible and takes his place in the sanctuary.

Prayer. When the *Magnificat* is finished, the celebrant sits and puts on his biretta. The acolytes again come to him and stand on each side as before ; he uncovers, rises and sings *Dominus vobiscum* and the collect. If there are commemorations, the cantors may sing the versicle for each, or the celebrant may do so himself. The cantors (or the celebrant) may sing the verse *Benedicamus Domino* ; the acolytes go back to the altar and set down their candles. The celebrant, still standing, says " in a lower tone " *Fidelium*, etc., then silently the Lord's Prayer, then in a low voice *Dominus det nobis suam pacem* and the anthem of the Blessed Virgin,[2] during which he kneels, except on Saturdays and Sundays and during all Eastertide. The celebrant then takes his biretta, goes to the altar, bows or genuflects, and all go out as they came in, unless Benediction or some other service follow immediately.

---

[1] Cf. pp. 84 and 107. The singers are incensed in a body (like the people) with three simple swings for each side.

[2] See p. 197, n. 3.

CHAPTER XX

PONTIFICAL VESPERS

§ 1. VESPERS IN THE PRESENCE OF A BISHOP AT THE THRONE

THERE is a difference between Vespers celebrated by a bishop and Vespers celebrated by a priest when a bishop is present.

The first case is when a bishop assists at Vespers celebrated by a priest, and uses the throne.[1] It is supposed in this case, first that the Bishop is the Ordinary or other greater prelate (as described at p. 31) since these alone have, normally, the right to use a throne ;[2] secondly, that the Bishop will the next morning, in the same way, assist at High Mass.

Preparations. The church and altar are prepared as usual for Vespers, except that no lectern is placed before the seat of the celebrant. Further the throne is covered with a canopy and cloths of the colour of the Office. A faldstool or kneeling-desk is prepared in the middle of the sanctuary, and another in the chapel of the Blessed Sacrament.[3] These are adorned as always in such cases (see p. 139, n. 2). Near the throne are the three stools for the assistant deacons and priest. Four or six candles stand at the entrance of the sanctuary, and are lighted. It is supposed in the liturgical books that the Chapter is present, as when the Ordinary assists at High Mass (p. 140).

The celebrant (supposed to be a canon) vests in the sacristy, wearing on this occasion an amice under his cope ;[4] his assistants wear only surplice and cope. The servers are those for solemn Vespers. All go in procession to the sanctuary, say the prayer *Aperi, Domine* before the altar, and go to their places to await the Bishop. The celebrant goes to the sedile. His assistants in copes stand on either side of him, not facing him, lest they turn their back to the throne, but looking in the same direction as he does.

Arrival of Bishop. Meanwhile the canons go to the door of the church to receive the Bishop. The Bishop wears cappa magna and biretta.[5] They offer him holy water, and he signs himself and sprinkles them. He goes to the chapel of the Blessed Sacrament and there prays for a

---

[1] C.E. II. ii, 4–11.

[2] But the Ordinary may allow the use of his throne to certain other bishops (see p. 153, n. 2).

[3] The Sanctissimum should not be reserved at the High Altar during pontifical functions.

[4] C.E. II. ii, 4.

[5] If the bishop assists in mozetta he cannot (apart from special indult) use the throne. He occupies the first place in choir and the only difference that his presence makes is that he is incensed (by the first assistant of the celebrant) with three double swings after the celebrant has been incensed with two.

short time. He comes to the sanctuary and kneels again at the faldstool or kneeling-desk. Two canons in choir dress serve as his assistant
deacons. They kneel on either side of him, rather behind the faldstool.
As the Bishop enters the sanctuary the celebrant and his assistants
stand. He blesses them ; according to the general rule the assistants
genuflect, the celebrant bows low. While the Bishop kneels at the
faldstool those in choir and sanctuary (except the celebrant and his
assistants) kneel too.

Beginning of Vespers. The Bishop rises, bows to the altar, blesses
the celebrant and his assistants and goes to the throne. Here he sits
for a moment and puts on his biretta. All in choir sit at the same time,
the assistant deacons on either side of the throne on the stools prepared
for them. Then the Bishop rises and all with him. He hands his
biretta to the first assistant deacon, who receives it with the solita
oscula ; all say silently the *Pater noster* and *Ave Maria.* Vespers then
proceed as usual. The celebrant bows to the Bishop and intones *Deus
in adiutorium meum intende.* All the pre-intonation of antiphons and
so on is as usual (p. 193). The Bishop takes no part in this. The first
and second assistants in copes sit one on either side of the celebrant,
the others (if there are others) at the benches or stools in the middle of
the sanctuary. In going to and fro in the sanctuary everyone genuflects to the altar, then to the Bishop, except the celebrant and canons,
who bow to him. As soon as the first psalm is intoned the canon who
is to be A.P. (i.e., the highest of the presbyteral canons) comes from
the choir to his place by the Bishop.

Chapter. The Chapter is not read by the celebrant, but by a member
of the choir invited for that purpose by the M.C.[1] He comes out,
makes the usual reverence to altar and Bishop and sings the Chapter
at the place where the subdeacon at Mass sings the Epistle. Meanwhile the Bishop and all others uncover and stand. The hymn and
antiphon for the *Magnificat* are intoned by the first assistant in cope
to the celebrant as usual. During the antiphon before the *Magnificat*
the thurifer brings the thurible to the throne, genuflecting as usual first
to the altar, then to the Bishop, then kneeling.

Incensation. The Bishop puts on and blesses the incense, the A.P.
presents the boat. The celebrant with all the assistants in copes goes
to the altar, making the usual reverence to the Bishop on the way.
The thurifer brings him the incense here ; he incenses the altar as
usual, having first kissed it. He is then incensed with two double
swings by the first assistant in cope, while he stands, not at the sedile
but at the Epistle corner of the altar. The thurifer takes the thurible
to the A.P., who incenses the Bishop with three double swings. The
A.P. then returns to his place in choir. All (including the incensation
of the assistants at the throne and the choir) proceeds as usual [2] to the
versicle *Benedicamus Domino.* The verse *Fidelium animae* is not sung.

[1] " Ab aliquo cantore " (C.E. II. ii, 7).
[2] As there is no lectern a cleric holds the book for the celebrant when he sings
the prayer " stans versus Altare a latere Epistolae " (C.E. II. ii, 10).

The chaplains with book and hand-candle come to the throne, the Bishop wearing his biretta gives his blessing in the episcopal form, singing first the verses *Sit nomen Domini*, etc. [If he is an archbishop, his cross his held before him (the cross-bearer kneeling) and he is uncovered.[1]] The faldstool is brought again to the middle. The Bishop goes to it and prays there for a little time, all in choir kneeling too, except the celebrant and his assistants, who stand and bow. The Bishop, accompanied by canons, goes to the chapel of the Blessed Sacrament and then leaves the church. As soon as he has left the sanctuary, the celebrant and the rest go to the sacristy. The anthem of the Blessed Virgin is not said.

§ 2. VESPERS IN PRESENCE OF A BISHOP WHO IS NOT THE ORDINARY

EXCEPT in the case of the Ordinary or a greater prelate (occupying the throne), there is no special ceremony when a bishop assists at Vespers. A bishop other than the Ordinary, dressed in rochet and mantellettum, has the first place in choir. He is treated as the person of greatest dignity, incensed first, after the celebrant, with three double swings (in the absence of a greater prelate), and so on.

§ 3. VESPERS BY THE ORDINARY, WHO WILL SING MASS THE NEXT DAY

THIS is the case of greatest solemnity.[2] It is supposed that the whole celebration of a feast is one thing, beginning at the first Vespers the evening before. If then the Bishop of the diocese, or other greater prelate, intends to celebrate all the feast himself, there are special ceremonies at the first Vespers. There is another rite, slightly modified, if the Bishop celebrates Vespers on other occasions, not as the first part of a solemnity to be continued by his High Mass the next morning.[3] This will be described below (§ 4, p. 217). The Ceremonial says: " If the Bishop will solemnly celebrate Mass the following day, Vespers are carried out with more solemnity than if he were not to do so." [4] There follows a list of feasts on which this connected celebration of Vespers and Mass should especially be carried out.[5] But the Bishop may use the same solemnity at the second Vespers, if he has sung the High Mass in the morning, at least on certain greatest days of all.[6]

Preparations. The things to prepare beforehand are much the same as those for Pontifical High Mass at the throne, except that the secre-

---

[1] The bishop will give the blessing at the throne " if from there he can be seen by the people," otherwise at the altar (C.E. II, ii, 11).

[2] C.E. II. i.

[3] Namely in the same church and at the same altar.

[4] C.E. II. i, 2.

[5] Christmas, Epiphany (not Easter, because its first Vespers are part of the morning service on Holy Saturday), Ascension, Pentecost, SS. Peter and Paul, Assumption, All Saints, Dedication and Titular of the church, Patron of the city (*ib.*).

[6] Easter, Christmas, Titular of the church and Patron of the city.

tarium is not needed, and the vestments are different. It is supposed that the Sanctissimum is not reserved at the time on the High Altar.

In the chapel of the Blessed Sacrament the frontal and conopaeum are of the colour of the Office ; before its altar a kneeling-desk or fald-stool is prepared, arranged as for Pontifical High Mass (p. 153), six candles on the altar are lit, at least for the moments when the Bishop comes here, before and after the ceremony.

The High Altar has a frontal of the colour of the Office, and six (not seven) candles are lit on it. The Bishop's vestments are laid out on the altar. They lie on a veil or altar cover spread over the linen altar cloths. The vestments in order are : a cope and stole of the colour of the Office, the pectoral cross,[1] girdle, alb, amice and near by the Bishop's morse (*formale*) on a salver. All are covered with a veil of the colour of the Office. The precious mitre stands on the Gospel side the golden mitre on the Epistle side. The crozier is near the altar. The veils for the mitre-bearer and crozier-bearer are on the altar near the precious mitre. On the credence are placed the acolytes' candles lit, the hand-candle, a Vesper book (*Vesperale, Antiphonarium*) for the Bishop's use, which is covered with silk of the liturgical colour; the Pontifical Canon, if it will be needed for the blessing ; another anti-phonary or other book for the subdeacon who pre-intones the antiphons, the thurible and incense boat.[2]

In middle of the sanctuary a faldstool stands with cushions, as described on p. 8. The throne is covered with hangings of the liturgical colour ; if the Bishop will kneel at the throne [3] there must be a cushion there for him to kneel on. On either side of the throne is a stool, of plain wood, for the assistant deacons, on the Bishop's right a third stool for the assistant priest. On the opposite side of the sanctuary is a stool for the subdeacon who will pre-intone and will sing the Chapter (p. 210). On the canon's stalls their vestments are prepared ; namely, copes for the dignitaries, chasubles for the canon priests, dalmatics for the deacons, tunicles for the subdeacons. Near at hand are two dalmatics for the deacons at the throne, and a cope for the A.P. On each vestment an amice is laid.

At the entrance of the choir are large candles burning, either four, six or at most seven, according to the feast.

In the sacristy are prepared four copes, less adorned than the others, for the chaplains who will bear the mitre, crozier, book and hand-candle.

[If the prelate is an archbishop, the amice, alb, girdle and tunicle for the subdeacon who will bear his cross are laid out in the sacristy, or behind the choir.]

[1] But generally the Bishop will use over the alb the same pectoral cross that he wears (by usage) over the cappa on arriving. In this case it is taken off before he vests and put on again after the alb and girdle.

[2] Unless (as is more convenient) these are in the sacristy. There may also be a second credence near the throne for the things needed there. If the celebrant is an archbishop a stand for his cross is prepared near the throne.

[3] In the case of stanzas in certain hymns (see p. 192).

Assistants and Servers. The persons who assist at this ceremony are (besides the Bishop himself) the Chapter, arranged in orders as dignitaries, priests, deacons and subdeacons; two assistant deacons at the throne, who on this occasion wear dalmatics; an assistant priest, who should be the canon first in rank, and who wears a cope. A canon subdeacon who will pre-intone. He will be the subdeacon of the Mass on the following day or another canon, according to the custom of the church. There are two Masters of Ceremonies, two acolytes, a thurifer, two cantors (who wear copes or cottas according to custom) and other servers to bring the vestments to the throne. There are also the four chaplains or servers who carry the mitre, crozier, book and candle; they may wear copes. There are no other assistants in copes (*pluvialistae*).

General Rules for Assistants. Before going through the ceremony in detail it may be useful to note in general the office of each assistant and server.

The function of the A.P. is to hold the book whenever the Bishop sings from it, to offer the incense boat and spoon, incense the Bishop and present the ring. He intones the third antiphon.

The assistant deacons vest and unvest the Bishop; the first puts on the Bishop's mitre, the second takes it off. They walk on either side of the Bishop, holding the ends of his cope (with the orphreys turned in), when he incenses the altar, and every time he goes from one place to another; they hold back the cope when he blesses, puts on incense, or performs any other action at which it would otherwise be inconvenient.

When they are not occupied these three have their places on the stools by the throne.

The subdeacon pre-intones the antiphons and sings the Chapter. He should be one of the canons of that order, vested in tunicle. However, the Ceremonial does not require absolutely that this function be performed by the subdeacon of the Mass on the following day. It says, " the subdeacon, or other person, according to the custom of the church," [1] from which it appears that he may be another canon or dignitary.

The first M.C. stands near the throne at the Bishop's left, and sees that all is done rightly; the second looks after the inferior ministers, accompanies the subdeacon at the pre-intoning, and stands by his stool, at his right, when he sits there opposite the Bishop.

General Rules for Servers. The four servers of the mitre, crozier, book and hand-candle have much the same functions as at Pontifical High Mass. The book-bearer will bring the Antiphonary to the throne when it is wanted, and hand it to the A.P. Afterwards he takes it away and holds it till it is wanted again, or he puts it on the credence if there is a long interval. The bearer of the candle attends and holds it by the Bishop, on the book-bearer's right, when he sings or reads.

----

[1] C.E. II. i, 7.

The bearers of mitre and crozier come to the throne and hand these when they are wanted. These four sit on the bottom step of the throne, without their burdens, while the psalms are sung.

The acolytes and thurifer have the same office as always at Vespers, with the changes that follow from the special ceremonies of a pontifical Office. The acolytes stand on each side of the throne before the Bishop at the Collect and commemorations only. They do not put their candles on the altar step nor extinguish them, The candles are left lighted on the credence before the function and when they are not in use. While the psalms are sung they, and all other servers, sit on the altar steps at the Epistle side.

The Bishop wears the golden mitre only while he sits during the five psalms. At all other times the precious mitre is used.

Once for all—every time that anyone goes from one part of the choir or sanctuary to another, he genuflects first to the altar, then to the Bishop. Everyone who comes up to the throne for any purpose genuflects to the Bishop, at the foot of its steps, before going up. The exception is that canons bow, instead of genuflecting, to the Bishop. The assistant deacons and priest are canons, according to the Ceremonial.

Arrival of Bishop. The Bishop (in rochet and cappa) is received at the door of the church by the canons in their robes. He uncovers, takes holy water himself and sprinkles those around, goes to the chapel of the Blessed Sacrament and says a prayer (first removing his skull-cap), then to the faldstool in the middle of the choir, all as in the secretarium before his Mass (p. 158). While the Bishop is received by the canons the four servers of book, hand-candle, mitre and crozier put on their surplices and copes in the sacristy. [So does the subdeacon who will carry the archbishop's cross, if there is one.] These then come and wait at the credence.

While the Bishop prays at the faldstool in the sanctuary, the canons go to their stalls and put on the vestments, each according to his order. The A.P. and the assistant deacons also vest at the stalls, then go to wait by the throne. The A.P. at first waits at the stall nearest to the throne on that side. The M.C. frees the Bishop's cappa from the fald-stool ; [1] the Bishop bows to the altar, goes to the throne and sits there, blessing the choir as he passes. The faldstool is then put aside until it is wanted again at the end.

Vesting of Bishop. The precious mitre and crozier are taken by their bearers, with the veils. They come and stand by the throne aside. The Bishop takes off his biretta, handing it to the first assistant deacon, and stands. The deacons take off his pectoral cross and cappa. They hand the cappa to the servant, who lays it aside, and also loosens the train of the Bishop's cassock.

The servers (directed by the second M.C.) bring each vestment to the deacons. They aid the Bishop to put on the amice, alb, girdle,

---

[1] While the Bishop kneels before the faldstool his cappa is spread over it (p. 158, n. 3).

pectoral cross,[1] stole, cope, morse.   The Bishop sits and the first deacon
puts on the precious mitre.   The A.P. puts on the ring, if the Bishop

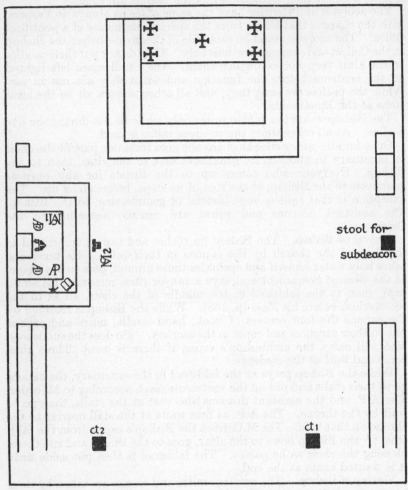

FIG. 30. PONTIFICAL VESPERS AT THE THRONE : PRE-INTONING THE
FIRST ANTIPHON

is not already wearing it.[2]   The Bishop, seated, rests a little.[3]   The
A.P. now goes to his stool by the throne.

The second assistant deacon takes off the mitre, hands it to the

---

[1] The first deacon first presents the cross to be kissed by the Bishop.
[2] The Bishop does not wash his hands at Vespers.
[3] C.E. II. i, 5.

bearer, who carries it to the altar, here changes it for the golden mitre, and comes back to the throne. During all this time, since the Bishop entered the church, the organ is played.

Beginning of Vespers. The Bishop rises, and the organ is silent. Turned towards the altar he says silently *Pater noster* and *Ave Maria*. The Bishop intones *Deus in adiutorium meum intende,* he and all making the sign of the cross. While the choir sings *Gloria Patri,* etc., all bow towards the cross on the altar. Meanwhile the subdeacon who is to

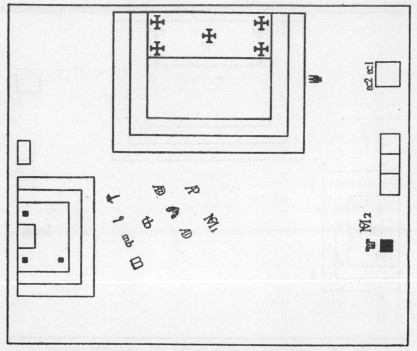

FIG. 31. PONTIFICAL VESPERS AT THE THRONE : GOING TO INCENSE
THE ALTAR

pre-intone comes from his stool, accompanied by the second M.C., who hands him an antiphonary or other book containing the music (if necessary), and goes to the middle of the sanctuary. He comes to the Bishop with the usual reverences and pre-intones to him the first antiphon, singing its text, as far as the asterisk, in a low voice. The A.P. (if necessary [1]) holds the book and the Bishop intones this anti-phon. The A.P. returns to his stool. The subdeacon and second M.C. now go to their place opposite the Bishop. The cantors come to the

---

[1] Cf. C.E. I. xx, 4, and II. i, 7. As the antiphon is pre-intoned, the Bishop will not, ordinarily, need the book to intone it.

middle and intone the first psalm, singing its first verse. They then bow to that side of the choir which will sing the second verse. The Bishop sits when the first psalm has been intoned, the first deacon puts on the golden mitre. The Bishop remains seated during the five psalms. All sit in their places after the Bishop. Vespers proceed as usual. The subdeacon pre-intones the antiphons. The first is pre-intoned to the Bishop, as already said, the second to the first assistant deacon, the third to the assistant priest, fourth to the first canon in choir, fifth to the second assistant deacon. When one of the assistants

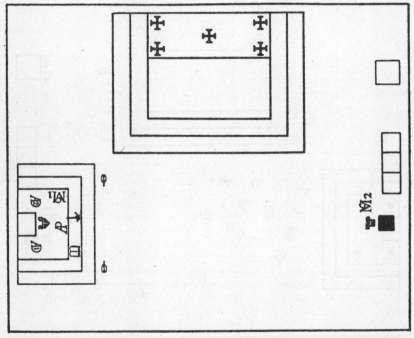

FIG. 32. PONTIFICAL VESPERS AT THE THRONE : THE COLLECT

intones an antiphon his co-assistants and they alone rise with him ; when the canon in choir does so the members of the choir rise.[1] At the verse *Gloria Patri* the Bishop bows, wearing the mitre ; all others uncover and bow. The same rule applies to the verse *Sit nomen Domini benedictum* in the psalm *Laudate pueri*. During the last antiphon, after the fifth psalm, the bearers of book, candle, mitre and crozier rise and genuflect to the Bishop. Those of the book and candle go to fetch these from the credence ; the mitre-bearer brings the precious mitre from the altar, the crozier-bearer stands by the crozier. The servers who sat on the altar steps also rise and go to the credence.

[1] All the choir, according to C.E. II. i, 10. But see p. 192, n. 2.

The Bishop rises, and all with him. He stands wearing the mitre, the others uncover before standing. The subdeacon, at the place (at a distance from the altar steps) where the Epistle is read, chants the Chapter ; the second M.C. hands him the book, conducts him, and stands at his side.

Hymn. The subdeacon comes to the Bishop and pre-intones the hymn. The Bishop sits and the second assistant deacon takes off the mitre. The Bishop rises ; the A.P. holds the book (if necessary [1]), the Bishop intones the first line of the hymn. [At the first stanza of the hymns *Veni, Creator* and *Ave maris stella* all kneel when he intones, and the Bishop himself kneels after he has sung the first line. For this a cushion is placed before the throne, and the first deacon takes off the skull-cap.] The mitre-bearer takes the golden mitre to the altar and brings back the precious mitre. The acolytes go to uncover the table of the altar and they replace the cover after the incensing.[2] During the doxology stanza of the hymn all bow towards the altar.

Magnificat. The cantors come out and sing the versicle. The subdeacon pre-intones the antiphon of the *Magnificat* to the Bishop. The Bishop intones it, then sits and is covered with the precious mitre. All in choir sit. Meanwhile the thurifer has come with the thurible and the crozier-bearer with the crozier ; they stand near. Sitting, the Bishop puts on and blesses incense, the A.P. assisting, the thurifer kneeling. The cantors intone the *Magnificat.* At once the Bishop rises, wearing his mitre, and makes the sign of the cross (all do so too) ; he takes the crozier from its bearer (solita oscula) and goes to the altar. He is preceded by the A.P., the assistant deacons go on either side holding the ends of his cope ; the train-bearer follows holding the train, lastly, the bearers of mitre, crozier, book and candle. The first M.C. goes by the A.P. and signs to the choir (except the dignitaries and canons) to kneel. As the Bishop passes he blesses the clergy.

Incensation. Before the altar the Bishop gives his crozier to its bearer, and the second assistant deacon takes off the mitre. The Bishop and assistants bow low to the altar, and go up to it ; the Bishop kisses the altar. He takes the thurible from the A.P. and incenses the altar in the usual way (p. 111), reciting meantime with his assistants the *Magnificat,* if this is the custom.[3] The assistant deacons hold the cope on either side, the A.P. goes to stand at the Epistle end, on the ground. Then the Bishop gives the thurible back to the A.P. (who goes up to receive it and then hands it to the thurifer), again takes the mitre [4] and crozier at the Epistle corner, reverences to the cross at the middle, and goes back to the throne by the shorter way (preceded by the thurifer and A.P.), blessing the clergy as before. At the throne he gives away the crozier and is incensed by the A.P. (with three double

[1] Cf. p. 213, n. 1.
[2] This cover is supposed by C.E. II. i, 13, which directs that the acolytes before the incensation fold it back on the table of the altar (" illamque conduplicant usque ad medium ") and afterwards spread it again.
[3] Other altars are not incensed when *the* Bishop sings Vespers (S.R.C. 3110[6]).
[4] It is put on by the first assistant deacon.

swings). The assistant deacons hold the cope. The Bishop blesses the A.P. and sits. The second deacon takes off his mitre ; he rises, takes again the crozier and stands, holding it with both hands, as at the Gospel of Mass, while the rest of the *Magnificat* is sung. The subdeacon has come to the side of the A.P. He now takes the thurible and incenses the assistant priest and deacons at their place by the throne, bowing and making two double swings to each. He then incenses the canons, each in order, bowing to each separately before and after. He hands the thurible to the thurifer, who incenses him (with two double swings), the rest of the choir and the people. The singers should not begin the *Gloria Patri* till this is ended. The organ may be played between the verses of the *Magnificat*, or at the end of the verse *Sicut locutus est*, etc. While the antiphon is sung after the canticle the Bishop hands the crozier to its bearer, and sits wearing the mitre. All sit with him. Meanwhile, after the incensation of the altar, the acolytes fold back the veil on the table of the altar, so that it is once more covered.

Prayer. The acolytes now bring their candles to the throne [1] ; the A.P. takes the antiphonary from its bearer. The second deacon takes off the mitre. The Bishop rises, turns towards the people, sings *Dominus vobiscum*, and—having turned to the altar—the Collect, while the A.P. holds the book and the candle-bearer the candle. If there are commemorations, the A.P. hands the book to its bearer till the time comes for the Bishop to sing each collect. The cantors in the middle sing the versicles. Then they sing *Benedicamus Domino*. Meanwhile the acolytes go back to the credence during the singing of the second *Dominus vobiscum* after the prayer or prayers.

Pontifical Blessing. The pontifical blessing follows. The Bishop sits and is covered with the precious mitre. The book-bearer brings the Canon (or the Antiphonary, if it contains the form) to the A.P. ; the crozier-bearer is at hand. The A.P. holds the book before the Bishop ; he rises and the assistant deacons hold the ends of his cope. He sings the verses *Sit nomen Domini*, etc., then lifts his hands and eyes, joins the hands, takes the crozier in his left (after the words *Benedicat vos omnipotens Deus*) and makes the sign of the cross thrice over the people, singing the form *Benedicat vos.*[2] All kneel, except the canons in their places, the assistant deacons and priest. [If the celebrant is an archbishop, the subdeacon of the cross brings this and holds it, kneeling before him, so that the figure of our Lord is turned towards the archbishop. He does not wear the mitre when blessing and bows to his cross before he blesses.]

Unvesting. The verse *Fidelium animae* and the anthem of the Blessed Virgin are not said. After the blessing the Bishop unvests at

[1] C.E. II. i, 17 directs the (second) ceremoniar to conduct the acolytes to and from the throne.
[2] If the Bishop cannot well be seen at the throne, he may go to the altar to give the blessing (C.E. II. i, 18). He then gives it as he would at Mass, kissing the altar first. The indulgence is not pronounced at Vespers.

the throne, assisted by the deacons.   Servers take each vestment and
put it back on the altar, as at the beginning directed by the second M.C.
The A.P. goes back to his place in choir.   The canons unvest and put
on their robes again.   Meanwhile the organ is played.   The four
bearers of mitre, crozier, book and candle go to the sacristy and there
take off their copes.   The faldstool is brought back to the middle of the
sanctuary.   The cappa is put on the Bishop.   He goes to the faldstool
and prays there.   Meanwhile the assistant deacons take off their
dalmatics at the stalls.   The Bishop goes to the chapel of the Blessed
Sacrament, prays there, then leaves the church accompanied by the
canons.

§ 4. WHEN THE BISHOP DOES NOT SING MASS THE NEXT DAY

In this case the following changes are made in the ceremony : [1]

The assistant priest and deacons wear their usual choir dress.   Only
four or six canons in choir will wear copes, the others have choir dress.
The canons who are in vestments will occupy the first stalls near the
throne and remain there all through the ceremony.

The clerics who act as mitre-bearer, etc., do not wear copes.

The antiphons are not pre-intoned by a subdeacon, but by a canon
or other person (in choir dress), according to the custom of the church.
The first is pre-intoned to the Bishop and intoned by him, the others
to the canons who are vested, in order of dignity (beginning with the
highest).

The Chapter is read by one of the cantors, at his place in choir, or
at the usual place, according to custom.   The A.P. does not hold the
book, but its bearer does so.   The A.P. incenses the Bishop ; a cleric
who is not a canon incenses all others.   All the rest is as above (§ 3).

§ 5. PONTIFICAL VESPERS AT THE FALDSTOOL

As in the case of Mass, a bishop who is not the Ordinary of the diocese,
that is, an auxiliary or extern bishop, does not use the throne.[2]   If he
celebrates Vespers, he does so at a faldstool on the Epistle side of the
sanctuary, and the whole ceremony is considerably modified.[3]

Preparations.   The preparations to be made in this case are the
following :

The altar is arranged as for Vespers at the throne.   It has a frontal
of the colour of the Office ; the Sanctissimum should not be reserved
here.

On the altar the bishop's vestments are laid out in the middle,
namely, the cope, stole, pectoral cross,[4] girdle, alb, amice.   These are

---

[1] C.E. II. ii.   These Vespers are sometimes called semi-pontifical.
[2] But see p. 153, n. 2.
[3] There is much diversity of opinion among authors on many points of detail
regarding Vespers at the faldstool ; hence there is room for approved local
custom in this ceremony.
[4] Unless the same cross will be used that the bishop wears on arriving.

covered with a veil of the liturgical colour. The precious mitre stands on the Gospel side, the golden mitre on the Epistle side. The six candles are lit.

On the credence the acolytes' candles stand (unless the bishop is to vest in the sacristy), lighted, also the hand-candle, an Antiphonary, which should be covered with silk of the liturgical colour, and the Pontifical Canon for the blessing at the end.

In the sanctuary, before the altar, there is a cushion, of the colour of the Office, on which the bishop will kneel before Vespers begin. On the Epistle side of the sanctuary the faldstool is placed. It should be covered with the colour of the Office.[1] At the end of the choir nearest the altar [2] are two benches covered with green for the assistants in copes, one on either side, so that they sit facing the altar ; or they may have two rows of stools. There must be benches or seats for the other servers, either on each side after the manner of choir stalls, or in some other convenient place.

In the sacristy the copes for the assistants are laid out ; a faldstool or a chair is prepared in the middle, on which the bishop will sit on arriving, if he is to vest in the sacristy.

Assistants. The following persons assist at the ceremony, besides the bishop himself. There are always two assistants in copes, who attend the bishop, one on either side, as do the deacons when Vespers are sung at the throne. Besides these there may be two or four others, in copes, according to the feast.[3] All the copes are of the colour of the Office. Those who wear copes also have the biretta. There are two cantors in surplice. There is no assistant priest.

There are, further, two Masters of Ceremonies, two acolytes, a thurifer, three servers who bear the book, hand-candle and mitre,[4] a train-bearer and, if possible, other servers, who assist at the vesting of the bishop.

[It may be that the bishop vests in the sacristy.[5] In this case his vestments are laid out there. Having vested and wearing the precious mitre the bishop goes into the church between the first two assistants, at the end of the procession, the train-bearer holding his train behind. In this case the golden mitre alone stands on the altar. The acolytes' candles are prepared in the sacristy ; they come at the head of the procession, following the thurifer. Before the altar the bishop's mitre is removed (by the first assistant) and he kneels there to say the prayer *Aperi, Domine*, then goes to the faldstool.]

Procession to Sanctuary. If he vest at the faldstool, the following order is observed :

[1] For the arrangement of the faldstool, see above, pp. 8 and 176.
[2] These benches are sometimes some distance back. Separate stools are more convenient (see fig. 27, p. 194). Domestic chairs are not allowed.
[3] See p. 198.
[4] There is no crozier.
[5] Ordinarily the bishop will vest in the sanctuary ; in churches where there is a Chapter or if he is to officiate in presence of a greater prelate he vests in the sacristy.

The assistants put on their surplices and copes in the sacristy ; all the others vest in surplice. The bishop comes to the sacristy, bows to the cross there and sits on a chair till the procession is ready. He wears rochet and mantellettum. When the assistants are vested they come before the bishop, form in a straight line and bow to him. The first and second stand at his side, right and left. The procession goes to the sanctuary, first the thurifer, with hands joined, then the acolytes, also with joined hands, the choir, the first M.C., assistants in copes, if there are more than two, the bishop between the first and second assistants.[1] Then follow the three bearers of book, hand-candle and mitre. The second M.C. walks at the side of, or before, the first assistant. Before leaving the sacristy all bow to the cross there. At the door all take lustral water, uncovering at the time ; the first assistant offers it to the bishop. In the sanctuary all take off the biretta again, the assistants form one line, with the bishop in the middle. Before the altar the bishop bows,[2] all the rest genuflect. The bishop kneels on the cushion prepared and says the prayer *Aperi, Domine* ; the assistants kneel on each side. All then rise, bow or genuflect, as before, bow to the choir, first to the Gospel side, and go to the faldstool. The bishop sits covered, facing the people ; the assistants stand before him and bow. The first two go to his sides, facing the people, the others to the bench near the entrance of the sanctuary. The M.C. takes the assistants' birettas. The bishop uncovers and hands his to the first assistant, who receives it with the solita oscula and gives it to the first M.C. The birettas are put aside, on the credence or other convenient place.

Vesting of Bishop. The bishop takes off the pectoral cross, helped by the first assistant, and the mantellettum. Now the first assistant vests the bishop in amice, alb, girdle, pectoral cross, stole and cope, the other assistant helping. Each vestment is brought from the altar, where the second M.C. hands them to servers. The mitre-bearer receives the veil, and using it brings the precious mitre. The first assistant puts the mitre on the bishop. The other assistants (if there are more than two) come to the bishop, genuflecting first to the altar ; they stand in line before the faldstool, and bow, then form in two lines before him as at a procession.

Beginning of Vespers. The bearers of book and candle must now be at hand. The first assistant [3] takes off the bishop's mitre and gives it

---

[1] Menghini thinks it unsuitable that the bishop in mantellettum should come in procession with assistants in copes. He notes that at Rome the assistants and acolytes come first to the sanctuary and await the bishop there (Martinucci, II. ii, p. 548, n. 1). De Herdt, Favrin, Saraiva, Le Vavasseur and others are of the same opinion. If this is done the second M.C. heads the procession to the sanctuary. The first and second assistants in cope follow him, then the other vested assistants, the acolytes, and lastly the other servers. On arrival the first and second assistants take their places at each side of the faldstool. All the others go to their seats in the sanctuary.

[2] If the Sanctissimum is there reserved he genuflects.

[3] It appears that, in this ceremony, by Roman usage, the first assistant always puts on and takes off the mitre.

to its bearer. The bearer takes it to the altar and changes it for the golden one. The bishop turns to the altar (by the left) and says silently the *Pater noster* and *Ave Maria*. As soon as he stands, all in choir uncover and stand too. The first two assistants change places and stand at the bishop's sides (the first on his right), the others behind him (he has turned his back to them). The bishop makes the sign of the cross as he sings *Deus in adiutorium meum intende;* the assistants holding the ends of the cope. The candle and book (if necessary[1]) are held before him by their bearers, on the other side of the faldstool. When the choir has ended the response to this, the first assistant comes to the bishop, bows and pre-intones the antiphon of the first psalm.[2] The bishop then intones it; the assistant bows again, and returns to

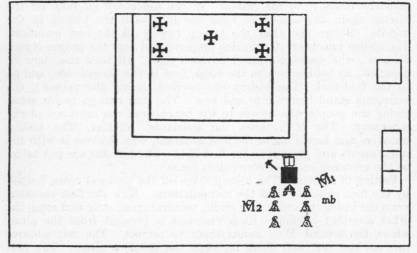

FIG. 33. PONTIFICAL VESPERS AT THE FALDSTOOL:
" DEVS IN ADIVTORIVM "

the bishop's right. The cantors stand in the middle and intone the first psalm. They then take their place in the choir stalls at the end near the people, so that they can easily come forward each time to intone the psalms. The bearers of book and candle retire, and put these on the credence. As soon as the psalm is intoned the bishop turns by the right towards the people and sits on the faldstool; the first assistant puts on the golden mitre. All the assistants in copes (the first and second having come before the bishop in front of the others) bow to the bishop, genuflect at the middle to the cross, salute one another and go and sit at the stool or benches prepared for them (the

[1] Cf. C.E. I. xx, 4; II. i, 7.
[2] The bishop is standing facing the altar across the faldstool. The first assistant comes before him, on the other side of the faldstool, a little to his left and faces him.

first assistant occupying the inmost one on the Epistle side ; the second the inmost on the Gospel side) facing the bishop.[1] They sit and cover themselves. All in choir sit. At the *Gloria Patri* all, except the bishop, uncover and bow ; he bows wearing the mitre. The last of the assistants in cope pre-intones the second and remaining antiphons to members of the choir beginning with the highest in rank. The cantors

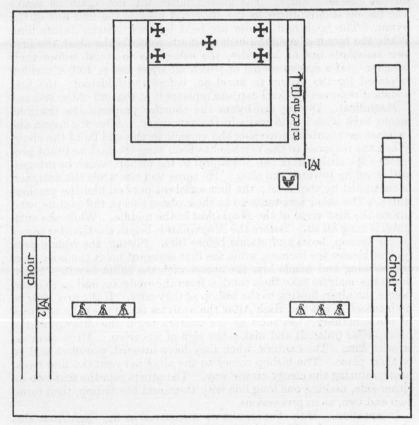

FIG. 34. PONTIFICAL VESPERS AT THE FALDSTOOL : DURING THE PSALMS

intone the first verse of each psalm. In going to the middle they genuflect each time before the altar and bow to the bishop.

Chapter. At the end of the fifth psalm all the assistants in copes come to the bishop (first genuflecting to the altar), bow to him, and stand before him in line, except the first two at his sides. The bishop

[1] Or the first and second assistants may sit at the sedile on the Epistle side, the first being nearer the bishop.

rises and all in choir rise with him.   He turns to the altar,[1] still wearing
the mitre.   The first cantor reads the Chapter, at his place, now behind
the bishop.   When *Deo gratias* has been answered the first assistant
pre-intones the hymn to the bishop.   Immediately afterwards the
latter turns by his right and sits and the first assistant takes off the
mitre.   (The mitre-bearer takes this to the credence and exchanges it
for the precious mitre.   The golden mitre will not again be used.)
The bishop stands, turns to the altar and intones the first line of the
hymn.   The book and candle are held by their bearers before him.
While the hymn is sung the bishop stands towards the altar, the first
two assistants are at his sides, the others go to stand before their
benches.   [If a stanza occurs at which all kneel (see p. 192) a cushion
is placed for the bishop to kneel on, before the faldstool ; the first
assistant removes his skull-cap and replaces it at the end of the stanza.]

Magnificat.   During the hymn the thurifer prepares the thurible,
comes back with it and waits in the sanctuary.   After the hymn the
two last assistants in cope sing the versicle in the middle of the choir.
When the response to the versicle has been sung the first assistant pre-
intones the antiphon of the *Magnificat* to the bishop, which he intones,
still standing towards the altar.   He turns and sits while the antiphon
is continued by the choir ; the first assistant puts on him the precious
mitre.   The other assistants go to their place, except the cantors, who
intone the first verse of the *Magnificat* in the middle.   While the antiphon is sung all sit.   Before the *Magnificat* is begun the thurifer comes
to the bishop, bows and stands before him.   Sitting, the bishop puts
on and blesses the incense, while the first assistant holds the boat, asks
the blessing and hands him the spoon with the solita oscula.   Meanwhile the acolytes take their candles from the credence, and go to stand
before the altar, bowing to the bishop as they pass.   If the first altar to
be incensed is not the High Altar the acolytes stand near the entrance
of the sanctuary.   As soon as the cantors begin the *Magnificat* the
bishop rises (mitred) and makes the sign of the cross.   All in choir do
so with him.   The cantors, when they have intoned, genuflect and go
to their place.   The bishop comes to the altar between the first assistants, saluting the clergy on the way.   The others join the first two on
either side, making one long line with them and the bishop, then form,
two and two, as in processions.

Incensation.   If the Sanctissimum is reserved at the High Altar this
alone is incensed.   The bishop's mitre and skull cap are taken off, he
genuflects with all the others, goes up, kisses the altar, takes the
thurible from the first assistant and incenses the altar as usual.   But
if, as should be, the Sanctissimum is reserved at another altar, that
altar is incensed first.   In this case the bishop and the assistants in
cope bow to the High Altar, the others genuflect ; all then go in procession to the altar of the Blessed Sacrament.   If it is the custom,

---

[1] Most authors direct the bishop to turn to the altar for the Chapter, but
De Herdt (*Praxis Pont.* III, 437)—with whom Ab Appeltern agrees—says that
he does not turn to the altar " because he is not about to read or sing anything."

some of the principal members of the choir may accompany this procession. The thurifer goes first with the thurible and boat, then the acolytes, first M.C., assistants in copes, except the first two, the bishop between the first assistants, train-bearer with the mitre-bearer at his right, the members of the choir who accompany the bishop. The bishop wears the mitre ; those in vestments wear the biretta on leaving the choir.

At the altar of the Blessed Sacrament six candles burn, at least for this time of incensing ; the altar is uncovered. On arriving before the altar all take off the biretta. The acolytes stand right and left, the assistants part on either side to allow the bishop, with the first two, to come before the altar. The first of these takes off the mitre and skull-cap. The bishop genuflects, goes up to the altar between the assistants, kisses it, then incenses it as at Mass. The procession is formed again ; all genuflect, the skull-cap and mitre are put on the bishop and the procession returns to the High Altar. On the way the biretta is worn by those in vestments.

If other altars are to be incensed [1] this is done, in the same way (except the reverence to the altar will be a bow and the skull-cap is not removed), before they come back to the High Altar. The bishop always incenses without the mitre. When they come back to the High Altar the acolytes go to put their candles on the credence. The bishop kisses and incenses the High Altar. He gives the thurible to the first assistant, who hands it to the thurifer. At the Epistle corner the mitre is put on the bishop. He bows to the altar, and goes directly to the faldstool. He stands here facing the people. All the assistants stand before him facing him ; the first takes the thurible and incenses him with three double incensings. The thurifer holds back the right end of this assistant's cope meanwhile. The bishop then sits, the first two assistants come to his sides, the first takes off his mitre ; he stands and faces the altar for the rest of the *Magnificat*.

The other assistants return to their bench, except the last assistant in cope who now incenses the canons in choir, next the assistants beside the bishop, then the others, with two swings for each, bowing before and after. Then he finishes the incensation of the clergy in choir who are not canons. He gives the thurible to the thurifer, who incenses him, the servers at the credence and the people. The choir must take care that they do not sing the *Gloria Patri* verse of the *Magnificat* till the incensing is finished. The organ may be played between the verses, or after the verse *Sicut locutus est ad patres nostros*. As soon as the verse *Sicut erat in principio* is finished the bishop turns and sits and is covered with the mitre. All in choir sit with him. But the first two assistants stand, one on either side of the faldstool. Towards the end of the antiphon after the *Magnificat* the other assis-

---

[1] In Rome, at Vespers *at the faldstool*, it is usual to incense the altar of the Blessed Sacrament and any altar at which an important relic is exposed. Incense is put in once only by the celebrant ; the thurifer may add some later if the thurible is not smoking properly.

tants rise, come to the middle, genuflect, then go to stand in line before
the bishop.

Prayer. The acolytes, at the same time, take their candles from the
credence and come to stand at each side of the faldstool. The bearers
of book and candle also come to the bishop. Then the first assistant
takes off the mitre, the bishop rises and faces the altar.

The first assistants should now change places behind the bishop, so
that the first is on his right. The others are in two lines behind him.
The book-bearer holds the Antiphonary before him ; the other holds
the candle at the book-bearer's right. Both are on the other side of the
faldstool, between the acolytes. The bishop, standing and facing the
altar, with joined hands, sings *Dominus vobiscum* and the Prayer. If
there are commemorations the choir sings the antiphon of each ;

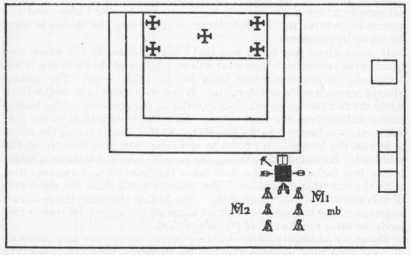

FIG. 35. PONTIFICAL VESPERS AT THE FALDSTOOL. THE PRAYER

meanwhile the last two assistants in cope go to the middle, genuflect,
and standing there sing each versicle. The bishop then sings the
prayer. When the commemorations are finished he again sings
Dominus vobiscum ; the last two assistants in the middle sing *Benedicamus Domino.* The acolytes go back to the credence and put down
their candles ; the bearers of book and candle go with them. The
second M.C. takes the Canon and puts it in the middle of the altar,
with the hand-candle by it, for the blessing which will now follow.
The verse *Fidelium animae* is not sung. The bishop sits and the first
assistant puts on his mitre. The first two assistants again change
places ; the others go to their bench. The bishop goes to the altar,
bowing to the choir on the way.

Pontifical Blessing. The assistants at his sides hold the ends of his
cope. In front of the altar, with mitre on, he and the assistants in

copes bow ; [1] the others genuflect. The bishop goes up to the altar, kisses it, and sings the verses *Sit nomen Domini*, etc. He turns to the people and blesses them with the form *Benedicat vos omnipotens Deus.* The first and second assistants stand at his sides holding the cope while he sings the verses, then kneel in front of him (unless they are canons) on the edge of the foot-pace, as he gives the blessing. The other assistants in cope kneel at the foot of the altar. All in choir kneel too, except canons, who bow low. Then the bishop comes from the altar between his assistants (having turned at the foot and, with his assistants, bowed to it), bows again to the choir in passing and goes back to the faldstool. A server takes the book and hand-candle to the credence.

Unvesting. The bishop sits between the assistants at his sides. He now unvests, the first assistant taking off his mitre and the other vestments in order, while the second helps. The cushion is placed in the middle of the lowest altar step. An attendant brings the mantellettem ; it is put on the bishop and his pectoral cross over it. His train is fastened so that it does not hang down. He goes before the altar, bowing to the choir on his way, there bows to the altar, while the others genuflect and kneel ; he kneels there on the cushion for a short time. The first two assistants kneel at his sides. All the servers kneel behind the bishop.

The bishop rises, all make the usual reverence to the altar and the choir, and the procession goes out in the order in which they came.[2]

If the bishop unvests in the sacristy, the procession is formed as soon as he has given his blessing. In this case the acolytes go first with lighted candles.

The anthem of the Blessed Virgin is not sung when a bishop celebrates Vespers.

In the sacristy the bishop (all having, as usual, bowed to the cross) either sits for a moment while the assistants bow to him, or he unvests at the chair there prepared.

---

[1] Supposing the Sanctissimum not to be reserved there.

[2] If the bishop unvests at the faldstool, it is better that he should return to the sacristy accompanied only by the M.C., and that the assistants who are still in vestments should retire in a separate procession after the bishop has left in the order in which they came (cf. p. 219, n. 1).

CHAPTER XXI

OTHER EVENING SERVICES

§ 1. COMPLINE [1]

COMPLINE is the simplest and, therefore, in many ways, the best liturgical evening service for a small church having but one priest. While the prayers of Compline are most suitable for evening devotion, and the chants are both beautiful and easy to sing, it has hardly any ceremonies.

The rules for Compline are simply one particular case of the Divine Office sung in choir without solemnity. However great the feast, there are never solemnities at Compline, as at Vespers. It is one of the lesser hours, of the same rank as Prime, Terce, Sext and None.

Some authors say that not so many candles should be lit on the altar as for Vespers.[2] However, there seems no reason against lighting the six lit for most public services. The covering over the altar cloths may remain.[3]

Assistants. The persons who take part in the Office are the celebrant (called *hebdomadarius*),[4] a reader (*lector*), two cantors and a choir. But it is possible to reduce the number if necessary The reader may be one of the cantors ; if there is no liturgical choir (in surplices, before the altar), Compline may be sung by singers in other parts of the church, or the verses of the psalms may be sung alternately by trained singers and the congregation. If there are no cantors before the altar, the responsory, versicle and so on may be sung by one or two singers away from the sanctuary. Incense is not used.[5]

Beginning of Compline. The only vestments worn are cassock and surplice, except that the celebrant and clergy present wear the biretta when seated. The celebrant is not to wear a cope.[6] He comes to the altar, in choir dress, behind the cantors, followed by the others. All genuflect before the altar if the Sanctissimum is there reserved, otherwise the celebrant bows low. All kneel to say the prayer *Aperi, Domine* silently.[7] They rise, make the same reverence to the altar as before, and go to their places, the reader to the middle of the choir. The celebrant will go to the first place in the choir, or to the sedile.[8]

---

[1] Cf. C.E. II, iv.

[2] So De Herdt, ii, p. 493, § 384. There does not seem to be any rule of the S.R.C.

[3] The altar is not incensed nor otherwise used. It may, however, be uncovered, especially if Benediction follows at once.

[4] This is the special name for the officiating priest at the Divine Office. It is, however, convenient to use the general name celebrant for all functions.

[5] C.E. II. iv, 3.

[6] *Ib.*, §§ 4–5.

[7] Unless Compline follows Vespers immediately.

[8] If there is no place in choir.

If there is no liturgical choir and no stalls, benches are prepared for the reader and cantors on either side.

All stand at their place. The reader stands in the middle before the altar. He turns to the celebrant, bows towards him and sings *Iube, domne, benedicere.* He stays bowed while the celebrant gives the blessing, *Noctem quietam et finem perfectum,* etc. The choir answers *Amen.*[1] Then the reader sings the short lesson, *Fratres, sobrii estote,* etc. As he chants the last words of this, *Tu autem, Domine, miserere nobis,* he genuflects, bows to the choir and goes to his place. The celebrant sings the verse *Adiutorium nostrum in nomine Domini* ; as he does so, he and all make the sign of the cross. All say *Pater noster* silently right to the end. The celebrant, bowing straight before him, says the *Confiteor,* not singing it, but reciting on one note.[2] He strikes his breast thrice at the words *mea culpa, mea culpa, mea maxima culpa.* He turns towards the choir at *vobis, fratres* and *vos, fratres.* The choir answer *Misereatur,* while the celebrant still bows. Then he stands erect ; the choir together say the *Confiteor,* they turn to the celebrant and bow as they say *tibi, pater* and *te, pater* ; they strike the breast at *mea culpa,* etc. The celebrant answers *Misereatur vestri,* etc. The choir do not stand erect till he has finished this. Then he says *Indulgentiam,* etc., all making the sign of the cross. If there is no choir before the altar, the part of the choir may be taken by the cantors or by the reader. If the reader takes this part he should stay at the middle till the end of the prayer *Misereatur.* The celebrant. sings the verse *Converte nos, Deus, salutaris noster,* he and all making— if customary—the sign of the cross with the thumb on the breast. Then, making the sign of the cross in the usual way, he sings *Deus in adiutorium meum intende.* The choir or singers answer.

Psalms. The cantors sing the fragment of the antiphon assigned for the day and the first verse of the first psalm. If there are no cantors this may be sung by the reader or by one or two persons among the singers. At the end of the first half of this verse the choir takes up the psalm and all sit ; those who wear the biretta cover themselves. They remain seated till the end of the antiphon after the three psalms. The first half of the first verse of each psalm is intoned by the cantors. At the verses *Gloria Patri,* all uncover and bow.

Hymn. After the repetition of the antiphon, all uncover and rise. They now stand to the end, except while the antiphon of the *Nunc dimittis* is sung after this canticle. The hymn is sung, having been intoned by either the celebrant or the cantors. All bow to the altar at its last verse. The celebrant sings the Chapter, and the choir answers *Deo gratias.* The cantors come to the middle and sing the verses of the short responsory *In manus tuas,* the choir or people answering. The reader may take the part of cantor, or the verses

---

[1] C.E. II. iv, 3 says that the organ is not played, " unless in some churches it is the custom to celebrate this Office more solemnly, in which case the organ may be used." This will generally be the case in England.

[2] " Voce recta et paulisper depressa." (*Cantorinus,* 1912.)

may be sung by one or two among the singers. The versicle *Custodi nos, Domine, ut pupillam oculi* is sung by those who sang *In manus tuas.* The cantors (or other persons, as before) sing the part of the antiphon *Salva nos*, and the first part of the first verse of the canticle *Nunc dimittis*, etc. It is usual to make the sign of the cross at the opening words of this. During the antiphon that follows all sit. They rise again as soon as it is finished.

Prayer. If the " Preces " follow, all stand while they are sung, except on weekdays, when ferial preces have been said at Vespers. In this case all kneel during the preces. The celebrant sings *Dominus vobiscum* and the prayer.[1] He sings again *Dominus vobiscum*, the cantors sing the verse *Benedicamus Domino*, the celebrant says the blessing *Benedicat et custodiat nos*.[2] He makes the sign of the cross on himself as he sings the names of the Divine Persons : all do so with him. He begins the anthem of the Blessed Virgin. This is said standing on Saturdays and Sundays and during Paschal time ; otherwise kneeling. According to the Ceremonial the anthem should be recited in a low voice ;[3] it is, however, generally sung, and this practice is allowed. There is no rule that the celebrant should stand before the altar during the anthem, but it is a common and lawful custom. The celebrant sings (or says, if the anthem were recited only) the versicle and prayer of this anthem. He says the collect standing. Then he says, or sings,[4] the verse *Divinum auxilium*, and lastly *Pater noster*, *Ave Maria*, and *Credo*, silently. For these all present stand or kneel according as they were standing or kneeling for Our Lady's anthem. The prayer *Sacrosanctae et individuae Trinitati* may be said, kneeling, at the end.[5]

§ 2. MATINS AND LAUDS

EXCEPT in Holy Week (for which see pp. 275–278), probably the only occasion on which Matins will be sung in smaller churches is on Christmas night before midnight Mass. Lauds will hardly ever occur.

The general rules for Matins sung in choir are these.[6] The persons who take part are the celebrant, two cantors, lectors for the nine lessons. There may be a M.C. to supervise the whole ceremony. All wear only cassock and surplice (with biretta) during the first part of Matins. The celebrant puts on a cope of the colour of the Office before the ninth lesson. This cope should therefore be laid out beforehand on the credence or other suitable place. There should be a lectern in the middle of the choir and before this the lessons are sung.

The ceremonies are those of every part of the Divine Office sung in choir, adapted to the special form of Matins. The procession should

---

[1] To the simple ferial tone, without inflection.
[2] " Recta sed gravi et protracta voce ". (*Cantorinus.*)
[3] C.E. II. iii, 15.
[4] " Voce recta et paululum depressa." (*Cantorinus.*)
[5] Compline has a slightly different form during the Triduum Sacrum and the Easter octave (cf. Roman Breviary).
[6] C.E. II. vi.

come in this order : M.C., cantors, celebrant (in choir dress), clergy ; those of higher rank before the others.[1]

Beginning of Matins. All kneel [2] while the prayer *Aperi, Domine* is said silently at the beginning, during the verse *Venite adoremus et procidamus ante Deum* in the Invitatory psalm, during the verse *Te ergo quaesumus*, etc., in the Te Deum. All stand while the *Pater, Ave* and *Credo* are said at the beginning, during the Invitatory and hymn till the first verse of the first psalm ; also during the versicle, the Lord's Prayer and absolution in each nocturn after the psalms. The choir should also stand during the blessing given before the first lesson of each nocturn and before the ninth lesson ; during the others they sit. They stand while the fragment of the Gospel is read at the beginning of the seventh lesson (on Christmas night also before the eighth), during the whole ninth lesson read by the celebrant, and during the *Te Deum.* All the rest of the time the choir sit. The rules for bowing and uncovering are those of every hour of the Divine Office, namely, at the *Gloria Patri*, the last verse of the hymn (Doxology), the Holy Name and so on (see p. 29).

The celebrant has his place at the chief place in choir, or at the sedile. He intones the hymn and the first antiphon (both being pre-intoned to him by the first cantor). He stands always to bless, even when the others sit. The sign of the cross is not made at the blessings before the lesson.

Psalms and Lessons. The cantors sing the Invitatory (before the lectern). One of them pre-intones the hymn and first antiphon to the celebrant and each succeeding antiphon to a different one of the clergy in choir (beginning with the person of highest rank). Both cantors intone each psalm, in the middle of the choir, before the lectern. The first eight lessons are chanted by eight separate members of the choir. If there are not eight the same person may chant several. The cantors sing the versicles after the psalms of each nocturn. During the eighth responsory the celebrant puts on the cope. The cantors may also put on copes at the same time.[3] The acolytes should light their candles before the ninth lesson. They come and stand on either side of the celebrant, facing one another. He chants this lesson at his place. If other priests are present, before the ninth lesson the celebrant turns and bows to one of them (the first in rank) and asks him for the blessing. Otherwise (without bowing) he says *Iube, Domine, benedicere*, and gives the blessing himself. No one who is not a deacon may read the Gospel at the beginning of a lesson. If the lector is not ordained deacon the celebrant supplies this part. The celebrant intones the first words *Te Deum laudamus*, pre-intoned to him by the first cantor.

At Lauds the ceremonies are the same as at Vespers. There are the same distinctions as to assistants in copes and so on. The altar is

[1] C.E. II. vi, 2.
[2] The celebrant (with the M.C. and chanters) may kneel at the foot of the altar for this and then go to his place.
[3] C.E. II. vi, 15.

incensed during the *Benedictus*.   But at Lauds only the altar of the choir is incensed.

§ 3. NON-LITURGICAL SERVICES

IN many churches in England it is the custom to form the service on Sunday evening of English prayers, or the Rosary, and English hymns, followed by a sermon, and then Benediction.   Since such prayers and hymns are not liturgical services,[1] but private devotions, it is obvious that there are no liturgical rules for them, except negative ones.   The priest who conducts such cervices is free to arrange them in any way he likes, as long as he violates no general rule.   He will, naturally, continue the custom of the church, unless he has good reason to change it.

He must, however, observe the rules which forbid certain ceremonies used only at liturgical functions.   There are other points that may be noticed, since they make for reverence and decorum.

At non-liturgical services the priest who conducts them does not wear a stole or other vestment, except cassock and surplice, with the biretta under the usual conditions.   He may light some candles on the altar, though there should not be as many as at Benediction or during Exposition of the Blessed Sacrament.   Two are generally sufficient.

He may conduct the prayers from a stall in the choir or kneeling before the altar.   He may kneel at a desk here.   The Rosary and prayers in general are said kneeling ; hymns are usually sung standing.[2]

In the case of vernacular devotions only approved forms may be used.[3]   Nor may hymns be sung except those approved by the Ordinary.

§ 4. SERMONS

IN preaching members of religious Orders which have a distinct dress wear their habit.   Other priests wear a surplice.   It is the common custom in England and Ireland to preach in a stole of the colour of the day.[4]   If the sermon comes between vernacular prayers or hymns the stole should be put on immediately before it begins and taken off again as soon as the sermon is finished.   The preacher may wear a biretta, which he will take off if he mentions the Holy Name and under the usual other conditions (for which see p. 22).   In quoting the Bible he should use an approved translation of the Vulgate.[5]

---

[1] Nothing in the vulgar tongue is liturgical, except the questions, Creed and Lord's Prayer at Baptism, the questions at marriage, the penitent's part of confession, and sometimes (*reductive*) a sermon or publication of indulgence.

[2] The people are more likely to join in the hymns if all stand.

[3] Cf. C.J.C. 1259.   For England the *Manual of Prayers* is approved.   The prayers in the various editions of the *Garden of the Soul* are also approved by the bishops.   The prayers in the collection *Preces et Pia Opera Indulgentiis Ditata* (Vatican Press, 1938) are approved by the Holy See.

[4] There is no authority for the stole, except recognized custom.   (Cf. S.R.C. 2682[21], 3157[6], 3185).

[5] C.J.C. 1327–1348, contains important new rules as to the duty of, and faculties for, preaching.

CHAPTER XXII

BENEDICTION AND EXPOSITION OF THE BLESSED SACRAMENT

§ 1. GENERAL RULES

THE part of Benediction which begins at the *Tantum, ergo Sacramentum* and ends with the actual benediction is found in the liturgical books, i.e. in the Ceremonial of Bishops (II. xxxiii, 24 *seq.*), in the Roman Ritual at the end of the procession of the Blessed Sacrament, and in the Clementine Instruction which regulates the Forty Hours' Prayer, and is a strictly liturgical function. The part preceding the *Tantum* is not found in the liturgical books and, accordingly, is regulated by decisions of S.R.C., by the directions of the Ordinary and by local usages which are in accordance with the general principles of Sacred Liturgy and with the rubrics concerning Exposition of the Most Holy Sacrament.

Permission must be obtained from the Ordinary for Benediction given in its solemn form (i.e. with the monstrance). It is not lawful to give it on any day, at the discretion of the rector of the church. The Code of Canon Law, c. 1274, gives the general law about Benediction (which in its solemn form involves " exposition " in the sense of c. 1274 [1]): In all churches which have the faculty of reserving the most holy Eucharist . . . " public exposition, i.e. with the monstrance, may take place on the feast of Corpus Christi and within the octave during Mass and at Vespers ; at other times, however, only for a just and grave cause, especially a public one, and with the permission of the Ordinary of the place, even though the church belongs to an exempt religious Order." When leave is given by the Ordinary the days on which this service may be held are specified. They usually include Sundays and holy days of obligation.

Since the first part of Benediction is not a strictly liturgical service, there are, naturally, considerable local differences in its forms in different countries. For England we have authoritative rules made by the Hierarchy,[2] which rules must be observed [3] exactly in England,

---

[1] Pontifical Commission for the Authentic Interpretation of the Code (6 March, 1927).

[2] These rules are contained in the *Ritus Servandus in Solemni Expositione et Benedictione SS. Sacramenti* (Burns, Oates and Washbourne, new edition, 1928), pp. 9–15. In Ireland there is a book entitled " *Benedictionale* " *seu Ritus servandus in expositione et benedictione SS. Sacramenti*, edited by Rev. J. O'Connell (1922 and 1930). It gives (unofficially) the general laws that govern Exposition and Benediction, a synopsis of the rite and the chants and prayers for use at Exposition and Benediction throughout the year. There is also an edition of this book prepared for use in England (1930).

[3] The ceremonial part of R.S. was submitted for approbation to S.R.C., and though its directions in some details go beyond the common law, it was formally

as far as they go. They still allow some latitude as to the details of what is sung, and in the ceremonies.

Preparations. The first preparation is that a throne, with a canopy over it, must be placed on or near the altar ; generally it is placed in a high position over the altar. On this throne the monstrance will stand. The throne should be, ordinarily, a movable structure. It may be permanent only when it does not interfere with the correct liturgical construction of the altar. Hence it may not be permanent if it is erected on or too near the tabernacle or if it prevents the altar cross of proper size from standing in front of it.[1] The throne should not as a rule be *on* the tabernacle ; but it must not be too distant from the altar. If it is placed behind the altar, it must nevertheless appear to be joined to it, so as to form one moral whole with the altar.[2] If there is a permanent ciborium or canopy over the altar, then there need not be a throne [3] for Benediction. The monstrance is placed on the table of the altar [4] which is the most hallowed place in the church.

The interior of the throne may not be lighted with electric light (S.R.C. 4275).

At least twelve candles must burn on the altar during Benediction. More are allowed.[5] In Paschaltide the Paschal candle is not to be lighted.[6] The veil which covers the altar cloths during the day should be removed. For exposition of some length it is better to remove the altar cross ; for short exposition this is not necessary unless the position of the throne should require it.[7] It is not allowed to place a cushion on the lowest altar step, unless a bishop or prelate gives Benediction.[8] Still less is a kneeling-desk allowed. The monstrance may stand (sideways) on the altar before Benediction begins. It should be covered with a white veil while not in use.[9]

On the throne a corporal is placed, on which the monstrance will stand. The burse and tabernacle key (which must, however, be kept under careful supervision) are on the altar.

In the sacristy cassocks and surplices must be ready for the servers ; the charcoal [10] is lighted before Benediction and the thurible prepared.

The torches are lit, according to the number used, as indicated

---

approved in these words : " Praesens Caeremoniale legibus liturgicis conforme est ; ideoque approbari potest et observandum est " (S.R.C. March 29, 1912).

[1] The cross may not stand in the throne. Cf. S.R.C. 3576[2], 4136[2], 4268[4].

[2] S.R.C. 4268[5]. " The most holy Sacrament ought never to be placed outside the hallowed altar, which represents Christ himself " (R.S. § 1).

[3] Cf. R.S., p. 13, §§ 1-2. " *Benedictionale*," p. 2, II. 2.

[4] Cf. C.E. II. xxxiii, 22, 24, 33 ; R.R. IX. v, 5 ; I.C. § xxxi.

[5] Cf. S.R.C. 3480, 4257.[4]

[6] S.R.C. 3479[3]. If Benediction immediately follows Vespers at which the Paschal candle was lighted it may remain lighted for Benediction (S.R.C. 4383).

[7] Cf. I.C. § 5 ; S.R.C. 2365[1]. R.S. § 3, however, directs that the cross be removed.

[8] S.R.C. 4268[9].   [9] S.R.C. 4268[7].

[10] A good quantity of well lighted charcoal should be used, otherwise the incense—the smoke of which is a symbol of prayer—will not burn properly and is wasted.

below. Further, the vestments are laid out for the celebrant and his ministers (if he has any), as described below.

Assistants. The persons who take part in Benediction are the following : the celebrant, who must be a priest ; at least one assistant, who will bring the humeral veil, ring the bell, etc. (M.C.),[1] at least two torch-bearers and a thurifer.

It is well, if possible, that another priest or deacon expose the Blessed Sacrament.[2] The celebrant may be further assisted by a deacon and subdeacon ; but there may not be assistants in copes, except when Benediction immediately follows Vespers in which these assistants took part. Various combinations are possible. There may be one priest who will give Benediction, and one priest or deacon to expose the Sanctissimum, or there may be a priest, deacon and sub-deacon. In this case the deacon exposes the Sanctissimum. Or there may be a celebrant, deacon, subdeacon and a priest to expose.

On more solemn occasions the number of torch-bearers may be increased. There may be four, six or, on an exceptional occasion, even eight.

Vestments. The colour of the vestments for Benediction is white. But if it follows a liturgical Office immediately and the celebrant does not leave the altar, if he is already wearing a cope of the colour of the Office, he may give Benediction in this (unless the colour of the Office be black).[3] But he must put on a stole under the cope, which will be of the same colour. In any case the humeral veil is always white. The celebrant at Benediction, then, wears a surplice, stole and cope. He may wear amice, alb, girdle, stole and cope ; this should always be his dress, if there are assistants in dalmatic and tunicle.[4] These assistants wear amice, alb, girdle and dalmatic or tunicle. If the deacon will expose the Sanctissimum, he wears the stole diaconally, from the left shoulder to under the right arm. The priest or deacon who exposes the Blessed Sacrament, if he is not one of the two assistants, wears a surplice, and, at the moment of opening the tabernacle and exposing, as also when he replaces the Sanctissimum, a stole. He may carry the stole, over his arm, to the altar or it may be left on the credence beforehand. This stole will be of the colour worn by the celebrant.[5]

§ 2. THE RITE OF BENEDICTION

THE servers come to the sanctuary holding their torches, preceded by the thurifer with burning charcoal, but without incense in the thurible.

---

[1] It is difficult to dispense with this server (here called M.C.), since neither a torch-bearer can leave his torch, nor the thurifer his incense to bring the humeral veil to the celebrant, ring the bell or take the biretta.

[2] It is actually prescribed in England in a church served by several priests (R.S., *Praemonenda*, § 3).

[3] S.R.C. 1615[6], 2562, 3175[3], 3799[2], 3949[7].

[4] S.R.C. 3201[6], 3799.[1] If the celebrant has a right to the rochet, he wears it and an amice under the cope.

[5] S.R.C. 4268[8].

They are followed by the M.C., the priest who exposes (if he assists), then the celebrant, who, if he has two assistants, walks between them, while they hold the ends of his cope, turning in the orphreys so that the lining does not show unduly.

Before the altar the torch-bearers part on either side to allow the celebrant to pass them, the thurifer goes over to the Epistle side of the sanctuary and stands before the credence. The celebrant with his assistants comes before the altar. On entering the sanctuary, if there are clergy in choir, otherwise at the foot of the altar, all take off the biretta. The M.C. takes the birettas and hands them back at the end. The deacon, if there is one, takes the celebrant's biretta (with the solita oscula) and then hands it to the M.C. The birettas are put aside till the end. Before the altar all genuflect on the ground, then kneel in silent prayer for a moment.

Exposition of Sacred Host. The priest who exposes the Sanctissimum now does so. He may be the celebrant himself. He goes up to the altar, takes the corporal from the burse, puts this aside, and spreads the corporal on the mensa as at Mass. Next he unveils the monstrance and places it on the corporal towards the Gospel side. He takes the tabernacle key, opens the tabernacle and genuflects on one knee. If the celebrant himself does so, he genuflects straight in front of the tabernacle door, placing his hands on the table of the altar. If it is another priest or deacon, he should stand back a step towards the Epistle side, so as not to turn his back to the celebrant ; then he genuflects towards the tabernacle. No one else makes any reverence at this moment, since they all already kneel.[1] The priest who exposes takes the little vessel which contains the Sanctissimum (the *lunula*) from the tabernacle, puts it on the corporal, shuts the tabernacle door and places the Sanctissimum in the monstrance. He genuflects again to the Sanctissimum as before. If the monstrance is to be put into a throne over the altar, a stand or small ladder (if necessary) is brought forward by a server and put in position. The priest then mounts and places the monstrance on the corporal which lies on the throne.[2] He descends, once more genuflects, and returns to his place at the foot of the altar. An assistant priest in stole and surplice now takes off the stole and puts it somewhere near, till he uses it again later.

Incensation. As soon as the Sanctissimum is exposed, it is incensed. The celebrant and his assistants bow, not low,[3] rise, the thurifer comes forward and hands the incense boat to the deacon, or to the M.C. The celebrant—turned towards the Epistle corner—puts on incense as usual, but nothing is kissed, nor does he bless it, because the Blessed Sacrament is now exposed and is alone to be incensed. The celebrant kneels, takes the thurible from the deacon or M.C. and incenses the Sanctissimum three times with the double swing.[4] He hands the

---

[1] Cf. S.R.C. 4179[2].

[2] In some churches he carries the monstrance to the back of the altar and mounts by steps from there to reach the throne.

[3] " Inclinatio mediocris " (S.R.C. 4179[1]).   [4] Cf. p. 26.

thurible back to him from whom he received it. All remain on their knees, except for such chants as *Te Deum, Regina caeli,* or *Magnificat.* The thurifer stands before the credence, gently swinging the thurible (at his side) with the right hand to keep the charcoal alight.

Hymns and Prayers. While the Blessed Sacrament is being exposed the hymn *O Salutaris* is usually sung. This custom, not usual in Rome, is to be maintained in England.[1] When that hymn is finished, and before the *Tantum, ergo, Sacramentum* is begun any approved hymn, litany or antiphon may be sung either in Latin or in the vernacular. Liturgical texts, however—such as *Te Deum, Lauda Sion,* an Introit or communion antiphon and (it would seem) the liturgical litanies—may be *sung* only in Latin.[2] Prayers (provided that they have ecclesiastical approbation—see p. 230) may be recited aloud ; these may be in the vulgar tongue. This is the moment at which special prayers ordered by the Bishop of the diocese to be said at Benediction occur. Throughout England at the principal Benediction on Sundays and holy days of obligation the prayer *O blessed Virgin Mary, Mother of God,* composed by Pope Leo XIII, is to be said after the *O Salutaris,* or at latest before the *Tantum ergo.*[3] But on the second Sunday of each month, instead of this, the *Hail Mary,* Cardinal Wiseman's prayer *O merciful God, let the glorious intercession of thy saints assist us,* and *O most loving Lord Jesus,* are said here.[4] In Wales at every Benediction a prayer for the conversion of that country [5] is prescribed. In England on the feast and during the octave of Corpus Christi no prayer is to be said before the Blessed Sacrament exposed, except the prayer of the feast, which occurs after the *Tantum ergo.*[6] Then follows the hymn *Tantum ergo.* This may be intoned by the celebrant. As the words of the second line, *Veneremur cernui,* are sung, all bow moderately.[7] At the beginning of the second verse, *Genitori Genitoque,* the Sanctissimum is incensed, as before.[8] After this hymn the versicle *Panem de caelo praestitisti eis* is sung by one or two cantors, or by the celebrant. The choir answers.[9] The celebrant

---

[1] R.S. § 6.

[2] S.R.C. 3124[7], 3537[3], 4235[8], 4268[10], and cf. 3496[1]. Cf. "*Benedictionale*," p. 3, § 2. For England, R.S. (*Praemonenda* § 5) mentions the hymns *Jesus, my Lord, my God, my All* and *Sweet Sacrament Divine* ; while the bishops at their Low Week meeting in 1934, approved of the following additional hymns in English at Benediction and Exposition : *Soul of my Saviour ; O Bread of Heaven ; Jesus, the Only Thought of Thee,* and *O Godhead Hid, Devoutly I Adore Thee* (cf. *Clergy Review,* April 1942, p. 191).

[3] R.S. p. 43.

[4] R.S. p. 44.

[5] R.S. Appendix.

[6] R.S. § 7.

[7] Cf. S.R.C. 4179[2].

[8] This second incensation is prescribed even though the first has taken place but a short time before. In this case incense is not again put into the thurible (unless this be necessary) but the priest immediately receives the thurible and incenses the Blessed Sacrament (S.R.C. 4202[1]).

[9] In Eastertide and during the octave of Corpus Christi "Alleluia" is added to this versicle and response. It should not be added (outside the canonical Office) to other versicles sung before the *Tantum* at Benediction unless it be expressly prescribed, as e.g. to *Gaude et laetare* of *Regina caeli* (S.C.R. 3764[18] ; cf. 1334[6]).

stands, without first bowing.[1] With joined hands and bowing his head at *Oremus*, he sings the prayer of the Blessed Sacrament, *Deus qui nobis sub Sacramento mirabili*, etc. Meanwhile the assistants hold the book before him, or he may sing the prayer from memory. No other prayer may be added after the *Tantum ergo* [2] unless this be prescribed by the Holy See (as at the Forty Hours' Prayer).

Benediction. When the prayer is finished, the priest or deacon who exposed the Sanctissimum puts on the stole again. He goes to the throne, genuflects *in plano*, takes the monstrance and puts it on the corporal on the altar. The celebrant receives the humeral veil from a server (the M.C.). He goes up to the altar, making no reverence first. Here he, with the priest who exposes, genuflects on one knee. Then the priest who exposes hands the monstrance to him, both standing, or the celebrant may take the monstrance from the altar having first turned it around.[3] The other priest or deacon then goes back to kneel at his place.

If there is no second priest or deacon, the celebrant himself goes to the throne and takes the monstrance, putting it on the altar. Then he kneels on the edge of the foot-pace and so receives the humeral veil.

In giving Benediction the celebrant holds the monstrance through the ends of the humeral veil, turns by his right to the people, and makes the sign of the cross once over them, not lifting the Host above the level of his own eyes and not moving his feet.[4] Meanwhile he neither sings nor says any words aloud.[5] He then turns back to the altar by his right so as to complete the circle. Either the assistant priest or deacon now comes to him, receives the monstrance, both standing, and then genuflecting; or the celebrant himself places it on the altar, then genuflects.

While the celebrant gives Benediction nothing may be sung, but the organ may be played gravely and reverently.[6] The Sanctus bell may be rung. It is usual to ring the bell three times, once as the celebrant turns to the people, once in the middle of the blessing, once as he turns back to the altar. It is not necessary to ring the bell if the organ is played meanwhile, though this may be done. Instead of the Sanctus bell, or together with it, the bell of the church outside may be rung in the same way.[7] If deacon and subdeacon assist at Benediction they should go up to the foot-pace with the celebrant, kneel on its edge, bowing on either side before him, and hold the ends of his cope while he gives the blessing. If the deacon has exposed the Sanctissimum he may hand the monstrance to the celebrant and take it back (both standing while doing so). He will then genuflect with the

---

[1] S.R.C. 4179[3].
[2] S.R.C. 4194[10], 4350[2].
[3] S.R.C. 3975[4].
[4] Cf. S.R.C. 1563[2].
[5] S.R.C. 2464, 2722[3].
[6] S.R.C. 2464, 3058[2]; cf. C.E. II. viii, 70.
[7] There is no rubric requiring the incensation of the Blessed Sacrament by the thurifer during the act of benediction. If it be the custom it may be done (S.R.C. 2956[9], 3108[6]).

celebrant when the monstrance is replaced on the altar. All then come down (the celebrant keeping a little towards the Gospel side) to kneel again on the lowest step. The humeral veil is removed. The prayers *Blessed be God* may then (if it is the custom) be said in English.

Conclusion of Benediction. Afterwards the priest who has exposed or the deacon, or the celebrant himself, goes to the altar, genuflects, takes the Sanctissimum from the monstrance, replaces it in the taber-nacle, genuflects, shuts and locks the tabernacle, removes the monstrance from the corporal, covers it with its veil, folds the corporal, replaces it in the burse, comes back to his place and takes off the stole. When he genuflects the others, who are kneeling, make no other rever-ence than is already contained in their position.[1] While the Sanctisi-simum is put back in the tabernacle the antiphon *Adoremus in aeternum sanctissimum Sacramentum*, with the psalm *Laudate Dominum omnes gentes* (Ps. 116) may be sung by custom. The antiphon is sung before and after the psalm. But any other text, a hymn or suitable anthem may take the place of this.

When the tabernacle is closed all stand. All bow at the *Gloria Patri* of the psalm (if it be sung). When the singing ends all genuflect on one knee, on the ground, and go back to the sacristy as they came.

In Rome it is the custom that a priest in surplice and stole should come first, carrying with him the burse and tabernacle key, preceded by thurifer and two torch-bearers. He opens the tabernacle, exposes the Sanctissimum on the throne and incenses it. Hymns and litanies or such chants are sung. At the end of all that the celebrant in a cope with assistants and torch-bearers comes from the sacristy, the *Tantum ergo* is sung, and all proceeds as above.

This method will hardly occur in England, except in the case of exposition of the Sanctissimum lasting some time.

§ 3. BENEDICTION BY A BISHOP

In this case there should always be deacon and subdeacon, also, if possible, a priest or other deacon to expose and replace the Sanctis-simum ; and a number of attendants to act as bearers of mitre, crozier, book, hand-candlestick and bishop's train. A cushion is placed for the bishop on the lowest step of the altar. The bishop will use his precious mitre and (if customary) his crozier. He will, normally, vest in the sacristy.

The bishop's mitre is taken off before the altar,[2] his skull-cap as soon as the tabernacle is opened. The bearer of the hand-candlestick holds it near the bishop when he reads or sings anything from a book. The thurifer does not kneel when presenting the thurible to have incense put in. The bishop gives the blessing, making the sign of the cross

---

[1] S.R.C. 4179[2].

[2] If the Sanctissimum is already exposed, the ministers uncover when they come in sight of the Blessed Sacrament, and the deacon removes the bishop's mitre and skull-cap. All make a prostration before the altar.

thrice with the monstrance in the same way as when he blesses with his hand. There is no other difference. The skull-cap is replaced when the tabernacle is shut at the end, the mitre after the final genuflection.

If the Bishop assists at Benediction wearing his cappa magna, he kneels in the centre of the sanctuary, or to one side, at a faldstool or at a kneeling-desk (covered and with cushions, as usual—see p. 8). Assisted by the senior of the presbyteral canons he puts in incense and going to the foot of the altar incenses the Sanctissimum at the usual times and then returns to his place. The celebrant—not the Bishop—sings the prayer and gives Benediction.

If the Bishop assists in rochet and mozzetta he kneels at the first place in choir or at a kneeling-desk and takes no special part in the function.

§ 4. BENEDICTION WITH THE CIBORIUM

THIS is a little ceremony which may be held any day for a just cause.[1] The priest who celebrates it wears only surplice and stole. He may, however, wear a cope. He may give this Benediction immediately after Mass, wearing the Mass vestments except the maniple, which he takes off first. At least six candles should be lit on the altar. There is no throne ; the altar cross remains. A thurifer may attend. If possible there should be two torch-bearers. If not, it is laudable to light two candles in the sanctuary before the altar on the lowest step at each side. On arriving at the altar, after the usual genuflection, the priest spreads the corporal, opens the tabernacle, genuflects again and leaves it open, so that the people may see the veiled ciborium. He may bring this forward in the tabernacle, that it may be better seen. He must not place it on the altar.

The usual hymns may be sung ; the *Tantum* with the versicle and prayer must be either sung or recited. If incense is used,[2] the priest incenses as soon as he has come back to his place after having opened the tabernacle ; and again at the verse *Genitori Genitoque*. For the blessing the priest receives the humeral veil, goes up to the altar, genuflects, takes the ciborium and places it on the corporal before the tabernacle. He takes it with the left hand covered by the veil, and arranges the other end of the veil over it with the right and so holds the ciborium with both hands. He turns and gives the blessing with one sign of the cross, saying nothing. He replaces the ciborium momentarily on the corporal (until he has freed his hands from the veil), or directly in the tabernacle, and genuflects. He comes down to say the prayers *Blessed be God* (if customary). Then he goes up to the

---

[1] Cf. "*Benedictionale*," p. 7. Permission of the Ordinary is not required for this simplest form of Benediction. C.J.C. 1274, § 1.

[2] The Blessed Sacrament may be incensed ; but this is not necessary, nor does the S.R.C. appear to desire it : " The omission of incensing is more conformable to the practice of the Church in Benediction with the sacred pyx " (= ciborium) (2957, cf. 4202[1]).

altar, genuflects, moves the ciborium further into the tabernacle, closes its door, and replaces the corporal in the burse, etc., as at Benediction given with the monstrance.

§ 5. EXPOSITION OF THE BLESSED SACRAMENT

THE best-known case of exposition is that of the Forty Hours' Prayer, for which see pp. 349–359. But it may happen, on other occasions, that the Ordinary allows or commands exposition for some space of time, that the people may have this special opportunity of saying prayers.[1] When the exposition lasts for some hours the Blessed Sacrament should not remain in the tabernacle at the altar of the exposition. If this is its customary place, it should be removed, temporarily, to another altar.

For exposition of some hours the Blessed Sacrament should be placed in a throne above the altar. It is better that any fixed image over the altar should be veiled; other images are to be removed, and relics may not be put on. The altar and tabernacle are vested in white, and it is better to remove the cross.[2] Twenty wax candles, or at least twelve,[3] are to burn during the exposition. Flowers may be used, but with great restraint. Neither they nor the candles should be near the throne; the Sacred Host ought to stand out in a detached manner.

The ceremonies are the same as those of Benediction. Indeed this exposition may be considered as one long Benediction service, with an interval between the exposing of the Sanctissimum and the blessing and reposition at the end. During this interval the priest who has exposed and his servers may go away.

The Blessed Sacrament is exposed by a priest or deacon in surplice and white stole. If the exposition begins immediately after Mass the celebrant of Mass may place the Sanctissimum on the throne. In this case he wears the Mass vestments, except the maniple, which should be first taken off. If possible, two priests or clerks in surplices should watch kneeling in the sanctuary all the time of exposition. Priests and deacons should wear a white stole. In England it will not always be possible to observe this. But someone should be in the church, kneeling before the Blessed Sacrament all the time outside the sanctuary. People may relieve one another at intervals.

While the Blessed Sacrament is exposed the *O salutaris* may be sung.[4] As soon as It is placed on the throne It is incensed. The priest who exposed will now generally retire, making a prostration on both knees. This rule is observed by everyone who comes to the church, passes

[1] C.J.C. 1275.

[2] R.S. (§ 3) prescribes this for England.

[3] Local legislation (e.g. synodal law) may prescribe a greater number.

[4] This does not seem of obligation. Neither the decrees of the S.R.C. nor Roman books on ceremonies say anything about a hymn or prayer at the time of exposition, though they require the "Tantum ergo" at the end. The rule of the *Ritus Servandus* (p. 14, § 6) is for Benediction. Therefore, at the beginning of exposition any approved Latin hymn may be sung; or it may be begun in silence.

before the altar, or rises to leave. But, according to the general principle, if someone is occupied in the sanctuary he will make the prostration only on entering and leaving. While passing, during the time he is there, he genuflects on one knee only. No one should enter the sanctuary unless vested in surplice ; women may not enter it at all.

During all the time of exposition the Sanctus bell may not be rung at Mass, even at a side altar. Holy Communion should not be given from the altar of exposition, unless there is no other way.[1] No one may wear a biretta or skull-cap. No one bows to the choir, but its members are incensed as usual.

All the solita oscula of mere courtesy, but not those inherent in the rite of the Mass (e.g. at the Epistle, Gospel and for the altar, the paten and chalice), are omitted. The hours of the Divine Office may be said or sung, but not the Office for the dead. If, during the Office, a veil is placed in front of the Sanctissimum,[2] the members of the choir may wear the biretta when seated ; but, even then, it is better not to do so.[3] Sermons may be preached, but only on the subject of the Holy Eucharist. During a sermon a veil must be placed before the Sanctissimum ; the preacher may not cover his head.[4] No one should sit with his back to the altar.

During the time that no liturgical function is celebrated private prayers may be said aloud and hymns may be sung. Either may be in Latin or in the vulgar tongue. The texts must be approved.[5] Translations of liturgical texts are not allowed, since these must be sung in Latin.[6]

While the Blessed Sacrament is exposed, even more than at any other time, reverence should be shown by everyone in church.

When the time of exposition is over Benediction is given. The celebrant enters, with or without deacon and subdeacon or assistant priest, to put back the Blessed Sacrament. All make a prostration before the altar, then kneel. The usual form of Benediction may be used (without, of course, the rite of taking the Sanctissimum from the tabernacle, since It is already exposed), or only the latter part, from the *Tantum ergo.* The Sanctissimum will not be incensed on the arrival of the celebrant, but only at the verse *Genitori Genitoque.*[7] The closing of the tabernacle after Benediction ends the exposition.

§ 6. TO REMOVE THE BLESSED SACRAMENT

If, for any reason, the Sanctissimum is to be carried from one altar to another, this is done by a priest or deacon [8] in surplice and white

---

[1] S.R.C., 3448[1], 3482, 4353, and cf. S.R.C. July 27, 1927.
[2] This is generally a little banner of white silk on a staff.
[3] S.R.C. 2552.[1]
[4] Cf. S.R.C. 1352. He should wear a surplice, even if a Regular (see below, p. 352).   [5] See p. 230,
[6] S.R.C. 3537[3]. Cf. " *Benedictionale,*" p. 3.
[7] S.R.C. 4202[2].
[8] A deacon may always do so, even if priests are present (S.R.C. 4194[3] ; cf. C.J.C. 1274, § 2).

stole. He is accompanied by three servers, of whom two carry torches,[1] the third the small canopy (*umbella*) used on these occasions.[2]

A corporal must first be spread on the altar to which the Sanctissimum will be brought. On the altar from which it is taken there is another corporal, unless the priest brings this with him. By this altar a white humeral veil and the *umbella* are made ready. On both altars two candles should be lighted. The torch-bearers may come from the sacristy holding their torches, or these may be ready for them to take at the altar to which they first go. The bearer of the canopy goes first, then the torch-bearers, then the priest or deacon.

At the altar from which the Sanctissimum will be taken all génuflect, then kneel for a moment. The priest rises, spreads the corporal, opens the tabernacle, genuflects and takes out the ciborium or pyx and places it on the corporal. Then he kneels and receives the humeral veil from a server. With this he holds the ciborium or pyx. The torch-bearers go in front with the torches, the other server walks behind the priest, holding the canopy open over him.

On the way to the other altar the priest should recite psalms.[3] He goes straight up to the altar and places the ciborium on the corporal there and genuflects. The torch-bearers kneel ; the *umbella* is closed and put aside. Then the priest kneels on the edge of the foot-pace and the veil is taken from him. He opens the tabernacle, puts the ciborium in it, genuflects again and closes the tabernacle. The servers rise ; the torches are extinguished. The priest comes down the steps and all genuflect together and go back to the sacristy.

[1] In case of necessity one torch-bearer is sufficient. (Cf. Instruction of the Congregation of the Sacraments, Ascension Day, 1938).

[2] Cf. p. 17. The umbella is always used at Rome. If the church does not possess one, it must be dispensed with. But, where the Sanctissimum is reserved not on the High Altar, this umbella becomes a necessary article of furniture, which should be procured.

[3] The psalms are not specified. Ps. 115 (Credidi), 147 (Lauda Ierusalem), 121 (Laetatus sum), 112 (Laudate pueri), 116 (Laudate Dominum), or others from the office of Corpus Christi are suitable. They are recited with the servers, if these are clerics who know them.

APPENDIX

THE WAY OF THE CROSS

THOUGH the pious exercise of the Way of the Cross is not a liturgical function it is much in use in our churches, and so it is well to indicate the correct method of carrying it out.

When the Stations of the Cross are made privately all that is required is that the person making them should move from Station to Station and meditate even briefly on the Passion of our Lord. No vocal prayers are necessary, though they may, of course, be used, but meditation on the Passion in general or on some part of it is essential.

When the Stations are made publicly those taking part in the exercise should, if possible, follow the priest from Station to Station, the men preceding the women. This, however, is almost always impossible in our churches which are filled with seats, and so it is permitted [1] that the people remain in their places, answering the prayers, kneeling, standing and genuflecting when the priest does so, and that only the priest and his assistants move from Station to Station.

The outline of the form which is to be followed when the Stations are made in public is indicated by Pope Clement XII in the instruction (§ 5) which he issued on 3 April 1731 on the exercise of the Way of the Cross. At each Station a cleric or a priest is to "read aloud the consideration corresponding to each mystery and Station and having recited a *Pater* and *Ave* and made an act of contrition he continues his way, and from one Station to another the *Stabat mater* or another prayer is sung."

Following this instruction the usual way of making the Way of the Cross solemnly, according to Roman usage and the practice of the Franciscan Fathers, is as follows : The priest, vested in surplice and violet stole,[2] is accompanied by two acolytes in surplice carrying the usual acolytes' candles and a cross-bearer.[3] Having bowed to the image of the sacristy they go in procession to the altar. The priest goes to the foot of the altar, the cross-bearer stands in the middle of the sanctuary between the acolytes. The priest bows low to the cross or genuflects to the Sanctissimum and kneels on the lowest step ; the acolytes and the cross-bearer remain standing.[4] The priest recites the preparatory prayers of whatever form of the Stations is followed. The priest then rises, reverences once more and then all go in procession to the first Station. There they stand in a line, the cross-bearer between the acolytes, the priest nearest the altar and directly in front of the

---

[1] The Sacred Penitentiary, 14 December 1917.

[2] Cf. *Ephemerides Liturgicae*, vol. vii, pp. 21–25.

[3] The Roman practice is to use a large cross made of wood, painted black and having no figure.

[4] The priest may be accompanied by two chanters. These remain all the time with him, one on each side.

Station (or, if room permits, the priest may stand before the acolytes). The priest, having bowed or genuflected to the cross of each Station, says the versicle " We adore thee, O Christ, and we bless thee," to which his assistants and the people answer, " Because by thy holy Cross thou hast redeemed the world." The priest then reads the consideration which is proposed for the particular Station. If a prayer based on the consideration follow he (but not the acolytes and crossbearer) may kneel for it. In any case he kneels for the *Pater, Ave* and short act of contrition which follow the meditation. In some places the *Gloria Patri* [1] is added and the prayer for the dead (" May the souls of the faithful departed, through the mercy of God, rest in peace. R̰. Amen.") Between the Stations the hymn *Stabat Mater* is usually sung. This hymn consists of ten stanzas of two strophes each. As the stanzas ought not to be broken up the best arrangement is to sing one entire stanza after each two Stations (beginning after the first Station). The seventh stanza is then sung after the thirteenth Station and as the priest returns to the foot of the altar the remaining stanzas—or the last (tenth) only—may be sung. If there are concluding prayers in the form of the Way of the Cross which is used (no such prayers are essential for the gaining of the indulgences) the priest recites them kneeling at the foot of the altar. He then rises, receives the cross from the crossbearer, ascends to the foot-pace and with the cross blesses the people, saying the usual form *Benedictio Dei*, etc. He descends to the foot of the altar, restores the cross to the cross-bearer and, having reverenced to the altar or the Sanctissimum, returns in procession to the sacristy.

[1] It should be omitted during the Triduum Sacrum.

PART IV

THE LITURGICAL YEAR

CHAPTER XXIII

ADVENT TO HOLY WEEK

§ 1. ADVENT

THE colour of the season in Advent is violet. The *Gloria in excelsis* at Mass and *Te Deum* at Matins are not said, except on feasts.[1] But *Alleluia* is said in the Office, as usual, and on Sundays at Mass. At Mass of the season the ministers do not wear dalmatic and tunicle, but folded chasubles, except on the third Sunday and Christmas Eve. From 17 December (*O Sapientia*) to Christmas, private votive Masses and private daily Mass for the dead are not allowed.

During Advent (and Lent) the altar is not to be decorated with flowers or other such ornaments ; nor is the organ played at liturgical Offices. But the organ may be played at Benediction since it is for the most part a non-liturgical function ;[2] and it is tolerated, even at Mass, if the singers cannot sing correctly without it. In this case it should be played only to accompany the voices, not as an ornament between the singing.

The exceptions to this rule are the third Sunday of Advent—mid-Advent, " Gaudete " (and the fourth Sunday of Lent—mid-Lent, " Laetare "). On these two days in the year the liturgical colour is rosy (*color rosaceus*).[3] On both days the ministers wear dalmatic and tunicle, the altar is decorated as on Sundays outside Advent (or Lent) and the organ is played. On the week-days after the third Sunday (Monday, Tuesday, Thursday), when the Mass is that of the Sunday, repeated,[4] the colour may be rose, the ministers wear dalmatic and tunicle, the organ is played. The same rule applies to Christmas Eve (see below, p. 246).

[1] According to the general rule, when the " Gloria in excelsis " is not said, the form " Benedicamus Domino " is used at the end of Mass, instead of " Ite, missa est".

[2] There is no law requiring the organ at any time. If a priest thinks well to mark the season by complete silence of the organ at all services during this time he may do so, and does well.

[3] For lack of rosy vestments the usual violet may be used (violet dalmatic and tunicle).

[4] Wednesday, Friday and Saturday are Ember days and have a Mass of their own.

§ 2. THE FOLDED CHASUBLES

THE rules for the use of folded chasubles[1] are these. They are worn in cathedrals and the chief churches [2] by the deacon and subdeacon, instead of dalmatic and tunicle, on days of fasting and penance, except vigils of Saints' days and Christmas Eve, which have dalmatic and tunicle. Folded chasubles therefore are used on Sundays and week-days of Advent and Lent, when the Mass is of the season. Except from this the third Sunday of Advent and the week-days (Monday, Tuesday and Thursday) on which its Mass may be repeated. Except also the fourth Sunday of Lent, Maundy Thursday and (for the deacon) Holy Saturday at the blessing of the Paschal candle and Mass. Folded chasubles are used further on Ember days (except those in the Whitsun octave), on Whitsun Eve before Mass (not at the red Mass), on Candle-mas at the blessing of candles and procession.[3] From this it follows that the folded chasuble is always violet, except on Good Friday, when it is black. But the violet colour does not always involve folded chasubles. On Christmas Eve, on the three Sundays Septuagesima, Sexagesima, Quinquagesima and (for lack of rosy vestments) in some churches on mid-Advent and mid-Lent the ministers wear violet dalmatic and tunicle.

The folded chasubles (not the colour violet) are the test for the organ to be silent.[4]

The chasubles are now folded about half-way up in front.[5] The ministers wear the same vestments as usual, with this one exception. The folded chasubles are taken off when they have some special office to perform. During the last collect the subdeacon takes off his, assisted by the second acolyte, who then lays it on the sedilia. He sings the Epistle in alb and maniple. When he has received the celebrant's blessing and has handed the book to the M.C., he goes to the sedilia and puts on the folded chasuble again, assisted by the second acolyte.[6] He then moves the Missal.

The deacon goes to the sedilia as soon as the celebrant begins to read the Gospel. Here, assisted by the first acolyte, he takes off the folded chasuble, which is laid there. Formerly he folded it lengthwise and put it over his shoulder. It is difficult to do so with the badly made and generally stiff chasubles so much in vogue since the eighteenth century. He is therefore allowed to use instead a broad band of violet silk (black on Good Friday), incorrectly called a " broad stole." [7] As it is not really a stole there is no cross on it.[8] The deacon puts it on

[1] " Planetae plicatae " in the Missal (R.G. xix, 6) and C.E. II, xiii, 3.
[2] Which include collegiate and parish churches (S.R.C. 3352[7]).
[3] Missal, R.G. xix, 6.   [4] S.R.C. 2365[4].
[5] " Plicatae ante pectus " (R.G. xix, 6). The old rule was that they should be folded up the sides as far as the shoulders, thus making them exactly the size of the Baroc chasuble now common.
[6] C.E. II. xiii, 8.
[7] The Missal uses this expression : " aliud genus stolae latioris." The Italians call this strip " stolone."
[8] S.R.C. 3006[7].

over the real stole, from the left shoulder to under the right arm, where he gathers it together with the ends of the girdle. He then takes the Evangeliarium and puts it on the altar as usual. He remains so vested till after the Communion. Then, when he has carried the Missal to the Epistle side, he goes again to the sedilia, takes off the " broad stole " and puts on the folded chasuble, assisted as before by the first acolyte.[1] In putting on and taking off this garment he does not kiss it. It is not really a stole at all. The deacon must wear his stole all the time beneath it. There is no reason why he should not carry out the original plan, namely, to fold his chasuble (or use one previously folded) and wear that in a long strip across his shoulder, if he can do so.[2]

All this rule about folded chasubles need not be observed in smaller churches.[3] If they are not used the subdeacon wears only amice, alb, girdle, maniple ; the deacon wears amice, alb, girdle, maniple, stole. In this case neither makes any change during Mass ; the " broad stole " is not used.

§ 3. CHRISTMAS AND EPIPHANY

CHRISTMAS EVE is a privileged vigil of the first class. If then Christmas Day falls on a Monday, an exception is made to the general rule, that in such cases the vigil is on the Saturday. The Office of 24 December is made up from that of the fourth Sunday of Advent and that of the vigil. At Matins the Invitatory is of the vigil, the hymn, the antiphons, the psalms and versicles of the Sunday ; the lessons of the first and second nocturn are of Sunday with their responses, those of the third (with the preceding verse) of the vigil, without the ninth lesson of Sunday. All the rest of the Office and the Mass are of the vigil, with commemoration of Sunday (but the Gospel of this is not read at the end of Mass). On Christmas Eve the colour is violet ; the ministers wear dalmatic and tunicle. There is only one prayer (unless the vigil occur on a Sunday, then this is commemorated).

The colour for CHRISTMAS is white. On that day (beginning at midnight) every priest may say Mass three times. No special privilege is needed for this (C.J.C. 806, § 1). Three Masses are provided in the Missal, one for the night, one for dawn, one for the day. If a priest says Mass once only, he should choose the one which best corresponds to the hour at which he says it. The same rule will apply to a priest who says two Masses. If he says three he must say the three provided, in their order, at whatever time he says them.[4]

It is not allowed (without special indult) to say a purely private Mass in the night.[5] One Mass only is allowed at midnight, the conventual

---

[1] C.E. II. xiii, 9.
[2] Both the Missal (R.G. xix, 6) and the Ceremonial (II. xiii, 9) propose this first, as the normal way. It is followed in some churches.
[3] Missal (R.G. xix, 7).
[4] But if he sings the third Mass, he may say the first and second later.
[5] C.J.C. 821, § 2.

or parochial one.[1] It should be, if possible, a High Mass ; but a sung, or even a Low Mass is allowed, if it is the one at which the people attend, and is said in default of High Mass. It may not begin before midnight. People are allowed to receive Holy Communion at the midnight Mass, unless the Bishop, for some reason, forbids this.[2] If they do so there is no special rule concerning the Eucharistic fast. The common law remains, that they must be fasting from midnight. It is, however, considered respectful not to eat or drink for some hours before Communion.[3]

If Matins are said or sung in church before midnight Mass, see the rules at pp. 228–229. The celebrant, when he intones the hymn *Iesu redemptor omnium* at Matins, should extend, raise and join the hands, bowing towards the altar.[4]

If a priest says three Masses he must not take the ablutions at the end of the first or second. For the manner of purifying the chalice in this case see pp. 59–60.

At all sung Masses on Christmas Day the celebrant and his ministers kneel on the lowest step in front of the altar or at the Epistle side (or they may kneel before the sedilia) while the choir sings the words *Et incarnatus est de Spiritu Sancto ex Maria virgine : et homo factus est.* If they have not yet left the altar they descend to the second step and kneel and bow on the edge of the foot-pace.

A special clause is inserted in the *Communicantes* prayer of the Canon. In this clause the celebrant says *noctem sacratissimam celebrantes* at the first Mass (at whatever hour he may celebrate) ; at the second and third Masses and during the Christmas octave he says *diem sacratissimum.*

At the Gospel of the third Mass the deacon who reads it, and all, except the subdeacon who holds the book and the acolytes, genuflect at the words *Et Verbum caro factum est*—the deacon towards the book, all others towards the altar. But when, at High Mass, the celebrant reads the Gospel, he does not genuflect. The last Gospel of this third Mass is that of the Epiphany.

Epiphany. The EPIPHANY is, liturgically, one of the three greatest feasts of the year. It is celebrated as a double of the first class with a privileged octave of the second order. Its colour is white. Matins of the Epiphany begin with a special form. The Invitatory is not said, nor *Domine, labia mea aperies,* nor *Deus in adiutorium.* After the silent *Pater noster, Ave Maria* and Creed, the Office begins at once with the first antiphon. This occurs only on the feast itself, not during the octave.

In the Mass a genuflection is made at the words of the Gospel

---

[1] In all religious or pious houses having an oratory with the faculty of keeping habitually the Blessed Eucharist one priest may celebrate three Masses (or only one) on the night of the Nativity. Those present at it will satisfy the precept of hearing Mass and Holy Communion may be given (C.J.C. 821, § 3).

[2] Cf. C.J.C. 821, § 3 ; 867, § 4 ; 869.

[3] When the Holy See permitted an evening Mass on Christmas Eve or non-fasting Communion during the war a fast of four hours was prescribed.

[4] C.E. II. xiv, 5.

Procidentes adoraverunt eum, under the same conditions as noted above for Christmas ; that is, the celebrant does not genuflect when he reads this Gospel if the deacon will sing it later.

In cathedrals and the principal church of each place, after the Gospel the movable feasts of the year are announced. If this is done a white cope is prepared in the sacristy for the priest or deacon who will do so. A lectern stands on the Gospel side of the choir, or the pulpit may be used. The lectern or pulpit is covered with a white veil. The priest or deacon who will announce the feasts goes to the sacristy during the Gradual and puts on the cope over his surplice. He comes out, makes the usual reverences to altar, celebrant and choir, and announces the feasts. The form for doing so, with the chant, is in the Pontifical at the beginning of its third part.

§ 4. CANDLEMAS

CANDLEMAS (the Purification of the Blessed Virgin Mary, February 2) is a double of the second class. On this day candles are blessed and distributed, and a procession is made with them before the principal Mass. The colour of the day is white, but violet is the colour for the blessing of candles and procession. The candles are blessed and the procession made on February 2, even if the feast is transferred.[1]

Supposing first the normal conditions, that is, that High Mass will be celebrated with deacon and subdeacon, the ceremony is arranged in this way : [2]

Preparations. The preparations are : On the credence, all required for High Mass, as usual, covered with a violet veil, also the holy water and sprinkler, and a basin of water, some stale bread (or soap) and a towel for the cleansing of the celebrant's hands after the distribution of the candles. Near by is the processional cross. If another priest will assist to give out the candles a violet stole is required for him. On the sedilia the Mass vestments (white, normally, chasuble, dalmatic tunicle, two stoles and three maniples) are laid out , these, too, should be covered with a violet veil. Near the altar a table stands at the Epistle side, so that the celebrant standing there can easily sprinkle and incense the candles on it. This table is covered with a white cloth, on which the candles lie. They are then covered with white or violet.[3] The altar is prepared for Mass, the six candles are lit. Over the white frontal there should be another of violet. Over the white conopaeum (if the Blessed Sacrament be in the tabernacle) the violet one is put. No flowers or other such ornaments stand on the altar ; the altar-cards are not placed on it till the beginning of Mass. The Missal, covered

---

[1] February 2 may be Septuagesima or a following Sunday or a local double of the first class may fall on that date. In this case the feast is transferred ; the Mass is of Sunday (violet) or occurring feast, and all noted above about changing to white is to be ignored. Lighted candles are not held during the Gospel and from the beginning of the Canon to the Communion.

[2] Cf. C.E. II. xvi, xvii, M.R. I.

[3] " Aliqua mappa munda " is the direction of M.R.I. i.

with violet,[1] stands open at the Epistle side. At the blessing of candles and procession the organ should not be played. Following the usual procession of servers,[2] the celebrant comes from the sacristy in amice, alb, girdle, violet stole and cope, between the ministers, who wear folded chasubles [3] (no maniples), the deacon with his stole. If it is a Sunday the usual Asperges ceremony is first carried out, in violet vestments. The celebrant and ministers bow, as usual, to the choir, bow or genuflect to the altar, go up to it ; the celebrant kisses it (the ministers do not genuflect while he does so) ; then they stand at the Epistle side, the ministers on each side of the celebrant.

Blessing of Candles. They no longer now hold the ends of the cope. The M.C. uncovers the candles. With joined hands all the time (even at *Oremus*, at which, however, the celebrant bows to the cross) the celebrant sings *Dominus vobiscum* and the prayers provided in the Missal for the blessing of candles, all in the simple ferial tone.[4] As he signs the cross over the candles he lays his left hand on the altar and the deacon raises the right side of the cope. While these prayers are said all in choir stand ; the thurifer goes to prepare the thurible, if he has not come with it at the beginning. When the fifth prayer is ended, the thurifer approaches, with (on his right) the first acolyte who carries the holy water and sprinkler. The celebrant puts on and blesses incense as usual, the deacon assisting and holding the incense boat. Meanwhile the subdeacon raises the right end of the cope. When the incense is blessed the deacon hands the sprinkler to the celebrant (solita oscula). He sprinkles (in the centre, to his left and to his right) the candles, saying in the subdued voice the entire antiphon *Asperges me, Domine* only (not the psalm). Then he incenses the candles with three simple swings—towards the centre, to his left and to his right— saying nothing. The thurible and holy water are put back in their places.

Distribution of Candles. The celebrant and ministers go to the middle of the altar, turn to the people, not changing their places. The deacon remains at the celebrant's left. The priest highest in rank— even a bishop, if he be not a " greater prelate " (p. 31)—comes to the altar (not wearing a stole). The M.C. hands him a candle, which he gives to the celebrant, both standing. He kisses the candle first ; the celebrant does so on receiving it ; neither kisses the other's hand. The celebrant gives this candle to the subdeacon, who lays it on the

---

[1] The Roman texts always suppose that books are covered in the colour of the Office (cf. C.E. I. xii, 15). This is often not observed in England. If such a cover is used, it should be changed to white for the Mass.

[2] A M.C., thurifer and acolytes at least are required. There may be others, and clergy. The subdeacon will carry the cross at the procession of candles.

[3] Folded chasubles are not of obligation, except in the principal churches (R.G. xix, 6, 7) ; otherwise the ministers may wear only amice, alb, girdle and the deacon his stole (cf. p. 245).

[4] That is without inflection (*recto tono*), prolonging and softening the final note of the prayer and of the conclusion (cf. O'Connell *The Celebration of Mass*, III. p. 59).

altar or gives it to the M.C. to put on the credence. The celebrant now receives another candle from the deacon and hands this to the priest from whom he received his own.[1] This priest kneels to take it, kissing first the candle, then the celebrant's hand. If he is a canon or prelate he stands and kisses only the candle. He then goes back to his place. The ministers kneel before the celebrant, who gives them candles in the same way. In every case the person who takes the candle kisses it first, then the celebrant's hand.[2] The ministers hand their candles to an acolyte, who puts them on the credence.

The clergy in choir now come up in order and kneel on the foot-pace. The celebrant hands to each a candle in the same way. Canons and prelates do not kneel to receive theirs, nor do they kiss the celebrant's hand, but they do kiss the blessed candle.[3] If canons are present the ministers (unless they, too, are canons) receive their candles after them. The servers and singers also come up to take their candles. This should be arranged so that the singing is not interrupted. The M.C. must see that the candles are brought from the table to the celebrant and handed to him by the deacon.

If the people receive candles, the celebrant, with his ministers, goes to the Communion rail or entrance of the choir and distributes them. Each person kisses first the candle, then the celebrant's hand. Another priest, in surplice and violet stole, may assist in distributing the candles.

During the distribution, beginning as soon as the celebrant has received his candle, the choir sings the antiphon *Lumen ad revelationem gentium*, etc., with the canticle *Nunc dimittis*, as in the Missal and Gradual. The antiphon *Exsurge, Domine*, etc., is sung immediately after the distribution has been completed. Towards the end of the distribution the candles of those in choir are lighted by the acolytes. After the distribution the celebrant washes his hands at the Epistle side of the altar *in plano*; the acolytes serve him, as at Mass, the ministers holding the ends of the cope. Then, ascending by the shorter way and standing at the Epistle side as before, he sings *Oremus* (with hands joined) and the collect *Exaudi, quaesumus Domine* as in the Missal. [If Candlemas comes after Septuagesima, and falls on a weekday, when the celebrant has sung *Oremus*, the deacon adds *Flectamus genua*; all genuflect except the celebrant; the subdeacon, rising first, sings *Levate*, and all rise.] Meanwhile the M.C. or servers light the candles of the celebrant and deacon.

Procession. The procession follows: [4] If the thurifer has laid aside

---

[1] In no case may the deacon or subdeacon give the celebrant his candle. If no other priest is present, a candle is laid on the altar by the M.C. The celebrant takes this from the altar himself, standing, and kisses it (cf. M.R. I, ii, § ii, 2).

[2] This is the rule for things already blessed.

[3] C.E. II. xvii, 2.

[4] If the blessing of the candles is carried out the procession may not be omitted (except when the Blessed Sacrament is exposed). The arbitrary mutilation of a rite is quite unlawful.

the thurible he takes it again during this last prayer. The celebrant, still standing at the Epistle corner, puts on and blesses incense, assisted by the deacon. Then the subdeacon goes to the credence and takes the processional cross ; the acolytes, carrying their candles, go with him and stand at his side by the entrance of the choir, facing the altar. The subdeacon bearing the cross and the acolytes with him do not genuflect. The thurifer goes to stand behind the subdeacon, so as to be first in the procession. The M.C. hands the celebrant's candle to the deacon, who gives it (solita oscula) to the celebrant. Then he gives the deacon his candle, lighted. The celebrant and deacon, at his right, turn towards the people. The deacon sings *Procedamus in pace* ; the choir answers *In nomine Christi. Amen.* The celebrant and deacon come down the altar steps, all genuflect ; [1] the celebrant and deacon put on their birettas. The procession goes in this order : first, the thurifer, then the subdeacon bearing the cross between the acolytes, the choir, clergy, celebrant, with the deacon at his left holding the cope (all carrying their lighted candles in the outside hand). The M.C. may walk at the right of the celebrant (holding the cope) or in front of him. The procession passes around the church, or goes outside,[2] according to the custom of the place. Meanwhile the choir sings the antiphons *Adorna thalamum tuum Sion*, and *Responsum accepit Simeon*, from the Gradual.[3] One of these may be omitted, if there is not time for both. During the procession the church bells should be rung. If Mass is being said at the same time at a side altar, the Sanctus bell should not be rung. On entering the church, if the procession has gone without, the choir sings the responsory *Obtulerunt pro eo Domino par turturum.* If the procession has not left the church this is sung as it comes back to the sanctuary.[4] If the Mass is to be that of the feast, during the procession the sacristan or some assistant removes the violet antependium and conopaeum, the violet cover of the Missal or Missal-stand and the violet veil over the credence, leaving the white coverings, puts on the altar-cards and may put on flowers (if their use is customary). When the procession returns to the sanctuary the clergy genuflect, two and two, bow to each other, and go to their places. The celebrant and deacon come before the altar, hand their candles to the M.C., and make the usual reverence. The thurifer goes to the sacristy to prepare the thurible for Mass, the acolytes put their candles on the credence, the subdeacon puts the cross near, and goes to the celebrant's left. The celebrant and ministers then go to the sedilia. They take off the violet vestments and vest for

---

[1] Except the subdeacon with the cross and acolytes. The celebrant, canons and prelates bow only, if the Sanctissimum is not reserved on the altar.

[2] In the first case it turns to the right outside the sanctuary, goes around and returns to the altar ; in the second case it goes down the church directly to the door (M.R. I. ii, § iii, 5).

[3] Martinucci-Menghini, I. ii, p. 167, § 65, and Vavasseur (II, p. 244) say that the singers do not hold lighted candles. It is a question whether they can do so conveniently while singing from books (see p. 265, n. 1).

[4] " In ipso cancellorum presbyterii ingressu " says M.R. I. ii, § III, n. 7.

Mass, assisted by the M.C. and acolytes. They come to the altar and begin Mass.[1]

Mass. During Mass the candles are held lighted by those in choir during the Gospel, and from after the *Sanctus* to the end of the Communion. The M.C. will see that they are lit in time, first during the Epistle or Gradual, the second time after the choir is incensed at the Offertory. At the sung Gospel the celebrant also holds his candle lit. The M.C. hands it to him (solita oscula), after he has signed himself, at the words *Sequentia sancti Evangelii.* Each time, when the period in question is ended, everyone blows out his candle and lays it down. After the Gospel the celebrant gives his back to the M.C.

If the Mass is not of the Purification the violet ornaments and vestments are retained after the blessing and the candles are not lit nor held during Mass.

If *the Blessed Sacrament be exposed* the candles are blessed at an altar away from the high altar and the procession is omitted.[2]

§ 5. FUNCTIONS IN SMALL CHURCHES

CANDLEMAS is the first of the days concerning which there is a special document, describing how the ceremonies are to be carried out in small churches.

Memoriale Rituum. This document is the MEMORIALE RITVVM of Pope Benedict XIII. In 1725 Benedict XIII issued a *Memoriale Rituum pro aliquibus praestantioribus sacris functionibus persolvendis in minoribus ecclesiis parochialibus.*[3] This considers the ceremonies of six days in the year only, namely, the blessing of candles and procession at Candlemas, the blessing and distribution of ashes on Ash Wednesday, the blessing of palms and procession on Palm Sunday, the ceremonies of Maundy Thursday, Good Friday, Holy Saturday.[4]

By small churches those are meant in which it is not possible to celebrate these functions with the assistance of deacon and subdeacon, of several clerics (or servers) and a competent choir ; the rites described in the document are simplified for the case of a celebrant and three or four servers only. The Memoriale Rituum was not originally issued for all such small churches of the Roman rite throughout the world, but for the smaller parish churches of the city of Rome. Nor is there any general law imposing it on other churches. However, since the Roman diocese is the mistress of all, this document forms the natural standard for similar cases everywhere. Indeed, on at least three occasions the Congregation of Rites has answered a question from

---

[1] The same priest who blesses the candles must celebrate the Mass. Only the Bishop of the diocese may bless the candles and not celebrate the Mass that follows.

[2] Cf. S.R.C. 2621[9].

[3] The M.R. forms a little book in six parts (tituli). A new typical edition was issued in 1920. An English translation of it by Rev. Leonard A. Clark (third edition, 1926, Burns Oates and Washbourne) has been published.

[4] There is one titulus for each of these six days.

some other diocese by saying that the Memoriale Rituum of Benedict XIII is to be followed.[1] The first provincial Synod of Westminster ordered its use in small churches.[2]

The manner of celebrating the rites in this document is exceedingly simple. It supposes as a minimum the assistance of three servers only (four for Holy Saturday). A choir is not necessary, but "if a sufficient number (at least two) of chanters be available, who are capable of properly doing their business, singing may be used in these functions."[3] The Mass which follows is usually a Low Mass, but if circumstances permit it may be a sung Mass.[4] The Mass must be said or sung by the same priest who performs the first part of the function.

Obligation of Blessings. The blessing of candles, ashes and palms is obligatory in cathedral and collegiate and parochial churches. It must take place immediately before (the principal) Mass and in connection with it. It is not of parochial right and may, therefore, take place in the churches of religious and in oratories in which the Blessed Sacrament is reserved. In such oratories and in smaller churches the solemn rite as given in the Missal should be followed when possible, but if the want of clergy or other reasons should make the more solemn rite not feasible, the simpler form of the Memoriale may be followed without indult.[5]

In the following accounts of these days, besides the instructions of the Memoriale Rituum, we add directions for other servers and for the choir, in the case where these can attend.

Rubrics of M.R. It will be noticed below that in some cases, where the description of the ceremonies with deacon and subdeacon does not seem sufficiently explicit in the Missal, Ceremonial of Bishops and other liturgical authorities, the rubrics of the Memoriale Rituum (which are much more detailed than those of the Missal) are quoted to illustrate the point. It is of course true that this document describes a different order. Its rules apply to the case in which there are no deacon and subdeacon, and then (in the first place) only to the smaller parish churches at Rome. But the points in question are such as are not affected by the presence or absence of sacred ministers. The ceremonies of the Memoriale Rituum are intended to be those of the normal full rites simplified. It would be strange if Benedict XIII had intended to make changes in indifferent points common to both cases. Since then his decree is put forth by the same authority as the other liturgical books, we may, no doubt, consult it (with due regard to the necessary modifications) when other documents fail. In the same way all the

---

[1] S.R.C. 2915[1], 2970[5], 4049[1].

[2] Decr. xviii, no. 19 (2nd ed., p. 21).

[3] *Memoriale* (1920), introduction (p. 7).

[4] The introduction to the new edition of the *Memoriale* supposes this when it adds to what is above quoted about the chanters " but in this case (i.e. if singing be used), unless an assisting cleric sing the Epistle, it will suffice if the Epistle be read by the celebrant, and he may sit at the *Kyrie, Gloria* and *Credo*."

[5] This is *not* so in reference to the ceremonies of Maundy Thursday, Good Friday and Holy Saturday (cf. p. 275, *infra*).

approved books of ceremonies quote the rules of the Ceremonial of Bishops (*mutatis mutandis*) for services celebrated by a priest. In the case of processions we apply general rules, noted for some other procession, perhaps in another book (e.g. the Roman Ritual or the Ceremonial), whenever an explicit exception does not occur.

§ 6. CANDLEMAS IN SMALL CHURCHES [1]

THE following preparations must be made beforehand :

On the credence the chalice, with its ornaments, are prepared for Mass.[2] The Mass vestments are made ready at the sedile. If the Mass is of the Purification the colour is white. The holy water and sprinkler are on the credence, the cruets for Mass, a plate with bread, with which to cleanse the celebrant's hands after the distribution of candles and another vessel of water with a dish and towel for this purpose. The Memoriale also requires that a copy of that book be at the credence, from which the celebrant and ministers will recite the chants in the procession. All on the credence is covered with a violet veil.

The altar is covered with a white frontal,[3] and over it a violet one, easily removed, for the blessing of candles. The tabernacle is covered with a violet conopaeum over the white (if the Mass be of the feast) and the Missal-stand has a violet cover over the white one. At the Epistle corner of the altar is a table with a white cloth, on which are the candles to be blessed, covered with a clean cloth (" aliqua mappa munda "). The processional cross and flowers (if customary to use them) are near. In the sacristy are the surplices for the servers (three, according to the Memoriale), the amice, alb, girdle, violet stole and cope for the celebrant, the thurible and incense boat.

If it is a Sunday the Asperges ceremony is held first, in violet vestments.

Blessing of Candles. According to the Memoriale Rituum the function is carried out by the celebrant and three servers only. Of these three one, the first, brings the thurible when it is required at the blessing ; he then lays it aside and, in due time, takes the processional cross and goes in front of the procession. The other two stand on either side of the celebrant during the blessing (the second uncovers the candles at the beginning of it), answer the prayers, hand him the sprinkler for the holy water, assist when he puts on and blesses incense, and finally walk on each side of him, presumably holding the ends of his cope,[4] in the procession. These two, and the celebrant, hold their candles lighted during the procession and recite the chants.

If no other priest is present the first server after the blessing lays a candle on the altar at the centre ; the celebrant goes there, standing takes it, kisses it, and then gives it to the server to keep, till he requires

---

[1] M.R. Tit. I.

[2] If one of the servers is not at least tonsured the celebrant himself must see to this.

[3] Supposing that the Mass is of the Purification. See p. 248, n. 1.

[4] The M.R. does not say this.

it again for the procession. If a priest is present, he gives the candle to the celebrant, who receives it before the altar facing the people, both standing. Before giving it the other priest kisses the candle, the celebrant does so when he receives it. Neither kisses the hand of the other. But this second priest receives his candle from the celebrant in the usual way, kneeling, kissing first the candle, then the celebrant's hand.

There is no difficulty about the blessing. The celebrant—with hands joined—says all the prayers in order, as they are in the Missal, the servers at his side answer. The Memoriale says that, when the candles are blessed, the celebrant sitting with his head covered at the 'Gospel side of the foot-pace may preach to the people about the meaning of the ceremony. When he has taken his own candle, he stands before the Missal at the Epistle side and there recites with the servers the antiphon *Lumen ad revelationem* with the *Nunc dimittis*,[1] etc. Then he gives the candles to the people (having, with the servers, reverenced to the altar before going to the Communion rail).[2] The servers accompany him, right and left, and hand him the candles to distribute. The first brings them from the table. The celebrant then goes back to the altar, washes his hands—the first server pouring the water, the others handing the towel. Then, returning to the Missal, he says the antiphon *Exsurge, Domine*, etc. (unless there be a choir to sing it), *Oremus* and the prayer.[3]

Procession. Finally, taking at the Epistle corner his lighted candle from a server (the other servers, except the first, taking theirs) he turns to the people and says or sings *Procedamus in pace*. The servers (or singers) answer *In nomine Christi. Amen*. The celebrant and servers descend and reverence to the altar. The celebrant puts on his biretta, then carries his candle in the right hand. So the little procession goes, the cross before, borne by the first server.[4] During the procession (unless there be chanters to sing them) the celebrant recites with his assistants the antiphon *Adorna*, and as the procession re-enters the church (if it remains inside, then as it re-enters the sanctuary) *Responsum*. When it comes back to the altar, all make the usual reverence, the celebrant goes to the seat and there takes off the cope and stole, putting on Mass vestments, assisted by the second and third servers. While he does so the first server takes off the violet

---

[1] If there are singers they chant these. The celebrant does not read them but at once distributes the candles (M.R. I. ii, § ii, 3).

[2] M.R. I. ii, § II, 6 says first to the men, then to women. This is not usual in England. If there be clerics present they receive their candles—those of higher rank first—before the people and kneeling on the foot-pace.

[3] If it be after Septuagesima and not a Sunday the celebrant says *Flectamus genua*, he and all genuflecting, and the second server—as he rises before all others—adds *Levate*, when all stand.

[4] The cross-bearer—who does not genuflect before the altar before leaving—leads the procession either without or within the church, according to custom. In the first case he leads it straight down to the door ; in the second he turns to the right outside the sanctuary and going around returns to the altar (M.R. I. ii, § iii, 5). If the people take part in the procession they follow the priest.

frontal, conopaeum and Missal-stand cover so as to expose the white one, removes the violet veil from the credence, and puts vases of flowers between the candles on the altar if their use be customary.[1] Low Mass (or a sung Mass) follows. If the Mass is that of the Purification the servers (and presumably the people) hold the candles lighted during the Gospel, and from after the *Sanctus* to the Communion (inclusive).

More Solemn Form. To this simple ceremony it is possible to make the following additions : There may be a M.C., thurifer, cross-bearer and two acolytes. These acolytes cannot well be the two servers who stand at the celebrant's side (his assistants), because these should walk on either side of him in the procession, whereas the acolytes go in front on either side of the cross. Other servers in surplices may attend, to carry blessed candles and make a longer procession. They may come out from the sacristy in the usual order and stand in the sanctuary during the blessing. All receive candles, but the acolytes, thurifer and cross-bearer cannot carry theirs in the procession. The acolytes hold, not the blessed candles, but those of their office, in candlesticks. Incense will be put on and blessed by the celebrant before the procession begins.

All may be sung as when there are deacon and subdeacon. The celebrant in this case will sing the prayers,[2] the choir answering. He will sing *Procedamus in pace* before the procession. During the procession the choir sings the antiphons provided in the Gradual.

If the procession is not made, the candles should not be blessed.[3] They are blessed and distributed primarily in order to be held during the procession. Indeed, in many countries the candles are given back to the church afterwards. But in England people keep them for use at sick calls, or to burn around the bed of a dying person.

Other candles may be blessed at the same time, not distributed, but used in the course of the year on the altar.

§ 7. SEPTUAGESIMA AND LENT

THE time from Septuagesima to Ash Wednesday partakes in many ways, but not in all, of the character of Lent. The colour of the season is violet from Septuagesima to Easter.[4] The *Te Deum* is not said at Matins, nor the *Gloria in excelsis* at Mass, except on feasts. At the end of Mass the deacon (or celebrant) says *Benedicamus Domino* instead of *Ite, missa est.* In no case is the word *Alleluia* used at all from Septuagesima till it returns at the first Easter Mass on Holy Saturday. On all days (except in the ferial Masses of Tuesday, Thursday and

---

[1] If he be at least tonsured he arranges the chalice on the altar, otherwise the celebrant must take it with him when he is vested for Mass.

[2] These have a long conclusion and are sung to the simple ferial tone (cf. p. 259, n. 1). The prayer after the distribution has a short conclusion and so is sung to the second ferial tone.

[3] It is not lawful to mutilate a ceremony merely to suit one's own convenience.

[4] Except on Mid-Lent Sunday (rosy), Maundy Thursday (white for Mass), Good Friday (black), and Holy Saturday (partly white), as will be noted.

Saturday), even feasts, a Tract takes the place of the *Alleluia* and its verse after the Gradual. In the Office at the end of the response to *Deus in adiutorium—Laus tibi, Domine, rex aeternae gloriae* is said instead of *Alleluia*. But from Septuagesima to Ash Wednesday, although violet is the colour, the ministers use dalmatic and tunicle. The organ may be played then, as during the rest of the year.[1]

From Ash Wednesday to Easter (except on *Laetare* Sunday and Maundy Thursday) the ministers in Masses *de tempore* in greater churches wear folded chasubles ; the organ is silent [2] till the Mass of Holy Saturday (except on mid-Lent).

From Ash Wednesday to the Wednesday of Holy Week there is a special prayer called *Oratio super populum* added in ferial Masses after the post-Communion prayers. The celebrant sings *Oremus*. The deacon turning to the people sings *Humiliate capita vestra Deo*, and the celebrant, turned to the altar, sings the prayer, in the simple ferial tone. In private Masses the celebrant says *Oremus* and *Humiliate*, etc., bowing once towards the cross.[3]

On Ash Wednesday and the three following days the Office is said as on other ferias of the year, though they have special prayers, anti-phons at the *Magnificat* and *Benedictus* and ferial "preces." The Lenten order of the Office does not begin till the first Sunday of Lent.

During Lent private Votive Masses and private Requiem Masses are not allowed. A private Requiem Mass is, however, allowed on the first free day of each week (except in Holy Week).

On mid-Lent Sunday, the fourth of Lent (*Laetare*) rosy-coloured vestments are used, the altar is decorated as for Sundays outside Lent, the organ is played.[4]

Passiontide. During the last fortnight of Lent, from Passion Sunday (Passiontide), the verse *Gloria Patri* in the Office of the season is omitted at the invitatory of Matins, at all responsories, at the Asperges and at the Introit and Lavabo of Mass *de tempore*. The psalm *Iudica me* in Masses *de tempore*, and the Suffrage in the Office are not said. Before the first Vespers of Passion Sunday all statues and pictures (including crucifixes) in the church and sacristy are to be covered with a plain opaque violet veil. No figure or ornament is allowed on these veils. The images are not to be uncovered on any pretext (except the crosses on Good Friday, see p. 294), till the veils are removed at the *Gloria in excelsis* on Holy Saturday. But the Stations of the Cross may remain uncovered.[5]

At High Mass on Lady Day (25 March) the celebrant and ministers come to kneel before the altar, on the lowest step at the Epistle side

[1] This is the general rule, that the organ may be played when the ministers wear dalmatic and tunicle, even if the colour be violet (S.R.C. 2365[4]).

[2] It may be played during *Gloria in excelsis* on Maundy Thursday.

[3] Some authors prescribe one bow to the cross at *Oremus* and another towards the book at *Humiliate*.

[4] The rule is the same as for mid-Advent (see p. 244).

[5] The veiling of crosses and images applies to those on altars or throughout the church which are objects of worship, not to those which are merely ornamental.

(facing north) or at the centre, while the choir sings *Et incarnatus* . . . *et homo factus est*, as at Christmas (see p. 247).

§ 8. ASH WEDNESDAY

THE rite of blessing the ashes is similar to that of blessing candles at Candlemas.[1]

Preparations. The colour is violet for both blessing and Mass. The frontal and conopaeum are violet. Flowers are not used. The altar-cards may either be on the altar from the beginning of the function, or they may be put in their place before Mass begins. The Missal, covered with violet, stands open on the Epistle side ; near it, between the book and the end of the altar, is a vessel containing the ashes (finely powdered and dry) made by burning palms or other foliage blessed on last Palm Sunday. This vessel—"of silver or other ornamental material "[2]—is covered with a lid of similar material or with a violet veil. On the sedilia are the three maniples, and a chasuble for the celebrant. At the credence everything is prepared for Mass, as usual. There is, moreover, the vessel of holy water and sprinkler, the broad stole for the deacon (if the ministers wear folded chasubles), water in a vessel, a basin, towel and plate with dry bread (or soap), that the celebrant may wash his hands after the distribution of ashes. If another priest will assist in distributing the ashes, a violet stole and a second vessel for ashes are made ready for him.

In the sacristy everything is prepared for Mass as usual, except the maniples and the celebrant's chasuble, which are at the sedilia. The celebrant vests in violet stole and cope ; the deacon in violet stole ; he and the subdeacon in folded chasubles.[3]

The function begins after None.[4]

Blessing of Ashes. The procession comes to the sanctuary as usual. The celebrant, between the ministers, goes up to the altar and kisses it in the middle. The ministers do not genuflect. They go to the Missal at the Epistle side and stand there, the celebrant between the ministers, who do not hold the ends of his cope. The ashes are uncovered by the M.C. While the choir sings the antiphon *Exaudi nos, Domine*, etc., the celebrant reads it in a low voice, with joined hands. Meanwhile those in choir sit. Then all stand and remain standing while the ashes

---

[1] C.E. II. xviii, xix ; M.R. Tit. II.

[2] M.R. (cf. C.E. II. xviii, 1).

[3] The folded chasubles are not necessary, except in cathedrals and larger churches. Otherwise the deacon need wear only alb and stole, the subdeacon only the alb (cf. p. 245).

[4] For the convenience of the people it is permitted to bless the ashes early in the morning, outside Mass, before the solemn blessing takes place. A priest vested in surplice and violet stole does this, reciting *Dominus vobiscum* and the four prayers of blessing found in the Missal and sprinkling (but not incensing) the ashes. These ashes may be distributed at any time by a priest vested in surplice and violet stole, or in Mass vestments if the distribution is immediately before or after a private Mass. The priest who blesses ashes outside the solemn blessing may not impose them on himself.

are blessed. The celebrant sings the four prayers, as in the Missal. He chants them in the ferial tone,[1] with joined hands, and does not turn to the people at *Dominus vobiscum.* At the word *Oremus* he bows to the cross. The ministers are at his sides. Meanwhile the thurifer goes to prepare the thurible, and returns with it. When the celebrant blesses the ashes, he lays his left hand on the altar and makes the sign of the cross over them with the right. The deacon holds up the end of the cope. Incense is put on and blessed—the deacon, as usual, saying *Benedicite, Pater Reverende*—the ashes are sprinkled thrice (in the centre, to the celebrant's left and to his right) with holy water, then incensed with three simple swings as always on such occasions. While sprinkling the ashes the celebrant says the entire antiphon *Asperges me, Domine,* without the psalm. He incenses them, saying nothing. The thurible is taken back to the sacristy. While the ashes are distributed the choir sings the antiphons appointed in the Missal and Gradual.

Distribution of Ashes. If another priest is present he gives the ashes to the celebrant. In this case he does not wear a stole. He comes to the altar when the blessing is finished. The celebrant, with the ministers, also comes to the middle and turns to the people ; the ministers change places, passing behind him, so that the deacon shall be on his right as they face the people. The M.C. gives the vessel with ashes to the deacon to hold. The priest who gives the ashes to the celebrant takes some from the dish between the forefinger and thumb of his right hand, and sprinkles them in the form of a cross or with his thumb dipped in them makes the sign of the cross on the celebrant (standing bowed). The rubrics do not define exactly the place where the ashes are put.[2] It is usual, in the case of priests and of all who are tonsured, to put the ashes at the place of the tonsure. Lay people receive them on the top of the head or on the forehead. In the case of women they should be put on the hair or forehead (when this can be conveniently done), not on the headdress. In making the cross with ashes the verse *Memento homo quia pulvis es et in pulverem reverteris* is said.

If no other priest is present the celebrant stands [3] facing the altar, and puts the ashes on himself, in the form of a cross, saying nothing. Neither of the ministers may give the ashes to the celebrant. The celebrant next gives the ashes to the priest from whom he himself received them. This priest kneels on the edge of the foot-pace (if he is a prelate or canon he stands and bows). The deacon hands the dish to the M.C., and kneels before the celebrant ; he and the subdeacon

---

[1] Those with a long conclusion are sung to the simple ferial tone (no inflection) ; those with a short conclusion to the second ferial or semifestal tone (an inflection of a minor third at the end of the prayer and of the conclusion) (Cf. O'Connell, *The Celebration of Mass,* III. p. 59 ; and cf. p. 249, n. 4, *supra*).

[2] The Missal simply says " cineres imponit in capite " ; M.R. says " in modum crucis imponit in capite."

[3] S.R.C., Nov. 1, 1931.

receive the ashes. If canons or prelates are present they receive ashes before the ministers, unless these, too, are canons.

The ashes are then distributed to the clergy in choir, in order. They come before the altar two by two (if their number is unequal the last group is of three). They kneel there—unless they are prelates or canons, in the dress of their rank, when they stand, bowed—while the celebrant puts the ashes on their tonsure or forehead, in the form of a cross, saying to each *Memento*, etc. The deacon holds the vessel of ashes meanwhile at the celebrant's left.

Ashes are then given in the same way to the servers. Lastly they are given to the people at the Communion rail. To do so the celebrant goes there between the ministers having first reverenced at the foot of the altar. The Roman books direct that men should kneel separate from women.[1] This is not the usage in England. When the distribution begins and as long as it continues the choir sings the antiphons (repeating them if necessary) and responsory which are given in the Missal.

While the ashes are distributed the clergy in choir sit as soon as all in their order have received them. If another priest assists, or alone gives out the ashes to the people, the M.C. must put some of them into a vessel for his use, and he will wash his hands after the celebrant.

Final Prayer. When the distribution is over the celebrant goes to the Epistle corner of the altar, and there *in plano* washes his hands. The first acolyte holds the plate with bread (or soap), the second the water and dish, with the towel over his arm. The ministers at the celebrant's sides hold the ends of his cope. Then ascending by the shorter way to the Epistle corner of the altar, the celebrant sings (with joined hands) *Dominus vobiscum* and the last prayer, as in the Missal. The ministers stand at his side as before. They then go straight to the sedilia, without reverence to the cross, and there the celebrant takes off the cope, putting on the maniple and chasuble ; the ministers put on their maniples. The M.C. and acolytes assist them.

Mass. Mass follows as usual and must be celebrated by the priest who blessed the ashes.[2] The subdeacon removes his chasuble to sing the Epistle and afterwards puts it on again. When the celebrant reads the verse *Adiuva nôs* in the Tract he does not genuflect. He says the Gospel, then, returning to the middle, kneels there, between the ministers, while the choir sings the entire verse *Adjuva nos . . . nomen tuum.* The deacon takes off the folded chasuble (if he wears it) and puts on the " broad stole "[3] before he takes the Gospel book to put it on the altar. He puts on the chasuble again after the Communion (see p. 245).

After the last Postcommunion the celebrant sings *Oremus*, the deacon, with joined hands, turns to the people, sings *Humiliate capita*

---

[1] M.R. II. ii, § 11, 4.
[2] Only the Bishop of the diocese may bless ashes and not celebrate the Mass that follows.
[3] If he does not use the folded chasuble, neither does he use a " broad stole."

vestra Deo, then turns back to the altar. The celebrant sings the *Oratio super populum.*[1]

If the Blessed Sacrament be exposed the ashes must be blessed at an altar away from that of the Exposition (S.R.C. 4057[6]).

§ 9. ASH WEDNESDAY IN SMALL CHURCHES

THE Memoriale Rituum (Title II) in its description of this ceremony has almost the same account as is already given above.[2] That is to say, the ministers have so little to do on Ash Wednesday that the description above will do for this case too, with the obvious exception that their part is left out. The servers assist at the incensing and sprinkling of ashes. A server holds the vessel of ashes by the celebrant while he distributes them. According to the Memoriale Rituum the celebrant, with the servers, recites the antiphons, if there is no one to sing them,[3] as soon as he himself has received the ashes. If there is a choir they will sing the same parts as when there are deacon and subdeacon.

---

[1] What is left of the blessed ashes is to be thrown into the sacrarium afterwards.

[2] The rubrics of the present edition of M.R. are very detailed and speak for themselves.

[3] The ant. *Exaudi nos,* at the beginning of the blessing, is recited alone in a low tone by the celebrant, if it is sung by the choir (M.R.).

CHAPTER XXIV

THE FIRST PART OF HOLY WEEK

§ 1. PALM SUNDAY [1]

THE normal rites of Palm Sunday suppose that the celebrant is assisted by deacon and subdeacon, that the Mass is a High Mass.

The persons who take part in the service are the celebrant, deacon and subdeacon, three other deacons who will chant the Passion, two Masters of Ceremonies,[2] thurifer, two acolytes, torch-bearers, clergy in choir who receive palms and form the procession. It is supposed that the singers are among these.

Preparations. The following preparations are made beforehand :

The altar is prepared for Mass, with the cross (veiled in Passiontide), six candles and Missal open at the Epistle side.

The altar-cards may be on the altar from the beginning of the ceremony, or may be placed there by one of the Masters of Ceremonies while the celebrant vests for Mass. If it is the custom, branches of palm or olive may decorate the altar between the candles in the place where flowers are put on feasts.[3]

At the credence everything for High Mass is prepared as usual.

Further, another vessel of water, basin and towel (with some soap if necessary) are put here, that the celebrant may wash his hands after distributing the palms ; the so-called " broad stole " for the deacon, if he uses a folded chasuble ; also the holy water and sprinkler. The processional cross (covered with violet) stands near the credence, and by it a violet ribbon to tie a palm to it. Near the altar, at the Epistle side,[4] a table is prepared, covered with a white cloth and on this the palms [5] are laid out.

The sedilia should be covered in violet. On it the chasuble and three maniples are laid. If lecterns will be used for the singing of the Passion, they may be set up beforehand or brought out during the Tract of the Mass. Three are used, in a line at a little distance from

---

[1] C.E. II. xxi ; M.R. tit. III.

[2] The chief office of the second M.C. will be to attend to the deacons who sing the Passion.

[3] The M.R. (III. i) prescribes this for the smaller churches of Rome : " Rami palmarum, loco florum, inter candelabra."

[4] The rubric in the Missal (on Palm Sunday) says : " in the middle before the altar, or at the corner of the Epistle." It is now always at the Epistle side.

[5] The rubrics of the liturgical books speak of " palmae seu rami olivarum " (C.E.) ; " rami palmarum et olivarum, sive aliarum arborum " (Missal). The prayers of the blessing use similar terms. C.E. (II. xxi, 2) also speaks of little crosses made of palm leaves. C.E. directs that palms be used at least for the Bishop and other important persons.

one another, at the place where the Gospel is sung. They may be bare or covered in violet.

In the sacristy the vestments are laid out for the celebrant and ministers. The celebrant will wear amice, alb, girdle, violet stole and cope ; the deacon amice, alb, girdle, violet stole and folded chasuble ; the subdeacon amice, alb, girdle and folded chasuble. In the sacristy, or other convenient place, the vestments are prepared for the three deacons who will sing the Passion. They wear amice, alb, girdle, violet maniple and (ordinary) stole. The book—covered in violet— out of which the Passion will be sung will be at hand for the deacon who acts as Narrator.

The ceremony begins after Terce. The Asperges (at which the *Gloria Patri* is omitted) takes place first. Then the acolytes bring maniples to the ministers and help them to put them on.

Blessing of Palms. The celebrant goes up to the altar between the ministers. He kisses it in the middle. All go to the Epistle side and M.C. uncovers the palms. Here the celebrant stands between the ministers and reads the first antiphon *Hosanna filio David* in a low voice. Meanwhile it is sung by the choir ; and during the chant the clergy in choir sit. Then all stand ; the celebrant at the same place, not turning to the people and with hands still joined, sings *Dominus vobiscum,* and the collect, in the simple ferial ,tone. As soon as he begins, the subdeacon comes down from the foot-pace to his place behind the celebrant. He stands here, facing the altar, and assisted by the second acolyte he takes off his chasuble and the second M.C. hands him the book of lessons. When the collect is finished, he comes to the middle, accompanied by the second M.C. They genuflect to the altar, bow to the choir, as usual, and go to the place where the Epistle is sung, some distance away from the foot of the altar. All in choir sit. The subdeacon sings the lesson. He again makes the usual reverences to the altar and choir, comes to receive the celebrant's blessing, kissing his hand, as at Mass, puts on again the folded chasuble and goes back to the celebrant's left. The celebrant may read the lesson, one of the responsories, say the *Munda cor meum* and read the Gospel, all at the Epistle side.[1] After the lesson the choir sings one of the responsories provided " for a Gradual." [2] The deacon goes down to the sedilia when the subdeacon has been blessed, takes off the folded chasuble and puts on (a rolled-up chasuble or) the " broad stole," assisted by an acolyte. The second M.C. hands him the book of lessons. He puts this in the middle of the altar, as at High Mass goes to the right of the celebrant and assists as usual while incense is put on and blessed. The subdeacon then goes down to the middle and waits there. The deacon kneels on the edge of the foot-pace and

[1] The celebrant keeps his hands joined all the time, bows low towards the cross while reciting *Munda* and *Dominus sit,* and does not kiss the book at the end of the Gospel.

[2] Rubric of the Missal. During the chanting of the lesson and the responsory the clergy in choir sit. They stand for the Gospel and what follows.

says the *Munda cor meum.* He asks and receives the celebrant's blessing, as at Mass. He sings the Gospel exactly as at High Mass, the subdeacon holding the book, the thurifer, acolytes with candles and M.C. accompanying him. He incenses the book ; the celebrant stands facing him at the Epistle side. The celebrant afterwards kisses the book and is incensed, as at Mass. The deacon takes off the " broad stole " and maniple, and puts on the folded chasuble. The subdeacon takes off his maniple ; the maniples are put at the sedilia. The ministers stand again on either side of the celebrant. The celebrant, at the Epistle side, chants the prayer that follows in the Missal (in the simple ferial tone) and the Preface, keeping his hands joined. The choir answers. The choir sings *Sanctus* ; the celebrant and ministers say it in a low voice, bowing. The prayers for blessing the palms follow. They are sung with hands joined and in the ferial tone,[1] by the celebrant. When he makes the sign of the cross over the palms with his right, he rests his left on the altar, and the deacon holds up the end of the cope. Incense is put on and blessed, the palms are sprinkled thrice with holy water—in the centre, to the celebrant's left and to his right—while the celebrant says in the subdued voice *Asperges me, Domine* (without the psalm) ; the palms are incensed thrice (with simple swings) by the celebrant in silence, as on all similar occasions. When the palms have been incensed the thurifer takes the thurible back to the sacristy, unless the procession will follow very soon. The celebrant sings *Dominus vobiscum* and the final prayer of the blessing.

Distribution of Palms. When the palms are blessed the distribution follows. The celebrant and ministers come to the middle of the altar, and turn so as to face the people. If the clergy are present the highest in rank (not wearing a stole) comes to the foot-pace, takes a palm from the M.C., kisses it and hands it to the celebrant, who kisses it on receiving it, then gives it to the subdeacon to lay on the altar. Both stand ; neither kisses the hand of the other. The celebrant then first gives a palm to this priest. He receives it kneeling on the foot-pace, and kisses first the palm, then the celebrant's hand. If he is a canon or prelate he stands to receive his palm, and does not kiss the celebrant's hand. If no other priest be present, the deacon lays a palm on the altar. Standing, the celebrant takes it thence, kisses it and hands it to the subdeacon, who lays it again on the altar.[2] The ministers kneeling (unless they are canons) on the top step now receive their palms from the celebrant (handed to him by the M.C.). If the Chapter is present the ministers receive them after the canons, [3] unless they too are canons. They place their palms on the altar, or hand them to an acolyte. The deacon now stands at the left of the celebrant. He takes palms from an acolyte or the M.C. and hands them to the

---

[1] See p. 259, n. 1.

[2] Neither of the ministers (even though a priest) may give the palm to the celebrant.

[3] The canons receive the palm standing. They kiss it but not the celebrant's hand.

celebrant for distribution. The subdeacon on the right holds the end of the cope. Palms are given to the clergy in choir. They come up two and two (if there is an uneven number the last group is of three) and take the palms from the celebrant, as they kneel on the edge of the foot-pace, kissing first the palm, then the celebrant's hand. Those in choir sit as soon as all in their order have received palms. Palms may now be given to the servers and then to the people at the Communion rail or entrance of the sanctuary, beginning on the Epistle side. The celebrant does this, with the ministers at his sides, having first at the foot of the steps reverenced to the altar. Or it may be done by another priest, who will wear a surplice and violet stole and begin the distribution at the same time as the celebrant. When the distribution begins, and until it ends (repeating them if necessary) the two antiphons *Pueri Hebraeorum* are sung by the choir. While the palms are distributed a server ties one to the processional cross.

The celebrant and ministers go back to the altar, reverence to the cross and go to the Epistle side ; the celebrant washes his hands (at the credence if he had gone down to distribute palms to the people, otherwise at the Epistle corner of the foot-pace), then standing between the ministers (having returned *per breviorem* if he had been *in plano*) he sings—with hands joined—*Dominus vobiscum* and the prayer.

Procession. While he does so the procession is formed. The thurifer brings the thurible to the sanctuary, if he has put it away, and comes to the top step at the Epistle corner. Incense is put in and blessed as usual, the ministers assisting. The subdeacon takes the processional cross. Preceded by the thurifer he goes with the acolytes to stand at the entrance of the sanctuary, facing the altar. Neither the cross-bearer nor the acolytes with him genuflect.

The deacon takes the celebrant's palm from the M.C. and gives it to the celebrant with the solita oscula. Then he takes his own. The thurifer stands behind the cross-bearer, so as to be in front of him when all turn round ; the deacon turns to the people, at the celebrant's right, and sings *Procedamus in pace*. The choir answers *In nomine Christi. Amen.* The procession moves off in this order : First the thurifer with smoking thurible, then the subdeacon carrying the cross between the acolytes with their candles, then the singers,[1] and the clergy in choir. These come out from their places two and two, genuflect before the altar and join those before them. The M.C. may go immediately before the celebrant, or at his right (holding the cope). Before leaving the altar the celebrant and deacon, having come down from the foot-pace, make the usual reverence. The deacon takes the celebrant's biretta from the M.C. and hands it to him with the solita oscula, then takes his own. Both celebrant and deacon cover themselves. The

---

[1] Some authors (e.g. Martinucci, I. ii, p. 184, § 74) say that the singers do not carry palms. This seems to be only because they think that a man cannot both hold a palm and a book to sing from. There is no reason why the singers should not hold palms, if they can do so conveniently. Indeed, the rubric of the Missal says : " omnes cum ramis in manibus " ; so does the C.E. II. xxi, 8.

deacon walks at the celebrant's left, holding the end of the cope in his right, his palm in his left. In the procession everyone holds the palm in the outer hand. Meanwhile the choir sings all or some of the antiphons appointed. During the procession the church bells should be rung.

Gloria, Laus. The procession goes outside the church and turning by the right proceeds some distance. The doors are then closed. On the return of the procession the order before the church doors is this: The subdeacon (holding the cross facing forward as usual) with an acolyte on either side is immediately before and facing the doors, the thurifer stands to the right of the first acolyte. The celebrant and

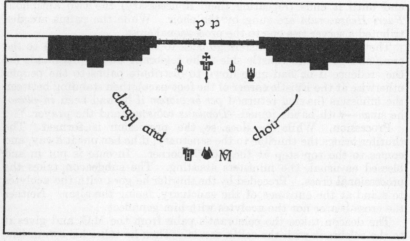

FIG. 36. PALM SUNDAY : THE PROCESSION BEFORE THE
CHURCH DOORS

The ministers wear folded chasubles. The deacon is at the celebrant's
left, except while actually ministering to him

deacon (both covered) stand behind the subdeacon, also facing the door, but at some distance from it. The choir and clergy form lines, one on either side, between the celebrant and the door ; or they make a wide semicircle around.

Meanwhile two or more cantors [1] remain inside. They should separate themselves from the rest of the choir when the procession leaves the church. These cantors inside, facing the closed doors, sing the first verse of the hymn *Gloria, laus et honor*. The celebrant and those without repeat the same verse. The cantors within sing the following verses,[2] those without after each repeat the first, *Gloria,*

---

[1] Missal rubric : " duo vel quatuor cantores " ; C.E. II. xxi, 8 : " aliqui cantores."

[2] They may sing all of them or some only (so the rubrics of the Missal, Ceremonial and *Memoriale*).

laus et honor tibi sit, Rex Christe redemptor, etc. When all is sung, the subdeacon strikes the door with the lower end of the processional cross. It is opened by those within. The procession enters, singing the responsory *Ingrediente Domino*.

Return of Procession. If it is impossible that the procession go outside the church this ceremony must be performed at the entrance of the sanctuary. If there are gates to the sanctuary, they are shut, instead of the church doors.[1] Outside the church all who have birettas may wear them (except the subdeacon, the M.C., acolytes and thurifer). It is better that they (except the celebrant and deacon) should uncover during the singing of the hymn *Gloria, laus*. Inside the church only the celebrant and deacon wear the biretta. They too uncover when they enter the choir. Before the altar the thurifer genuflects and either takes the thurible to the sacristy, or waits at the side for the beginning of Mass. The subdeacon with the cross and acolytes do not genuflect ; they go to the credence. The subdeacon here puts the cross near, and comes to the sedilia, where he waits for the celebrant and deacon. The acolytes put their candles on the table and stay there. The members of the choir genuflect, two and two, bow to each other and go to their places. The M.C., celebrant and deacon come to the altar, genuflect (if the Sanctissimum is not there the celebrant bows low), and go to the sedilia. Here the deacon takes the celebrant's palm (solita oscula) and hands it, with his own, to the M.C., who puts them on the credence. The subdeacon is already at the seat. They vest for Mass, the celebrant putting on maniple and chasuble ; the ministers their maniples.

Mass. The Mass—which must be celebrated by the priest who blesses the palms [2]—is celebrated according to the rules for Passiontide (p. 257) with the following special points. The celebrant, when he reads the Epistle, does not genuflect. When the subdeacon reads it he, the celebrant, deacon and all in choir genuflect at the words *Ut in nomine Iesu* to *infernorum*. Having sung the Epistle and received the blessing the subdeacon resumes the folded chasuble and stands on the deacon's right, as at the Introit. While the Tract is sung the celebrant (having read it) and ministers may sit at the seat.

Chanting of Passion. The chief feature of this Mass is that the Passion is not sung by the deacon who assists the celebrant, but by three other deacons. Of these three deacons one sings all the narrative ; he is called the Narrator. Another sings the words spoken by our Lord, and is called Christus. The third sings whatever is spoken by the crowd or by anyone else. He is generally called the Synagoga.[3] In case of necessity the celebrant himself—at the Gospel corner of the

---

[1] If the entrance to the sanctuary has no gates the subdeacon strikes the floor with the cross ; the opening of the doors must be left to pious imagination.

[2] Only the Bishop of the diocese may bless the palms if he is not going to celebrate the Mass that follows.

[3] So in editions of the Passion for use in Holy Week the three parts are generally marked : " N, C (or +), S."

altar and wearing the chasuble—may sing the words of Christ ; there
are then but two deacons of the Passion.[1] The choir (of clerics or even
laymen, but not of nuns) may sing the words said by the crowd (the
" Turba ") ; [2] but this does not dispense with the Synagoga deacon,
though it reduces what he has to sing to very little.   He will then take
the part of Pilate, or of any other one person who speaks.

While the Gradual is sung, the deacons of the Passion go to the
sacristy, or other place where their vestments are laid out, and vest in
amice, alb, girdle, violet maniple and stole from the left shoulder, as
always worn by deacons.   If lecterns are used, these are meanwhile
set up in a straight line, at a little distance from one another, at that
place in the sanctuary where the Gospel is sung at High Mass and the
books (if more than one is used) of the Christus and Synagoga deacons
laid on them.[3]   The lecterns may be covered with violet cloths.

The Ceremonial of Bishops (II. xxi, 15) does not suppose that lecterns
be used.[4] It directs that the three deacons sing from one book, held
by three servers, one standing before each deacon, who pass it to one
another as the parts change.   In this case, the deacons of the Passion
come out towards the end of the Tract, the Narrator holding the book
(the opening towards his left).   The second M.C. goes before them,
then the Narrator, the Synagoga, and the Christus one after the other.
Each wears his biretta.   The three servers follow one beside the other,
with hands joined.   The deacons uncover at the entrance of the choir,
handing their birettas to the M.C. or to the three servers.   They form
a line (the Narrator in the centre, the Christus on his right, the Synagoga
on the Narrator's left), genuflect and then bow to the choir.   Then
they go to stand at the usual place for singing the Gospel.   The three
servers stand facing them, the Narrator is in the middle here, the
Christus at his right, the Synagoga at his left, the second M.C. at the
left of the Synagoga deacon, a little behind him.   •

If lecterns are used, the three servers need not accompany the
deacons ; if they do they stand behind the lecterns.   If three books
are used the Narrator brings his book with him, the other two are
arranged beforehand on the lecterns.

The Narrator begins at once *Passio Domini nostri Iesu Christi
secundum Matthaeum.*   Without further ceremony they sing the
Passion, with joined hands.   All in choir and in church stand as they
do so ; and all hold their palms, except the deacons of the Passion and

---

[1] It is even allowed, if the subdeacon is ordained deacon, that the ministers of
Mass take off the folded chasubles (the subdeacon puts on a deacon's stole) and
sing two parts of the Passion at the usual place, the celebrant singing the
" Christus " at the altar.   But there must be three men, ordained deacon, to sing
the Passion.   Otherwise the celebrant (not holding his palm until the deacon
sings the Gospel) reads it aloud at the Gospel side, the deacon and subdeacon by
him as at the Introit, and the deacon sings the last part only (cf. M.R. III, ii,
§ IV, 4).

[2] S.R.C. 2169 and 4044[2].

[3] Unless this was done before the service began (see p. 262).

[4] But S.R.C. (3804[3]) permits their use and the use of three books.

servers who hold the book. Meanwhile the celebrant, deacon and sub-deacon—holding their palms—stand at the Epistle corner of the altar, as at the Introit. The celebrant reads the Passion in a low voice. He does not genuflect when he reads the words *emisit spiritum*. When

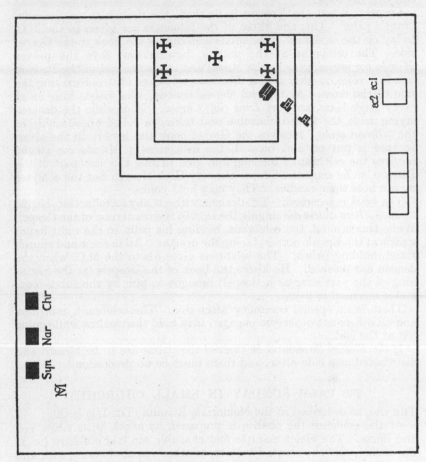

FIG. 37. PALM SUNDAY (AND GOOD FRIDAY) : THE PASSION
The ministers wear folded chasubles

he has finished, he and the ministers (who go one behind the other as at the Collect of the Mass) turn to face the deacons of the Passion, and stand there in line holding their palms in the right hand. At the Holy Name they bow to the cross. As the words *emisit spiritum* are sung by the Narrator they kneel where they are, facing towards the altar ; the deacons of the Passion kneel facing their books. Everyone

in church kneels and pauses for a short time. On a signal from the
M.C. the Narrator rises first [1] and all rise with him. The deacons of
the Passion continue the text to the part to be sung by the deacon of
the Mass. Then they leave the sanctuary as they came, the Narrator
carrying his book.

Gospel. When the Passion is finished, the deacon takes the celebrant's palm. This and those of the ministers are given to the M.C.
to lay on the credence. The subdeacon carries the book to the Gospel
side. The celebrant at the middle, bowing low, says the prayer
Munda cor meum, goes to the Missal and reads the end of the Passion
in a low voice, neither saying *Dominus vobiscum*, etc., nor making the
sign of the cross. At the end the subdeacon, who assists him, as at
every High Mass, answers *Laus tibi, Christe*. Meanwhile the deacon,
laying aside the folded chasuble and taking a rolled-up chasuble or
the " broad stole," receives the Gospel book and lays it on the altar.
Incense is put on and blessed, the deacon says *Munda cor meum*,
receives the celebrant's blessing and goes to sing this last part of the
Passion, as he sings the Gospel at every High Mass. But the acolytes
do not hold their candles. They may hold palms.

The book is incensed. The deacon, without any introduction, begins
at once *Altera autem die* singing the text to the usual tone of the Gospel.
While this is sung, the celebrant, holding his palm in the right hand,
stands at the Epistle corner, facing the deacon. All in choir and church
stand, holding palms. The celebrant gives his to the M.C. when the
deacon has finished. He kisses the book of the Gospels (at the beginning of the part sung as a Gospel) brought to him by the subdeacon,
and is incensed as usual.

There is no special ceremony after this. The celebrant, ministers
and all others not otherwise engaged may hold their palms while going
out at the end.

If the Blessed Sacrament be exposed the palms are to be blessed and
distributed at a side altar, and there must be no procession.[2]

§ 2. PALM SUNDAY IN SMALL CHURCHES

THE rite, as described in the Memoriale Rituum (Tit. III) is this :

At the credence the chalice is prepared, as usual, with violet veil
and burse. The violet maniple and chasuble are laid out here (or at
the sedile), also the cruets for Mass, another vessel of water, dish and
towel to wash the hands after the distribution of palms, and a copy of
the Memoriale Rituum to use if the chants are to be recited in procession. The altar is vested in violet, the Missal is covered in violet silk,
palms instead of flowers stand between the candles.[3] At the Epistle
corner is a table covered with a white cloth, on which are the palms to
be blessed. The processional cross stands near, veiled in violet ; and
at hand a violet ribbon with which to tie a blessed palm to it. In the

---

sacristy three surplices are prepared for the servers, a surplice, amice, alb, girdle, violet stole and cope for the celebrant, also lighted charcoal for the thurible and the holy water.

There are supposed to be only three servers and the celebrant. If a choir is available, the Memoriale indicates what may be sung.

Blessing of Palms. The first server comes first to the altar, holding the holy-water vessel and sprinkler. He is followed by the celebrant between the other two. The Asperges is performed as usual. The celebrant goes up to the altar between the second and third servers, kisses it in the middle, goes to the Epistle side and here, standing between these two servers, he says, "in a loud and even voice," [1] (if there is no choir) the first antiphon, *Hosanna filio David.* The servers continue it with him. If the choir sings the antiphon the celebrant recites it by himself in a low tone. He says (with joined hands) *Dominus vobiscum* and the collect, lesson, one of the responsories (*Collegerunt pontifices* or *In monte*),[2] *Munda cor meum* (bowing) and Gospel, all at the same place. He kisses the book after the Gospel saying *Per evangelica,* etc. The celebrant continues, saying *Dominus vobiscum,* the prayer and the Preface (all the time with joined hands) and, bowed and with the servers, the *Sanctus.* The five prayers in the Missal follow in order. While he says them the first server goes out and brings the thurible. While he says the fifth prayer the third server takes the holy water from the credence. Assisted by the servers the celebrant puts on and blesses incense, sprinkles the palms (in the centre, to his left and to his right) saying in the subdued voice, *Asperges me,* without the psalm, and incenses the palms with three single swings, saying nothing. Then he adds *Dominus vobiscum* and the sixth prayer. Sitting, the celebrant now may preach to the people.[3]

Distribution of Palms. The first server then takes a palm and puts it on the altar. Standing before the altar the celebrant takes it for himself, kisses it, and gives it to the first server to put, for the present, on the credence. If another priest is present he gives the palm to the celebrant. Both stand, the celebrant with his back to the altar, facing the other priest. The priest who gives the palm kisses it first ; the celebrant does so on receiving it. Neither kisses the hand of the other. Having taken his palm, the celebrant goes to the Epistle corner and there recites with the servers the two antiphons, *Pueri Hebraeorum.* If the choir sings them the celebrant proceeds at once to the distribution of the palms. He comes to the middle, and gives palms to the servers. If another priest is present he receives his first.

The celebrant descends, reverences to the altar and distributes the palms to the people at the Communion rail, beginning at the Epistle side. Everyone receives the palm kneeling, and kisses first the palm then the celebrant's hand. The Memoriale says that palms are to be

---

[1] M.R. III. ii, § i, 6.
[2] He says one responsory with the servers ; if the choir sings, it, he recites it alone at the same time (M.R.).
[3] M.R. III. ii, § I, 19.

given first to men, then to women. The celebrant washes his hands at the Epistle corner *in plano*, the servers assisting. He goes by the shortest way to the Missal at the Epistle corner and says *Dominus vobiscum* and the prayer before the procession. Meanwhile the first server ties a palm branch to the processional cross. He then hands their palms to the celebrant and the other servers, and (if there are no chanters) copies of the book from which they will recite the antiphons during the procession.

Procession. The celebrant, standing in the middle with his back to the altar and holding his palm in the right hand, says (or sings) *Procedamus in pace* ; the servers (or choir) answer *In nomine Christi. Amen.* The celebrant (or a chanter) begins the antiphon *Cum appropinquaret*, and continues it with the servers. Meanwhile the first server has taken the processional cross and stands with it at the entrance of the sanctuary, facing the altar. He turns without first genuflecting. The procession proceeds, first the cross-bearer, next singers, if there are any, then the celebrant (having made due reverence before the altar) covered, between the other two servers, reciting the antiphons alternately (if there is no choir). They go outside the church. The second and third servers go in (if there are no chanters). The door is shut, they stand inside, facing the door. The cross-bearer stands without, facing the door, the celebrant behind him.

Gloria, Laus. The servers within recite (or chanters sing) wholly or in part the hymn *Gloria laus*, the celebrant [1] (or singers) without in reply repeat the first verse each time. When this is finished the first server knocks at the lower part of the door with the foot of the cross. It is opened by those within. The cross-bearer enters, followed (by the singers and) by the celebrant, who (if there are no chanters) begins the responsory *Ingrediente Domino.* The second and third servers join him on either side as he enters and recite with him the responsory (unless it be sung). So they go up the church. Before the altar the first server puts aside the cross and takes the palms from the celebrant and others. If the responsory is not finished by the time they arrive before the altar, they stand there first to finish it. The celebrant goes to the seat and vests for Mass, assisted by the servers. Then he is to sit for a little.[2] The first server (if a cleric) takes the chalice to the altar ; otherwise the celebrant himself must see to it. Mass follows as usual.

Mass. The Passion is read at the Gospel side. The celebrant does not say *Munda cor meum*, etc., till before its last part. While he reads the Passion the servers may hold their palms. At the end of the Gospel the celebrant, saying *Per evangelica*, etc., kisses the book and the server answers *Laus tibi, Christe*. During the Communion antiphon the first server (if a cleric) takes the chalice from the altar to the credence. After Mass the servers arrange everything.

---

[1] " Tecto capite " (M.R.).

[2] M.R. III. ii, § iv, 2. This constant provision, that the celebrant, being tired, is to sit and rest in the middle of ceremonies, need not be observed if he is not tired.

§ 3. THE FUNCTION WITH CHOIR

ACCORDING to what we have noted above about churches where the deacon and subdeacon cannot assist, if this ceremony is to be made more solemn, after the manner of a sung Mass (which sung Mass will follow it), the following additions may be made. There may be more servers, a M.C., cross-bearer, thurifer,[1] two acolytes, the two who accompany the celebrant,[2] and others who will carry palms in the procession, of whom some will serve as torch-bearers at Mass. All will be sung, as when there are ministers. Two or more cantors sing the *Gloria laus* within the church, the rest of the choir answering without.

At the Mass the celebrant reads the first part of the Passion, in an audible voice, at the Gospel side. He comes to the middle of the altar, puts on and blesses incense,[3] says *Munda cor meum*, goes back to the book on the Gospel side, incenses the book, and sings the last part of the Passion in the usual Gospel tone. The acolytes do not hold candles at this Gospel. All the rest of Mass follows the rules of Missa Cantata. A lector may read the first lesson at the blessing of palms and the Epistle at Mass.

§ 4. PRIVATE MASS ON PALM SUNDAY

IN a private Mass on Palm Sunday the celebrant says the Passion at the Gospel side. He bows his head when crossing the centre of the altar (and does not genuflect even if the Blessed Sacrament be present.)[4] He does not say *Munda cor meum* till before its last part. He begins the Passion with joined hands : *Passio Domini nostri Iesu Christi secundum Matthaeum* with no other ceremony. At the words *emisit spiritum* he kneels for a short time before the book. All in church kneel too. After the words *contra sepulchrum* he goes to the middle, there says *Munda cor meum* etc., as usual, goes back to the book and finishes the Passion, not making the sign of the cross. At the end he kisses the book, at the beginning of the part read as the Gospel ; the server answers *Laus tibi, Christe*. At the end of a private Mass, instead of the Gospel of St. John, the celebrant reads the Gospel *Cum appropinquasset*, otherwise read at the blessing of palms.

§ 5. MONDAY, TUESDAY AND WEDNESDAY IN HOLY WEEK

DURING Holy Week (indeed, during the Easter octave too, that is, from the first Vespers of Palm Sunday to the second Vespers of Low Sunday) no other Office or Mass may be said than those of the season. No feast is commemorated from Maundy Thursday to Easter Tuesday.

---

[1] If the thurifer attends the procession, incense is put on and blessed first; he goes in front of the cross.

[2] As far as the ceremonies are concerned, if there are a M.C., thurifer, and acolytes, these two assistants are not really needed. The acolytes may wash the celebrant's hands after the distribution of palms.

[3] Presuming that there is an indult for the use of incense at Sung Mass.

[4] S.R.C. 3975[2].

On the Monday, Tuesday and Wednesday following Palm Sunday everything is done according to the rules for Passiontide (p. 257), and as noted further in the Missal and Breviary (or Holy Week book). On Tuesday the Passion according to St. Mark is read or sung at Mass, on Wednesday the Passion according to St. Luke. Whether the Passion be read or sung, the same rules are observed as on Sunday (pp. 267–270).

NOTE : BINATION IN HOLY WEEK

IF a priest has the right and duty of saying two Masses on Palm Sunday, usually he can obtain from the Ordinary [1] permission to omit the reading of the Passion (except the last part) in *one* of the Masses (at choice). In this case he reads the last part (*Altera autem die*) as the Gospel, saying as usual beforehand *Munda cor meum* and prefacing the pericope with *Dominus vobiscum,* + *Sequentia sancti Evangelii,* etc.

[1] The faculty is given in the quinquennial faculties.

CHAPTER XXV

TRIDVVM SACRVM

§ 1. GENERAL RULES

THE Triduum Sacrum is the three days, Maundy Thursday, Good Friday and Holy Saturday. It begins with Matins of Maundy Thursday (Tenebrae) said or sung on the evening of Wednesday, and ends with the first Vespers of Easter, which occur during the Mass on Holy Saturday. The carrying out of the ceremonies of the Triduum is of obligation in cathedral, collegiate, conventual and parochial churches. They are not of obligation, as a general rule, in other churches or oratories. By leave of the Ordinary these functions *may* take place in non-parochial churches where the Blessed Sacramant is reserved. They may also be held in the chapels of convents or institutions where the Blessed Sacrament is reserved—provided they are carried out according to the rite of the Missal.[1] In cathedral churches they are to be performed according to the directions of the *Caeremoniale Episcoporum* and the Missal. Wherever possible they are to be carried out in all other churches and oratories according to the form of the Missal. Where this more solemn form is not feasible, the simpler form of the *Memoriale Rituum* may be used in *parochial* churches. In non-parochial churches (e.g. the churches of religious, the chapels of convents and institutions) this simpler form may be used *only by Papal indult.*

During the Triduum Sacrum special rules are to be observed :

The Office is double in rite. It contains no *Deus in adiutorium*, etc., at the beginning of any hour. The verses *Gloria Patri* and *Sicut erat in principio* are not said at any time, not even at the end of psalms. There are no Chapters, hymns, or short responsories. At the end of each hour the antiphon *Christus factus est* is said, with a further clause in the Office of Friday and another again in the Office of Saturday. Then *Pater noster* is said silently, the *Miserere* aloud, and the prayer *Respice, quaesumus Domine*, without *Dominus vobiscum* or *Oremus*. The conclusion of this prayer, *qui tecum vivit et regnat*, etc., is said silently. Except Tenebrae, the Divine Office is not sung, but recited in monotone. On these three days the morning Office may be celebrated only once in each church. Private Masses are forbidden.[2]

For further rules to be observed from the Mass of Maundy Thursday to that of Holy Saturday, see pp. 285, 286.

§ 2. TENEBRAE

THE office of Tenebrae is simply Matins and Lauds said, as usual, the evening before. Matins and Lauds of these three days have special rules and are commonly called by this name.

Tenebrae, therefore, of Maundy Thursday is said on the evening of

---

[1] Cf. C.J.C. 1193. [2] Cf., however, *infra*, pp. 278, 332.

Wednesday ; Tenebrae of Good Friday on the evening of Thursday ; Tenebrae of Holy Saturday on the evening of Friday.

The directions which follow [1] apply to all three days. The differences between the three cases are noted here.

Preparations. These preparations are to be made beforehand :

The six candles on the altar should be of unbleached wax ; the candlesticks the plainer ones used for Good Friday. On Wednesday evening the altar cross is veiled in violet as during Passiontide ; on Thursday evening it is veiled in black, or violet, according to the usage for the function of Good Friday [2] ; on Friday evening it is unveiled. The frontal is violet on Wednesday evening ; there is none on Thursday and Friday. The altar has no other decoration. The Sanctissimum should be removed. On the Epistle side of the choir, at about the place where the Epistle is read, the hearse [3] stands, bearing fifteen candles of unbleached wax.[4] An extinguisher should be near. In the middle of the choir a lectern stands, uncovered, with a Breviary for the lessons. At Tenebrae on Wednesday the altar carpet may be violet. In the other two cases there should be no carpet before the altar at all. The candles on the altar and all those of the hearse are lighted for the function.

The procession to the choir should proceed in this order : the M.C., the two cantors, celebrant, the choir, those of greater dignity before the others. All wear choir dress (cassock and plain surplice, except for prelates or canons). The celebrant has neither stole nor cope. He occupies the first place in choir. At Tenebrae on Friday no reverences are made to the choir ; in many churches this rule is observed on all three days.[5]

The singing of Tenebrae may not be accompanied by the organ.

Matins. The Ceremonial (II. xxii, 6) does not suppose that the antiphons be pre-intoned, at Tenebrae. But in many churches, especially at Rome, this is done, as usual (see pp. 193, 194). The prayer *Aperi, Domine* is said, all kneeling. All stand while *Pater noster, Ave Maria* and the Apostles' Creed are said silently. The first antiphon is sung by the choir. The cantors intone the first psalm either at their places or in the middle of the choir ; all sit, put on the biretta, and continue it. Everything proceeds as usual at Matins (see pp. 228–230), except that the verses *Gloria Patri* and *Sicut erat* are not sung at the end of the psalms.[6]

---

[1] C.E. II. xxii. [2] Cf. M.R. V. i, 2.

[3] The hearse is a tall staff supporting a triangle on which are fifteen spikes or sockets for candles. Originally the word means a harrow. The Tenebrae hearse is so called because it looks like a harrow (a triangle with spikes). Such triangles of candles were erected on the stand where a coffin rests in church ; so this too is still called a hearse.

[4] All the candles should be unbleached. There is no authority for using a white candle in the centre.

[5] S.R.C. 3029[11] ; cf. 3059[27], which contradicts the other decision.

[6] The former special cadence for the end of the last verse of each psalm has disappeared from the Vatican edition. But the last words of the psalm may be sung more slowly to mark the conclusion.

At the end of the first psalm the M.C. or a server appointed for this purpose, goes to the hearse and—having reverenced to the altar and (except on Friday) to the clergy in choir—extinguishes the lowest candle on the Gospel side.

At the end of the second psalm he extinguishes the lowest candle on the Epistle side. So he extinguishes a candle after every psalm, going to the alternate sides to do so. There are fourteen psalms in Tenebrae, nine at Matins and five at Lauds. When the last psalm of Lauds is finished, he will have extinguished all the candles, except the one in the middle at the summit of the triangle.

At the end of the third psalm of each nocturn of Matins the versicle and response appointed are sung, the versicle by the cantors. Then all stand and say the Lord's Prayer silently. All sit again and put on the biretta. The lessons are sung at the lectern in the middle. The M.C. should go to each lector, beginning with those of lower rank, accompany him to the lectern (having made due reverence to the altar and—except on Good Friday—to the clergy) and stand at his left behind while he chants, holding his biretta. The lessons are chanted without asking first for a blessing, and without the final clause *Tu autem, Domine, miserere nobis*. While chanting the lector lays his hands on the book. There should be nine lectors chosen beforehand. The celebrant does not sing the last lesson. The lessons of the first nocturn (Lamentations of Jeremias) have a special tone. Any or all of these may be sung by the choir. In this case no one goes to the lectern. At the end of each lesson the lector and M.C. repeat the reverence to the altar, and (except on Friday) to the choir, and the M.C. conducts the lector back to his place.

Lauds. Lauds follow immediately after the ninth responsory ; the choir remain seated. All stand when the *Benedictus* begins. The *Benedictus* has twelve verses. During the last six of these (beginning with *Ut sine timore*) the same server who put out the candles on the hearse puts out one of the six candles on the altar, beginning with the farthest candle on the Gospel side. Next time he puts out the farthest on the Epistle side, and so on alternately. On Wednesday evening, as soon as the last candle on the altar is extinguished, all the lamps in the church are put out, except those which burn before the tabernacle. The lamps are not lit again till the *Exsultet* on Holy Saturday.

As soon as the M.C. or server has put out the last candle on the altar, he goes to the hearse and takes from it the candle which remains there burning. He does not extinguish it, but carries it to the Epistle side of the altar. He holds it here in his right hand, resting it on the Epistle corner of the table of the altar, facing the Gospel side while the antiphon at the end of the *Benedictus* is sung, during which all in choir sit.

Christus Factus Est. As soon as the antiphon *Christus factus est* begins, all kneel ; the server puts the candle behind the altar, so that its light is not seen,[1] then kneels near it.

---

[1] If the altar is against the wall, so that the candle cannot be put behind it, or the altar is between the choir and nave, a small screen or a lantern should be

On Wednesday evening the antiphon is *Christus factus est pro nobis obediens usque ad mortem.* On Thursday evening the choir adds to this, without pause, *mortem autem crucis.* On Friday evening they add the third clause, *Propter quod et Deus exaltavit illum, et dedit illi nomen quod est super omne nomen.*

After the antiphon *Pater noster* is said silently. Then the psalm *Miserere* is recited, aloud, but in a low voice. The celebrant, still kneeling, recites aloud, and with head somewhat bowed, the prayer *Respice, quaesumus Domine, super hanc familiam tuam.* But he says the conclusion *qui tecum vivit et regnat,* etc., silently. All remain kneeling from the beginning of the antiphon *Christus factus est.*

At the end the M.C. strikes the bench or a book to make a sound ; everyone in choir does so too. The server takes the candle from behind the altar, and holds it up so as to show the light. Then the noise ceases and the server may extinguish the candle and put it on the credence, or take it with him to the sacristy. When he has shown the light, all rise and leave the church silently, as they came. The hearse is taken away and put back for the next Tenebrae.

§ 3. TENEBRAE IN SMALL CHURCHES

No special provision is made for this ; but there is no reason why a church in which Vespers or Compline are celebrated should not have Tenebrae on these days. It is permissible to sing Tenebrae on one of the three days only.

In a small church the rules, as given above, will be carried out as far as possible. Indeed, there is no great difficulty in any point. Only one server is absolutely necessary, to put out the candles. If there are no choir stalls, the celebrant will sit at the sedile. The choir and people may sing alternate verses of the psalms. Any nine men in cassock and surplice may read the lessons, including the celebrant. If nine cannot be procured, the same lector may read more than one lesson. The celebrant may sing the versicles, if there is no other cantor.

§ 4. MAUNDY THURSDAY MORNING [1]

THE morning services of Maundy Thursday and Good Friday correspond, so that neither may be held, unless the other is held also. Only one Mass may be celebrated in each church ; all the other priests receive Communion at this.[2] But bishops (provided that they are not bound to celebrate in the cathedral) and abbots *nullius* may say private Mass in a private chapel ; the superiors of Regulars may say Mass, without the procession and reservation, in order to give Communion to their brethren, but only privately in an oratory, or, if there be none, in the church, with doors shut. In churches where not even the simple rites of the Memoriale Rituum can be carried out, the Ordinary may

made ready in the corner near the Epistle side, so as to hide the light. The server puts the candle behind or into this.

[1] C.E. II. xxiii ; M.R. Tit. IV.   [2] Cf. C.J.C. 862.

allow one Low Mass to be said (at an hour earlier than the Mass at the cathedral) on Maundy Thursday. This permission must be renewed each year, unless legitimate custom excuses.

On Maundy Thursday the colour of the Office is violet ; that of the Mass is white. It is in part a festal Mass.

Preparations. The following preparations are made beforehand :

The High Altar is vested in white, the best frontal and conopaeum being used, as for a great feast. The altar cross is veiled in white ; there are six candles of bleached wax, lighted. Flowers, in moderation, may be used.[1]

On the credence all is prepared as usual for High Mass. Two altar-breads are placed on the paten. A second chalice is prepared with its paten, a pall, veil of white silk sufficiently large to cover this chalice fully, and white silk ribbon. The rattle (*crotalus*) is laid on the credence, if it will be used.[2] The white cope is prepared near the credence ; white stoles for the priest and deacons who will receive Holy Communion are made ready. The processional cross stands near the credence, veiled in violet ; and the canopy to carry over the celebrant during the procession. Candles for those who walk in the procession are laid in some convenient place.

The Place of Repose. In another part of the church, the place is prepared at which the Sanctissimum will be reserved till the Mass of the Presanctified on Good Friday. It will generally be a side chapel with an altar.[3] The place of repose is not used as an altar. No Mass is said on it. All that is essential is the casket (*capsula, urna*) in which the Sanctissimum is reserved, and a table or space in front on which the chalice can be set down before it is enclosed in the casket.[4] This is often made in a special form, like an urn. It must be so enclosed that the chalice within cannot be seen.[5] It has a lock and a key. Inside a corporal is spread. Before the service begins, and till the Sanctissimum is enclosed here, the urn should be left open. This urn may be the tabernacle of a side altar. The place of repose is decorated with precious hangings and lights.[6] The Memoriale Rituum (IV. i) makes mention of flowers. Relics or pictures are not allowed. The "locus aptus," whether it be really an altar or a temporary table without an altar stone, should have a white frontal. On the table before

---

[1] Cf. M.R. IV. ii, § iv, 4.

[2] Cf. p. 281, n. 2.

[3] " Locus aptus in aliqua Capella Ecclesiae vel Altari " (Missal) ; "aliquod sacellum intra ecclesiam " (C.E.) ; " locus ipse ab Altari majori distinctus " (M.R.). Cf. Instruction of the Congregation of the Sacraments (§ 111) of 26 March 1929.

[4] However, the C.E. II. xxiii, 2, 13, does call the place of repose an altar. So does the rubric of the Missal on Maundy Thursday (after the Mass). This is because, as a matter of fact, a side altar will nearly always be used. It is often called the sepulchre (M.R. and S.R.C. 3939 ; 2873[2]) and sometimes in English " the altar (or place) of repose."

[5] S.R.C. 3660[1].

[6] No liturgical book mentions a cross at the place of repose.

the urn a corporal is spread, as the Sanctissimum is to be placed on it ; near this is the key of the urn. If necessary, steps are provided that the deacon may go up to put the Sanctissimum in the urn.

Reservation of Blessed Sacrament. Somewhere else, if possible outside the church or in the sacristy, a suitable place is prepared where the ciborium containing the Sanctissimum, in case of sick calls, will be kept.[1] The proper place is "some chapel near the church, or the sacristy itself, or some safe and becoming press in the sacristy, or even a suitable place in the presbytery apart from domestic and everyday use and free from all danger of irreverence." [2] Where no such suitable place is available, the pyx may be left from the Mass of the Maundy Thursday to the Mass of the Presanctified in the urn of the place of repose (behind the chalice), and from after the Mass of the Presanctified it is to be put in some more remote and quiet chapel within the church, with a lamp burning before it. If no place except the place of repose is available the pyx may remain in the urn up to Holy Saturday, with a lamp burning, but with the lights and ornaments of the place of repose removed. If in any church the function of Maundy Thursday is not held, the ciborium may remain at its altar until the evening of that day, then—until Holy Saturday—it is to be removed to one of the places mentioned above.[2]

In the sacristy all is prepared for High Mass, with white vestments. An amice, alb, girdle and white tunicle are laid out for the second subdeacon who will carry the cross ; also violet stoles for the celebrant and deacon to use when they strip the altar.

[**Preparations for Maundy.** If the Maundy [3] (washing of feet) is to be performed, further preparations are necessary. This ceremony, if possible, should not be held before the High Altar, but in a side chapel, in the sacristy or a hall near the church. Here there should be an altar or table [4] with violet frontal, a cross covered with violet, four or six candles of bleached wax, the Missal covered in violet. At the Epistle side a credence stands, covered with a white cloth, on which are a large white cloth with strings to tie (an apron) for the celebrant, the book of lessons (covered in white), two vessels of water and two basins,[5] thirteen towels on a plate or in a basket, a plate containing the coins to be given to those whose feet are washed (if they are poor people), another vessel of water, dish and soap with which the celebrant washes his hands afterwards. On the Gospel side is a long bench on which the thirteen men will sit, and a large vessel into which the water may be poured after use. There may be other benches or seats for the clergy who assist at this ceremony.]

[1] There a (movable) tabernacle, with a corporal within, is made ready. In front of it another corporal is spread. Near by are prepared the key, the (white) conopaeum for this tabernacle and the lamp that will be lighted when the Sanctissimum is present.

[2] Instruction of the Congregation of the Sacraments, 26 March 1929.

[3] See p. 286.

[4] It need not be a real (consecrated) altar ; nor need it have an altar-stone.

[5] Two are needed only if one is not large enough to wash thirteen feet (p. 287).

Assistants. On Maundy Thursday besides the usual ministers and servers required for every High Mass, there should be a cross-bearer, who is to be a second subdeacon vested (without maniple), or, if a sub-deacon is not available, a server in surplice ; a second thurifer for the procession ; as many torch-bearers as attend on the greatest feasts ; clergy to walk in the procession holding candles. The canopy is carried by canons, priests or clerics in choir dress, or by laymen. Confrater-nities may walk in the procession in their dress, holding candles.

The Mass. The service begins after None. High Mass is celebrated as usual, with the following exceptions :

The psalm *Iudica me* is not said, nor the *Gloria Patri* at the Introit and Lavabo. *Gloria in excelsis* is sung. When the celebrant has intoned this, the church bells are rung ; then not again, on any condi-tion, till the *Gloria* of Holy Saturday. After the intonation of the *Gloria*, the organ may be played for a little time, or the *Gloria* may be accompanied on the organ.[1] The Sanctus bell (and other small bells, if customary) may also be rung for a short time when the celebrant has intoned the *Gloria*. It is not rung again. From now on till the Mass of Holy Saturday a wooden clapper or rattle may be used, if customary, instead of the bell.[2] There is a special *Communicantes*, *Hanc igitur* and *Qui pridie*. The torch-bearers remain before the altar to the end of Mass. The kiss of peace is not given.

Second Sacred Host placed in Chalice. After they have said *Agnus Dei* with the celebrant, the ministers change places, genuflecting before and after. The M.C. (if he is a cleric) then brings the second chalice to the altar with its paten, pall and veil. When the celebrant has made his communion, the subdeacon covers the chalice of Mass and sets it aside on the Gospel side, not outside the corporal. The ministers genuflect and again change places. The deacon uncovers the second chalice and presents it to the celebrant on the corporal. The three sacred ministers genuflect and the celebrant takes the second Host he has consecrated and places It carefully in this chalice. The deacon covers the chalice with the pall, then over this he puts the paten, upside down, covers all with the silk veil, and ties the veil around the stem with the ribbon. He places it on the middle of the corporal, and by it the ciborium from which Holy Communion will now be distri-buted.[3] The celebrant and ministers genuflect. The ministers go to

[1] The organ may not be played at any other time during the Mass (S.R.C. 3515[4], 3535[7]).

[2] The C.E. and Missal do not mention this wooden instrument (*crotalus*) at all. The M.R. speaks of it, but only for the Angelus after Mass. Many authors disparage its use (e.g., Martinucci, I. ii, p. 199, n. 2). It is not commanded. It may be used. If it is, it is rattled whenever, on other days, the bell would be rung—at the *Sanctus*, before and at the Elevation.

[3] Most authors suppose that the Hosts to be distributed at Communion are consecrated at this Mass (and this is more conformable to liturgical tradition). So they direct the M.C. to bring the ciborium from the credence at the Offertory. But in many churches the Sanctissimum will be taken from the tabernacle where It is already reserved. The deacon opens the tabernacle after he has arranged the second chalice.

the ends of the foot-pace, the deacon at the Epistle side, the subdeacon at the Gospel side. and stand there on the step below facing each other. The celebrant turns partly towards the people, facing towards the Epistle corner, so as not to turn his back to the Sanctissimum.

Communion. The subdeacon bows low ; the deacon bows somewhat and sings the *Confiteor.* Meanwhile a server has given stoles to the priests and deacons in choir. Holy Communion is distributed according to the usual rule (see pp. 119–121). The ministers of Mass receive Communion first, then priests, deacons and others in ·Orders, the acolytes of the Mass, then all the others. All come up two and two, or in groups of four, kneel before the foot-pace where the acolytes hold the Communion cloth stretched across (p. 120). Afterwards the celebrant goes down to the Communion rails to give Communion to the people, accompanied by the ministers on either side. The deacon holds the paten under the chin of each communicant. Torch-bearers go and kneel at either end of the rail. After Communion no one sits, because the Sanctissimum is exposed on the altar.

The rest of Mass is celebrated according to the rules when the Blessed Sacrament is exposed (pp. 61, 124). The deacon sings *Ite, missa est* ; the blessing is given ; the celebrant says the last Gospel, not signing the altar, but himself only, when commencing it.

During the last Gospel the cross-bearer gets the cross.[1] Two thurifers bring the thuribles from the sacristy. Candles are given out to all in choir, unless the singers find it impossible to hold both a candle and an open book. A server takes the birettas of the sacred ministers to the place of repose ; another removes the Missal and its stand and the altar cards from the altar.

Procession to Place of Repose. When Mass is ended, the celebrant and ministers descend to the foot of the altar, genuflect on both knees and go to the sedilia. Here the ministers take off their maniples, assisted by acolytes. The celebrant, assisted by the M.C., takes off the chasuble and maniple, puts on the cope. At the sedilia the celebrant and ministers must take care not to turn their backs on the Blessed Sacrament. The acolytes take their candles and go on either side of the cross-bearer, to the entrance of the sanctuary, where they wait facing the altar. The celebrant and ministers come to the altar, prostrate and kneel on the lowest step. The two thurifers come forward, the celebrant puts incense into both thuribles, not blessing it, and kneeling, incenses the Sanctissimum with one.[2] The thurifers stand on either side of the altar. The M.C. takes the humeral veil and puts it on the celebrant, the subdeacon attaches it in front. The canopy-bearers

---

[1] A second subdeacon (if available) vested in amice, alb, cincture and white tunicle, will carry it.

[2] In cases of processions when there are two thurifers, it is convenient to distinguish them as first and second. The first is the one whose thurible is used by the celebrant to incense the Sanctissimum. He will naturally be the thurifer of the Mass ; his thurible will receive incense after the other one. The second thurifer merely walks by his side swinging a thurible.

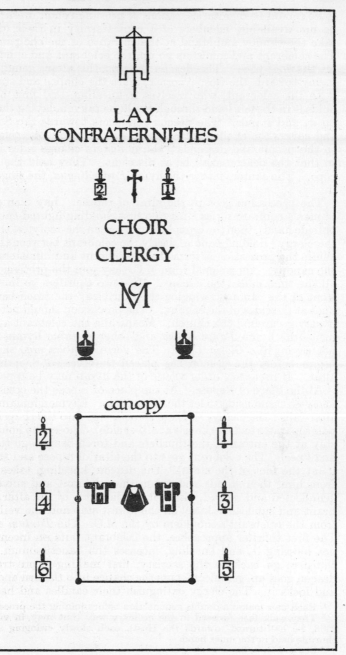

FIG. 38. MAUNDY THURSDAY : THE PROCESSION

(who should be dignitaries, canons or priests in choir dress ; or, if these be not available, members of a confraternity in their official dress) take the canopy and stand at the entrance of the choir or sanctuary. The celebrant and ministers go up, the celebrant and subdeacon kneel on the foot-pace. The deacon goes to the altar, genuflects, partly facing towards the Gospel corner, takes the chalice and standing gives it to the celebrant, who receives it kneeling, and first bowing. He holds it in the left hand through the humeral veil, laying the right hand on it, and stands. The deacon genuflects towards the Sanctissimum and covers the chalice with the end of the veil. The celebrant turns to the people and descends ; the ministers change sides behind him, so that the deacon shall be at his right. They hold the ends of the cope. The cantors intone the hymn *Pange lingua*, the singers continue it.

The procession goes to the altar of repose. Lay men or members of men's confraternities [1] may go first, holding lighted candles (in the outside hand), then the cross-bearer between the acolytes, the chanters,[1] the clergy [1] holding candles, lastly the celebrant between the ministers. While the procession is formed the celebrant and ministers wait under the canopy. On a signal from M.C. they join the procession and walk all the time under the canopy. The two thurifers go immediately in front of the canopy, swinging the thuribles,[2] the torch-bearers in two lines at the sides of the canopy. The procession should not go outside ; it may go around the church. Meanwhile the celebrant and ministers recite the hymn *Pange lingua* and other suitable hymns or psalms,[3] not saying the *Gloria Patri*. The verse *Tantum ergo* should not be begun before the deacon has placed the Blessed Sacrament on the altar. If necessary other verses of the hymn may be repeated.

At the Place of Repose. At the place of repose the cross-bearer and acolytes stand aside to let the others pass. Laymen remain outside the altar-rails ; the clergy—if there is room—go into the chapel where each pair separates and one kneels at either side. Those who hold the canopy stay at the entrance, the thurifers and torch-bearers go to either side and kneel. The celebrant goes to the altar of repose and stands before it (at the foot of the steps). The deacon, kneeling, takes the chalice from him, then stands and, when the celebrant and subdeacon have genuflected and adored, places it on the table of the altar. The celebrant and subdeacon kneel on the lowest step and the veil is removed from the celebrant's shoulders by the M.C. The *Tantum ergo* is sung. The first thurifer approaches, the celebrant puts on incense as usual, not blessing it, and kneeling, incenses the Sanctissimum. Then the thurifers go back to the sacristy, first making a prostration. The deacon goes up, genuflects, puts the chalice into the urn and then shuts and locks it. The clergy extinguish their candles and hand them to

---

[1] Each pair makes a double genuflection before joining the procession.
[2] They walk face forward in the ordinary way (but may, in view of S.R.C. 2368, be half-turned towards the Host), each slowly swinging at his side a thurible held in the inner hand.
[3] See p. 241, n. 3.

servers, the torch-bearers put out their torches and leave them aside. All make a prostration and leave the place of repose to go back to the choir. The celebrant, ministers, cross-bearer and acolytes remain meanwhile where they are. They then rise, prostrate (except the cross-bearer and acolytes) and go to the sacristy. The celebrant and ministers wear the biretta on the way (when outside the chapel).

Vespers. Meanwhile Vespers are said in choir. The altar is covered with a violet frontal, the altar cross with a violet veil. The six candles remain alight. Vespers are recited, not sung, according to the rubrics in the Vesperal. There are no ceremonies, except that all stand at the *Magnificat*, and kneel during the antiphon *Christus factus est* and all that follows.

While the *Miserere* is said at the end of Vespers, a priest in surplice and white stole takes the ciborium containing the Blessed Sacrament from the altar to the place where it is to be kept during the Triduum Sacrum. The rules for this case are observed as usual [1] (p. 240). He leaves the tabernacle open and the conopaeum should be at once removed.

Stripping of Altars. At the end of Vespers the celebrant and ministers come back to the altar, the celebrant and deacon wearing violet stoles over the alb. The acolytes go before them, without candles. They hand the birettas they have worn to the M.C., bow to the choir, as usual. All, except the celebrant, genuflect to the altar ; he bows low. The celebrant begins the antiphon *Diviserunt sibi*, not singing it. The choir continue the antiphon and the psalm *Deus, Deus meus*. The celebrant, ministers and acolytes go up to the altar. The acolytes take away the altar-cards, flowers, etc., and put them on the credence. The celebrant and ministers take off the three altar cloths and hand them to the acolytes to put aside. The acolytes take away the frontal, the tabernacle veil (if not already removed) and the carpet. They leave only the cross, now covered with violet, and the six candles. They remove the covering of the credence and of the sedilia. They extinguish the candles and the sanctuary lamp. If there are other altars in the church, the celebrant, ministers and acolytes go to strip them in the same way (beginning with the one nearest on the Gospel side). In going the sacred ministers wear the biretta. The choir does not recite the antiphon after the psalm till the sacred ministers return to the High Altar. The other altars may be stripped by other priests in surplice and violet stole, assisted by servers. If anyone passes before the place of repose he makes a prostration. All leave the church and unvest in the sacristy as usual.

From now till the Mass of the Presanctified the Blessed Sacrament at the altar of repose is treated as if It were exposed. In passing It everyone makes a prostration. At least six candles burn continually there. If possible two clerks in surplice watch, kneeling all the time. Priests and deacons while watching wear a white stole. In any case

---

[1] The small canopy (umbella) is used over the Blessed Sacrament in this procession.

someone must watch all the time the church is open. If necessary, for safety, the chalice containing the Sanctissimum may be put in the tabernacle used throughout the year during the night. It must be replaced at the altar of repose early on Friday morning.

From now till Saturday no lamps in the church are lit. No bells are rung. Holy water should be removed from all stoups and thrown into the sacrarium.[1] A small quantity is kept for blessing the fire on Holy Saturday or for a sick call. The holy Oils should be burned (in the sanctuary lamp) and the new oil procured from the Bishop as soon as possible on Maundy Thursday. The High Altar is quite bare, having neither altar cloth nor frontal. The tabernacle is unveiled, open and empty.

The Maundy. If the MAUNDY is performed it may follow immediately the stripping of the altars, or be done later in the day.[2]

Thirteen men wait at the place prepared.[3]

The ceremony is done by a celebrant (" Prelatus seu Superior " according to the Missal) in violet stole and cope, deacon and subdeacon in white vestments with maniples, acolytes who carry their candles lighted, a thurifer, M.C. and four servers [4] who will hand what is wanted at the time.

The procession comes to the place appointed in the usual order.[5] The men whose feet are to be washed stand as it enters. The members of the choir, clergy and singers go to the benches or seats prepared for them. The celebrant and ministers go to the altar, make the usual reverences, ascend and, if it is really an altar, the celebrant kisses it. The acolytes remain below, or in front, holding their candles. The deacon takes the book of lessons from the credence, brings it to the altar and lays it there, as at Mass, when he is about to sing the Gospel.

All now follows exactly as at the Gospel of High Mass. The subdeacon goes down and waits for the deacon before the altar. Incense is put on and blessed by the celebrant, standing at the altar, the deacon kneels to say *Munda cor meum*, takes the book and receives the celebrant's blessing. He sings the Gospel *Ante diem festum* (it is the same Gospel as at Mass), first singing *Dominus vobiscum* and announcing *Sequentia*, etc. The choir answer as at Mass. The book is incensed. After the Gospel the subdeacon takes it to the celebrant to kiss. He says, as usual, *Per evangelica*, etc. The deacon incenses the celebrant. All stand during the Gospel.

Then the acolytes put their candles at the credence and the thurifer

---

[1] S.R.C. 2682[54].

[2] This ceremony is generally now performed in cathedrals and religious houses only.

[3] In many places it is the custom to select poor men. No special dress is appointed for them ; it would be proper that they should be dressed uniformly in e.g. the costume of some confraternity.

[4] The acolytes could be two of these ; if necessary, the M.C. and thurifer might be the other two.

[5] Thurifer, acolytes, choir, servers, celebrant between the ministers. For the things to prepare see above, p. 280.

takes away the incense. The ministers join the celebrant ; all come from the altar together to the credence. The ministers take off their maniples, the celebrant takes off the cope and puts on the white cloth that is to serve as an apron, assisted by the acolytes and M.C. The men whose feet are to be washed sit and take off their shoes and socks, each from his right foot.

One server takes a basin, another a vessel of water, a third the towels, a fourth the plate with coins. They go to the first man whose feet are to be washed in this order : first, the servers with the water and basin ; the celebrant, between the ministers, with hands joined, all three wearing birettas ; the other two servers bearing the towels and plate with coins.

In passing the altar all make the usual reverence. They come to the first of the thirteen. The server with the water stands at his left, the server with the basin at his right. The celebrant kneels before him, the ministers stand on either side of the celebrant. The subdeacon holds the man's right foot, the server pours a little water over it, into the basin held by the other server. The celebrant rubs the foot a little with his hand. Meanwhile the deacon takes the first towel and unfolds it. He hands this to the celebrant, who dries the foot and kisses it. He hands the towel to the man. The deacon holds the plate with coins, the celebrant takes one and gives it to the man, who takes it, kissing the celebrant's hand. They then pass to the next and repeat the same ceremony for each. If the water fails in the vessel the servers bring the other vessel and basin. The water used is poured into the large jar at the end of the row of men. As each man's foot is thus washed he puts on his sock and shoe again.

As soon as the washing begins the choir sings the antiphon *Mandatum novum*, with the psalm verse, and the other antiphons and verses, provided in the Gradual, as long as the ceremony lasts. The celebrant. when he has washed the feet of the last, goes back to the credence. Here he washes his hands, assisted by the acolytes. He takes off the apron and puts on the cope. The ministers accompany him. They go to the altar. Standing there at the Epistle corner, between the ministers, the celebrant chants the *Pater noster* (continued silently), the versicles and prayer, in the simple ferial tone. All then go back to the sacristy or other place as they came.

§ 5. MAUNDY THURSDAY IN SMALL CHURCHES [1]

THE altar is prepared as for feasts, with white frontal and tabernacle veil (conopaeum).[2] The altar cross is covered with white. The six candles are lit. The Missal is at the Epistle side, open. At the credence all is prepared for Mass. Two altar breads are placed on the paten. There is another chalice with its pall, paten, a white silk veil (sufficiently big to cover the chalice fully) and ribbon. If necessary

---

[1] M.R. Tit. IV.
[2] There may be flowers (M.R. IV. ii, § iv, 4), but they should be used on the high altar at all times with great restraint.

the ciborium with altar breads for the Communion is placed here, also a white humeral veil and the rattle (*crotalus*) if this be used.[1] The processional cross, covered with violet, stands near; and a small canopy (*umbella*) and two torches are at hand.

The place of repose for the reservation of the Blessed Sacrament is prepared in another part of the church, as described above (p. 279) and " in some becoming place near the sacristy or outside the church "[2] is made ready a (movable) tabernacle with a white conopaeum and within a corporal, to receive the ciborium; and a lamp to be lighted before it in due time. In the sacristy white Mass vestments are laid out for the celebrant, also a white cope, violet stole, the surplices for the servers (supposed to be only three by the Memoriale Rituum), the thurible and incense boat and candles or torches[3] to be carried by people in the procession.

The six altar candles are lit.

Mass. The Memoriale Rituum supposes that a Low Mass is said. The *Iudica* psalm is omitted; so is *Gloria Patri* at the Introit and Lavabo. At the *Gloria in excelsis* the church bells are rung, and, if customary the Sanctus bell may be rung also. No bell is sounded again until the *Gloria* of Holy Saturday. At the *Sanctus* and Elevation the rattle may be sounded. During the prayers before Communion the first server (if a cleric) brings the second chalice, with its coverings, from the credence and puts it on the altar.[4] After his Communion the celebrant—having covered the chalice of the Mass and put it aside to his left—puts the second consecrated Host into the second chalice, lays the pall over the chalice, on the pall the paten upside down, and the veil over all.[5] He genuflects before and after doing this. He uncovers the ciborium (if necessary takes it from the tabernacle) and genuflects. From now he acts as if the Blessed Sacrament were exposed, genuflecting each time he comes to the middle or leaves it, not turning his back to the Sanctissimum (see p. 61). He stands towards the Gospel side, looking towards the Epistle side, while the first server, kneeling at the Epistle corner, says the *Confiteor*. The celebrant then adds *Misereatur* and *Indulgentiam*. Holy Communion is given as usual, first to the servers, unless priests (or other clerics) are present. Coming back to the altar the celebrant puts the ciborium in the tabernacle and closes it. After the ablutions the chalice used at Mass (without the burse and corporal) is put on the credence by the first server, if he is a cleric. While Mass is being finished the candles at the place of repose are lighted, candles or torches are handed to the members of pious

---

[1] See p. 281, n. 2.

[2] M.R. IV. i, " In Sacristia," 8.

[3] " Funalia sive candelae pro processione " are required (M.R. IV. i, " In Sacristia," no. 7). As all three servers are otherwise occupied, these can be held only by members of the congregation (cf. M.R., Tit. IV. cap. ii, § I, 20).

[4] If one server is not a tonsured cleric the celebrant must see to this himself before Mass.

[5] He does not tie this with the ribbon until he goes later to take the chalice in procession to the altar of repose (M.R. IV. ii, § II, 5).

confraternities who will take part in the procession or to some of the men of the congregation [1] ; the canopy is made ready. At the beginning of the last Gospel the celebrant does not sign the table of the altar.

Procession to Place of Repose. When Mass is ended, the celebrant descends to the foot of the altar and genuflects on both knees to the Sanctissimum in the chalice ; then at the sedile he takes off the chasuble and maniple and puts on the cope, assisted by the servers. He must not turn his back to the Blessed Sacrament while doing this. The first server brings the thurible from the sacristy. The celebrant comes to the middle, genuflects on both knees on the ground, and kneels on the lowest step for a short time. He rises and puts on incense ; he does not bless it, nor do the solita oscula occur. Kneeling on the lowest step he incenses the Sanctissimum with the usual three swings. He gives the thurible back to first server ; the second brings the humeral veil and puts it on his shoulders. He goes up to the altar and genuflects. It is at this moment that the Memoriale Rituum says he is to tie the ribbon round the stem of the chalice. He takes the chalice in his left, holding it through the humeral veil ; he lays his right hand on it, the second server spreads the end of the veil over the hand and chalice. The celebrant turns his back to the altar and begins to recite the hymn *Pange lingua* (unless there are chanters to intone and sing it). The procession goes to the place of repose in this order : First the banner used when Viaticum is taken to the sick [2] (if the church has such a banner) ; then confraternities or pious men carrying lighted candles ; the processional cross borne by the third server ; chanters (if present) ; the clergy, if any, carrying candles ; the first server swinging the thurible ; the celebrant carrying the Blessed Sacrament. At his left the second server walks, who holds back the edge of the cope. Immediately behind him the small canopy is carried by a member of the congregation or of a confraternity,[3] who holds it over to him. The celebrant and second server, as they go, recite the *Pange lingua* (even though it is being sung [4]) and other hymns, psalms or canticles, if time permits.

At the Place of Repose. At the chapel where the place of repose is prepared all divide,[5] so that the celebrant may pass. The thurifer goes to the Epistle side. The celebrant goes straight up to the altar or table and places the chalice on it, and genuflects. He comes down, kneels, and the humeral veil is taken off. He puts on incense, without a blessing, and, kneeling on the lowest step, incenses the Sanctissimum. Meanwhile the servers and people recite (or chanters sing) the last two

---

[1] Cf. M.R. IV. ii, § I, 20.

[2] M.R. IV. ii, § II, 8.

[3] The M.R. does not say who carries the canopy ; but no server remains to do so. The large canopy may be used, borne by four or more men.

[4] If there are singers the hymn is sung up to the verse *Tantum, ergo* (exclusively). Then, if necessary, the second and following stanzas may be repeated. The last two stanzas are reserved for use at the altar of repose.

[5] Clerics of higher rank are nearest the altar ; laymen remain outside the altar rail.

verses of the hymn *Tantum ergo* and *Genitori*. The celebrant goes up to the altar, genuflects, puts the Sanctissimum in the casket, genuflects again, closes and locks the casket. He comes down, kneels for a short time at the foot of the steps, then rises, prostrates, as do all the others, and goes back to the altar, wearing his biretta (when he gets out of sight of the Sanctissimum). One of the servers brings with him to the high altar the humeral veil.

Removal of Ciborium. At the High Altar the celebrant first takes the ciborium and carries it to the place prepared for it.[1] In doing this he observes the usual rules for taking the Blessed Sacrament from one place to another (p. 240). The first server, having put the humeral veil on the celebrant, carries the small canopy over the Blessed Sacrament ; the other two carry torches.

The celebrant then goes to the sacristy, takes off the white vestments and puts on a violet stole over the alb, crossing it in front. The candles at the high altar are extinguished.

Stripping of Altars. He comes to the High Altar with the three servers, bows low (the servers genuflect) and begins the antiphon *Diviserunt sibi vestimenta mea* ; he continues this and the psalm *Deus, Deus meus* alternately with the servers.[2] Meanwhile he goes up to the altar and takes off the three altar cloths. The servers help him to do so, and they take from the altar the frontal, flowers and carpet,[3] so as to leave only the altar cross and six candles, extinguished. In the same way all other altars in the church are stripped. Coming back to the High Altar the celebrant finishes the psalm and repeats the antiphon.

Having bowed low to the cross (while the servers genuflect) he goes to the sacristy and unvests. The violet veil is replaced on the crucifix of the altar.

The arrangement of the place of repose and the rules for watching there are the same as at p. 285. So also the other rules about taking away the holy water and so on.

§ 6. SUNG MASS

To the simplicity of this rite the following additions may be made.

The Mass may be a Sung Mass, with the full complement of servers. Instead of the three clerks, there may be a M.C., cross-bearer, thurifer, two acolytes, two, four or six torchbearers.

The torch-bearers will remain to the end of Mass. The procession will be formed as when there are deacon and subdeacon (above, p. 284) only without these two.

---

[1] Only when no other place is available may the ciborium be put into the urn at the altar of repose (M.R. IV. ii, § III, 4). Then it is placed behind the chalice. (Cf. above, p. 280.)

[2] The celebrant is supposed to know this psalm, and the " Pange lingua," by heart. If there are chanters or clerics in choir they alone recite the psalm and repeat the antiphon.

[3] If this cannot be done conveniently now it is done afterwards. For the ceremonial stripping it suffices to uncover the greater part of the table of the altar (M.R. IV. ii, § iv, 4).

When the celebrant has intoned *Gloria in excelsis Deo*, the organ may be played for a short time, while the bells are rung. At the procession the *Pange lingua* is sung. Vespers may be recited before the Sanctissimum is removed from the High Altar.

§ 7. GOOD FRIDAY MORNING [1]

THE morning office of Good Friday may not, cannot be held unless that of Maundy Thursday was held the day before.

It consists of five parts : 1. The " Mass of the Catechumens " ; 2. The litanical or " bidding " prayers ; 3. The Worship of the Cross ; 4. Mass of the Presanctified ; 5. Vespers. All follow one another without interruption. The colour of the day is black.

Preparations. The following preparations must be made beforehand : The altar is entirely bare. It has no frontal nor conopaeum. The tabernacle is open and empty ; the six candles are of unbleached wax and are not lighted till the Mass of the Presanctified. The candlesticks should be, if possible, neither gilt nor of silver, but dark in colour. The altar cross (of wood) is covered with a violet or black veil according to custom.[2] It will be used for the worship of the cross. Normally, it would stand on a foot like those of the candles ; but it should be removable from this foot. Its veil must be so fixed that it can be undone by the celebrant in three stages (below, pp. 294–295). There is no carpet before the altar. On the second step are three cushions covered with violet cloth, on which the celebrant and ministers will lie when they are prostrate.

The credence has a white cloth covering only the top of the table. On it are placed the Missal, covered with black, on its stand ; the book of lessons also covered with black ; one altar cloth slightly bigger than the table of the altar (which, therefore, will not hang down fully at the sides) ; a black burse containing a corporal and purificator ; the black chalice veil ; cruets as for Mass ; the broad stole for the deacon, if he will use this ; the little purifying bowl with its purificator (in case the celebrant should need to purify his fingers) ; the acolytes' candles of unbleached wax, not lit ; a taper ; the rattle, if it is used.

Near the credence are a long strip of carpet of violet cloth and a silk cushion of the same colour, to put under the cross during the worship, a white veil ornamented with violet silk to cover the cushion, the processional cross veiled in violet.[3] The sedilia are bare. If lecterns are used for the Passion, these—uncovered—may be placed where the Gospel is usually read ; or they may be brought just before the Passion.

At the chapel where the Sanctissimum is reserved a corporal is spread on the altar in front of the casket, its burse (white) lies near and the key of the casket. The white humeral veil is on a credence nearby ; the torches and candles that will be used at the procession, with a taper for

[1] C.E. II. xxv, xxvi ; M.R. Tit. V.
[2] M.R. V. i.
[3] Whichever colour is used to veil the altar cross, all other crosses in the church keep the violet veils of Passiontide till they are uncovered.

lighting them ; the canopy to carry over the Blessed Sacrament is placed in the chapel in some convenient place (outside the altar rail).

In the sacristy black vestments are laid out for the celebrant and ministers as for Mass [1] ; the vestments for the three deacons of the Passion and their book or books, as on Palm Sunday (p. 263), but black ; the vestments for the subdeacon who will bear the processional cross, namely, amice, alb, girdle, a black folded chasuble, no maniple.[2] If needed, a surplice and black stole for another priest, who will hold the cross for the people to worship at the Communion-rails. Two thuribles are prepared.

The persons who take part in the ceremony are the celebrant, deacon and subdeacon ; three deacons who sing the Passion ; another sub-deacon in tunicle, or server in surplice, who will carry the processional cross ; the M.C., possibly a second M.C. ; two thurifers, two acolytes, two, four or six torch-bearers ; the men who will carry the canopy.

"**Mass of the Catechumens.**" The service begins after None. All ceremonial kisses are left out to-day, even those of the chalice and paten ; no one bows to the choir.[3]

The procession comes to the church in this order : the first thurifer without the thurible, the acolytes holding no candles, the members of the choir, unless they are already in their places, the other servers, M.C., subdeacon, deacon, celebrant. Before the altar all genuflect except the celebrant, who bows low. Then the celebrant between the sacred ministers kneels before the altar and all three prostrate themselves, lying on the ground with their arms on the cushions. All others kneel. After a few moments the M.C. and acolytes rise. The acolytes take one altar cloth from the credence and spread it on the altar.[4] The M.C. places the Missal at the Epistle corner and opens it at the beginning of the service. They kneel again. When the celebrant and ministers have lain prostrate for about the time it would take to say the *Miserere*, they rise on a signal from the M.C. ; the thurifer and acolytes take away the cushions, the ministers go up to the altar. The celebrant kisses the altar ; they go to the Epistle corner and stand there as for the Introit. All in choir sit. A lector goes to the credence and there takes the book of lessons ; accompanied by the (second) M.C. he goes to the middle of the choir, genuflects, goes to the place where the Epistle is

---

[1] Folded chasubles for the ministers, if they use them (see p. 245). All that follows as to taking off the folded chasubles, the deacon's broad stole and so on, supposes, of course, that these are used in the church. If not, the subdeacon wears only a black maniple over the alb, the deacon a black stole and maniple. During the service they have only to take off their maniples before creeping to the cross and to put them on again as soon as they have done so (p. 295).

[2] Supposing that the cross is borne by a subdeacon. Otherwise a server will bear it, vested in cassock and surplice.

[3] That is to say, certainly no one bows from the uncovering of the cross till None on Holy Saturday (S.R.C. 3059[27]) ; moreover bowing may be omitted altogether to-day, if such is the custom of the church (S.R.C. 3029[11]).

[4] It is unfolded fully *lengthways* along the table of the altar, but it is left folded along the centre, so that it is doubled along the back of the altar, while the part of the table towards the front of the altar remains uncovered. This is the direction of M.R. (V. ii, § i, 5), neither the Missal nor C.E. speak thus.

read, and there chants the first lesson (the prophecy) without any title. He goes again to the middle, genuflects, takes the book back to the credence and goes to his place. Meanwhile the celebrant in a low voice reads this lesson and the Tract that follows, laying his hands on the book at the Epistle of Mass. *Deo gratias* is not said after any lesson to-day. When the lector has finished, the choir sings the Tract. The celebrant and ministers may sit at the sedilia. At the end of the Tract they return to the book by the shortest way and the ministers stand in line behind the celebrant. All in choir stand. He sings *Oremus* (opening and rejoining his hands); the deacon genuflects, singing *Flectamus genua*, all genuflect with him except the celebrant; the sub-deacon rises, singing *Levate*, all rise with him. The celebrant with out-stretched hands sings the collect in the simple ferial tone.[1] This is the order observed on all such occasions. During the collect the subdeacon goes to the credence and takes off the folded chasuble, assisted by an acolyte. He then takes the Epistolary and sings the second lesson (without a title) as he sings the Epistle at Mass. He does not go after-wards to kiss the celebrant's hand, but resumes his folded chasuble. The celebrant reads this lesson and the Tract in a low voice. The deacon does not answer *Deo gratias*. All in choir sit while the sub-deacon sings and during the Tract sung immediately afterwards. The celebrant (having read the Tract) and ministers may sit also.

Singing of Passion and Gospel. Towards the end of the Tract the three deacons of the Passion come from the sacristy and sing the Passion. Everything is now done exactly as on Palm Sunday (see pp. 267—270), except that there are no palms to hold and that the cele-brant reads the entire Passion, including the last part which is sung as a Gospel (and before which, bowed, he says *Munda cor meum*), at the Epistle corner. When the first part of the Passion is finished, the deacon takes off the folded chasuble and puts on a rolled-up chasuble or the " broad stole " at the credence.[2] He brings the book of lessons to the altar, lays it on the table and kneeling on the edge of the foot-pace says *Munda cor meum*. He does not ask for the celebrant's blessing. He sings the last part of the Passion as the Gospel at Mass (not signing the book or himself at the beginning). The Acolytes stand on either side of the subdeacon with joined hands, not holding candles. There is no incense; the celebrant does not kiss the book afterwards. The subdeacon gives it at once to the M.C.

If there is to be a sermon it may be preached at this moment.

Bidding Prayers. The BIDDING PRAYERS follow. The celebrant stands at the Epistle corner, the ministers in line behind him. All stand. After each summons to prayer by the celebrant[3] *Flectamus genua* follows and *Levate*, as above. The tone is simple ferial.

---

[1] Cf. p. 259, n. 1.

[2] He wears the broad stole from now to after the celebrant's Communion; then he puts it off and takes back his folded chasuble (p. 245).

[3] While singing the long invitation to prayer (*Oremus*, etc.) the celebrant holds his hands joined, at *Oremus* he opens and rejoins them and while singing the collect itself he holds them extended.

The prayer for the Emperor is left out. At the prayer for Jews the genuflection is not made nor is *Oremus*, etc., said.

The WORSHIP OF THE CROSS [1] follows. Towards the end of the collects the acolytes, or other servers, spread the violet carpet in front of the altar, at the middle, in such a way that one end covers the lowest step, and the rest is spread along the sanctuary to its entrance. On the lowest step they lay the cushion and the white cloth over it.

Unveiling of Cross. When the collects are ended the celebrant and ministers go directly to the sedilia. All in choir sit. The celebrant and subdeacon take off their chasubles (only). They come back to the altar, the celebrant stands at the hinder corner of the Epistle side, on the ground beside the steps, having the subdeacon at his left. Both face the people. The deacon goes to the altar accompanied by the M.C. ; both genuflect. The deacon takes the cross from the altar (detaching it from its base) and brings it to the celebrant covered with its veil. The celebrant holds it so that the figure of our Lord is towards the people. An acolyte brings the Missal from the altar and holds it before the celebrant open at the text *Ecce lignum crucis*. The deacon stands at the celebrant's right. Assisted, if necessary, by the ministers, the celebrant unveils the upper part of the cross about as far down as the cross-piece (exclusively), holding it meanwhile in his left hand. He lifts it with both hands to the height of his face and chants, on notes low in pitch, *Ecce lignum crucis* ; the ministers join him as he continues *in quo salus mundi pependit*. The choir answers *Venite adoremus*, everyone in church kneeling, except the celebrant. All rise ; the celebrant goes to stand on the foot-pace at the Epistle corner, facing the people between the ministers, as before. He uncovers the right arm of the cross and the head of the figure of Christ,[2] raises the cross a little higher, then sings as before, except that he does so in a higher pitch. All kneel during the answer. The third time he goes to the middle of the altar, uncovers the whole cross, handing the veil to the subdeacon (who gives it to the second acolyte to put on the credence), raises it still higher, and sings again in a still higher pitch.[3] When the answer is sung, all remain kneeling ; the celebrant, accompanied by the M.C., descends on the Gospel side, carries with both hands the cross to the carpet prepared, kneels there and lays it so that the upper part rests on the cushion. He rises and genuflects to the cross with the M.C. All rise at the same moment. He goes to the seats, where the ministers (having genuflected on the foot-pace to the cross) meet him.

As soon as the celebrant has completely uncovered the altar cross, servers unveil the processional and all other crosses (only) in the church and sacristy. After the last *Venite adoremus* the choir begins to

[1] This is what our fathers before the Reformation called " Creeping to the Cross."

[2] So the rubric of C.E. (II. xxv, 23) and M.R. (V. ii, § ii, 5). The Missal speaks of uncovering the right arm only.

[3] " Ecce lignum crucis " begins on *fa*. It may be sung conveniently a tone higher each time, beginning first on E♭ (*do* = B♭), next on F (*do* = C), next on G (*do* = D).

sing the Reproaches (*Improperia*) and the hymn *Pange lingua*, with the verse *Crux fidelis* repeated, as in the Gradual. They may sing all or part of this, according to the time occupied by the worship of the cross.[1]

Worship of Cross. At the seats the celebrant and ministers take off their maniples,[2] then their shoes, assisted by the M.C. and acolytes. The ministers remain standing at the seats ; the celebrant, with the M.C. at his left, goes first to worship the cross. He kneels at the end of the carpet on which the cross rests, prays for a moment,[3] rises, kneels again in adoration for a moment about half-way up the carpet, then a third time immediately before the cross. This third time he bends and kisses the feet of the crucified. The M.C. kneels each time with him but does not kiss the cross.[4] Both rise, genuflect towards the cross [5] and go back to the sedilia. Here the celebrant puts on his shoes,[6] maniple and chasuble. He may wash his hands if this is necessary. He is assisted by the M.C. and, if he washes his hands, by the acolytes. He sits and puts on his biretta.

The ministers now go to worship the cross in the same way ; the second M.C. may accompany them if there is a second M.C. The deacon is on the right, he kisses the cross first. They come back to the sedilia and put on shoes and maniples, and the subdeacon his folded chasuble. If the Chapter is present the ministers go to worship the cross after the canons, unless they are canons themselves.

All the members of the choir now come in turn to creep to the cross, those of higher rank before the others. They may all take off their shoes first.[7] They come in groups of two, make the three genuflections, (on both knees), the man on the right kisses the cross first. The servers do so after the choir.

The most convenient and orderly way to arrange the creeping to the cross is that there should be three pairs at least before the crucifix all the time. As the first pair kneel to kiss it the second pair make their second genuflection in the middle of the carpet, the third pair at the same time make their first at the end of the carpet. All rise, the first pair genuflect (on one knee) to the cross and go to their places ; the second pair now becomes the first. Meanwhile a new pair has come to the end of the carpet. All make the (double) genuflection together as before, each pair in their place.

When each pair has kissed the cross they rise and genuflect on one knee to it (at the same moment as the two who come next kneel for their third adoration), one on either side, and go to their places.

---

[1] The singing should end when the Creeping to the Cross ends. There is no justification for singing while the procession goes to the place of repose, and to do so spoils the ceremony.   [2] S.R.C. 2326[4].

[3] Cf. C.E. II. xxv, 25 ; xxvi, 11. The celebrant may recite, for example, the versicle *Adoramus te, Christe, etc.* No rubric prescribes a prostration before the cross.

[4] The M.C. will come to worship the cross himself later, as first of the servers.

[5] From this moment till the beginning of the function of Saturday everyone genuflects towards the cross *in actu functionis* (only).

[6] It is useful to provide a shoe-lift for him and the ministers.

[7] M.R. V. ii, § ii, 15.

As laics may not enter the sanctuary to venerate the cross, after the clergy have done this or while they do so a priest in surplice and black stole may take a cross to a place near the entrance of the choir and place it on another carpet and cushion, that the people may come to it there. This priest genuflects to the cross before carrying it and when he has laid it down. A server may kneel by the cross and wipe the feet of the figure each time when they have been kissed.

Another way, also allowed, is that a priest in surplice and black stole take a crucifix, either the one that has served hitherto or a smaller one, to the Communion rails and there let the people kiss it. They come up

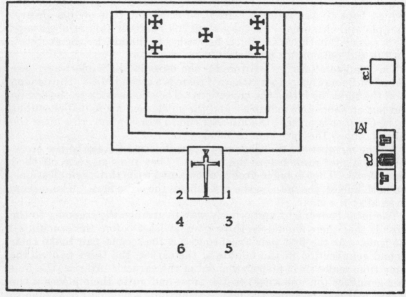

FIG. 39.   CREEPING TO THE CROSS

as to Communion. He may wipe the feet of the figure with a cloth each time.

Reproaches. While the creeping to the cross proceeds the celebrant and ministers read the Reproaches (dividing them in the way indicated in the Missal), sitting with head covered. The second acolyte brings the Missal from the altar and holds it before them. They read the text alternately, the celebrant saying the verses, the ministers answering each time *Agios o Theos, Popula meus, Crux fidelis,* and so on. When they have finished, the acolyte puts the Missal back on the altar.

Towards the end of the creeping to the cross an acolyte lights the six candles on the altar and those of the acolytes. The acolytes unfold the altar cloth and cover with it the front part of the table which had hitherto been uncovered, and place the purifying bowl on the altar near the tabernacle. The Missal open on its stand is placed by the M.C. near the centre of the altar on the Gospel side. The deacon goes to spread the corporal on the altar (genuflecting to the cross before and after), laying the purificator near it on the Epistle side. He makes the usual reverence to the celebrant when passing him ; the subdeacon stands uncovered meanwhile at the sedilia.

When the creeping to the cross is ended, the deacon, accompanied by the M.C., puts it back on the altar in its usual place. Both genuflect to the cross before he takes it. He kneels to lay hold of the cross and carries it with both hands, raised. He genuflects again to it when he has put it on the altar. As the deacon kneels to take up the cross all in choir kneel too, including the celebrant and subdeacon, who kneel at the sedilia. They remain on their knees till the cross is placed on the altar. The acolytes take away the cushion and carpet.

Procession to the Place of Repose. If another subdeacon is to carry the processional cross he will go out towards the end of the worship of the cross and will vest in amice, alb, girdle and folded chasuble (if the folded chasuble is used in the church), without maniple. Otherwise a server in surplice carries the processional cross. Two thurifers go to prepare the thuribles. They take the thuribles, with burning charcoal, but without incense, straight to the place of repose, and wait there. Other servers go to the chapel and there light the torches which will be carried on the way back to the high altar. The men who hold the canopy also wait there.

The cross-bearer, between the acolytes with lighted candles, stands at the entrance of the choir. The celebrant and ministers come before the altar. It will be convenient, if possible, that the members of the choir come out to the middle and stand here, in the inverse order to that in which they will go in procession.[1] All genuflect except the cross-bearer and acolytes. They turn and go by the shortest way, and in silence, to the place of repose, the celebrant and ministers (*unus post alium*) covered.

At the Place of Repose. Here the cross-bearer and acolytes stand aside, to let the others pass. The thurifers are at the Epistle side. The clergy will be within or without the chapel according to the space available, and those arriving first will remain farthest from the altar. The ministers stand at either side at the entrance to the place of repose to let the celebrant come between them. All three uncover and give their birettas to the M.C.[2] and advance to the foot of the altar. All make a prostration ; the celebrant and ministers kneel on the lowest step before the place of repose. All kneel with them. They pray here a short time. Candles are distributed to the clergy and lighted. The torch-bearers light and take their torches. Meanwhile the deacon goes

---

[1] In the procession those of highest rank will be towards the end, nearest the celebrant.

[2] He hands them to a server to take to the sedilia at the high altar.

up to the casket, genuflects,[1] opens it, genuflects again, and comes back to his place. The thurifers come to the celebrant ; he puts incense into both thuribles, not blessing it (nor are the solita oscula made). He kneels again, the deacon hands him the first thurible, he incenses the Sanctissimum as usual.

The M.C. puts the white humeral veil on the celebrant. He and the ministers go up. The celebrant and subdeacon kneel on the edge of the foot-pace. The deacon genuflects, takes the chalice from the urn (leaving the urn open and empty), and hands it to the celebrant, who bows, receives it kneeling, and holds it in the left hand through the veil. He lays the right hand on it ; the deacon arranges the end of the veil so that it shall cover the hand and chalice and then genuflects. The celebrant rises and turns to the people. The ministers change places behind him, and stand at his sides. The cantors intone the hymn *Vexilla regis*, the choir continues.

Procession to High Altar. The procession returns to the High Altar singing the hymn. The cross-bearer goes first between the acolytes, then the clergy and members of the choir holding lighted candles in the outside hand. If not all hold candles, those who do so will walk behind the others, so as to be near the Sanctissimum. The celebrant carries the chalice under the canopy between the ministers, the thurifers walk immediately in front swinging the thuribles. The torch-bearers walk on either side of the canopy. In the choir and sanctuary all remain kneeling with lighted candles to the celebrant's Communion (inclusive). The torch-bearers remain kneeling at each side of the sanctuary.

At the High Altar the acolytes, without genuflection, go and place their candles on the credence, and the cross-bearer retires to the sacristy. The deacon, kneeling *in plano* before the celebrant at the foot of the altar, takes the chalice from him. The celebrant genuflects ; the deacon rises, goes up to the altar and places the chalice on the corporal there. He genuflects and unties the veil over the chalice, but leaves it covered.

As soon as the deacon has taken the Sanctissimum, the celebrant and subdeacon kneel on the lowest step. The M.C. takes the humeral veil and puts it on the credence. The celebrant and subdeacon rise, the deacon stands at the celebrant's side. Incense is put on, not blessed ; the Sanctissimum is incensed, the ministers holding the ends of the chasuble, if necessary.

The second thurifer takes his thurible to the sacristy ; this is not wanted again. When the procession has left the place of repose, all candles there should be put out.

Mass of the Presanctified. The celebrant and ministers go up to the altar. They genuflect before it ; the subdeacon goes to the right of the deacon, and genuflects again when he is at that side. The deacon uncovers the chalice and gives the veil to the M.C., who takes it to the

---

[1] As always when the celebrant is present the deacon withdraws a little to the Epistle side to make each genuflection.

credence. The deacon then takes off the paten and pall. He holds the paten over the corporal ; the celebrant takes the chalice and lets the consecrated Host slip from it on to the paten. He should not touch the Host with his fingers ; if he does he must purify the fingers at once in the little vessel provided for that purpose. He puts the empty chalice on the corporal in its usual place, takes the paten with both hands, and lets the Sanctissimum slip from it on to the corporal, not making the sign of the cross with the paten. He puts the paten on his right, on the corporal. The first acolyte brings the cruets on the dish, genuflecting before he comes up. The deacon takes the chalice in his left, does not wipe it, stands it on the pall. The subdeacon hands the wine cruet to the deacon, who pours wine into the chalice. The subdeacon pours in a little water, as at Mass. The water is not blessed ; the celebrant does not say the prayer *Deus qui humanae substantiae*. The acolyte takes back the cruets, again genuflecting at the foot of the altar. The subdeacon goes to the celebrant's left, genuflecting before he goes and when he arrives. The deacon hands the chalice to the celebrant, who places it on the corporal. The deacon covers it with the pall. There are no oscula, the sign of the cross is not made with the chalice. The thurifer comes up, first genuflecting.

Incensation. The celebrant puts incense into the thurible, does not bless it, takes the thurible from the deacon, genuflects and incenses the chalice and Host, as at the Offertory in Mass, saying the prayer *Incensum istud*, etc. He genuflects and incenses the cross thrice, saying *Dirigatur*, etc., again genuflects and incenses the altar, while continung the prayer, as at Mass. The M.C. removes the Missal momentarily. All genuflect each time in passing the middle, the Blessed Sacrament being present. The celebrant gives the thurible to the deacon, saying *Accendat in nobis*. He is not incensed. The thurifer takes away the thurible ; it will not be used again. The celebrant (saying nothing) washes his hands, as before the Blessed Sacrament exposed, that is, turning so as not to have his back to the middle.[1] The subdeacon holds the water and dish, the deacon the towel. Or the acolytes may serve at the washing of hands.[2] In this case, the ministers stand in line, as at the Collect. The celebrant comes to the middle ; the ministers do so too, behind him in line. All genuflect. The celebrant bows and with joined hands laid on the altar says the prayer *In spiritu humilitatis*[3] ; he kisses the altar, genuflects, turns to the people on the Gospel side, says the *Orate fratres*, etc., turns back the same way, not completing the circle and genuflects again. No answer is made.

Pater Noster. He sings the Lord's Prayer in the ferial tone, his hands joined up to *dicere* and then extended (as at Mass). The ministers stand in line behind him. When the choir has answered *Sed libera nos a malo*, he says *Amen* silently, then sings the prayer *Libera*

---

[1] " Aliquantulum extra Altare in cornu Epistolae " (Missal, C.E., M.R.). See p.125 .

[2] Cf. p. 123.

[3] " Submissa sed intelligibili voce " (C.E. II. xxvi, 19 ; M.R. V. ii, § iv, 11).

nos, Domine in the simple ferial tone, that is, without any inflection of the voice.[1] During this prayer he keeps his hands extended. He does not take the paten nor make the sign of the cross. The choir sings *Amen*.

The celebrant and ministers genuflect. They kneel on the foot-pace behind him ; the M.C. kneels on a step at the Gospel side. The celebrant passes the paten under the Host, holds the paten in the left hand which he rests on the altar, takes the Sanctissimum in the right and elevates It over the paten. He lifts It so that it may be seen by the people, but does not lift the paten.[2] When the Elevation is ended, the ministers rise and stand at the celebrant's sides. The deacon at the right uncovers the chalice. The celebrant lays the paten on the altar, does not genuflect, lowers the Host over the chalice and at once breaks It, as at Mass, saying nothing. He puts the fraction in the chalice ; not making the sign of the cross. The deacon covers the chalice ; all three genuflect. The ministers change sides and genuflect again on arriving.

Communion of Celebrant. The celebrant, bowing over the altar, says the prayer *Perceptio corporis* (alone) silently, his hands joined on the altar. He genuflects with the ministers, takes the paten with the Sacred Host, says silently the prayers *Panem caelestem accipiam*, *Domine non sum dignus* (thrice, striking his breast), *Corpus Domini*, as usual, and receives Holy Communion, making the sign of the cross with the Host, as at Mass, the ministers bowing low. He stands a moment in meditation. Then the subdeacon uncovers the chalice, all three genuflect, the celebrant (saying nothing) gathers up the fragments on the corporal with the paten and puts them into the chalice. The first acolyte brings up the cruets, genuflecting before he comes up. The celebrant drinks the wine with the fraction, not making the sign of the cross with the chalice, saying nothing. Meanwhile the ministers stand at his sides and bow.

Conclusion of Service. Then all in choir stand,[3] and extinguish their candles. The torch-bearers rise, genuflect and retire. The subdeacon pours wine and water into the chalice over the celebrant's fingers.[4] He drinks this as usual. The ministers change places, genuflecting in the middle. The deacon goes to the credence, takes off the broad stole and puts on his folded chasuble. Having genuflected at the foot of the altar, he comes to the right of the celebrant. The Missal is not carried across. The M.C. sees that a server leaves the chalice veil on the table of the altar towards the Gospel side. The subdeacon dries the chalice, covers it with the paten and pall, puts the corporal into the burse and this on the chalice, with purificator, paten, pall and veil, all as usual, then carries it to the credence. He comes back to the celebrant's left, genuflecting before going up the steps. The celebrant bowing and with

---

[1] Cf. p. 259, n. 1.
[2] Cf. C.E. II. xxvi, 20.
[3] Martinucci lets them stand now to the end (I. ii, p. 233, § 93). Le Vavasseur says they sit, rising as the celebrant goes out (ii, § 355).
[4] The usual first pouring of wine alone into the chalice is omitted.

joined hands laid on the edge of the table of the altar says silently the prayer *Quod ore sumpsimus* ; the subdeacon closes the Missal. The M.C. gets the birettas. The acolytes, without candles, come before the altar. The sacred ministers come down the steps ; all genuflect and go to the sacristy, not bowing to the clergy in choir, the celebrant and ministers covered.

When the celebrant and ministers have left the church, the choir recite Vespers, as the day before (p. 285). Meanwhile two servers take from the altar the Missal and altar cloth, leaving only the cross and six candles alight. Everything is taken from the credence and put away in the sacristy. After Vespers the candles are put out.

All the ornament of the place of repose is taken away after Mass of the Presanctified.[1]

§ 8. GOOD FRIDAY IN SMALL CHURCHES

THE preparations are : at the High Altar six candles of unbleached wax, not lighted, the cross (in wood) covered with a violet or black veil,[2] which can easily be removed, a violet cushion at the second altar step in the middle. The credence is covered with a white cloth, not bigger than the top of the table ; on it are placed one altar cloth a little larger than the size of the table of the altar, the Missal on its stand, a black burse with corporal and purificator, the black chalice veil, the purifying bowl with its little towel, cruets as for Mass. Near the credence are a violet carpet, violet cushion and white veil ornamented with violet silk on which to rest the cross, the processional cross veiled in violet. At the altar of repose a corporal is spread before the urn; its key is at hand ; near by are a white humeral veil, the canopy, torches and candles for the procession and a taper. In the sacristy three surplices are prepared for the servers ; a surplice, an amice, alb, girdle, black maniple, stole and chasuble for the celebrant ; the thurible, with fire at hand.

The Memoriale Rituum supposes, as usual, that only the celebrant and three servers take part in the function. However there must be one man or more to hold the canopy in the procession, and others to accompany the Blessed Sacrament with lighted candles.

"**Mass of the Catechumens.**" A sign is given with the rattle, the servers vest, the celebrant washes his hands and vests. He goes to the sanctuary, following the three servers, with hands joined, and head covered. Before the altar he takes off his biretta, bows low, then kneels and prostrates, lying prone with his arms on the cushion, for about the time it would take to say the *Miserere*.

The first and second servers meanwhile spread the one altar cloth on the altar,[3] the third puts the Missal on its stand at the Epistle corner.

---

[1] S.R.C. 4081[6].
[2] M.R. V. i.
[3] M.R. V. ii, § i, 5, adds the direction that they fold the altar cloth in half lengthwise, so that it is doubled on the back part of the altar, the near half of the altar being bare,

The celebrant rises, a server takes away the cushion. He goes up to the altar and kisses it in the middle. He goes to the Missal and there reads the first lesson, with the Tract.[1] He says *Oremus*, genuflects, saying *Flectamus genua*, and all genuflect with him. The second server rising says *Levate*. The celebrant, and all with him, rise. The celebrant with hands extended says the first collect. Then he reads the second lesson, Tract and the Passion, with hands joined, at the Epistle side. At the same place he says, bowed, the prayer *Munda cor meum*, and the last part of the Passion ; he does not kiss the book at the end.

After the Passion a sermon may be preached.

Bidding Prayers. The celebrant, at the Epistle corner, reads the collects, as they stand in the Missal (his hands joined during each admonition, extended for each prayer itself). After each admonition he says *Oremus*, then, genuflecting, *Flectamus genua* ; the second server, rising before all others, says *Levate*, the celebrant, and all with him, rise. The collect for the Emperor is not said ; there is no genuflection at that for the Jews and *Oremus* etc., is not said. Towards the end of these collects the first and third servers spread the violet carpet on the steps at the entrance to the sanctuary, and there on the first or second step the violet cushion and on this the white veil ornamented with violet silk.

Worship of the Cross. When the prayers are finished, the celebrant, descending to the floor by the shortest way, at the same Epistle corner takes off the chasuble (only). He goes to the middle, genuflects, ascends the altar and takes the veiled altar cross. The first server holds the Missal. The celebrant descends on the Epistle side and stands on the ground beside the steps, at the Epistle corner, facing the people and holding the cross. The server holds the Missal open before him. He unveils the upper part of the cross (up to the cross-piece exclusively) with his right hand, holds it up with both hands and " reads in a grave voice (or sings) " [2] the words *Ecce lignum crucis* ; the servers say (or sing) the rest with him, namely, *in quo salus mundi pependit*. All kneel, except the celebrant. The servers say (or chanters sing) *Venite adoremus* and then rise. The celebrant goes to stand on the foot-pace at the Epistle corner, uncovers the right arm of the cross and the head of the figure of our Lord, lifts it higher, and says the same words as before in a higher voice.[3] The servers continue with him and answer as before. The third time he stands on the foot-pace in the middle uncovers the whole cross, lifts it higher still, and says the words still higher. The servers continue with the celebrant and reply as before. The Missal is put back on its stand on the altar, the processional cross and all others in the church are uncovered. The celebrant, carrying the cross raised with both hands, comes to the place where the carpet

---

[1] Should the function be carried out with music, a cleric (if present) will sing the lesson and chanters the Tract, the celebrant meantime reading them in a low tone. The same will be done with the subsequent lesson and Tract (M.R.).

[2] M.R. V. ii, § ii, 4.

[3] " Magis elevans crucem et vocem " (*ib.*, 5).

is prepared, passing on the Gospel side, kneels there and lays the cross on the cushion. The Memoriale Rituum says that if necessary he attaches it with cords. He rises, genuflects towards the cross, goes by his right to the seat and takes off his maniple and shoes, assisted by the servers. He comes alone to worship the cross. He kneels on the carpet, at a suitable distance away, adores for a moment,[1] rises, comes forward, kneels again midway between the place of the first adoration and the cross, then a third time immediately in front of the cross. As he does so the third time he kisses the feet of the Crucified. He rises, genuflects to the cross, goes to the sedile and puts on his shoes and maniple and remaining seated puts on his biretta. The three servers take off their shoes (if they wish to do so) [2] and come forward, kneeling thrice in the same way in prayer and kissing the feet of the Crucified. They may do so together in a group of three, the one on the right kissing first, then the one in the middle, lastly the one on the left ; or the first server may advance alone followed by the two others. The person on the right always kisses the cross first. They go back and put on their shoes.

The people come up and worship the cross—first members of confraternities in their dress,[3] then men, then women, all in pairs—" devoutly and gravely." [4] The Memoriale Rituum makes no provision for any other manner of worshipping the cross. But there seems no reason why, if another priest is present, he should not take the cross to the Communion rails for the people to worship there, kneeling in line, as when they come to Communion. He would wear a surplice and black stole. Or the celebrant himself may do so, saying the Reproaches afterwards.

While the people worship, the celebrant, sitting with biretta, recites the Reproaches, alternately with the second and third servers, in a clear voice. The text and the manner of reciting it in verses are printed in the book. They recite all or part of the Reproaches according to the number of persons taking part in the worship of the cross. If there are singers they begin the Reproaches when the celebrant goes to worship and then he and the servers when ready recite them in a low voice while they are being sung. Meanwhile the first server is to assist at the worship of the cross by the people and see that all is done in order. He may wipe the feet of the crucifix each time when they have been kissed.

Procession to the Place of Repose. Towards the end of the Creeping to the Cross the first server lights the six altar candles ; the third removes the Missal-stand, the second and third servers unfold the altar cloth and spread it full out. The second server brings to the altar the burse and purificator. He spreads the corporal (if he is a cleric) and lays the purificator near it, on the Epistle side, and puts the purifying bowl and its towel or purificator near the corporal. The third server places the Missal—opened—near the centre on the Gospel side, turned

---

[1] See p. 295, n. 3.   [2] M.R. V. ii, § II, 15.
[3] " Sodales cum saccis " (ib., 16).   [4] Ib.

towards the middle, as during the Canon of Mass. When the worship of the cross is ended, the celebrant puts it back on the altar, genuflecting towards it before he lifts it from the cushion, and again after he has put it in its place. All should kneel while the celebrant replaces the cross on the altar. The second and third servers take away the cushion, veil and carpet used for the cross. The first server brings the thurible with burning charcoal from the sacristy and carries it to the altar of repose. The celebrant at the sedile puts on the chasuble, comes to the altar bare-headed, and genuflects. The third server takes the processional cross. The procession goes, by the shortest way, to the place of repose, in this order : First the processional banner (if used) then members of a confraternity in their dress or other " pious men," [1] the processional cross borne by the third server, chanters (if present), the clergy (if any), the celebrant (covered), having at his left, and a little before him, the second server.

At the Place of Repose. At the place of repose all part on either side to allow the celebrant to pass, lay persons remaining outside the altar rails of the chapel, and those of greater dignity being nearer to the altar. The thurifer is at the Epistle side. The celebrant, having uncovered when he came in sight of the most holy Sacrament, first genuflects on both knees on the ground before the altar of repose, then kneels on the lowest step and prays silently for a short time. Meanwhile lighted candles are given to men and the canopy is got ready. All genuflect when the celebrant does so, kneel with him, and remain kneeling till the procession starts back. The celebrant rises, opens the urn, genuflects, comes down, puts incense into the thurible (the second server assisting), not blessing it, kneels on the lowest step and incenses the Sanctissimum. He gives the thurible back to the thurifer, goes up, genuflects, takes the chalice from the urn and places it on the altar. He genuflects again and closes the urn if the ciborium with consecrated particles remains in it.[2] He then comes to kneel on the edge of the foot-pace. Here he receives the humeral vein from the second server, rises, genuflects, takes the chalice in his left hand, holding it through the veil, lays the right on it and covers all with the end of the veil assisted by the second server. He turns and (if there are no singers) begins to recite in a loud tone the hymn *Vexilla Regis*[3] ; he says this during the procession alternately with the second server. All rise, genuflect, and form themselves for the procession to the High Altar.

Procession to the High Altar. It goes, by the shortest way in this order : the banner as before, the men, now holding lighted candles in the outside hand, the cross, the clergy (if any), the thurifer swinging the thurible at his right side, the celebrant under the canopy (held over him by one man or more) having the second server at his left before him.

If the Blessed Sacrament remains in the urn, four candles are left

---

[1] M.R. V. ii, § III, 2.   [2] Cf. p. 290, n. 1.
[3] If there are chanters (in surplice) they follow the cross ; the celebrant then either recites the hymn in a low tone with the server or joins in the singing. The people may laudably join in it also (M.R.).

burning there, otherwise all are extinguished when the procession has gone. When the procession arrives before the altar, the banner is put aside outside the Communion rails, the processional cross near the credence. Laymen stay outside the rails, holding candles and kneeling till after the celebrant's Communion ; the canopy remains outside the rails and is put away.

The celebrant goes straight up to the altar, places the chalice on the corporal, genuflects and comes down the steps. Kneeling on the lowest step the second server takes from him the humeral veil. The celebrant rises, puts incense in the thurible, assisted by the second server, not blessing it, kneels and incenses the Sanctissimum in the usual way.

Mass of the Presanctified. The celebrant rises, goes up to the altar, genuflects, undoes and removes the veil from the chalice, takes from it the paten and pall, placing the paten on the corporal in the middle, in front of the chalice and the pall on the Epistle side outside the corporal. He lets the consecrated Host slip from the chalice on to the paten, not touching It with his fingers. If he does so, he must purify the fingers in the vase for that purpose. He takes the paten with both hands and lets the Host slip from it on to the corporal, in the middle (again careful not to touch It himself), saying nothing and not making the sign of the cross. He lays the paten on the corporal, on the Epistle side.

Meanwhile the third server brings the cruets to the altar, genuflecting before he goes up to the foot-pace. He places them at the Epistle corner and stands by them. The celebrant genuflects and, going towards the Epistle corner, takes wine and water from the server, and pours them into the chalice, as at Mass, holding the chalice in his left hand (or standing it on the pall). He does not wipe the chalice nor bless the water ; nor does he say the prayer *Deus, qui humanae substantiae*. He places the chalice on the corporal at the Epistle side, returns to the centre, genuflects and then sets the chalice in the centre of the corporal in its usual place, not making the sign of the cross with it. He covers it with the pall. Standing in the middle, he puts incense in the thurible, without blessing. The first server, still holding the thurible, comes up for this purpose, first genuflecting ; the second assists.

Incensation. The celebrant takes the thurible from the second server, genuflects and incenses the *oblata*, as usual, saying *Incensum istud*, etc. He genuflects, incenses the cross while reciting *Dirigatur*, etc., genuflects again and incenses the altar (genuflecting whenever he passes the centre), continuing the prayer. While he does so the second server accompanies him and the third removes and replaces the Missal. He gives the thurible back, saying *Accendat in nobis*, etc. He is not incensed ; the thurible is laid aside. He comes down the steps, not turning his back to the Sanctissimum, and washes his hands, standing a little outside the altar at the Epistle corner (on the top step or *in plano*), facing the people, and not reciting the psalm *Lavabo* ; the third server pours the water, the second holds the towel. The celebrant goes to the middle, genuflects and, bowing with hands joined on the altar,

306 THE LITURGICAL YEAR

says, in a low but audible voice, the prayer *In spiritu humilitatis*. He kisses the altar, genuflects, turns to the people on the Gospel side and says *Orate fratres*, etc. No answer is made. He turns back by the same way, not completing the circle, and again genuflects.

Pater Noster. He says (or sings in the ferial tone) the Lord's Prayer, as at private Mass. The servers (or singers) answer *Sed libera nos a malo*. He says *Amen* silently ; then aloud (or in the ferial tone), with hands still extended, he says the prayer *Libera nos, quaesumus Domine*. The servers (or singers) answer *Amen*. He genuflects, uncovers the chalice, slips the paten under the Host, holds the paten in his left hand, resting on the altar, and with the right elevates the Host, so that it can be seen by the people. He leaves the paten on the corporal and immediately lowering the Sacred Host breaks It into three parts over the chalice, as at Mass, but saying nothing. The fraction is put into the chalice without words or sign of the cross.

Communion of Celebrant. He covers the chalice, genuflects and, bowing with hands joined on the altar, says silently the prayer *Perceptio corporis tui*, etc., omitting the two preceding prayers. Again he genuflects, takes the paten in his left hand, the Host in the right, says the prayers *Panem caelestem accipiam* and *Domine, non sum dignus* thrice, striking his breast, and so makes his Communion, as at Mass. He makes the sign of the cross with the Host and says *Corpus Domini nostri*, etc. He pauses awhile in prayer silently, then uncovers the chalice and genuflects. He gathers the fragments on the corporal with the paten, puts them in the chalice, and leaves the paten aside on the corporal. He takes the chalice with both hands [1] and drinks the wine, with the consecrated fragment, not making the sign of the cross with the chalice, saying nothing. The second server brings the cruets to the altar and pours wine and water over the celebrant's fingers. He drinks this one ablution. The first server brings the black chalice veil from the credence and puts it on the altar towards the Gospel side. Meanwhile all rise and put out their candles. The celebrant wipes the chalice with the purificator, and covers it and veils it in the usual manner. The first server, if tonsured, takes it to the credence. The celebrant, bowing with hands joined, says silently the one prayer *Quod ore sumpsimus*, etc. He comes down to the ground before the altar, genuflects with the servers, puts on his biretta and follows them to the sacristy.

Removing the Ciborium. The Memoriale Rituum supposes that the ciborium with consecrated particles for the sick may, if no other place is available, be placed in the urn on Maundy Thursday (p. 290, n. 1). If so, it is now removed. The celebrant, in surplice and white stole, goes to the place of repose. In front of him are the first server, carrying a white humeral veil and burse with corporal, and the other two holding candles (torches). He takes the Blessed Sacrament to a tabernacle, if possible, in the sacristy,[2] or in a remote chapel of the church. In doing

---

[1] So M.R. V. ii, § IV, 22. Authors ignore this departure from the normal practice.

[2] See p. 280.

so he observes the usual ceremonies for such occasions (see pp. 240, 241). A lamp must burn before the place where It is now reserved. If no other place is possible It may stay at the place of repose in the urn.[1] In this case a lamp is left there.

Then the altar candles are extinguished, and the altar and credence are stripped without ceremony.

§ 9. THE FUNCTION WITH CHOIR

IF this simplest possible rite of Good Friday is to be amplified after the manner of a Sung Mass, according to what is said above (pp. 252–253) the following additions will be made. There will be a greater number of servers ; a M.C., cross-bearer, thurifer (or two thurifers), two acolytes, two, four or six torch-bearers for the procession. Men will be appointed to carry the canopy.

The first and second lessons may be sung by lectors. The Passion will be read by the celebrant at the Epistle side, as the Memoriale Rituum describes. But in a Sung Mass he goes to the middle to say the *Munda cor meum* and sings the last part at the Gospel side.[2]

All else may be sung. The celebrant will sing his part as when there are ministers ; the choir will sing the answers, Reproaches, and so on. Vespers may be recited (not sung) after the Mass of the Presanctified.

In some churches a ceremony is made of stripping the altar after Vespers to-day, as on Maundy Thursday. This is nowhere prescribed.

§ 10. HOLY SATURDAY MORNING [3]

THE Holy Saturday service, longest of any that is usually celebrated in a parochial church, consists of five parts : 1. The Blessing of New Fire and the Paschal Candle ; 2. The Prophecies ; 3. The Blessing of the Baptismal Water and Baptism ; 4. The Litanies ; 5. The First Easter Mass and Vespers.

The colour of the Praeconium Paschale (*Exsultet*) and Mass is white, of all the rest violet.

Preparations. In the SACRISTY three amices, albs and girdles are laid out for the celebrant and ministers ; a violet stole and cope for the celebrant ; the deacon's violet stole, folded violet chasubles for deacon and subdeacon [4] ; also white Mass vestments, with tunicle for the subdeacon, but not the deacon's maniple, stole and dalmatic (which are needed at the church door). The thurible, the vessel of holy water [5] and sprinkler, the five grains of incense [6] on a silver salver or plate, the

---

[1] M.R. V. ii, § V, 9.
[2] M.R. V. ii, § I, 11.
[3] C.E. II. xxvii, xxviii ; M.R. Tit. VI.
[4] In greater churches where folded chasubles are available.
[5] Some lustral water should have been kept when the stoups were emptied on Maundy Thursday. If there is none, some must be blessed before the ceremony on Holy Saturday.
[6] The grains of incense are now generally enclosed in little wooden or metal cases, having spikes which can be stuck into the candle, like large nails with spaces in the head where the incense is put. It is quite possible, however, to

processional cross are also made ready. If the church has no font the
acolytes' candles (bleached) are in the sacristy till Mass.

Outside the Door of the Church or, if necessary, in the porch, a fire
(of coal or preferably of charcoal) is prepared in a brazier. This is lit,
just before the ceremony begins, with a spark struck from a flint [1] ; near
the fire are tongs and charcoal to be lighted from the fire and then put
in the thurible. Near at hand (sometimes inside the porch) is a table
covered with a white cloth ; on this are a white dalmatic, maniple and
stole for the deacon and subdeacon's violet maniple ; a Missal covered
with violet, a taper. By the side of this table, supported on a stand,
is the reed [2] holding the triple candle. It may be adorned with flowers.

It is convenient to have a lectern to the left of where the fire will be
placed.

The **High Altar** is vested in the best white frontal, which is then
covered with a violet one. The tabernacle is unveiled, open and empty.
The altar is covered with three altar cloths. The cross is unveiled.
There are six altar candles, not lit, and a Missal, covered in violet, at
the Epistle corner open on its stand (covered with a violet cover over
a white one). In front of the altar the carpet used on feasts is spread,
then covered with a violet one. Or the foot-pace and steps may be left
bare till the Mass.[3]

Near the altar on the Gospel side is the PASCHAL CANDLE [4] in its
candlestick (*in plano*), not lighted. In it in the form of a cross are
prepared five holes in which to insert the grains of incense ; the candle
is placed with these holes facing the Epistle corner of the altar (where
the celebrant will stand during the *Exsultet*).[5] By its side, turned in the
direction in which the Gospel is sung, is a lectern covered with a rich
white veil. A foot or stand in which to put the reed with the triple
candle is at hand (it may be placed to the left of the lectern), and (if
necessary) steps by which the deacon may reach the Paschal candle
when he lights it.

The CREDENCE is covered entirely with a white cloth. On it are
placed all things necessary for a festal High Mass with white vestments ;

---

obtain large grains or to stick several incense grains together, by warming them,
so as to make one larger grain. Five such larger grains may be made. By
warming them again they can be stuck to the candle.

[1] So the rubric of the liturgical books ; and the first prayer of the blessing of
the fire refers to its origin from a flint.

[2] According to the rubric the candles should be arranged on the reed in
triangular formation, not in the form of a trident as one commonly sees. " Cum
tribus candelis in summitate illius," says the Missal, " triangulo distinctis."

[3] If, as is usual, further ornaments, vases of flowers (see p. 321), and so on,
will be used on the altar at the first Easter Mass, these should be prepared beforehand in the sacristy or other convenient place, from which they will be brought
during the litanies.

[4] The candle—which should contain at least 65 per cent. of beeswax—need
not be renewed each year, but only when not enough remains to last until the
end of Paschaltide (S.R.C. 3895[1]).

[5] Cf. S.R.C. 4198[7]. Once it has been blessed the cross of incense grains should
face the congregation. (*Ib.*)

the book containing the *Exsultet* chant,[1] covered with white ; the altar-cards, and over all a violet veil.[2] If the church has a font, the alcoytes' candles of bleached wax are on the credence, not lighted. Near the credence are three violet cushions, to be. used when the Litanies are sung, and a bare lectern for the Prophecies.

The SEDILIA are vested as for feasts, and then covered again with violet. On them are the violet chasuble and maniple for the celebrant, the violet maniples for the celebrant and deacon, the subdeacon's biretta.

The font (if there is one) is emptied into the sacrarium and cleaned beforehand. It is then filled with clear water. It may be adorned with flowers and these may be strewn on the ground. Near the font is a table covered with a white cloth, on which are the two holy-oil stocks containing Chrism and the Oil of Catechumens ; a second aspersory (empty) and its sprinkler ; a vessel to take the water from the font and pour into this aspersory ; a violet stole for the priest who will sprinkle the people, a jug of water and basin for washing hands, bread and cotton-wool on a plate, two towels ; a large vessel to receive some of the water from the font which will be used as lustral water at Eastertide [3] ; a book containing the rite,[4] covered with violet, placed on a lectern (if one is available). If Baptism is to be administered after the blessing of the font, there will be needed, further, salt, a Ritual, the holy Oils, the shell or ladle used to pour the water over the child, a towel to dry the child's head, a white stole and cope, the white robe and candle given after Baptism. The candle will be lit, when the time comes, from the Paschal candle. A taper may be provided for this purpose.

If the Blessed Sacrament is reserved in the sacristy or a side chapel, everything is prepared that It may be brought to the usual place at the end of the ceremony ; namely a white burse with corporal, the key, a white humeral veil, the small canopy.

Assistants. The following persons take part in the ceremony : the celebrant, deacon and subdeacon,[5] a M.C., thurifer, two acolytes, at least two other servers at the blessing of the font,[6] torch-bearers during the Mass at the end. The choir attends throughout.

The function begins after None.

Blessing of New Fire. The celebrant, ministers and servers vest during None. The celebrant wears violet stole and cope, the ministers

---

[1] This will generally be a Missal.

[2] Which may be a humeral veil.

[3] See p. 319.

[4] Usually a Missal.

[5] The same deacon must serve throughout the function (S.R.C. 2684[8], 2965[3]). But the usage that another priest bless the fire and grains of incense is permitted (S.R.C. 2684[8]). In this case he must do so privately, without the sacred ministers, according to the form of the Memoriale Rituum.

[6] They may be those who will serve as torch-bearers. It will be more convenient to have four. They will also be needed to prepare the altar for Mass.

folded chasubles,[1] the deacon his stole. They do not wear maniples. During the ceremony the deacon when handing anything to or receiving anything from the celebrant uses the ceremonial kiss (solita oscula).

The procession comes from the sacristy and goes to the place where the fire has been lit. Three servers walk in front, namely, the first acolyte in the middle carrying the holy water and sprinkler, at his right, the thurifer carrying the thurible (quite empty) and the incense boat with incense in it, on the left the second acolyte holding the plate with the five grains of incense. Behind them comes the subdeacon (of the Mass) holding the cross. He walks alone. Then the choir and clergy who assist; lastly the celebrant, with hands joined, having the deacon at his left, both wearing the biretta. The M.C. walks at the celebrant's right holding, with the deacon, the cope. If they pass the High Altar, all in passing genuflect, except the subdeacon, who has the cross, and the celebrant, who uncovers and bows low. At the entrance of the church; or wherever the fire may be, they stand around it (the clergy of higher rank being nearest the celebrant). The subdeacon holds the cross with his back to the door (or to the High Altar). The first acolyte puts the aspersory on the table, and takes and opens the Missal (if a lectern is not used). On the other side of the fire the celebrant faces the cross, having the deacon at his right and the first acolyte at his left, who holds the book open.[2] The M.C. stands near the deacon, the second acolyte (with the grains of incense) and thurifer near the M.C.

The celebrant and deacon take off their birettas, which they give to the M.C. to put aside for the time. The celebrant reads (or chants in the ferial tone [3]) Dominus vobiscum and the three collects appointed in the Missal for the blessing of the fire. To each the choir answers Amen. During the first two of these collects he makes the sign of the cross over the fire at the points marked; the deacon holds back the end of his cope. The deacon does this each time the celebrant blesses, sprinkles, or incenses the fire.

Blessing the Grains of Incense. Towards the end of the third prayer the acolyte who holds the grains of incense comes with them before the celebrant; he blesses the grains, reciting the prayer without any introductory Oremus. While he does so, the thurifer takes some burning charcoal from the fire, and puts it in the thurible, using the tongs.[4] When the prayer for blessing the grains of incense is finished, the first acolyte shuts the book, puts it back on the table, and takes the holy water and sprinkler. The celebrant puts incense into the thurible and

---

[1] If these are used; otherwise the sacred ministers are in albs (the deacon with his stole).
[2] If a lectern is used the first acolyte keeps the aspersory and stands between the thurifer and second acolyte.
[3] Cf. p. 259, n. 1.
[4] The most convenient arrangement is this, if the fire is not of charcoal: Most churches possess a little wire basket with a long handle for lighting charcoal. The thurifer puts charcoal in this and lays the basket over the fire before the blessing begins. The charcoal in it takes fire and is blessed with the rest. The thurifer lifts the basket from the fire and empties its charcoal into the thurible.

blesses it with the usual formula (*Ab illo benedicaris*), the deacon assisting. The M.C. holds the end of the cope. The deacon hands the sprinkler, the celebrant sprinkles thrice [1] first the grains and then the fire, saying *Asperges me, Domine*, etc., without the psalm. He incenses the grains with three simple swings. Then he incenses the fire in the same way, saying nothing. Meantime all lights in the church are extinguished so that subsequently they may be lighted from the blessed fire.

The first acolyte puts the holy water on the table. The deacon goes

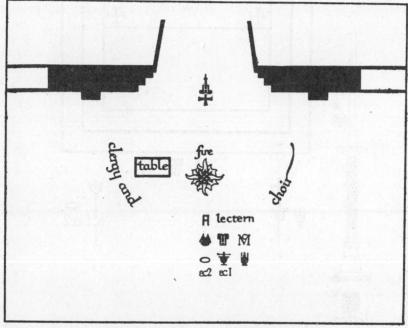

FIG. 40. HOLY SATURDAY : BLESSING THE FIRE
(The ministers wear folded chasubles)

there, bowing first to the celebrant. Here, assisted by the first acolyte and M.C., he takes off the violet chasuble and stole and puts on the white maniple, stole and dalmatic. He comes back to the celebrant's right. The subdeacon puts on his own violet maniple. The first acolyte lights a taper from the blessed fire.

Procession to High Altar. The celebrant again puts incense (in generous quantity) into the thurible and blesses it, as usual. The deacon takes the reed with the triple candle in both hands. The M.C.

---

[1] In the usual way : in the centre, to his left, to his right. The incensation with three simple swings is done in the same manner.

hands his biretta to the celebrant. The procession is formed in this order : first, the thurifer (carrying the thurible open) with the second acolyte at his right holding the plate with grains of incense (held aloft with both hands) ; the subdeacon with the cross ; the choir and clergy ; the deacon holding the reed with both hands, with the first acolyte at

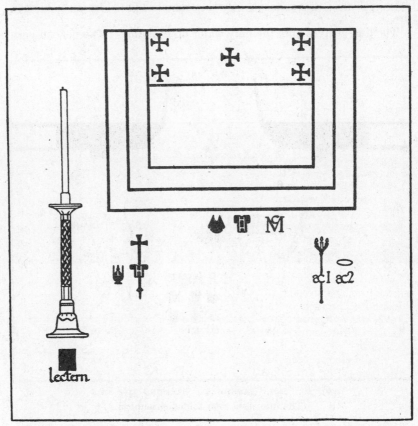

FIG. 41.   HOLY SATURDAY :   BEFORE BLESSING THE PASCHAL CANDLE

his left holding the lighted taper ; the celebrant, with joined hands and covered, having the M.C. at his left.

While the procession goes to the altar, a server carries the deacon's biretta, violet stole and folded chasuble to the sedilia. The table with all on it, is taken away (to the sacristy) ; the holy water used for the fire poured into the sacrarium.

As soon as the celebrant is inside the church, the procession waits, at a sign from the M.C. The deacon lowers the reed and the first acolyte lights one of the three wicks of the triple candle from the taper held by him. Then the deacon holds the reed erect and genuflects. All genuflect with him, except the subdeacon who has the cross. The celebrant takes off his biretta and genuflects. Genuflecting the deacon sings *Lumen Christi*, to the notes given in the Missal. He must sing this at a low pitch, since he will sing it again twice, each time higher. All rise while the choir at the same pitch, answers *Deo gratias*. The procession goes forward. At the middle of the church the same ceremony is repeated ; the acolyte lights the second wick and the deacon sings at a higher pitch. The procession goes forward. When it arrives in the sanctuary before the altar the acolyte lights the third wick, the deacon sings again the same words yet higher,[1] all genuflect as before.

Before the altar the thurifer goes to stand at the Gospel side, the second acolyte with the grains of incense at the Epistle side. The subdeacon with the cross stands at the side of the thurifer. The first acolyte puts out the taper, hands it to the M.C. (who lays it on the credence), takes the reed with the triple candle from the deacon, and stands on the left of the second acolyte. The deacon comes to the right of the celebrant at the foot of the altar steps ; he takes the latter's biretta and hands it to the M.C. who lays it aside. The group at this moment is formed as fig. 41.

All genuflect, except the celebrant (who bows low), cross-bearer and first acolyte (holding the reed). The celebrant goes up to the altar and kisses it, goes to the Epistle corner, and stands there facing the Missal. The deacon remains below. The M.C. brings the book containing the *Exsultet* to the deacon.

Exsultet. The deacon, holding the book, goes up to the celebrant,[2] kneels on the foot-pace, turning towards him, and says *Iube, domne, benedicere*. The celebrant turns to him and gives the blessing, as in the Missal. The form is the same as for the Gospel, except that he says *suum paschale praeconium*, instead of *evangelium suum*. He makes the sign of the cross over the deacon, lays his hand on the book ; the deacon kisses it.

The deacon comes down the steps and stands in the middle at the foot of the altar. All genuflect (the deacon on the lowest step), except the subdeacon and first acolyte. All go to the lectern. Each turns (by his left) and goes straight to his place, as marked here at fig. 42.

The deacon stands in the middle, before the lectern, facing in the same direction as when he sings the Gospel at solemn Mass.[3] At his right is the subdeacon with the cross, then the thurifer. At his left are the first acolyte with the reed, then the second acolyte with the grains of incense. The M.C. stands behind the deacon at his right. All face the same way as the deacon. The subdeacon turns the cross, so that

---

[1] Each time he sings on one note, dropping a minor third on the last syllable (do-la). He may rise a minor third each time : E-C♯, G-E, B♭-G.

[2] The deacon does not lay the book on the altar nor say *Munda cor meum*.

[3] S.R.C. 4057[3] and 4198[8].

it may face the celebrant.[1] The deacon puts the book on the lectern opens it and incenses it, as at the Gospel, but does not sign it nor himself.

Then, with hands joined, he begins to sing the Praeconium. As soon as he does the celebrant turns to face him and all in choir stand. The thurifer takes away the thurible, comes back and stands with hands

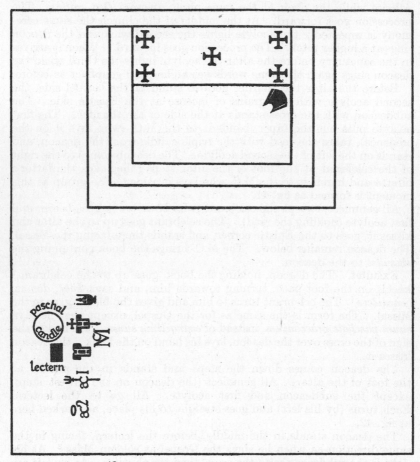

FIG. 42.   HOLY SATURDAY : PRAECONIVM PASCHALE

joined. During the chant the M.C. turns the pages. The choir answers the responses to the part which has the form of a Preface. When the deacon has sung the words *curvat imperia* he stops. He takes the grains of incense, goes to the candle, accompanied by the M.C.

[1] S.R.C. 4198².

and the acolyte who held them.   He fixes the grains in the candle, in the direction of the celebrant,[1] in the form of a cross, thus :

$$1$$
$$4 \quad 2 \quad 5$$
$$3$$

He comes back to the lectern and continues the chant.   The second acolyte puts the dish which contained the grains on the credence ;   takes the taper there and comes back.   The taper is not alight.

Lighting of Candle and Lamps.   When the deacon has sung *rutilans ignis accendit*, he stops again, takes the triple candle from the first acolyte, and with one of the wicks lights the paschal candle.[2]

He comes back to the lectern and continues.   The acolyte fixes the triple candle in the base provided for it, and goes back to his place. When the deacon has sung *apis mater eduxit*, he pauses ;   the second acolyte lights the taper at the triple candle and goes to light all the lamps [3] in the church, beginning with those before the High Altar. Meanwhile the choir and clergy may sit, rising again as soon as the deacon continues.   When the lamp or lamps before the High Altar are lit, the deacon continues and sings to the end.   If the Holy See is vacant, he leaves out the clause for the Pope.   If the see of the place is vacant, he leaves out that for the Bishop.   Otherwise the name of the local Ordinary is to be inserted by everyone, even by exempt Regulars.   All the clause about the Emperor, beginning *Respice etiam ad devotissimum imperatorem nostrum*, to *cum omni populo suo*, is now always omitted.   After the clause for the Bishop the deacon goes on at once to the end, *Per eundem Dominum nostrum*, etc.   The choir answers *Amen*.

As soon as the Praeconium is ended, all in choir and church sit.   The deacon closes the book and leaves it on the lectern.   The subdeacon hands the processional cross to the thurifer, who takes it to the place where it is laid aside, near the credence.   The deacon and subdeacon, with the two acolytes and M.C., come to the middle, genuflect before the altar and go to the sedilia.   The celebrant goes there by the shortest way.

Here the celebrant takes off the cope and puts on violet maniple and chasuble.   The deacon takes off the white vestments and puts on a violet maniple, stole and folded chasuble.   A server takes the white vestments to the sacristy ;   also the violet cope, if the church has no font.

The Prophecies.   The celebrant and ministers go by the shorter way to the Epistle corner of the altar, and stand there, as at the Introit

---

[1] During the Praeconium the cross formed by the grains is to face the celebrant, but after the function it is to face the people (S.R.C. 4198[7]).

[2] He may have to use steps.   If so a server or the M.C. must put them in place. The M.C. may take down the candle to be lighted.   M.R. (VI. ii, § II, 9) says that the candle is to be lighted by means of a taper lighted from the triple candle, and this is certainly easier to do.

[3] The altar candles are not lighted until the Mass.

of Mass (see fig. 7, p. 115). Meanwhile, if necessary, an uncovered lectern for the prophecies is placed in the middle of the choir. The lector who reads the first prophecy comes to it, conducted by the (second) M.C. or an acolyte. He genuflects to the altar, bows to the choir on either side, and chants the prophecy (without any title), to the tone appointed, resting his hands on the lectern or book. The server, who accompanied him stands at his left, a little behind him, holding his biretta. At the end of his chant the lector waits (when there is no Tract) to genuflect at *Flectamus*, rises at *Levate*, then reverences to the altar and choir, and returns to his place. While the lector chants the celebrant reads the prophecy (and the Tract, when it occurs) in a low voice with hands on the book. They are read without any title and without *Deo gratias* at the end. When he has finished he may go to sit at the sedilia, with the ministers.[1] Towards the end of the chanted prophecy (or of the Tract, when it occurs) the ministers stand in line behind the celebrant, as at the Collect of Mass. When the singing of the prophecy terminates all in choir rise ; the celebrant, bowing towards the altar cross, sings *Oremus* ; the deacon genuflects as he sings *Flectamus genua*. All do so with him, except the celebrant

The subdeacon rising sings *Levate*. All rise and stand while the celebrant sings in the simple ferial tone [2] the collect with hands extended. Each of the twelve prophecies is sung in the same way. After the fourth, eighth and eleventh the choir sings the Tract. Meanwhile all continue seated (as long as the sacred ministers sit). After the twelfth, *Flectamus genua* is not said and no one genuflects. The members of the choir and all in church sit during the prophecies, stand as soon as the ministers are in line behind the celebrant (as soon as they rise, if they were seated), genuflect at *Flectamus genua*, rise at *Levate* and stand during the collect.

It is forbidden to leave out the prophecies. All must be sung entirely. It is forbidden for the lector to sing only a part of each and to stop when the celebrant has read the whole.[3]

If there are not twelve lectors the same person may sing several prophecies. It is better that he should not sing two consecutively. The lectors follow in order of rank, beginning with those of lower rank. If there are no clergy to chant the prophecies the celebrant will read them in a clear voice.

Blessing of the Baptismal Water. If the church has no font, the whole of this part is omitted. The ceremony continues at once with the litanies (p. 320).

Towards the end of the twelfth prophecy the acolytes light their candles at the credence. A server, who may be the thurifer, takes the Paschal candle from its candlestick. Another server (not the subdeacon) takes the processional cross. After the prophecy the lectern is removed from the middle of the choir.

---

[1] They go and return *per breviorem*.   [2] Cf. p. 259, n. 1.
[3] S.R.C. 2436[4], 3104[8].

The server who carries the Paschal candle stands at the entrance of the choir. In front of him, as they face the altar, are the cross-bearer and acolytes with their candles.

The celebrant and ministers go directly to the sedilia and take off their maniples. The celebrant also takes off the chasuble and puts on a violet cope. The procession goes to the baptistery. The Paschal candle (alight) is borne first, then the cross between the acolytes, then

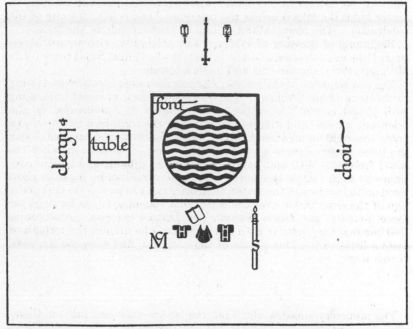

FIG. 43. HOLY SATURDAY : BLESSING THE FONT
(The ministers wear folded chasubles)

the choir and clergy, the M.C., the celebrant between the ministers who hold the ends of the cope.

Procession to Baptistery. All genuflect to the altar before setting out, except the celebrant (who bows low), candle-bearer, cross-bearer and acolytes. On the way to the font the Tract *Sicut cervus* is sung. The celebrant and ministers wear their birettas.

At the entrance to the baptistery the candle-bearer, the cross-bearer and acolytes stop outside and the three latter turn towards the celebrant. The choir also stay outside in two lines. The celebrant and ministers uncover and hand their birettas to the M.C. The celebrant, between the ministers, outside the entrance of the baptistery, standing with joined hands, sings *Dominus vobiscum* and the collect appointed in the

Missal (*Omnipotens sempiterne Deus, respice* . . .) to the simple ferial
tone. A server holds the Missal open before him. Then the bearer
of the candle, the cross-bearer and acolytes go into the baptistery.
The choir and clergy follow them, if there is room there. The celebrant
and ministers enter last. The cross-bearer and acolytes should stand
opposite the celebrant, facing him, on the other side of the font. The
cross is turned towards him. The celebrant stands before the font,[1]
having the deacon at his right and the subdeacon at his left. At the
right of the deacon is the server who holds the Paschal candle. A
server holds the Missal before the celebrant,[2] at his left, in front of the
subdeacon. The clergy stand in line at another side of the font.

Beginning of Blessing of Water. The celebrant, with joined hands
sings *Dominus vobiscum* and the collect, in the simple ferial tone. The
M.C. puts down the birettas and holds a towel.

The last sentence of the prayer, *Per omnia saecula saeculorum*, is sung
to the tone of the Preface. The Preface follows, in ferial tone, sung
with joined hands. After the words *gratiam de Spiritu Sancto*, the
celebrant pauses, and divides the water in the form of a cross, i.e., he
holds the right hand stretched out, with fingers joined, and so—with
the little finger—traces a cross in the water. The deacon takes the
towel from the M.C. and hands it to him to dry his hand. He continues to sing. After the words *inficiendo corrumpat* he lays the right
hand on the surface of the water, then dries it, as before. He makes the
sign of the cross thrice over the water (not touching it), as he sings *per
Deum+vivum, per Deum+verum, per Deum+sanctum*. After *cuius
Spiritus super te ferebatur* with the right hand he divides the water and
casts a little to the four points of the compass, first towards the east,
in this way :

$$1$$
$$3 \quad 4$$
$$2$$

The ministers stand aside, that the water may not fall on them.
The celebrant dries his hand as before. As he sings *Bene+dico te* he
again signs the cross over the water, not touching it. After *in nomine
Patris et Filii et Spiritus Sancti* he changes the tone to a lower key and
continues chanting on one note, as when singing a lesson. After *tu
benignus aspira* he breathes thrice over the water in the form of a cross.

Immersion of Paschal Candle. After *purificandis mentibus efficaces*,
he takes the Paschal candle from the deacon (who has taken it from the
server). Singing again in the Preface tone he plunges the lower end
of the candle a little into the water, as he sings *Descendat in hanc
plenitudinem fontis virtus Spiritus Sancti*. He takes out the candle,
plunges it again a little deeper and sings the same words in a higher key.
He takes out the candle and plunges it in this time to the bottom,
singing again the third time, still higher. Holding the candle in the

---

[1] " Celebrans accedit prope Fontem facie ad Orientem conversa, si ita fieri
possit (ob commoditatem enim praestat ut habeat Fontem a dextris) " (M.R.).

[2] Or it may be placed on a lectern, and this is preferable.

water he breathes three times on the water in the form of the Greek letter Ψ, then continues : *Totamque huius aquae substantiam regenerandi foecundet effectu.* Then he takes the candle from the water, hands it to the deacon, who gives it to the server. The server dries it with a towel. The celebrant continues in the tone of the Preface to the words *novam infantiam renascatur.* Then he lowers the voice and ends *Per Dominum nostrum*, etc., reading, not chanting. The choir answer *Amen.* Each time that the celebrant performs any action the ministers raise the ends of the cope.

Sprinkling. The celebrant and ministers stand away from the font. Another priest (or priests) in surplice and violet stole (handed to him at this moment by the M.C.), or the celebrant himself, now sprinkles the people with the water. A server first fills the aspersory with water from the font. The celebrant receives the water first from the deacon, unless another priest is to sprinkle the people. If another priest assists, he comes to the celebrant and hands him the sprinkler, bowing and with the solita oscula. The celebrant makes the sign of the cross on his forehead with the water, sprinkles the priest and ministers (who bow and make the sign of the cross), then hands him the sprinkler. The priest sprinkles the choir and clergy (as at the Asperges but in silence) then goes round the church, sprinkling the people, accompanied by a server who holds the aspersory. Meanwhile the celebrant and ministers may sit, and put on their birettas. The priest who sprinkles the people comes back to the font, gives the vessel, sprinkler and stole to the M.C., who lays them aside ; then goes to his place again as before. If there is no other priest to do this, the celebrant does the sprinkling after having taken the water himself. He is accompanied by the ministers, M.C. and a server holding the vessel. While the people are sprinkled, a server (or the sacristan) takes from the font some of the water in a vessel (or vessels) and from this fills the holy-water stoups in the church ; part of this blessed water is put aside for the blessing of houses, the Asperges on Easter Day, etc.

Infusion of Holy Oils. A server takes the stocks of holy Oils,[1] stands at the right of the deacon and hands them to him. The celebrant, standing at the font as before, pours a little of the Oil of Catechumens into the water in the form of a cross, saying aloud (not singing) : *Sanctificetur et foecundetur*, etc. He hands the stock back to the deacon, who gives it to the server. In the same way he takes the Chrism, pours a little in the form of a cross saying *Infusio Chrismatis*, etc.

[1] The holy Oils should be those blessed by the Bishop the preceding Maundy Thursday. Rectors of churches are bound to procure these in time for this ceremony, if possible. If they have not done so, if they will have the new Oils in a short time, and if no one will be baptized during this function, they may omit this part of the ceremony now. It will then be supplied later *privately* by a priest in surplice and violet stole (S.R.C. 2436³, 2650³, 3879). But if the newly blessed Oils cannot be soon got or a Baptism must take place before they arrive, the Oils of the last year may be used for the blessing of the font (S.R.C. 2773¹, ², 3092, 3879 ; cf. C.J.C. 734). Baptism may not be administered with the water until the holy Oils have been added.

He takes both stocks in his right hand and pours from both at once, saying the form *Commixtio Chrismatis sanctificationis*, etc., making three crosses over the water as he says the last words, where crosses are marked in the Missal. He then mixes the oil and water together, stirring all round with the right hand extended. He wipes his hand on cotton-wool, then washes his hands (using bread to cleanse them) and dries them, the deacon presenting the towel.

Baptism. If Baptism is to be administered, it follows now. The sacrament is administered, in every way as usual (beginning in the porch of the church [1]), except that the ministers assist on either side and hand what is wanted to the celebrant. If they have worn folded chasubles they keep them during the Baptism. The candle given after Baptism is lighted at the Paschal candle. After baptizing, the celebrant (who had put on a white stole and cope after the anointing of the child with Oil of Catechumens) resumes the violet vestments. Finally, the celebrant washes his hands with bread and water. Servers hold the vessel, basin and towel, the ministers hold the ends of the cope.

While the font is being blessed, a server, or the sacristan, lays three violet cushions before the altar, on the highest step for the prostration during the litanies. A stool may be set in the middle of the choir, with a book from which the cantors will sing the litanies. If this would hinder the procession returning, it should be placed there later.

Litanies. The litanies should begin while the procession returns to the altar. The procession comes back in the same order in which it went to the font. Meanwhile two cantors in surplices, walking immediately behind the cross, sing each petition with its response. The whole petition and response are repeated by the choir. Before the altar all genuflect (except the candle-bearer, the cross-bearer and acolytes) separate to let the celebrant, ministers and servers pass, then kneel in their places. The server who carried the Paschal candle puts it back in its candlestick. The acolytes put their candles on the credence, the cross-bearer puts the processional cross aside.

The celebrant, between the ministers, arrives before the altar ; they genuflect, he bows. All three go to the sedilia. The celebrant takes off the cope (only), the sacred ministers take off the folded chasubles, if they have worn them. The M.C. and acolytes aid them and then the acolytes take these vestments and carry them to the sacristy. The celebrant and ministers at his sides kneel on the lowest step and prostrate, lying on the steps with their arms and face downward on the cushions at the edge of the foot-pace.

The two cantors kneel in the middle of the choir before the stool, if there is one there. The litanies continue, having gone on without interruption since the procession left the baptistery.

If the church has no font, the litanies (duplicated) follow at once after the prophecies. In this case a server lays the cushions on the steps during the last prophecy ; when this prophecy is over, the lectern is taken away from the middle and a stool with a book containing the text

---

[1] The bearer of the Paschal candle remains in the baptistery.

of the litanies is put in its place. The celebrant and ministers, at the end of the last collect, go to the sedilia and there take off chasubles and maniples ; they come to the altar, reverence to the cross, and prostrate on the steps, leaning on the cushion. Two cantors kneel at the stool and begin the litanies.

Peccatores. When the cantors arrive at the petition *Peccatores, te rogamus audi nos*, the celebrant and ministers rise. The M.C. and servers rise with them. All make the usual reverence to the altar, and go to the sacristy, not bowing to the choir.[1] The celebrant and ministers walk one behind the other, wearing birettas. The acolytes do not carry candles. If the font has been blessed, their candles remain on the credence ; if not, they will find them and light them in the sacristy.

If the sacristy is very far away, the celebrant and ministers may go to the sedilia to vest for Mass. In this case the white vestments must be brought there beforehand.

Preparation of Altar for Mass. As soon as the sacred ministers have left the sanctuary, servers prepare the altar for the Mass. They take off the violet frontal, so as to show the white one under it. They take away the cushions and violet carpet, if there is one. If there has been no carpet, they now lay down one adorned as for the greatest feasts. They put on the altar the Missal covered with white, and the altar cards. They decorate the altar as for the chief feast of the year. According to the Ceremonial of Bishops and the Memoriale Rituum this means that they may put vases of flowers between the candles.[2] They light the six candles on the altar. All violet coverings in the sanctuary are taken away. Meanwhile, in the sacristy, the celebrant and ministers vest for High Mass, in white, assisted by the M.C. and acolytes.

First Easter Mass. As the cantors sing the petition *Agnus Dei*, etc., the procession comes from the sacristy. The acolytes come first.[3] If their candles were in the sacristy they carry them lighted ; if not, their hands are joined. The M.C. follows, then the subdeacon, deacon and celebrant, one behind the other, wearing birettas. They uncover at the entrance of the choir, but do not bow to the members of the choir, since these are kneeling. They should arrive before the altar as the petition *Christe, audi nos* is sung.

As soon as the choir has answered *Christe, exaudi nos* they rise and sing the *Kyrie, eleison*, as at High Mass. The two cantors go back to their place. The celebrant and ministers make the usual reverence to the altar and begin Mass. The psalm *Iudica me* is said, with the verses *Gloria Patri* and *Sicut erat*. Then the confession as usual. The sacred ministers go up to the altar and incense it, as at every High Mass. The thurifer must bring the thurible in time for this, unless he has brought it at the head of the procession before Mass. There is no Introit. The celebrant, having been incensed at the Epistle corner, says the *Kyrie*,

---

[1] Because the choir kneels. See p. 23.
[2] C.E. I. xii, 12 ; M.R. VI. ii, § VI, 2.
[3] Or the thurifer may lead the procession with the thurible.

eleison with the ministers. He comes to the middle and intones *Gloria in excelsis Deo.*

The sanctuary bell and church bells are rung.[1] All the violet veils over pictures and statues in the church and sacristy are taken down. The choir begins the *Gloria* as soon as the celebrant has intoned it. It is accompanied. From now the organ is played throughout Mass, as on feasts.

Chanting of Alleluia. High Mass proceeds as usual, with the following notable exceptions : When the celebrant has read the Epistle he does not go on at once to read the Gradual. He waits till he has blessed the subdeacon after the chanted Epistle. Then, at the Epistle corner (the deacon and subdeacon standing in a semicircle as for the Introit) he sings *Alleluia* thrice, to the tone in the Missal, with hands joined, raising the pitch of his voice each time. The choir answers, repeating *Alleluia* at the same pitch. The celebrant reads, and they sing the Gradual and Tract.

Offertory. At the Gospel the acolytes stand on either side of the subdeacon or lectern, in their usual place, but do not hold candles. Incense is used as usual. The Creed is not sung. The celebrant sings *Dominus vobiscum* and *Oremus* at the Offertory as usual, but the Offertory antiphon is not said nor sung. The organ is played to the beginning of the Preface. If the Sanctissimum is normally reserved at the High altar a ciborium with particles and the pyx with the Host for Benediction are brought up at the Offertory. They are consecrated at this Mass and put in the tabernacle by the deacon after the Communion.[2] At the Lavabo *Gloria Patri* is added to the psalm. The Easter Preface is sung, with the clause *in hac potissimum nocte,* as noted in the Missal. The Paschal form of the *Communicantes* prayer is said, again with the form *noctem sacratissimam celebrantes.* The Paschal form of the *Hanc igitur* prayer is said. The *Agnus Dei* is not said. The kiss of peace is not given, so the subdeacon does not then go up to the altar. After the celebrant has put the consecrated Particle into the chalice the deacon covers it. Both genuflect ; the deacon goes to the left of the celebrant and genuflects on arriving. With him the subdeacon genuflects, and then goes to the right of the celebrant, not genuflecting on arrival. Meanwhile the celebrant says the three usual prayers before his Communion. Holy Communion may be distributed to the faithful at this Mass.[3]

Vespers. As soon as the Communion of priest and people is over the choir sit. Instead of the Communion antiphon the cantors begin Vespers, intoning the antiphon *Alleluia, alleluia, alleluia.* It is con-

---

[1] They are rung as long as the celebrant says the " Gloria." The church bells may be still rung while the choir sings the " Gloria." But these may be rung only if the church (where there are several) is the chief one or, if it is not, if the chief church has already rung its bells.

[2] This is, strictly, only necessary if there will be Communion of the people during Mass. After Mass the Sanctissimum will be brought back to the tabernacle.

[3] C.J.C. 867, § 3.

tinued by the choir. The cantors intone the first verse of the psalm, *Laudate Dominum omnes gentes*. This is sung, as usual, with *Gloria Patri*, etc. ; the antiphon is repeated.

The thurifer must bring the thurible from the sacristy in time for the incensing at the Magnificat, which will now occur.

While the choir sings the psalm, the celebrant, at the Epistle corner, says it, with the antiphon, alternately with the ministers. They stand as at the Introit. With joined hands the celebrant then intones the antiphon *Vespere autem sabbati*. The melody is in the Missal. The choir continue it, while the celebrant and ministers recite it in a low voice. Then two cantors intone the *Magnificat*. The celebrant makes the sign of the cross and goes to the middle, with the ministers, who stand at his sides. The thurifer comes up, incense is put on and blessed, the altar is incensed as usual. While he incenses, the celebrant may recite the *Magnificat* alternately with the ministers. At the end of the incensing the deacon, having the subdeacon at his left, incenses the celebrant, who stands at the Epistle corner, as at Mass. The deacon, accompanied by the thurifer at his left, incenses the choir as usual. Meanwhile the subdeacon goes to the Epistle corner and stands at his place as for the Introit. When he has incensed the choir the deacon comes to the Epistle side of the altar and incenses the subdeacon, who turns towards him. The deacon then goes to his place, as at the Introit, and is incensed by the thurifer, to whom he has handed the thurible after having incensed the subdeacon. The thurifer incenses the servers and people (p. 205). When the antiphon after the *Magnificat* has been sung the celebrant goes to the middle, the ministers go behind him and stand there in line. He sings *Dominus vobiscum*, then, at the Epistle corner, with hands extended, the prayer *Spiritum nobis, Domine, tuae caritatis infunde*, etc., which prayer serves as both Post-communion of Mass and collect of Vespers.

Mass ends as usual, except that at the verse, *Ite, missa est* and at its response *Alleluia* is added twice, to the tone provided in the Missal.

After Mass the white conopaeum is put on the tabernacle and the Sanctissimum is brought back thither. The reed with the triple candle is taken away.

Holy Communion may be distributed during and immediately after Mass.[1]

§ 11. HOLY SATURDAY IN SMALL CHURCHES

THE function consists of five parts : 1. The Blessing of New Fire and the Paschal Candle ; 2. The Prophecies ; 3. The Blessing of Baptismal Water and Baptism ; 4. The Litanies ; 5. The First Easter Mass and Vespers.[2]

Preparations. Outside the main door of the church, or (if necessary) in the porch, a table is set covered with a white cloth. On it are placed

---

[1] See p. 332.　　[2] M.R. Tit. VI.

a small book-stand [1] (as used on the altar) with a Missal open at the beginning of the blessing of the fire ; also a dish, if possible of silver, with the five grains of incense ; an empty thurible and the incense boat with incense ; the aspersory with holy water and a sprinkler ; a white maniple, stole and dalmatic ; a taper.   Near this table is a small fire (preferably of charcoal), lit just before the ceremony from a flint, in some convenient vessel ; tongs to take charcoal for the thurible ; the reed with triple candle.[2]

The High Altar is prepared, with the cross unveiled, six candles of bleached wax, and the Missal at the Epistle corner, open, on a stand covered with a violet cover over a white one.   The altar has a white frontal and over this a violet one.   On the Gospel side of the sanctuary is the Paschal candle (with five holes in it in the form of a cross [3] prepared for the grains of incense) in a candlestick, in front of it a lectern (in plano) covered with white [4] for the Praeconium (Exsultet) ; a stand in which to place the reed with the triple candle (it may be placed to the left of the lectern) ; if necessary steps by which the celebrant may reach the Paschal candle, to put in the grains of incense and to light it.   The sanctuary lamp and other lamps in the church are ready to be lit.

The credence is covered with a white cloth.   On it are a Missal (or other book) for the Praeconium, the chalice arranged for Mass, with white veil and burse, the cruets, dish and towel, a taper, the altar-cards and bell.   The whole is covered with a violet (humeral) veil.   At the sedile the violet maniple and chasuble are made ready.

In the sacristy the surplices are laid out ready for the four [5] servers, amice, alb, girdle, violet stole and cope, for the celebrant [6] ; a white maniple, stole and chasuble ; a white humeral veil ; canopy and torches for the carrying of the Blessed Sacrament back to the altar at the end ; the processional cross.

If there is a baptistery and font, a table is prepared there and covered with a white cloth ; on it are an empty aspersory [7] and sprinkler, vessels to take some of the water from the font ; the stocks containing Oil of Catechumens and Chrism ; a basin and water with bread on a plate, to wash the celebrant's hands, cotton-wool, and two towels ; a lectern with a Missal on it open at the rite of the blessing of the font. If Baptism is to be administered, a copy of the Ritual will be required, further a white stole and cope, salt, the holy Oils, the ladle or shell to

---

[1] A lectern, if available, is more convenient.

[2] Cf. p. 308, n. 2.

[3] This cross should face towards the people (M.R. VI. i).

[4] M.R. says the lectern is to be " pulchre ornatum " ; C.E. (II. xxvii, 1) that it is to be covered with a white silk or a cloth of gold veil.

[5] For Holy Saturday M.R. requires a minimum of four servers.

[6] If a violet cope is not available, the celebrant carries out the blessing in alb and stole.

[7] If the church possesses only one aspersory, it is used first for the fire, emptied into the sacrarium during the procession up the church, taken to the baptistery and used again for baptism water.

pour the water, a towel to dry the child's head, the white robe and candle given after Baptism.

Blessing the New Fire. Before the service begins the fire is lit outside the church with a flint.[1] The four servers vest in cassock and surplice in the sacristy ; the celebrant vests there in amice, alb, girdle, violet stole and cope.

The procession goes to the place of the new fire in this order : the first server with hands joined, then the third server bearing the processional cross, lastly the celebrant, wearing the biretta, between the second and fourth servers, who hold the ends of his cope. If they pass before the High Altar, all genuflect, except the celebrant, who uncovers and bows low. · At the door of the church the cross-bearer stands with his back to it (or to the altar, if this ceremony takes place in the porch). In front of him is the table. The celebrant stands on the other side of this table, with the fire at hand. The cross is held so as to face him. The second and fourth servers are at his sides.

Standing so the celebrant, with hands joined, says *Dominus vobiscum*, and, reading from the Missal on its stand or held by a server, the three prayers for blessing the fire, then the fourth prayer for blessing [2] the grains of incense (which are on the table). When he makes the sign of the cross, the second server, at his right, raises the end of the cope. The servers answer these and all prayers during the whole ceremony.

While he blesses the grains of incense the first server, who now becomes thurifer, takes charcoal from the fire with tongs [3] and puts them into the thurible. The celebrant puts incense on and blesses it as usual, the second server assisting, holding the boat and handing the spoon with the solita oscula. The fourth comes round to the priest's right and lifts the end of the cope. The celebrant sprinkles [4] thrice first the fire and then the grains of incense, saying *Asperges me, Domine*, etc., not the psalm. He incenses the fire and grains each with three simple incensings, saying nothing.

Assisted by the fourth server the celebrant now takes off the violet stole and cope and puts on the white maniple and the stole, wearing this like a deacon, from the left shoulder to under the right arm ; lastly the white dalmatic. Meanwhile the second server lights a taper from the blessed fire. The fourth takes the plate with the grains of incense. The celebrant again puts incense into the thurible (held by the first server) and blesses it. Then he takes the reed with the triple candle.

Procession to High Altar. The procession enters the church in this order : first the thurifer and server with grains of incense, side by side, the thurifer to the left ; next the cross-bearer (i.e., the third server), then the celebrant with the reed, having the second server carrying the lighted taper at his left. While this procession goes up the church the sacristan or an extra server takes the violet vestments and the biretta

---

[1] Cf. p. 308, n. 1.
[2] This prayer is not preceded by *Oremus*.
[3] Cf. p. 310, n. 4.
[4] Cf. p. 311, n. 1.

to the sacristy or sedile. What remains of the holy water is poured
into the sacrarium, if the aspersory is needed in the baptistery.

As soon as the celebrant is within the church the procession pauses.
The second server lights one wick of the triple candle from the taper ;
the celebrant then holds the reed erect and genuflects. All genuflect
with him, except the cross-bearer. He says aloud (or sings) *Lumen
Christi*, and rises. All rise while the servers (or chanters) answer *Deo
gratias*. The procession goes forward. At the middle of the church it
pauses again, and the second server lights the second wick of the triple
candle ; all is done as before, except that the celebrant raises his voice
to say or sing *Lumen Christi*. The procession goes on till the celebrant
arrives before the altar steps, the others parting that he may pass.
Here the third candle is lit in the same way, the celebrant raising his
voice still higher to say *Lumen Christi*. When they rise with the celebrant this third time, all stand in a straight line, with him in the middle,
before the altar thus : the thurifer is at the Gospel corner, the third
server with the cross beside him to his right, then the celebrant, on his
right the second server, and to his right the fourth with the grains of
incense. The second server puts the taper on the credence and takes
the Missal. He hands this to the celebrant, who hands him in return
the reed. The server holds the reed. The celebrant, with the book
closed in his hands (its opening towards his left hand), kneels on the
lowest altar step. He does not say *Munda cor meum*, but only the
prayer *Iube, Domine, benedicere. Dominus sit in corde meo et in labiis
meis, ut digne et competenter annuntiem suum Paschale Praeconium.
Amen.* He rises and genuflects [1] (on the step) as do all the others
(*in plano*), except the cross-bearer. All go to the lectern before the
Paschal candle and stand there in this order. The celebrant is in front
of the lectern. At his right are the cross-bearer, then the thurifer ; at
his left the server holding the reed, then the server with the grains of
incense (fig. 44, p. 327).

Exsultet. All look in the same direction as the celebrant, facing the
book. The processional cross is turned towards him. He places the
book on the lectern and incenses it, as the Gospel book is incensed at
High Mass ; the thurifer takes away the thurible, then returns and
stands where he had been. All in church stand. The celebrant, with
hands joined, reads the Praeconium " in a clear voice (or singing)." [2]
The servers (or singers) answer the versicles which occur in the Praeconium. When he has said *et curvat imperia*, he pauses and puts the
five grains of incense into the candle,[3] in this order :

$$1$$
$$4 \quad 2 \quad 5$$
$$3$$

The server who holds the dish assists. If necessary, the celebrant
goes up the steps. Then the fourth server, who has held the grains of

---

[1] While he acts as deacon he genuflects to the altar.
[2] M.R. VI. ii, § II, 6 : " clara voce (vel cantans)."
[3] The cross formed by the grains should face the people (M.R.).

incense, goes to put the empty plate on the credence and takes there a
taper ; then comes back to his place as before.   The celebrant continues
to recite (or sing) the *Exsultet*.

Lighting of Candle and Lamps.   When he has said *rutilans ignis
accendit*, he pauses again and lights, with the aid of a taper, the Paschal

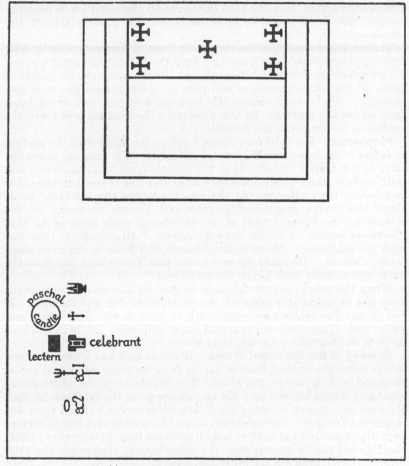

FIG. 44.   HOLY SATURDAY IN A SMALL CHURCH :
PRAECONIVM PASCHALE

candle from the triple candle.   He continues the Praeconium.   After
the words *apis mater eduxit*, he pauses, while the fourth server goes to
light the lamps with the taper that had been lit from the triple candle.
The celebrant waits only till the lamps before the High Altar are lit,
if there are many in the church.   He then continues the *Exsultet* to the

end.   If the Holy See is vacant, he omits the clause for the Pope ; if the local see is vacant, he omits that for the Bishop.   In any case he omits all the clause for the Emperor.   After *gubernare et conservare digneris* he goes on at once to the end : *Per eumdem Dominum nostrum,* etc.

When he has finished the Praeconium the celebrant closes the book. The second server fixes the reed in the stand provided for it near the lectern, the third puts the cross aside on the Epistle side of the sanctuary.

The celebrant goes to the sacristy.   In front of him walk, side by side, first the thurifer and fourth server ; then the second and third servers. All genuflect to the altar before going.   In the sacristy the celebrant takes off the white vestments and puts on a violet maniple, stole and chasuble.   Or he may change the vestments at the seat or credence assisted by the servers.   In this case only the thurifer will leave the sanctuary to put away the thurible.

Prophecies.   The celebrant comes back to the altar with the servers as before.   He bows low, the servers genuflect.   He goes up, kisses the altar in the middle and stands at the Epistle corner.   The second and third servers stand before the lowest altar step, right and left, the other two before the credence.   At the Epistle corner the celebrant reads aloud the twelve prophecies, prayers and Tracts, observing all the rubrics in the Missal ; that is, he genuflects, each time as he says *Flectamus genua* ; a server answers *Levate.*   All genuflect, then rise with the celebrant.   He extends his hands and bows to the cross while saying *Oremus.*   He reads the prophecies and Tracts with hands on the book, the collects with hands stretched out.[1]

When the prophecies are finished, he goes by the shorter way to the credence or sedile and takes off the violet chasuble and maniple.   If the church has no font he comes back at once to the altar in alb and violet stole ; the litanies begin and are duplicated.   If there is a font he puts on the violet cope and sits awhile.

Blessing of the Baptismal Water.   If the church has a font, the first server takes the lighted Paschal candle from its candlestick and comes to stand with it before the altar.   The third takes the processional cross and stands before him ; the two others go to the celebrant's sides. He rises and begins to recite the Tract *Sicut cervus,*[2] unless there are chanters to sing it.   The celebrant bows, the second and fourth servers with him, genuflect to the altar and all go to the font, in this order : First, the Paschal candle-bearer, then the cross-bearer, afterwards the celebrant covered, between the other two servers, slowly reciting the Tract with them (unless it is sung).

All stop outside the baptistery.   The cross-bearer turns round and

---

[1] M.R. VI. ii, § III, 3, gives directions for this part if the function be a sung one.

[2] Unless there are chanters present, the celebrant will need to have the M.R. or some other book containing the Tract, as he is to recite it with the servers on the way to the font ; and a book for the recitation of the litanies on the way back.

faces towards the celebrant. The fourth server takes the book from the table there and holds it before him. With joined hands he says *Dominus vobiscum* and the prayer *Omnipotens sempiterne Deus, respice*. The servers answer.

Beginning of Blessing. Then the server with the Paschal candle and cross-bearer go into the baptistery. They stand on one side of the font facing the celebrant and other servers, who enter after them and stand on the other. The celebrant before the font facing eastwards,[1] if possible, says the prayer appointed and continues the Preface, reciting all with hands joined. The second and fourth servers stand at his sides. While saying the Preface he performs all the actions appointed in the rubrics of the Missal. After saying *gratiam de Spiritu Sancto*, he divides the water, in the form of a cross, with the right hand extended, the little finger tracing the cross ; then wipes his hand on a towel offered by the second server. After *non inficiendo corrumpat*, he lays the right hand palm downwards touching the water, and again dries it as before. At the words *per Deum+vivum, per Deum+verum, per Deum+sanctum*, he makes the sign of the cross thrice over the water, not touching it. After *cuius Spiritus super te ferebatur* with the right hand he divides the water and throws a little to the four points of the compass, beginning at the east, in this order :

$$1$$
$$3 \quad 4$$
$$2$$

The servers stand aside, so that no water shall fall on them. He continues to read : *Haec nobis praecepta* in a lower tone. After *tu benignus aspira*, he breathes thrice over the water, in the form of a cross.

Immersion of Paschal Candle. After *purificandis mentibus efficaces*, he takes the Paschal candle and plunges its lower end a little into the water saying *Descendat in hanc plenitudinem fontis virtus Spiritus Sancti*. He draws out the candle, plunges it again deeper, repeating the same words in a higher tone ; draws it out and plunges it in once more, this time to the bottom of the font, repeating the words yet higher. Then, still holding the candle in the water, he breathes thrice over the water in the form of the Greek letter Ψ, continues *Totamque huius aquae substantiam regenerandi foecundet effectu* and then takes out the candle. He hands it back to the first server, who dries it with a towel. He says the conclusion, *Per Dominum nostrum*, etc., in a lower voice. The servers answer *Amen*. Each time the celebrant performs any action the second server at his right raises the end of the cope. The same server now fills the aspersory with water from the font. He hands the sprinkler to the celebrant with the usual oscula. The celebrant dips the sprinkler into the aspersory, makes the sign of the cross with the water on his own forehead, then sprinkles the servers and bystanders. Between the second and fourth servers (the second holding the aspersory) he goes round the church, sprinkling the people.

[1] M.R. VI. ii, § IV, 8.

The second and fourth servers.[1] having come back to the font, put some of the water from it into a vessel, from which to fill the holy-water stoups in the church, and for the blessing of houses and other things.

Infusion of Holy Oils. The celebrant at the font takes the stock of Oil of Catechumens and pours a little into the font, in the form of a cross, saying aloud *Sanctificetur et fœcundetur*, etc. He then takes the stock of Chrism, pours some of that into the water, in the form of a cross, saying aloud *Infusio Chrismatis*, etc. Then he takes both stocks in his right hand and pours from both together in the form of a cross (thrice), saying *Commixtio Chrismatis salutis*, etc. He mixes up all the water and Oils with the right hand. Then he wipes his hands on cotton-wool offered by the second server. The fourth brings the vessel of water, basin and bread ; the celebrant washes his hands and dries them.

Baptism. The Memoriale Rituum says that Baptism is to be administered at this moment if there is anyone to be baptized. The celebrant, having washed his hands, goes, preceded by the cross-bearer and accompanied by the second and fourth servers (the first bearing the candle remains in the baptistery), to the porch of the church where those to be baptized and their sponsors are. He carries out the rite of Baptism as given in the Ritual up to the anointing with the Oil of Catechumens (inclusive) outside the rails of the baptistery. Then he changes the violet stole and cope for white ones, and entering the baptistery carries out the baptism rite, as in the Ritual. Then he washes his hands and changes again to violet stole and cope. The procession goes back to the altar in same order as it came. As it moves off the celebrant begins the recitation of the litanies with his assistants, who repeat fully each invocation and response. The server who has borne the Paschal candle puts it back in its candlestick ; the processional cross is put aside, in its usual place. The celebrant before the altar, between the second and fourth servers, takes off his biretta and bows ; they genuflect. He takes off the violet cope before the altar but retains the stole. He kneels [2] on the lowest step ; the servers kneel at his sides or behind him.

Litanies. So he recites the litanies, reading them from a book (Missal) placed on a stool before him. He says each clause entire ; the servers repeat it. When he says the petition *Peccatores, te rogamus audi nos*, the first and third servers begin to prepare the altar for Mass. The others remain on their knees and continue to answer. The first and third servers take away the violet frontal, showing now the white one ; they remove the violet cover of the Missal-stand and the violet veil at the credence. They light the six candles ; and put vases of flowers between them if this be the custom.[3]

---

[1] Or the sacristan may do this.

[2] If there are chanters they begin and continue the singing of the litanies, in which the celebrant takes no part, but on arriving at the altar removes his cope and prostrates on a cushion prepared for him on the altar steps until the chanters reach the invocation *Peccatores*. Then he retires to vest for Mass.

[3] M.R. VI. ii, § VI, 2. The first server, if a cleric, brings the chalice (veiled in white) from the credence to the altar, and arranges it there.

When the celebrant has said the petition *Christe, exaudi nos*, and the servers have answered it, they rise and go to the sedile or to the sacristy. Here the celebrant takes off the violet stole and vests in white for Mass.

First Easter Mass. The celebrant, following the servers, comes out to the altar and begins Mass.[1] He says the preparatory prayers, as usual, the psalm *Iudica me*, with *Gloria Patri*, etc. He goes up to the altar, says *Kyrie, eleison* at the middle, and then says (or intones) *Gloria in excelsis Deo*. The sanctuary bell and other bells within the church are rung if it is customary ; the outer bells are also rung if the church (where there are several) is the chief one, or if the bells of the chief church have already rung. All images and statues are unveiled. After the celebrant has read the Epistle, he says (or sings) *Alleluia* three times, raising his voice each time. The servers (or singers) repeat *Alleluia* after him, each time in the same tone of voice. He goes on with the Gradual and Tract.

The Creed is not said. He says *Dominus vobiscum* and *Oremus* at the Offertory, as usual ; but he does not read an Offertory verse. If the Sanctissimum is to be consecrated, a ciborium and pyx with the altar-bread for Benediction are brought up at the beginning of the Offertory. In the Paschal Preface *in hac potissimum nocte* is said ; *noctem sacratissimam* in the proper *Communicantes*. There is also a proper *Hanc igitur*. *Agnus Dei* is not said, nor is the kiss of peace given. When the celebrant has made his Communion, there may be Communion of the faithful.

Vespers. After the ablutions,[2] instead of the Communion antiphon, standing at the Epistle corner, he says the first antiphon of Vespers, *Alleluia, Alleluia, Alleluia*. He begins the psalm, *Laudate Dominum omnes gentes*, and continues it alternately with the servers. Then he says the antiphon *Vespere autem sabbati*, etc., and the *Magnificat*, alternately with the servers and repeats the antiphon.[3] He goes to the middle, kisses the altar, turns and says *Dominus vobiscum*, and at the Epistle corner the Postcommunion. Mass ends as usual, except that to *Ite, missa est* and to the response, *Alleluia* is added twice.

After Mass the Sanctissimum is brought back to the tabernacle (having on it the white conopæum). In doing so the priest observes the usual rule, as at pp. 240–241.

§ 12. THE FUNCTION SUNG

In this case there will be, if possible, a M.C., cross-bearer, thurifer, two acolytes, and four other servers who, in the earlier part of the service,

---

[1] If there are singers the celebrant will begin Mass when they have sung the concluding *Christe, exaudi nos* of the litanies and begin the solemn singing of the *Kyrie* of the Mass (there being no Introit).

[2] If the first server is a cleric he takes the chalice to the credence.

[3] If the servers cannot answer, he says all himself. If there are singers they sing all these while the celebrant recites them in a low tone himself alone or alternately with the servers. He intones the antiphon *Vespere*.

attend on the celebrant [1] and serve as torch-bearers during the Mass.

The preparations are made as in the Memoriale Rituum, except that the violet vestments used at the fire may afterwards be laid out at the sedile. The celebrant may change his vestments each time there.

At the blessing of the fire the acolytes stand on either side of the celebrant. They may bring the grains of incense, thurible and holy water with them, as in the function with ministers.

The litanies may be chanted by two cantors ; if so, the celebrant will lie prostrate before the altar, rising and going to the sacristy to vest at the petition *Peccatores, te rogamus audi nos.*

All will be sung by the celebrant, cantors and choir, as at the normal service with ministers. The prophecies and Tracts may be sung by lectors, while the celebrant recites them in the subdued voice.[2] Incense may be used throughout, at Mass and Vespers, if the celebrant has by indult permission to use incense at a Sung Mass. The organ may accompany the singers once the celebrant has intoned the *Gloria in excelsis.*

The Mass that follows will be a Sung Mass. according to the usual rule, with the exceptions for this day. Vespers will be sung, as when there are ministers.

APPENDIX

PRIVATE MASS AND HOLY COMMUNION ON HOLY SATURDAY

APART from Apostolic indult a private Mass is not allowed on Holy Saturday. When it is allowed by indult it may be said only *after* the Liturgy of the day ; it is celebrated without the Prophecies and Litanies and without an Introit, and the celebrant recites the Vespers at the end with the server. Holy Communion may be given only within the Mass or immediately after.[3] Hence it may not be given in a church or oratory in which the Liturgy of the day does not take place. It is forbidden to distribute Holy Communion, in the Mass vestments, after a solemn, sung or conventual Mass,[4] and so the celebrant must retire from the sanctuary at the end of Mass and come out again (without delay) in surplice (or alb) and white stole to give Holy Communion ; or another priest may administer it.

---

[1] Other servers besides the thurifer and acolytes are useful to bring and hold things at the fire and font. The M.C. will direct them and send them for what is wanted.

[2] In this case, after the "Exsultet," the book is taken from the lectern, the veil is removed from the lectern and the latter is placed in the middle of the choir or sanctuary.

[3] C.J.C 820, 867, § 3.

[4] S.R.C. 4177³.

CHAPTER XXVI

EASTER TO ADVENT

§ 1. EASTERTIDE

EASTERTIDE (*Tempus Paschale*) begins with Mass on Holy Saturday and ends after None and Mass on the Saturday before the feast of the Blessed Trinity, which feast is kept on the first Sunday after Pentecost. It is altogether a wrong conception that Eastertide does not begin till Low Sunday. The right way to conceive it is that, although the season begins with the first Easter Mass on Holy Saturday, the Easter octave, which has its own further peculiarities, falls over the normal Paschal-tide, and causes further changes in the Offices. So any octave, occurring in a season of the Church, is liable to modify the rules for the season. In this case it so happens that the Easter octave occurs at the very beginning of Eastertide. The colour of the season is white.

Eastertide Office. Eastertide has its own hymns at Matins, Lauds, Vespers. In all hymns of the common (iambic dimeter) rhythm the last verse is changed to

> *Deo Patri sit gloria,*
> *Et Filio qui a mortuis*
> *Surrexit, ac Paraclito,*
> *In sempiterna saecula.*

When the Suffrage would be said, at Lauds or Vespers, it is replaced by the commemoration of the Cross, as in the *Ordinarium Divini Officii* in the Breviary.

To all versicles in the Divine Office and to *Panem de caelo praestitisti eis* at Benediction, and to their responses, *Alleluia* is added. But *Alleluia* is never added to *Adiutorium nostrum in nomine Domini, Domine, exaudi orationem meam, Dominus vobiscum*, or to their responses. Nor does it occur at the " preces " of Prime and Compline.

In the responsories after the lessons at Matins *Alleluia* is added after the first part (the response) each time it is said, not after the versicle. At Prime, Terce, Sext, None and Compline the short responsories are changed, so that the whole first part (the response), normally divided by an asterisk, is put before that asterisk. The second part now consists of *Alleluia, Alleluia*. This second part (*Alleluia, Alleluia*) alone is repeated after the versicle. The versicle which follows the short responsory obeys the usual rule for this time, having *Alleluia* at the end, as also its response. At Prime the versicle of the short responsory is *Qui surrexisti a mortuis*.[1]

---

[1] Except in the octaves of Ascension and Pentecost, which have their own forms in the Breviary.

During Eastertide *Alleluia* is added to all antiphons of the Office, if they do not already so end, also to the Invitatory at Matins. At the end of Matins *Te Deum* is said on ferias.

Eastertide Mass. At Mass the Sundays of the season have their own Proper, interspersed with *Alleluia*. In these the Introit has *Alleluia* in the middle of the antiphon and again two or three times at the end. The Offertory has *Alleluia* at the end once, the Communion antiphon twice.

If a Mass such as may occur either in Eastertide or not (such as the Masses of Commons of Saints [1]) is said in this season, at the end of the antiphon of the Introit *Alleluia* is added twice, and once at the end of the Offertory and Communion antiphon.[2]

During Eastertide in all Masses (except those for the dead), instead of the Gradual and *Alleluia*, the Great Alleluia is said. This is formed thus : *Alleluia* is said twice. When it is sung the second time it has the Iubilus [3] at the end. Then follows an Alleluiatic verse. The tone changes. *Alleluia* is said again with a Iubilus, a second Alleluiatic verse, then *Alleluia* with its Iubilus as before this verse.[4] In Masses which may occur in Eastertide a form of the Great Alleluia is provided to take the place of the Gradual.

The hymn *Gloria in excelsis Deo* is said throughout Eastertide, even on weekdays, except in the Rogation Masses, Requiems, and certain votive Masses. Whenever the *Gloria* is said at Mass the dismissal at the end is *Ite, missa est*.

During this season (to Whit-Sunday inclusive) the chant for the sprinkling of holy water before Mass is *Vidi aquam* instead of *Asperges me*.

Lighting of Paschal Candle. During Eastertide the Paschal candle is lit at High or Sung Mass (or at a Low Mass which takes the place of a solemn one) and at sung Vespers : on the three more solemn days of the Easter octave, on Saturday *in albis* and on all Sundays (and if customary, on other days and at other solemnities).[5] It is also to be lighted at solemn Mass or solemn Vespers which are celebrated in the presence of the Blessed Sacrament solemnly exposed during Paschaltide.[6] It is not lit at Requiems, nor at the Office for the dead, nor at any service held with violet vestments (as Rogation Masses), nor at Mass on the vigil of Pentecost, nor at Benediction.[7]

After Ascension Day (see p. 339) the Paschal candle is not again used, except at the blessing of the font on Whitsun eve.

---

[1] Apostles and martyrs have a special common for Eastertide.
[2] *Alleluia* is added twice to the Communion verse in the first Mass of Martyrs in Paschaltide.
[3] The long neum on the syllable " a " at the end of " alleluia".
[4] But see p. 335 for the Easter octave.
[5] M.R. VI. ii, § VII, 6. And up to the Gospel (inclusive) on Ascension Day.
[6] S.R.C. 4383.
[7] Unless Vespers immediately preceded and it was lit at that Office (S.R.C. 4383[1]).

§ 2. THE EASTER OCTAVE

THE first week of Paschaltide is the Easter octave, which has its own further rules. This octave begins at the Mass on Holy Saturday and ends after None and Mass on the Saturday after Easter day (*sabbatum in albis*). Low Sunday, although it is the octave day of Easter, conforms to the normal rules of Eastertide.

Easter Day is the greatest feast of the year.[1] No feast may be kept on it or during its octave. The Monday and Tuesday of this octave are also doubles of the first class, but are kept with less solemnity.

On Easter Day no Mass for the dead may be said, not even if the body is present. On the Monday and Tuesday a Mass for the dead may be said only at the funeral. On these days no votive Mass may be said. A solemn votive Mass for a grave cause may be sung on the other days of the octave.

During the Easter octave there is only one nocturn at Matins. There are no versicles except at Matins. There are no chapters nor short responsories, nor hymns in any part of the Office. There are no antiphons to the psalms at Prime, Terce, Sext, None. At Compline there is no antiphon at the beginning of the psalms ; at the end *Alleluia, Alleluia, Alleluia, Alleluia* is sung. After the psalms of each Office the antiphon *Haec dies quam fecit Dominus*, etc., is sung, all standing. At Lauds and Vespers this is intoned by the celebrant. The first assistant, in cope, pre-intones it to him.

At the end of Lauds and Vespers *Alleluia, Alleluia* is added to the verse *Benedicamus Domino*.

At Mass (till Friday) there is a Gradual, formed in the usual way, the first verse being *Haec dies*. After the Alleluiatic verse the Sequence *Victimae paschali* follows.

At the end of Mass *Alleluia, Alleluia* is added to *Ite, missa est* and to its response.

On Easter Day, if the church has a font, the sprinkling of lustral water before Mass is made with water from the baptismal font kept from the day before (p. 319).

§ 3. ST. MARK AND THE ROGATION DAYS

ON four days a procession should be made, while the Litanies of the Saints are sung, to beg the blessing of God on the fruits of the earth. These days are the feast of St. Mark (25 April) [2] and the three Rogation

---

[1] It may fall on or between 22 March and 25 April.

[2] There is no inherent connection between St. Mark and the procession. 25 April (vii kal. maias) was the date of a pre-Christian procession of the same kind at Rome (the so-called Robigalia). That day occurs at just the time when the harvest (in Italy) should ripen. The pagan procession was replaced by a Christian one before the feast of St. Mark began to be kept on that day. The Rogation days are later and originally Gallican. They are said to have been introduced by St. Mamertus, Bishop of Vienne, about the year 470. They were not kept at Rome till the time of Leo III (795–816).

days, namely, the Monday, Tuesday and Wednesday before Ascension Day. On St. Mark's feast the litanies are called " greater " (*litaniae maiores*), being sung with more solemnity ; [1] on the Rogation days they are " lesser " (*minores*).

If 25 April is Easter Day the feast of St. Mark is transferred beyond the Easter octave, but the procession and litanies are transferred to the Tuesday in the octave. If St. Mark occurs in the Easter octave the procession is made (even on the Monday of Easter week), although the feast is transferred.

Mass of the Rogations. Rogation Monday is a greater weekday, Tuesday an ordinary weekday, Wednesday the eve of the Ascension. On all three days the Rogation Mass may be displaced by that of a feast, according to the usual rules. IN CATHEDRALS AND COLLEGIATE CHURCHES, where several Conventual Masses are said, that of the feast is said after Terce, that of Rogation after None, neither commemorating the other. On Wednesday the Mass of Ascension eve is said, in addition, after Sext, without commemoration of either feast or Rogations. On the days of the Litanies, IN CHURCHES THAT ARE NOT CATHEDRAL OR COLLEGIATE : (i) *if the procession is held,* the Mass following it will be that of the Rogations, *Exaudivit* (except on a double of the first class, when it will be of the feast, with a commemoration of Rogations, under one conclusion), with a commemoration of the occurring Office ; (ii) *if the procession is not held* (a) the Mass will, normally, be of the occurring Office, with a commemoration of the Rogations (unless there be another Mass, sung, of the Rogations), (b) a private Mass of the Rogations *may* be said on Rogation Monday (provided no double of the first or second class occurs) ; on Rogation Tuesday it is said only if the occurring Office is ferial ; on Wednesday it may not be said at all.

In general [2] on the days of the Litanies at every Mass (whatever its rite), which is not the Mass of the Rogations or a Requiem Mass, a commemoration of the Rogations must be made.

Procession of the Rogations. Normally on these four days the procession should be made after None, if possible to another church, where the Rogation Mass is sung. But on St. Mark's feast, if the procession ends at a church dedicated to him, the Mass of his feast is said there. If it is not possible to end the procession at another church it may come back to the one from which it set out.

There should be only one general procession in each place, at which all the clergy, secular and regular, take part. [3] It sets out from the principal church of the place. If a general procession through the town is not possible, each church may make its own procession inside the building.

The same priest should, if possible, preside at the procession and

---

[1] Also because the litanies on 25 April are a much older tradition than the Rogation days.

[2] The exceptions, in greater churches, have just been noted above.

[3] For the order of the procession, see p. 346.

sing the Mass which follows it.   However, in case of real difficulty, this rule is not urged.

The rules for the procession are these.[1]

Preparations. At the church from which it sets out all is provided for a procession, with violet [2] vestments, that is : the processional cross, acolytes' candles, surplices as required, vestments for the celebrant and ministers, namely, amice, alb, girdle, stole, violet dalmatic and tunicle for the ministers, violet stole and cope for the celebrant. If there are no ministers, the celebrant may wear a surplice under the cope.   A book containing all that the celebrant will chant must be provided.   The High Altar is vested in violet.

At the church at which the procession will arrive all is prepared, as usual, for High Mass with violet vestments (the chasuble and three maniples).   If the priest of the procession will sing the Mass (as he should), he and the ministers vest for Mass at the sedilia.   In this case the maniples and his chasuble will be laid out there.   On St. Mark's feast, if the church is dedicated to St. Mark, the frontal and vestments will be red.

Beginning of Procession. The procession takes place after None.[3] If None is said publicly,[4] the celebrant and ministers go meanwhile to the sacristy to vest for the procession.   Otherwise they and the clergy come out at the appointed time, following the cross-bearer and acolytes. The cross-bearer and acolytes do not genuflect before the altar, they go to stand at the Gospel side of the sanctuary facing the Epistle side. All the members of the choir (the clergy) genuflect as usual, and go to their places.   They stand till the celebrant is before the altar.   The celebrant and ministers wear the biretta, but uncover as they enter the choir.   They bow to the choir on either side, and genuflect at the foot of the altar (the celebrant bows low if the Sanctissimum is not at the altar).   They kneel on the lowest step ; all kneel with them.

A short prayer is said in silence.   Then all stand and the cantors begin the antiphon *Exsurge, Domine* [5] ; it is continued by the choir. The psalm verse is sung with *Gloria Patri* and *Sicut erat ;* the antiphon is repeated.   Meanwhile the cross-bearer and acolytes go to stand at the entrance of the choir, facing the altar.   All the others kneel again as soon as the antiphon has been repeated.

Two cantors—kneeling in the middle of the choir—begin the Litanies of the Saints.   They sing *Kyrie, eleison ;* the choir repeats the same words.   In the same way each petition is sung entire by the cantors, repeated entire by the choir.

When *Sancta Maria, ora pro nobis* has been sung and repeated, all rise ; the procession sets out.   The cross-bearer goes in front between

---

[1] Cf. C.E. II. xxxii ; R.R. IX. iv.

[2] The colour for the procession is always violet, whatever be the colour for the Mass that follows (cf. R.R. IX. iv, 1).

[3] In cathedral or conventual churches ; in other churches at any convenient hour, but in the morning.

[4] *Fidelium*, etc., is not added when the procession follows.

[5] R.R. IX. iv, 1.

the acolytes. The cantors follow, then come the clergy, the M.C., and the celebrant between the ministers, who hold the ends of his cope. The celebrant and ministers wear the biretta during the procession outside the choir ; all the clergy, outside the church. The M.C., or a server, carries the book from which the celebrant will chant the prayers. The church bells are rung as the procession starts.

If the litanies are finished (exclusive of the prayers) before the procession arrives at its final place, they may be repeated, beginning again at *Sancta Maria, ora pro nobis.* Or penitential and Gradual psalms may be sung. It is not allowed to sing joyful chants. The prayers which follow the litanies must not be sung till the procession arrives at the church where it ends.

Visit to Churches on the Way. The procession may visit other churches on the way. In this case, it is received by the clergy of each church. The rector (in choir dress, without stole) may offer holy water to the celebrant and ministers at the door. The procession will go up the church till it arrives in the choir and the celebrant is before the altar. All then kneel awhile in silent prayer. The celebrant rises and all rise with him. The cantors sing the antiphon for a commemoration of the Titular of the church ; the corresponding versicle and response are sung. The celebrant sings in the second ferial tone [1] the prayer of that Saint, in the short form, ending *Per Christum Dominum nostrum.* Since it is Eastertide, *Alleluia* is added to the antiphon, versicle and response. Meanwhile the singing of the litanies is interrupted. The litanies are then resumed, and the procession proceeds.

Conclusion of Procession. At the church at which the procession is to end it is received by the clergy, and holy water is offered at the door to each member of the clergy on the side near the rector as he passes in (who in turn passes it to the person beside him) and to the celebrant and ministers, as above. All come to the choir, the celebrant and ministers before the altar. The usual reverence is made. The cross-bearer puts aside the cross near the credence ; the acolytes put their candles on it. All kneel. If the litanies are not finished they are sung to the end. Then, all kneeling, the celebrant sings *Pater noster*, etc. The cantors intone the psalm, which is sung alternately by the choir. The celebrant sings the versicles, as in the text, the ministers holding the book before him. He alone rises, sings *Dominus vobiscum* and the prayers. Then he kneels and sings again *Dominus vobiscum*. He adds the verses *Exaudiat nos omnipotens et misericors Deus*, and in a lower tone *Et fidelium animae per misericordiam Dei requiescant in pace.* The choir answers *Amen* each time.

The celebrant and ministers go to vest for Mass at the sedilia or sacristy. Mass of the Rogations [2] follows.[3] It has no *Gloria in excelsis*

---

[1] See p. 259, n. 1.

[2] It is always—even if it be the only Mass celebrated that day—the Mass of the Rogations, except on a double of the first class. Then the Mass is of the feast, with a commemoration of the Rogations under one conclusion (cf. p. 336).

[3] The Paschal candle is not lighted (cf. p. 334).

nor Creed, even on a Sunday or in the Easter octave. The prayers [1] are sung in the (simple) ferial tone. The *Alleluia* has a special form, *Alleluia* once only, with Iubilus, and one verse, *Alleluia* not repeated. The Preface is of Eastertide, according to the usual rule. At the end the deacon sings *Benedicamus Domino*, not adding *Alleluia*, even in the Easter octave.

Where it is not possible to go out the procession goes around the church.

Everyone who is bound to say the Divine Office is bound to say the Litanies of the Saints, with the following psalm and prayers, on these days, if he does not take part in the procession. They should be said after Lauds (when these are not anticipated); but they may not be anticipated the day before. They should follow *Benedicamus Domino* at the end of Lauds. The verse *Fidelium animae* and the anthem of the Blessed Virgin are then not said.

In churches where the procession cannot be held, it is recommended that the litanies be said or sung before the chief Mass, all kneeling. In this case the invocations are not doubled as-(outside Holy Saturday) this occurs only in procession.

§ 4. ASCENSION DAY

ON Ascension Day the Paschal candle is lit for the principal Mass. It is extinguished after the first Gospel and taken away after Mass. It is not used again, except at the blessing of the font on Whitsun eve.

§ 5. WHITSUN EVE

THIS day no other Office or Mass may be said but those of the eve. In all churches which have a font it must be blessed to-day. This is a strict obligation, even though a sufficient supply of the water blessed on Holy Saturday is still available.

Preparations. The morning function begins (after None) with six prophecies. For these violet vestments are used, as on Holy Saturday. The celebrant uses maniple, stole and chasuble, the ministers maniples and folded chasubles (and the deacon his stole), till the blessing of the font (or till the Mass, if there is no font). The altar is vested in red, and over this a violet frontal. The tabernacle (if the Blessed Sacrament be present) is clothed with the violet conopaeum over the red one. The Missal is open at the Epistle corner on its stand covered with violet over red. All is prepared for Mass (with red vestments) at the credence, then covered with a violet veil over the red one. Near the credence are three violet cushions for the celebrant and ministers at the litanies.

---

[1] In cathedral and collegiate churches where there is only one conventual Mass and in other churches where there is only one Mass, in the Mass of the Rogations occurring commemorations are made (including that of the vigil of the Ascension). Should an occurring commemoration be of a feast of double rite, the common prayer (*Concede*) will be omitted. In all other cases the Mass of the Rogations is celebrated without any commemoration, but with the second and third prayers of the season.

Red Mass vestments must be laid out in the sacristy, as well as the violet ones.

If there is a font, a violet cope is laid at the sedilia. The acolytes' candles stand on the credence, not lit ; near it are the Paschal candle (unlighted and without its candlestick) and the processional cross.

A lectern stands in the middle of the choir for the prophecies.

The altar candles are not lit till the beginning of Mass.

At the font everything is prepared as on Holy Saturday (p. 309).

Beginning of the Function. The celebrant and ministers come to the altar following the acolytes (without candles). The celebrant kisses the altar, then goes to the Epistle corner and stands there. The ministers stand around as at the Introit of Mass. The first prophecy is begun. The prophecies are not announced by titles. Six members of the choir or clergy [1] should chant them in turn, each coming to the lectern when summoned by the M.C. or a server. They chant them as on Holy Saturday, the server standing at the reader's left, behind him, holding his biretta. Meanwhile the celebrant reads the prophecy at the altar in a low voice, with hands on the book. When he has finished each, he and the ministers may go to sit at the sedilia until the chanting of the prophecy is nearly completed (going and returning *per breviorem*). Then he sings the prayer (simple ferial tone [2]) at the altar, with uplifted hands. He begins with the word *Oremus*, but the deacon does not sing *Flectamus genua*, nor does anyone genuflect, because it is Paschal time. During the prayer the ministers stand in line, as at the collects of Mass. The prophecies are six of the twelve read on Holy Saturday [3] ; the second, third and fourth are followed by a Tract sung by the choir. During this the celebrant and ministers may sit. The prayers are not those of Holy Saturday, but are special ones suitable to this vigil.

The clergy and others in choir and church sit during the prophecies and Tracts, stand during the collects.

Procession to Font. If there is a font, the Paschal and acolytes' candles are lit during the last (sixth) prophecy. The server who will carry the Paschal candle must now hold it, near the credence. After the last collect the celebrant and ministers go to the sedilia and take off their maniples ; the celebrant changes the chasuble for a violet cope. They come back to the altar, and the procession goes to the font as on Holy Saturday, that is to say, the Paschal candle is borne in front, then the processional cross between the acolytes, the choir, M.C., celebrant between the ministers.

At the baptistery everything is done exactly as on Holy Saturday. It will be sufficient here to refer to the directions for that day (pp. 316–320). The Tract sung on the way to the font is the same as on Holy Saturday, but the prayer before entering the baptistery is proper to the day. Baptism should follow, if possible, as on Holy Saturday.

---

[1] The same lector may, if necessary, chant more than one prophecy.
[2] Cf. p. 259, n. 1.
[3] The Whitsun prophecies, 1, 2, 3, 4, 5, 6, are nos. 3, 4, 11, 8, 6, 7, of Easter Eve.

The procession comes back to the altar singing the litanies.[1]

Litanies. When it arrives at the sanctuary, the server holding the Paschal candle takes this to the sacristy, and there extinguishes it. The celebrant takes off his cope, the ministers their chasubles ; they then lie prostrate before the altar ; all others kneel during the rest of the Litanies (p. 321). At the petition *Peccatores, te rogamus audi nos* the celebrant and ministers go to the sacristy, with the M.C. and acolytes, to vest for Mass. They put on red Mass vestments. Meanwhile servers take away the violet coverings from the altar, tabernacle and Missal-stand, leaving them vested in red ; the six candles are lit, the altar is adorned as for feasts. All other violet coverings are taken away from the sanctuary.

Mass. Mass begins as on Holy Saturday. The preparatory prayers are said. The celebrant goes up to the altar and incenses it. There is no Introit. He says the *Kyrie, eleison,* then intones *Gloria in excelsis Deo.* The organ may not be played this morning till this point. It may now be played, as on Holy Saturday ; the sanctuary bell and church bells are rung. The acolytes do not carry candles at the Gospel, but stand on either side of the subdeacon or lectern with joined hands, There is no Creed. The Pentecost Preface, *Communicantes* and *Hanc igitur* are said.

§ 6. WHITSUN EVE IN SMALL CHURCHES

THE Memoriale Rituum makes no provision for this occasion ; but it is easy to see what should be done from the directions for Holy Saturday.

The celebrant will read the prophecies, in a clear voice, at the Epistle corner of the altar, vested in violet Mass vestments. He changes to violet stole and cope, and goes to bless the font. Before him a server bears the Paschal candle, another the processional cross ; he walks between two others, who hold the ends of the cope. At the font he does all exactly as on Holy Saturday (see pp. 328–330), alone the prayer before entering the baptistery is different. He comes back to the altar. The Paschal candle is put away in the sacristy. Kneeling before the altar, in alb and stole, the celebrant recites the litanies (if there are no singers to chant them ; if there are the celebrant prostrates during them and at *Peccatores* leaves to vest for Mass). At *Peccatores* the violet frontal is taken away, the altar is decked for a feast in red and the candles are lighted. At the end of the Litanies (after *Christe, exaudi nos*) the celebrant goes to the sacristy to put on red Mass vestments, comes to the altar, and begins Mass, as on Holy Saturday. At the *Gloria* the bells are rung.

If it is desired to make a ceremony of this, on the lines of a Sung Mass, this can be done in the same way as on Holy Saturday (p. 331).

---

[1] Where there is no font, at the end of the prophecies and prayers, the sacred ministers go directly to the sedilia. The celebrant removes his chasuble and maniple ; the deacon and subdeacon their maniples. All three prostrate before the altar and the Litanies are begun.

But in most small churches with one priest the function of Whitsun Eve will be performed in the simplest manner.

§ 7. PRIVATE MASS ON WHITSUN EVE

A PRIEST who says private Low Mass on this day, that is to say, every priest except the one who celebrates the principal Mass of the day, leaves out the prophecies, blessing of the font and litanies. He begins Mass exactly as usual. For this purpose an Introit is provided in the Missal at the end of the Mass. *Gloria in excelsis* is said (the bells are not rung), not the Creed. There are no special ceremonies.

§ 8. WHIT SUNDAY

THIS is a double of the first class with a privileged octave of the first order. No other feast may displace it, nor occur during the octave. Feasts may be commemorated during the octave, except on Monday and Tuesday.

The colour of the feast and octave is red.

At the verse of the Great Alleluia, *Veni, Sancte Spiritus, reple tuorum corda fidelium*, etc., all genuflect. At Low Mass the celebrant genuflects as he says these words. At High or Sung Mass he does not genuflect then, but goes to kneel (between the ministers) on the edge of the foot-pace while they are sung by the choir. The sequence *Veni, Sancte Spiritus* follows.

Matins has only one nocturn. At Terce the hymn *Veni, Creator Spiritus* is said, instead of *Nunc Sancte nobis Spiritus*.[1] The hymn *Veni, Creator Spiritus* is also the Vesper hymn. Whenever this is sung, all kneel during the first stanza. The hymn should be intoned by the celebrant.[2] In churches which have a font water from it (withdrawn before the Holy Oils are added) is used for the Asperges, instead of ordinary lustral water, on Whit Sunday, as at Easter (p. 319).

9. THE SEASON AFTER PENTECOST

THIS season begins at the first Vespers of the Blessed Trinity on the Saturday after Whit Sunday and lasts till Advent. It contains at least twenty-three Sundays, and may have as many as twenty-eight.[3] The Offices for twenty-four are provided in the Breviary and Missal. If Easter falls early, so that there are more, the Offices for these are taken from those which were omitted after Epiphany. But, in every case, the Mass and Office of the twenty-fourth Sunday (containing the

---

[1] Because it was at the third hour that the Holy Ghost came down on the Apostles, the hour of Terce (Acts ii, 15).

[2] This hymn always keeps its Paschal doxology (last stanza) whenever it may be sung or said.

[3] There are twenty-three Sundays after Pentecost when there are only fifty-two Sundays in the year and Septuagesima falls on the seventh Sunday after Epiphany. In this case the Office and Mass of the twenty-third Sunday are said on the Saturday before it; those of the twenty-fourth are always said on the last, whatever happens. There are twenty-eight Sundays after Pentecost when Septuagesima falls on the third Sunday after Epiphany.

Gospel about the Day of Judgment) is said on the last Sunday after Pentecost.

The colour of this season is green. It has no liturgical peculiarities ; but many great feasts occur during it.

§ 10. CORPUS CHRISTI

THE Thursday after the feast of the most Holy Trinity is Corpus Christi. It will occur between 21 May and 24 June. It is now restored as a holiday of obligation.[1] It is celebrated as a double of the first class with a privileged octave of the second order. On Corpus Christi and during its octave *Alleluia* is added to the versicle *Panem de caelo praestitisti eis* and to its response, whenever they are sung or said.

The external solemnity (which in some places is transferred to the following Sunday) consists of the Mass of the feast and one general procession of the Blessed Sacrament.[2] In some countries exposition of the Blessed Sacrament is held on the feast and every day of the octave. Canon 1274, § 1, of the Code gives permission for all churches (in which the Sanctissimum is reserved) to have public exposition on the feast of Corpus Christi and within the octave during (the principal) Mass and at Vespers. The authority of the Ordinary is not necessary for this.

General Rules for the Procession. The procession should be a general one for the whole town. That is to say, there should be only one in each town, setting out from the principal church and returning to it, in which the clergy of all the other churches, secular and regular, take part. It should go out from the church into the streets, the houses in which are to be ornamented with draperies and sacred images.

In England it is generally not possible to carry the Blessed Sacrament through public streets ; nor may this be done without special leave of the Ordinary. There is, then, usually no general procession in this country. Each church will have its own procession inside the church. Where a large garden or private grounds belonging to a religious house or to a Catholic can be used the procession may be made through these grounds.

The procession normally should be held in the morning, immediately after the Mass, with a Host which has been consecrated at the solemn Mass.[3] It is, however, allowed, and it is not unusual, to put it off till the afternoon, for reasons of convenience.

Route of Procession. It should be held with every possible solemnity. The Corpus Christi procession is the chief public joyful solemnity of the kind in the year. If the procession passes over much ground, there may be one or two places (not more) of repose, arranged like altars,[4]

---

[1] C.J.C. 1247, § 1. The feasts of the Immaculate Conception and St. Joseph, added by this canon, are not holidays of obligation in England. In Ireland the former feast is, the latter is not a holiday, of obligation.

[2] C.J.C. 1291.

[3] C.E. II. xxxiii, 15, 17, and all rubricians suppose this.

[4] C.E. II. xxxiii, 22. The purpose of the stops is not to give Benediction, but to rest the celebrant. On these " altars "—which are decorated with wax candles and flowers (with no statutes or relics)—there should be some form of baldachin

at which it stops. According to the Ceremonial of Bishops the Sanctis-simum should be placed on these " altars " and incensed, the *Tantum ergo* sung, with the usual versicle and response and prayer, but, strictly, Benediction should not be given. However, the Congregation of Rites allows Benediction to be given at altars of repose, not more than twice, if such is the ancient custom.[1]

The route over which the procession passes should be ornamented with flowers and green leaves ; draperies, banners and pictures may be hung along the way.[2] In the procession itself there may be no scenic representations or people dressed in fancy costumes to represent saints or angels, nor anything theatrical or profane.[3] Nor may relics and statues be carried.[4] Not more than two thurifers are allowed.[5] The Congregation of Rites tolerates the custom that children (boys) scatter flowers on the way ; but it is a very undesirable practice. They may not walk among the clergy nor between the clergy and the celebrant carrying the Sanctissimum.[6]

Dress of Clergy. The secular clergy should wear the surplice only, regulars wear the habit of their order, canons (if within their own diocese) and prelates their robes. If the cathedral Chapter assists, the canons ought to wear vestments of their three orders, that is subdeacons in tunicles, deacons in dalmatics, priests in chasubles ; dignitaries in copes.[7] These are put on after the Communion of the Mass and should be worn immediately over the rochet and an amice without stole or maniple, as when the Ordinary sings High Mass (pp. 155, 159). The colour of the vestments is white. If the cathedral Chapter is not present the clergy may be divided into groups wearing these vestments.[8] If the clergy are so vested the processional cross is borne by a sub-deacon in amice, alb, girdle and tunicle ; otherwise by a server in surplice only. If the canopy is borne within the church [9] by four, six or eight of the clergy—as the Ceremonial directs—these wear white copes in a cathedral church, in other churches they wear choir dress. The Host borne in the procession should be consecrated at the preceding Mass. The celebrant of Mass [10] should carry it all the time, without giving place to another priest. He must carry the monstrance in his hands, walking. No other manner is allowed.[11]

§ 11. PREPARATION

IN the church and sacristy all is prepared for High Mass, with white vestments, as usual. The church should be adorned as sumptuously as possible. In the sacristy two thuribles are prepared, torches and

---

or throne under which the monstrance will be placed and a corporal spread on which to stand it.

[1] S.R.C. 2609, 3086[4], 3448[2], 3621[3].   [2] C.E. II. xxxiii, 2.
[3] *Ib.* 12.   [4] S.R.C. 1361[7].
[5] *Ib.* 3448[10].   [6] *Ib.* 3324, 3935[1].
[7] C.E. II. xxxiii, 5.   [8] Cf. S.R.C. 2362[1].
[9] Outside it is borne by laymen of distinction (cf. C.E. II. xxxiii, 13, 21).
[10] The only exception is if the Bishop of the place should himself carry the Blessed Sacrament.   [11] Cf. S.R.C. 4389.

candles to distribute to those who take part in the procession. At the credence, beside all that is needed for Mass, another white humeral veil, more adorned, may be laid out for the celebrant in the procession. There will be a white cope (not a heavy one) for him; the monstrance (light in weight) covered with a white veil; a second altar bread (in the lunette) to be consecrated at Mass and carried in the procession; the book with prayers for Benediction [1]; if necessary cords of white silk to put around the celebrant's shoulders, by which the weight of the monstrance may be relieved while he holds it. In the sanctuary, the processional cross is by the credence. In the choir, or by the Communion rails, is the canopy for the procession. There may be four lanterns, containing candles, to carry on either side of the canopy. Candles are prepared for the clergy and others who walk in the procession.

§ 12. THE CEREMONY [2]

HIGH Mass begins as usual. The colour is white; there is a Sequence, *Lauda Sion*. At the Offertory the second altar bread is brought in the lunette. The torch-bearers remain kneeling after the Elevation. After the Communion the monstrance is brought to the altar. When the subdeacon has covered the chalice the celebrant and ministers genuflect; they change places behind him and genuflect again. The deacon puts the Blessed Sacrament into the monstrance [3] and stands it on the corporal. The celebrant and ministers genuflect again; they change places, as before. The rest of Mass is celebrated as before the Blessed Sacrament exposed (see pp. 61, 124). Towards the end of Mass all is prepared for the procession. Candles are given out to the clergy and others and lighted.

After Mass. After Mass the celebrant and ministers come down the steps, make a prostration and go to the sedilia. Here, not turning their back to the Sanctissimum, they take off the maniples; the celebrant also takes off the chasuble and puts on the white cope. They are assisted by the M.C. and acolytes. They come back to the altar, prostrate on both knees and kneel there for a short time. Meanwhile the Missal and altar cards have been removed from the altar.

The cross-bearer takes the cross and goes to stand at the entrance of the choir, between the acolytes with their candles. Those who will carry the canopy stand by it outside the choir.[4]

Incensation of Blessed Sacrament. The celebrant bows, rises and puts incense on the two thuribles (not blessing it), assisted as usual

---

[1] The *Ritus Servandus* in England); " *Benedictionale* " in Ireland.

[2] C.E. II. xxxiii; R.R. IX. v. For this ceremony—especially if many are to take part in the procession—at least two M.Cs. will be needed. The formation and direction of a procession needs the attention of more than one M.C.

[3] Ho should not touch the Sanctissimum; if he does, he must at once wash his fingers in the little vessel, by the tabernacle.

[4] The person of highest rank holds the first pole on the right of and before the celebrant; the second in rank the first on the left; the third the second pole on the right, and so on.

by the deacon who omits the solita oscula. With one of them he incenses the Sanctissimum. If necessary, a scarf or cord is now arranged by the M.C. around the celebrant's neck to help him to sustain the monstrance.

If there is room in the sanctuary and choir it is best that the clergy now come out from their places and kneel before the altar, in the inverse order of the procession, so that they can rise, prostrate, turn round and go at once in the procession. (Should the number taking part be large the M.C. or one of his assistants will begin the formation of the procession before the end of Mass.) The celebrant receives the humeral veil from the deacon or M.C. He and the ministers rise and go to the edge of the foot-pace. He and the subdeacon kneel here. The deacon goes to the altar, takes the monstrance, and hands it to the celebrant, who receives it kneeling and bowing. The deacon then genuflects. The celebrant and subdeacon rise. The ministers change places behind him. The cantors intone the hymn *Pange lingua* (if there are no cantors the celebrant intones it), and the procession sets forth, all rising and prostrating first.[1]

It should go in this order :

Order of Procession. First a banner of the Blessed Sacrament, borne by a clerk in surplice.[2] Then religious associations (*piae uniones*), confraternities [3] and Tertiaries [4] in that order. After them lay Religious (i.e., Brothers). Then come clerical Religious (members of a congregation), then Regulars, next monks, and finally Canons Regular.[5] Next the processional cross of the secular clergy between the acolytes with their candles ; the choir of singers ; seminarists ; assistant priests and parish priests ; the Chapter and dignitaries ; the two thurifers, swinging their thuribles [6] ; then the celebrant, holding the monstrance under the canopy. He goes between the ministers, who hold the ends of his cope. At the sides of the canopy go the torch-bearers. Lanterns with candles may be carried at the sides of the canopy, if the procession goes out. Prelates, if any are present, follow the canopy ; those of highest rank nearest the Sanctissimum. At the end of the procession come such laymen as are not members of any of the religious societies who are taking part officially in the procession.[7]

---

[1] Except, of course, the cross-bearer and acolytes.

[2] Martinucci, I. ii, p. 273, § 40.

[3] In processions of the Blessed Sacrament confraternities of the Blessed Sacrament have precedence over other confraternities in the procession itself, in carrying the canopy and in bearing torches beside the Sanctissimum (C.J.C. 701, § 2 ; S.R.C. 4143).

[4] These three classes enjoy precedence in a liturgical procession only when walking as a body, behind their own cross or banner, and in the dress and insignia of their society (C.J.C. 701).

[5] C.J.C. 106, 491 ; C.E. II. xxxiii, 5.

[6] It is better to walk straight, not backwards or sideways (see p. 284). Each thurifer swings his thurible by the inside hand. From time to time a M.C. puts in fresh incense.

[7] The rubrics do not suppose women to take any part in a liturgical procession. If they do—by legitimate custom—they should come at the very end (after the

All go bareheaded and all carry lighted candles (in the outside hand) ; those who have birettas carry them in their hands. The masters of ceremonies must see that good order and decorum are observed by all who take part in the procession.

During the procession hymns and canticles (in Latin) to the Blessed Sacrament and suitable psalms are sung.[1] The same hymn may be repeated. The celebrant and ministers recite psalms or hymns, in the subdued voice.

Benediction on the Way. At the places of repose the deacon takes the monstrance and sets it on the altar, observing the usual rules (see p. 234). The celebrant (having taken off the humeral veil) puts incense on one thurible and incenses the Sanctissimum. Meanwhile the *Tantum ergo* is sung. The versicle *Panem de caelo*, etc., with its response,[2] and the prayer *Deus, qui nobis sub Sacramento mirabili* follow. If Benediction is to be given at these places of repose, it follows as usual. The procession sets out again.

Return of Procession. Finally it arrives back at the High Altar of the church from which it set out. At the foot of the altar the celebrant standing gives the monstrance to the deacon kneeling and then genuflects to the Blessed Sacrament ; then the deacon sets the monstrance on the altar. The *Tantum ergo* is sung with versicle, response,[2] and prayer. The Sanctissimum is incensed and Benediction is given as usual. The Sanctissimum is put in the tabernacle (unless Exposition [3] follows), and then all who carry candles extinguish them.

§ 13. ALL SOULS

THE Office of All Souls, said on 2 November (or 3 November if All Saints fall on a Saturday), is no longer an extra Office (except at Vespers), to be said after that of the octave of All Saints. It is now the Office of the day, having all the normal parts. The colour of the day is black.

On All Souls every priest may now say three Masses for the dead.[4] The text of these Masses is provided in the Missal under the date.

If a priest is saying only one Mass he will say the first one, for this is the Mass of the day ; if he is *singing* a Mass he will use the formulary

---

Blessed Sacrament). If a band is tolerated by the Ordinary it must go at the head of the procession and may not play in the church. If soldiers in arms take part as a guard of honour to the Blessed Sacrament they walk *at the sides,* not in the procession (Cf. S.R.C. 1633).

[1] The Roman Ritual (IX, v) gives as suitable after the *Pange lingua* : (a) *Sacris solemniis*, (b) *Verbum supernum*, (c) *Salutis humanae Sator*, (d) *Aeterne Rex altissime*, and then *Te Deum, Benedictus, Magnificat.* The chanters will see that the strophe *Tantum ergo Sacramentum* of *Pange lingua* is not sung when the procession is moving, but is reserved to be sung when it stops.

[2] With " Alleluia " throughout the octave of Corpus Christi.

[3] Even if Exposition follows, Benediction is given at the end of the procession. For the Exposition the deacon places the monstrance in the throne after the Benediction.

[4] C.J.C. 806.

of the first Mass and may in this case anticipate the second and third Masses. The Missal in a rubric at the end of the first Mass explains about the purification of the chalice at the time of the ablutions in the first and second Masses ; and in a rubric given after the Offertory verse of the second Mass it directs what is to be done in putting in the wine and water at the second and third Masses.

The priest who says three Masses may accept a stipend for only one,[1] applying this Mass according to the will of the donor, the second he must apply for all the faithful departed and the third for the intentions of the Pope.

If the three Masses are said immediately one after another the prayers in the vernacular are said after the last Mass only.

[1] Whichever one of the three Masses he wishes.

PART V

OCCASIONAL FUNCTIONS

CHAPTER XXVII

THE FORTY HOURS' PRAYER

§ 1. GENERAL DIRECTIONS

ONE of the best-known popular devotions in Catholic churches is that exposition of the Blessed Sacrament, lasting part of three days, which we call the devotion of the Forty Hours' Prayer.[1] It is to be held yearly—on days appointed by the Ordinary—with the greatest possible solemnity, in all parish churches and in those in which the Blessed Sacrament is habitually reserved.

The laws which now regulate this devotion were promulgated finally in 1731, but the devotion itself is older. Going back, it seems, in its first origin to mediaeval customs, such as watching by the Easter sepulchre, then later connected with special prayers of expiation at Carnival time, it was begun in Milan in 1527 and ten years later revived in that city by the preaching of a Capuchin friar, Padre Giuseppe da Ferno. It was then that the two special notes of this' devotion were instituted, namely, that it should last, as nearly as possible, for forty consecutive hours, and that it should begin in another church at the exact moment when it ended in one, and so be kept up all the year round.[2] The idea of exposing the Blessed Sacrament for forty consecutive hours has been variously explained, for instance, as a memory of our Lord's forty days' fast. But the common explanation is that it is in memory of the forty hours during which His body lay in the tomb, between his death and resurrection.[3]

Clementine Instruction. In 1575 S. Charles Borromeo issued a detailed instruction for the due ordering of the Prayer in Milan. On 25 November 1592 Clement VIII (1592–1605) issued his constitution *Graves et diuturnae*, formally recognising the devotion and ordering the practice of it in Rome. On 21 January 1705 Clement XI (1700–1721)

---

[1] " Oratio (Supplicatio) Quadraginta Horarum." Not uncommonly called by the Italian form " Quarant' Ore."

[2] An excellent account of the history of the devotion will be found in H. Thurston, S.J., *Lent and Holy Week* (Longmans, 1904), chap. iii. pp. 110–148.

[3] Neither in the period commemorated nor in the period of the exposition is the number forty hours exact. From three in the afternoon of Good Friday to sunrise (conventionally 6 a.m.) on Easter Day is thirty-nine hours. But St. Augustine calls it forty, counting in the ninth hour (2–3 p.m.) of Friday (*De Trinitate*, iv, 6; Migne, P.L., xlii, 894–895). Still less are there exactly forty hours of exposition. From Mass on one day to Mass on the third day will be more like forty-eight hours, unless the last Mass is said eight hours earlier than the first, which is hardly possible.

published directions for its observance in the churches of Rome. They were republished by Clement XII (1730–1740) on 1 September 1731. This document, written in the Italian language, is the *Instructio Clementina*, by which the Forty Hours' Prayer is still regulated.[1]

The Clementine Instruction, in itself, applies only to churches in the city of Rome. It was published for them, and has strict force of law only in their case. However, as always happens, other dioceses follow the example of the mother Church. Several times the Congregation of Rites has expressed its wish that in the arrangements of this devotion, wherever held, the Instruction should be observed as far as possible and any bishop may order its observance in his diocese.[2] The indulgences attached to the Prayer are to be gained only on condition that at least the substance of that Instruction remain, though later popes (e.g., Pius X in 1914) have conceded modifications of the law of the Instruction in several points without loss of the *spiritual* privileges.[3]

The essence of the devotion was originally that the Blessed Sacrament remain exposed day and night for about forty hours without interruption, that is to say, from High Mass on one day until after High Mass on the third day.

At the beginning and end of the exposition there should be a procession of the Blessed Sacrament. On the second day of exposition there is to be a votive High Mass,[4] at another altar in the same church.[5]

Modifications of Clementine Instruction. Only in few places does the exposition begin at another church immediately it ends in the former one, so as to continue in some church of the city or diocese all the year round. In others arrangements are made by the Ordinary by which the Forty Hours' Prayer is held at different churches at such intervals as are possible and convenient throughout the year. There is no longer any special connection between this devotion and the time of Carnival immediately preceding Lent.

[1] The *Instructio Clementina*, in Italian with a parallel Latin translation and a long commentary by A. Gardellini, is contained in vol. iv of the Decrees of S.R.C. It was brought into line with the Pianine reform of the Roman Missal by an Instruction of S.R.C. of 27 April 1927. An English version of it (entitled *The Rubrics of the Forty Hours' Prayer*) with a commentary, bringing it up to date and elucidating its provisions, has been edited by Rev. J. O'Connell and published by Burns, Oates and Washbourne (1927). The Instruction is cited in the following pages as I.C.

[2] S.R.C. 2403, 3049[1], 3332[1-3], 4015[5].

[3] This is the real question in this matter always, not so much whether exposition arranged in a certain manner be lawful, as whether exposition so arranged can be considered a case of the Forty Hours' Prayer and so share its liturgical and spiritual privileges (see p. 358). Otherwise there is no reason against a church having exposition for one, two, three or any number of days, by permission of the Ordinary, and observing the general rules for exposition as explained above, pp. 239, 240.

[4] Usually the Mass for peace. The devotion began as a prayer specially for peace (see Thurston, *Lent and Holy Week*, pp. 114–121).

[5] The three Masses for the Prayer must be High Masses. A Sung Mass (much less a Low Mass) will not do, apart from Apostolic indult, and enjoys no liturgical privileges if celebrated in connection with the Prayer (I.C. § XV; cf. S.R.C. 4268[1]).

A further concession is that the Blessed Sacrament may be exposed, not continuously day and night for forty hours, but by day for three days, being put in the tabernacle at night. This arrangement may be followed whenever there is grave difficulty in watching through the night.[1]

General Directions for the Prayer. The general instructions of Clement XII's document for the Forty Hours are these :

A sign (e.g., a shield) or banner should be placed over the door of the church, bearing a symbol of the Blessed Sacrament, that people may see that the Forty Hours are being held there. The exposition should be made at the High Altar of the church. If there is a picture over the altar it is to be covered with a red or white hanging. In the same way all pictures close to the altar are to be covered. No relics or statues of saints are to be placed on the altar. Over the altar in a prominent place is prepared a throne draped in white, according to the usual rule for Exposition. If the altar has a permanent ciborium or canopy over it, a canopy is not necessary over this temporary throne. Around the throne or place where the monstrance will stand, wax-candles [2] are to burn continually during the time of exposition. At least twenty such candles should burn all the time. Flowers may be placed on and around the altar [3] (but they should not be too near the place where the monstrance will stand). While Mass is said at the altar of exposition an altar cross is not necessary, but is allowed. No light may be placed behind the monstrance, so as to shine through the Sanctissimum.[4]

The windows near the altar may be darkened to foster recollection in prayer. Whatever colour may be used for the Mass of Exposition, the altar frontal is to be white. A bench is to be prepared, which will be placed near the lowest step of the altar after the first Mass, at which priests and clerics kneel during the exposition. This bench may be covered with red or green. Clerics wear cassock and surplice while watching ; priests and deacons a white stole also, if customary. If possible two priests or clerics should watch all the time. Lay people who watch do so outside the sanctuary. During the exposition, if anyone has duty in the sanctuary, he must wear a surplice. Women (even Religious) are not to go into the sanctuary. The Blessed Sacrament reserved in the tabernacle should be removed, if possible, to another altar, so that people may make their Communion there. They should not receive Holy Communion from the altar of exposition, unless this is unavoidable. If private Masses are said during the exposition at any altar, the Sanctus bell is not rung at all. Requiem Mass should not be said at this time, unless All Souls is one of the days.[5] Private Masses are said according to the calendar of the day ; in them the collect of the Votive Mass of the Blessed Sacrament, with its Secret and Postcommunion, are added at the end of the commemorations

---

[1] See p. 358.   [2] Cf. p 7.
[3] In Rome they are not used for the Prayer.
[4] I.C. § VI ; S.R.C. 2613[5]. Electric light is forbidden on the altar or within the throne of exposition (S.R.C. 4086, 4097, 4206, 4210[1], 4275).
[5] Regarding the Prayer on All Souls' Day, see O'Connell, p. 17.

(but before *orationes imperatae* or votive prayers) even on the more solemn feasts of the Church.[1] When the rubrics permit, during the Prayer it is becoming to celebrate a votive Mass of the Blessed Eucharist, but such a Mass has no special liturgical privileges.

Sermons are discouraged during the Forty Hours. But sermons about the Holy Eucharist are tolerated. The preacher wears a surplice (even if a Regular), and may, outside Rome, use a (white) stole ; he preaches bareheaded. He must stand near the altar of exposition, so that no one shall turn his back to it.

If Palm Sunday (or Candlemas) occurs during the Forty Hours, there is to be no procession with palms (or candles). These may—if it is really necessary—be blessed and distributed in a side chapel ; or, if this is not possible, the whole ceremony should be omitted.[2] So also on Ash Wednesday. From the morning of Maundy Thursday to the morning of Holy Saturday the Prayer is not permitted.[3]

The day before exposition begins the church bells should be rung, with special solemnity, at the Angelus, and again half an hour before sunset and at the first hour of the night. During the exposition the bells should be rung every hour day and night.[4]

§ 2. THE FIRST DAY

THE Mass this day—celebrated after None—is normally the solemn votive Mass of the Blessed Sacrament, with *Gloria in excelsis* and Creed, the Preface of the birth of our Lord and the last Gospel of St. John.[5]

The Votive Mass. But this Mass is not to be sung if the day is a Sunday of the first class or a feast of the first class. The other days on which it is forbidden are Ash Wednesday, Holy Week and the eves of Christmas and Pentecost.[6] On these days the Mass of the day is to be sung, with the Collect, Secret and Postcommunion of the Blessed Sacrament added (under one conclusion) unless the feast of the day be of the same mystery as the Blessed Eucharist. The Preface will be that of the Mass of the day ; if there be none proper it will be the Preface of the Nativity (because of the commemoration of the Blessed Sacrament). The last Gospel will be that from the impeded votive Mass of the Blessed Sacrament, unless a Sunday, a weekday, vigil, or octave having a strictly proper Gospel occur. The colour of the vestments is that of the Mass. At the procession the celebrant wears a cope of the colour of the Mass.

In the Mass of the first day of the Prayer a commemoration is made

---

[1] See p. 61.   [2] S.R.C. 2621[9].
[3] S.R.C. 1190, 3574[5].
[4] So I.C. (§§ X, XI) for Rome.
[5] Cf. O'Connell : *The Celebration of Mass*, I. pp. 93, *seq.*
[6] The votive Mass may be excluded also on the ground of identity of mystery or, in certain churches, because the Mass of the day must be celebrated (*ib.*, p. 95).

of only (*a*) a double of the second class, (*b*) any Sunday, (*c*) a greater weekday (i.e., any weekday of Advent or Lent ; Ember days), (*d*) Rogations, (*e*) the vigil of Epiphany, (*f*) any privileged octave. An *oratio imperata* is said if it is *pro re gravi.*

Preparations. All is made ready for the exposition, as described in the former paragraph. The altar picture is covered, the candles are arranged at the sides of the throne, but are not yet lighted (except the six altar candles for Mass). A corporal is laid on the throne. The altar cross is in its place. Whatever the colour of the Mass may be, the altar is vested in white (p. 351). The usual preparations for High Mass are made, according to the colour that will be used. Beside these, a cope of the colour of the chasuble is laid out near the credence ; also the monstrance, covered with a white veil, and a book containing the prayers to be sung at the end (the *Ritus Servandus* or the " *Benedictionale* ") are made ready. A second altar bread is laid on the paten.[1] The bench at which the priests and clerks who watch will kneel is ready, but is not put before the altar till the end of the ceremony. White stoles for priests and deacons are prepared.

The canopy to carry over the Sanctissimum is made ready near the altar rails. The processional cross is by the credence. In the sacristy provision should be made for two thurifers and as many torches or lanterns as will be used in the procession. Candles to be held by the clergy in the procession will be at hand, either in the sacristy or at some convenient place in the church.

Besides the celebrant, ministers and servers for High Mass, a cross-bearer will be required,[2] two thurifers, a number of torch-bearers, men to hold the canopy.

The Mass of Exposition. High Mass [3] is celebrated as usual, to the Communion. Two Hosts are offered and consecrated. After the Communion, when the subdeacon has covered the chalice, the ministers genuflect, change places behind the celebrant and genuflect again. The M.C. brings the monstrance to the altar. The celebrant, aided by the deacon, puts the Sanctissimum in the monstrance. He stands it on the corporal. From now Mass continues as before the Blessed Sacrament exposed (see pp. 61, 124).

Towards the end of Mass the other candles on the altar are lighted, and candles are given out to the members of the choir (the clergy), and are lighted.

After Mass the celebrant and ministers having genuflected at the altar in the centre,[4] come down the altar steps, make a prostration and go to the sedilia.[5] Here, assisted by the M.C. and acolytes, they take off

---

[1] It is supposed that the Host to be exposed will be consecrated at the Mass. This is not absolutely necessary but is more correct.

[2] Not a subdeacon, but a server in surplice (I.C. § XX).

[3] See p. 350, n. 5.

[4] Or they may descend *per breviorem.*

[5] It is the celebrant of the Mass who is to carry the Sacred Host. Only a Cardinal or the Bishop of the diocese may do so, if he has not celebrated the Mass of Exposition.

their maniples, the celebrant exchanges the chasuble for a cope. In so doing they should not turn the back to the altar.[1] The altar cross, cards and Missal are removed.

Meanwhile two thurifers bring thuribles from the sacristy, leading out a procession of the torch or lantern bearers. On entering the sanctuary, or before leaving it, everyone prostrates before the Sanctissimum exposed, according to the usual rule.

Incensation of Blessed Sacrament. At the sedilia,[2] when he is vested, the celebrant puts incense on the two thuribles, not blessing it. He does so facing the Blessed Sacrament ; he is assisted, as always, by the deacon (who omits the solita oscula), while the subdeacon holds the end of the cope.

The celebrant and ministers then come to the altar and prostrate. The celebrant incenses the Sanctissimum, using the thurible of the first thurifer.

Procession. Meanwhile the procession[3] is formed in the sanctuary or choir. The men who are to carry the canopy stand by it outside the choir.

When the Sanctissimum is incensed, the M.C. puts the white humeral veil on the celebrant, the subdeacon ties it. All go up to the foot-pace, the celebrant and subdeacon kneel on its edge, the deacon genuflects (a little towards the Epistle side) takes the monstrance, and hands it to the celebrant. He receives it kneeling, first bowing. When he has handed the monstrance, the deacon genuflects. The sacred ministers stand, the celebrant turns towards the people, the ministers change places behind him, so that the deacon shall now be on his right. The cantors intone *Pange lingua*. The celebrant descends at once and goes under the canopy.

As soon as the celebrant and ministers have gone to the altar, the cross-bearer takes the cross and goes to stand at the farther end of the choir. The acolytes with their candles stand at his sides. The members of the choir should already be kneeling in the centre (if there is room there) All now rise, prostrate (except the cross-bearer and acolytes), turn, and so the procession begins.

It goes in this order :

First, confraternities of laymen, then the cross-bearer between the acolytes, then the (surpliced) singers, and lastly the clergy,[4] all holding lighted candles in the outside hand. The thurifers go immediately in

---

[1] If the deacon and subdeacon are wearing folded chasubles they retain them. But if there is an interval before the procession and they leave the sanctuary, they must change into white dalmatic (with stole) and tunicle.

[2] I.C. § XIX.

[3] The procession must be held unless it be quite impossible to carry it out or its omission is permitted by Papal indult. If the procession is to be a large one, an assistant M.C. should begin its formation earlier—any time after the Consecration of the Mass. When a procession is held within the church, normally it turns to the right outside the sanctuary, goes down the church on the Gospel side and returns by the centre passage.

[4] For details of the order of the procession, see p. 346 (Corpus Christi).

front of the canopy,[1] the torch-bearers at each side of it.[2] At the entrance of the sanctuary the celebrant goes between the ministers under the canopy ; they hold the ends of his cope. During the procession they should recite suitable psalms and hymns together in the subdued voice.

The procession is not to go outside the church, unless the church is very small. In this case it may go round the square or place just outside.[3] Meanwhile the *Pange lingua* is sung ; the church bells are rung.[4]

Return of Procession. When the procession comes back to the High Altar the cross-bearer and acolytes enter the sanctuary, put aside the cross and the candles (on the credence), and kneel before the credence when the Blessed Sacrament arrives. The choir and clergy—without any reverence to the altar—file into their places. As the Blessed Sacrament passes, all fall on their knees. The canopy remains outside the sanctuary.

Before the altar (*in plano*) the deacon kneels, bows and takes the monstrance from the celebrant, and waits standing while the celebrant genuflects. The celebrant than kneels on the lowest step—the subdeacon on his left—and the deacon puts the monstrance on the throne. The deacon may place the monstrance on the altar, and another priest or deacon in surplice and white stole may put it on the throne.

The subdeacon unfastens the celebrant's humeral veil ; the M.C. takes it from him. Now (not before) the stanzas *Tantum ergo* and *Genitori Genitoque* are sung. At this last stanza the celebrant incenses the Blessed Sacrament, as at Benediction. The two thurifers may now go to the sacristy.

Litanies. Meanwhile two cantors come to kneel in the middle of the choir or sanctuary. They begin the Litanies of the Saints.[5] These are sung through, the choir answering each petition. The petitions are not sung twice. The cantors sing the first half (e.g., *Sancta Maria*), the choir answers the second half (*Ora pro nobis*). After the litanies the celebrant, still kneeling, intones *Pater noster*. It is continued silently ; he sings *Et ne nos inducas in tentationem ;* the choir answers *Sed libera nos a malo.* The cantors intone the psalm *Deus in adiutorium meum intende,* which is continued by the choir, each side singing an alternate verse. The celebrant, kneeling, sings *Salvos fac servos tuos,* and the verses which follow.

He stands and sings *Dominus vobiscum,* and the prayers, to the simple ferial tone.[6] The ministers hold the book. Then, kneeling

---

[1] See p. 346, n. 6; p. 284, n. 2.

[2] I.C. (§ XX) directs that eight priests (in surplice) carry torches, walking before the thurifers.

[3] I.C. § XXI.

[4] I.C. § XX.

[5] The Litanies (of which there is a special form for the Prayer) and the following prayers for the Forty Hours are in the English *Ritus Servandus,* pp. 31–40 ; in the Irish " *Benedictionale,*" pp. 14–24.

[6] Cf. p. 249, n. 4 ; 259, n. 1.

again, the celebrant sings *Domine, exaudi orationem meam.* The cantors sing *Exaudiat nos omnipotens et misericors Dominus.* The celebrant sings in a low tone, *Fidelium animae per misericordiam Dei requiescant in pace.* Rɉ. *Amen.*

The clergy extinguish their candles. All remain for a short time praying silently. They rise, prostrate and go to the sacristy (the sacred ministers remaining uncovered until they are at a distance from the altar).

The Blessed Sacrament remains exposed. There must always be people who watch in the church, taking hours, or shorter periods by turn. If possible there should be two priests, deacons or clerics in Holy Orders who kneel at the bench in the sanctuary. Priests and deacons wear surplice and white stole, other clerics surplice only.

§ 3. THE SECOND DAY

On this day a solemn votive Mass for peace is to be sung,[1] not at the altar of exposition but at another altar in the church (not, however, at one on which the Blessed Sacrament is reserved in the tabernacle [2]). It should be High Mass.[3] The vestments are violet, the *Gloria in excelsis* is not said. The Creed is sung even on week-days. The Collect, Secret and Postcommunion of the Blessed Sacrament are added (unless a commemoration of a mystery identical with the Blessed Sacrament occurs in the Mass) with their own conclusion after the prayers prescribed by the rubrics but before an *oratio imperata pro re gravi.* The same commemorations are to be made as in the Mass of the first day (p. 353). The Preface will be that proper to an occurring commemoration (e.g., that of the Blessed Trinity on a Sunday) or that proper to the season (e.g., Paschal-tide) or (if there be none proper) the common Preface, according to the general rules. The Gospel of St. John is said at the end, unless an occurring commemoration has a proper Gospel.

But on those days on which the votive Mass of the Blessed Sacrament at the exposition may not be said (see p. 352) neither may this votive Mass for peace occur. On such days the Mass of the day must be said, with the Collect, Secret and Postcommunion for peace, under the same conclusion.[4] Even on the more solemn feasts there will be a commemoration of the Blessed Sacrament under its own conclusion, and, if other commemorations prescribed by the rubrics occur, after these. The Creed will be sung, even if it is not proper to the Mass of the day, unless the rite of the Mass of the day be simple only (e.g. Ash Wednesday).

---

[1] In the Missal, the Mass "Da pacem, Domine." But the Bishop may substitute for this another suitable votive Mass, at his discretion (S.R.C. 3049[4]).
[2] I.C. § XIV.
[3] Cf. p. 350, n. 5.
[4] A prayer is added to the prayer of the Mass of the day *under one conclusion,* when it represents an impeded votive Mass.

§ 4. THE THIRD DAY

HIGH Mass [1] of Deposition follows the general rules of that of exposition
on the first day (p. 352). It is a solemn votive Mass of the Blessed
Sacrament sung at the altar of exposition. All must be prepared
beforehand for the Mass and procession, as on the first day (see p. 353).
The rules for days on which the votive Mass may not be said are the
same as on the first day (p. 352). On these days the Mass of the day
is said, with the Collect, Secret and Postcommunion of the Blessed
Sacrament, after those of the Mass, under one conclusion. The chief
difference is that this Mass of Deposition is all sung before the Blessed
Sacrament exposed. Therefore, during the whole Mass the rules for
that occasion are to be observed (see pp. 61, 124).[2]

The procession follows at the end of Mass. But this time the litanies
are sung before the procession.

Litanies. The celebrant and ministers go to the sedilia, to change
their vestments, as on the first day. Meantime the crucifix (if used),
the Missal and altar cards are removed ; a corporal spread on the altar ;
the tabernacle key and monstrance veil put near it. The sacred
ministers come back to the altar, prostrate and kneel on the lowest
step. The cantors, kneeling in the middle of the choir, begin the
Litanies of the Saints. They are sung as on the first day. The prayers
follow as before, down to the versicle *Domine, exaudi orationem meam*
and its response (inclusive).

Towards the end of the litanies, or during the prayers that follow,
the two thurifers go to the sacristy and return with thuribles. They
make the usual prostration before going and on returning. The cross-
bearer gets the cross, the acolytes their candles and stand at the
entrance to the sanctuary. The torch-bearers and canopy-bearers
make ready. Candles are distributed to the clergy and others. The
procession is formed. When the response to *Domine, exaudi orationem
meam* has been sung, the celebrant rises and puts incense in both
thuribles, not blessing it. Taking the first thurible he incenses the
Sanctissimum. He receives the humeral veil and goes up the steps
with the ministers. Here the deacon gives him the monstrance, as on
the first day.

Procession. The procession goes round the church singing *Pange
lingua.* The celebrant and ministers recite suitable psalms and hymns
meanwhile. They come back to the altar, the deacon puts the monstrance on the corporal on the table of the altar. The stanzas *Tantum
ergo* and *Genitori Genitoque* are sung. The Blessed Sacrament is
incensed at this last stanza. The cantors sing the versicle *Panem de
caelo*, etc. Then the celebrant, standing, sings (without *Dominus
vobiscum*) the prayer *Deus quo nobis sub Sacramento mirabili*, and adds

---

[1] See p. 350, n. 5.
[2] In this Mass such solita oscula as are merely marks of reverence to the
celebrant, but not part of the rite itself, are omitted. Hence, e.g., the kissing
of the paten and chalice at the Offertory, of the paten and the celebrant's hand
after the *Pater Noster*, are not omitted.

at once the other prayers, which on the first day are sung at the end of the litanies (including the verse *Fidelium*). The celebrant gives Benediction according to the usual rules (see pp. 233 *sqq.*). The Sanctissimum is put back in the tabernacle by the deacon or by an assistant priest (It is to be consumed at a subsequent Mass on that day or on the following morning). The clergy who hold lighted candles extinguish them. All rise, genuflect and go to the sacristy as after every Benediction.

§ 5. MOFIDICATIONS OF THE RULES OF THE CLEMENTINE INSTRUCTION

WHEN the full requirements of the Clementine Instruction cannot be carried out (if, for example, the adoration must be interrupted at night) the Ordinary may permit a modification of the form of the Supplication, i.e., the Sacred Host may be exposed in the morning or towards midday on the first day and put into the tabernacle in the evening, exposed again on the mornings of the second and third days, and the adoration brought to a close at midday or in the evening of the third day. In such a case the spiritual privileges of the Prayer (i.e., the indulgences, including that of the privileged altar) are not lost:[1] It is very doubtful, however, if this form of Exposition enjoys the *liturgical* privileges of the Forty Hours' Prayer. It would seem that it does not.[2]

In this case of interrupted adoration, the Exposition may begin, as described above, with High Mass, procession,[3] etc. In the evening the Sanctissimum is replaced in the tabernacle by a priest or deacon in surplice and white stole. He may give Benediction, if the Ordinary so allows.

On the second day a priest, vested in the same way, exposes the Sanctissimum and incenses It. Meanwhile *Pange lingua* and prayer *Deus qui nobis* may be sung or recited, but Benediction is not given. This exposition of the Blessed Sacrament should be done early in the morning. Later Mass may follow. It may be the (private) votive Mass for peace, if the calendar of the day permits, or, if the Ordinary allows,[4] a solemn votive Mass. The Blessed Sacrament is put in the tabernacle in the evening as the day before.

The third day some authors say that there should be no Mass to take the place of the Mass of Deposition, since the deposition is made in the evening.[5] If there is a special Mass it may not be at the altar of the Exposition ; nor may it be a votive Mass of the Blessed Sacrament, unless the rubrics allow a private votive Mass that day, or the Ordinary permits a solemn votive Mass, or there is an apostolic indult. In the

---

[1] Holy Office, 22 January 1914 ; *Preces et Opera* (1938), no. 140.
[2] Cf. S.R.C. 4268[1] (a reply to a query from Westminster in 1911).
[3] By permission of the Ordinary (cf. C.J.C. 1292).
[4] Cf. *Additiones* of the Missal II. 3.
[5] E.g., Martinucci I. ii, p. 124, § 24.

evening of this day there may be the procession, or *Pange lingua* is sung, preceded by the litanies, as after the Mass of Deposition in the case of the exact observance of the Instruction.[1] Benediction is given and the devotion ends.

[1] This is the usual practice in England. In his Pastoral Letter of Trinity Sunday, 1936, the Archbishop of Westminster gave the following instructions for the (interrupted) Forty Hours' Prayer in the diocese of Westminster : (*a*) The three Votive Masses prescribed by the Clementine Instruction are to be celebrated ; if possible they should be sung Masses : (*b*) *Benediction* is to be given each evening. On the first and second evenings the Litanies of the Saints shall be sung or recited with the versicles and collects which follow, then the *Pange lingua*, collect *Deus qui nobis* and Benediction. On the third evening the Litanies are to be sung and the Procession shall also take place. (*c*) In the morning of the second and third days, when the Blessed Sacrament is exposed, *incense* must be used and the *O Salutaris* must be sung or recited.

CHAPTER XXVIII

CANONICAL VISITATION AND CONFIRMATION

§ 1. GENERAL PRINCIPLES

ONE of the chief duties of a diocesan bishop is to know his clergy and people, to see that everything concerning the worship of God in his diocese is in order, to decide disputed matters, and correct any possible abuses. The opportunity for all this is his Canonical Visitation of churches, parishes and religious institutions.[1]

The Council of Trent explains the purpose of Canonical Visitation : " The chief object of all Visitations is to maintain right and orthodox doctrine, to drive out heresies, defend good and correct bad manners, to incite the people to religion, peace and innocence by sermons and warnings, to arrange all things according to the need of the place, time and occasion by the prudence of the Visitor, for the good of the people."[2]

The Ordinary should make the visitation himself,[3] or (if he is legitimately prevented) by a delegate. There is no special law as to who this delegate shall be. The Ordinary may send any priest he chooses to appoint, his vicar-general, a rural dean, or other. But, since in most countries the opportunity of the visitation is used for the administration of Confirmation, either the Ordinary will come himself or he will send an auxiliary bishop.

The Council of Trent desires the visitation to be made once a year, or (in the case of a large diocese) once every two years.[4] The new Code of Canon Law says that the Bishop is to visit yearly his diocese either completely or in part so that at least every five years he shall have visited the entire territory. The Ordinary may, however, visit oftener and at any time that he thinks fit.

All persons, places and objects belonging to the diocese are visited ; that is, the clergy and Catholics who live in each parish or mission, all churches and chapels, including the churches of Regulars, as far as they do diocesan work. The Code [5] says : " to the ordinary episcopal visitation are subject persons, things and pious places, although exempt, which are contained within the ambit of the diocese, unless it can be proved that a special exemption from the visitation had been granted them by the Apostolic See. The Bishop may visit exempt Religious, however, only in cases laid down in law." The Ordinary

---

[1] C.J.C. 343–346.
[2] Conc. Trid. Sess. XXIV, de Reform, c. 3.
[3] In default of the Ordinary, the Metropolitan. C.J.C. 274, 5°.
[4] Conc. Trid. Sess. XXIV, de Ref. c. 3.
[5] Canon 344. Regarding the visitation of Religious, see canons 512, 513, 631, 690, 1261, 1491.

also visits all convents of nuns,[1] religious and pious institutions, such as schools, orphanages, almshouses and so on. He examines the objects of divine worship, the furniture of the church, vessels and vestments. He inquires into the conduct of services, the administration of sacraments, administration of ecclesiastical property in all its forms. He examines the books of the parish, the register of baptisms, marriages, confirmations and funerals. He makes any inquiries that seem opportune to him concerning the life of the clergy and people. He allows the people an opportunity of speaking to him, that they may expose any question or make any complaint.

The entertainment of the Bishop and those who accompany him and the travelling and other expenses are to be provided for in accordance with legitimate local usage.

The Ordinary may bring other co-visitors with him, to whom he delegates part of the duty.

There is no suspensive appeal (*appellatio suspensiva*) from any decision made by the Ordinary in those matters which concern the object and end of the visitation ; that is to say, no such appeal as can impede the execution of what he decides. But a devolutive appeal (*appellatio devolutiva*) is allowed, namely, the decision may be deferred to a higher court, after it has been obeyed. In other matters the Bishop must proceed, even at the time of the visitation, in accordance with law.

There are differences in the ceremony of visitation, according to whether it is made by the Ordinary or by his auxiliary bishop. There are further modifications according to the rank of the Ordinary. In the first place we consider the visitation of the church of the parish, next that of convents and institutions, lastly that of the churches of exempt Regulars.[2]

§ 2. BEFORE THE VISITATION

NOTICE of the visitation will be sent in due time to the rector of the church and he may be sent a questionary to answer about the affairs of his parish. In most cases the day and hour of the function are arranged by agreement with him, so that both may be convenient for the people who will attend and the candidates for Confirmation.

According to the practice in England the visitation is announced to the people beforehand, generally on the Sunday before it takes place, if not earlier. Notice is given that the faithful will have an opportunity of seeing the Bishop privately in the sacristy or other convenient place. The hymn *Veni Creator* is sung or recited, with the versicle *Emitte*

---

[1] All convents of religious women are subject to visitation by the Ordinary, whether they have a regular Superior or not. But those under regular Superiors are examined by him for certain specified matters only (cf. canon 512).

[2] The ceremonies for Canonical Visitation are in the Pontifical (" Ordo ad visitandas parochias " in Par III). There is a booklet in use in England entitled *Order of the Episcopal Visitation of Parishes, with the Rite of Confirmation* (Burns and Oates, 1931). It is an excerpt from the Roman Pontifical giving the prayers in Latin and English, with the rubrics in English.

Spiritum tuum, its response and the prayer *Deus qui corda fidelium*, after the chief Mass on the Sunday before the visitation.

§ 3. VISITATION BY THE ORDINARY

SUPPOSING the Ordinary to be a bishop [1] the following are the ceremonies of his visitation.

The general order is always the same, namely, reception of the Bishop at the doors of the church, procession to the altar, prayers for him, his blessing (possibly Mass), his sermon to the people, proclamation of the indulgence he grants, prayers for the dead, visitation of the tabernacle and altar (possibly Benediction), Confirmation, visitation of the church and its furniture, of the sacristy, its vessels, holy Oils and vestments, the opportunity for the faithful to speak to the Bishop, examination of the mission books and accounts, instructions to the clergy, last visit to the Blessed Sacrament.

In the details, the vestments worn and so on, greater or less solemnity may be used.[2] If the visitation takes place in the morning, either the Bishop himself may say or sing Mass, or the rector of the church may do so in his presence. In this case the Mass is said after the Bishop has given his blessing. His address to the people is normally made after the Gospel of the Mass.

The Preparations. The following preparations must be made :

The church and High Altar are decorated as for a feast. If Mass will be celebrated the altar is vested in the colour of the day ; otherwise it is vested in white for the Benediction (if this should take place) and Confirmation. At the Epistle corner of the altar, facing that corner, a Pontifical (or other book) open at the prayers for the reception of the Bishop is ready on the Missal stand. The Canon—open at the form for a bishop's blessing—is placed on the centre of the altar, leaning against the tabernacle or cross. The altar cards are not put on.[3]

At the door of the church a small carpet is laid, and on it a priedieu with a (green) cushion is placed for the Bishop. If the processional canopy will be carried over the Bishop, it is prepared by the door. If there are not enough servers to make a procession to the door, a table must stand there, on the right just inside the door, on which are placed the incense boat, a crucifix (covered with a white veil) which the Bishop will kiss, the vessel of lustral water and sprinkler.

In the sanctuary a carpet is laid before the altar steps. On it is a kneeling-stool covered with two cushions, one on which the Bishop will kneel, the other on which he will rest the arms. The colour of this covering and the cushions is green for a bishop, red for a cardinal.

If Mass is not to be said a faldstool (covered in white) or chair is

---

[1] For the changes in the rite when he is an archbishop, see p. 369.

[2] For example, in the more solemn form the Bishop puts on amice, stole and cope (with morse) for the Absolution and for the visitation of the tabernacle ; in the simpler form he uses a stole only, worn over the rochet.

[3] If Mass is to be celebrated in the presence of the Bishop they are put on just before it begins.

placed on the foot-pace on the Gospel side, where the Bishop will sit while preaching. If Mass is to be celebrated the faldstool is at hand on the Gospel side of the sanctuary.

On the ordinary credence are prepared : a white burse (containing a corporal), the tabernacle key, a white stole for the rector, the bell.

If *Mass is to be celebrated by the Bishop* : on the credence, in addition, are made ready the chalice prepared for Mass, the Bishop's maniple, and the cruets. If *Mass is to be said in the Bishop's presence*, the cruets are made ready with the things on the credence ; and the vestments and chalice for the celebrant are prepared in the sacristy. The Missal and altar cards are ready near the altar.

At an extra credence (near the ordinary one) are laid out the special requisites for the Bishop [1] : his mitres, the hand-candle, a salver, the Pontifical (Part III), a book for the Absolution for the dead, the form for the publication of the Indulgence, a card or book containing the music of the *Confiteor*, if this is to be sung. Nearby (at the sedilia or other convenient place) are an amice, white stole, cope and morse for the Bishop (stole only, if he will follow the simpler rite) ; a black stole, cope and simple morse (or stole only) for the Absolution ; a white humeral veil.

If *the Bishop is to celebrate Mass* : vestments (amice, alb, cincture, stole and chasuble) are prepared near the credence (they will later be transferred to the table of the altar).

Aside in the sanctuary is a black cloth (or a catafalque) for the Absolution for the dead.

If *Confirmation is to be administered* the following additional things are put on either credence : the Chrism, a supply of cotton wool, the ewer and basin (with some lemon and dry bread) with towels, and a gremial veil (for which an amice serves). Nearby is the crozier.

In the sacristy : a white cope for the rector (if the rite will be the more solemn one), the aspersory, the thurible and boat, the processional cross, and a small crucifix on a salver and covered with a white veil.

For the Bishop's visitation, towards the end of the function, the keys of the Baptistry, of the aumbry for the Holy Oils, and of any reliquaries that are to be inspected, are at hand.

The vessels, vestments and furniture that the Bishop will examine must be ready for this purpose, also whatever books he will see, either in the sacristy or the priest's house.

Assistants. All the clergy of the church go to the door to receive the Bishop. There should also be a thurifer, cross-bearer and acolytes, two other servers to carry the holy water and crucifix, four servers to hold the book, candle, mitre and crozier, torch-bearers.[2] The rector of the church wears a surplice ; or he may, for greater solemnity, go to the door in surplice, and white cope.

The procession may go to the house where the Bishop awaits it and

---

[1] Normally the pontifical ornaments and vessels, etc., will be brought by the Bishop and arranged beforehand by his chaplain or by the M.C.

[2] If the Bishop wears the cappa, a train-bearer will be needed.

conduct him thence to the church. Meanwhile the canticle *Benedictus* is sung.

Reception of the Bishop. But in England and Ireland the Bishop, with his chaplain, is usually received at the door of the church. The Ordinary wears rochet and mozzetta, or the cappa magna. The rector, clergy and servers go to meet him at the door.[1] The cross-bearer and acolytes stand on the left of the entrance, the thurifer, aspersory-bearer, and crucifix-bearer on the right. The rector holds the small crucifix for the Bishop to kiss. Meanwhile the Bishop, uncovered, kneels on the kneeling-stool there prepared. The Bishop rises. The rector hands him the sprinkler, kissing it first, then the Bishop's hand. The Bishop sprinkles himself on the forehead with holy water, then sprinkles the rector and those who are around. All genuflect (except the cross-bearer and acolytes) and make the sign of the cross. The rector receives back the sprinkler. The thurifer kneels before the Bishop, holding up the thurible. The rector takes the spoon and hands it (with the solita oscula), saying *Benedicite, Pater reverendissime* (to a cardinal *Benedicite eminentissime ac reverendissime Pater*). The Bishop puts on incense and blesses it. The thurifer rises ; the rector takes the thurible and incenses the Bishop (covered) with three double swings, bowing low before and after.

The procession now goes up the church. The thurifer goes first, than the cross-bearer between the acolytes, then the choir, servers, clergy, the Bishop's chaplain, the rector of the church, lastly, the Bishop himself (uncovered).[2] A canopy may be carried over him by men chosen for that purpose. If the Bishop is in cappa his train is held by a server. As the Bishop goes up the church he blesses the people, who kneel as he passes. Meanwhile the antiphon *Sacerdos et Pontifex*, or the responsory *Ecce Sacerdos magnus*, is sung or recited.

Prayers for the Bishop. Before the altar the Bishop kneels at the faldstool. The cross and acolytes' candles are put aside in the usual place. The aspersory-bearer leaves the aspersory on the credence. The thurifer makes ready the thurible for the Absolution (unless Mass intervenes). All kneel, except the rector, who (having put on a white stole, if he is not already in cope) stands at the Epistle corner of the altar (on the top step), facing the Gospel side. He then sings or says the following versicles, the choir singing the answers, or the servers saying them : [3]

℣. *Protéctor noster áspice Deus,*
℟. *Et réspice in fáciem christi tui.*[4]
℣. *Salvum fac servum tuum.*

[1] They may go in this order : The crucifix-bearer having on his left the thurifer, and on his right the aspersory-bearer. These are followed by the cross-bearer between the acolytes (with their candles). Then come the singers ; next the servers ; then the clergy and lastly the rector.

[2] If he has co-visitors they (in choir dress) follow him.

[3] The text is given, since there may be difficulty in finding it.

[4] The " christus " is the (anointed) bishop. The prayer—*Deus humilium*—is sung in the second ferial tone (cf. p. 259, n. 1).

Rℓ. *Deus meus, sperántem in te.*
Vℓ. *Mitte ei, Dómine, auxílium de sancto,*
Rℓ. *Et de Sion tuére eum.*
Vℓ. *Nihil profíciat inimícus in eo,*
Rℓ. *Et fílius iniquitátis non appónat nocére ei.*
Vℓ. *Dómine, exaudi oratiónem meam,*
Rℓ. *Et clamor meus ad te véniat.*
Vℓ. *Dóminus vobíscum,*
Rℓ. *Et cum spíritu tuo.*

Oremus

Deus humílium visitátor, qui eos patérna dilectióne consoláris, praeténde societáti nostrae grátiam tuam, ut per eos in quibus hábitas tuum in nobis sentiámus advéntum. Per Christum Dóminum nostrum.

Rℓ. *Amen.*

The rector takes off his stole, or the cope if he has worn one.
The Bishop goes up to the altar and kisses it in the middle. He says or sings the form for his blessing, the clergy or choir answering :

Vℓ. *Sit nomen Dómini benedíctum,*
Rℓ. *Ex hoc nunc et usque in saeculum.*
Vℓ. *Adiutórium nostrum in nómine Dómini,*
Rℓ. *Qui fécit caelum et terram.*
Benedícat vos omnípotens Deus, Pa+ter et Fi+lius et Spiritus+ Sanctus.

Rℓ. *Amen.*

Meanwhile the rector and all in church kneel.
Mass and Sermon. If Mass is to be said, it follows now. If the Bishop will say Mass, he is vested before the altar.[1] If it is to be said in his presence, the celebrant goes to the sacristy to vest. The Bishop kneels at the kneeling-stool in the centre of the sanctuary or on the Gospel side of it.

For the ceremonies of Low Mass by a bishop see pp. 67–69. For Low Mass in his presence see pp. 64–66.[2]

After the Gospel of the Mass the faldstool or a chair is placed on the foot-pace at the Gospel side. The Bishop sits there and addresses the people.[3]

Meanwhile the celebrant sits at the sedile. After the address the Indulgence is proclaimed, as below.

If Mass is not said, as soon as the Bishop has given his blessing he sits on the faldstool or chair on the foot-pace and addresses the people.

[1] While he reads the psalms of preparation at the priedieu the (second) M.C. arranges the vestments on the altar and servers prepare to bring them from there for the vesting (see p. 67).
[2] It is unlikely that the Bishop will desire High Mass to be sung in his presence, and still less likely that he will himself sing High Mass. However, the rules for both these functions may be found above, chaps. xv and xvi.
[3] Or the Bishop may defer his address until after Mass. In either case it is after the sermon that the Indulgence will be imparted.

After the address a priest or server stands before him, below the altar steps, and (moderately bowed) sings or says the *Confiteor*. This may be done by the rector of the church. No change is made in the text of the *Confiteor* ; but he who says it genuflects to the Bishop as he says *tibi, pater* or *te, pater*. The Bishop stands during the *Confiteor*, then sits for the publication of the indulgence.

The Indulgence. The rector then, standing near the Bishop, bows to him and reads the formula of indulgence, first in Latin, then in English :

Reverendíssimus in Christo Pater et Dóminus, Dóminus N.[1] Dei et Apostólicae Sedis grátia huius sanctae N.[2] Ecclésiae Epíscopus, dat et concédit ómnibus hic praeséntibus centum dies de vera indulgéntia in forma Ecclésiae consuéta. Rogáte Deum pro felíci statu sanctíssimi ,Dómini nostri N.[3] divina providéntia Papae N.,[4] Dominatiónis suae reverendíssimae et sanctae Matris Ecclésiae.

The Right Reverend Father and Lord in Christ, N. by the grace of God and of the Apostolic See Bishop of this holy Church of N. gives and grants to all persons here present one hundred days of true indulgence, in the customary form of the Church. Pray to God for the good estate of His Holiness N.[5] by Divine Providence Pope, of His Lordship the Bishop, and of holy Mother Church.

For an ARCHBISHOP :

Reverendíssimus in Christo Pater et Dóminus, Dóminus N. Dei et Apostólicae Sedis grátia huius sanctae N. Ecclésiae Archiepíscopus, dat et concédit ómnibus hic praeséntibus ducentos dies de vera indulgéntia in forma Ecclésiae consuéta. Rogáte Deum pro felíci statu sanctíssimi Dómini nostri N. divína providéntia Papae N., Dominatiónis suae reverendíssimae et sanctae matris Ecclésiae.

The Most Reverend Father and Lord in Christ, N. by the grace of God and of the Apostolic See Archbishop of this holy Church of N. gives and grants to all persons here present two hundred days of true indulgence, in the customary form of the Church. Pray to God for the good estate of His Holiness N. by Divine Providence Pope, of His Grace the Archbishop and of holy Mother Church.

For a CARDINAL [and ARCHBISHOP] :

Eminentíssimus et reverendíssimus in Christo Pater et Dóminus, Dóminus N. Tituli sancti N. sanctae Romanae Ecclesiae (presbyter) Cardinalis N. [et Archiepíscopus] N. dat et concédit ómnibus hic praeséntibus trecentos dies de vera indulgéntia in forma Ecclésiae consuéta. Rogáte Deum pro felíci statu sanctíssimi Dómini nostri N. divína Providéntia Papae N. Dominatiónis suae eminentíssimae ac reverendíssimae et sanctae Matris Ecclésiae.

[1] The Bishop's Christian name only.
[2] The name of the diocese in adjective form (gen. sing.).
[3] The Pope's name only (gen.).
[4] The Pope's number (gen.).
[5] The Pope's name and number.

The Most Eminent and Right Reverend Father and Lord in Christ N.[1] *Cardinal (priest) of the holy Roman Church, of the title of Saint N. [and Archbishop of N.] gives and grants to all persons here present three hundred days of true indulgence, in the customary form of the Church. Pray to God for the good estate of His Holiness N. by Divine Providence Pope, of His Eminence the Cardinal and of holy Mother Church.*

Meanwhile two servers take the Pontifical and candle, they genuflect before the altar, then before the Bishop, and stand by him.[2] The Bishop, standing uncovered, reads or sings the form *Precibus et meritis*, etc. ; then *Indulgentiam, absolutionem*, etc. Lastly, *Et benedictio Dei*— with his biretta on (unless he be an archbishop, when his cross will be held before him)—*omnipoténtis Pa+tris et Fi+lii et Spiritus+Sancti descéndat super vos et máneat semper*. To each form the answer is *Amen*. All kneel during the prayer and blessing.

Absolution for the Dead. The prayers for the dead follow.[3]

If the church has no churchyard or cemetery immediately around it, the following form of the Absolution has been approved.[4]

A catafalque is set up in the choir, or a black cloth is spread on the ground in the middle. The Bishop, having put on a black stole over his rochet (or vested in amice, black stole, cope, simple morse and simple mitre), stands *in plano* somewhat to the Epistle side, facing the catafalque or cloth. The servers hold the book and hand-candle before him. Others have lustral water and incense at hand.

He recites with those around *De profundis*, with the antiphon *Si iniquitátes observáveris Dómine, Dómine quis sustinébit* before and after.[5]

Then he uncovers (if mitred) and says the following versicles and prayers. Those around answer them :

℣. *Kyrie, eléison,*
℟. *Christe, eléison,*
℣. *Kyrie, eléison. Pater noster* (continued silently).

While he says the Lord's Prayer, the Bishop puts incense into the thurible and blesses it with the usual form (the rector having asked the blessing, saying *Benedicite, Pater Reverendissime*). The rector, at his right, hands him the spoon and takes it back, kissing neither the spoon nor the hand. The thurifer kneels. The rector presents the sprinkler and the Bishop, remaining in his place, thrice sprinkles the

---

[1] It is usual to say the cardinal's Christian name first, then, after " Cardinalis " his surname.

[2] The book in front, the hand-candle at his left.

[3] If there is a cemetery adjoining the church, for the rite of the Absolution there, see *Pontificale*, Pars III, or *Order of the Episcopal Visitation of Parishes*, pp 15, *sqq.*

[4] Reply of Cardinal Barnabo (1866).

[5] Only the first two words of the antiphon are said before the psalm.

catafalque or black cloth with lustral water and incenses it thrice.[1]
He continues :

℣. *Et ne nos indúcas in tentatiónem,*
℟. *Sed líbera nos a malo.*
℣. *In memória aetérna erunt iusti,*
℟. *Ab auditióne mala non timébunt.*
℣. *A porta inferi*
℟. *Erue, Dómine, ánimas eorum.*
℣. *Réquiem aetérnam dona eis, Dómine,*
℟. *Et lux perpétua luceat eis.*
℣. *Dómine, exaudi oratiónem meam,*
℟. *Et clamor meus ad te véniat.*
℣. *Dóminus vobíscum.*
℟. *Et cum spíritu tuo.*

Oremus :

Deus qui inter apostólicos sacerdótes [2]. . . .
Deus véniae largítor et humánae salutis amator. . . .
Deus cuius miseratióne ánimae fidélium requiéscant,[3] . . . . And
he recites these three prayers under one conclusion (*Per eundem
Christum Dominum nostrum.* ℟. *Amen.*)

℣. *Réquiem aetérnam dona eis, Dómine.*
℟. *Et lux perpétua luceat eis.*
The cantors (or the Bishop himself) :
℣. *Requiéscant in pace.*
℟. *Amen.*

While this verse is sung the Bishop makes the sign of the cross over
the catafalque or cloth.

This is the end of the prayers for the dead in churches which have
no cemetery attached. The catafalque or cloth is removed.

Visitation of the Blessed Sacrament. The Bishop, standing before
the altar, is vested in white stole and cope (with precious morse),[4] and
kneels on a cushion at the foot of the altar before the tabernacle, with
head uncovered. If the Blessed Sacrament is reserved in a side
chapel, the Bishop (mitred) is conducted thither.

The rector of the church puts on a white stole, and takes from the
credence the burse and tabernacle key. He goes up to the altar,
spreads the corporal, opens the tabernacle, genuflects, and pulls aside
the curtains of the conopaeum that the ciborium may be visible. He
again genuflects, descends, and takes off the stole.

---

[1] He sprinkles in the centre, to his left and to his right. He incenses in the
same way with simple swings of the thurible.
[2] In this case the words *seu sacerdotali* are added after *Pontificali* in this
prayer as given in the Pontifical.
[3] In this case, if no one has been buried in the church, the words *hic et* (before
ubique) are omitted in this prayer as given in the Pontifical.
[4] Or he may wear only a white stole, if he is following the simpler form of the
ceremony.

The Bishop—assisted by the rector—puts incense into the thurible and incenses the Sanctissimum, as usual. The *Tantum ergo* is then begun. After the words *veneremur cernui* the Bishop goes up to the altar, genuflects, takes out the ciborium and other vessels containing the consecrated Particles, uncovers them, inspects them and the inside of the tabernacle. He re-covers the vessels, leaves them on the corpora. and comes back to kneel before the altar or on the edge of the foot-pace, receives the humeral veil and gives Benediction (a triple blessing) with the ciborium,[1] while *Genitori*, etc., is sung, and then descends *in plano*. The rector resumes the stole, puts the vessels back into the tabernacle, making the usual genuflections, shuts the tabernacle, folds the corporal, and puts aside his stole. The Bishop resumes his skull-cap.

Visitation of Church and Sacristy. The Bishop is then unvested. In rochet and mozetta (or cappa) he now goes round the church, attended by the rector and other clergy. He examines the chapels, altars, ornaments, confessionals, pulpit, font, the seats for the people, the notices at the church doors, and any other article of furniture or ornament he may wish to inspect.

He is conducted to the sacristy and here examines the relics, stocks of holy Oils, vestments, vessels and furniture [2]; and he may bless vestments,[3] etc. Then he may administer the sacrament of Confirmation (see pp. 373–376), or this may be done immediately after the visitation of the Blessed Sacrament.

The Bishop will then give an opportunity to the people to speak to him privately, either in the sacristy or other convenient place.

Generally in the presbytery the Bishop examines the books of the church. He writes the word *Visum* with his signature and the date at the last used page of the registers. He examines the account books and others concerning the mission or school. He asks any questions he may think fit. Then the rector and clergy receive his instructions.

Finally the Bishop, in private dress, is conducted to the church again that he may make a visit to the Blessed Sacrament before his departure.[4]

§ 4. VISITATION BY AN ARCHBISHOP

IF the Ordinary is an archbishop, the following alterations in the ceremony must be made. The processional cross is not used ; instead of it the archiepiscopal cross is carried before his Grace. If the Archbishop does not bring this archeipiscopal cross with him, the processional cross of the church may take its place.

---

[1] The verse *Panem*, etc., and the prayer *Deus qui nobis* are not sung. The Bishop may recite the Divine Praises after the Benediction.

[2] A list of all objects and persons examined at the Visitation, drawn up by Pope Benedict XIII (1724–1730), is printed in Martinucci-Menghini, II. ii, pp. 371–385.

[3] Or he may do all this at another time.

[4] The Pontifical directs the Bishop at this last visit to stand at the Epistle corner of the (high) altar, and say—with the clergy—*De profundis*, *Pater noster*, the versicles and prayer *Deus cujus miseratione* for the dead.

It is not carried before the procession on the way to the door to meet the Archbishop. It should be placed by the door beforehand. As the procession comes up the church, the cross is carried immediately before the rector of the church and the chaplain, who walk in front of the Archbishop. It is always carried so that the figure of our Lord shall face the Archbishop. Acolytes do not go on either side of the cross.

While the Archbishop gives the first blessing (after the prayers for him at the altar) the cross-bearer holds the cross before him, facing him. The bearer kneels on the lowest altar step. This is done again while he gives the indulgence, namely, while he says the prayers *Precibus et meritis*, etc. The cross is borne in the same way before the Archbishop if he goes to the cemetery, and in other processions. The form for proclaiming the indulgence is slightly modified, as also for a cardinal (p. 366).

§ 5. VISITATION BY AN AUXILIARY BISHOP

THE auxiliary bishop wears rochet and mantellettum when he arrives at the door of the church. He does not kiss a crucifix, nor is he incensed. The rector of the church offers him holy water, handing him the sprinkler, with which he signs himself only.

In the rest of the ceremony the following changes occur :

The prayers for the Ordinary are not said by the rector. The bishop kneels for a short time at a faldstool or kneeling-desk before the altar. Then, if Mass is said, it follows at once. Otherwise the bishop, standing or sitting, addresses the people. No indulgence is published. The prayers for the dead follow, either in the cemetery or before a catafalque or black cloth in the sanctuary, as above (pp. 367–368). For the examination of the vessels containing the Sanctissimum, the bishop puts on a white stole over his rochet (if he does not wear amice, stole and cope), then he kneels before the tabernacle, the rector opens it, the bishop examines the vessels and tabernacle, as above. He may give Benediction. The bishop unvests ; wearing rochet and mantellettum, he goes round the church inspecting everything. He inspects the sacristy and its furniture, and gives the people an opportunity of speaking to him, all as above (p. 369). Confirmation may follow. He examines the books and gives instructions to the clergy. He signs the books in the same way as the Ordinary.

§ 6. VISITATION OF OTHER BUILDINGS AND INSTITUTIONS

AFTER the visitation of the church, the Bishop, if he desire to do so, will inspect the school, orphanage, or any other religious institutions in the parish. He may inspect the buildings, interview the teachers or officials, examine the account books and other documents, and so satisfy himself as to the good state of the school or institution in every respect.

§ 7. VISITATION OF CONVENTS

ALL convents of religious women are subject to visitation by the Ordinary.[1] The visitation of a convent may, or may not, take place at the occasion of the visitation of the church. Notice of it will be given to the Superior beforehand, and prayers will be said by the nuns for the blessing of God. Unless the order is subject to a regular Superior, a copy of the rules and constitutions is sent to the Ordinary before the visitation.

At the convent the Bishop may, if he think fit, carry out the ceremonies used at the visitation of churches. He may say or assist at Mass, address the nuns, and say the Absolution for the dead. He will inspect the tabernacle and ciborium, if the chapel has the right of reserving the Blessed Sacrament. The convent chaplain will attend as the rector of the church.

The Bishop will then interview each member of the community in order, beginning with the youngest. If the community is enclosed, a table with a crucifix, writing materials and a list of the nuns will be placed before the grating of the enclosure. Here the Bishop will sit and will see each nun separately and privately. He will ask any questions he thinks fit as to the manner in which the rule is kept and the lives of the nuns, and will give such advice as he thinks needed.

The Bishop then visits the buildings, beginning with the outer premises. If the community is enclosed, the Bishop enters the enclosure.[2] The community of an enclosed order receives the Bishop at the door of the enclosure. At the entrance a kneeling-stool is placed, on which the Bishop kneels to kiss a crucifix handed to him by the Superior. The nuns then form a procession, with their processional cross, to conduct him to their choir, singing meanwhile *Veni, Creator*. In the choir the versicles and prayers are said as at the visitation of a church (if the visitor is the Ordinary). The Bishop may then address the nuns and give them his blessing. The nuns go to their cells, except the Superior and four others, chosen by the Chapter, or appointed by the Bishop, to accompany him. He inspects every part of the convent. The books and accounts are presented outside the enclosure, and are examined by the Bishop or by someone appointed by him. The whole community assembles at the end to receive his final address and blessing.

§ 8. VISITATION OF THE CHURCHES OF EXEMPT REGULARS

WHEN the Ordinary or his delegate visits the church of a Religious Order exempt from his jurisdiction,[3] all the ceremonies are carried out as above with the following exceptions :

The Ordinary visits the church, clergy, objects, services, only in so far as they concern the people living around, and so the diocese. If

---

[1] Cf. C.J.C. 344, 512, 513.

[2] C.J.C. 600 says that at least one cleric or religious man of mature age should accompany him.

[3] The laws for canonical visitation and other matters of the kind affecting bishops and Regulars are drawn up in the Constitution *Firmandis* of Benedict

the church has the rights and duties of a parish, the Bishop examines all that concerns these.   If it is not a parish church and has no parochial rights or duties, it is not subject to episcopal visitation.   In a parish church served by Regulars he does not inspect every altar, but only that at which the Blessed Sacrament is reserved.   He visits the confessional, pulpit, font (if there is one), because these are used for the parish or people.   He examines in the sacristy all that is used for public or parochial functions and services.   He visits the schools, in the same way as those of the diocesan clergy, the property of the parish (not that of the Order).   He makes a personal visitation of those members of the Order who are engaged in parish work, not with a view to see whether they are faithful to their rule (for this is the business of their regular Superiors), but to see whether they fulfil faithfully the duties they owe to the people, and so to the diocese. From this point of view the Ordinary may inquire into the life and manners of these priests, since that affects the parish as well as their rule.   The Bishop examines the parish registers and signs them, as in the case of other churches.

" In one word, whatever the bishop may inquire and demand of a secular parish priest, all that he must inquire and demand of a Regular parish priest, excepting only what belongs to the observances of his religious Order." [1]

§ 9. THE FIRST VISITATION OF THE ORDINARY

THE first visitation of the Ordinary should be held with more pomp. The following additions to the ceremony may be made where possible :

If there is a separate chapel of the Blessed Sacrament, a kneeling-desk is prepared there, and a faldstool at the Epistle side at which the Bishop will unvest.   In the sanctuary on the Gospel side of the High Altar a throne is prepared covered with white hangings.

The Bishop wears the cappa on arriving, and has a train-bearer.   He is received at the door of the church, or gate of the churchyard, by all the clergy, the rector wearing surplice and white cope.   He is escorted to the altar under a canopy held by servers in surplice, or distinguished members of the congregation.   The rector takes off his cope after the versicles and prayer for the Bishop before the altar.

The Bishop goes to the throne to preach, or, if this is not convenient,[2] to the altar, where the indulgence is proclaimed and he gives the blessing *Precibus et meritis*.   He is assisted by two deacons in choir dress, who then vest him, at the throne, in black stole and cope and white mitre.   He comes down between them and performs the Absolu-

---

XIV (18 November 1744 ; printed in *Decreta Quator Conciliorum Provincialium Westmonasteriensium*, 2nd ed., Burns and Oates, s.a., pp. 366–379), and, for England and Scotland in particular, in the Constitution *Romanos Pontifices* of Leo XIII (8 May 1881 ; *ib.*, pp. 345–365).   Cf. C.J.C. 344, § 2 ; 512 ; 513, etc.

[1] Const. *Firmandis*, § 11 (*loc. cit.*, p. 372).

[2] The difficulty of preaching from the throne is that it faces sideways across the church, so that the people often cannot well see or hear the Bishop.

tions either at the cemetery or in the middle of the choir. The rector now acts as assistant priest and (without the solita oscula) hands him the lustral water sprinkler and incense spoon, holding the boat. Going back to the throne he there changes his vestments to a white stole and cope and golden mitre. He goes with the assistants to the altar of the Blessed Sacrament, the tabernacle is opened by the A.P. (the rector), who then assists at the incensing. The Bishop examines the tabernacle. He may give Benediction according to the rules of chap. xxii, § 3 (p. 237).

If the Blessed Sacrament is reserved at the High Altar the Bishop goes to the throne to be unvested. If it is in a side chapel he unvests at a faldstool there. He continues the visitation in cappa. The canopy is not used as he departs.

Confirmation may be administered after the prayers for the dead and the general inspection, as above (pp. 367–369).

The four chaplains of mitre, crozier, book, candle, and the train-bearer assist throughout.

§ 10. THE SACRAMENT OF CONFIRMATION

IN most parish churches in England and Ireland Confirmation [1] is administered by the Ordinary, or his auxiliary bishop, on the occasion of the canonical visitation. But this is not always the case.

Preparations. The following preparations must be made :

Each person to be confirmed should have a card on which are written his name and the name he will take in Confirmation (in Latin, in the nominative case). A godfather is required for men, a godmother for women. Only one sponsor is to stand for each person confirmed ; and each sponsor is to stand for only one or two persons, unless the minister decide otherwise for a just cause. [2] The sponsors must be themselves confirmed, and fulfil the other conditions laid down in the Code of Canon Law c.c. 795 and 796. They will contract spiritual relationship with their godchildren. The sponsor stands during the Confirmation at the right behind the candidate.

The Bishop may confirm with simple rite—in the church or, for a reasonable cause, in any becoming place [3]—wearing only a white stole over his rochet [4] and the mitre. In solemn administration he wears amice, pectoral cross,[5] white stole and cope, and cloth of gold mitre. The Bishop will use the crozier and, if he is the Ordinary, the morse also. The vestments are laid on the centre of the altar in the inverse order, namely, cope,[6] stole, amice. The golden mitre is placed on the Gospel

---

[1] The rite is in the Pontifical (Part i, first chapter) and in the English *Ritus Servandus*, pp. 76–79 ; *Benedictionale*, p. 85. Cf. C.J.C. 780–800.

[2] C.J.C. 794.   [3] C.J.C. 791.

[4] A stole should never be worn over the mozzetta or mantellettum (S.R.C. 4355, I, ad. 4). At private Confirmation, for a just cause, the mitre need not be used.

[5] Usually the Bishop's pectoral cross is taken off before he vests and is put on again over the alb before the stole.

[6] If the Bishop is the Ordinary the morse, on a salver, will be placed on the altar near the vestments.

side. But if the Bishop also uses the precious mitre (for other cere-monies at the visitation), this is put on the Gospel side, the golden one on the Epistle side.

Before the ceremony the crozier—in a stand or leaning against the wall—is on the Epistle side of the sanctuary. Near by are prepared the veils for the bearers of mitre and crozier. The altar is vested in white (unless Mass is to be celebrated and the colour of the Office is not white). The six candles are lit.

On the credence are the hand-candle, the vessel of water, basin and towels to wash the Bishop's hands, a plate containing bread and lemon, a plate with cotton-wool,[1] the Pontifical (or *Ritus Servandus* or " *Bene-dictionale* "), the stock of Chrism, a linen gremial.[2]

A faldstool or chair is placed either in the middle of the foot-pace or on the ground before the middle of the altar steps, and is covered with white.

Assistants. The following persons assist the Bishop : two priests, of whom one stands at his right, takes the cards [3] and tells the Bishop the Confirmation names ; the other, on his left, wipes the foreheads of the candidates after the anointing. Three servers are required to hold the mitre, book and hand-candle. If the Bishop uses the crozier a fourth is required to carry this.[4] If he is the Ordinary a fifth will carry his train. The two acolytes wash the Bishop's hands. The god-parents must be ready somewhere near the altar rails.

No one who has been confirmed may leave the church till the Bishop has given his blessing at the end.[5]

Arrival of Bishop. The Bishop, when he arrives at the church for the Confirmation, will wear rochet and mozetta or mantellettum. If Confirmation takes place during the Visitation it may follow at once after the Absolution for the dead and the visitation of the Sanctissimum.

If Confirmation does not follow Visitation the Bishop on arrival will kneel in prayer for a short time before the altar at the faldstool (or at a kneeling-stool) prepared there.

Address to Candidates. He rises and is vested for Confirmation as above. Wearing the golden mitre he sits on the faldstool (or chair) and addresses or catechizes the candidates. He holds the crozier in his left hand while so doing. When finished he hands the crozier to its bearer,[6] who takes it with the solita oscula. The Bishop

---

[1] This should be prepared in balls, one for each confirmand (or for each two or three if they are numerous) and there should be a (silver or glass) dish to receive the balls after use.

[2] If necessary an amice may be used for this.

[3] There should be a basket or some other receptacle to hold these cards when received from the confirmands.

[4] The bearers of mitre and crozier wear white veils (*vimpae*) over their shoulders through which they hold these ornaments. They put on the veils just before they first hold them.

[5] There is a special rubric in the Pontifical to this effect. It is to prevent any doubt as to the integrity of the sacrament.

[6] The crozier-bearer always receives the crozier (kneeling, if the prelate be the Ordinary or a higher prelate) directly from the Bishop, and directly hands it to

washes his hands, the acolytes kneeling if he is the Ordinary, the priest at his right hands him the towel and when he has dried his hands, takes off the mitre. The Bishop stands facing the candidates and joins his hands. The book-bearer holds the book before him (standing), the other server holds the candle at the Bishop's left. The Bishop says the first versicle *Spiritus Sanctus superveniat in vos et virtus Altissimi custodiat vos a peccatis.* R/. *Amen.* The other versicles and the prayer follow, as in the Pontifical. The assisting priests answer. During the prayer the Bishop stretches his hands over the candidates. Meanwhile the candidates kneel in places in front of the church, or at the Communion rails. After the prayer the Bishop sits and the mitre is put on by the first assistant priest. A gremial veil (an amice fulfils the purpose) is placed on the Bishop's lap and fastened. The vessel with Chrism is brought to the Bishop and held by a server at his left.

The Confirming. Each candidate now comes forward, genuflects and kneels before the Bishop.[1] The godparent lays his right hand, without glove, on the candidate's right shoulder.[2] The candidate hands his card to the priest at the Bishop's right, who says the Confirmation name to the Bishop.[3] The Bishop, holding the crozier in his left hand, dips the thumb of the right hand into the Chrism, makes the sign of the cross once with it on the candidate's forehead, laying the hand on his head, and says the form of Confirmation, making the sign of the cross three times over the person confirmed at the words *In nomine Patris*, etc. He then lightly strikes the candidate on the left cheek saying *Pax tecum.* There is no answer to this. The candidate rises, giving place to the next. He stands before the priest on the Bishop's left, who wipes away the Chrism from his forehead with cotton wool. The candidates pass before the Bishop from his right to his left. When the Chrism has been wiped off, each person who has been confirmed genuflects and returns to his place.

After the Confirming. When all are confirmed the Bishop gives away his crozier and washes his hands, using bread and lemon. The acolytes who bring the water and these, kneel. Meanwhile the choir sings (or the assistant clergy say) the antiphon *Confirma hoc,* with the *Gloria Patri,* etc., and antiphon repeated. The gremial is removed and the mitre is then taken off by the priest at the Bishop's right. The Bishop rises, turns towards the altar, and sings or says, with hands joined, the versicles *Ostende nobis, Domine, misericordiam tuam,* etc. (the book-bearer and candle-bearer standing before him). The choir

him, with the usual ceremonial kisses. He holds the crozier with both hands, the crook turned forward (except when handing the crozier to the Bishop).

[1] If there are many candidates, they may kneel at the Communion rail. The Bishop then confirms, standing, passing along the rail between the two priests.

[2] The Pontifical says that the candidate puts his foot on the right foot of the godparent. This is now obsolete. It supposes that the candidates stand to receive the sacrament (cf. S.R.C. 2404[6]).

[3] In what case? The bishop uses the vocative. Usually the priest says the name in the nominative and leaves the Bishop to decline it.

sings the responses, or those around say them. The persons confirmed
remain on their knees till the end of the service. The Bishop, with
hands still joined, says or sings in the second ferial tone the prayer
Deus qui apostolis tuis. R₂. *Amen.* Then *Ecce sic benedicetur omnis
homo qui timet Dominum.* He turns, receives the crozier and makes
the sign of the cross over the confirmed, saying *Bene+dicat vos Dominus
ex Sion,* etc. The Bishop sits, receives the mitre, and addresses the
sponsors on their duties to their spiritual children. Usually he recites
the Creed, Lord's Prayer and " Hail Mary " with the confirmed. He
may, in conclusion, give a simple blessing [1] to all those present with his
right hand, saying nothing ; or use the usual form *Sit nomen Domini.*

The parish priest notes the confirmations in a special book, and also
in his Baptism register.[2]

Confirmation Administered by a Parish Priest. When a bishop is not
available, a parish priest may now[3] give Confirmation to any person
within his parish who is in real danger of death from a grave illness.
The form of administration is given in the Appendix of the Roman
Ritual.[4] The priest will need a server to hold the book during the
prayers (said with joined hands) and at the imposition of hands and
anointing. The chrism is carried in a white silk bag. The P.P. wears
a surplice and white stole. He begins by telling those present (from
whom heretics must be excluded) that a bishop is the ordinary minister
of Confirmation, and that a priest administers it as a delegate of the
Pope. All the prayers are said facing the sick person. For the prayer
Omnipotens, the verses, and the prayer *Adiruple,* the priest extends
both hands towards the sick person. During the anointing the Sponsor
puts his right hand on the right shoulder of the invalid. The priest
anoints the latter on the forehead with the thumb of the right hand and
at the same time places this hand on the head of the invalid. He
makes the triple sign of the cross over the latter at *In nomine,* etc., and
then strikes him lightly on the left cheek. He then wipes the chrism
from the invalid's forehead with cotton wool ; cleanses his own hand
with bread crumb and water (all these are later disposed of in the
Sacrarium) ; and continues *Confirma,* etc. Later he enters the
particulars of the administration in the parochial Confirmation register
—adding " Confirmatio collata est ex Apostolico indulto, urgente
mortis periculo ob gravem confirmati morbum "—and in the baptismal
register. He is to notify the diocesan Ordinary at once, explaining the
circumstances of the case. If the invalid was from another parish, the
P.P. of this is to be notified also. If Confirmation be given with the
last sacraments, it follows confession and precedes Holy Viaticum.

---

[1] The Pontifical says nothing of this blessing, but some rubricians mention it.
[2] C.J.C. 798.
[3] S. Cong. Sacr., Sept. 14, 1946.
[4] The new form issued by the Congregation simply adapts the rubrics of the
form of the Pontifical and R.R. to the case of one sick person.

CHAPTER XXIX

THE CEREMONIES OF THE RITUAL

§ 1. THE ENGLISH RITUAL

BY ritual in this case is meant the book, the " Rituale." There is a *Rituale Romanum*, published (after there had been many books of the same kind) by Pope Paul V (1605–1621) in the constitution " Apostolicae Sedi " of 17 June 1614. It was revised and published again in 1752 by Benedict XIV (1740–1758) and has had further revisions by Leo XIII (1878–1903) in 1884, by Pius X (1903–1914) in 1913 and by Pius XI in 1925, bringing it into conformity with the Code of Canon Law (1918) and the rubrics of the Missal (1920). The Ritual contains the texts and ceremonies for all sacraments administered by a priest, the rite of funerals, blessings, liturgical processions, the liturgical litanies, exorcism, and the forms for keeping parish registers. A large and constantly growing appendix gives some further information about points connected with the administration of some of the sacraments and the forms for other blessings, not included in the original book of Paul V. This book is used exclusively in many dioceses. It forms the ultimate standard for all Rituals. But it is not imposed by law on all dioceses of the Roman rite. In many parts of the Church local Rituals are still allowed and used. This is the case in England. In this country we have our own Ritual with the title : *Ordo Administrandi Sacramenta et Alia Quaedam Officia Peragendi.*[1] This is the book we use ordinarily. A priest in England may, and indeed should, possess a copy of the *Rituale Romanum* for study and reference. He will normally administer sacraments and sacramentals from the English *Ordo Administrandi* which may be imposed on him by the authority of his bishop.[2] However, to a great extent, the difference is merely theoretical ; for our *Ordo Administrandi* conforms to the Roman Ritual throughout, except that, in one or two ceremonies, such as particularly the marriage rite, we have some forms peculiar to English dioceses. Otherwise the differences between our *Ordo* and the Roman book are rather of the nature of additions to it (as the title page of the *Ordo* states). In any case in practice the immediate norm and standard for us in England is this English book.

[1] Published in 1915 by Burns, Oates and Washbourne and brought up to date in part by a supplementary leaflet issued in 1925. In Ireland there is a local ritual entitled *Rituale Parvum*, edited by Rev. J. O'Connell, and published by Jas. Duffy & Co. The first edition appeared in 1919 and the second in 1929.

[2] In his preface to *Ordo Administrandi* His Eminence Cardinal Bourne merely recommends the book to the clergy—" Reverendo Clero Sacra ministranti impense commendamus.' S.R.C. (D.3792⁹) has decided that the Roman Ritual may be used everywhere and in all functions even though there is a proper diocesan Ritual different in some points only from the Roman.

The ceremonies of the Ritual here discussed are those of Baptism, Penance, the receptions of converts, Holy Communion, sick calls, Extreme Unction and the last rites, Marriage, churching of women, and various blessings. The funeral rites are described in the next chapter (pp. 406–425). No detailed description of these ceremonies is necessary. They are all exceedingly simple ; the Ritual gives exact rubrics throughout. From these rubrics alone it is possible to perform the ceremonies correctly. However, some notes about the necessary preparations and certain special points will be found useful.

§ 2. BAPTISM [1]

THE common case is that of the solemn [2] baptism of infants. Children should be brought to church to be baptized as soon after birth as possible, i.e., as is safe and reasonably convenient. Unless there is grave danger of the child's life, it is to be brought to the church and there baptized solemnly by the parish priest of the place in which it is born, or a priest authorized by him or by the Ordinary.[3]

Sponsors. The child should have one godparent ; or at most a godfather and a godmother. Not more than two are allowed. To act validly as a sponsor the person must be a Catholic, appointed by the parents or guardians of the child (or, failing them, by the priest who baptizes), intending to act as sponsor and must at the actual baptism touch the child physically. To act lawfully the sponsor must be at least fourteen years of age and know the rudiments of the faith.[4]. Members of religious Orders may not without express leave from their Superior be godparents lawfully ; nor priests, unless they have leave from their Ordinary ; nor the child's parents. The godmother holds the child during the whole ceremony. The godfather stands by her side, answers the questions in the child's name, touches the child physically (generally by putting his hand on its shoulder) at the moment when the priest pours the water, and holds the lighted candle given (theoretically) to the child at the end. If there is only one godparent, he or she must do all that otherwise is done by either. In our time the duties of the godparent towards the child are much reduced from what they were in the Middle Ages.[5] There remains a general duty of looking after the child's spiritual welfare, especially in default of its parents. Spiritual relationship does not now involve any temporal obligation.

[1] R.R. Tit. II ; C.J.C. 737–779.
[2] Solemn Baptism means with all the ceremonies of the Ritual ; private Baptism is the essential matter and form, with or without some of the ceremonies prescribed by the Ritual. C.J.C. 737, § 2.
[3] The Ordinary may allow baptism in a house for very special reasons (cf. R.R. II. i. 45). A deacon may baptize solemnly, by leave of the Ordinary or of the parish priest of the place ; but then the salt and water that are used must have been blessed by a priest (R.R. II. i, 15 ; ii, 27).
[4] The sponsor must be able to recite the Creed and *Our Father* during the ceremony.
[5] These duties are given in R.R. II. i, 38.

Place of Baptism. It is usual to fix a time for solemn baptisms, generally on Sundays after noon. But the priest will be ready to baptize at other times, if the request is reasonable. Solemn Baptism is a public ceremony of the Church, at which anyone may be present. It supposes three distinct places, the narthex or porch of the church, in which the first part of the rite takes place (till the priest lays his stole on the child and says *N. ingredere in templum Dei*, etc.) ; the nave or other part of the church, outside the baptistery, where the ceremony continues till he has changed the stole ; the baptistery, where it is concluded. The baptistery should be either a separate chapel, or it should at least have a railing round it. If there is no visible distinction (as there ought to be) between these three places, the priest and god-parents must move nearer to the font each time, crossing an imaginary line of division.

Preparations. Near the font there should be a table covered with a white cloth, unless the font is so made that the necessary objects can be placed on it. Here are prepared : the stocks containing Oil of Catechumens and Chrism,[1] a vessel with the salt, the shell or ladle used for pouring the water, a towel to wipe the child's head after baptism, cotton-wool to use after the annointings, the white robe, a wax candle,[2] the white stole (unless the priest wears a stole white on one side and violet on the other), a vessel of water and a towel, with bread on a plate, for washing the priest's hands after Baptism.

There ought to be at least one server, to hand the things and especially to answer ; but often the priest baptizes without one, answering the versicles and saying *Amen* himself. In the baptistery or sacristy the register of baptisms must be ready to be filled up immediately afterwards.

At the Church Door. The priest first washes his hands in the sacristy, then vests in surplice and violet stole ; he carries the Ritual with him. The server or servers vest in surplice. The priest with them goes to where the godparents wait with the child, in the porch or narthex. The child should be borne by the godmother[3] on her right arm. The priest must first ascertain the child's name ; it should be the name of a Saint.[4] He then begins the rite, as in the Ritual or *Ordo Administrandi.*

[1] The first synod of Westminster desires that a place should be arranged in the baptistery, where the holy Oils may be kept permanently (Decr. xvi, no. 2, *ed. cit.*, p. 15). R.R. (II. i, 53) directs that the Oils be kept in the church in a special place, which is to be decent, clean, safe and locked. It is best to have an ambry (with a white and violet curtain hung before it) and marked clearly "Olea Sacra." A distinct ambry should contain the other requisites for Baptism. The font should be kept locked (R.R. II. i, 46).

[2] No rubric orders this candle to be lighted till it is given to the godfather. It may, however, very suitably stand in a candlestick and burn during the whole ceremony. St. Charles Borromeo required two lighted candles on the altar of the baptistery, or on the table, all the time.

[3] Usually the godmother carries the child throughout the entire ceremony. She need not, however, do so, except at the actual baptism.

[4] If it is not, the priest should himself add the name of a saint and enter both names in the register (R.R. II. i, 30 ; cf. n. 70).

The questions must be asked and answered in Latin, then, if necessary, repeated in the vulgar tongue. The priest may have to prompt the godparent as to the answers. If the child receives several Christian names, all may be said at the first question and at the actual baptism. Otherwise the first, name is sufficient. The gender of all prayers. is changed, according to the sex of the child, except in the exorcism *Exorcizo, te, omnis spiritus immunde,* where all is neuter, agreeing with *plasma.*

The sign of the cross (and the imposition of the hand) is to be made by physically touching the child (or its dress), when the part of the body to be signed is definitely mentioned (e.g., the head) ; otherwise the sign is made *over* the child.

The salt may have been already blessed. In this case it is not blessed again. But it must have received the special blessing for baptism.

Entering the Church. After the prayer *Aeternam ac justissimam pietatem,* the priest lays the left end of his stole momentarily on the child as he says *N. ingredere in templum Dei,* etc. and introduces him into the church. Walking by the side of the child and godparents or before them, he says with them the Creed and Lord's Prayer. The priest says these in Latin ; the godparents may use the vulgar tongue.[1] Standing near, but outside the baptistery, with his back to it, he says the exorcism *Exorcizo te, omnis spiritus immunde.* He then moistens his own right thumb with his tongue, and with the thumb touches the lobes of the ears and the nostrils of the child, saying the forms *Ephpheta,* etc. There is no direction to make the sign of the cross here. He wipes his thumb with a towel. For the anointing with Oil of Catechumens the godmother uncovers the child's breast and loosens its dress behind.[2] All anointing is done on the bare skin and in the form of a cross ; but it is not necessary to open the dress very far down. After the anointing the priest wipes the child and his own thumb with cotton-wool. He then changes the violet stole for a white one, or turns the stole so that the white side is now seen ; he enters the baptistery, followed by the godparents and child.

The Baptism. At the moment of pouring the water and baptizing, the godmother holds the child's head over the font,[3] the godfather lays his right hand, bare, on its shoulder. The child had better be held with its face sideways, so that the water flows over its bare skin, and yet is not poured over its features. The priest pours[4] three distinct times in the form of a cross, as he says the words marked with a cross in the book. There is no *Amen* to the form. The priest must see that the water touches the skin of the child. He, or the godparents, wipe the child's head with a towel, used for this purpose only. If Baptism

---

[1] S.R.C. 3535[10].

[2] It is advisable to warn the godmother or nurse about this before the ceremony begins.

[3] Over that part of it into which the water when it has been used is to flow.

[4] " Abluenda est pars capitis superior " (*Ordo,* p. 7).

is given under condition, he uses the form N. *si non es baptizatus*, etc., as in the Ritual.

Anointing with Chrism. The anointing with Chrism follows. The child is anointed at the top of the head in the form of a cross (at the words *ipse te liniat*) ; then the priest wipes the place and his thumb with cotton-wool. Instead of a complete white garment, it is now usual to lay a white cloth on the head of the child, as the rubric implies.[1] The priest gives the candle, lighted, to the godfather. If there is no godfather the godmother holds the candle. Lastly he dismisses the child with the form N. *vade in pace*, etc. He wipes his hands with bread, and washes them. The entry in the Baptism register is made at once, in the baptistery or sacristy.[2] If the child belongs to another parish the priest who has baptized it is to inform the child's parish priest as soon as possible of the baptism. A note of the baptism must be made in the child's parish also.[3] The priest is to warn the sponsors of the (diriment) impediment to marriage that spiritual relationship creates. The water used for the baptism and that used to wash the priest's hands is poured into the sacrarium and all is put away.

§ 3. BAPTISM OF SEVERAL CHILDREN TOGETHER

THE Ritual gives the forms for this. The boys are to be placed on the right of the girls [4] and the priest begins each action with the boys. The book gives plainly the forms to be said in the plural for all, and those said in the singular to each child separately. If boys and girls are addressed together, the masculine plural is used, according to the normal rule of Latin grammar. When the priest has to lay his hand on them, he does so, for a moment, on each ; then says the prayer with hand outstretched, but not touching any one child. For the entry into the church the stole is laid on the first child only, the others follow in.

§ 4. THE BAPTISM OF ADULTS

THE Roman Ritual has a much longer form for the solemn baptism of grown-up people, but the Ordinary for a grave and reasonable cause may permit the form for infants to be used in the baptism of adults. In addition, for the *conditional* baptism of adult *heretics* the form of private baptism may be used.[5] The only differences in the baptism of adults according to the form for infants are that the catechumen answers the questions himself, stands between his godparents, and lays his head over the font. While the priest pours the water the god-

---

[1] " Linteolum candidum loco vestis albae " (R.R. II. ii, 24).
[2] If the child be illegitimate, C.J.C. 777, § 2 directs how the entry is to be made.
[3] Congregation of the Sacraments, 29 June 1941.
[4] This is the better interpretation of the rubric (R.R. II. ii, 28). The priest is to begin each action with the boys, and he will more naturally move from left to right along the row or circle of children.
[5] R.R. II. i, 26, 28. In England the conditional baptism of converts is to be carried out privately, with lustral water and without ceremonies (First Synod of Westminster, D. XVI. 8°).

parents lay their right hands on his shoulder. It is recommended that the minister and subject be fasting from midnight. The neophyte should then (unless there are urgent and grave causes to the contrary) hear Mass and make his first Communion.[1]

§ 5. PRIVATE BAPTISM

IN case of danger of death anyone may baptize, even a heretic or pagan. It is sufficient that he administer the essential matter and form and have the implicit intention of doing what Christ instituted. Naturally a Catholic should be preferred, if possible. A man is preferred to a woman ; but anyone else to the parents.[2] A priest may administer " private " Baptism (i.e., Baptism without the full rite) as well as a layman ; indeed, if he is at hand the priest should obviously be preferred. If possible, a priest or deacon should wear a surplice and a white stole. Private Baptism may be given only in the case of real necessity, i.e. if the child (or adult) is in danger of dying before the full rite is completed. If it were possible to go through the whole rite, the case would not be one of necessity at all, and so there would be no excuse for private Baptism. But it may well happen that, after the essential matter and form, the child still survives, at least for a time. In this case, if a priest or deacon baptizes, and if he has the Chrism, white robe and candle at hand, he should go on with the ceremonies to the end, anointing with Chrism, giving the robe and the candle.[3] Obviously these ceremonies are not repeated, if there is a later supplying of ceremonies. For private Baptism any natural water may be used validly, and lawfully in case of need. But baptismal water is to be preferred, if it is at hand. There may be a godparent ; but it is not necessary.[4] All the ceremonies that precede the actual baptism are omitted. Private Baptism should be entered in the register as such.

§ 6. SUPPLYING THE CEREMONIES OF BAPTISM

AFTER private Baptism, administered in case of urgent danger, the child, if it survives, must later be brought to the church that the ceremonies may be supplied. The form for doing this is in the Ritual. There must be a godparent, as at Baptism ; but he does not contract the spiritual relationship unless he had been sponsor at the actual Baptism. Everything is done as at Baptism, except, of course, the interrogation *Vis baptizari* and the Baptism itself. The three places are used for the three parts of the rite. All follows as at Baptism, with certain verbal alterations (noted in the Ritual) necessary to the circum-

---

[1] C.J.C. 753. Baptism of adults is, when convenient, to be announced to the Bishop beforehand, that Baptism may, if he wishes, be more solemnly administered by himself or his delegate. R.R. II. iii, 2.

[2] R.R. II. i, 16.

[3] R.R. II. ii, 29.

[4] R.R. II. i, 31. There should be two witnesses, or at least one (n. 16).

stance. After the questions about faith, which, normally, come immediately before the actual Baptism, the priest simply omits the Baptism and goes on at once to the anointing with Chrism, unless this has already been performed.

§ 7. CONDITIONAL BAPTISM

IN this case, the normal rite is exactly the same, with the one exception of the sacramental form, which becomes *N. si non es baptizatus (baptizata) ego te baptizo*, etc. But in the case of grown-up converts from heresy, conditional Baptism may, with the permission of the Ordinary, be given privately without ceremonies,[1] as noted below (pp. 385 *sqq.*).

§ 8. BLESSING THE FONT

IF it is necessary to bless baptismal water [2] in the course of the year, not on Holy Saturday or Whitsun Eve, the priest uses the short form in the Ritual. The font must be filled with clean water beforehand, the stocks of Oil of Catechumens and Chrism placed near it. A towel will also be needed, a vessel of water and basin, with bread, to wash the priest's hands afterwards. There should be a cross-bearer, two acolytes and thurifer. It will be well to have two other servers also, if possible, to answer, assist and hand things to the priest. The priest wears surplice and violet stole, or stole and cope for greater solemnity. The procession goes to the baptistery in the usual order. Here the cross-bearer and acolytes stand opposite the priest, as on Holy Saturday (p. 318). The thurifer is by his side. The priest and all [3] kneel, facing the altar of the baptistery, if it have one, or the High Altar of the church. The priest says the Litany of the Saints, either in the usual form, or the shorter form of Holy Saturday (not doubling the petitions). He rises and makes the sign of the cross over the water as he says twice *Ut fontem istum*, etc.[4] He kneels again till he has said the final *Kyrie, eleison*. Then all rise. The priest recites aloud the *Pater* and *Credo* and then the verses, prayer and exorcism. The ceremonies which follow are described clearly in the rubrics.[5] After he has breathed on the water the priest puts on and blesses incense, then incenses the water thrice with three simple swings (in the centre, to his left and to his right).[6] The holy Oils are poured into the water [7] and mixed, as on

---

[1] R.R. II. i, 26, 28. In England this form of Baptism is of obligation *in casu*.

[2] Ordinary water may be added (in less quantity) to baptismal water, even many times. R.R. II. i, 6.

[3] Except, of course, the cross-bearer and acolytes.

[4] This is the special petition inserted twice, before : " Ut nos exaudire digneris."

[5] And compare the rite of Holy Saturday (pp. 318 *sqq.*).

[6] Incense is not used at the solemn blessing on Holy Saturday and Whitsun eve ; so it may seem strange that it should be used now. The usual explanation is that it is a substitute for plunging the Paschal candle.

[7] If he has but little Oil he may dip his thumb or a silver rod into it and therewith make the sign of the cross in the water (*Ordo Adm.*, no. 6, p. 63).

Holy Saturday.   At the end he washes his hands, using bread, and the water in which he has washed them is poured into the sacrarium.

§ 9. THE SACRAMENT OF PENANCE [1]

THERE should be, at each church, fixed days and hours at which confessions are heard.   The clergy wait at these times so that people know that, coming then, they can make their confession without special appointment.[2]   But at other times, too, priests who have care of souls must be ready to hear the confession of those who demand this reasonably.

Normally the proper place for hearing confessions is the confessional in the church.   Confessions of men may be heard anywhere for a reasonable cause.   The confessions of women are not to be heard outside the confessional, except in case of sickness or other real necessity.[3]

To administer the sacrament of Penance the priest wears a surplice and violet stole.   (Regulars wear the stole only, over their habit.) This is the normal dress for confessions heard in church.   In other cases the priest should wear at least the stole.[4]   In case of necessity, naturally, he may hear confession in any dress.   Penance is the only sacrament administered sitting.   The priest sits as a judge at his tribunal.

In many countries it is usual for the penitent to begin by asking the priest's blessing.   The Roman Ritual speaks only of the penitent making the sign of the cross and says nothing about seeking a blessing. The English *Ordo Administrandi* says that he should do so, and suggests the form of blessing *Dominus sit in corde tuo*, etc., or a similar one.[5] It is also usual for the penitent to say either the *Confiteor*, or some similar prayer, before telling his sins.   The Ritual suggests the *Confiteor* or the short form *I confess to almighty God and to you, Father*.[6]   The form of absolution is given in the Ritual.   The prayers *Misereatur* and *Indulgentiam* before the absolution and the prayer *Passio* after it may be omitted for a just cause.[7]   From *Indulgentiam* till he makes the sign of the cross at the end of the absolution form (or, if he does not say *Indulgentiam*, from *Dominus noster Iesus Christus*) the priest holds the right hand raised towards the penitent.   This is the remnant of the old imposition of hands at Penance.   He makes the sign of the cross over the penitent where the cross is marked, at the invocation of the

---

[1] R.R. III. ;   *Ordo Administrandi*, Tit. III.

[2] Conc. prov. Westm., I, Decr. xix, no. 8, p. 23.

[3] R.R. III. i, 9.

[4] R.R. (III. i, 10) says : " Superpelliceo, et stola violacei coloris utatur, prout tempus vel locorum feret consuetudo."   In Ireland the usage is to wear the stole only.

[5] *Ordo Adm.*, Tit. III. cap. ii, § 13, p. 67.   At the end of the telling of their sins penitents should say at once : " For these and all my sins, I am sorry," or some such words, thus indicating in a becoming way that they have finished and giving external expression to their sorrow (which is part of the matter of the sacrament).

[6] R.R. III. i, 15.   [7] R.R. III. ii, 4.

Holy Trinity ; then continues *Passio Domini nostri*, etc., with hands joined. In the form the word *Deinde* is part of it [1] ; the word *suspensionis* is used only when the penitent is tonsured. A bishop makes the triple sign of the cross when absolving. In case of urgent necessity, in danger of death, the short form of absolution is *Ego te absolvo ab omnibus censuris et peccatis, in nomine Patris, et Filii+et Spiritus Sancti. Amen.*

§ 10. RECEPTION OF CONVERTS (IN ENGLAND) [2]

THERE are two very different cases of reception of a convert into the Church, whether he is already baptized or not. A third case is if he has received doubtful baptism in some heretical sect.

Theoretically there is all the difference in the world between the first and second cases. If a man has never been baptized, is a Jew, Moslem or Unitarian,[3] he has never been a member of the Catholic Church. So he becomes a Catholic in the normal way, by Baptism. It would seem that nothing more is needed. He must, of course, be instructed first. He must, when receiving the sacrament, have the necessary intention and dispositions, faith and repentance for his sins. Otherwise it should suffice that he be baptized, since really he is in the same state as the infant presented for baptism. He makes his profession of faith by saying the Apostles' Creed in the baptism ceremony, which is exactly the purpose for which it is put there. The baptism should be in the form for adults unless the Ordinary for a grave and reasonable cause permits the use of the infant form.[4]

But in England we have a law modifying this simple position in two ways. First, we may use the form of baptism for infants,[5] secondly, independently of the Creed said at the baptism ceremony, a grown-up convert must make the usual profession of faith, as do those already baptized.[6]

The case of a convert already baptized differs entirely in principle. He has once been a Catholic. He became so when he was baptized, no matter who baptized him. But since then he has incurred excommunication for frequenting the conventicle of an heretical sect. All that is needed then, in principle, is that he now be absolved from that excommunication. The process of his reception is a negative rather

---

[1] It is printed as part of the form in the typical editions of the Roman Ritual of 1913 and 1925.

[2] For the United States, see pp. 388-392.

[3] Some Unitarians do baptize, with the form of Mat. xxviii, 19. Supposing they pour water and have the implicit intention of doing what Christ instituted, their baptism is valid.

[4] R.R. II. i, 26.

[5] Cf. the general law of R.R. II. i, 28, which allows the Ordinary to permit private Baptism (i.e., Baptism without the full ceremonies) in the case of an adult *heretic* who is to be baptized *conditionally*. This private Baptism is of obligation in England (I West., xvi. 8).

[6] *Ordo Adm.*, Tit. III. cap. iv, no. 1, following the Instruction of the Holy Office, 20 June, 1859, p. 72. There is now (1943) a modified form of the profession.

R.R.

than a positive one. The priest who receives him takes away the impediment of excommunication, and so restores him to the rights given, all unconsciously, by the heretical minister who baptized him. In England there is no supplying the ceremonies for converts.

In the case of a man doubtfully baptized no one of course can say which of these two processes really takes place. We baptize again conditionally as a precaution for the one case, and absolve him from excommunication and hear his confession for the other.[1]

In the case of all grown-up converts the priest who will receive them must first report the case to the Ordinary, using the form provided for that purpose, and must obtain leave and faculties to receive the convert.

(i) **Convert not already baptized.** If the convert is CERTAINLY NOT BAPTIZED, he makes no abjuration of heresy, but (in England) he does make the public profession of faith, if he is grown up. Then he is baptized publicly with the full form used for children. He has, of course, no confession to make, since sins committed before Baptism are not valid matter for the sacrament of Penance, but are absolved in Baptism. Children, in this case, are simply baptized.

(ii) **Convert already baptized.** If the convert is CERTAINLY ALREADY BAPTIZED, there can be no question of baptizing him again. It would be a grave sacrilege to attempt to repeat Baptism. In this case he makes his profession of faith, abjures heresy, is absolved from excommunication and other censures. Then he makes his first confession and Communion.

(iii) **Convert doubtfully baptized.** The commonest case in England is that of converts DOUBTFULLY BAPTIZED. Such a convert makes his profession of faith and abjures heresy. He is then baptized conditionally (the condition is expressed), privately with lustral water (not baptismal water). Then comes the absolution from excommunication. But if it seems more convenient, the private Baptism may follow the absolution from censures. Then the convert makes his first confession.[2]

The order for converts certainly already baptized is the same, except, of course, that the conditional baptism is omitted.

In all cases the reception of a convert is to take place before a priest appointed by the Ordinary, and at least two witnesses (in order that the abjuration may be juridical which is required by C.J.C. 2314, § 2). These must also be present at the Baptism (even private), unless, for grave reason, the Bishop dispenses.

Children[3] who are received from heretical sects, and are either certainly or doubtfully baptized, do not make any abjuration, nor are they absolved from censures which they cannot have contracted. They make a simple profession of faith, either the Apostles' Creed or the form

---

[1] Both sacraments, Baptism and Penance, are given conditionally, and one of the two is certainly invalid. No one can say which.

[2] Conc. prov. Westm., I, Decr. xvi, § 8, pp. 15–16 ; *Ordo Adm., loc. cit.,* nos. 1, 3, 5, pp. 72–74. The confession must be made in the case of conditional Baptism (Conc. prov. Westm., I).

[3] Boys under fourteen, girls under twelve (or, probably, fourteen in the matter of censures).

used for adults, without the abjuration. If necessary they are then baptized conditionally.[1]

In the case of babies who cannot speak or understand even the simplest profession of faith,[2] if they are certainly baptized, there is nothing to do but to see that henceforth they are brought up as Catholics and in due time receive the sacraments. Such children have never ceased to be Catholics since they became so at their Baptism.

The ceremony for the reception of a convert NOT BAPTIZED is very simple.[3] The priest wears a surplice and violet stole. In his presence and that of two witnesses the convert makes his profession of faith (in England), as in the Ritual, but leaving out the last clause, *With a sincere heart*, etc. Then (having reminded him to make an act of at least attrition for his sins) he is baptized publicly in the usual form (for infants).

The other two cases (of CONDITIONAL baptism, or NONE) may be described together.[4]

"Veni, Creator" and Profession of Faith. The priest, vested in surplice and violet stole,[5] sits before the altar (on the Epistle side of the foot-pace or ground, if the Sanctissimum is reserved there) facing the convert kneeling before him. With head covered he addresses the convert, exhorting him to thank God for the gift of faith, which in future he is to show forth by deed. Then the priest rises and kneels before the altar ; all present kneel with him. So they say the hymn *Veni, Creator* alternately. The priest (alone) stands to say the prayer after the hymn. He sits again and puts on the biretta ; kneeling before him the convert reads the profession of faith,[6] as in the *Ordo Administrandi*.[7] The priest holds a book of the Gospels on his knees, which the convert meanwhile touches.[8] They remain in the same position while the priest says the psalm *Miserere* or *De profundis*, at his discretion. He then takes off his biretta, stands facing the altar, and says *Kyrie, eleison* and the versicles and prayer which follow. The convert or people present should answer ; if no one can, he must answer himself.

Conditional Baptism. After this prayer is the right time for conditional Baptism (in England, according to the *Ordo Administrandi*), if it is to be administered. The priest goes with the convert to the sacristy, the two witnesses following. There, in their presence (having

---

[1] *Ordo Adm., loc. cit.*, no. 2, pp. 72–73.

[2] Such a case may occur when a whole family joins the Church.

[3] In this case, too, the *Veni, Creator* may precede and the *Te Deum* follow the reception, but the psalm *Miserere*, etc., are not recited—it would seem—since these form part of the rite of absolution from censure (cf. R.R. III. iii).

[4] *Ordo Adm.*, Tit. III, cap. v, pp. 75–87.

[5] Instruction of Holy Office of 20 July 1859.

[6] If the convert cannot read the priest slowly reads for him the profession of faith so that he may understand it and may be able to pronounce it distinctly with the priest (*Ordo*). As the form is a very difficult one the priest who instructs the convert should coach him in it before the day of his reception.

[7] There is a booklet—" Form for the Reception of a Convert " published by C.T.S. containing the entire rite in Latin and English.

[8] There is no direction to kiss the book at the end.

reminded the convert to make at least an act of attrition for his sins), he baptizes the convert, pouring lustral water over his head into a vessel, and saying the form *Si non es baptizatus*, N. *ego te baptizo in nomine Pa+tris et Fi+lii et Spiritus+Sancti.* For this he wears momentarily a white stole.

Absolution from Censure. Returning to the church the priest (having resumed the violet stole) sits at the seat having his back to the altar, with head covered. The convert kneels before him. So he absolves him from excommunication, using the form in the book *Auctoritate apostolica*, etc. In case of doubt as to whether the convert has incurred excommunication by professing heresy, the priest inserts the word *forsan* after *incurristi*, as directed in the note. He then imposes a penance for this absolution.

Te Deum. The convert may make his confession now or after the *Te Deum*.[1] All standing, the priest says *Te Deum laudamus*, alternately with the convert and those present. They kneel, as always, at the verse *Te, ergo, quaesumus*, etc. Still standing, while the others kneel, the priest says the verses and prayer that follow. He turns to the convert and makes the sign of the cross over him, as he gives the blessing at the end. He sits and again speaks to the convert about his duties as a Catholic, as is directed in the rubric.

Confession. Lastly, if he has not already done so, the convert makes his confession. Since it is his first, it will be a general confession of his whole life. If the convert has just received conditional Baptism, the absolution will be conditional also; but this condition is not expressed in words. If the confessor have power to grant plenary indulgence to the convert, he will do so after the confession and absolution. The convert says the *Confiteor* (in Latin or English); the confessor may use the form given on p. 73 of the *Ordo Administrandi*.

The convert will attend Mass and make his first Communion immediately, if possible, after his reception and Baptism, or confession.[2]

§ 11. RECEPTION OF CONVERTS (IN THE UNITED STATES)[3]

Those who are to be received into the Church fall into one of three classes: the unbaptized, the baptized, and the doubtfully baptized.

An adult who has never received Baptism, or whose reception of it was certainly invalid, has never been a member of the Catholic

[1] There is a practice that the convert should make his confession, then receive conditional Baptism, then make a general statement repeating that he wishes to confess all the sins he has already told, then be absolved (cf. *Ordo*, p. 73, n. 3). If so, the priest must, of course, be the same throughout. But there is no necessity to confess before Baptism. It is often better that the convert should make his confession last of all, partly because he need not confess to the priest who receives him (there is, indeed, no general law of the Church commanding him to go to confession at once), partly because the witnesses and other people may then go away before his confession.

[2] C.J.C. 753, § 2.

[3] The 1944 Benziger *Rituale Romanum* contains a "Supplementum Ritualis Romani ad Usum Cleri Americae Septentrionalis Foederatae," a section of which [pp. (16) ff.] is entitled "The Reception of Converts and Profession of Faith."

Church. He therefore becomes a Catholic in the normal way, by Baptism. Neither abjuration from heresy, nor absolution from censures or from sins is required. He must, of course, be instructed first. He must, when receiving the sacrament, have the intention of receiving the sacrament; he must likewise have the requisite dispositions, faith and repentance for past sins.[1] Otherwise it suffices that he be baptized, since really he is in the same state as the infant presented for Baptism. He makes his profession of faith by saying the Apostles' Creed in the baptism ceremony. This is precisely the purpose for which it was put there. The Baptism should be conferred in the form prescribed for adults, unless the Ordinary for a grave and reasonable cause permits the use of the infant form.[2]

The case of a convert already validly baptized differs entirely in principle. He has once been a Catholic. He became so when he was validly baptized, no matter who baptized him. But since then he has incurred excommunication by frequenting the conventicle of an heretical sect. All that is needed then, in principle, is that he now be absolved from that excommunication. The process of his reception is a negative rather than a positive one. The priest who receives him takes away the impediment of excommunication, thereby restoring him to the rights given, all unconsciously, by the heretical minister who baptized him. The Roman Ritual provides for the supplying of the ceremonies omitted in the heretical baptism. While this supplying of ceremonies is dependent on the judgment of the Ordinary, the obligation to supply the omitted ceremonies prevails when the Ordinary has issued no specific decision regarding the matter.[3]

In the case of a person doubtfully baptized, no one can say which of these two processes really takes place. The priest baptizes conditionally as a precaution for the one case, and hears his confession for the other. Both sacraments, Baptism and Penance, are administered conditionally, and the one or the other, as the case requires, is certainly valid.

Merely having instructed a convert does not confer on the priest the right to receive that convert into the Church. If the convert is to be received into the Church through solemn Baptism, the local Ordinary is the one to administer the sacrament.[4] If the local Ordinary has by statute or through diocesan custom relinquished his right to baptize adults, then the (proper) pastor of the person to be baptized is the ordinary minister of the sacrament. In cases where there is a question of abjuration of heresy, and absolution from the censure of excommunication in the external forum, it is again the local Ordinary who can receive the abjuration of former errors and

[1] S.C.S. Off., inst. (ad Vic. Ap. Tche-Kiang), 1 aug. 1860—*Fontes*, n. 963.
[2] *E.g.*, Synodus Fargensis I, Statutum 213,3: "Conversi ad fidem juxta normas in sacra doctrina traditas recipiantur: ob consuetudinem autem jamdudum in Diocesi vigentem indulgemus ut caeremoniae praescriptae pro baptismo infantium adhibeantur in baptismo adultorum."
[3] "Ubi vero debita forma et materia servata est, omissa tantum suppleantur, nisi rationabili de causa aliter loci Ordinario videatur."—Tit. II, cap. 3, n. 12.
[4] Cf. canon 744: "Adultorum baptismus, ubi commode fieri potest, ad loci Ordinarium deferatur, ut, si voluerit, ab eo vel ab eius delegato solemnius conferatur."

absolve from the censure. This power of the Ordinary, however, can be delegated either wholly or in part,[1] and such general delegation is the usual practice in the United States.

In accordance, therefore, with their condition, there are three methods of receiving converts.

(i) If the convert has never been baptized, or if his previous baptism was certainly invalid, he is baptized unconditionally. Abjuration is not necessary, nor absolution, since censures bind only subjects of the Church, and sins committed before baptism are not valid matter for the sacrament of Penance.

(ii) If the convert has already been validly baptized, there can be no question of baptizing him again. It would be a grave sacrilege to attempt to do so. In this case the convert makes his abjuration or profession of faith and is absolved from censures. Then the ceremonies omitted in the heretical baptism are supplied, unless the Ordinary has ruled otherwise.

(iii) If the convert has been doubtfully baptized, this procedure is to be followed:

(x) abjuration or profession of faith;

(y) conditional baptism;

(z) sacramental confession with conditional absolution.

In all cases, the abjuration of former errors and profession of faith must be made in the presence of the bishop or his delegate and two witnesses.[2]

Converts under the age of fourteen do not make any formal abjuration,[3] nor are they absolved from censures which they have not incurred. They make a simple profession of faith: the recitation of the Apostles' Creed is sufficient. If necessary, they are baptized conditionally.

In the case of babies who cannot speak or understand even the simplest profession of faith, if they are certainly baptized, there is nothing to be done except to see that henceforth they are brought up as Catholics and in due time receive the sacraments. Such children have never ceased to be Catholics since they became so at Baptism.

THE CEREMONY for the reception of a convert never before validly baptized is very simple. Baptism is solemnly administered, in the manner prescribed by the Roman Ritual[4] for the reception of adult converts.[5] As previously noted, however, permission to substitute the form for infants is frequently granted by the local Ordinaries.

THE CEREMONIES for the reception of converts already baptized and of converts doubtfully baptized need not be separately described.

According to the Instruction of the Holy Office issued July 20, 1859, the priest, vested in surplice and violet stole and wearing the biretta, sits on the Epistle side (if the Blessed Sacrament is reserved

[1] Canons 2314, 2; 199, 1.
[2] Canon 2314,2.
[3] S.C.S. Off. litt. 8 mart. 1882—*Fontes*, n. 1073.
[4] Tit. II, cap. 4.
[5] All persons except infants under seven years of age, or who do not yet have the use of reason, are to be baptized according to the form for adults.

in the tabernacle), otherwise in front of the tabernacle. The convert, accompanied by two witnesses, kneels before him and, touching the book of Gospels with his right hand, pronounces the profession of faith. If he cannot read, the priest is to read it to him slowly, so that the convert may understand it and may be able to pronounce it distinctly after the priest. The formula to be recited by the convert is the one sent to the bishops of the United States by His Excellency, the Most Reverend Amleto G. Cicognani, D. D., Apostoli Delegate, under date of March 26, 1942, beginning "I. . . . years of age, born outside the Catholic Church, have held and believed errors contrary to her teaching. Now, enlightened by divine grace, I kneel. . . ."[1] This 1942 formula supplants the formula contained in the Instruction of 1859.

The profession of faith having been made, the convert remains kneeling, while the priest, still seated, recites the *Miserere* or the *De Profundis,* adding *Gloria Patri* at the end. The priest then takes off his biretta, stands facing the altar, says *Kyrie eleison* and the versicles and prayer which follow.

After this, if there is no question of conditional baptism, *i e.*, if the convert has already been validly baptized, the priest, seated pronounces the absolution from excommunication according to the form provided by the Roman Ritual,[2] inserting the word *forsan* if he is in doubt of its incurrence.

Then the priest imposes some salutary penance, such as prayers or a visit to a church.

It is to be noted that converts already validly baptized are clearly bound to receive the sacrament of Penance if they know themselves guilty of grievous sin. The time of their reception into the Church offers a suitable occasion for them to fulfill this obligation.

Likewise, as previously mentioned, the Roman Ritual provides for the supplying of the ceremonies omitted in the Baptism conferred by the heretical minister. If the Ordinary has decreed that this supplying of ceremonies is to be omitted, then the ceremony of reception of those already validly baptized ends with the sacramental absolution of the convert.

In the case of the reception into the Church of those doubtfully baptized, the Instruction of 1859 states that the profession of faith be followed by conditional Baptism.[3] The proper method and form

---

[1] The complete formula is to be found in the 1944 Benziger Ritual already referred to—pp. (16) ff.; in Bouscaren, *Canon Law Digest* (Milwaukee: Bruce, 1934-1943), II, 182-184; in *The American Ecclesiastical Review*, CVI (1942), 355-357.

[2] In the Benziger Ritual, this formula is to be found in the section entitled "Supplementum Ritualis Romani ad Usum Cleri Americae Septentrionalis Foederatae," p. (19).

[3] The "Supplementum" seems to insert the conditional absolution from censures between the profession of faith and the administration of conditional baptism. In his *The Reception of Converts* (C. U. Ph. D. dissertation, 1944), the Reverend Joseph G. Goodwine, J. C. D., judges that in the case of the doubtfully baptized the conditional absolution from censures is unnecessary, though the practice of conditional absolution from censures prevails in England and Ireland. Goodwine, pp. 109 ff.

of administering conditional baptism is to be determined from diocesan statutes and faculties. In the absence of any legislation by the local Ordinary, baptism is to be conferred according to the form for adults, with the words *si non es baptizatus (a)* prefixed to the *ego te baptizo* . . .

Conditional baptism is to be followed by sacramental confession with conditional absolution.[1] Since this is the convert's first confession, it will be a general confession.

Finally, converts should be admonished to attend Mass and to receive Holy Communion as soon as possible.

§ 12. HOLY COMMUNION

THE normal time for distributing Holy Communion is at the moment appointed in Mass. The rite in this case is described above, pp. 55–56.

But no priest may make any difficulty against giving people Communion at other times, if their request is reasonable, that is if they have a serious (not necessarily a very grave) reason, and if they satisfy the law, being in a state of grace and fasting from midnight.[2]

The rite of distributing Holy Communion out of Mass is this : [3]

A server is needed to say the *Confiteor*. If possible, he should wear a surplice and kneel in the sanctuary ; but often it is necessary that someone in the church (a man rather than a woman) should say the prayers. Two candles are lighted on the altar ; the dust-cloth is removed ; the Communion-plate [4] is made ready on the credence ; the purifying bowl on the altar near the tabernacle.

The priest washes his hands and vests in surplice and white stole or stole of the colour of the day.[5] He comes from the sacristy (following the server), covered, with hands joined or carrying the burse (of the same colour as the priest's stole) containing a corporal and the tabernacle key. Obviously, Communion in this way can be given only from an altar where the Blessed Sacrament is reserved. At the foot of the altar the priest uncovers and he and the server genuflect and kneel for a moment's prayer. The server puts the biretta on the credence and then kneels at the Epistle side and says *Confiteor*. Meanwhile the priest goes up to the altar, spreads the corporal, opens the tabernacle, genuflects (with his hands laid on the altar), takes the ciborium and places it on the corporal. He uncovers it—laying the veil outside the corporal, the lid within it—genuflects again, partly turns to the people, not turning his back to the Sanctissimum, and says *Misereatur*. The server answers *Amen*. Then, making the sign of the cross over the

[1] The condition is not to be expressed in words.

[2] Cf. R.R. IV. i, 13, 16.

[3] R.R. IV. ii.

[4] An Instruction of the Congregation of the Sacraments (26 March 1929) directs that a plate—of silver or of metal gilt, and entirely smooth on its inner surface—be used, in addition to the cloth, for the Communion of the people. It is held by each communicant (or it may be carried by a server) and afterwards purified by the priest into the chalice or (outside Mass) into the ciborium.

[5] On All Souls' Day white or violet is used instead of black.

people, he says *Indulgentiam*, to which the server again answers *Amen*.[1]
Both these prayers are said in the plural, even if there be only one
communicant. The priest turns to the altar, genuflects, takes the
ciborium in his left hand ; with the thumb and forefinger of the right
he takes a consecrated Particle and holds it over the ciborium. So he
turns to the people, this time with his back to the middle, and says
aloud *Ecce Agnus Dei*, etc., and *Domine, non sum dignus*, etc., three
times.[2] The form is always masculine (*dignus*), even if only women
are present. Carrying the ciborium and Particle in the same way, he
goes to the Communion rail and gives each person Communion with
the usual form (*Corpus Domini nostri*, etc.), said for each communicant,
beginning at the Epistle end. He makes the sign of the cross with each
sacred Particle over the ciborium before placing it on the tongue of
the communicant. When all have received, he takes the Communion-
plate from the last communicant, goes back to the altar, places the
ciborium and the plate on the corporal, genuflects (with at least the
right hand within the corporal) and then says aloud at once *O sacrum
convivium*, with its versicle, response and prayer, the server answering.
In Eastertide and throughout the octave of Corpus Christi *Alleluia* is
added to the antiphon, versicle and response ; the prayer is *Spiritum
nobis, Domine* in Paschaltide. Each prayer has the long conclusion
and the Easter one (*Spiritum*) has *ejusdem*, since the prayer makes
reference to the Holy Ghost. While saying these prayers, the priest
purifies the thumb and index of his right hand and the Communion-
plate (if he sees any particles of the Sacred Species on it) into the
ciborium, and then puts the plate outside the corporal to be removed
by the server. He then washes the thumb and index of the right hand
in the little vessel for that purpose by the tabernacle, and wipes them
on the purificator by it. He covers and veils the ciborium, puts it in
the tabernacle, genuflects, closes and locks the tabernacle. Then he
gives the blessing. He says *Benedictio Dei omnipotentis*, facing the
altar, raising his eyes to the cross and extending, raising and joining
his hands ; he bows his head to the cross at the words *Dei omnipotentis*,
then turns fully to the people and makes the sign of the cross over them
as he continues : *Patris et Filii+et Spiritus Sancti*.[3] The server
answers *Amen*. The blessing is always in the plural. The priest
turns back to the altar by the same way, not completing the circle,
folds the corporal and puts it back in the burse. He takes the burse

[1] If there is no server one of the communicants should say the *Confiteor* and
answer the prayers. If there is no one who can do this the priest—standing
bowed—must himself say the *Confiteor* and the responses. He omits " tibi,.
Pater " and " te, Pater."·
[2] Meantime the server takes the Communion plate to the first communicant,
unless he himself is going to Communion or is to carry the plate during the distribution. If he does he walks before the priest and holds the plate under the chin
of each communicant. After the distribution he takes the plate back to the
altar and leaves it on or near the corporal to be purified.
[3] When a bishop gives Holy Communion outside Mass, he gives the blessing
in the usual episcopal way, saying *Sit nomen Domini*, etc., and making the triple
cross.

and key, comes down the steps, genuflects with the server, puts on the biretta and goes back to the sacristy.

Communion may be given in this way either entirely apart from Mass or immediately before or after private Mass. In this case the priest wears the Mass vestments. If they are black he does not give the blessing. Neither, if he says Mass with black vestments in Eastertide or within the octave of Corpus Christi, does he add *Alleluia* after the antiphon or versicle, but he does say the prayer *Spiritum* at Easter.

§ 13. MATRIMONY [1]

THE ideal, when Catholics marry, is that they should receive the Nuptial Blessing. This blessing is always given in the Nuptial Mass (or other Mass which takes its place, on days when a Nuptial Mass may not be said ; see p. 396). It is not allowed to give *the* Nuptial Blessing without Mass. The parties are to be strongly urged to go to confession beforehand and receive Holy Communion at the Nuptial Mass.

General Rules for Nuptial Blessing. The Nuptial Mass may not be said, nor the blessing given, in the case of mixed marriages, nor in the case of widows who have already received it,[2] nor in the times of forbidden solemnity, namely, from the first Sunday of Advent to Christmas Day, from Ash Wednesday to Easter Day (both inclusive).[3] In the case of Catholics, when the woman has not already received the Nuptial Blessing, and outside the forbidden time, there is in England an indult by which a special form of blessing (not *the* Nuptial Blessing) may be given, if Mass is not said.[4]

We have also a third form to be used for Catholics who marry in the forbidden time, or when the wife has already received the Nuptial Blessing.[5] If people are married during the forbidden time, or if it is not convenient to them to have the Nuptial Mass and Blessing at the moment of their marriage, these may always be added later, when the forbidden time is over. In the case of mixed marriages none of these forms may be used.

Banns. The banns of marriage are to be proclaimed beforehand at Mass or at other services which are well attended, on three successive Sundays or on a holiday of obligation, should it occur (or the Ordinary may, instead, allow a notice to be hung in the porch for eight days, which must include two days of obligation). The form is given in the

---

[1] R.R. VII.

[2] The point is not the woman's widowhood, but that she has already received the nuptial blessing. So if she did not receive it at her former marriage, it may be given (cf. R.R. VII. i, 18).

[3] Unless the Ordinary dispense (R.R. VII. i, 19). " Tempus prohibitum " does not mean time when it is forbidden to marry, but when it is forbidden to " solemnize " marriage, that is to celebrate Nuptial Mass and give the nuptial blessing. The blessing is also excluded on All Souls' Day.

[4] The Bishops of the United States, by Indult, can grant permission for the Nuptial Blessing outside of Mass and similarly for the special prayers outside of Mass, when the Nuptial Blessing is not permitted.

[5] *Ib.*, pp. 207–208.

Ritual.[1] If the persons live in different places the banns must be announced in both. For mixed marriages the banns are not called without the authority of the Ordinary.[2] It is possible, for a sufficient reason, to obtain dispensation from the proclamation of banns from the Ordinary. Marriage should take place in the parish church ; in other churches or oratories (public or semi-public) only by leave of the Ordinary of the place or of the parish priest. The Ordinary may allow it to be celebrated in a private chapel or house only in an extraordinary case and always with a just and reasonable cause. Marriages may be allowed by the Ordinary in the churches or oratories attached to seminaries or convents only in case of necessity and with due precautions.

Form of Marriage. Besides the priest two witnesses must be present. In England we must also obey the law of the land which requires the presence of the government official (registrar) and the declarations made afterwards before him and two witnesses.[3] Sometimes the registrar is present in the church during the ecclesiastical function, sometimes he waits in the sacristy. The witnesses of both declarations, those made in the church during the marriage, and those made before the registrar, should be the same persons. The priest who marries the people must be the same who presides at the civil declarations afterwards.

Rite of Marriage. The essential rite is the same in all cases :

The priest wears surplice and white stole. If he is to celebrate Mass immediately afterwards, he may wear the vestments except the maniple. There should be a server in surplice who carries the holy water. On the credence, or on a small table near the entrance to the sanctuary, a salver or plate is laid, on which the ring will be placed while it is blessed.

The priest stands with his back to the altar at the entrance of the sanctuary or choir. The man and woman to be married kneel [4] (outside the sanctuary) before him, the man at the woman's right. The witnesses stand behind, or on either side. The priest first asks the question of the man : N., *wilt thou take* N.,[5] *here present*, etc., as in the Ritual. The man answers *I will*. The priest asks the question of the woman, and she answers. The man and woman then join right hands.[6]

---

[1] R.R. VII. i, 8 ; *Ordo Adm.*, p. 197.

[2] C.J.C. 1026.

[3] By order of the bishops (in England) the religious ceremony must precede the civil one. In Ireland there is only one ceremony, the religious one, as the priests acts as registrar for the State.

[4] The custom, in many places, in the United States is for the bridegroom and bride to stand until after the placing of the ring on the bride's finger, and then kneel for the blessing.

[5] The Roman Ritual by the single letter N. seems to indicate that only the Christian name is used. It is, however, permissible to use both the Christian name and surname and this is the practice in many places.

[6] In some places the person who " gives the bride away " places her right hand in her husband's at this moment. The rubric of the English ritual speaks of the " giving away."

The man first says the form, *I, N., take thee,* N., *for my lawful wife,* etc., repeating it in short phrases after the priest. The woman, in the same way, says the form appointed for her. After this they keep the hands joined while the priest makes the sign of the cross over the persons, saying *Ego coniungo vos in matrimonium, in nomine Patris+ et Filii et Spiritus Sancti. Amen.* He then sprinkles them thrice with lustral water.

The husband puts the ring on the salver or plate held by the server. The priest blesses the ring with the form in the Ritual and sprinkles it thrice (i.e., in the form of a cross) with lustral water. The husband takes the ring from the priest and says, in short phrases after the priest, *With this ring I thee wed,* etc. As he says the words, the husband puts the ring on the third finger of the woman's left hand.

The priest says the versicles *Confirma hoc Deus,* etc., and the prayer, the server answering.[1] That is the end of the essential rite.

Nuptial Mass. If NUPTIAL MASS is to follow, the priest assumes the maniple and Mass begins. The newly-married kneel close to the altar, but outside the sanctuary.[2]

The Nuptial Mass is the votive Mass "Pro sponso et sponsa," in the Missal. It is a privileged votive Mass, yet of simple rite only.

It is said with white vestments, without *Gloria in excelsis* or Creed (even though an occurring commemoration should require it).

Apart from the forbidden times, when no such Mass may be said and no Nuptial Blessing given (except by permission of the Ordinary), this Mass may be said any day, except Sundays and holidays of obligation (even the suppressed ones, now called days of devotion), or doubles of the first or second class, or within the octaves of Epiphany, Easter, Pentecost and Corpus Christi; or on privileged weekdays and vigils; or on All Souls' Day. On these days the Mass of the day is said; the prayers of the Nuptial Mass are added to the prayer of the Mass of the day (except on All Souls' Day) under one conclusion; other occurring commemorations and *orationes imperatae* are added and the prayers of the Blessing are said in the usual place. The rubrics of the Missal suppose that the husband and wife make their Communion at this Mass. It is said as usual, with two exceptions. After the *Pater noster,* before the prayer *Libera nos,* the priest genuflects, goes to the Epistle corner and turns to the husband and wife, who remain kneeling. The server holds a Missal (or other book containing the form of blessing) before the priest. With joined hands he says the two prayers *Propitiare Domine* and *Deus,*

---

[1] When more than one pair are married at the same time, having first received the consent of each pair and duly celebrated their union, and having said to each pair *Ego conjungo vos,* etc., the priest blesses the rings and carries out the other blessings once for all in the plural.

[2] In this country, the custom for the newly married is to assist at the Nuptial Mass at kneelers, placed in the sanctuary .

qui potestate virtutis tuae, as in the Missal. He returns to the centre of the altar, genuflects and goes on with Mass. The server puts the book back on its stand (or on the credence). Again after *Benedicamus Domino* (or *Ite, missa est*) the priest turns, this time at the middle of the altar. The husband and wife remain kneeling and the priest says the prayer *Deus Abraham* in the Missal. The server again holds the book before him. The server puts back the book and takes the lustral water. The priest now addresses the husband and wife on the duties of married life.[3] Then he sprinkles them with lustral water-(thrice, i.e., in the centre, to his left and to his right), turns to the altar and ends Mass as usual. The Leonine prayers may be omitted after this Mass.[4]

The rector of the church or whoever takes his place (even though the parties were married in presence of another priest) must at once enter the marriage in the register, and add a note about it to the entry of baptism of each person in the baptismal register; or, if they were not baptized in his church, he must send a statement to the rector of the church where they were baptized, that he may make this entry.[5]

§ 14. CHURCHING [6]

ONLY the mother of a child which has been born in legitimate wedlock has a strict right to receive the blessing after childbirth. The imparting of this blessing is not reserved to the parish priest. The mother comes to the church at a convenient time after the birth of the child. The priest wears a surplice and white [7] stole. There should be a server carrying lustral water. The mother holds a lighted candle. She kneels in the porch or by the door of the church.[8] The priest, standing before her, sprinkles her thrice with lustral water, then says the prayers in the Ritual. After the psalm *Domini est terra* and its antiphon, the woman rises and he gives her the left end of his stole to hold and introduces her into the church saying *Ingredere,* etc. The woman goes to the altar (that of the Blessed Sacrament or of the Lady Chapel or another according to custom) and kneeling there gives thanks to God for the favours bestowed on her. Standing with his back to the altar (inside the rails or on the foot-pace) the priest continues the prayers.

---

[3] The rubric at the end of this Mass in the Missal says he should do so.

[4] The Blessing may be given to more than one pair at the same time. In that case no change—it would seem—is to be made in the prayers (S.R.C. 3 March 1936).

[5] R.R. VII. ii, 7.

[6] R.R. VII. iii.

[7] As the colour of Candlemas.

[8] "Foris ad limina genuflectentem " says the Roman Ritual.

Finally he sprinkles the woman again thrice with lustral water, saying the blessing *Pax et benedictio*, etc.

When more than one woman is churched at the same time the stole is handed to the first, the others follow her and the priest into the church ; the formula of introduction and the subsequent prayers and the blessing are all said in the plural.

§ 15. BLESSINGS [1]

THERE are blessings which any priest may use ; others, called consecrations, used only by a bishop ; and a third class which may be given by a priest if he has permission from the Ordinary or has an apostolic indult.[2] To this third class belongs the blessing of vestments.[3]

The general rule for blessings is that the priest wears a surplice and a stole of the colour of the day unless another colour is expressly prescribed (e.g., if there is an exorcism the colour will be violet). The priest stands uncovered while blessing ; he nearly always uses the form *Adiutorium nostrum, Dominus vobiscum* and a prayer or prayers, and he ends by sprinkling the person or thing thrice (i.e., in the form of a cross) with lustral water. Sometimes incense is also used.

The blessing of lustral water [4] (with salt) should normally be made on Sunday before the chief Mass. Then follows the Asperges ceremony.

§ 16. SICK CALLS

THE ceremonies to be noted in connection with sick calls are those of the sacraments then administered.[5]

If there is time, a dying man will receive the sacraments of Penance, Holy Eucharist and Extreme Unction.

Preparations. If these sacraments are to be administered in one visit,[6] the priest will take with him the Blessed Sacrament in the small pyx used for this purpose, the Oil of the Sick in its stock. By the sick man's bed (in a position where the patient can easily see it) a table will be prepared, covered with a white cloth, having on it two wax candles burning (if possible, blessed candles), lustral water and a sprinkler,[7] a wineglass with a *little* water to drink. It is suitable that

---

[1] R.R. VIII. and Appendix.

[2] C.J.C. 1147.

[3] The forms for blessing vestments are also in the Missal among the blessings which follow the Masses and prayers for the dead. C.J.C. 1304, 3⁰, gives the faculty of blessing vestments, etc., to parish priests for the churches and oratories within their parish and to rectors of churches for their own churches. Other priests (who are not Religious) require a special faculty from the Ordinary.

[4] In the Missal : *Ordo ad Faciendam Aquam Benedictam*, first among the blessings ; also in R.R. VIII. ii. ; *Ordo Adm.*, Tit. XI. cap. i, pp. 240–244 ; *Rituale Parvum*, pp. 203–208.

[5] For prayers, advice and help in general to be given to the sick, see R.R. V. iv ; *Ordo Adm.*, Tit. V. cap iv, pp. 125–137.

[6] The liturgical books suppose that Extreme Unction is not given at the same time as Communion (see p. 402). It is, however, often necessary to do so.

[7] Unless the priest brings holy water with him. The best kind of sprinkler is a small branch of box, yew, or some such plant.

a crucifix also stand on the table. If Extreme Unction will be administered at the same visit, a plate with cubes of dry bread, water to wash the priest's hands, a towel and cotton-wool [1] should be on the table.

The first Synod of Westminster, in 1852, recommended that a case containing all these things be sent beforehand to the house, or brought by the priest when he comes.[2] A Communion cloth (a clean napkin or handkerchief will do) should be spread under the chin of the sick person at the moment of Communion. In England it is rarely possible to carry the Blessed Sacrament to the sick publicly (except, of course, in a religious house or a Catholic institution having an oratory).[3] In a small, quiet district, where the house is not very far from the church, the priest may be able to wear his cassock, surplice, stole and a cloak covering all. In many large towns, and where the distance is great, he must take the Sanctissimum in his usual dress, with no external sign. He carries the burse or pocket which contains the pyx concealed within his coat, hanging by its strings round his neck. The Oil of the Sick is carried in another bag,[4] also a little vessel of lustral water is brought, unless it is already prepared at the house. It is convenient, in this case especially, to use a stole white [5] on one side and violet on the other. He wears this round the neck under his coat while carrying the Sanctissimum. When the Blessed Sacrament is carried privately the burse or pocket which contains the pyx should also contain a small corporal [6] and purificator, such as are used for sick calls.

Communion of a Sick Person. In the church two candles are lighted on the altar. The priest (in surplice and white stole) spreads

---

[1] The priest usually brings this with him. It is useful to have a small plate or glass dish ready to hold it.

[2] Decr. xviii, no. 12, p. 20.

[3] The rubrics of the Ritual suppose, normally, a public procession to take the Blessed Sacrament to the sick, with torches, the priest in surplice, stole (even cope) and humeral veil, under a canopy (R.R. IV. iv, 6, 12, 13). But the note on p. 102 of *Ordo Administrandi* says that this public procession may not be held (in England) without leave from the Bishop. A new rubric added to R.R. (IV. iv. 29) gives directions for the private carrying (for a proper reason) of the Blessed Sacrament to the sick. The priest is to wear at least the stole and is to be accompanied by at least one person; the pyx is to be carried in a little bag which is to be hung from the priest's neck and laid on his breast. On arriving in the sick-room the priest is to put on a surplice if he had not previously worn it.

[4] The rubric (R.R. V. ii, 2) supposes the vessel of Oil of the Sick to be carried in a little bag of violet silk; only in the case of a long journey or when, for example, the priest must ride to the sick call so that there is danger of spilling the Oil, does it direct that the bag be hung around the priest's neck. This rubric does not suppose that the priest is at the same time carrying the Blessed Sacrament. It is supposed that a server accompanies the priest, carrying the lustral water (R.R. IV. iv, 13; *Ordo Adm.*, Tit. V, cap. vi, p. 140). In England this is often not possible. If an ecclesiastic goes with the priest, he carries the holy Oil.

[5] To take Communion to the sick a white stole is always worn, whatever the colour of the day (R.R. IV. iv, 12). The rule for this case is different from that of other distributions of Communion out of Mass (p. 391).

[6] The pyx may be wrapped up in it.

the corporal,[1] opens the tabernacle, takes a consecrated Particle and lays It in the pyx, arranges the pyx as he will carry it, and having washed his fingers replaces the ciborium in the tabernacle. He goes directly to the sick man's house, speaking to no one on the way, reciting the psalm *Miserere* and other psalms and canticles. At the door of the house (unless people carrying lights had accompanied him) he is met by a person who holds a (blessed) lighted candle and who genuflects as the door is opened. Entering the sick-room the priest says *Pax huic domui*, to which the answer is *Et omnibus habitantibus in ea*. He first sees that the candles on the table are lighted, then spreads the corporal on the table, puts the pyx on it and genuflects. If Extreme Unction is to be administered, he lays the Oil and cotton-wool on the table also (p. 403). If he has brought the Blessed Sacrament privately he now vests in surplice and white stole.[2] All present in the room kneel. He sprinkles the sick man and the room,[3] saying *Asperges me, Domine*, etc., with the versicles and prayer in the Ritual. If no one else can answer, the priest must answer himself. If the sick man will now make his confession,[4] the other people leave the room, genuflecting to the Sanctissimum when they rise from their knees. The priest changes his stole to violet and hears the sick man's confession, sitting so as not to turn his back to the Sanctissimum. The friends of the sick man may and ought now to return. Either the man himself or someone else in his name says the *Confiteor* in Latin or in English (otherwise the priest himself must say it in Latin) ; the priest changes his stole to white, stands before the table, opens the pyx. He genuflects, turns partly and says *Misereatur* and *Indulgentiam* in the singular. He genuflects again, takes a Sacred Particle in the right hand, holding It over the pyx held in the left, turns and says *Ecce Agnus Dei* (showing the Host to the patient) and *Domine, non sum dignus*, thrice.[5] The sick man says the same words in a low tone at least once. Meanwhile the cloth is spread on the bed beneath his chin. The priest gives him Holy Communion, saying either the usual form, *Corpus Domini nostri*,

---

[1] O'Kane (p. 382) considers two cases. He thinks it well to keep the small pyx always ready, containing the Sanctissimum, in the tabernacle. In this case he says the priest may open the tabernacle and take it out, wearing the dress in which he will go to the sick man's house. But, if he has to take a Particle from the ciborium and put it in the pyx, then he should be vested in surplice and stole, changing afterwards to the dress in which he will go out.

[2] Even when the priest takes the Sanctissimum secretly, he must vest in cassock surplice and white stole at the house (cf. R.R. IV. iv, 29). If necessary, he must send these vestments beforehand, or take them with him. Only a most urgent reason would allow a priest to give Communion in his outdoor dress.

[3] The rubric in the administration of Extreme Unction (R.R. V. ii, 4) says that the priest sprinkles the patient, room and those around, and in the form of a cross (i.e., straight in front, to his left and to his right).

[4] If possible, the confession should be heard at another visit beforehand. The Ritual supposes this, and it prevents the danger that the man may be unfit to receive the Holy Eucharist when It has been brought to him.

[5] If death were imminent and delay be dangerous the priest may omit some or all of the prayers preceding *Misereatur*, etc. (R.R. IV. iv, 21) and need not supply them later, if the patient survives.

or, if Holy Communion is given as Viaticum, the form *Accipe frater* (or *soror*) *Viaticum Corporis Domini nostri Iesu Christi, qui te custodiat ab hoste maligno et perducat in vitam aeternam. Amen.*[1]

Returning to the table he washes the forefinger and thumb of the right hand in the water there provided and dries them with the purificator, and if the pyx is empty he may purify it into the water. This purification is in due time put into the sacrarium or, if this be not available, into the fire, or it may be given to the patient to drink. He then says *Dominus vobiscum* and the prayer *Domine sancte, Pater omnipotens*, in the Ritual. If any Particle remains in the pyx [2] he genuflects, takes the pyx in both hands, blesses the man with it, saying nothing. If no Particle remains he gives the blessing with the hand, using the form *Benedictio Dei omnipotentis*, etc.,[3] in the singular (unless more than one had received). If Extreme Unction, etc., immediately follows the blessing (with the Sanctissimum or the priest's) is postponed until the end of the whole ceremony.

Public Procession of the Blessed Sacrament. When Holy Communion is carried publicly to the sick (e.g., in a college or convent) the priest wears surplice, white stole and humeral veil, and a small canopy (*umbella*) should, when possible, be carried over the Blessed Sacrament. The ciborium itself may be carried or some Particles (one more than the number required for the sick) may be transferred to a veiled pyx. R.R. supposes an acolyte to lead the procession, one to carry the aspersory and the burse (containing a corporal and a small purificator), a third to carry the Ritual and ring a bell all the time, and torch-bearers. Usually, however, the holy water will be made ready on the table in the sick room, and the corporal (spread), purificator and book put there also beforehand, and one server will precede the priest carrying a light and ringing the bell to mark the passing of the Lord, while a second carries the canopy. In convents should a server not be able to accompany the priest, two of the sisters may carry lights, but they must *follow* the priest (a third sister may precede the little procession if it is necessary to guide it to the rooms of the sick). In the sick room the priest puts off the humeral veil on his arrival and resumes it before blessing the patient at the end of the ceremony.

Return to the Church. When the Blessed Sacrament is carried back publicly to the church the priest on the way recites the psalm *Laudate Dominum de caelis* and other psalms and hymns. On arrival he places the pyx or ciborium on the altar, genuflects, kneels on the foot-pace or on the lowest step, and says *Panem*, etc., then rising says *Dominus*

---

[1] This form is used whenever Communion is given as Viaticum, that is, as long as the sick person is in danger of death from any cause, external or internal. It is noteworthy that the rubric in the older editions of R.R. which directed that Holy Communion be given as Viaticum when it was probable that the sick person would not again be able to receive it no longer appears in the Ritual of 1925.

[2] R.R. IV. iv, 12, 23, 27 says that more than one Particle ought to be taken to the house of the sick person unless the journey thither be too long or too difficult. This rubric, however, supposes that the Blessed Sacrament is carried publicly in procession. [3] See p. 392.

vobiscum and the prayer *Deus, qui nobis* (with the short conclusion), even in Paschal-tide.[1] Then (having announced the indulgences that are granted to those who accompany the Blessed Sacrament) he blesses those present with the pyx wrapped up in the humeral veil, saying nothing. He then replaces the Blessed Sacrament in the tabernacle.

If the Blessed Sacrament has to be carried back privately the priest may laudably recite the psalms on the way, and it would seem that he should say *Panem de caelo* and the prayer before closing the Tabernacle door. If anyone had accompanied him he may bless him with the Sanctissimum before replacing it.

Communion of Several. If Communion is given to several people in one room, the words are said once only for all (*Misereatur, Indulgentiam* and the prayer *Domine sancte* being said in the plural), except the actual form of administration (*Accipe frater* or *Corpus Domini*) said to each. If Communion is distributed to several sick people who are in the same house or hospital but in different rooms,[2] the greeting, the sprinkling and the prayers before Communion are recited (in the plural) once only, viz., in the first room. In all the other rooms the priest says only *Misereatur tui . . . Indulgentiam . . . Ecce Agnus Dei . . ., Domine, non sum dignus* (once only) *. . . Accipe frater (soror) . . .* or *Corpus Domini . . .* and in the last room he adds the versicle *Dominus vobiscum* with its response and the prayer *Domine sancte . . .* said in the plural. In the last room also, if a consecrated Particle be left, he imparts the Eucharistic blessing. He then completes the prayers in the church in the usual way.[3]

With the Ordinary's or parish priest's leave, granted for a grave cause, a deacon may give Holy Communion, using all the forms and blessing as above[4]; in case of necessity the permission may be presumed.

§ 17. EXTREME UNCTION [5]

NORMALLY this sacrament will be administered after confession and Communion. But the Ritual does not suppose that it be given usually at the same visit as when the sick man receives Holy Communion. The ideal is that the three sacraments be administered at three successive visits, though it is provided that the man " if he wish to confess " should do so again, immediately before the anointing. Extreme Unction may be given to those who are unconscious or delirious, if there is no fear of profaning the sacrament. It may not be given to those who are manifestly impenitent, or excommunicate, nor to children under the age of reason, nor to any who are not in danger of death

---

[1] *Alleluia* is added to the verse and the response in Paschaltide and within the octave of Corpus Christi.
[2] It will be necessary to have a table with two lighted candles and a corporal spread on it in each room ; and also the vessel for the purification of the priest's fingers, unless a server carries this from one room to another.
[3] S.R.C., 9 Januarii 1929 ; cf. *Rituale Parvum*, p. 101.
[4] R.R. IV. iv, 28.
[5] R.R. V. i, ii.

through sickness or old age at the time. It is not given more than once in the same danger of death. It may be given again, if the person has partly recovered, and then again falls into danger.

Preparations. If, then, Extreme Unction be given at a separate visit, a table is prepared near the bed, covered with a white cloth, on which are placed a crucifix, a candle, lighted and held by a server during the anointing [1] (if its light be necessary), also cotton-wool divided into six parts, bread, water to wash the priest's hands and a towel, lustral water and a sprinkler. The priest arrives in cassock, surplice and violet stole, bearing the Oil of the Sick. He may also bring the lustral water and cotton-wool. (The Ritual supposes him to be accompanied by a server who carries a cross, the aspersory and the book.) In England he will generally come in outdoor dress and vest at the house.

Arrival of Priest. Arriving at the sick-room he says *Pax huic domui*, etc., lays the stock of holy Oil on the table, vests if he is not already vested, gives the sick man a cross to kiss, performs the Asperges ceremony (sprinkling the patient, room, and those around in the form of a cross), saying Asperges, etc., but not *Miserere* nor *Gloria Patri*. Then, if necessary, he hears the confession, instructs the man about the sacrament, encouraging him, and begins the rite of Extreme Unction, saying *Adiutorium nostrum*. If there is no one to answer, the priest himself must do so.

But often it will be necessary to give Extreme Unction immediately after Viaticum, at the same visit. In this case, having finished the prayer *Domine sancte*, the priest puts on a violet stole, and, omitting the greeting and sprinkling, at once presents the cross to the patient to kiss.

Opening Prayers. The priest says the opening prayers facing the sick man, and makes the sign of the cross over him where it is marked in the book. When he has said the prayer *Exaudi nos, Domine sancte*,[2] the sick man, server, or other person says the *Confiteor* in Latin or the vulgar tongue. In case of necessity the priest must say it himself. The priest, turned towards the sick man, says *Misereatur* and *Indulgentiam* in the singular. He then tells those present to pray for the sick man. They may say the seven penitential psalms and Litanies, or other suitable prayers, while the priest administers the sacrament. He says *In nomine Pa+tris et Fi+lii et Spiritus+Sancti*, etc., making the sign of the cross over the man, and then holds his right hand extended over the patient's head during the remainder of this prayer.

The Anointings. He then dips the thumb of the right hand into the stock of Oil of the Sick. If there is a server in Holy Orders present he will wipe away the Oil after each anointing. Otherwise the priest does

---

[1] If there is no server the candle may stand in a candlestick on the table. If Extreme Unction is given immediately after Communion a third candle is not needed, the two used during Communion continue burning.

[2] The *Confiteor* with *Misereatur* must be repeated even though they had been recited a short time previously for the Communion.

so himself. The most convenient way (unless there is someone to hold the plate containing the wool) is to hold a small piece of cotton-wool between the forefinger and second finger of the right hand, and to wipe the place anointed each time immediately with it.[1] Only in case of grave necessity (e.g., in the case of contagious disease of a serious character) is it allowed to anoint with an instrument. This may be a small pencil of wood, or piece of cotton-wool. There must be a separate pencil or piece for each anointing, lest the infection return to the vessel of oil. These pieces of wood or wool are burned afterwards and the ashes thrown into the sacrarium.

The priest makes the sign of the cross with the Oil on each organ and limb, saying the form once only for the pairs of organs (spreading it out over the two anointings). According to the rite the eyes (closed), the ears (the lobes), nostrils, mouth (with closed lips), hands and feet are anointed. The right organ or limb is anointed first. For any reasonable cause the anointing of the feet may be omitted. For each organ the priest says the form in the Ritual. He ought to know these forms by heart. The hands of priests are anointed on the back, those of laymen on the palms. The nostrils are anointed either with one anointing on the tip or preferably with two on the sides ; the feet preferably above.[2] If any organ is not anointed it is not lawful to anoint another part of the body instead. If a limb or organ is mutilated or wanting, the nearest part of the body to it is anointed, with the form for that limb. The priest then wipes his fingers with dry bread and washes them (the bread and water are later to be thrown into the sacrarium or into the fire). He continues the prayers in the Ritual, facing the sick man. He should then address the man, saying suitable words to prepare him for death (if death is imminent) or warning him to bear his sickness patiently. The Ritual instructs the priest to see that the sick man has a crucifix (to look at and to kiss from time to time) and holy water.

Anointing in Immediate Danger of Death. If there is immediate danger of death, the priest, omitting all that goes before the anointing, at once anoints the organs ; then if the person remains alive he says the prayers which had been omitted. If the danger is very urgent he anoints one of the senses or preferably the sick man's forehead, saying the one formula, *Per istam sanctum Unctionem indulgeat tibi Dominus quidquid deliquisti. Amen* ; afterwards he must supply (unconditionally) the anointings of each of the senses, if the person still lives.[3] In doubt whether the man is still alive he begins with the condition *Si vivis*. If the man dies during the rite the priest does not proceed further with the rite.[4]

---

[1] The cotton-wool used for this must later be burned and the ashes thrown into the sacrarium.

[2] The English *Ordo* in a note to the rubric (p. 110) says : " Ad nares Unctio fit in parte inferiore : ad pedes, in parte superiore."

[3] R.R. V. i, 21.

[4] R.R. V. i, 13.

Extreme Unction to Several. If Extreme Unction be given to more than one person at the same time the prayers which precede and follow the anointings are said once in the plural. The crucifix is given to each person to kiss and the anointings (with their forms) are, naturally, done for each one. In the second prayer which follows the anointing, at N. the names may be omitted.

§ 18. THE APOSTOLIC BLESSINGS FOR THE MOMENT OF DEATH [1]

EVERY priest who attends a sick person has now [2] the faculty and the duty to impart to him the Apostolic Blessing, which will enable him to gain a plenary indulgence at the moment of death. To impart this indulgence validly the form given in the Ritual must be used. The blessing may be given to anyone in danger of death from any cause. It may be given even to those who are unconscious (and then nothing need be done by the person to whom it is imparted) or delirious or insane. It may not be given to the excommunicated, the impenitent or those who die in manifest mortal sin.

The priest wears a surplice and violet stole. The sprinkling (with *Asperges*, etc., but without the psalm and *Gloria Patri*) is done unless it had been carried out for Viaticum or Extreme Unction immediately before. If the sick man has not been previously to confession he should receive the sacrament of Penance or at least make an act of contrition. The priest, if time will allow, is to instruct him about the blessing and he must see [3] that the patient (a) invokes the name *Jesus* (at least mentally), (b) and willingly accepts the sufferings of his illness in expiation for his past life and offers himself to God ready to accept whatever is pleasing to Him, and patiently undergo even death itself in satisfaction of the punishments which he has merited by his sins. The priest is also to console the patient by reminding him of the divine generosity, etc.[4]

The *Confiteor*, *Misereatur* (*tui*), etc., are to be repeated for the blessing even though they were said shortly before for Viaticum or Extreme Unction.

The Ritual gives two shorter forms of imparting the blessing in case of imminent danger of death. Should the blessing be given to several together all the prayers, etc., are said once only, changing the singular into the plural wherever necessary.

[1] R.R. V. vi.

[2] C.J.C. 468, 2 (cf. R.R. V. vi, 2).

[3] The invocation of the Holy Name and resignation to death are conditions necessary for the future gaining of the indulgence, if the patient be of sound mind and conscious when he receives the blessing. The best time to secure the necessary resignation is during his confession, when the priest can speak to him about it.

[4] R.R. V. vi, 4.

CHAPTER XXX

FUNERALS

§ 1. THE COMPLETE RITE

AS in the case of marriage, so in that of funerals, there are really several rites which follow one another. The complete function, as supposed normally by the Ritual [1] and Missal, consists of these five offices : 1. The bringing of the body to the church ; 2. Matins and Lauds for the Dead ; 3. Requiem Mass ; 4. The Absolution ; 5. The burying. In general these complete funeral rites are of obligation.[2] While the Office of the dead may be omitted for a reasonable cause, the prayers which follow the Absolution may never be omitted. The Exequial Mass may be omitted (on the day of the funeral) only if it be liturgically impeded or, the omission be *necessary*. The Absolution, too, is of obligation after the funeral Mass.

The bringing of the body to the church, the Office for the dead, Requiem Mass, burying, are different functions, which may be performed by different priests. But if the Absolution follows Mass immediately it must always be carried out by the priest who has said the Mass. Only the Bishop of the place (or a " greater prelate " [3]) is allowed to give the Absolution without having said the Mass before it.[4]

The right and duty of celebrating a funeral belong ordinarily to the parish priest of the church in whose district the man lived, even when he died somewhere else. The rector may delegate another priest to perform the function.

As far as possible, funerals should not be held on doubles of the first class, and especially not on Sundays or holidays of obligation. They should be put off to the next day. But if this cannot be done the funeral may be held on such days, as long as it does not interfere with the solemnity of the day.

General Rules for the Exequial Mass. The funeral Mass may not take the place of the Chapter Mass, Conventual Mass, or *Missa pro populo*.[5] On the following days even *the* Exequial Mass (i.e., Mass sung *de die obitus* and in the church in which the funeral takes place) is forbidden, namely, Christmas Day, the Epiphany, Easter Sunday, Ascension Day, Whit Sunday, Trinity Sunday, Corpus Christi, feasts

---

[1] R.R. VI. (cf. C.J.C. 1203–1242).
[2] R.R. VI. i, 4 ; C.J.C. 1215.
[3] See p. 31.
[4] Cf. S.R.C. 3029[10], 3798[2].
[5] Neither may it be celebrated in a church in which there is only one Mass on Palm Sunday, Purification, Ash Wednesday and vigil of Pentecost if the palms, candles, ashes or font are blessed ; nor on the feast of St. Mark or Rogation days in such a church if the procession is held.

of the Sacred Heart, Kingship of Christ, the Immaculate Conception, Annunciation, Assumption, both feasts of St. Joseph (19 March and Wednesday after the second Sunday after Easter), Birthday of St. John Baptist, St. Peter and St. Paul, Dedication of St. Michael the Archangel, All Saints ; also all days to which the solemnity of these feasts is transferred ; the Dedication and Titular Saint of the church where the funeral takes place ; the chief Patron of the place ; (for religious institutes) the Titular or Founder ; the last three days of Holy Week ; during solemn exposition of the Blessed Sacrament, whether for the Forty Hours' or other solemn exposition.[1] If, then, it is necessary to bury a man on these days, the funeral service must be held in the afternoon or evening without Mass ; nor may the church bells be tolled. On all other days the Exequial Mass (and in case of a poor person, a Low Mass celebrated for the funeral) is allowed. In England [2] when High Mass or Sung Mass is impossible because of the shortage of sacred ministers or of a choir, one Low Mass is allowed for the funeral on all the days on which the Exequial Mass may be celebrated.[3] When the Exequial Mass is impeded by the rubrics it may be celebrated on the nearest subsequent day which is not similarly impeded. Low (private) Mass for the dead person, even when celebrated in the church or public oratory where the funeral takes place, in the presence of the body, is forbidden on all doubles of the first and second classes and all days of obligation, including Sundays ; on All Souls' Day ; on the vigils of Christmas, Epiphany and Pentecost ; on Ash Wednesday and the days of Holy Week and within privileged octaves.[4] From the Mass of Maundy Thursday to that of Holy Saturday, and while the Blessed Sacrament is exposed in the church, a funeral (without Mass) may be held, only if absolutely necessary, without singing or solemnity. The church is not to be adorned with any sign of mourning, the bells are not to be rung, the Office is not said.

On all other days the funeral rites, with Mass, are allowed.

Preparations. For the complete ceremony the following preparations must be made :

In the sacristy plain surplices are laid out, a black stole, a black cope, the lustral water and sprinkler, processional cross, acolytes' candles, which if possible should be of unbleached wax. The altar is prepared for Requiem Mass. The frontal is black unless the Blessed Sacrament is there reserved, in which case the frontal and tabernacle veil (conopaeum) are violet. The altar candles should be of unbleached wax ; the carpet covers only the foot-pace ; the Missal-stand and sedilia are bare or covered in black.

---

[1] The list is given in the current *Ordo Recitandi.*
[2] Rescripts of 7 March 1847 and 12 May 1864.
[3] In Ireland, when for want of priests solemn Mass cannot be celebrated Low Mass may be said as the funeral Mass on all days except doubles of the first and second class, feasts of obligation, privileged weekdays, vigils and octaves (Rescript of 29 June 1862).
[4] For a full explanation of the rubrics about Requiem Masses, see O'Connell, "The Celebration of Mass," I, pp. 135 *sqq.*

In the middle of the church, outside the choir in every case, a hearse or trestles are set up on which the coffin will be laid, so that it is possible to go all round it. Candles, usually six, of unbleached wax, stand around on the ground. They are lit just before the coffin is placed on the trestles. Candles of bleached wax are prepared to be distributed to the clergy during the Mass and Absolution, if this be the custom.

Conducting the Corpse to the Church. The priest, with servers and clergy, goes first to the house where the coffin waits.[1] It may await them in some house other than that of the death.[2] The officiating priest wears surplice, black stole, and (for greater solemnity) black cope ; he wears his biretta when walking. The processional cross is carried in front between the two acolytes with lighted candles,[3] then the singers or clergy in order. At the end of the procession comes the celebrant, immediately preceded by a server carrying the aspersory. If he wears the cope he should be assisted by two servers in surplice who hold its ends. The officiating priest (even within the church) and clergy (outside the church) wear the biretta on the way. At the house, where the coffin waits it will be more convenient if, at once, the procession is formed in the order in which it will return to the church (as below). The coffin should be already brought to the door of the house, with the feet foremost. Candles are handed to the clergy and lighted ; all uncover. Standing before the coffin (at the foot of the corpse) the priest sprinkles it with lustral water three times, first in front of him, then at his left, lastly at his right. He hands back the sprinkler and recites *Si iniquitates* and the psalm *De profundis* with those around. Instead of the verses *Gloria Patri* and *Sicut erat*, at this and all psalms at funerals, the verses *Réquiem aetérnam*✱*dona ei,*[4] *Dómine, Et lux pérpetua*✱*luceat ei*[5] are substituted. Then the whole antiphon *Si iniquitates* is said.

The procession now goes to the church. Confraternities of laymen go first ; the cross is borne before the clergy, that is, all who wear cassock and surplice. Regular clergy go before the secular clergy, all walking two and two, holding lighted candles (in the outside hand). The officiating priest goes immediately in front of the coffin. He does not hold a candle. Behind the priest the coffin is carried by bearers, or it may be drawn on a hearse. Men should walk on either side of it holding lighted candles. If there are wreaths of flowers (which are only tolerated by usage) they should be carried behind the coffin ; then

[1] The body of a tonsured cleric or cleric in minor orders is vested in cassock, surplice and biretta ; that of a subdeacon, deacon or priest in violet Mass vestments of his order (R.R. VI. i, 12–16).

[2] Or even, in case of necessity, at the entrance to the church (S.R.C. 3481[1]).

[3] The acolytes, if available, may on occasions of greater solemnity accompany the cross. The Roman Ritual makes no mention of them.

[4] The prayers special to the funeral rite are said in the singular ; those of the Mass and Office, are, generally speaking, in the plural.

[5] If the rite is carried out for more than one person, in this verse *Requiem* and in all the other verses and prayers (except *Non intres*), the singular is changed into the plural.

come the lay mourners. The church bells are tolled as soon as the procession leaves the house. As soon as it starts the priest recites the antiphon *Exsultabunt,* the cantors begin the psalm *Miserere,* and the clergy continue it. This and all other psalms on the way to the church are to be recited " devote, distincte, gravique voce." If the way is long, so that the *Miserere* is finished before they arrive at the church, they recite the Gradual psalms or others from the Office for the dead. The lay mourners behind the coffin pray for the dead man silently. The procession should go to the church by the shortest way. As soon as it arrives at the church the psalm is interrupted, the verse *Requiem aeternam dona ei* is said at once, then the antiphon *Exsultabunt.*

Arrival at the Church. As they come up the church the cantor begins the responsory *Subvenite, Sancti Dei.* The choir continues it. This is sung. If the Office or Mass is to follow, all go to their places in choir.[1]

The coffin is set on the hearse or trestles prepared, the candles around are lighted. The body of a layman, clerk in minor orders, subdeacon or deacon, is set with the feet towards the altar, that of a priest with the head towards the altar.[2] A black pall is laid over the coffin and wreaths of flowers may be placed around.[3] In the case of a priest or deacon a violet stole and biretta may be placed on the coffin, a biretta alone for subdeacons and clerics in minor orders. Any suitable symbol of the dead man's rank or office may be placed here if it is not grotesque or irreverent.

As soon as the clergy are in their places in choir they put out their candles ; the cross-bearer sets the cross near the credence. It may not be stood at the head of the coffin. The acolytes take their candles to the sacristy.[4]

Office of the Dead. The Office for the dead should follow. The priest who will officiate at this takes his place in the first stall. He wears a surplice and black stole.[5] The Office for the dead consists of (Vespers), Matins (with three nocturns) and Lauds. All antiphons are doubled when the body is present. But the Ritual contemplates that not all this Office be said always. For a reasonable cause Lauds may be omitted, or only one nocturn of Matins said.[6] The Ritual supposes

---

[1] In the shorter form, when the Absolution follows at once, the clergy and choir will go to stand around the coffin.

[2] This is the rule when the body is present physically or morally (that is, at the funeral ceremony when, for some exceptional reason, the body cannot be brought to the church). When the body is not present, either physically or morally, the foot of the catafalque is always nearest the altar.

[3] At the funerals of baptized children who die before the use of reason the rubric (R.R. VI. vii, 1) prescribes the use of flowers " in signum integritatis carnis et virginitatis " ; the use of flowers at other funerals is alien to the mind of the Church and should be strongly discouraged. The national flag may be used instead of a pall for soldiers, sailors or airmen.

[4] Namely, in the complete rite, when the Office or Mass will follow. If the Office does not follow at once, see p. 413, § 2, *infra.*

[5] He may wear a black cope also.

[6] The first nocturn when the body is present (R.R. VI. iii, 16).

that the body is brought to the church in the morning, that Requiem Mass follows after the Office. The Mass should always be said, if possible.[1] If another priest presides at the Office the celebrant of Mass, with deacon and subdeacon, goes to the sacristy and vests during Lauds or the last part of the Office. At the end of the Office *Pater noster* and the following prayers are sung or said kneeling (the priest who presides standing while he sings or says *Dominus vobiscum* and the

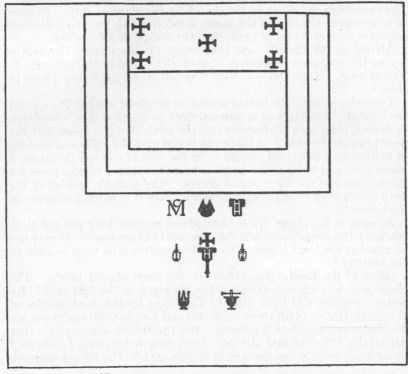

FIG. 45. FUNERAL : BEFORE GOING TO THE HEARSE

prayer *Absolve*). The prayer will be *Absolve* or any other suitable one from those given at the end of Vespers for the dead. At N. the baptismal name of the deceased (the religious name for Religious of either sex) is said and *Sacerdotis* is added in the case of a priest. It is not followed by the versicles *Requiem*, etc., if Mass or Absolution immediately follows.[2]

The Exequial Mass. Mass is then celebrated according to the rules for a Requiem (pp. 63, 122–124). If the same priest celebrates the Office and Mass he cannot go to vest till the Office is finished.

[1] R.R. VI. i, 4, 7. But a festal Mass may not be said before a dead body.
[2]. R.R. VI. iii, 5.

A funeral oration may (with permission of the Ordinary) be preached after Mass. The preacher wears neither surplice nor stole.

The Absolution. After Mass follows the ABSOLUTION.[1] The celebrant of Mass with the ministers goes to the seat. Here the celebrant takes off his chasuble and maniple and puts on a black cope. The ministers take off their maniples. If Mass is sung without ministers there are none at the Absolution, a server carries the cross, and the M.C. or a server replaces the deacon.

The subdeacon takes the cross and stands between the acolytes ; the thurifer, with a server carrying the aspersory on his right ; the celebrant, deacon and M.C. (with the book) first stand before the altar in the order shown in fig. 45.

All make the usual reverence to the altar, turn and go to the coffin. The clergy, holding lighted candles, go after the cross, two and two. The celebrant and deacon (now on the celebrant's left) do not hold candles. The subdeacon, with the cross, and the acolytes stand at the head of the coffin, some way from it.[2] If the dead man is not a priest, this means that they stand at the end farthest from the altar, facing the celebrant at the other end. In the case of a priest's funeral they stand at the end nearest the altar ; the celebrant is then at the other end. The clergy with their candles stand in a line on either side, leaving room for the celebrant and ministers to go round the coffin. Those of higher rank are nearer to the celebrant. The celebrant stands at the foot of the coffin facing the cross at the other end [3] ; when he moves the deacon holds the end of his cope at his left. The M.C. is at his right. The thurifer and bearer of holy water are at the deacon's left. When all are in their places the celebrant says or sings in the ferial tone *Non intres,*[4] the deacon holding the book before him. At the end all answer *Amen.*

"Libera." Then the cantors begin the responsory *Libera me, Domine* ;[5] the choir continues. During the repetition of *Libera* the celebrant puts incense in the thurible, the deacon assisting as usual (having passed to the celebrant's right), omitting the solita oscula. The incense is blessed with the usual form, the deacon having said *Benedicite, Pater reverende.* The M.C. holds the right end of the cope. When the responsory is finished, the cantor and clergy on the Gospel side sing *Kyrie, eleison* ; the cantor and the clergy on the other side answer *Christe, eleison* ; all together sing *Kyrie, eleison.* The celebrant intones *Pater noster,* which all continue silently.

---

[1] When the Absolution is given immediately after Mass it must be given by the celebrant. Only the Bishop of the diocese or a " greater prelate " (p. 31) may give it if he has not celebrated the Mass.

[2] To allow space for the celebrant to pass between them and the hearse.

[3] The rubric of the Missal says : " aliquantulum versus cornu Epistolae, ita ut Crucem Subdiaconi respiciat."

[4] No change is made in this prayer whatever the sex of the dead person.

[5] The chant for this and all the funeral rite is in the Vatican Gradual and *Liber Usualis* (edited by the Solesmes monks), in the Roman Ritual and in the *Missae Defunctorum* issued by the Vatican Press (1919).

Sprinkling and Incensation of Coffin.   The deacon takes the sprinkler, dips it in the lustral water, and hands it to the celebrant, not kissing it or his hand.   The celebrant and deacon at his right, who holds the end of the cope, reverence to the altar and go round the coffin, beginning at the right-hand side as one faces it.   The celebrant sprinkles it with lustral water first towards the feet, next in the middle, then towards the head—not bowing, not pausing.   As he passes the cross he bows

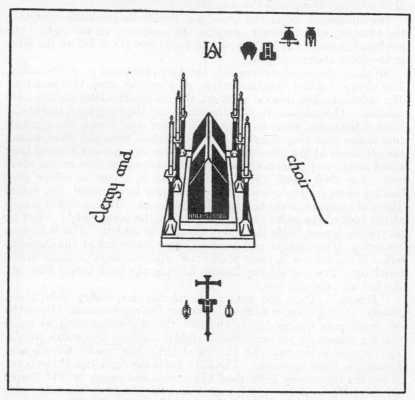

FIG. 46. FUNERAL: THE GROUP AROUND THE HEARSE

low to it; the deacon genuflects.[1]   Coming back the other side, he sprinkles in the same way.   Then the celebrant hands the sprinkler to the deacon, who gives it back to the server.   The deacon takes the thurible and hands it to the celebrant, without kissing it or his hand. They again reverence to the altar, go round the coffin as before, incensing it with single swings of the thurible (three on each side). The celebrant gives the thurible back to the deacon, who hands it to the thurifer and takes the book, which he holds before the celebrant.

[1] If the deacon is a canon in his own capitular church, he bows low.

The celebrant with joined hands chants *Et ne nos inducas in tentationem*, and the other versicles, the choir answering, then the prayer (*Deus cui proprium est*) in the ferial tone (*recto tono*).[1] At N. he inserts the baptismal name of the deceased (except in the case of Religious of both sexes, when the religious name is used) and adds *Sacerdotis* if the body is that of a priest.

At the Graveside. If the coffin is taken at once to the place of burial, the procession is now formed, as when going from the choir to the coffin for the Absolution. The thurifer leads if the grave is to be blessed ; otherwise the aspersory-bearer leads. As the coffin is carried to the cemetery the choir sings the antiphon *In paradisum deducant te angeli*. If the distance is great, other suitable psalms may be sung after this antiphon. At the grave the coffin is laid by its side and all stand around, in the same order as during the Absolution. If the grave is not already blessed, the celebrant blesses it, using the prayer *Deus cuius miseratione*.[2] He then puts on incense, blessing it as usual, and standing where he is sprinkles the coffin and the grave (together) thrice with holy water, and incenses both. If the cemetery or grave is already blessed, neither is sprinkled or incensed. The celebrant then intones the antiphon *Ego sum*, the choir sings (or the celebrant recites) the *Benedictus*. The celebrant sings *Kyrie, eleison* to the simple tone, on one note, falling a half tone on the last syllable. The choir, in the same tone, answers *Christe, eleison* and *Kyrie, eleison* ; the priest then intones *Pater noster*. While this is said silently, he sprinkles the coffin (thrice), not going around it. The other versicles and prayer follow, as in the Ritual. The celebrant makes the sign of the cross over the coffin while saying *Requiem aeternam*, etc.

Return to the Church. Then the procession leaves the grave, and the coffin is lowered into it.[3] On the way back to the church or sacristy the celebrant recites the antiphon *Si iniquitates* ; all say the *De profundis* and at the end *Requiem aeternam* in the plu ral. Then the antiphon *Si iniquitates* is said in full. In the sacristy th celebrant says *Kyrie, eleison, Pater noster, A porta inferi*, etc., as after Lauds for the dead, and the last prayer *Fidelium Deus omnium conditor et redemptor, Requiem aeternam*, etc., *Requiescant in pace*, the choir answering.

§ 2. MODIFICATIONS OF THE FUNERAL RITE

VARIOUS changes may be made in this ceremony, according to the necessity of time and place.[4]

[1] R.R. VI. iii, 5.

[2] If no other body is already buried in this grave the clause of the prayer that is in brackets must be changed into the singular, as is indicated in the Ritual.

[3] The Ritual does not suppose that the clergy remain while the body is lowered into the grave. It is, however, usual in England and Ireland to do so. It is also not unusual for the priest at the grave, when the liturgical prayers have been said and the coffin lowered, to say " De profundis " in English and other English prayers for the dead.

[4] When because of special local conditions changes have to be made in the funeral Liturgy the general principle is that as far as possible the rite, as set forth

The first change is that, if the body is brought to the church in the evening, Vespers of the dead (as given in *Rituale Romanum*, VI, iv) may be recited.[1] The psalm *Lauda* is not recited at the end of Vespers. The Office is terminated by *Pater noster*, etc., and the prayer suitable to the occasion (with a long conclusion) chosen from those assigned in the Ritual (or Breviary). Vespers are followed by Matins and Lauds or at least Matins (or one nocturn of it). If Lauds are not said, *Pater noster* and the other prayers which come at their end are said, kneeling, after Matins or the one nocturn which may be said. If the Office is not said at all on the arrival of the body, then after the singing of *Subvenite*, when the body is in its place, the prayers as at the end of Lauds (i.e., *Pater noster*, etc.) are said. These prayers are preceded by *Kyrie, eleison, Christe, eleison, Kyrie, eleison* and the conclusion to the prayer *Absolve* will be short [2] (*Per Christum Dominum nostrum*). At the end are added *Requiem* (in the singular) and *Requiescat*.

After Mass and the Absolution, if the body is not taken at once to be buried, the antiphons *In paradisum* and *Ego sum*, with the *Benedictus* and all that follows, are sung or said in the church. If the body is buried another day, or later, it is not necessary to repeat these prayers at the grave ; but this may be done. The whole funeral service may be repeated another day, or at another church, if the burying is delayed.

If it is not possible to bring the body in procession from the house to the church, the priest meets it at the entrance of the churchyard, or at the door of the church, there sprinkles it with lustral water, and says the *De profundis* and (if the procession lasts for some time) the *Miserere* with their antiphons, as above.[3] If the distance to the altar is short, the antiphon *Exsultabunt* and the *Miserere* may be omitted and *Subvenite* begun at once on entering the church.

§ 3. PRIVATE FUNERALS

UNDER this title (*exequiae privatae*) the *Ordo Administrandi Sacramenta* provides the shortest possible ceremony.[4] This may take place at any time of the day. The priest, in surplice and black stole, and uncovered, receives the body at the door of the church or churchyard. He sprinkles it thrice with lustral water and says *De profundis* with the antiphon *Si iniquitates* and as he goes before it to the place in front of the altar he says *Subvenite sancti Dei, Pater noster*, etc. Immediately after the prayer *Absolve, quaesumus Domini* [5] he adds *Non intres in* in R.R. VI. iii, and the prescription of C.J.C. 1215 are to be followed (S.R.C. 4357).

---

[1] *Pater* and *Ave* are not said at the beginning if Vespers immediately follow the arrival of the body and the responsory *Subvenite*.

[2] Being outside the Office (cf. R.R. VI. iii, 5).

[3] S.R.C. 3481[1].

[4] *Ordo Adm.*, VI. iii, n. 6, p. 171.

[5] It would seem (and it is the view of Martinucci and Vavasseur) that when the Absolution *immediately* follows the arrival of the body (the Office and Mass being omitted) after *Subvenite Non intres* should be said at once. But *Ordo Adm.* (p. 171) apparently prescribes *Pater noster*, etc., and the prayer *Absolve* before the Absolution is begun.

iudicium and the full Absolution. As the coffin is carried to the cemetery he says *In paradisum deducant te angeli.* He may say this as it is borne from the church. He will accompany the coffin to the cemetery (in England generally in a carriage). With him is a server who holds the lustral water and sprinkler and, if the grave is not yet blessed, another with incense. At the cemetery he blesses the grave, if it is not yet blessed, says the *Benedictus* with its antiphon *Ego sum,* and the rest of the prayers in the Ritual.

It may even be that the body cannot be brought to the church at all. The priest accompanies it from the house to the grave, saying first *De profundis* and *Miserere* (if there is time), with their antiphons, *Subvenite,* the Absolution, then *In paradisum* and all that follows.

§ 4. OFFICE FOR THE DEAD WHEN THE BODY IS NOT PRESENT

IT is allowed under privileged conditions to say the Office and Requiem Mass for a deceased person on the third, seventh and thirtieth days after either his death or burial, on the anniversary of death or burial and on the first convenient day after having received news of the death.[1]

The Privileged Requiem Mass. On these days in any church *one* Requiem Mass—either Solemn, Sung or Low—is permitted except on : doubles of the first and second class ; Sundays and holydays of obligation (even suppressed) ; the eves of Christmas and Pentecost and Epiphany ; during the octaves of Christmas, Epiphany, Easter, Ascension Day, Pentecost, Corpus Christi and of the feast of the Sacred Heart ; Ash Wednesday, and all Holy Week ; on All Souls' Day and during the time of solemn Exposition of the Blessed Sacrament.

If this privileged Requiem Mass be *liturgically* impeded on the correct date, it may be anticipated on or postponed to the nearest day not similarly impeded, provided that it be a *sung* Mass.

If the Absolution[2] is to follow, a catafalque is set up in the place where the coffin would be placed, or the funeral pall or a black cloth is spread on the floor to represent the coffin.[3] The Office of the dead is said or sung, either Matins and Lauds, or Matins only, or one nocturn and Lauds, or one nocturn.[4] The antiphons are doubled. At Matins the Invitatory is said. Then the Requiem Mass is said or sung. The Mass is that appointed in the Missal.[5]

The Absolution. The Absolution follows at the catafalque or pall spread on the ground, as when the body is present, except that the

[1] For a detailed exposition of the rubrics which regulate these privileged Masses, see O'Connell, " The Celebration of Mass," I, pp. 150 *sqq.*
[2] R.R. VI. v. The Absolution is of obligation only at a funeral.
[3] This cloth should not be spread till just before the Absolution. In this simpler form of the Absolution (i) the cross-bearer and acolytes do not take part, (ii) the celebrant stands all the time on the foot-pace (cf. O'Connell, III, 187, 188).
[4] The first nocturn is said on Monday and Thursday ; the second on Tuesday and Friday ; the third on Wednesday and Saturday.
[5] The Mass for anniversaries or other according to the rubric in the Missal after the burial Mass. For a deceased bishop or priest the Mass on an anniversary will

prayer *Non intres in iudicium* is omitted.[1] The clergy stand around with lighted candles, the subdeacon or a server holds the processional cross at the head of the coffin ; the celebrant at the foot says the same prayers, sprinkles the catafalque with lustral water and incenses it, all as above in the case of funerals. The only other difference is in the final prayer.[2] Then the celebrant makes the sign of the cross over the catafalque, saying *Requiem aeternam*, etc. The cantors sing *Requiescat in pace*. ℞. *Amen.* The celebrant chants *Anima, eius*, etc., all as in the Ritual. They go back to the sacristy in order, reciting—for all the faithful departed—the *De profundis* with the antiphon *Si iniquitates*, and, in the sacristy, add the last prayers which are given in the Ritual.

If the Office is for a woman the gender is changed in the prayers. If it is for several people the plural is used ; if for a bishop, priest or deacon, this rank is expressed in the prayers, after the man's name.

§ 5. PONTIFICAL ABSOLUTION AT THE THRONE [3]

ACCORDING to the normal rule, after Pontifical High Mass for the dead (pp. 186–189) the Bishop proceeds to make the Absolution, either over the coffin or (if the body is not present) over a catafalque or over a black cloth spread on the ground.

Supposing, first, that the Bishop uses the throne and that the hearse or catafalque is erected in the usual place, namely in the centre of the church, outside the choir, the following ceremonies are observed :

A faldstool covered with black is placed at the foot of the hearse,[4] on either side of it are stools for the assistant deacons, if they attend, on the right is a third stool for the A.P.

Vesting of Bishop. As soon as Mass is finished the Bishop goes to the throne and sits there. The two assistant deacons are at his side. Candles are distributed to the clergy ; the Bishop's candle is held for him by a server at the right of the first assistant deacon. The deacon and subdeacon of the Mass take off their maniples at the seat and come to the Bishop. Four servers [5] attend to take the Mass vestments, and

be the first one given for All Souls' Day but with the prayer proper to the person for whom the Mass is offered (cf. O'Connell, " The Celebration of Mass," I, pp. 136, 137).

[1] Nor in the case of a catafalque (unless the body be " morally " present) is the position changed for a priest. The head is supposed to be away from the altar, so the cross-bearer stands at that end, the celebrant between the catafalque and the altar.

[2] It is " Absolve, quaesumus Domine", or the collect of the appropriate Mass (with the short conclusion), or other suitable prayer.

[3] C.E. II. xi, 10–12.

[4] That is to say, between the hearse and the altar for a layman, and always in the case of Absolution at a catafalque when the body is present neither physically nor morally. Only in the case of a priest or bishop whose body is present physically or morally (p. 409, n. 2) is the faldstool at the end nearer the door of the church.

[5] Four would be the number if one takes each vestment, chasuble, dalmatic, tunicle, maniple. If there are not four they may take each vestment to the altar, leave it there (where the second M.C. will arrange it) and return for another.

another server brings the black cope. The three chaplains of the mitre, book and candle [1] will assist at the Absolution. The mitre-bearer comes and stands by the deacon of Mass. The subdeacon takes off the Bishop's maniple and gives it to a server; the deacon of Mass takes his mitre and gives it to the mitre-bearer; the Bishop rises, the deacon, assisted by the subdeacon, takes his chasuble, dalmatic and tunicle.

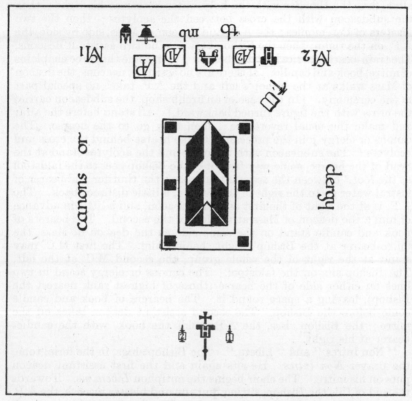

FIG. 47. FUNERAL : PONTIFICAL ABSOLUTION

They give these to the servers who lay them on the altar, where they are arranged by the second M.C. The ministers of Mass then vest the Bishop in a black cope and simple morse. The Bishop sits and the deacon puts on him the simple mitre.

If there is to be a funeral oration, it is preached now, while the Bishop sits at the throne. The preacher does not ask his blessing, but genuflects first to the altar, then to the Bishop.

[1] The Bishop never uses a crozier at funeral rites.

R.R.   E E

Procession to the Hearse. After the sermon, if there is one, the subdeacon takes the processional cross, the acolytes take their candles. [If the prelate is an archbishop in his own province, the subdeacon carries the archiepiscopal cross immediately before him, according to the general rule.] The thurifer takes the thurible and incense boat ; another server takes the lustral water and sprinkler. The assistant priest now comes to the Bishop's right. The procession goes to the altar, first the thurifer with the holy-water bearer at his right ; then the subdeacon with the cross between the acolytes ; then the two Masters of Ceremonies ; the A.P. and deacon of Mass, side by side, the A.P. on the right ; then the Bishop between the two assistant deacons. The train-bearer carries his train behind ; then come the three chaplains of mitre, book and candle. If there are no assistant deacons, the deacon of Mass walks at the bishop's left and the A.P. takes no special part in the ceremony. [In the case of an archbishop, the subdeacon carries the cross with the figure turned backward.] All stand before the altar and make the usual reverences ; then they go to the hearse. The canons or clergy join the procession to the hearse behind the cross and acolytes.[1] The subdeacon with the cross and the acolytes stand at the head of the hearse, some way from it [2] ; the Bishop goes to the faldstool at the foot,[3] between the assistant deacons ; the thurifer and bearer of lustral water go to the right of the Bishop, a little distance back. The A.P. is at the right of the first assistant deacon, and a little in advance of him ; the deacon of Mass at the left of the second. The bearers of book and candle stand on the same side as the deacon of Mass, the mitre-bearer at the Bishop's right, behind him. The first M.C. may stand at the right of the whole group, the second M.C. at the left. The Bishop sits on the faldstool. The canons or clergy stand in two lines on either side of the hearse (those of highest rank nearest the Bishop), leaving a space round it. The bearers of book and candle come before the Bishop. The second assistant deacon takes off the mitre ; the Bishop rises, the A.P. holds the book, with the candle-bearer at his right.

" Non Intres " and " Libera." The Bishop sings, in the ferial tone, the prayer *Non intres.* He sits again and the first assistant deacon puts on his mitre. The choir begins the antiphon *Libera me.* Towards the end of this the Bishop, sitting, puts on and blesses incense, the A.P. assisting and omitting the solita oscula. The thurifer kneels, as usual. Then the second assistant deacon takes off the mitre and hands it to the mitre-bearer. When the responsory is finished the Bishop rises,

---

[1] If the archbishop's cross is carried before him, and if his Chapter attends, the canons walk between the cross and the archbishop.

[2] To allow space for the Bishop and his assistants to pass between them and the hearse.

[3] In figure 47 it is supposed that the Sanctissimum is not present or that the catafalque is a long way down the church. If, however, the Sanctissimum is present and the catafalque is not a long distance away, the Bishop and his assistants will take their places somewhat to the Epistle side, in order to avoid directly turning their backs to the Sanctissimum.

the cantors sing *Kyrie, eleison*, etc. ; the Bishop intones *Pater noster*.
The A.P. hands him the sprinkler and he goes round the hearse sprinkling it with lustral water between the assistant deacons,[1] who hold
back the cope. Then, having come back to the faldstool, he takes the
thurible from the A.P. and incenses the hearse. The Bishop sprinkles
and incenses in the same way as a priest, and bows to the processional
cross as he passes it (p. 412).[2] When this is finished, the bearers of
book and candle come before him. The A.P. holds the book. The
Bishop sings the verses *Et ne nos inducas in tentationem*, etc., as usual ;
lastly, he makes the sign of the cross over the hearse as he sings *Requiem
aeternam dona ei, Domine*. The first assistant deacon holds the end
of the cope while he does so. The cantors sing *Requiescat in pace*.
R̸. *Amen*. Nothing more is added. The Bishop sits, the first
assistant deacon puts on his mitre. The procession goes to the throne
as it came and the Bishop is there unvested.[3]

Absolution if Body Absent. If there is no catafalque, a black cloth
is spread in front of the throne. In this case the cross is not carried.
The ministers of Mass go to the seat, take off their maniples, go to the
throne and vest the Bishop, then return to the sedilia and stand there
during the Absolution. But if there are no assistant deacons, then
the ministers of Mass take their place at the throne, standing one on
either side of the Bishop. The Bishop stays at the throne ; the
procession to the altar is not made.[4] The clergy do not stand around
the cloth. The acolytes hold their candles one on either side of the
throne before the Bishop.[5] He puts on incense and blesses it at the
throne. He sprinkles and incenses the cloth from the throne, not
going round it, but doing so thrice each time, once in the middle,
once at his left, lastly at his right. At the end of the Absolution the
deacon and subdeacon go to the throne and aid the Bishop to
unvest.

Only *the* Bishop or a " greater prelate " (p. 31) may perform the
Absolution, without having first sung the Mass.[6]

[1] If the Sanctissimum be present and the catafalque be not a long way from
the altar the Bishop and his assistants genuflect to the Sanctissimum before the
sprinkling and before the incensation.
[2] If there are no assistant deacons the deacon of the Mass accompanies the
Bishop, on his right, and holds back the cope.
[3] Should the Bishop go to the sacristy to unvest, it would seem that the prayers
Si iniquitates, De profundis, etc., should be recited.
[4] At the Absolution *when the body is not present* (physically or morally) it is
a moot point as to whether the Bishop should say the *Non intres* or not. The
Pontifical (part iii) prescribes it ; the Ceremonial (II. xi, 12), says nothing about
it and when a priest officiates it is not said. It would seem that when the Absolution is more solemn (given at a " castrum doloris " on an important occasion)
and given by *the* Bishop, the *Non intres* is said ; not otherwise (so Martinucci
teaches).
[5] Cf. C.E. II. xi, 12 ; *Pontificale*, iii (*De Officio Solemni post Missam pro
Defunctis*).
[6] Cf. S.R.C. 3029[10] and 3798[2]. He may do so whether he presides at the throne
or—in mozetta—in the first stall in choir (S.R.C. 4355, ii, 3) ; and even if he were
not present at the Mass.

§ 6. PONTIFICAL ABSOLUTION AT THE FALDSTOOL

The ceremony in this case is almost the same as when the Bishop uses the throne, except that the faldstool at the Epistle side takes its place. Another faldstool is placed at the foot of the hearse, outside the choir. There is no A.P. There are no assistant deacons ; so the deacon of Mass is at the bishop's left. He assists when incense is put on and blessed, he hands the holy-water sprinkler, puts on and takes off the mitre. The first M.C. is at the bishop's right. Meanwhile the sub-deacon holds the cross at the head of the hearse. The deacon walks at the bishop's right when he goes round the hearse. The book-bearer holds the book with the candle-bearer at his right.

If there is no catafalque, a black cloth is spread before the faldstool at the Epistle side. The second faldstool is not used. The Bishop does everything here as at the throne (above, p. 419). but he goes to the Epistle corner of the altar (after the blessing of the incense) to chant the prayers ; and from the foot-pace sprinkles and incenses the cloth.[1] The ministers of Mass are at his sides.

§ 7. THE FIVE ABSOLUTIONS

In certain cases of special solemnity the Absolution at the hearse is performed by five prelates.[2] These cases are the funerals of greater prelates,[3] of (Catholic) sovereigns or the lord of the place.[4]

General Rules. The five Absolutions follow Pontifical High Mass for the dead. There are, then, besides the bishop who sings the Mass, four other bishops. The ceremony may be performed only once for one person. It should take place at the occasion of the funeral if possible, or (failing that) soon afterwards, on the third, seventh or thirtieth day, not later. It is not done at anniversaries. It is generally performed at the cathedral church ; but the Ordinary may appoint another for the purpose. The five who perform the Absolutions should be bishops or prelates having the right to use pontificals. If so many cannot be procured, the other four may be priests. Those of highest rank available will be chosen. At the cathedral they will naturally be dignitaries or canons.

According to the Ceremonial of Bishops the five Absolutions are performed at the funeral of the Ordinary, which funeral is supposed to be celebrated by the highest dignitary of the Chapter, normally not a bishop. It is then clear that the ceremony may be carried out when no bishop is present. It is, however, usual, in this case, for the Chapter to invite a bishop to sing the Mass and preside at the Absolutions.

Besides the faldstool at the foot of the coffin, i.e., between it and the main door of the church (if the body be present and be that of a bishop

---

[1] C.E. II. xi, 10–12 ; cf. O'Connell, " The Celebration of Mass," III, 187, 188.
[2] This ceremony is in the Pontifical, at the end of part iii : " De Officio quod post Missam Solemnem pro Defunctis Agitur." Cf. C.E. II. xi, 13–24.
[3] C.E. II. xi, 13 mentions the Pope, Cardinals, Metropolitans, Ordinaries. This list corresponds with that of " Greater Prelates."
[4] " Dux magnus aut Dominus loci " (ib.).

or prelate ; otherwise between the hearse and the altar), prepared for the celebrating bishop, four plain bare stools are set up at its corners, and behind them a bench covered with violet or black on both sides for the canons.

Vesting of Prelates. Supposing, in the first case, that five bishops will perform the ceremony, the four who assist, besides the celebrant of the Mass, go to the sacristy to vest at the end of Mass or of the funeral oration. Meanwhile the bishop-celebrant goes to the throne or faldstool.

The four other bishops vest in amice over their rochet, black stole and black cope, simple mitre. They wear no train. They come from the sacristy, each attended by a mitre-bearer and a servant or server, who carries a lighted candle.[1] The second M.C. comes first, then the bishops, two and two, those of higher rank behind. On the outer side of each are his mitre-bearer and server with a lighted candle, each in surplice. The prelates form in a straight line before the altar ; the servers stand behind them. In the middle of their line they leave space for the celebrant. They take off their mitres and hand them to the bearers. In this ceremony the assisting bishops always take off the mitre themselves. They bow to the bishop-celebrant at the throne or faldstool. The subdeacon goes to take the processional cross, the acolytes take their candles'; other servers bring the thurible, lustral water and a Pontifical. These stand behind the line of bishops. The first M.C. now invites the bishop-celebrant to join the others. He comes, with his assistant deacons, and takes his place in the middle. The deacons stand behind him. Meanwhile the deacon of Mass and A.P. stand near the altar. The four bishops bow with the celebrant, then put on their mitres.

Procession to Hearse. The procession goes to the hearse in this order : first the thurifer with the server carrying the lustral water at his right ; then the subdeacon of the Mass (*paratus*) holding the cross (processional or archiepiscopal) between the acolytes ; the clergy and canons carrying lighted candles in the outer hand ; the four bishops, two and two, those of higher rank behind, with their servers at their sides, as when they came in ; the A.P. with the deacon of Mass at his left ; the bishop-celebrant between his assistant deacons. The server who holds his candle is at the right of the first assistant deacon. The train-bearer follows, holding the celebrant's train ; then come the three chaplains of mitre, book and hand-candle.

All stand around the hearse in the usual way, the subdeacon with the cross and acolytes at the head, the bishop-celebrant with his attendants at the foot before his faldstool, the clergy or canons around. The four other bishops are at the four stools prepared, in order of rank, the first (or senior) at the right of the celebrant, the second at the right of the cross at the other end, the third at the celebrant's left, the fourth at the left of the cross. The bishops and canons sit. At the right of each assisting bishop is his mitre-bearer, at his left the server with his

---

[1] If the assistants be not bishops they themselves carry their candles.

candle. Then the second assistant deacon takes the mitre from the
celebrant, the other bishops take off theirs, handing them to the bearers.
All stand.

"**Non Intres.**" The celebrant chants the prayer *Non intres* [1] in the
ferial tone, the A.P. holding the Pontifical. All sit again and put on

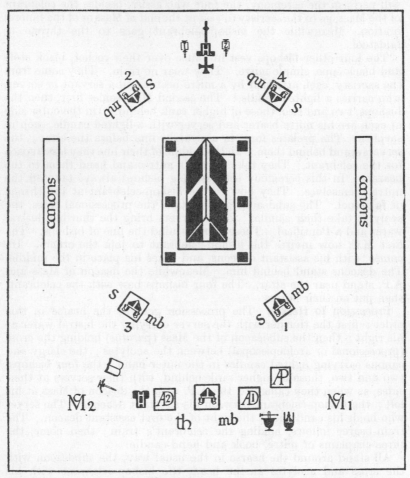

FIG. 48. THE FIVE ABSOLUTIONS
(THE BODY OF A BISHOP OR PRELATE BEING PRESENT)

their mitres. The first assistant deacon puts on the celebrant's mitre.
If the four assistants are bishops the A.P. now goes to join the other

[1] Even, in the case of the five Absolutions, if the body be not present (cf.
C.E. II. xi, 15, 17 ; cf. also p. 419, n. 4).

canons.[1] The choir sings the responsory *Subvenite, Sancti Dei.*[2] Meanwhile the deacon of Mass goes to the first (or senior) of the assisting bishops with the thurifer and bearer of lustral water and stands at his right.

First Absolution. Towards the end of the responsory (when the verse *Requiem aeternam* is begun) this bishop puts on and blesses incense, as usual, the deacon assisting.[3] The cantors sing *Kyrie, eleison,* etc. As soon as they begin all stand (uncovered). The first assistant bishop chants *Pater noster,* and then, continuing it silently, accompanied by the deacon on his right, he goes round the hearse twice (beginning on his right), first sprinkling it, then incensing—three times on each side, as usual. He does not wear the mitre while so doing (the deacon having removed it) ; he bows as he passes each of the other bishops and to the cross. Then having given back the thurible to the deacon (who hands it to the thurifer), he sings the verses *Et ne nos inducas,* etc., and the prayer *Deus, cui omnia vivunt,* as in the Pontifical (the book-bearer holding the book [4]). All sit again and the prelates put on the mitre (the deacon puts on that of the absolving prelate). The choir sings the second responsory, *Qui Lazarum resuscitasti.*

Second, Third and Fourth Absolutions. Meanwhile the deacon goes to the second bishop ; all is done by him as before. He blesses incense, sprinkles and incenses and sings the verses and prayer *Fac, quaesumus Domine.* The choir sings the responsory *Domine, quando veneris* ; and the third bishop performs the Absolution. His prayer is *Inclina, Domine, aurem tuam.* The choir sings *Ne recorderis peccata mea* ; and the fourth (or junior) bishop makes his Absolution, singing at the end the prayer *Absolve, quaesumus Domine.*

The Final Absolution. The A.P. comes to the celebrant. Then follows the last responsory *Libera me, Domine ;* and the bishop-celebrant performs the last Absolution as usual, except that he, too, bows to the other bishops as he passes them. The A.P. assists with incense and holy water, and holds the book while he sings. The candle-bearer attends. No versicle or prayer follows after *Requiescat in pace.* All go to the altar as they came, the assisting bishops to the sacristy, the bishop-celebrant to the throne, where he is unvested.

If Assistants are not Bishops. If the assistants who make the Absolutions are not bishops and have no use of Pontificals, the following exceptions occur.[5] They carry their own candles and have no mitre-bearers. They come in wearing the biretta, uncover and bow to the choir as usual ; then make the proper reverence to the Bishop at the throne or faldstool. They wear the biretta while going to the hearse

---

[1] Because he has no further function till the Absolution by the celebrant.
[2] The five responsories, each with its versicles and prayer, are printed in order in the Pontifical. The *Liber Usualis* gives the chants.
[3] The deacon asks the blessing, saying *Benedicite, reverendissime Pater.*
[4] The hand-candle-bearer holds the candle at the fifth Absolution only.
[5] C.E. II. xi, 24.

and coming from it, and while they sit on the stools there. They uncover to bow. While each makes the Absolution he hands his biretta and candle to the second M.C. or to a server to hold. If the presiding bishop is the Ordinary the priests do not bless the incense ; but he does so for each of them.[1] They bless incense if he is not the Ordinary.

§ 8. THE FUNERAL OF INFANTS

INFANTS who die without baptism may not be buried with any liturgical ceremony. When baptized infants die under the age of reason (seven years), there is a special rite for their funeral.[2] There are no signs of mourning ; no prayers for the dead child are said. The colour is white. If the bells are rung at all they are rung joyfully. A crown of sweet-smelling flowers is put on the child's head as a sign of his bodily integrity and virginity.[3]

The priest goes to the house, to bring the coffin to the church, with a cross-bearer and a server who carries lustral water. He may be accompanied by clergy ; there may be acolytes who go on either side of the cross. The cross is borne without its shaft.[4] The celebrant wears surplice, white stole, and he may wear a white cope.

At the House. At the house he sprinkles the coffin, then intones the antiphon *Sit nomen Domini* [2] the choir chants or recites the psalm *Laudate, pueri, Dominum*. When the antiphon after this psalm has been said the procession goes to the church in the same order as for a grown-up person. On the way they recite the psalm *Beati immaculati*, and (if there is time) *Laudate Dominum de caelis*. The verses *Gloria Patri* and *Sicut erat* are said at the end of these psalms.

If the priest cannot go to the house to bring the coffin to the church, he may meet it and carry out this rite at the gate of the churchyard or door of the church.

At the Church. When the procession arrives at the church, the psalm is interrupted ; at once they say or sing *Gloria Patri* and *Sicut erat*.

Candles may be lighted around the coffin, placed in the usual place before the altar, outside the choir.[5] But they are not distributed to the clergy. If it is morning either the Mass of the day, or, if the rubrics permit, a private votive Mass, a suitable votive Mass—not for the child, but for some other intention (e.g., in thanksgiving for the blessing conferred on him ; to beg consolation for his parents) may be celebrated. In the evening votive Vespers of the Angels, or those of the little Office of our Lady, may be said or sung.[6]

---

[1] To assist at this the A.P. (sitting on his stool) stays by the Ordinary all the time.
[2] R.R. VI. vii.   [3] R.R. VI. vii, 1.
[4] The liturgical books make a special point of this. Not the whole processional cross with the long shaft, but a smaller hand-cross is carried. The processional cross should be so made that its upper part can be detached from the shaft for the funeral of infants.   [5] Or, preferably, in the mortuary chapel.
[6] S.R.C. 3481[2].

Then, instead of the Absolution, all stand around the coffin, the celebrant in white stole or white stole and cope. The cross (without shaft) is held at the head of the coffin, the celebrant stands at the feet. The psalm *Domini est terra* is said or sung, with the antiphon *Hic accipiet*.[1] The prayers *Kyrie, eleison*, etc., follow, as in the Ritual. While *Pater noster* is said silently the priest sprinkles the coffin three times before him. He does not go round it ; nor is it incensed.

At the Graveside. After the prayer *Omnipotens et mitissime Deus* the coffin is carried to the grave. Meanwhile the choir in procession sings the psalm *Laudate Dominum de caelis*, with the antiphon *Iuvenes*. Incense and lustral water are taken in this procession. At the grave the celebrant says *Kyrie, eleison*, and the following prayers. After the collect *Omnipotens sempiterne Deus, sanctae puritatis amator*, he puts incense into the thurible and blesses it. Then he sprinkles the coffin and grave together with lustral water and incenses them, not moving from his place. The procession returns to the church, and the body is buried.[2] On the way to the church they sing or recite the psalm *Benedicite*, with the antiphon *Benedicite Dominum*. Before the altar the celebrant says *Dominus vobiscum*, and the prayer *Deus qui miro ordine*. All go to the sacristy.

If the body is not to be taken to the grave at once, all these prayers are said in the church.

If the priest does not accompany it to the grave, they may be said or sung at the door of the church, before it is taken farther.

If all the prayers have been said in church, it is not necessary to repeat them at the grave ; but they may be repeated.

[1] R.R. supposes these prayers to follow immediately after the arrival of the body in the church. It makes no reference to the celebration of Mass.

[2] As in the case of adults, it is supposed that the celebrant and clergy have left the grave before the actual burial.

INDEX

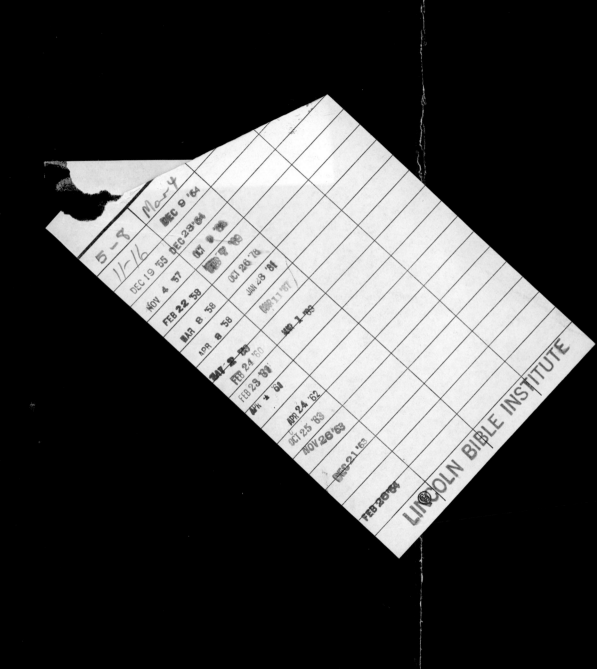